appeared around 1800 in Paris. Early "velos" were powered by pushing on the ground with the feet and were not steerable until 1818. Velos were powered using treadles and rods by 1840 and by foot pedals in 1861, and finally, a chain was used in approximately 1869, creating a machine that is recognizable as a modern bicycle.

In other situations, an invention's date was established by determining when the device or process was first depicted in illustrations or mentioned in writings. In yet other cases, the date a patent was issued is employed. Obviously, the date of recent discoveries are accurate as a result of better recordkeeping and documentation.

In some cases, two dates are shown matching the two places that those events/discoveries (or variations of the technology) took place. This may be useful in understanding the time that elapsed for a given technology in moving from one locale to another (technology diffusion) or in evolving separately in two different societies.

Event	Date	Event	Date
Cities	5000 BC	Crayons (Crayola)	1902
Clock (mechanical)	1300	Crop rotation (theory)	1804
Clock (pendulum)	1656	Crystal radio	1901
Clock (water)	1400 BC	Cuisinart	1973
Cloning (fish)	1981	Diaper (disposable)	1951
Coca-Cola	1866	Dinosaurs (era)	245 to 65 MYA
Codes/Cyphers	1623	Disk (floppy)	1970
Coffee	1400	DNA discovered	1953
Coins	700 BC	DNA evolves	1.8 BYA
Coliseum	70	Drill (bow)	20,000 BC
Compact discs	1982	Drill (dental)	1790
Compass	300 BC	Dynamite	1867
Computer (mechanical)	1832	Earth Day	1970
Computer (electromechanical)	1942	Electric generating station	1882
Computer (electronic)	1946	Electrocardiogram (EKG)	1924
Computer (digital/binary)	1938	Electroencephalogram (EEG)	1929
Computer (personal)	1975	Elevator (electric)	1887
Computer (programmable)	1941	E-mail	1987
Concrete	200 BC	Embryo transplant (cattle/human)	1950/1983
Contact lens	1887	Erector set	1901
Container shipping (ships/trucks)	1954	Escalator	1911
Contraception (pill)	1956	Fastener (Velcro)	1948
Contraceptives	2000 BC	Fas†	1933
Contracts (written)	2700 BC	Fax	
Copper	6400 BC	Fe†	
Copying (Xerography)	1937	Fil	
Crank handle	100 BC		

k of book)

SOCIETY, ETHICS, AND TECHNOLOGY

Third Edition

Morton E. Winston
The College of New Jersey

Ralph D. Edelbach
The College of New Jersey

THOMSON
™
WADSWORTH

Australia • Canada • Mexico • Singapore • Spain
United Kingdom • United States

Publisher: Holly J. Allen

Philosophy Editor: Steve Wainwright

Assistant Editors: Lee McCracken, Barbara Hillaker

Editorial Assistant: John Gahbauer

Technology Project Manager: Julie Aguilar

Marketing Manager: Worth Hawes

Marketing Assistant: Andrew Keay

Marketing Communications Manager: Laurel Anderson

Executive Art Director: Maria Epes

Print Buyer: Barbara Britton

Permissions Editor: Sarah Harkrader

Production Service: Matrix Productions, Inc.

Copy Editor: Frank Hubert

Cover Designer: Chris Wallace

Cover Image: Colin Anderson/Brand X Pictures/ Getty Images

Compositor: International Typesetting and Composition

Text and Cover Printer: Webcom

Library of Congress Control Number: 2005924548

ISBN 13: 978-0-534-52085-4
ISBN 10: 0-534-52085-5

Thomson Higher Education
10 Davis Drive
Belmont, CA 94002-3098
USA

Asia (including India)
Thomson Learning
5 Shenton Way
#01-01 UIC Building
Singapore 068808

Australia/New Zealand
Thomson Learning Australia
102 Dodds Street
Southbank, Victoria 3006
Australia

Canada
Thomson Nelson
1120 Birchmount Road
Toronto, Ontario M1K 5G4
Canada

UK/Europe/Middle East/Africa
Thomson Learning
High Holborn House
50–51 Bedford Row
London WC1R 4LR
United Kingdom

For Carla, Margaret, and Molly Winston

MORTON E. WINSTON

To my grandsons, Ryan C. and Kyle T. Edelbach

RALPH D. EDELBACH

Contents

Part II: *Contemporary Technology and the Future*   153

Preface

The idea for this book began at The College of New Jersey in 1993 with the decision to introduce a new general education core course entitled "Society, Ethics, and Technology" (SET). Among the ideas that influenced the development of this course were the discussions of the "New Liberal Learning," the development of a vigorous "Science, Technology, and Society" (STS) movement under the auspices of the National Association for Science, Technology, and Society (NASTS), and the New Liberal Arts (NLA) program that was sponsored during the 1980s through grants made by the Sloan Foundation.

These trends made it clear that general education at the undergraduate level should include courses and curricula that help students to understand the profound role that science and technology play in shaping modern society, and which provide them with a method for evaluating the benefits and risks associated with technological change. The course and this reader were developed under the assumption that scientific and technological literacy remains an essential aspect of what it means to be an educated person in the twenty-first century.

The positive response to the earlier editions of this reader encouraged us to prepare this updated and revised third edition, which includes thirteen new readings by authors such as: David Landes, Rosalind Williams, Thomas Friedman, Max More, Lee Silver, Michael Sandel, and Robert Kates, among others. We have kept the basic organization of the book the same as in the earlier editions, but have expanded the topics covered in Part II of the book to provide better coverage of topics such as globalization, transhumanism, nanotechnology, privacy, human cloning, genetically engineered foods, and energy alternatives. However, as we noted in the preface to the earlier editions, the range of topics and issues related to the social and ethical implications of technological change is so broad, and is changing so quickly, no printed anthology can possibly do justice to all the topics that might be covered in courses dealing with these issues. We believe that the four-month subscription to InfoTrac on-line library that can be bundled with new copies of this text and which allows students and instructors to access more than 30 million articles from over 5,000 journals going back to 1980, provides an invaluable resource to be used along with this book.

The editors are grateful to our reviewers for comments on the earlier editions. Thanks to David Kaplan for helping us identify topics and readings for the second edition. Thanks also to the reviewers of this edition: Ralph Acampora, Hofstra University; Rob Faux, University of Minnesota; Micheal Pelt, Oakland City University; and Richard Volkman, Southern Connecticut State University. We also thank Steve Wainwright, philosophy editor at Wadsworth, for his encouragement, as well as Aaron Downey at Matrix Productions, and Frank Hubert, our copyeditor, for their assistance in bringing out this third edition.

M.W. & R.E.
March 2005

How to Use This Book

This book is designed for use in standard fifteen-week undergraduate Science, Technology, and Society (STS) courses. Such courses are intended to provide an interdisciplinary bridge between the humanities, particularly ethics, the social sciences, and the natural sciences and engineering by developing a framework for analyzing the social, environmental, and ethical implications of contemporary science and technology. A principal goal of these courses is to empower students to think critically about contemporary technological issues, such as privacy on the Internet, genetic engineering, and global warming, and to learn to accept the social responsibilities of educated citizens in a global technological society.

The key bridge idea that links science and technology with ethics and social science together is the dictum that "Ought Implies Can, but Can Does Not Imply Ought." The first half of this statement asserts that one cannot be obliged to do something that one cannot do, while the second half says that just because one can do something does not mean that one ought to do it. Science and technology, by enlarging the domain of what we humans know how to do, are continually enlarging the class of actions we can perform. As a consequence of this expansion of our power to do more things, we are obliged to ask ourselves whether we ought to be doing all the things that science and technology now allow us to do. "Ought questions" are ethical questions, and to answer these sorts of questions, one needs to understand how ethical values and traditional moral standards can be applied to evaluating past and present scientific and technological innovations.

The introductory essay, "Children of Invention," which has been written especially for this volume, provides students with a conceptual framework for thinking about the relationship between scientific and technological innovation and the social and ethical issues that such innovations can create when new technologies are deployed and diffused in society. All too often, new technologies are developed and deployed without proper reflection as to their likely consequences for society. One reason for this is ignorance about the nature of technology and the processes by which new technologies are developed and deployed. Addressing the need for students to be scientifically and technologically literate has long been a primary goal of the STS movement, and it is also a primary goal of this book.

However, another reason for the failure to evaluate technology ethically is that traditional ethical theories were primarily intended to evaluate persons and their actions rather than sociotechnical practices employed by many persons in society. To correct for this, it is necessary for students to understand at least a little bit about ethics and to be familiar with the essential features of the major traditional ethical theories, such as ethical egoism, utilitarianism, natural law, and Kantian deontological ethics. It is also necessary to explain how these theories can be adapted to the evaluation of technology and to provide a method for applying familiar ethical principles to particular controversial issues surrounding contemporary science and technology. It is unusual to find books that serve these multiple purposes.

The introductory essay attempts to provide an ethical framework through which students can approach the evaluation of technology. It is advisable to assign the introductory essay early in courses for which this book is adopted because it provides students who are new to STS with a comprehensive overview of the subject matter as well as a concise introduction to the ethical and social aspects of technology. The selections in Part I convey general perspectives on the historical, social, and philosophical aspects of technology, while those in Part II deal with several issues in specific fields of contemporary technology.

In selecting readings for this text, the authors have tried to provide current selections on a number of standard STS topics, such as computers, automation, robotics, the Internet, genetic engineering, artificial reproduction, population, energy, and environmental policy issues. We have departed slightly from the standard set of topics by also including several articles dealing with the phenomenon of globalization. Each selection is preceded by a brief introduction describing the topic and major themes of the reading, mentioning something about its author, and providing several focus questions for students to keep in mind while reading the essay. Usually, at least one of these focus questions asks the reader to compare the view in the present reading with that found in another selection that presents a competing or complementary perspective. This allows instructors to design their syllabus using such topical links instead of the standard organization.

However, one of the problems with edited readers is that no matter how careful the editors are in selecting the texts to be included, it is inevitable that some topics or issues will be omitted or given only cursory treatment and that some readings will soon become obsolete. This problem is especially difficult with respect to the field of science, technology, and society studies because, given the dynamic nature of contemporary science and technology, new discoveries and developments are occurring constantly, and their impacts on society need to be addressed and examined. Thus, even if the selections of an edited anthology are current at the time of publication, they soon lose their currency and must be updated with new materials.

Although it is possible to use this book as a stand-alone course reader dealing with social and ethical issues related to technology, it is specially designed to be used along with InfoTrac College Edition, a searchable online full text library containing more than 18 million articles from over 5,000 publications. By combining this text with InfoTrac, students and instructors can supplement the readings in this book with virtually any number of additional current readings dealing with the topics and issues that specifically interest them. Each reading introduction contains a set of suggested keywords that can be used in conjunction with InfoTrac, or other Web-based libraries, to search for articles on related themes or topics. By combining the readings in this book with the InfoTrac virtual library, it is possible for instructors to design their own units on topics or issues that are not addressed by the readings in this textbook. Instructors can choose a topic to discuss, search InfoTrac for suitable articles and references on that topic, and then ask students to access InfoTrac and retrieve and read the indicated selections. It is of course also possible to assign the task of searching InfoTrac to students and ask them to prepare reports on these supplementary course topics.

InfoTrac is easy to learn, and combining the readings in this book with the InfoTrac online library gives instructors considerable freedom in adapting this book to their particular course design and personal interests. Students will find that their InfoTrac subscription is useful not only for the course for which they bought this book but for other courses as well. We believe that the combination of the *Society, Ethics, and Technology* reader with an InfoTrac subscription provides an exceptional resource for STS courses.

If this text was ordered with the InfoTrac option, a four-month subscription is bundled with the book. To access your InfoTrac account, point your web browser to:

http://www.infotrac.thomsonlearning.com/

After you enter your account ID number, fill in your registration information. Once registered, you can search the database for specific entries on precisely defined topics by subject or keyword, journal, or date of publication (using Boolean operators, wildcards, and nested operators), or you can use the Easy Search to quickly compile a list of citations related to your topic. There is a complete online help index with InfoTrac that will guide you as you go.

The combination of a traditional print-media course reader together with the InfoTrac College Library transforms this text into what might be termed a "CyberReader"—a literary amphibian that exists both in the print world and in cyberspace. To provide additional linkage between the text and the World Wide Web, the book is also supported by a course website:

http://www.tcnj.edu/~set/set.htm

that contains hyperlinks to various other sites on the web dealing with topics and issues addressed in the reader. These links are continually updated, but instructors may also want to create their own websites for their courses and link them to the *Society, Ethics, and Technology* site that supports this book. The site also provides the e-mail addresses of the authors, who welcome comments and suggestions about this text.

M.W. & R.E.

April 2005

Children of Invention

IF NECESSITY IS THE MOTHER OF INVENTION, who is the father, and who, or what, are invention's children? Necessity, of course, is a matter of degree: We actually only *need* air, water, and food to survive. Shelter, clothing, and a few material possessions are also nice, as are companionship, affection, security, and several other psychological goods that we crave as social animals. But we humans learned how to satisfy these basic biological needs millions of years ago. Why then did we embark on the long journey that transformed us from cave dwellers into cosmonauts? What was it that made possible the ascent from the Stone Age to the Space Age?

Clearly, the leading answer to these questions is superior intelligence. But in what specific respects is human intelligence superior to that found in other species? Is it our capacity to learn from observation and experience and to transmit what we learn to others? Is it our ability to create and use language? Or might it be these general cognitive capacities for culture and language, together with our unique ability to discover new solutions to old problems and better ways of making and doing things—in short, our unique capacity as a species to form science and technology? Coupled with our needs and desires, which provide the motives that propel us to discover and invent, our scientific and technological creativity has guided the development of civilization through the development of theories, tools, inventions, and technologies that have transformed the ways we live and work.[1]

For most of us, a world without technology is inconceivable. The inventions that it has given are all around us. In fact, most of us spend most of our lives in completely artificial environments, wrapped in a technological cocoon that provides us with much more than merely food and protection from the elements. We are so wrapped up in our technological culture, in fact, that it takes an effort to distance ourselves from it to understand how technology has transformed human existence from its natural state. Such a historical perspective also helps us to see how contemporary technologies, such as genetic engineering and the Internet, are now changing us in even more dramatic ways, creating new opportunities for humans to flourish, new ways of life, and also, in some cases, new social and ethical problems. These social and ethical issues arising from technological innovation are the "children of invention" that this book is about. To understand these issues, however, it is first necessary to get a clear view of their source—*technology*.

The Scope of Technology

When one ordinarily thinks of technology, what most likely comes to mind are artifacts, the manufactured objects, machines, structures, and devices that are the useful end products of technological design. Then, perhaps, one thinks of the less familiar but potentially more impressive machines and industrial processes tucked away in factories that manufacture the various gadgets and widgets that we use. Finally, one might visualize the scientists, engineers, and technicians in white laboratory coats, hard at work in the laboratories of the Research and Development Division, designing the next generation of technological devices and processes.

While it is true that technology is involved in each of these contexts—end-use, manufacturing, and design—we take the even broader view that technology consists not only of artifacts and the tools and processes needed to produce them. It also consists of the entire social organization of people and materials that permits the acquisition of the knowledge and skills needed to design, manufacture, distribute, use, repair, and eventually dispose of these artifacts. Technology is not a collection of things but rather is a systematic and rational way of doing things; it is, in general, *the organization of knowledge, people, and things to accomplish specific practical goals.*[2]

Technology includes not only the obvious candidates, the mechanical, structural, and electronic technologies that direct the purposeful organization of materials, but the also less obvious *invisible technologies* that control the purposeful organization of people. Few would doubt that the mechanical, chemical, and electrical know-how that goes into the design of the motors, transmissions, wheels, and dashboard of an automobile qualifies as technology, but so also does the assembly line, a technology for organizing the manufacturing environment, and the classroom, a technology for education. Looking farther afield, the monetary system, the banks, and the stock and commodity markets are technologies for the distribution of value that, whatever their faults, have long since displaced the competing technologies of barter and stuffing gold coins in a mattress. Free-market capitalism and centralized planned economies are competing technologies for organizing social production. Even governmental systems, ranging from varieties of representative democracy to theocracy and dictatorship, are competing political technologies for managing concerted societal action and resolving political conflicts. People ask, "Is there a better way to run the government?" no less frequently than "Is there a better way to design a mousetrap?" Both questions are requests to find a better technology.

The word *technology* is itself of fairly recent coinage; Jahann Beckman of Gottingen first used it in 1789. Its root, *techne,* is the ancient Greek word for art, craft, or skill, which itself is derived from an earlier Indo-European root, *teks,* which means to weave or fabricate. (*Teks* is also the root of the word *textile*.) Recent archeological evidence suggests that the weaving of cloth predates the birth of agriculture and the dawn of civilization, going back to about 35,000 B.C., making it one of the first technologies. As the etymology suggests, a *techne* is a method or craft or skill used in making things, not the things themselves, which are rather called *artifacts*. For instance, a woven object made from animal hairs twisted together into long strands, dyed with vegetable colors, and interlaced by a weaver is an artifact. Let us say that this object functions primarily as a blanket; a person wraps

her- or himself in it to stay warm. A typical use or function of an artifact is called its *purpose, end,* or *valence,* and the knowledge of how to gather the fibers, twist them, dye them, and weave them are the individual *techniques* of which this particular technology is comprised.[3] Thus, the core meaning of the word *technology* refers to the ensembles of techniques by which humans make artifacts that serve certain useful ends. However, this original meaning is too restrictive for the contemporary context in which we think about the relationship between technology and modern society.

Technological Systems

Contemporary writers often speak of recent technologies as consisting of systems. Technological systems are complex things consisting of several distinguishable but interacting aspects: (1) techniques, human activity-forms, or sociotechnical practices; (2) resources, tools, or materials; (3) technological products, or artifacts; (4) ends, functions, or valences; (5) background knowledge and skills; and (6) the social contexts or organization in which the technology is designed, developed, used, and disposed of. These six aspects are present in every technological system.

The first aspect of technological systems is the *human activity-form*—that is, the particular skills, techniques, methods, practices, or ways of doing things. We know that animals other than humans are able to make and use tools (for instance, chimpanzees strip the branches off tree limbs to make sticks that can be used for gathering insects), but for the purposes of our characterization of the technological system, we can restrict activity-forms or techniques to those employed by human beings. Some human activity-forms employ natural objects rather than tools to achieve ends; for instance, if one throws a rock to try to kill an animal for food, one is employing a particular technique. But throwing rocks for hunting is a primitive and not very useful technique. Technologies for providing food have improved considerably. Nowadays, there are complex ensembles of techniques for doing just about everything from planting and harvesting crops to figuring out the orbit of a moon of Jupiter, from designing a house to conducting a leveraged hostile takeover, from cooking lasagna to programming a computer to sort sales data. Such complex techniques represent what is called procedural knowledge, or more commonly *know-how,* and is contrasted with factual or theoretical prepositional knowledge, or *know-that.* While both types of knowledge are necessary aspects of technological systems, techniques are their essence. Know-how forms the basis of technology since it provides the pattern for the sociotechnical practices that we humans use to create artifacts of all kinds and to build and maintain our technological infrastructures.

One of the main consequences of technology is that it increases our capacity to do things. Technologies, techniques, and tools extend, enhance, and sometimes even replace our natural powers such as sight, hearing, muscle movement, and even memory and thought. By using tools, we are able to accomplish things that we could not otherwise achieve, thus increasing our repertoire of human activity-forms. Tools are artifacts at our disposal that can be used to make other artifacts, but tools, even the *dawn stones* used by our distant ancestors, are themselves artifacts that have been transformed from their natural states in some way by means of human action.

The earth itself is, of course, not an artifact but has, for many centuries, been viewed by humans as a *resource well* into which we can dip at will to satisfy our needs and desires. Technology requires resources of various kinds as inputs to technological processes, and by employing specific techniques or human activity-forms, we act upon and transform these resources from their original or natural states. Once a *built environment* has been created, however, everything in it can serve as a resource to further technological development. The term *infrastructure* describes elements of the built environment that are available to create or apply new technologies.

By acting upon either natural or artificial resources, through techniques, we alter them in various ways and thus create *artifacts,* which form the third aspect of technologies. A clay pot is an example of a material artifact, which, although transformed by human activity, is not all that far removed

from its natural state. A plastic cup, a contact lens, or a computer chip, on the other hand, are examples of artifacts that are far removed from the original states of the natural resources needed to create them. Artifacts can serve as resources in other technological processes. This is one of the important interaction effects within the technological system: Each new technology increases the stock of available tools and resources that can be employed by other technologies to produce new artifacts.

The fourth aspect concerns the typical use or *valence* of an artifact or technique. Most artifacts have typical or intended uses, but in fact, every artifact can be embedded in multiple contexts of use or can serve multiple ends, a property referred to as *polypotency.* A toaster, for instance, designed to lightly burn slices of bread, can also be used as a hand warmer or as a murder weapon. There is a double ambiguity in the relations between artifacts and practices and between ends and practices, since the same artifacts can be used to achieve different ends, and different practices and their associated artifacts can be used to accomplish the same ends. For instance, I could have written this sentence with a quill pen, a pencil, a ballpoint pen, a typewriter, or a personal computer running text-editing software (in fact, I used the last). And I could have used my personal computer to play an adventure game or calculate my income tax instead of writing this sentence. Because artifacts are designed and created to serve certain intended functions, it is possible to talk about the ends of these objects, that is, their intended purpose, even though the objects themselves may often also be used in ways which were not intended by their designers. The *valences* of an artifact or technology are the ways it is typically used by most agents in most social contexts.

New technologies are developed in response to what we take to be our needs and desires. But as technologies develop, they tend to change our needs and desires. Several years ago, I had no need for zipdrives or CDs to save my written work, but now I do. Needs or ends come in two main varieties: *instrumental* and *intrinsic.* An instrumental end is one that is used to obtain or achieve something else that is perceived as valuable; that is, it is a means to another end or goal. An intrinsic end is something that is valued in and for itself. I have no intrinsic need for floppy disks, but I need them so that my writing on the screen will not disappear when I turn off my PC, and I need to write to do my job as a teacher and scholar, and I need to do my job to earn money, which I need to buy food and shelter for myself and my family so that we can survive. The only thing in this example that is an intrinsic end (at least for me) is the survival of my family and myself; everything else is an instrumental end that is only valuable to the degree that it helps me to achieve this intrinsic end.

The fifth aspect of technological systems is *knowledge-that,* or factual knowledge about what the universe consists of and how it operates. To employ our technologies, we need background knowledge of various kinds: knowledge about what resources to use and where to find them, knowledge about what techniques to employ to fabricate various artifacts, knowledge about the ends and purposes that are typically served by various techniques and objects, and knowledge about how all of these elements fit together in a systematic way. Both knowledge-how and knowledge-that have always been an important aspect of technologies, but since the scientific revolution of the seventeenth century, scientific knowledge—both factual and theoretical knowledge about the universe and the way it works—has come to play an increasingly important role in technological development.

The sixth aspect of technology is the *social context* or organization in which technologies are developed, distributed, and employed. A division of labor in which different individuals perform different tasks or occupy different roles to accomplish common or coordinated ends characterizes technological societies. The systems we use for organizing human labor represent a kind of technology that can be applied to the most important resource of all—ourselves. Complex systems that have become more or less institutionalized can be called *social artifacts.* Examples of social artifacts include the stock market, battalions or divisions in an army, baseball teams, hospitals, schools, and corporations. In each case, human resources are organized in a particular way, according to a plan or technique involving a division of labor in which different persons occupy

different roles, and their labor is coordinated to accomplish specific sorts of goals. It is important to see that technology encompasses not only material artifacts, but also the social and organizational forms, and even the cognitive techniques that produce the material and social infrastructure of human civilization. These *invisible technologies* frequently consist of formal, mathematical, or analytical techniques—for instance, the scientific method, statistical analysis, or procedures for creating a balance sheet, and many other specific high-order thinking skills that are the content of higher education. Becoming a scientifically or technologically educated person consists mainly in the acquisition of a fairly extensive repertoire of such cognitive techniques.

The social and psychological aspects of technological systems are the least obvious but also the most important. Technology is a human social construction. This is true in an obvious and straightforward sense when we speak of large technological structures, such as bridges, buildings, or dams, which obviously came into existence only by the coordination of the activities of numerous individuals, but it is equally true in the case of the lonely amateur inventor toiling in the attic. Inventions today are rarely the result of solitary creativity, but even when they are, the resources and techniques employed and the knowledge by which they are put to use are themselves the products of prior social processes. Even the inventor's own knowledge and abilities have been shaped by his or her education in society and by the repertoire of cognitive techniques acquired through this prior education. So there is really very little, only the raw materials and the laws of nature, which have not in some way resulted from a process of social production. Even when an inventor succeeds in inventing something new, it is still unlikely to be brought into production and placed on the market unless it has some social value or is of use to other people. So all technologies must be seen as embedded in social contexts of development, deployment, and use.

To summarize this discussion, we can define technological systems as *the complex of techniques, knowledge, and resources that are employed by human beings in the creation of material and social artifacts that typically serve certain functions perceived as useful or desirable in relation to human interests in various social contexts.*

Technological Revolutions

The use of technologies to satisfy our needs is a fundamental feature of human nature. All human societies we know of, both those presently existing and those that existed hundreds of thousands of years before the dawn of civilization, were technological to some degree. For almost all of our species' evolution, we lived in small, nomadic bands whose main means of livelihood were hunting, gathering, and scavenging. But we were also toolmakers and tool-users during this long period of human evolution, and tools were the principal means by which we satisfied our physiological needs for food, warmth, and shelter.

Our hominid ancestors first began chipping stones to make simple hand tools about 2.5 million years ago. Fire was used as early as 1.5 million years ago. If *Homo sapiens sapiens* (literally, the wise human who knows he or she is wise) really is wise, it is in large part because he or she is also *Homo faber* (human maker). Early human societies were organized as hunter-gatherer groups, gathering edible plants in season and supplementing their diet with the meat or marrow of hunted animals. Quite likely, these bands of hunter-gatherers were nomadic, following animal migrations and seasonal food plant distributions. As with the present-day hunter-gatherers, ancient nomadic societies were severely limited to only those objects they could take with them and thus tended to develop simple portable technologies for hunting, gathering, cooking, transportation, and defense. Perhaps surprisingly, life does not seem to have been especially hard for hunter-gatherers. The secrets of their success seem to have been populations that did not exceed the food supply, simple and limited material needs, and the ability to move to another area when the local food supply ran out. Nomadic hunter-gatherer societies persisted into the twentieth century in such diverse environments as the African desert, the tropical rain forest, and the arctic tundra. Remoteness might be the key to avoiding

conversion to more technologically intensive ways of life. For the rest of us, our lives are deeply dependent on far-flung and complex technological systems.

About 10,000 BCE, the first great technological revolution occurred in several fertile river valleys of Asia Minor and North Africa. During the Agricultural Revolution, humans learned how to domesticate animals and to plant, grow, and harvest crops to sustain their existence. This enabled humans to give up the nomadic lifestyle and to build permanent cities. *Civilization,* which means the building of cities, originates at this time, as do morality, law, religion, recordkeeping, mathematics, astronomy, class structures, patriarchy, and other social institutions that have since come to characterize the human condition. With the adoption of settled agriculture in the fertile river valleys, the history of humankind begins. Permanent houses could be built, tools and objects could be accumulated from year to year, and so humanity began the long climb toward the collections of miscellany and junk that now clutter people's closets, attics, and garages.

Settled agriculture had many advantages and a few disadvantages. The quantity of food that could be produced per acre was much higher, so population densities could also be much greater. With permanent dwellings, creature comforts could be made that did not have to be portable. With larger numbers of people together, specialization of activities could take place, and specialists were more likely to find better ways to do things. Larger concentrations of people could better share and perpetuate knowledge and band together to cooperate on projects that smaller groups could not attempt. Thus, we see that even at this early stage of technological development, the organization of people, of information, and of accumulated resources were essential aspects of emerging technological societies.

The disadvantages of settled agriculture sprang from the fact that society had put all its eggs in one basket and had committed itself to living in one place. A settled society is prey to flood, drought, and insects. Persistent weeds must be removed from fields before they displace crops. Houses and farm implements must be maintained. Crop seeds must be gathered and sown. In short, the settled farmer has more but must work harder to maintain the improved standard of living. Irrigated agriculture is even more technologically intensive and requires more complex social organization. Large irrigation projects demand larger groups to support them and must be maintained throughout the year, not just during the growing season. Irrigated farms produce more food per acre more reliably than dry farms that rely on uncertain rainfall, but they also require more work per person fed. At the extreme are rice paddies in the river deltas of southeast China where three crops are grown per year. They are the most productive farmlands but also the most labor intensive. The only exceptions to this unfortunate trend occur on large farms in industrialized countries where energy-intensive farm machinery substitutes for human labor and chemical fertilizers maintain soil fertility.

The second great technological revolution took place many centuries later, beginning during the eighteenth century in Europe. The Industrial Revolution replaced the muscle power of animals with coal-fired steam energy, and then later, about 100 years ago, with gasoline-driven internal combustion engines. The machine age caused profound changes in economic and social relations; the number of people needed to produce food declined as the number of people engaged in factory work increased. People migrated from rural areas to cities in search of higher paying factory jobs, and new inventions such as the cotton gin, the locomotive, and the telegraph laid the groundwork for the emergence of the technological society that we live in today.

The methods a society uses to produce goods have a profound effect on what life is like in that society, both for the producers of goods and for the consumers. Prior to the industrial age, production was organized by crafts. Individual crafters designed and produced each individual product, usually guided by traditional techniques that were occasionally modified by creative innovations. The relative value of the product was largely determined by the skill of the crafter. As a result, crafters were relatively autonomous, and production units often consisted of a single crafter and several apprentices.

When the invention of the steam engine made power available on a scale never previously possible, it became feasible to concentrate larger numbers of workers in one place and to have each worker perform only a small part of the production process, resulting in a much more specialized division of labor. Even more remarkable than the increased consolidation of people was the increased concentration and specialization of knowledge. In the early twentieth century, technological experts, working under the banner of "scientific management," studied the production process, learned what each worker knew about making the product, and then ordained the perfect way to produce a given product—what each worker would do and at what pace they would do it. Each worker needed fewer skills and could be paid less per item. However, cheaper workers making larger numbers of products using specialized machinery resulted in less expensive goods. Lower prices resulted in an increased standard of living for consumers. Factory work may have become onerous, but a salary could buy more than it could previously.

In the search for increased productivity, working conditions in early factories were often harsh and dangerous. In response to the many abuses that existed, employees often battled tyrannical bosses for the right to form unions and bargain collectively, many times suffering injuries or even death for their actions. The sacrifices made in such organizing drives secured improved working conditions and raised the standard of living for millions of workers and their families. Despite the growth of the factory system, crafts did not vanish entirely. They survived in niches where no one could think of an economical way of applying mass production techniques, or to produce distinctive goods of high quality, or in some cases, because traditional cultural values prevailed over the lure of newer technologies.

The Industrial Revolution was characterized by the development of a new kind of technological system: the factory system. It required far greater concentrations of power, labor, and raw materials than either agriculture or cottage industries. It also required the development of an infrastructure for transportation of raw materials to the factory site and finished products from the site. Railroads and canals were as essential a part of the Industrial Revolution as the factories themselves. The industrial system also required a large labor force near the factory, so society's living patterns were reorganized to include factory towns and to supply them with food and other necessities. Factories were often located near sources of power or raw materials, resulting in net population shifts away from agricultural lands.

The technologies of power production were driving forces of the industrial system, and each new source of power required industrialized society to provide an accompanying infrastructure to make the system work. Water power, an ancient technology, was limited in availability and location and required relatively little additional infrastructure beyond that already available in an agricultural and craft society. Coal could be more widely distributed, but coal-powered factories were large because efficient steam engines were large. Railroads and canals began to crisscross the countryside from mine to factory to market. Monetary supply and financial services had to expand to serve a system with increasing separation between producer and consumer.

Electricity is a more flexible source of power, capable of efficiently driving both large and small machines. Electricity permitted greater decentralization of industry, supported by a network of power grids that eventually reached nearly every house and factory in the United States. Oil and gasoline revolutionized the transportation and distribution of goods. Internal combustion engines fueled by gasoline and diesel oil made it possible to use smaller vehicles, and smaller vehicles continued the trend toward decentralization. However, gas- and oil-powered vehicles required more and better roads. The U.S. Interstate Highway System (and similar systems in other industrialized countries), built in the 1960s–1980s, are society's most recent contributions to an industrial technology system based on oil.

Many people believe that since the late twentieth century we have been going through a third great technological transformation—from the *machine age* to the *information age*. Called by various names—the Third Wave or the Knowledge Revolution—it is clear that computers, communications satellites, and ubiquitous, global, high-capacity communications technologies such as the Internet are already profoundly changing the way we live, play, and work. Over the last two decades, revolutionary developments in computing and communications technology have transformed the workplace faster than some would like but slower than its visionaries had hoped for. The earliest successes of computers in industry were in payroll, inventory, and similar routine and repetitive kinds of recordkeeping. The processes automated were well understood, straightforward, and implemented exactly as they had been done before the advent of computers. In some cases, they didn't even save time or resources, but they were the wave of the future. The next stage gave decision makers more and better information to enhance efficiency, competitiveness, and other factors that are reflected in the bottom line. Computers made it possible to gather and organize data on an unprecedented scale. Also successful were the attempts to use computers to improve scheduling and reduce inventory in the production process. Goods in inventory cost money to store and contribute nothing to profit until they are used or sold. Being able to predict exactly how much of which raw materials and parts will be needed at which steps of the manufacturing process, and being able to schedule their arrival in the factory at precisely the right place at precisely the right time, was the "just-in-time" manufacturing technique developed in Japan, which led to real gains in productivity. It also made possible the kinds of geographically distributed production systems characteristic of *globalization*. In fact, without computers and rapid worldwide communications, our present-day global marketplace would not be possible.

As computers and computer programmers got better, computers became capable of doing jobs that were formerly thought to require human intelligence. Typically, computers proved capable of doing far more than most people would have predicted and far less than their most vocal proponents claimed was possible. Although the conceptually most impressive achievements were in areas such as expert systems for medical diagnosis, the biggest successes of *artificial intelligence* were in the simpler applications, now so common that we take them for granted: automatic pilot, antilocking brakes, electronic fuel injection, and most important, more flexible, general purpose tools and machines for making other products. With flexible, modifiable, reprogrammable tools, it was no longer necessary to have long production runs to amortize the set-up time of the machinery. Computer-controlled machinery could switch quickly from one task to another, and customized production runs became in some cases economically viable. Supply could now more accurately follow demand, and both idle machinery and unproductive inventory were virtually eliminated in those industries adopting the new technology. More models and options could be made available to the consumer at substantially the same or lower price, unlike the early days of the assembly line when you could get a Model A Ford in any color you liked, as long as it was black.

Even more pervasive and far-reaching in its effects on society were the computer applications where the computer itself was the medium of interaction and communication. Computer word processing began in the late 1950s and early 1960s as a curious and amusing waste of computing resources that could only be tolerated in environments where the computers were severely underutilized; basically, only the development programmers at a computer manufacturer could afford to write word processing programs to help edit their computer programs. However, in about 1980, when the Apple II computer hit the streets at a retail price of under $2,000, and its more expensive imitator, the IBM PC, quickly followed, many people could afford to do word processing on a computer, and they soon did. Typewriters and typesetters hit the trash heap in record numbers, and the writing was on the wall that the secretarial pool would someday exit as well.

The now ubiquitous Internet also arose partly by accident. During the Cold War with the USSR, the threat of a nuclear attack on the United States seemed plausible, and the Department of Defense thought it prudent to establish electronic communications links between the supercomputers at the leading scientific laboratories so as to better share these resources. Soon it dawned on some people that having a decentralized communication system would allow those laboratories that survived a nuclear attack to still communicate with one another. The nuclear attack fortunately never happened, but no one who ever had access to the Internet (then called ARPANET or DARPANET) ever went back to using "snail mail" (the U.S. Postal Service) for anything from computer programs and data files to personal notes, messages, recipes, jokes, trivia, animated cartoons, and whatever other new uses the future may bring. During the 1980s, the Internet links expanded to most universities, and professors other than just those in computer science and engineering began using e-mail for both professional and personal communications. Then, in the mid-1990s, the Internet went commercial and everybody signed up for America Online to get onto the World Wide Web.

The key technologies for an information society are those that support recordkeeping and communication. Tapes, disks, and computers are supplanting paper and printing. Telephones, modems, faxes, and communications satellites carry the data that are the lifeblood of a technological system based on information. Aware that continued growth of information technology in the United States depends on adequate infrastructure, national leaders have proposed a national, federally funded, fiber optic communications network, the information society's equivalent of the interstate highway system. Industrial societies, in general, require better education of their workers than do agricultural societies; however, more than ever before, an information society requires an adequate infrastructure of education and educated individuals. The whole system seems in danger of collapsing if there are not enough sufficiently educated techies to maintain the computers.

Technology and Science

In the modern world, technology and science often go together, with science supporting technology and technology supporting science. Although they now share a great deal, their goals have been historically quite different. Traditionally, science was viewed as an elevated activity involving "pure contemplation" and the "value-free" pursuit of knowledge, whereas technology was associated with more practical concerns and with the arts. It was not until the beginning of the modern period in the seventeenth century that there was a decisive shift, when the view that scientific knowledge was valuable because it was useful in gaining mastery over nature became prominent.

This shift was largely due to the writings of several influential philosophers, such as René Descartes and Francis Bacon. Bacon's works, particularly *Novum Organon* (1620) and *New Atlantis* (1624), are notable for their contempt for traditional speculative philosophy and their emphasis on the importance of empirical methods of investigation through which the secrets of nature could be revealed by means of judicious experiments. In 1637, Descartes wrote the *Discourse on Method,* in which he proclaimed that "it is possible to attain knowledge which is very useful in life; and that, instead of speculative philosophy which is taught in the Schools, we may find a practical philosophy by means of which, knowing the force and the action of fire, water, air, stars, the heavens, and all other bodies that environ us, as distinctly as we know the different crafts of our artisans, we can in the same way employ them in all those uses to which they are adapted, and thus render ourselves masters and possessors of nature."[4] This change in the dominant view of the nature and bases of human knowledge set the stage for the modern belief in progress, which was expressed by Bacon as the belief that "the improvement of man's mind and the improvement of his lot are one and the same thing."[5]

Despite the merger of science and technology in the modern period, there remain some significant differences between the two enterprises. Technologists primarily seek to answer the question, "How?" "How can we keep warm in the winter?" or "How can we see distant objects that are invisible to the naked eye?" Engineers seek to design and produce useful material objects and systems that will function under all expected circumstances for the planned lifetime of the product. Science, on the other hand, may be considered a form of systematic inquiry, seeking to understand the underlying laws governing the behavior of natural objects. Scientists primarily try to answer the questions "What?" and "Why?" as in "What kind of thing is this?" and "Why does it behave the way it does?" In the early stages of a science, when little was known, the immediate goal of the science was to describe and classify the phenomena of the natural world. As more things became known, the sciences began asking, "How do these things change over time and interact with each other?" Scientists sought laws and principles that would enable them to predict and explain why things in nature behave as they do.

Science and technology have a symbiotic relationship, each one helping the other. Technology needs science to predict how its objects and systems will function so that it can tell if they will work. Science supplies predictive laws that apply to these objects and systems, a perfect match. However, although the laws of science are often simple, applying them to the complex objects of technology is often anything but simple. Sometimes the engineer must experiment with the complex objects that are the building blocks of a technology to find out what will happen. Perhaps the most important contribution that science makes to technology is in the education of engineers, supplying the conceptual framework upon which they build a body of more specific and practical knowledge.

Technology makes direct and obvious contributions to the progress of science. The laboratory equipment that the scientist uses is the product of technology. The biologist would discover little without a microscope, and the particle physicist even less without an accelerator. This direction of contribution is maintained throughout most of science. At the frontiers of science, however, the scientist may need equipment that has never been built before based on principles never used before in applied contexts. The design of the Tokamak (magnetic confinement torus) to study controlled nuclear fusion in hydrogen plasmas is without a doubt the product of technology, but it is technology that can only be done by the scientists who understand and can predict the behavior of high-temperature plasmas. Still, they do not do it alone; much of the design uses established technology, and this is the domain of the engineer.

But in recent years, the lines between the role of the scientist and that of the engineer or technologist have become increasingly blurred. Much of the current research agenda is dictated by the possible practical applications of new scientific knowledge. This merging of science and technology has led some writers, such as Bruno Latour, to speak of contemporary research as *technoscience*.[6] The complex relationship that presently exists between science and technology can be exemplified in the contemporary field of biotechnology.

Genetics is the science that studies inherited characteristics. Genetic engineering, by contrast, is the application of the knowledge obtained from genetic investigations to the solution of such problems as infertility, treatments for diseases, food production, waste disposal, or the improvement of crop species. Among genetic-engineering techniques are procedures that can alter the reproductive and hereditary processes of organisms. Depending on the problem, the procedures used in genetic engineering may involve artificial insemination, cloning, in vitro fertilization, species hybridization, or molecular genetics. Recent discoveries in molecular genetics have permitted the direct manipulation of the genetic material itself by the recombinant-DNA technique. Is this a scientific discovery or a technological one? Both know-that and know-how are essential elements of modern biotechnology, and both are a part of the training of every working geneticist and genetic-engineer.

The genome of an organism is the totality of genes making up its hereditary constitution. The Human Genome Project (HGP) was designed to map the human genome, and in 1990, the U.S. National Institutes of Health and the Department of Energy created the National Center for Human Genome Research. The goal is to determine the exact location of all the genes—about 35,000 of them, plus regulatory elements—on their respective chromosomes, as well as to establish the sequence of nucleotides—estimated to be about 6 million pairs—of all human genes. The HGP has been completed ahead of schedule at an estimated cost of $3 billion. It is highly doubtful that such a "big science" project would have been funded were it not for the expectation that it would result in

new medical technologies for the treatment of diseases that currently afflict many people. Recently, patents have been granted for the production of erythropoietin, a hormone that stimulates blood-cell formation; tissue-plasminogen activator, an anticlotting agent used to treat heart attacks; and alpha-interferon, which has been found effective in treating hepatitis C.

Biotechnology also has nonmedical commercial applications. In 1980, a ruling by the U.S. Supreme Court permitted the U.S. Patent and Trademark Office to grant a patent on a genetically engineered oil-eating bacterium. The bacterium was categorized as a "nonnatural man-made microorganism." Over the following eight years, some 200 patents were granted for bacteria, viruses, and plants that had been genetically modified. In 1988, a patent was granted on a mouse strain in which the cells had been engineered to contain a cancer-predisposing gene sequence. Technically referred to as a "transgenic nonhuman eukaryotic animal," each mouse of this type can be used to test low doses of cancer-causing substances and to test the effectiveness of drugs considered as possibly offering protection against the development of cancer. In the field of agriculture, a number of plants with genetically engineered traits have been patented, including maize (corn) plants rich in the amino acid tryptophan, cotton plants resistant to weed-killing herbicides, tobacco plants resistant to various insects, and potato plants resistant to various viruses.

The trial of O. J. Simpson has brought to light another application of DNA technology—its use in identifying the assailants in violent crimes when the victims are no longer able to do so themselves. Each person, with the exception of identical twins, has a unique DNA fingerprint that can be detected by matching patterns of restriction enzyme DNA fragments. Using this technique, it is possible to extract samples of DNA from dried blood, hairs, or semen and produce a near certain match, with the DNA pattern obtained from cells of the accused. But the same technology also raises issues about personal privacy and genetic discrimination.

Each new application of biological knowledge to human reproduction has raised profound and troubling ethical questions. Already it is possible for children to be produced artificially by the use of in vitro fertilization (IVF) or gamete interfallopian transfer (GIFT). It is now possible for a child to have different genetic, gestational, and social parents, greatly complicating questions of custody. While it is still necessary to employ women's wombs in the gestational process, it may not be long before we have developed artificial wombs or incubators that will enable us to gestate mammals, such as ourselves, in an extra-uterine environment.

We already have the ability to create plants and animals in the laboratory by splicing together strands of DNA taken from different organisms. How long will it be before we start applying these same techniques to ourselves? Germ-line genetic therapies offer the promise of eliminating many dreaded genetic diseases from the human gene pool, but they also raise the specter of our playing God by redesigning the human species to suit our dominant social values. Do we really want to live in a world where prospective parents can choose whether they will have a boy or a girl and choose other characteristics such as height, body type, hair and eye color, or perhaps even intelligence and beauty? Do we really want to know what genetic diseases we are harboring? What will become of the notion of human dignity if we begin to clone ourselves, as if a person were just another artifact built according to our specifications?

Technology and Ethics

In considering the ethical issues arising from technology, it is important to distinguish clearly between the specific products of technological development, such as clocks, internal combustion engines, digital computers, respirators, and nuclear bombs, and the typical ways that people use them, or what might be termed the associated *sociotechnological practices*. The fact that a particular device or technology, is available for human use does not, by itself, imply that we ought to adopt and use that technology, nor does it tell us how the technology should or should not be used. A gun, for instance, can be used in many ways: as a paperweight, for recreational target practice, for hunting, for personal protection, or for the commission of a crime. Although the gun itself has many uses, its valence lies in the practices of use typically associated with it, which may or may not match its intended purpose. We can and do make moral judgments concerning the various sociotechnological practices associated with different products of technology. We accept some uses as morally legitimate, find others morally questionable or problematic, and we take steps to restrict or outlaw certain other uses to which these devices may be put. In some cases, such as chemical or biological weapons, whose only valence is to produce mass death and destruction, we attempt to outlaw them entirely rather than to regulate their use. Other technologies are more benign, at least apparently so, and their introduction into society generates little concern or controversy.

Ethical concerns arising from technology can be divided into four kinds. The first and most basic kind concerns questions about how traditional ethical values and norms apply in new technological contexts. Technological innovations enlarge the scope of possible human action by allowing us to do some things we could not do before (such as, perform liver transplants) and to do things we could do before in different ways (for example, reheat food in microwave ovens). Each new technology thus raises the implicit ethical questions: "Should we employ this new technique/technology?" and if so, "How should we employ this new technique/technology?" In many cases, such questions are answered easily. However, in many other cases, decisions about whether, how, and when to use particular technologies can raise difficult and troubling ethical issues about how our traditional ethical values and rules apply in new technological contexts.

Ethical problems of this first kind are particularly evident in the field of medical technology where, for instance, the development and use of the respirator has made it possible to maintain heartbeat and respiration in patients who would certainly have died if this device were not available. Now that there is the option of placing a patient on such a device to prolong life, medical practitioners are faced with the moral choice about whether, and under what circumstances, they should do so, and whether, and under what conditions, they may ethically remove a patient from this device. Should patients with terminal illnesses be placed on respirators? What criterion should be used in determining when a person has died if that person's heart can be made to beat with the aid of a machine? Should physicians honor a patient's competent request to be removed from a respirator, even if that will bring death? Who makes such decisions for patients who are not able to decide for themselves? These are only a few of the difficult questions that present themselves when a life-prolonging technology such as artificial respiration comes into being. A different set of problems of this first kind arises with respect to modern computer and communications technologies that make it much easier to collect and analyze information about individuals. In this arena, people are asking how the traditional value we place on *privacy* can be protected in the digital age.

A second kind of ethical problem arises concerning some sociotechnical practices that, although innocuous in themselves when employed by individuals, raise serious concerns when their effects are aggregated across millions of users. There is, for instance, nothing intrinsically wrong in throwing empty bottles and cans into the trash to be carted off to the nearest landfill. But when millions of American households engage in this practice on a regular basis, we find that we are wasting recyclable resources and running rapidly out of space for new landfills. Similar sorts of *aggregation problems* arise with respect to causes of air and water pollution, overfishing, suburban development, and many other cases in which the aggregate and cumulative effects of individual sociotechnical choices threaten our collective long-term well-being.

A third class of ethical problems associated with technology concerns questions of *distributive justice* and social equality. New technologies generally benefit or advantage certain groups or members of society over others, namely those who have mastery over or access to the technology first. In many cases, we think that because such advantages are earned through hard work or special knowledge, they are therefore deserved. However, in other cases, we may feel that such restricted access to some technologies gives certain individuals or groups unfair advantages over others, and we seek to extend access to everyone in the society. Public libraries, for instance, were built to ensure that everyone could obtain access to books and learning. Today, we are putting computers and Internet connections into public schools for similar reasons. Questions of social justice and equality of opportunity thus can be occasioned by technological innovation.

A fourth and final kind of ethical question raised by technology concerns the scope of modern technology's power to alter the world. In earlier and simpler times, humans had not the power to do very much to disturb the balance of nature or affect the life prospects of other species or those of future generations of human beings. But when we entered the *nuclear age,* all that changed. With nuclear weapons, we now have the power to destroy virtually all life on Earth. Nuclear waste material from our reactors will last 10,000 years, posing a potential threat to unborn generations. Even apart from nuclear technology, we have been destroying natural habitats and thereby causing the extinction of other species at an alarming rate. Emissions from our cars and factories are filling the atmosphere with carbon dioxide, and we may be causing the earth to heat up. Issues and concerns of this type raise what are perhaps the most profound ethical questions about humankind's relationship to nature through technology. Should we continue down the course set for us by Bacon and Descartes, who advised us to seek knowledge so that we could become the masters of nature, or should we change this course toward stewardship and long-term sustainability?

When we consider these sorts of questions about how the products of technology ought to be used, we are really asking questions about how people ought to behave or act. Questions about whether to use products of technology or how such products should be used are ethical questions; that is, they are questions concerning what we *ought* to do rather than about what we *can* do. Ethical questions related to technology are basically no different from other ethical questions that we ask about human conduct; in each case, we must attempt to determine which action or policy, from among a range of alternative possible actions or policies, is the one we morally or ethically ought to choose. Viewed from the standpoint of technology, broadly defined, morality, ethics, and their cousin, law, are social techniques for regulating human behavior in society. They arose in human history at about the same time when most humans gave up the nomadic lifestyle and began building the permanent settlements that we call cities. Cities require the maintenance of high levels of social cooperation based on reliable expectations that others will act as they are required to. For instance, a simple commercial transaction, in which one person buys something from another at a mutually agreed upon price, presupposes that the buyer and seller cooperate in settling on a price and in exchanging the goods and money that the deal requires. Such economic exchanges are regulated by social custom and, in modern societies, by a complex system of laws that permits the drawing up of contracts legally binding individuals to the performance of the agreement terms. Other laws, such as those that prohibit theft of private property or forbid others from committing assault, rape, and murder, are part of a social contract that we make with one another allowing us to live together in mass societies with a reasonable degree of freedom and security.

Many people are skeptical about whether there is a single, universally correct moral viewpoint. However, almost everyone believes that there is a difference between right and wrong, and most people understand that difference and can use that understanding to guide their behavior. Ethical decision making, like most other things in the modern age, is something that can be rationalized and practiced in accordance with a technique. The technique of ethical decision making consists in a conscious attempt to get a clear view of the issues, options, and arguments that present themselves in any situation calling for an ethical judgment or decision. One should identify all of the *stakeholders*— that is, all of the individuals whose interests might be affected by a decision. One should identify all possible courses of action; review all of the arguments, developing their pros and cons in terms of their potential risks and rewards for all stakeholders;

and then, only after having carefully worked through such deliberations, make a rational choice from the available options that has the strongest set of moral reasons behind it.[7]

Moral reasons are those that involve ethical principles governing notions such as fairness, justice, equality, duty, obligation, responsibility, and various kinds of rights. In most ethical decisions, such reasons contend with other nonmoral reasons for actions based on prudence or self-interest, efficiency, and economy. From the moral point of view, ethical reasons ought always override nonmoral reasons for action. Ethical decisions concerning the use of technologies involving judgments of value and obligation, responsibility and liability, and assessments of risk and benefit can arise at various levels: the personal level of individual behavior, the level of institutional or organizational policy, and the social level of public policy. As individuals, we are the consumers and users of the products of technology in our everyday lives; as workers or students, we belong to and participate in institutions or organizations whose policies and practices can affect our health and well-being; and as citizens, we all must be concerned about the ethical issues we face because of modern technology.

Techno-Optimism Versus Techno-Pessimism

Our attitudes toward technology are complex and often ambivalent. We cannot but acknowledge and credit science and technology with delivering many wonders that have improved and extended our lives, and many people believe that these same agents will continue to solve our problems in the twenty-first century. Many people are, however, disturbed by what they view as technology being out of control and see technology as a threat to our traditional ways of life, to our environment, and even to our survival as a species. These two kinds of attitudes toward technology are often referred to as *techno-optimism* and *techno-pessimism*.

Techno-optimists tend to emphasize technology's benefits; they believe that science and technology are not the cause of society's current ills; they do not believe that technology needs to be controlled or regulated; and they have faith in "technological fixes" that will solve outstanding problems. Techno-pessimists, by contrast, tend to emphasize the risks and costs of technological changes; they believe that many social ills are attributable to technology; they think that technology needs to be controlled or is incapable of being controlled; and they do not have faith in "technological fixes."[8]

Although there are some techno-pessimists around still, even some extreme Luddites and anti-technologists, the dominant view of contemporary society seems to be techno-optimism. The modern idea of scientific and technological progress continues to hold sway not only for people in the developed countries but increasingly for those in the less developed nations of the world who tend to see development largely in terms of access to more sophisticated forms of technology. But although technological development can raise the standard of living, rapid technological and social change also brings with it social dislocation, confusion, and a sense of disappointment and alienation. Part of the problem is that technology has been allowed to assume an increasingly greater role in human affairs, without there being anyone in particular who is responsible for this change. Some writers see this as a problem, whereas others see uncontrolled or free technological innovation as the source of prosperity and human progress. These different reactions reflect broader differences among individuals in their general attitudes toward technology.

Among the ideas that are being questioned by critics of technology is the very idea of *progress*. Throughout most of history, societies believed strongly in tradition, and changes were presumed to be unwelcome and probably harmful. Kings sat comfortably (or uncomfortably) on their thrones, and when they were replaced through succession or conquest by other kings, it made little difference to the quality of life of the general populace. For most people as late as 1800, life was relatively little different from Roman times. Then came the steam engine, the railroad, and the automobile. Science finally had something worthwhile to say to technology, and off they went together in

an everwidening spiral of discovery and innovation. Individual productivity exploded in factory and farm. New crop varieties and chemical fertilizers enabled fewer farmers to produce more food than ever before. New products offered unimagined comfort and convenience to everyone. Medical advances improved health and increased life span. In the industrialized world, progress was more than an idea; it was an everyday fact of life, and the cornerstone of progress was technological innovation.

But in the industrialized world, over a century of uninterrupted belief in progress was disturbed by several rude surprises starting in the 1960s. Technology could put a man on the moon, but the Cuban missile confrontation reminded the world that we were only a button's push away from global nuclear war. The miracle chemical DDT that promised to end crop damage by insects was found to accumulate in ever-larger amounts as it progressed up the food chain until eagles and peregrine falcons could no longer reproduce. DDT was making their eggshells too thin to keep from cracking. It did not take a genius to realize that humans are also high on the food chain, and DDT was hastily banned. Mountain lakes in the northeastern United States and Europe were found to be too acidic to support fish anymore, and the problem was traced back to acid rain and to automobile emissions and the exhaust of coal-burning electric power plants. Asbestos, our modern weapon against the age-old danger of fire, turned out to cause lung damage in asbestos workers and possibly in people living and working in asbestos-lined buildings. Radioactive by-products of nuclear power plants piled up, and no one could think of a foolproof way to keep them isolated and sealed for the thousands of years they were a hazard. One too many reactors melted down (Chernobyl) and the world was worried. Once the myth of technology as an unmitigated blessing was destroyed, some people began looking for hazards posed by technology with as much fervor as had previously accompanied the search for benefits. They were not disappointed; there were heavy metals in the rivers and fish, farmland soil erosion and salinization, lead paint and pipes, houses built on industrial waste dumps, health problems of people processing radioactive materials, smog, ozone holes, radon, and global climate warming. Technology helped in the search for its own defects by supplying satellite photographs and instruments that could detect trace chemicals in parts per billion.

In the less developed countries of the world, the picture was often even worse. Some improvements in health care and new products trickled down, but they were expensive and too often trickled no further than to the privileged elite of the country. When genuine improvements in farm productivity did trickle down to the masses, they fueled population growth that soon ate up the entire surplus. Industrialization proved harder to copy than expected. Industrialization would not work without infrastructure, and infrastructure could not be paid for without the surplus productivity of industrialization. Throughout most of the underdeveloped world, per capita investment is losing the race with population.

Technological Citizenship

Many potential threats to human well-being have been identified, and others no doubt soon will be. Some may be false alarms that are best ignored; others may be early warnings for which action will someday have to be taken; and some may be urgent last calls for which the optimum time to respond has already passed. Moreover, understanding these problems requires a level of scientific and technological literacy that few of our children are achieving in standard curricula. If technology is responsible for many of our present problems, technology will likely enable us to overcome them, sometimes in the narrow sense of finding a technological fix, but more often in the wider sense that the technologies of democratic decision making and economic restructuring will be used to address and resolve outstanding social problems.

Good citizenship is a kind of moral virtue: Being a good citizen implies an understanding of mutual rights and responsibilities between oneself and other citizens and between citizens and the state or government. Among our rights as citizens are the

right to receive knowledge and information about technologies and how they might affect our lives, the right to express views and opinions about the development and use of technologies, and the right to participate in decisions concerning the development and deployment of potentially harmful technologies. To exercise any of these rights, however, citizens must first accept the responsibility to educate and inform themselves about the nature of the technologies that are changing their lives and to understand the ethical and public policy dimensions of the decisions in which they claim the right to participate.[9]

Technologies are not value neutral. Techniques are not developed and used for nothing, artifacts are not created without good reason, and social labor is not divided and organized for no purpose. In each case, there are human ends and values, which stand behind and direct the technological processes. Technology itself is perceived by most people as of positive value because they understand that through technology we are able to increase our powers and capabilities and are therefore better able to satisfy our needs and desires. But most people also realize that technological innovations are seldom all for the good, and there are almost inevitably trade-offs that need to be considered. A new drug may help cure a disease, but it may also produce undesirable side effects in some patients and may in the long run promote the spread of new and more drug-resistant forms of the disease; car ownership may enable one to move about freely and comfortably, but it also entails loan payments, insurance payments, repairs, gasoline, atmospheric pollution, car accidents, and other negative side effects.

One of the main themes of this book is that when we evaluate which new technologies to develop, which to deploy, and how to deploy them, we need to consider carefully the benefits and costs and the opportunities and risks that the technologies entail. Often, doing this sort of *cost-benefit analysis* is very difficult because of the manifold aspects that need to be considered, because the costs and benefits often have no common measurement scale (if they can be measured at all), and because uncertainty exists in predicting a technology's long-term societal consequences. For instance, inventors and innovators often have no idea how their inventions and innovations will ultimately be used or what their effects will be. Gutenberg, inventor of the printing press and movable metal type, was a devout Catholic who would have been horrified to know that his invention helped to stimulate the Protestant Reformation. Edison apparently believed that the phonograph would be mainly used for recording people's last wills and testaments and would undoubtedly be amazed by today's tapes and CDs. Given enough experiences of this kind, one gets the idea that every new technology has known and expected benefits and costs, but also unknown and unforeseen benefits and costs. They sometimes even produce consequences exactly the opposite of what they were intended to produce, "revenge effects." Powerful new technologies alter the social context in which they arise; they change the structure of our interests and values, they change the ways that we think and work, and they may even change the communities where we live. Who, until recently, would have thought that the chlorofluorocarbons, which have been used for decades as refrigerants, would be eating away the ozone layer in the upper atmosphere?

Another political feature of technological change is the way that technological change produces winners and losers in society. If technology is a source of power over nature, it is also a means by which some people gain advantage over others. Every technological revolution has witnessed the competition among technologies and the eventual replacement of one technology or technological system by another. Think of what happened to blacksmiths when the automobile came along, what happened to watchmakers when the quartz-electric digital watch came along, or what has been happening to bank tellers since the introduction of ATMs. In such processes of technological change, groups and individuals whose interests and livelihoods are connected to the older technology are usually the losers, whereas those whose interests are connected to the next wave of technological innovation are the winners. However, because the directions and effects of technological change are often

unpredictable, it is difficult to tell in all cases whether any particular individual or group will come out as a winner or a loser.

Similar social phenomena are occurring today in the midst of the information and biotechnology revolutions and the economic phenomenon known as *globalization*. Although the wealthier and better educated people in society largely remain favorably disposed toward new technologies such as computers, the Internet, gene-splicing, and robots and toward the globalization of production and distribution that these technologies have made possible, others see these developments as threatening to their jobs and livelihoods, even in some cases their ways of life. New technological elites are being created in each of these fields, while at the same time other people are becoming newly unemployed.

Population and Environmental Change

There is increasing evidence that our technological society is rapidly transforming the earth's environment, and probably not for the better. Hardly a day goes by that we do not hear of global environmental problems such as deforestation, species extinction, depletion of nonrenewable resources, desertification, overpopulation, acid rain, water pollution, ozone destruction, and atmospheric warming. In part, these problems represent the long-term and largely unforeseen effects of the Industrial Revolution, but in part, they are caused by the sheer weight of human population growth and the increasing demands it places on the earth's ecosystem. The earth's human population now stands at roughly 6 billion. Demographers predict that there is likely to be a doubling of the human population to nearly 11 billion persons sometime within the next fifty years so that by the middle of the twenty-first century, we will need twice the food, twice the water, and twice the resources we use now. At the same time, most of the world's population growth is taking place in the less developed countries, while rates of resource consumption of everything from oil to personal computers are highest in the more developed countries. Given these trends, many analysts are predicting a widening gap between the "have" and the "have-not" countries, accompanied by increasingly chaotic political, economic, and social conditions in the poorer nations where the environmental stress produced by population growth is greatest. Many believe it would be naïve to think that were such social unrest to grow and spread, the industrialized nations would not be affected.

Militarism, overpopulation, social inequality, poverty, environmental pollution, species extinction, global warming, and other threats are not unrelated. The links and dependencies between them are all too obvious when we take a moment to think about them. Worldwide arms sales consume about $500 billion annually, or about the same amount as the total income of the world's poorest 2 billion people. Poverty amidst abundance breeds resentment and social unrest, which in turn fuels repression by the ruling elites, who turn to the developed nations to supply them with weapons. The industrialized societies, to provide for their own population's overheated consumption habits, are depleting the earth's natural resources and returning to the environment industrial wastes and poisons that are polluting the water, the air, and the soil. It has been estimated that the average person from a developed country has a fifty times greater impact on the environment in terms of resource consumption and pollution than does a person in a developing country. The uncontrolled growth of population in the less developed countries will place extreme strain on their already overtaxed economies and environments.

The threats we presently face all seem to share certain characteristics that distinguish them from standard threats we faced throughout most of our history. First, these threats arise not mainly from the consequences of individual acts or omissions, or from forces beyond human control, but from our own collective action. Second, they do not involve direct harms, for the most part, but rather increased risks of harm that are distributed very broadly across individuals, often without their active participation or knowledge. Third, the threats affect not only the present but also the future, often the distant, incalculable future. Fourth, they do not

threaten only humans but other animals, the natural environment, and life itself. Fifth, they are also to some degree the result of technology—they are problems that have arisen in part because of new powers given to us by technological progress, powers we have not always learned to use wisely and responsibly. Sixth, they do not affect single communities or even single nations but threaten the whole of humankind.

Our previous ethics has not prepared us to cope with threats of these kinds. Traditional ethics has focused primarily on the moral requirements concerning individual action, on the direct dealings between persons, rather than on the remote effects of our collective action. This problem is particularly important with respect to widely distributed technologies such as the internal combustion engine, where the cumulative effects of individual decisions can have a major impact on air quality, even though no single individual is responsible for the smog. But traditional moral norms deal by and large with the present and near future effects of actions of individual human beings and do not prepare us to deal with cumulative effects and statistical deaths. Traditional ethics, above all, has been anthropocentric—the entire nonhuman world has been viewed as a thing devoid of moral standing or significance except insofar as it could be bent to satisfy human purposes. We have assumed that the natural world was our enemy and did not require our care (for what could we possibly do to harm it really?), and nature was not regarded as an object of human responsibility.

In the past, we have attempted to fashion our ethical theories in terms of these assumptions. The traditional maxims of ethics such as "Love thy neighbor as thyself," "Do unto others as you would have them do unto you," and "Never treat your fellow man as a means only but always also as an end in himself" are in keeping with the individualistic, present-oriented, and anthropocentric assumptions of our ethical traditions. Even the Christian ethic of universal love, which instructs us to be our brother's keeper, does not transcend the barriers of time, and community, and species. Even more modern ethical theories such as utilitarianism and

Kantian ethics do not provide particularly good guidance when it comes to the sorts of ethical concerns raised by technology. In part, this is because they were designed to evaluate individual actions of particular moral agents. But the sociotechnological practices that comprise our collective action are made up not only of many individual choices, such as the choice to have a child, or to eat a hamburger, or to invest in a mining stock, but they are also made up of the aggregate of these individual choices plus those of organized collectivities such as corporations and governments. In most cases, the individuals, business executives, or politicians who are making the choices that add up to our collective insecurity do not intend harm, and neither they nor we consequently feel any sense of responsibility for it.

While individuals view themselves as moral agents and consider themselves bearers of responsibility in all of the roles they participate in, the collectivities to which we belong do not. The threats we face are all in part the result of this diffusion of responsibility. How then should we citizens of the earth be responding to these environmental questions? Do people in richer countries have any responsibility to help those in poorer ones? Do we, in general, have any responsibilities to future generations concerning the long-term social and environmental effects of our present economic, lifestyle, and political choices?

These are essentially political issues. Political issues are ones in which different individuals and groups within society struggle to protect and enhance their interests against other individuals and groups who have different and often conflicting interests. Politics inevitably involves conflict and compromise. In democratic societies like ours, interest groups form around particular issues and each group tries to influence the outcome of decisions that will affect many people. However, one's ability to participate politically in decision making requires that one become informed about the technology involved and its likely or expected consequences and that one actively seek to have a voice in the way decisions are made.

All too often, decisions that involve complex or unfamiliar technologies are left to the discretion of elites—scientists, engineers, policy "wonks," and corporate and government officials—even though the consequences of their decisions will usually affect the interests of others who are not themselves members of these elites. These other interested but often silent parties are sometimes called *stakeholders*. We are all stakeholders in decisions concerning technology, but not infrequently, the scientific, political, or corporate elites make decisions about these questions in ways that primarily benefit themselves at the expense of other stakeholders. It is often relatively easy for elites to "manufacture consent" for policies that they prefer by selectively sharing information about the possible risks and benefits of a particular technology policy with the other stakeholders whose interests might be adversely affected by it.[10] For instance, in the 1950s, U.S. soldiers were ordered to witness nuclear explosions and were told that there was no risk of harm due to radiation. In fact, there was a risk, and years later, many of the soldiers who participated in these tests began developing lethal cancers.

To protect citizens against such unscrupulous practices, the government has established various special agencies, such as the Food and Drug Administration (FDA), the Environmental Protection Agency (EPA), and the Occupational Safety and Health Administration (OSHA), which are mandated to act as watchdogs looking out for the interests of the public and preventing people from being exposed to unnecessary or unreasonable risks without their informed consent. However, the operations of these very agencies often become politicized to some extent because they are funded by Congress and administered by the executive branch of government.

A second line of defense are the hundreds of nongovernmental organizations (NGOs), such as Common Cause, Greenpeace, the American Civil Liberties Union, and many less known organizations, who lobby decision makers to enforce and protect the stakeholder interests they represent and produce public information that may enable citizens to more effectively protect their own interests. Such public interest groups play an important role in American politics and provide a means, in addition to the ballot, by which ordinary citizens can participate in large-scale decisions that may affect their lives for good or for ill.

However, none of these groups could be effective without the support of an informed and attentive citizenry. In democratic societies, individuals and groups are given the right to inform themselves on the issues, associate with others having similar or common interests, and participate in the political discussions that determine which laws and policies will be enacted. If we fail as individuals to exercise these rights, that is, if we shirk our responsibilities as technological citizens, it is likely that others will end up making these decisions for us, and when they do, they may not always have our best interests at heart or in mind. If we accept the responsibility to educate ourselves about the issues and to participate in the public conversations about them, then we will have some voice in how things will be decided and some control over the future directions that our technological society will take. In the last analysis, there is no way for us to escape this responsibility, living as we do at the cusp of the third millennium, for we are all, in fact, the children of invention.

NOTES

1. For a rather long, but still incomplete, list of some of humankind's most significant inventions, see the Timeline of Significant Technological Innovations.

2. Compare this definition to that found in Rudi Volti, *Society and Technological Change*, 2nd ed. (New York: St. Martin's Press, 1992), in which technology is defined as "a system based on the application of knowledge, manifested in physical objects and organizational forms, for the attainment of specific goals" (p. 6).

3. Corlann Gee Bush introduces the term *valence* to describe the way in which tools and technological systems have "a tendency to interact in similar situations in identifiable and predictable ways." The term "end" usually refers to the purpose in the mind of the designer of the artifact. Often, the end is the same as the valence, but not always. See selection I.5.

4. René Descartes, "Discourse on the Method of Rightly Conducting the Reason and Seeking for Truth in the Sciences" (1637). In *The Philosophical Works of Descartes*, Vol. I, translated by Elizabeth S. Haldane and G. R. T. Ross (Cambridge, England: Cambridge University Press, 1970), p. 119.

5. Francis Bacon, "Thoughts and Conclusions." In Benjamin Farrington (ed.), *The Philosophy of Francis Bacon* (Chicago: University of Chicago Press, 1964), p. 93.

6. See Bruno Latour, *Science in Action* (Cambridge, MA: Harvard University Press, 1987).

7. For more on ethical decision making, see C. E. Harris Jr., *Applying Moral Theories*, 4th ed. (Belmont, CA: Wadsworth, 2002).

8. The terms *techno-optimism* and *techno-pessimism* were suggested by the discussion of pessimism and optimism about technology found in Mary Tiles and Hans Oberdiek, *Living in a Technological Culture: Human Tools and Human Values* (New York: Routledge, 1995), pp. 14–31.

9. The idea of technological citizenship is based on the work of Phillip J. Frankenfeld. See especially "Technological Citizenship: A Normative Framework for Risk Studies," *Science, Technology, and Human Values*, Vol. 17, No. 4 (1992): 459–484.

10. The idea of manufacturing consent is based on the work of Noam Chomsky. See especially Noam Chomsky, "The Manufacture of Consent." In James Peck (ed.), *The Chomsky Reader* (New York: Pantheon Books, 1987), pp. 121–136.

Part I

Perspectives on Technological Society

- Historical Perspectives
- Social Perspectives
- Philosophical Perspectives

Historical Perspectives

The Great Leap Forward

Although modern DNA research and the Human Genome Project show that we are closely related to many animals in genetic terms, there appears to be a huge gap between us and other living creatures inhabiting our planet. Being able to trace the evolution of life using modern science has shed light on the different stages through which various life forms have passed. However, Jared Diamond, with his background in physiology, considers the possibility that there was a major significant event that accounts for the fact that humans became the dominant species on Earth, with so much power and influence over everything else.

A MacArthur Foundation Genius Award recipient and Pulitzer Prize–winning author, Diamond proposes that a mutation of an upright walking ape occurred around 4 million years ago, which eventually led to modern humans—us. He discusses advances in various scientific fields that have permitted new insights into how different human societies evolved and possible reasons some thrived while others languished or failed.

Tool making and hunting techniques, art, culture, and other aspects of how early protohumans lived are examined in this article. Diamond also reviews Neanderthals, *Homo erectus, Homo sapiens,* and the ways in which their developments and skills contributed to our lives today. The seminal event that Diamond feels nudged our ancestors onto a unique path will not be disclosed here; you will have to read his article to discover it. This article builds a strong case for the view that what we are today has been influenced to a large extent by our distant relatives and dispels some commonly held beliefs about them.

Focus Questions

1. What are the major developmental stages humans went through since our distant relatives diverged from chimps and gorillas? Approximately when did those stages occur?
2. What are some of the similarities and differences between Neanderthals and more modern humans discussed by Diamond?
3. What are some of the possible reasons that Cro-Magnons replaced Neanderthals as the dominant species?
4. What was the unique human capability proposed by Diamond that made the "Great Leap Forward" possible? When did this probably occur and what made it possible?

Keywords

aboriginal Australians, aesthetic sense, anatomically modern, compound tools, Cro-Magnons, cultural variation, ecological role, hominid, *Homo erectus, Homo habilis, Homo sapiens,* Ice Age, Neanderthals, protohuman

ONE CAN HARDLY BLAME nineteenth-century creationists for insisting that humans were separately created by God. After all, between us and other animal species lies the seemingly unbridgeable gulf of language, art, religion, writing, and complex machines. Small wonder, then, that to many people Darwin's theory of our evolution from apes appeared absurd.

Since Darwin's time, of course, fossilized bones of hundreds of creatures intermediate between apes and modern humans have been discovered. It is no longer possible for a reasonable person to deny that what once seemed absurd actually happened—somehow. Yet the discoveries of many missing links have only made the problem more fascinating without fully solving it. When and how did we acquire our uniquely human characteristics?

We know that our lineage arose in Africa, diverging from that of chimpanzees and gorillas sometime between 6 million and 10 million years ago. For most of the time since then we have been little more than glorified baboons. As recently as 35,000 years ago western Europe was still occupied by Neanderthals, primitive beings for whom art and progress scarcely existed. Then there was an abrupt change. Anatomically modern people appeared in Europe, and suddenly so did sculpture, musical instruments, lamps, trade, and innovation. Within a few thousand years the Neanderthals were gone.

Insofar as there was any single moment when we could be said to have become human, it was at the time of this Great Leap Forward 35,000 years ago. Only a few more dozen millennia—a trivial fraction of our 6-to-10 million-year history—were needed for us to domesticate animals, develop agriculture and metallurgy, and invent writing. It was then but a short further step to those monuments of civilization that distinguish us from all other animals—monuments such as the *Mona Lisa* and the Ninth Symphony, the Eiffel Tower and Sputnik, Dachau's ovens and the bombing of Dresden.

From "The Great Leap Forward" by Jared Diamond, *Discover Magazine,* 1989. Copyright © 1989 by Jared Diamond. Reprinted by permission of the author.

What happened at that magic moment in evolution? What made it possible, and why was it so sudden? What held back the Neanderthals, and what was their fate? Did Neanderthals and modern peoples ever meet, and if so, how did they behave toward each other? We still share 98 percent of our genes with chimps; which genes among the other 2 percent had such enormous consequences?

Understanding the Great Leap Forward isn't easy; neither is writing about it. The immediate evidence comes from technical details of preserved bones and stone tools. Archeologists' reports are full of such terms as "transverse occipital torus," "receding zygomatic arches," and "Chatelperronian backed knives." What we really want to understand—the way of life and the humanity of our various ancestors—isn't directly preserved but only inferred from those technical details. Much of the evidence is missing, and archeologists often disagree over the meaning of the evidence that has survived.

I'll emphasize those inferences rather than the technical details, and I'll speculate about the answers to those questions I just listed above. But you can form your own opinions, and they may differ from mine. This is a puzzle whose solution is still unknown.

To set the stage quickly, recall that life originated on Earth several billion years ago, the dinosaurs became extinct around 65 million years ago, and, as I mentioned, our ancestors diverged from the ancestors of chimps and gorillas between 6 and 10 million years ago. They then remained confined to Africa for millions of years.

Initially, our ancestors would have been classified as merely another species of ape, but a sequence of three changes launched them in the direction of modern humans. The first of these changes occurred by around 4 million years ago: the structure of fossilized limb bones shows that our ancestors, in contrast to gorillas and chimps, were habitually walking upright. The upright posture freed our forelimbs to do other things, among which toolmaking would eventually prove to be the most important.

The second change occurred around 3 million years ago, when our lineage split in two. As background, remember that members of two animal species living in the same area must fill different ecological roles and do not normally interbreed. For example, coyotes and wolves are obviously closely related and, until wolves were exterminated in most of the United States, lived in many of the same areas. However, wolves are larger, they usually hunt big mammals like deer and moose, and they often live in sizable packs, whereas coyotes are smaller, mainly hunt small mammals like rabbits and mice, and normally live in pairs or small groups.

Now, all modern humans unquestionably belong to the same species. Ecological differences among us are entirely a product of childhood education: it is not the case that some of us are born big and habitually hunt deer while others are born small, gather berries, and don't marry the deer hunters. And every human population living today has interbred with every other human population with which it has had extensive contact.

Three million years ago, however, there were hominid species as distinct as wolves and coyotes. On one branch of the family tree was a man-ape with a heavily built skull and very big cheek teeth, who probably ate coarse plant food; he has come to be known as *Australopithecus robustus* (the "robust southern ape"). On the other branch was a man-ape with a more lightly built skull and smaller teeth, who most likely had an omnivorous diet; he is known as *Australopithecus africanus* (the "southern ape of Africa"). Our lineage may have experienced such a radical division at least once more, at the time of the Great Leap Forward. But the description of that event will have to wait.

There is considerable disagreement over just what occurred in the next million years, but the argument I find most persuasive is that *A. africanus* evolved into the larger-brained form we call *Homo habilis* ("man the handyman").

Complicating the issue is that fossil bones often attributed to *H. habilis* differ so much in skull size and tooth size that they may actually imply another fork in our lineage yielding two distinct *habilis*-like species: *H. habilis* himself and a mysterious "Third Man." Thus, by 2 million years ago there were at least two and possibly three protohuman species.

The third and last of the big changes that began to make our ancestors more human and less apelike was the regular use of stone tools. By around 2.5 million years ago very crude stone tools appear in large numbers in areas of East Africa occupied by the protohumans. Since there were two or three protohuman species, who made the tools? Probably the light-skulled species, since both it and the tools persisted and evolved. There is, however, the intriguing possibility that at least some of our robust relatives also made tools, as recent anatomical analyses of hand bones from the Swartkrans cave in South Africa suggest. . . .

With only one human species surviving today but two or three a few million years ago, it's clear that one or two species must have become extinct. Who was our ancestor, which species ended up instead as a discard in the trash heap of evolution, and when did this shakedown occur?

The winner was the light-skulled *H. habilis*, who went on to increase in brain size and body size. By around 1.7 million years ago the differences were sufficient that anthropologists give our lineage the new name *Homo erectus* ("the man who walks upright"—*H. erectus* fossils were discovered before all the earlier ones, so anthropologists didn't realize that *H. erectus* wasn't the first protohuman to walk upright). The robust man-ape disappeared somewhat after 1.2 million yeas ago, and the Third Man (if he ever existed) must have disappeared by then also.

As for why *H. erectus* survived and *A. robustus* didn't, we can only speculate. A plausible guess is that the robust man-ape could no longer compete: *H. erectus* ate both meat and plant food, and his larger brain may have made him more efficient at getting the food on which *A. robustus* depended. It's also possible that *H. erectus* gave his robust brother a direct push into oblivion by killing him for meat.

The shakedown left *H. erectus* as the sole protohuman player on the African stage, a stage to which our closest living relatives (the chimp and gorilla) are still confined. But around one million years ago *H. erectus* began to expand his horizons. His stone tools and bones show that he reached the Near

East, then the Far East (where he is represented by the famous fossils known as Peking man and Java man) and Europe. He continued to evolve in our direction by an increase in brain size and in skull roundness. By around 500,000 years ago some of our ancestors looked sufficiently like us, and sufficiently different from earlier *H. erectus,* to be classified as our own species, *Homo sapiens* ("the wise man"), although they still had thicker skulls and brow ridges than we do today.

Was our meteoric ascent to *sapiens* status half a million years ago the brilliant climax of Earth history, when art and sophisticated technology finally burst upon our previously dull planet? Not at all: the appearance of *H. sapiens* was a non-event. The Great Leap Forward, as proclaimed by cave paintings, houses, and bows and arrows, still lay hundreds of thousands of years in the future. Stone tools continued to be the crude ones that *H. erectus* had been making for nearly a million years. The extra brain size of those early *H. sapiens* had no dramatic effect on their way of life. That whole long tenure of *H. erectus* and early *H. sapiens* outside Africa was a period of infinitesimally slow cultural change.

So what was life like during the 1.5 million years that spanned the emergence of *H. erectus* and *H. sapiens*? The only surviving tools from this period are stone implements that can, charitably, be described as very crude. Early stone tools do vary in size and shape, and archeologists have used those differences to give the tools different names, such as hand-ax, chopper, and cleaver. But these names conceal the fact that none of these early tools had a sufficiently consistent or distinctive shape to suggest any specific function. Wear marks on the tools show that they were variously used to cut meat, bone, hides, wood, and nonwoody parts of plants. But any size or shape tool seems to have been used to cut any of these things, and the categories imposed by archeologists may be little more than arbitrary divisions of a continuum of stone forms.

Negative evidence is also significant. All the early stone tools may have been held directly in the hand; they show no signs of being mounted on other materials for increased leverage, as we mount steel ax blades on wooden handles. There were no bone tools, no ropes to make nets, and no fishhooks.

What food did our early ancestors get with those crude tools, and how did they get it? To address this question, anthropology textbooks usually insert a long chapter entitled something like "Man the Hunter." The point they make is that baboons, chimps, and some other primates prey on small vertebrates only occasionally, but recently surviving Stone Age people (like Bushmen) did a lot of big-game hunting. There's no doubt that our early ancestors also ate some meat. The question is, how much meat? Did big-game hunting skills improve gradually over the past 1.5 million years, or was it only since the Great Leap Forward—a mere 35,000 years ago—that they made a large contribution to our diet?

Anthropologists routinely reply that we've long been successful big-game hunters, but in fact there is no good evidence of hunting skills until around 100,000 years ago, and it's clear that even then humans were still very ineffective hunters. So it's reasonable to assume that earlier hunters were even more ineffective.

Yet the mystique of Man the Hunter is now so rooted in us that it's hard to abandon our belief in its long-standing importance. Supposedly, big-game hunting was what induced protohuman males to cooperate with one another, develop language and big brains, join into bands, and share food. Even women were supposedly molded by big-game hunting: they suppressed the external signs of monthly ovulation that are so conspicuous in chimps, so as not to drive men into a frenzy of sexual competition and thereby spoil men's cooperation at hunting.

But studies of modern hunter gatherers, with far more effective weapons than those of early *H. sapiens,* show that most of a family's calories come from plant food gathered by women. Men catch rats and other small game never mentioned in their heroic campfire stories. Occasionally they get a large animal, which does indeed contribute significantly to protein intake. But it's only in the Arctic, where little plant food is available, that big-game hunting becomes the dominant food source. And humans didn't reach the Arctic until around 30,000 years ago.

So I would guess that big-game hunting contributed little to our food intake until after we had evolved fully modern anatomy and behavior. I doubt the usual view that hunting was the driving force behind our uniquely human brain and societies. For most of our history we were not mighty hunters but rather sophisticated baboons.

To return to our history: *H. sapiens,* you'll recall, took center stage around half a million years ago in Africa, the Near East, the Far East, and Europe. By 100,000 years ago humans had settled into at least three distinct populations occupying different parts of the Old World. These were the last truly primitive people. Let's consider among them those whose anatomy is best known, those who have become a metaphor for brutishness: the Neanderthals.

Where and when did they live? Their name comes from Germany's Neander Valley, where one of the first skeletons was discovered (in German, *thal*—nowadays spelled *tal*—means "valley"). Their geographic range extended from western Europe, through southern European Russia and the Near East, to Uzbekistan in Central Asia, near the border of Afghanistan. As to the time of their origin, that's a matter of definition, since some old skulls have characteristics anticipating later "full-blown" Neanderthals. The earliest full-blown examples date from around 130,000 years ago, and most specimens postdate 74,000 years ago. While their start is thus arbitrary, their end is abrupt: the last Neanderthals died around 32,000 years ago.

During the time that Neanderthals flourished, Europe and Asia were in the grip of the last ice age. Hence Neanderthals must have been a cold-adapted people—but only within limits. They got no farther north than southern Britain, northern Germany, Kiev, and the Caspian Sea.

Neanderthals' head anatomy was so distinctive that, even if a Neanderthal dressed in a business suit or a designer dress were to walk down the street today, all you *H. sapiens* would be staring in shock. Imagine converting a modern face to soft clay, gripping the middle of the face from the bridge of the nose to the jaws, pulling the whole

mid-face forward, and letting it harden again. You'll then have some idea of a Neanderthal's appearance. Their eyebrows rested on prominently bulging bony ridges, and their nose and jaws and teeth protruded far forward. Their eyes lay in deep sockets, sunk behind the protruding nose and brow ridges. Their foreheads were low and sloping, unlike our high vertical modern foreheads, and their lower jaws sloped back without a chin. Yet despite these startlingly primitive features, Neanderthals' brain size was nearly 10 percent greater than ours! (This does not mean they were smarter than us; they obviously weren't. Perhaps their larger brains simply weren't "wired" as well.) A dentist who examined a Neanderthal's teeth would have been in for a further shock. In adult Neanderthals front teeth were worn down on the outer surface, in a way found in no modern people. Evidently this peculiar wear pattern resulted from their using their teeth as tools, but what exactly did they do? As one possibility, they may have routinely used their teeth like a vise, as my baby sons do when they grip a milk bottle in their teeth and run around with their hands free. Alternatively, Neanderthals may have bitten hides to make leather or wood to make tools.

While a Neanderthal in a business suit or a dress would attract your attention, one in shorts or a bikini would be even more startling. Neanderthals were more heavily muscled, especially in their shoulders and neck, than all but the most avid body-builders. Their limb bones, which took the force of those big muscles contracting, had to be considerably thicker than ours to withstand the stress. Their arms and legs would have looked stubby to us, because the lower leg and forearm were relatively shorter than ours. Even their hands were much more powerful than ours; a Neanderthal's handshake would have been bone-crushing. While their average height was only around 5 feet 4 inches, their weight was at least 20 pounds more than that of a modern person of that height, and this excess was mostly in the form of lean muscle.

One other possible anatomical difference is intriguing, although its reality as well as its interpretation are quite uncertain—the fossil evidence so far simply doesn't allow a definitive answer. But a

Neanderthal woman's birth canal may have been wider than a modern woman's, permitting her baby to grow inside her to a bigger size before birth. If so, a Neanderthal pregnancy might have lasted one year, instead of nine months.

Besides their bones, our other main source of information about Neanderthals is their stone tools. Like earlier human tools, Neanderthal tools may have been simple hand-held stones not mounted on separate parts such as handles. The tools don't fall into distinct types with unique functions. There were no standardized bone tools, no bows and arrows. Some of the stone tools were undoubtedly used to make wooden tools, which rarely survive. One notable exception is a wooden thrusting spear eight feet long, found in the ribs of a long-extinct species of elephant at an archeological site in Germany. Despite that (lucky?) success, Neanderthals were probably not very good at big-game hunting; even anatomically more modern people living in Africa at the same time as the Neanderthals were undistinguished as hunters.

If you say "Neanderthal" to friends and ask for their first association, you'll probably get back the answer "caveman." While most excavated Neanderthal remains do come from caves, that's surely an artifact of preservation, since open-air sites would be eroded much more quickly. Neanderthals must have constructed some type of shelter against the cold climate in which they lived, but those shelters must have been crude. All that remain are postholes and a few piles of stones.

The list of quintessentially modern human things that Neanderthals lacked is a long one. They left no unequivocal art objects. They must have worn some clothing in their cold environment, but that clothing had to be crude, since they lacked needles and other evidence of sewing. They evidently had no boats, as no Neanderthal remains are known from Mediterranean islands nor even from North Africa, just eight miles across the Strait of Gibraltar from Neanderthal-populated Spain. There was no long-distance overland trade: Neanderthal tools are made of stones available within a few miles of the site.

Today we take cultural differences among people inhabiting different areas for granted. Every modern human population has its characteristic house style, implements, and art. If you were shown chopsticks, a Schlitz beer bottle, and a blowgun and asked to associate one object each with China, Milwaukee, and Borneo, you'd have no trouble giving the right answers. No such cultural variation is apparent for Neanderthals, whose tools look much the same no matter where they come from.

We also take cultural progress with time for granted. It is obvious to us that the wares from a Roman villa, a medieval castle, and a Manhattan apartment circa 1988 should differ. In the 1990s my sons will look with astonishment at the slide rule I used throughout the 1950s. But Neanderthal tools from 100,000 and 40,000 years ago look essentially the same. In short, Neanderthal tools had no variation in time or space to suggest that most human of characteristics, *innovation*.

What we consider old age must also have been rare among Neanderthals. Their skeletons make clear that adults might live to their thirties or early forties but not beyond 45. If we lacked writing and if none of us lived past 45, just think how the ability of our society to accumulate and transmit information would suffer.

But despite all these subhuman qualities, there are three respects in which we can relate to Neanderthals' humanity. They were the first people to leave conclusive evidence of fire's regular, everyday use: nearly all well-preserved Neanderthal caves have small areas of ash and charcoal indicating a simple fireplace. Neanderthals were also the first people who regularly buried their dead, though whether this implies religion is a matter of pure speculation. Finally, they regularly took care of their sick and aged. Most skeletons of older Neanderthals show signs of severe impairment, such as withered arms, healed but incapacitating broken bones, tooth loss, and severe osteoarthritis. Only care by young Neanderthals could have enabled such older folks to stay alive to the point of such incapacitation. After my litany of what Neanderthals lacked, we've finally found something that lets us feel a spark of kindred spirit in these strange creatures of the Ice Age—human, and yet not really human.

Did Neanderthals belong to the same species as we do? That depends on whether we would have mated and reared a child with a Neanderthal man or woman, given the opportunity. Science fiction novels love to imagine the scenario. You remember the blurb on a pulpy back cover: "A team of explorers stumbles on a steep-walled valley in the center of deepest Africa, a valley that time forgot. In this valley they find a tribe of incredibly primitive people, living in ways that our Stone Age ancestors discarded thousands of years ago. Are they the same species as us?" Naturally, there's only one way to find out, but who among the intrepid explorers— male explorers, of course—can bring himself to make the test? At this point one of the bone-chewing cavewomen is described as beautiful and sexy in a primitively erotic way, so that readers will find the brave explorer's dilemma believable: Does he or doesn't he have sex with her?

Believe it or not, something like that experiment actually took place. It happened repeatedly around 35,000 years ago, around the time of the Great Leap Forward. But you'll have to be patient just a little while longer.

Remember, the Neanderthals of Europe and western Asia were just one of at least three human populations occupying different parts of the Old World around 100,000 years ago. A few fossils from eastern Asia suffice to show that people there differed from Neanderthals as well as from us moderns, but too few have been found to describe these Asians in more detail. The best characterized contemporaries of the Neanderthals are those from Africa, some of whom were almost modern in their skull anatomy. Does this mean that, 100,000 years ago in Africa, we have at last arrived at the Great Leap Forward?

Surprisingly, the answer is still no. The stone tools of these modern-looking Africans were very similar to those of the non-modern-looking Neanderthals, so we refer to them as Middle Stone Age Africans. They still lacked standardized bone tools, bows and arrows, art, and cultural variation. Despite their mostly modern bodies, these Africans were still missing something needed to endow them with modern behavior.

Some South African caves occupied around 100,000 years ago provide us with the first point in human evolution for which we have detailed information about what people were eating. Among the bones found in the caves are many seals and penguins, as well as shellfish such as limpets; Middle Stone Age Africans are the first people for whom there is even a hint that they exploited the seashore. However, the caves contain very few remains of fish or flying birds, undoubtedly because people still lacked fishhooks and nets.

The mammal bones from the caves include those of quite a few medium-size species, predominant among which are those of the eland, an antelope species. Eland bones in the caves represent animals of all ages, as if people had somehow managed to capture a whole herd and kill every individual. The secret to the hunters' success is most likely that eland are rather tame and easy to drive in herds. Probably the hunters occasionally managed to drive a whole herd over a cliff: that would explain why the distribution of eland ages among the cave kills is like that in a living herd. In contrast, more dangerous prey such as Cape buffalo, pigs, elephants, and rhinos yield a very different picture. Buffalo bones in the caves are mostly of very young or very old individuals, while pigs, elephants, and rhinos are virtually unrepresented.

So Middle Stone Age Africans can be considered big-game hunters, but just barely. They either avoided dangerous species entirely or confined themselves to weak old animals or babies. Those choices reflect prudence: their weapons were still spears for thrusting rather than bows and arrows, and—along with drinking a strychnine cocktail— poking an adult rhino or Cape buffalo with a spear ranks as one of the most effective means of suicide that I know. As with earlier peoples and modern Stone Age hunters, I suspect that plants and small game made up most of the diet of these not-so-great hunters. They were definitely more effective than baboons, but not up to the skill of modern Bushmen and Pygmies.

Thus, the scene that the human world presented from around 130,000 years ago to somewhat before 50,000 years ago was this: Northern Europe,

Siberia, Australia, and the whole New World were still empty of people. In the rest of Europe and western Asia lived the Neanderthals; in Africa, people increasingly like us in anatomy; and in eastern Asia, people unlike either the Neanderthals or Africans but known from only a few bones. All three populations were still primitive in their tools, behavior, and limited innovativeness. The stage was set for the Great Leap Forward. Which among these three contemporary populations would take that leap?

The evidence for an abrupt change—at last!—is clearest in France and Spain, in the late Ice Age around 35,000 years ago. Where there had previously been Neanderthals, anatomically fully modern people (often known as Cro-Magnons, from the French site where their bones were first identified) now appear. Were one of those gentlemen or ladies to stroll down the Champs-Elysées in modern attire, he or she would not stand out from the Parisian crowds in any way. Cro-Magnons' tools are as dramatic as their skeletons; they are far more diverse in form and obvious in function than any in the earlier archeological record. They suggest that modern anatomy had at last been joined by modern innovative behavior.

Many of the tools continue to be of stone, but they are now made from thin blades struck off a larger stone, thereby yielding roughly ten times more cutting edge from a given quantity of raw stone. Standardized bone and antler tools appear for the first time. So do unequivocal compound tools of several parts tied or glued together, such as spear points set in shafts or ax heads hafted to handles. Tools fall into many distinct categories whose function is often obvious, such as needles, awls, and mortars and pestles. Rope, used in nets or snares, accounts for the frequent bones of foxes, weasels, and rabbits at Cro-Magnon sites. Rope, fishhooks, and net sinkers explain the bones of fish and flying birds at contemporary South African sites.

Sophisticated weapons for killing dangerous animals at a distance now appear also—weapons such as barbed harpoons, darts, spear-throwers, and bows and arrows. South African caves now yield bones of such vicious prey as adult Cape buffalo and pigs, while European caves are full of bones of bison, elk, reindeer, horse, and ibex.

Several types of evidence testify to the effectiveness of late Ice Age people as big-game hunters. Bagging some of these animals must have required communal hunting methods based on detailed knowledge of each species' behavior. And Cro-Magnon sites are much more numerous than those of earlier Neanderthals or Middle Stone Age Africans, implying more success at obtaining food. Moreover, numerous species of big animals that had survived many previous ice ages became extinct toward the end of the last ice age, suggesting that they were exterminated by human hunters' new skills. Likely victims include Europe's woolly rhino and giant deer, southern Africa's giant buffalo and giant Cape horse, and—once improved technology allowed humans to occupy new environments— the mammoths of North America and Australia's giant kangaroos.

Australia was first reached by humans around 50,000 years ago, which implies the existence of watercraft capable of crossing the 60 miles from eastern Indonesia. The occupation of northern Russia and Siberia by at least 20,000 years ago depended on many advances: tailored clothing, as evidenced by eyed needles, cave paintings of parkas, and grave ornaments marking outlines of shirts and trousers; warm furs, indicated by fox and wolf skeletons minus the paws (removed in skinning and found in a separate pile); elaborate houses (marked by postholes, pavements, and walls of mammoth bones) with elaborate fireplaces; and stone lamps to hold animal fat and light the long Arctic nights. The occupation of Siberia in turn led to the occupation of North America and South America around 11,000 years ago.

Whereas Neanderthals obtained their raw materials within a few miles of home, Cro-Magnons and their contemporaries throughout Europe practiced long-distance trade, not only for raw materials for tools but also for "useless" ornaments. Tools of obsidian, jasper, and flint are found hundreds of miles from where those stones were quarried. Baltic amber reached southeast Europe, while

Mediterranean shells were carried to inland parts of France, Spain, and the Ukraine.

The evident aesthetic sense reflected in late Ice Age trade relates to the achievements for which we most admire the Cro-Magnons: their art. Best known are the rock paintings from caves like Lascaux, with stunning polychrome depictions of now-extinct animals. But equally impressive are the bas-reliefs, necklaces and pendants, fired-clay sculptures, Venus figurines of women with enormous breasts and buttocks, and musical instruments ranging from flutes to rattles.

Unlike Neanderthals, few of whom lived past the age of 40, some Cro-Magnons survived to 60. Those additional 20 years probably played a big role in Cro-Magnon success. Accustomed as we are to getting our information from the printed page or television, we find it hard to appreciate how important even just one or two old people are in preliterate society. When I visited Rennell Island in the Solomons in 1976, for example, many islanders told me what wild fruits were good to eat, but only one old man could tell me what other wild fruits could be eaten in an emergency to avoid starvation. He remembered that information from a cyclone that had hit Rennell around 1905, destroying gardens and reducing his people to a state of desperation. One such person can spell the difference between death and survival for the whole society.

I've described the Great Leap Forward as if all those advances in tools and art appeared simultaneously 35,000 years ago. In fact, different innovations appeared at different times: spear-throwers appeared before harpoons, beads and pendants appeared before cave paintings. I've also described the Great Leap Forward as if it were the same everywhere, but it wasn't. Among late Ice Age Africans, Ukrainians, and French, only the Africans made beads out of ostrich eggs, only the Ukrainians built houses out of mammoth bones, and only the French painted woolly rhinos on cave walls.

These variations of culture in time and space are totally unlike the unchanging monolithic Neanderthal culture. They constitute the most important innovation that came with the Great Leap Forward: namely, the capacity for innovation itself. To

us innovation is utterly natural. To Neanderthals it was evidently unthinkable.

Despite our instant sympathy with Cro-Magnon art, their tools and hunter-gatherer life make it hard for us to view them as other than primitive. Stone tools evoke cartoons of club-waving cavemen uttering grunts as they drag women off to their cave. But we can form a more accurate impression of Cro-Magnons if we imagine what future archeologists will conclude after excavating a New Guinea village site from as recently as the 1950s. The archeologists will find a few simple types of stone axes. Nearly all other material possessions were made of wood and will have perished. Nothing will remain of the multistory houses, drums and flutes, outrigger canoes, and world-quality painted sculpture. There will be no trace of the village's complex language, songs, social relationships, and knowledge of the natural world.

New Guinea material culture was until recently "primitive" (Stone Age) for historical reasons, but New Guineans are fully modern humans. New Guineans whose fathers lived in the Stone Age now pilot airplanes, operate computers, and govern a modern state. If we could carry ourselves back 35,000 years in a time machine, I expect that we would find Cro-Magnons to be equally modern people, capable of learning to fly a plane. They made stone and bone tools only because that's all they had the opportunity to learn how to make.

It used to be argued that Neanderthals evolved into Cro-Magnons within Europe. That possibility now seems increasingly unlikely. The last Neanderthal skeletons from 35,000 to 32,000 years ago were still full-blown Neanderthals, while the first Cro-Magnons appearing in Europe at the same time were already anatomically fully modern. Since anatomically modern people were already present in Africa and the Near East tens of thousands of years earlier, it seems much more likely that such people invaded Europe rather than evolved there.

What happened when invading Cro-Magnons met the resident Neanderthals? We can be certain only of the result: within a few thousand years no more Neanderthals. The conclusion seems to me inescapable that Cro-Magnon arrival somehow caused Neanderthal extinction. Yet many anthropologists recoil at this suggestion of genocide and invoke environmental changes instead—most notably, the severe Ice Age climate. In fact, Neanderthals thrived during the Ice Age and suddenly disappeared 42,000 years after its start and 20,000 years before its end.

My guess is that events in Europe at the time of the Great Leap Forward were similar to events that have occurred repeatedly in the modern world, whenever a numerous people with more advanced technology invades the lands of a much less numerous people with less advanced technology. For instance, when European colonists invaded North America, most North American Indians proceeded to die of introduced epidemics; most of the survivors were killed outright or driven off their land; some adopted European technology (horses and guns) and resisted for some time; and many of those remaining were pushed onto lands the invaders did not want, or else intermarried with them. The displacement of aboriginal Australians by European colonists, and of southern African San populations (Bushmen) by invading Iron Age Bantu speakers, followed a similar course.

By analogy, I suspect that Cro-Magnon diseases, murders, and displacements did in the Neanderthals. It may at first seem paradoxical that Cro-Magnons prevailed over the far more muscular Neanderthals, but weaponry rather than strength would have been decisive. Similarly, humans are now threatening to exterminate gorillas in central Africa, rather than vice versa. People with huge muscles require lots of food, and they thereby gain no advantage if less-muscular people can use tools to do the same work.

Some Neanderthals may have learned Cro-Magnon ways and resisted for a while. This is the only sense I can make of a puzzling culture called the Chatelperronian, which coexisted in western Europe along with a typical Cro-Magnon culture (the so-called Aurignacian culture) for a short time after Cro-Magnons arrived. Chatelperronian stone tools are a mixture of typical Neanderthal and Cro-Magnon tools, but the bone tools and art typical of Cro-Magnons are usually lacking. The identity of the people who produced Chatelperronian culture was debated by archeologists until a skeleton unearthed with Chatelperronian artifacts at Saint-Césaire in France proved to be Neanderthal. Perhaps, then, some Neanderthals managed to master some Cro-Magnon tools and hold out longer than their fellows.

What remains unclear is the outcome of the interbreeding experiment posed in science fiction novels. Did some invading Cro-Magnon men mate with some Neanderthal women? No skeletons that could reasonably be considered Neanderthal-Cro-Magnon hybrids are known. If Neanderthal behavior was as relatively rudimentary and Neanderthal anatomy as distinctive as I suspect, few Cro-Magnons may have wanted to mate with Neanderthals. And if Neanderthal women were geared for a 12-month pregnancy, a hybrid fetus might not have survived. My inclination is to take the negative evidence at face value, to accept that hybridization occurred rarely if ever, and to doubt that any living people carry any Neanderthal genes.

So much for the Great Leap Forward in western Europe. The replacement of Neanderthals by modern people occurred somewhat earlier in eastern Europe, and still earlier in the Near East, where possession of the same area apparently shifted back and forth between Neanderthals and modern people from 90,000 to 60,000 years ago. The slowness of the transition in the Near East, compared with its speed in western Europe, suggests that the anatomically modern people living around the Near East before 60,000 years ago had not yet developed the modern behavior that ultimately let them drive out the Neanderthals.

Thus, we have a tentative picture of anatomically modern people arising in Africa over 100,000 years ago, but initially making the same tools as Neanderthals and having no advantage over them. By perhaps 60,000 years ago, some magic twist of behavior had been added to the modern anatomy. That twist (of which more in a moment) produced innovative, fully modern people who proceeded to spread westward into Europe, quickly supplanting the Neanderthals. Presumably, they also spread east into Asia and Indonesia, supplanting the earlier people there of whom we know little. Some anthropologists think that skull remains of those earlier Asians and Indonesians show traits recognizable in modern Asians and aboriginal Australians. If so, the invading moderns may not have exterminated the original Asians without issue, as they did the Neanderthals, but instead interbred with them.

Two million years ago, several protohuman lineages existed side-by-side until a shakedown left only one. It now appears that a similar shakedown occurred within the last 60,000 years and that all of us today are descended from the winner of that shakedown. What was the Magic Twist that helped our ancestor to win?

The question poses an archeological puzzle without an accepted answer. You can speculate about the answer as well as I can. To help you, let me review the pieces of the puzzle: Some groups of humans who lived in Africa and the Near East over 60,000 years ago were quite modern in their anatomy, as far as can be judged from their skeletons. But they were not modern in their behavior. They continued to make Neanderthal-like tools and to lack innovation. The Magic Twist that produced the Great Leap Forward doesn't show up in fossil skeletons.

There's another way to restate that puzzle. Remember that we share 98 percent of our genes with chimpanzees. The Africans making Neanderthal-like tools just before the Great Leap Forward had covered almost all of the remaining genetic distance from chimps to us, to judge from their skeletons. Perhaps they shared 99.9 percent of their genes with us. Their brains were as large as ours, and Neanderthals' brains were even slightly larger. The Magic Twist may have been a change in only 0.1 percent of our genes. What tiny change in genes could have had such enormous consequences?

Like some others who have pondered this question, I can think of only one plausible answer: the anatomical basis for spoken complex language. Chimpanzees, gorillas, and even monkeys are capable of symbolic communication not dependent on spoken words. Both chimpanzees and gorillas have been taught to communicate by means of sign language, and chimpanzees have learned to communicate via the keys of a large computer-controlled console. Individual apes have thus mastered "vocabularies" of hundreds of symbols. While scientists argue over the extent to which such communication resembles human language, there is little doubt that it constitutes a form of symbolic communication. That is, a particular sign or computer key symbolizes a particular something else.

Primates can use as symbols not just signs and computer keys but also sounds. Wild vervet monkeys, for example, have a natural form of symbolic communication based on grunts, with slightly different grunts to mean *leopard, eagle,* and *snake.* A month-old chimpanzee named Viki, adopted by a psychologist and his wife and reared virtually as their daughter, learned to "say" approximations of four words: *papa, mama, cut,* and *up.* (The chimp breathed rather than spoke the words.) Given this capability, why have apes not gone on to develop more complex natural languages of their own?

The answer seems to involve the structure of the larynx, tongue, and associated muscles that give us fine control over spoken sounds. Like a Swiss watch, our vocal tract depends on the precise functioning of many parts. Chimps are thought to be physically incapable of producing several of the commonest vowels. If we too were limited to just a few vowels and consonants, our own vocabulary would be greatly reduced. Thus, the Magic Twist may have been some modifications of the protohuman vocal tract to give us finer control and permit formation of a much greater variety of sounds. Such fine modifications of muscles need not be detectable in fossil skulls.

It's easy to appreciate how a tiny change in anatomy resulting in capacity for speech would produce a huge change in behavior. With language, it takes only a few seconds to communicate the message, "Turn sharp right at the fourth tree and drive the male antelope toward the reddish boulder, where I'll hide to spear it." Without language, that message could not be communicated at all. Without language, two protohumans could not brainstorm together about how to devise a better tool or about what a cave painting might mean. Without language, even one protohuman would have had difficulty thinking out for himself or herself how to devise a better tool.

I don't suggest that the Great Leap Forward began as soon as the mutations for altered tongue and larynx anatomy arose. Given the right anatomy, it must have taken humans thousands of years to perfect the structure of language as we know it—to hit on the concepts of word order and case endings and tenses, and to develop vocabulary. But if the Magic Twist did consist of changes in our vocal tract that permitted fine control of sounds, then the capacity for innovation that constitutes the Great Leap Forward would follow eventually. It was the spoken word that made us free.

This interpretation seems to me to account for the lack of evidence for Neanderthal-Cro-Magnon hybrids. Speech is of overwhelming importance in the relations between men and women and their children. That's not to deny that mute or deaf people learn to function well in our culture, but they do so by learning to find alternatives for an existing spoken language. If Neanderthal language was much simpler than ours or nonexistent, it's not surprising that Cro-Magnons didn't choose to associate with Neanderthals.

I've argued that we were fully modern in anatomy and behavior and language by 35,000 years ago and that a Cro-Magnon could have been taught to fly an airplane. If so, why did it take so long after the Great Leap Forward for us to invent writing and build the Parthenon? The answer may be similar to the explanation why the Romans, great engineers that they were, didn't build atomic bombs.

To reach the point of building an A-bomb required 2,000 years of technological advances beyond Roman levels, such as the invention of gunpowder and calculus, the development of atomic theory, and the isolation of uranium. Similarly, writing and the Parthenon depended on tens of thousands of years of cumulative developments after the Great Leap Forward—developments that included, among many others, the domestication of plants and animals.

Until the Great Leap Forward, human culture developed at a snail's pace for millions of years. That pace was dictated by the slowness of genetic change. After the Great Leap Forward, cultural development no longer depended on genetic change. Despite negligible changes in our anatomy, there has been far more cultural evolution in the past 35,000 years than in the millions of years before. Had a visitor from outer space come to Earth before the Great Leap Forward, humans would not have stood out as unique among the world's species. At most, we might have been mentioned along with beavers, bowerbirds, and army ants as examples of species with curious behavior. Who could have foreseen the Magic Twist that would soon make us the first species, in the history of life on Earth, capable of destroying all life?

DAVID LANDES   I.2

The Invention of Invention

In his book *The Wealth and Poverty of Nations,* David Landes, Coolidge Professor of History and Professor of Economics Emeritus at Harvard University, explores the role of technology in determining the economic status of three major world regions, Europe, the Middle East, and the Orient, during the second millennium.

From his perspective as both a historian and economist, he identifies five major technologies that were highly developed and refined during the Middle Ages, although their beginnings predate this era. Landes proposes that various social and cultural conditions in those three societies encouraged the refinement of these and other technologies. In turn, these technologies had major impacts on the lives of citizens and also prompted subsequent technological advances.

As the title of this selection suggests, Landes believes that how a society encourages and supports the development of technology determines the power and influence it achieves as well as its sustainability. Although technological innovation is not the only driver of social and economic change, its importance cannot be discounted.

Focus Questions

1. Discuss ways in which this article suggests that technology challenges authority and aids in the redistribution of the power held by a few to a greater number of individuals. What long-range impacts did these technologies have, and what might have happened if such changes did not occur?
2. What factors not related to technology were at work in the societies examined in this article? Discuss how they either facilitated further technological development or were an impediment to it.
3. How does the focus of this article on five unique technological innovations compare with Cowan's view of technological systems in section I.3? Explain the differences and similarities in their perspectives by examining selected technologies from each historical period.
4. In what ways do the points made by Landes in this article compare with issues presented in the Globalization, Economics, and Human Rights section? Do the cultural factors discussed by Landes still operate in our present globalized world? Explain.

Keywords

division of labor, ecclesiastical authority, free market, institutionalized property rights, inventive society, key-machine, productivity, religious zealot, replication, secular authority, theocracy

WHEN ADAM SMITH CAME to write about these things in the eighteenth century, he pointed out that division of labor and widening of the market encourage technological innovation. This in fact is exactly what happened in the Europe of the Middle Ages—one of the most inventive societies that history had known. Some may be surprised: for a long time one saw these centuries as a dark interlude between the grandeur of Rome and the brilliance of the Renaissance. That cliché no longer holds in matters technological.[1]

A few examples:

1. *The water wheel.* It had been known to the Romans, who began to do interesting things with

it during the last century of the empire, when the conquests were over and the supply of slaves had shrunk almost to nothing. By then it was too late; order and trade were breaking down. The device may well have survived on Church estates, where it freed clerics for prayer. In any event, it was revived in the tenth and eleventh centuries, multiplying easily in a region of wide rainfall and ubiquitous watercourses. In England, that peripheral, backward island, the Domesday census of 1086 showed some 5,600 of these mills; the Continent had many more.

Even more impressive is the way waterpower technique advanced. Millwrights increased pressure and efficiency by building dams and ponds and by lining the wheels up to utilize the diminishing energy for a variety of tasks, beginning with those that needed the most power, and descending. At the same time, the invention or improvement of accessory devices—cranks, toothed gears—made it possible to use the power at a distance, change its direction, convert it from rotary to reciprocating motion, and apply it to an increasing variety of tasks: hence not only grinding grain, but fulling (pounding) cloth, thereby transforming the woolen manufacture; hammering metal; rolling and drawing sheet metal and wire; mashing hops for beer; pulping rags for paper. "Paper, which was manufactured by hand and foot for a thousand years or so following its invention by the Chinese and adoption by the Arabs, was manufactured mechanically as soon as it reached medieval Europe in the thirteenth century. . . . Paper had traveled nearly halfway around the world, but no culture or civilization on its route had tried to mechanize its manufacture."[2] Europe, as nowhere else, was a power-based civilization.

2. *Eyeglasses*. A seemingly banal affair, the kind of thing that appears so commonplace as to be trivial. And yet the invention of spectacles more than doubled the working life of skilled craftsmen, especially those who did fine jobs: scribes (crucial before the invention of printing) and readers, instrument and toolmakers, close weavers, metal-workers.

The problem is biological: because the crystalline lens of the human eye hardens around the age of forty, it produces a condition similar to far-sightedness (actually presbyopia). The eye can no longer focus on close objects. But around the age of forty, a medieval craftsman could reasonably expect to live and work another twenty years, the best years of his working life . . . if he could see well enough. Eyeglasses solved the problem.

We think we know where and when the first spectacles appeared. Crude magnifying glasses and crystals (*lapides ad legendum*) had been found earlier and used for reading.[3] The trick was to improve them so as to reduce distortion and connect a pair into a wearable device, thus leaving the hands free. This apparently first happened in Pisa toward the end of the thirteenth century. We have a contemporary witness (1306) who says he knew the inventor:

Not all the arts [in the sense of arts and crafts] have been found; we shall never see an end of finding them. Every day one could discover a new art. . . . It is not twenty years since there was

discovered the art of making spectacles that help one to see well, an art that is one of the best and most necessary in the world. And that is such a short time ago that a new art that never before existed was invented. . . . I myself saw the man who discovered and practiced it and I talked with him.[4]

These convex lenses were obviously not uniform or of what we would call prescription quality. But here medieval optical technology, however primitive, was saved by the nature of the difficulty: the lenses to correct presbyopia do not have to be extremely accurate. Their function is primarily to magnify, and although some magnify more than others, just about any and all will help the user. This is why people will occasionally borrow glasses in a restaurant to read the menu, and why five-and-dime stores can put out boxes of such spectacles for sale. The buyer simply tries a few and picks the most suitable. Myopes (short-sighted people) cannot do that.

That was the beginning. By the middle of the fifteenth century, Italy, particularly Florence and Venice, was making thousands of spectacles, fitted with concave as well as convex lenses, for myopes as well as presbyopes. Also, the Florentines at least (and presumably others) understood that visual acuity declines with age and so made the convex lenses in five-year strengths and the concave in two, enabling users to buy in batches and change with time.

Eyeglasses made it possible to do fine work and use fine instruments. But also the converse: eyeglasses encouraged the invention of fine instruments, indeed pushed Europe in a direction found nowhere else. The Muslims knew the astrolabe, but that was it. The Europeans went on to invent gauges, micrometers, fine wheel cutters—a battery of tools linked to precision measurement and control. They thereby laid the basis for articulated machines with fitted parts.

Close work: when other civilizations did it, they did it by long habituation. The skill was in the hand, not the eye-and-tool. They achieved remarkable results, but no piece was like any other; whereas Europe was already moving toward replication—batch and then mass production. This knowledge of lenses, moreover, was a school for further optical advances, and not only in Italy. Both telescope and microscope were invented in the Low Countries around 1600 and spread quickly from there.

Europe enjoyed a monopoly of corrective lenses for three to four hundred years. In effect they doubled the skilled craft workforce, and more than doubled it if one takes into account the value of experience.[5]

3. *The mechanical clock.* Another banality, so commonplace that we take it for granted. Yet Lewis Mumford quite correctly called it "the key-machine."[6]

Before the invention of this machine, people told time by sun (shadow sticks or dials) and water clocks. Sun clocks worked of course only on clear days; water clocks misbehaved when the temperature fell toward freezing, to say nothing of long-run drift as a result of sedimentation and clogging. Both of these devices served reasonably well in sunny climes; but north of the Alps one can go weeks without seeing the sun, while temperatures vary not only seasonally but from day to night.

Medieval Europe gave new importance to reliable time. The Church first, with its seven daily prayer offices, one of which, matins, was in spite of its name a nocturnal rite and required an alarm arrangement to wake clerics before dawn. (Hence our children's round, *Frère Jacques:* Brother Jacques has overslept and failed to sound the bells for matins.)* And then the new cities and towns had their temporal servitudes. Squeezed by their walls, they had to know and order time in order to organize collective activity and ration space. They set a time to wake, to go to work, to open the market, close the market, leave work, and finally a time to put out fires (*couvre-feu* gives us our word "curfew") and go to sleep.

All of this was compatible with the older devices so long as there was only one authoritative timekeeper; but with urban growth and the multiplication of time signals, discrepancy brought discord and strife. Society needed a more dependable

instrument of time measurement and found it in the mechanical clock.

We do not know who invented this machine or where. It seems to have appeared in Italy and England (perhaps simultaneous invention) in the last quarter of the thirteenth century. Once known, it spread rapidly, driving out the water clocks; but not solar dials, which were needed to check the new machines against the timekeeper of last resort. These early versions were rudimentary, inaccurate, and prone to breakdown—so much so that it paid to buy a clockmaker along with the clock.

Ironically, the new machine tended to undermine ecclesiastical authority. Although Church ritual had sustained an interest in timekeeping throughout the centuries of urban collapse that followed the fall of Rome, Church time was nature's time. Day and night were divided into the same number of parts, so that except at the equinoxes, day and night hours were unequal; and then of course the length of these hours varied with the seasons. But the mechanical clock kept equal hours, and this implied a new time reckoning. The Church resisted, not coming over to the new hours for about a century. From the start, however, the towns and cities took equal hours as their standard, and the public clocks installed in the towers and belfries of town halls and market squares became the very symbol of a new, secular municipal authority. Every town wanted one; conquerors seized them as specially precious spoils of war; tourists came to see and hear these machines the way they made pilgrimages to sacred relics. New times, new customs.

The clock was the greatest achievement of medieval mechanical ingenuity. Revolutionary in conception, it was more radically new than its makers knew. This was the first example of a digital as opposed to an analog device: it counted a regular, repeating sequence of discrete actions (the swings of an oscillating controller) rather than tracked continuous, regular motion such as the moving shadow of a sundial or the flow of water. Today we know that such a repeating frequency can be more regular than any continuous phenomenon, and just about all high-precision devices are now based on the digital principle. But no one could have known that in the thirteenth century, which thought that

---

* The English and German versions of the verse (and maybe others) traduce the meaning by saying that "morning bells are ringing." The point is, they are not ringing.

because time was continuous, it ought to be tracked and measured by some other continuity.

The mechanical clock had to meet the unsparing standards of earth and sun; no blinking or hiding its failures. The result was relentless pressure to improve technique and design. At every stage, clockmakers led the way to accuracy and precision: masters of miniaturization, detectors and correctors of error, searchers for new and better. They remain the pioneers of mechanical engineering—examples and teachers to other branches.

Finally, the clock brought order and control, both collective and personal. Its public display and private possession laid the basis for temporal autonomy: people could now coordinate comings and goings without dictation from above. (Contrast the military, where only officers need know the time.) The clock provided the punctuation marks for group activity, while enabling individuals to order their own work (and that of others) so as to enhance productivity. Indeed, the very notion of productivity is a by-product of the clock: once one can relate performance to uniform time units, work is never the same. One moves from the task-oriented time consciousness of the peasant (one job after another, as time and light permit) and the time-filling busyness of the domestic servant (always something to do) to an effort to maximize product per unit of time (time is money). The invention of the mechanical clock anticipates in its effects the economic analysis of Adam Smith: increase in the wealth of nations derives directly from improvement of the productive powers of labor.

The mechanical clock remained a European (Western) monopoly for some three hundred years; in its higher forms, right into the twentieth century. Other civilizations admired and coveted clocks, or more accurately, their rulers and elites did; but none could make them to European standard.

The Chinese built a few astronomical water clocks in the Tang and Sung eras—complicated and artful pieces that may have kept excellent time in the short run, before they started clogging. (Owing to sediment, water clocks keep a poor rate over time.) These monumental machines were imperial projects, done and reserved for the emperor and his astrologers. The Chinese treated time and knowledge of time as a confidential aspect of sovereignty, not to be shared with the people. This monopoly touched both daily and year-round time. In the cities, drums and other noisemakers signaled the hours (equal to two of our hours), and everywhere the imperial calendar defined the seasons and their activities. Nor was this calendar a uniform, objectively determinable datum. Each emperor in turn had his own calendar, placed his own seal on the passage of time. Private calendrical calculation would have been pointless.

These interval hour signals in large cities were no substitute for continuing knowledge and awareness. In particular, the noises were not numerical signifiers. The hours had names rather than numbers, and that in itself testifies to the absence of a temporal calculus. Without a basis in popular consumption, without a clock trade, Chinese horology regressed and stagnated. It never got beyond water clocks, and by the time China came to know the Western mechanical clock, it was badly placed to understand and copy it. Not for want of interest: the Chinese imperial court and wealthy elites were wild about these machines; but because they were reluctant to acknowledge European technological superiority, they sought to trivialize them as toys. Big mistake.

Islam might also have sought to possess and copy the clock, if only to fix prayers. And as in China, Muslim horologers made water clocks well in advance of anything known in Europe. Such was the legendary clock that Haroun-al-Raschid sent as a gift to Charlemagne around the year 800: no one at the Frankish court could do much with it, and it disappeared to ignorance and neglect. Like the Chinese, the Muslims were much taken with Western clocks and watches, doing their best to acquire them by purchase or tribute. But they never used them to create a public sense of time other than as a call to prayer. We have the testimony here of Ghiselin de Busbecq, ambassador from the Holy Roman Empire to the Sublime Porte in Constantinople, in a letter of 1560: ". . . if they established public clocks, they think that the authority of their muezzins and their ancient rites would suffer diminution."[7] Sacrilege.

4. *Printing*. Printing was invented in China (which also invented paper) in the ninth century

and found general use by the tenth. This achievement is the more impressive in that the Chinese language, which is written in ideographs (no alphabet), does not lend itself easily to movable type. That explains why Chinese printing consisted primarily of full-page block impressions; also why so much of the old Chinese texts consists of drawings. If one is going to cut a block, it is easier to draw than to carve a multitude of characters. Also, ideographic writing works against literacy: one may learn the characters as a child, but if one does not keep using them, one forgets how to read. Pictures helped.

Block printing limits the range and diffusion of publication. It is well suited to the spread of classic and sacred texts, Buddhist mantras, and the like, but it increases the cost and risk of publishing newer work and tends to small printings. Some Chinese printers did use movable type, but given the character of the written language and the investment required, the technique never caught on as in the West. Indeed, like other Chinese inventions, it may well have been abandoned for a time, to be reintroduced later.[8]

In general, for all that printing did for the preservation and diffusion of knowledge in China, it never "exploded" as in Europe. Much publication depended on government initiative, and the Confucian mandarinate discouraged dissent and new ideas. Even evidence of the falsity of conventional knowledge could be dismissed as appearance.[9] As a result, intellectual activity segmented along personal and regional lines, and scientific achievement shows surprising discontinuities. "The great mathematician Chu Shih-chieh, trained in the northern school, migrated south to Yang-chou, where his books were printed but he could find no disciples. In consequence, the more sophisticated of his achievements became incomprehensible to following generations. But the basic scientific texts were common property everywhere."[10] Basic texts, a kind of canonical writ, are not enough; worse, they may even chill thought.

Europe came to printing centuries after China. It should not be thought, however, that printing made the book and invented reading. On the contrary, the interest in the written word grew rapidly in the Middle Ages, especially after bureaucracy and the rise of towns increased demand for records and documents. Government rests on paper. Much of this verbiage, moreover, was written in the vernacular, shattering the hieratic monopoly of a dead but sacred tongue (Latin) and opening the way to wider readership and a literature of dissent.

As a result, scribes could not keep up with demand. All manner of arrangements were conceived to increase reading material. Manuscripts were prepared and bound in separable fascicles; that divided the labor of writing while enabling several people to read the book at the same time. And as in China, block printing came in before movable type, yielding flysheets more than books and once again copiously illustrated. So when Gutenberg published his Bible in 1452–55, the first Western book printed by movable type (and arguably the most beautiful book ever printed), he brought the new technique to a society that had already vastly increased its output of writing and was fairly panting after it. Within the next half century, printing spread from the Rhineland throughout western Europe. The estimated output of incunabula (books published before 1501) came to millions—2 million in Italy alone.

In spite of printing's manifest advantages, it was not accepted everywhere. The Muslim countries long remained opposed, largely on religious grounds: the idea of a printed Koran was unacceptable. Jews and Christians had presses in Istanbul but not Muslims. The same in India: not until the early nineteenth century was the first press installed. In Europe, on the other hand, no one could put a lid on the new technology. Political authority was too fragmented. The Church had tried to curb vernacular translations of sacred writ and to forbid dissemination of both canonical and noncanonical texts. Now it was overwhelmed. The demons of heresy were out long before Luther, and printing made it impossible to get them back in the box.

5. *Gunpowder.* Europeans probably got this from the Chinese in the early fourteenth, possibly the late thirteenth century. The Chinese knew gunpowder by the eleventh century and used it at first as an incendiary device, both in fireworks and in war, often in the form of tubed flame lances. Its use as a propellant came later, starting with inefficient bombards

and arrow launchers and moving on to cannon (late thirteenth century). The efficiency and rationality of some of these devices may be inferred from their names: "the eight-sided magical awe-inspiring wind-and-fire cannon" or the "nine-arrows, heart-penetrating, magically-poisonous fire-thunderer."[11] They were apparently valued as much for their noise as for their killing power. The pragmatic mind finds this metaphorical, rhetorical vision of technology disconcerting.

The Chinese continued to rely on incendiaries rather than explosives, perhaps because of their superior numbers, perhaps because fighting against nomadic adversaries did not call for siege warfare.* Military treatises of the sixteenth century describe hundreds of variations: "sky-flying tubes," apparently descended from the fire lances of five hundred years earlier, used to spray gunpowder and flaming bits of paper on the enemy's sails; "gunpowder buckets" and "fire bricks"—grenades of powder and paper soaked in poison; other devices packed with chemicals and human excrement, intended to frighten, blind, and presumably disgust the enemy; finally, more lethal grenades filled with metal pellets and explosives.[12] Some of these were thrown; others shot from bows. One wonders at this delight in variety, as though war were a display of recipes.

The Chinese used gunpowder in powder form, as the name indicates, and got a weak reaction precisely because the fine-grain mass slowed ignition. The Europeans, on the other hand, learned in the sixteenth century to "corn" their powder, making it in the form of small kernels or pebbles. They got more rapid ignition, and by mixing the ingredients more thoroughly, a more complete and powerful explosion. With that, one could concentrate on range and weight of projectile; no messing around with noise and smell and visual effects.

This focus on delivery, when combined with experience in bell founding (bell metal was convertible into gun metal, and the techniques of casting

were interchangeable), gave Europe the world's best cannon and military supremacy.[13]

As these cases make clear, other societies were falling behind Europe even before the opening of the world (fifteenth century on) and the great confrontation.* Why this should have been so is an important historical question—one learns as much from failure as from success. One cannot look here at every non-European society or civilization, but two deserve a moment's scrutiny.

The first, Islam, initially absorbed and developed the knowledge and ways of conquered peoples. By our period (roughly 1000 to 1500), Muslim rule went from the western end of the Mediterranean to the Indies. Before this, from about 750 to 1100, Islamic science and technology far surpassed those of Europe, which needed to recover its heritage and did so to some extent through contacts with Muslims in such frontier areas as Spain. Islam was Europe's teacher.

Then something went wrong. Islamic science, denounced as heresy by religious zealots, bent under theological pressures for spiritual conformity. (For thinkers and searchers, this could be a matter of life and death.) For militant Islam, the truth had already been revealed. What led *back* to the truth was useful and permissible; all the rest was error and deceit.[14] The historian Ibn Khaldūn, conservative in religious matters, was nonetheless dismayed by Muslim hostility to learning:

> When the Muslims conquered Persia (637–642) and came upon an indescribably large number of books and scientific papers, Sa'd bin Abi Waqqas wrote to Umar bin al-Khattab asking him for permission to take them and distribute them as booty among the Muslims. On that occasion, Umar wrote him: "Throw them in the water. If what they contain is right guidance, God has given us better guidance. If it is error, God has protected us against it."[15]

---

* The Chinese would seem to have been more afraid of rebellion from within than invasion from without. More modern armaments might fall into the wrong hands, and these included those of the generals. Cf. Hall, *Powers and Liberties*, pp. 46–47.

* For reasons well worth exploring in the context of the history of ideas and the invention of folklore, a number of scholars have recently tried to propagate the notion that European technology did not catch up to that of Asia until the late eighteenth century. The most active source at the moment is the H-World site on the Internet—a magnet for fallacies and fantasies.

Remember here that Islam does not, as Christianity does, separate the religious from the secular. The two constitute an integrated whole. The ideal state would be a theocracy; and in the absence of such fulfillment, a good ruler leaves matters of the spirit and mind (in the widest sense) to the doctors of the faith. This can be hard on scientists.

As for technology, Islam knew areas of change and advance: one thinks of the adoption of paper; or the introduction and diffusion of new crops such as coffee and sugar; or the Ottoman Turkish readiness to learn the use (but not the making) of cannon and clocks. But most of this came from outside and continued to depend on outside support. Native springs of invention seem to have dried up. Even in the golden age (750–1100), speculation disconnected from practice: "For nearly five hundred years the world's greatest scientists wrote in Arabic, yet a flourishing science contributed nothing to the slow advance of technology in Islam."[16]

The one civilization that might have surpassed the European achievement was China. At least that is what the record seems to show. Witness the long list of Chinese inventions: the wheelbarrow, the stirrup, the rigid horse collar (to prevent choking), the compass, paper, printing, gunpowder, porcelain. And yet in matters of science and technology, China remains a mystery—and this in spite of a monumental effort by the late Joseph Needham and others to collect the facts and clarify the issues. The specialists tell us, for example, that Chinese industry long anticipated European: in textiles, where the Chinese had a water-driven machine for spinning hemp in the twelfth century, some five hundred years before the England of the Industrial Revolution knew water frames and mules;[17] or in iron manufacture, where the Chinese early learned to use coal and coke in blast furnaces for smelting iron (or so we are told) and were turning out as many as 125,000 tons of pig iron by the later eleventh century—a figure reached by Britain seven hundred years later.[18]

The mystery lies in China's failure to realize its potential. One generally assumes that knowledge and know-how are cumulative; surely a superior technique, once known, will replace older methods. But Chinese industrial history offers examples of technological oblivion and regression. We saw that horology went backward. Similarly, the machine to spin hemp was never adapted to the manufacture of cotton, and cotton spinning was never mechanized. And coal/coke smelting was allowed to fall into disuse, along with the iron industry as a whole. Why?

> It would seem that none of the conventional explanations tells us in convincing fashion why technical progress was absent in the Chinese economy during a period that was, on the whole, one of prosperity and expansion. Almost every element usually regarded by historians as a major contributory cause to the industrial revolution in north-western Europe was also present in China. There had even been a revolution in the relations between social classes, at least in the countryside; but this had had no important effect on the techniques of production. Only Galilean-Newtonian science was missing; but in the short run this was not important. Had the Chinese possessed, or developed, the seventeenth-century European mania for tinkering and improving, they could easily have made an efficient spinning machine out of the primitive model described by Wang Chen. . . . A steam engine would have been more difficult; but it should not have posed insuperable difficulties to a people who had been building double-acting piston flame-throwers in the Sung dynasty. The crucial point is that nobody tried. In most fields, agriculture being the chief exception, Chinese technology stopped progressing well before the point at which a lack of scientific knowledge had become a serious obstacle.[19]

Why indeed? Sinologists have put forward several partial explanations. The most persuasive are of a piece:

- The absence of a free market and institutionalized property rights. The Chinese state was always interfering with private enterprise—taking over lucrative activities, prohibiting others, manipulating prices, exacting bribes, curtailing private enrichment. A favorite target was maritime trade, which the Heavenly Kingdom saw as a diversion from imperial concerns, as a divisive force and source of income inequality, worse yet, as an invitation to exit.

Matters reached a climax under the Ming dynasty (1368–1644), when the state attempted to prohibit all trade overseas. Such interdictions led to evasion and smuggling, and smuggling brought corruption (protection money), confiscations, violence, and punishment. Bad government strangled initiative, increased the cost of transactions, diverted talent from commerce and industry.

• The larger values of the society. A leading sociological historian (historical sociologist) sees gender relations as a major obstacle: the quasi-confinement of women to the home made it impossible, for example, to exploit textile machinery profitably in a factory setting. Here China differed sharply from Europe or Japan, where women had free access to public space and were often expected to work outside the home to accumulate a dowry or contribute resources to the family.[20]

• The great Hungarian-German-French sinologist, Etienne Balazs, would stress the larger context. He sees China's abortive technology as part of a larger pattern of totalitarian control. He does not explain this by hydraulic centralism, but he does recognize the absence of freedom, the weight of custom, consensus, what passed for higher wisdom. His analysis is worth repeating:

> . . . if one understands by totalitarianism the complete hold of the State and its executive organs and functionaries over all the activities of social life, without exception, Chinese society was highly totalitarian. . . . No private initiative, no expression of public life that can escape official control. There is to begin with a whole array of state monopolies, which comprise the great consumption staples: salt, iron, tea, alcohol, foreign trade. There is a monopoly of education, jealously guarded. There is practically a monopoly of letters (I was about to say, of the press): anything written unofficially, that escapes the censorship, has little hope of reaching the public. But the reach of the Moloch-State, the omnipotence of the bureaucracy, goes much farther. There are clothing regulations, a regulation of public and private construction (dimensions of houses); the colors one wears, the music one hears, the festivals—all are regulated. There are

rules for birth and rules for death; the providential State watches minutely over every step of its subjects, from cradle to grave. It is a regime of paper work and harassment [*paperasseries et tracasseries*], endless paper work and endless harassment.

The ingenuity and inventiveness of the Chinese, which have given so much to mankind—silk, tea, porcelain, paper, printing, and more—would no doubt have enriched China further and probably brought it to the threshold of modern industry, had it not been for this stifling state control. It is the State that kills technological progress in China. Not only in the sense that it nips in the bud anything that goes against or seems to go against its interests, but also by the customs implanted inexorably by the raison d'Etat. The atmosphere of routine, of traditionalism, and of immobility, which makes any innovation suspect, any initiative that is not commanded and sanctioned in advance, is unfavorable to the spirit of free inquiry.[21]

In short, no one was trying. Why try?

Whatever the mix of factors, the result was a weird pattern of isolated initiatives and Sisyphean discontinuities—up, up, up, and then down again—almost as though the society were held down by a silk ceiling. The result, if not the aim, was change-in-immobility; or maybe immobility-in-change. Innovation was allowed to go (was able to go) so far and no farther.

The Europeans knew much less of these interferences. Instead, they entered during these centuries into an exciting world of innovation and emulation that challenged vested interests and rattled the forces of conservatism. Changes were cumulative; novelty spread fast. A new sense of progress replaced an older, effete reverence for authority. This intoxicating sense of freedom touched (infected) all domains. These were years of heresies in the Church, of popular initiatives that, we can see now, anticipated the rupture of the Reformation; of new forms of expression and collective action that challenged the older art forms, questioned social structures, and posed a threat to other polities; of new ways of doing and making things that made newness a virtue and a source of delight; of utopias that fantasized better futures rather than recalled paradises lost.

Important in all this was the Church as custodian of knowledge and school for technicians. One might have expected otherwise: that organized spirituality, with its emphasis on prayer and contemplation, would have had little interest in technology. Surely the Church, with its view of labor as penalty for original sin, would not seek to ease the judgment. And yet everything worked in the opposite direction: the desire to free clerics from time-consuming earthly tasks led to the introduction and diffusion of power machinery and, beginning with the Cistercians, to the hiring of lay brothers (*conversi*) to do the dirty work. Employment fostered in turn attention to time and productivity. All of this gave rise on monastic estates to remarkable assemblages of powered machinery—complex sequences designed to make the most of the waterpower available and distribute it through a series of industrial operations. A description of work in the abbey of Clairvaux in the mid-twelfth century exults in this versatility: "cooking, straining, mixing, rubbing [polishing], transmitting [the energy], washing, milling, bending." The author, clearly proud of these achievements, further tells his readers that he will take the liberty of joking: the fulling hammers, he says, seem to have dispensed the fullers of the penalty for their sins; and he thanks God that such devices can mitigate the oppressive labor of men and spare the backs of their horses.[22]

Why this peculiarly European *joie de trouver*? This pleasure in new and better? This cultivation of invention—or what some have called "the invention of invention"? Different scholars have suggested a variety of reasons, typically related to religious values:

1. The Judeo-Christian respect for manual labor, summed up in a number of biblical injunctions. One example: When God warns Noah of the coming flood and tells him he will be saved, it is not God who saves him. "Build thee an ark of gopher wood," he says, and Noah builds an ark to divine specifications.

2. The Judeo-Christian subordination of nature to man. This is a sharp departure from widespread animistic beliefs and practices that saw something of the divine in every tree and stream (hence naiads and dryads). Ecologists today might think these animistic beliefs preferable to what replaced them, but no one was listening to pagan nature worshippers in Christian Europe.

3. The Judeo-Christian sense of linear time. Other societies thought of time as cyclical, returning to earlier stages and starting over again. Linear time is progressive or regressive, moving on to better things or declining from some earlier, happier state. For Europeans in our period, the progressive view prevailed.

4. In the last analysis, however, I would stress the market. Enterprise was free in Europe. Innovation worked and paid, and rulers and vested interests were limited in their ability to prevent or discourage innovation. Success bred imitation and emulation; also a sense of power that would in the long run raise men almost to the level of gods. The old legends remained—the expulsion from the Garden, Icarus who flew too high, Prometheus in chains—to warn against hubris. (The very notion of hubris—cosmic insolence—is testimony to some men's pretensions and the efforts of others to curb them.)

But the doers were not paying attention.

NOTES

1. The key piece is the seminal article of Lynn White, Jr., "Technology and Invention in the Middle Ages," *Speculum*, 15 (1940): 141–59.

2. Jean Gimpel, *The Medieval Machine*, p. 14. Cf. White, *Medieval Religion and Technology*, pp. 226–27. White also points out that whereas paper from Muslim lands (not mechanically produced) never shows watermarks, such trademarks appear in Italian paper by the 1280s, a sign of commercial enterprise.

3. On these glasses before eyeglasses, see the work of Zecchin, *Vetro e vetrai di Murano* (Venice, 1989), cited by Ilardi, "Renaissance Florence," p. 510.

4. The speaker is the Dominican Fra Giordano of Pisa, in a sermon at Santa Maria Novella in Florence in 1306. Quoted in White, "Cultural Climates,"

p. 174; also in reprint, 1978, p. 221. White cites the Italian original. I have made small stylistic changes in the translation. See also Rosen, "Invention of Eyeglasses"; and Ilardi, *Occhiali* and "Renaissance Florence."

5. Moses Abramovitz argues that a longer life span encourages investment in human capital and makes people readier to move to new places and occupations. How much more when the extra years can be the best—"Manpower, Capital, and Technology," pp. 55.

6. "The clock is not merely a means of keeping track of the hours, but of synchronizing the actions of men. The clock, not the steam-engine, is the key-machine of the modern industrial age . . . at the very beginning of modern technics appeared prophetically the accurate automatic machine. . . . In its relationship to determinable quantities of energy, to standardization, to automatic action, and finally to its own special product, accurate timing, the clock has been the foremost machine in modern technics; and at each period it has remained in the lead; it marks a perfection toward which other machines aspire"—Mumford, *Technics and Civilization*, pp. 14–15.

7. Cited in Lewis, *The Muslim Discovery of Europe*, p. 233.

8. Sivin, "Science and Medicine," p. 165, says that printing with movable type did not replace the older method until the twentieth century.

9. Cf. Hall, *Powers and Liberties, p. 49.*

10. Elvin, *Pattern of the Chinese Past*, p. 180.

11. Needham, "The Guns of Khaifeng-fu," p. 40.

12. Levathes, *When China Ruled the Seas,* p. 102.

13. On this point, note the development, as early as the sixteenth century, of a formal claim by victorious armies to all bells, or to the best bell, in and around a conquered place: "the right to the bells." Cipolla, *Guns, Sails, and Empires*, p. 30, n. 1.

14. In 885, all professional copyists in Baghdad were required to swear an oath not to copy books of philosophy. On the conflicts of Muslim science and Islamic doctrine, see Hoodbhoy, *Islam and Science,* especially chs. 9 and 10.

15. Ibn Khaldūn, *The Muqaddima: An Introduction to History* (London: Routledge and Kegan Paul, 1978), p. 373, cited in Hoodbhoy, *Islam and Science,* pp. 103–04. We have an analogous example of arrant cynicism and zealotry in Christian annals: when the French "crusader" army sent to repress the Cathar heresy broke into Béziers and was permitted (ordered) to put its inhabitants to the sword, the commander was asked how they might distinguish the good Christians from the heretics; to which he replied: "God will know his own."

16. White, *Medieval Religion and Technology*, p. 227.

17. Elvin, *Pattern of the Chinese Past*, p. 184.

18. *Ibid.*, p. 85. Elvin gives the figure as "between 35,000 to 40,000 tons and 125,000 tons," but says he prefers the higher estimate. He relies here on Yoshida Mitsukuni, a Japanese specialist writing in 1967. Subsequent work by Robert Hartwell, "Markets, Technology, and the Structure of Enterprise," p. 34, also advances the higher figure. In Hall, *Powers and Liberties*, p. 46, this becomes "at least 125,000 tons." That's the way of historical numbers—they grow.

19. Elvin, *Pattern of the Chinese Past*, pp. 297–98.

20. Cf. Goldstone, "Gender, Work, and Culture."

21. Balazs, *La bureaucratie céleste*, pp. 22–23.

22. Cited in White, *Medieval Religion and Technology,* pp. 245–46.

RUTH SCHWARTZ COWAN   I.3

Industrial Society and Technological Systems

As the Civil War came to an end, America began the transition from a preindustrial society into the industrial age. The period from 1870 to 1920 saw many changes in America, and at the end of that era, we had become the largest economy in the world—one that was far less dependent on nature than it once had been.

While we currently use many different technological systems, Ruth Schwartz Cowan, professor emeritas of history at the State University of New York, Stony Brook, discusses five developed during that fifty-year period to demonstrate the increasing complexity of life and the development of infrastructure we now largely take for granted. Eventually, this increasing complexity spread across the world. The characteristics of an industrialized society can now be found in even the most remote corners of the globe.

The increased levels of productivity in manufacturing, including agriculture, had economic as well as political ramifications. As these changes occurred, few thought about what was happening or what the long-range implications would be. Today's globalized world is vastly different from what it once was, with many people more reliant and interdependent on one another. Our lives are increasingly more intertwined than ever before.

Focus Questions

1. Explain the rationale behind Cowan's assertion that industrialization has made us less independent and more closely connected to many other people than ever before.
2. Consider the key points of this article in relation to the ethical issues raised in the Jonas piece (selection I.10). What new individual responsibilities might arise from the new networks extending far beyond the nuclear family?
3. If technology continues to improve the quality of life for many more people in the world, what might our future look like if the networks discussed by Cowan become larger and more common, linking even greater numbers of people throughout the world?

Keywords

balance of trade, entrepreneurs, hunter-gatherers, industrialization, infrastructure, international trade, investment banking, manufacturing, productivity, transportation

BETWEEN 1870 AND 1920, the United States changed in ways that its founders could never have dreamed possible. Although American industrialization began in the 1780s, the nation did not become an industrialized society until after the Civil War had ended. The armistice agreed to at Appomattox signaled, although the participants probably did not realize it, the beginning of the take-off phase of American industrialization. Having begun as a nation of farmers, the United States became a nation of industrial workers. Having begun as a financial weakling among the nations, by 1920 the

United States had become the world's largest industrial economy.

What did this transformation mean to the people who lived through it? When a society passes from preindustrial to industrial conditions, which is what happened in the United States in the years between 1870 and 1920, people become less dependent on nature and more dependent on each other. This is one of history's little ironies. In a preindustrial society, when life is unstable, the whims of the weather and the perils of natural cycles are most often to blame. In an industrial society, when life is unstable, the whims of the market and the perils of social forces are most often to blame. Put another way, this means that in the process of industrialization individuals become more dependent on one another because they are linked together in large, complex networks that are, at one and the same time, both physical and social: technological systems.

Industrialization, Dependency, and Technological Systems

Many Americans learned what it means to become embedded in a set of technological systems in the years between 1870 and 1920. Today we have become so accustomed to these systems that we hardly ever stop to think about them; although they sustain our lives, they nonetheless remain mysterious. In the late twentieth century, people have tended to think that, if anything, industrialization has liberated them from dependency, not encased them in it, but that is not the case. We can see this clearly by imagining how a woman might provide food for a two-year-old child in a nonindustrialized society.

In a hunter-gatherer economy, she might simply go into the woods and collect nuts or walk to the waterside and dig for shellfish. In a premodern agricultural community (such as the one that some of the native peoples of the eastern seaboard had created), she might work with a small group of other people to plant corn, tend it, harvest it, and shuck it. Then she herself might dry it, grind it into meal, mix it with water, and bake it into a bread for the child to eat. In such a community, a woman would be dependent on the cooperation of several other people in order to provide enough food for her child, but all of those people would be known to her and none of them would be involved in an activity in which she could not have participated if necessity had demanded.

In an industrialized economy (our own, for example), an average woman's situation is wholly different. In order to get bread for a child, an average American woman is dependent on thousands of other people, virtually all of them totally unknown to her, many of them living and working at a considerable distance, employing equipment that she could not begin to operate, even if her life (quite literally) depended on it and even if she had the money (which isn't likely) to purchase it. A farmer grew the wheat using internal combustion engines and petroleum-derivative fertilizers. Then the wheat was harvested and transported to an organization that stored it under stable conditions, perhaps for several years. Then a milling company may have purchased it and transported it (over thousands of miles of roads or even ocean) to a mill, where it was ground by huge rollers powered by electricity (which itself may have been generated thousands of miles away). Then more transportation (all of this transportation required petroleum, which itself had to be processed and transported) was required: to a baking factory, where dozens of people (and millions of dollars of machinery) were used to turn the flour into bread. Then transportation again: to a market, where the woman could purchase it (having gotten herself there in an automobile, which itself had to be manufactured somewhere else, purchased at considerable expense, and supplied with fuel)—all of this before a slice of it could be spread with peanut butter to the delight of a two year old.

The point should, by now, be clear. People who live in agricultural societies are dependent on natural processes: they worry, with good reason, about whether and when there will be a drought or a flood, a plague of insects or of fungi, good weather or bad. People who live in industrial societies are not completely independent of such natural processes, but are more so than their predecessors (many floodplains have been controlled; some droughts can be offset by irrigation). At the same time, they are much more dependent on other people and on the technological systems that other people have designed and constructed. The physical parts of these systems are networks of connected objects: tractors, freight cars, pipelines, automobiles, display cases. The social parts are networks of people and organizations that make the connections between objects possible: farmers, bakers, and truck drivers; grain elevators, refineries, and supermarkets.

Preindustrialized societies had such networks of course, but in industrialized societies, the networks are more complex and much denser—all of which makes it much harder for individuals to extricate themselves. A small change very far away can have enormous effects very quickly. Daily life can be easily disrupted for reasons that ordinary people can find hard to understand, and even experts can have difficulty comprehending.

People live longer and at a higher standard of living in industrial societies than in preindustrial ones, but they are not thereby rendered more independent (although advertising writers and politicians would like them to think they are) because, in the process of industrialization, one kind of dependency is traded for another: nature for technology. Americans learned what it meant to make that trade in the years between 1870 and 1920. We can begin understanding what they experienced if we look at some of the technological systems that were created or enlarged during those years.

The Telegraph System

The very first network that Americans experienced really looked like a network: the elongated spider's web of electric wires that carried telegraph signals. The fact that electricity could be transmitted long distances through wires had been discovered in the middle of the eighteenth century. Once a simple way to generate electric currents had been developed (a battery, or voltaic pile, named after the man who invented it, Alessandro Volta) many people began experimenting with various ways to send messages along the wires. An American portrait painter, Samuel F. B. Morse, came up with a practiceable solution. Morse developed a transmitter that emitted a burst of electric current of either short or long duration (dots and dashes). His receiver, at the other end of the wire, was an electromagnet, which, when it moved, pushed a pencil against a moving paper tape (thus recording the pattern of dots and dashes). The most creative aspect of Morse's invention was his code, which enabled trained operators to make sense out of the patterns of dots and dashes.

In 1843, after Morse had obtained a government subvention, he and his partners built the nation's first telegraph line between Baltimore and Washington. By 1845, Morse had organized his own company to build additional lines and to license other telegraph companies so that they could build even more lines, using the instruments he had patented. In a very short time, however, dozens of competing companies had entered the telegraph business, and Morse had all he could do to try to collect the licensing fees to which he was entitled. By 1849, almost every state east of the Mississippi had telegraph service, much of it provided by companies that were exploiting Morse's patents without compensating him.

Beginning around 1850, one of these companies, the New York and Mississippi Valley Printing Telegraph Company, began buying up or merging with all the others; in 1866, it changed its name to the Western Union Telegraph Company. In the decades after the Civil War, Western Union had an almost complete monopoly on telegraph service in the United States; a message brought to one of its offices could be transmitted to any of its other offices in almost all fairly large communities in the United States. Once the message was delivered, recipients could pick it up at a Western Union office. During these decades, only one company of any note succeeded in challenging Western Union's almost complete monopoly on telegraph service. The Postal Telegraph Company specialized in providing pick-up and delivery services for telegrams; yet even at the height of its success, it never managed to corner more than 25 percent of the country's telegraph business.

In 1866, when Western Union was incorporated, it already controlled almost 22,000 telegraph offices around the country. These were connected by 827,000 miles of wire (all of it strung from a virtual forest of telegraph poles, many of them running along railroad rights of way), and its operators were handling something on the order of 58 million messages annually. By 1920, the two companies (Western and Postal) between them were managing more than a million miles of wire and 155 million messages. Yet other companies (many of the railroads, for example, several investment banking houses, several wire news services) were using Western Union and Postal Telegraph lines on a contractual basis to provide in-house communication services (the famous Wall Street stock ticker was one of them).

As a result, as early as 1860, and certainly by 1880, the telegraph had become crucial to the political and economic life of the nation. Newspapers had become dependent on the telegraph for quick transmission of important information. The 1847 war with Mexico was the first war to have rapid news coverage, and the Civil War was the first in which military strategy depended on the quick flow of battle information over telegraph lines. During the Gilded Age (1880–1900), the nation's burgeoning financial markets were dependent on the telegraph for quick transmission of prices and orders. Railroad companies used the telegraph for scheduling and signaling purposes since information about deviations in train times could be quickly transmitted along the lines. The central offices of the railroads utilized telegraph communication to control the financial affairs of their widely dispersed branches. When the Atlantic cable was completed in 1866, the speed and frequency of communication between nations increased, thereby permanently changing the character of diplomatic negotiations. The cable also laid the groundwork for the growth of international trade (particularly the growth of multinational corporations) in the later decades of the century.

In short, by 1880, if by some weird accident all the batteries that generated electricity for telegraph lines had suddenly run out, the economic and social life of the nation would have faltered. Trains would have stopped running; businesses with branch offices would have stopped functioning; newspapers could not have covered distant events; the president could not have communicated with his European ambassadors; the stock market would have had to close; family members separated by long distances could not have relayed important news—births, deaths, illnesses—to each other. By the turn of the century, the telegraph system was both literally and figuratively a network, ranking together various aspects of national life—making people increasingly dependent on it and on one another.

The Railroad System

Another system that linked geographic regions, diverse businesses, and millions of individuals was the railroad. We have already learned about the technical developments (the high-pressure steam-engine, the swivel truck, the T-rail) that were crucial to the development of the first operating rail lines in the United States in the 1830s. Once the technical feasibility of the railroad became obvious, its commercial potential also became clear. The railroad, unlike canals and steamboats, was not dependent on proximity to waterways and was not (as boats were) disabled when rivers flooded or canals froze.

During the 1840s, American entrepreneurs had began to realize the financial benefits that railroading might produce and railroad-building schemes were being concocted in parlors and banks, state houses, and farm houses all across the country. By the 1850s, a good many of those schemes had come to fruition. With 9,000 miles of railroad track in operation, the United States had more railroad mileage than all other western nations combined; by 1860, mileage had more than trebled, to 30,000 miles.

The pre–Civil War railroad system was not yet quite a technological system because, large as it was, it still was not integrated as a network. Most of the existing roads were short-haul lines, connecting such major cities as New York, Chicago, and Baltimore with their immediate hinterlands. Each road was owned by a different company, each company owned its own cars, and each built its tracks at the gauge (width) that seemed best for the cars it was going to attempt to run and the terrain over which the running had to be done. This lack of integration created numerous delays and additional expenses. In 1849, it took nine transshipments between nine unconnected railroads (and nine weeks of travel) to get freight from Philadelphia to Chicago. In 1861, the trip between Charleston and Philadelphia required eight car changes because of different gauges. During and immediately after the Civil War, not a single rail line entering either Philadelphia or Richmond made a direct connection with any other, much to the delight of the local teamsters, porters, and tavern keepers.

The multifaceted processes summed up under the word "integration" began in the years just after the Civil War and accelerated in the decades that followed. The rail system grew ever larger, stretching from coast to coast (with the completion of the

Union Pacific Railroad in 1869), penetrating into parts of the country where settlement did not yet even exist. There were roughly 53,000 miles of track in 1870, but there were 93,000 miles by the time the next decade turned, and 254,000—the all-time high—by 1920. In that half century, the nation's population tripled, but its rail system grew sevenfold; the forty-eight states of the mainland United States became physically integrated, one with the other.

The form of the rail system was just as significant as its size. By 1920, what had once been a disjointed collection of short (usually north-south) lines had been transformed into a network of much longer trunk lines (running from coast to coast, east-west), each served by a network of shorter roads that connected localities (the limbs) with the trunks. Passengers could now travel from New York to San Francisco with only an occasional change of train and freight traveled without the necessity of transshipments. What had made this kind of integration possible was not a technological change, but a change in the pattern of railroad ownership and management.

From the very beginning of railroading, railroad companies had been joint-stock ventures. Huge amounts of capital had been required to build a railroad: rights of way had to be purchased, land cleared, bridges built, locomotives ordered, passenger cars constructed, freight cars bought. Once built, railroads were very expensive to run and to maintain: engines had to be repaired, passengers serviced, freight loaded, tickets sold, stations cleaned. Such a venture could not be financed by individuals, or even by partnerships. Money had to be raised both by selling shares of ownership in the company to large numbers of people and by borrowing large sums of money by issuing bonds.

As a result, both American stockbroking and American investment banking were twin products of the railroad age. Some of America's largest nineteenth-century fortunes were made by people who knew not how to build railroads, but how to finance them: J. P. Morgan, Leland Stanford, Jay Gould, Cornelius Vanderbilt, and George Crocker. These businessmen consolidated the railroads. They

bought up competing feeder lines; they sought control of the boards of directors of trunk lines; they invested heavily in the stock of feeder roads until the feeders were forced to merge with the trunks. When they were finished, the railroads had become an integrated network, a technological system. In 1870, there had been several hundred railroads, many of which were in direct competition with each other. By 1900, virtually all the railroad mileage in the United States was either owned or controlled by just seven (often mutually cooperative) railroad combinations, all of which owed their existence to the machinations of a few very wealthy investment bankers.

As railroad ownership became consolidated, the railroad system became physically integrated. The most obvious indicator of this integration was the adoption of a standard gauge, which made it unnecessary to run different cars on different sets of tracks. By the end of the 1880s, virtually every railroad in the country had voluntarily converted to a gauge of 4 feet, 8½ inches in order to minimize both the expense and the delays of long distance travel. On this new integrated system, the need for freight and passengers to make repeated transfers was eliminated; as a result, costs fell while transportation speed increased.

The railroad system had a profound impact on the way in which Americans lived. By 1900, the sound of the train whistle could be heard in almost every corner of the land. Virtually everything Americans needed to maintain and sustain their lives was being transported by train. As much as they may have grumbled about freight rates on the railroads (and there was much injustice, particularly to farmers, to grumble about) and as much as they may have abhorred the techniques that the railroad barons had used to achieve integration, most Americans benefited from the increased operational efficiency that resulted.

In the years in which population tripled and rail mileage increased seven times, freight tonnage on the railroads went up elevenfold. Cattle were going by train from the ranches of Texas to the slaughterhouses of Chicago; butchered beef was leaving Chicago in refrigerated railroad cars destined for urban and suburban kitchens. Lumber traveled from forests to sawmills by train; two-by-four beams to build houses on the treeless plains left the sawmills of the Pacific Northwest on flatcars. Some petroleum went from the well to the refinery by train; most kerosene and gasoline went from the refinery to the retailer by train. Virtually all the country's mail traveled by train, including cotton cloth and saddles, frying pans and furniture ordered from the mail-order companies that had begun to flourish in the 1880s.

Even as fundamental and apparently untransportable a commodity as time was affected by the integration of the rail system, for scheduling was an important facet of integration. People who were going to travel by train had to know what time their trains would leave, and if connections had to be made, trains had to be scheduled so as to make the connections possible. Schedules also had to be constructed, especially on heavily trafficked lines, to ensure that trains did not collide. But scheduling was exceedingly difficult across the long distances of the United States because communities each established their own time on the basis of the position of the sun. When it was noon in Chicago, it was 12:30 in Pittsburgh (which is to the east of Chicago) and 11:30 in Omaha (to the west). The train schedules printed in Pittsburgh in the early 1880s listed six different times for the arrival and departure of each train. The station in Buffalo had three different clocks.

Sometime in the early 1880s, some professional railroad managers and the editors of several railroad publications agreed to the idea, first proposed by some astronomers, that the nation should be divided into four uniform time zones. By common agreement among the managers of the country's railroads, at noon (in New York) on Sunday, November 18, 1883, railroad signalmen across the country reset their watches. The zones were demarcated by the 75th, 90th, 105th, and 120th meridians. People living in the eastern sections of each zone experienced, on that otherwise uneventful Sunday, two noons, and people living in the western sections, skipped time. Virtually everyone in the country accepted the new time that had been established

by the railroads, although Congress did not actually confirm the arrangement by legislation for another thirty-five years. Such was the pervasive impact of the integrated rail network.

The Petroleum System

In 1859, a group of prospectors dug a well in a farmyard in Titusville, Pennsylvania. Although they appeared to be looking for water, the prospectors were in fact searching for an underground reservoir of a peculiar oily substance that had been bubbling to the surface of nearby land and streams. Native Americans had used this combustible substance as a lubricant for centuries. The prospectors were hoping that if they could find a way to tap into an underground reservoir of this material, they could go into the business of selling it to machine shops and factories (as a machine lubricant, an alternative to animal fat) and to households and businesses (as an illuminant, an alternative to whale oil and candles).

The prospectors struck oil—and the American petroleum industry was born. Within weeks the news had spread, and hundreds of eager profiteers rushed into western Pennsylvania, hoping to purchase land, drill for oil, or find work around the wells. The Pennsylvania oil rush was as massive a phenomenon as the California gold rush a decade earlier.

The drillers soon discovered that crude petroleum is a mixture of oils of varying weights and characteristics. These oils, they learned, could be easily separated from one another by distillation, an ancient and fairly well-known craft. All that was needed was a fairly large closed vat with a long outlet tube (called a still) and a fire. The oil was heated in the still and the volatile gases produced would condense in the outlet tube. A clever distiller (later called a refiner) could distinguish different portions (fractions) of the distillate from each other, and then only the economically useful ones needed to be bottled and sent to market.

The market for petroleum products boomed during the Civil War: northern factories were expanding to meet government contracts; the whaling industry was seriously hampered by naval operations; railroads were working overtime to transport men and material to battlefronts. By 1862, some 3 million barrels of crude oil were being processed every year. Under peacetime conditions the industry continued to expand; by 1872, the number of processed barrels had trebled.

Transportation of petroleum remained a problem, however. The wells were located in the rural, underpopulated Appalachian highlands of Pennsylvania, not only many miles away from the cities in which the ultimate consumers lived, but also many miles away from railroad lines that served those cities. Initially crude oil had been collected in barrels and had been moved (by horse and cart or by river barges) to railroad-loading points. There the barrels were loaded into freight cars for the trip to the cities (such as Cleveland and Pittsburgh) in which the crude was being refined and sold. The transportation process was cumbersome, time-consuming, and wasteful; the barrels leaked, the barges sometimes capsized, the wagons—operating on dirt roads— sometimes sank to their axles in mud.

Pipelines were an obvious solution, but a difficult one to put into practice given that no one had ever before contemplated building and then maintaining a continuous pipeline over the mountainous terrain and the long distances that had to be traversed. The first pipeline to operate successfully was built in 1865. Made of lap-welded cast-iron pipes, two inches in diameter, it ran for six miles from an oil field to a railroad loading point and had three pumping stations along the way. This first pipeline carried eighty barrels of oil an hour and had demonstrated its economic benefits within a year. Pipeline mileage continued to increase during the 1870s and 1880s (putting thousands of teamsters out of business), but virtually all of the lines were relatively short hauls, taking oil from the fields to the railroads. Throughout the nineteenth century and well into the twentieth, the railroads were still the principal long-distance transporters of both crude and refined oil. After the 1870s, the drillers, refiners, and railroads gradually dispensed with barrels (thus putting thousands of coopers out of business) and replaced them with specially built tank cars, which could be emptied into and loaded from specially built holding tanks. As it was being constructed, the network of petroleum pipelines was thus integrated

into the network of railroad lines. It was also integrated into the telegraph network. Oil refineries used the telegraph system partly to keep tabs on prices for oil in various localities and partly to report on the flow of oil through the lines.

The most successful petroleum entrepreneurs were the ones who realized that control of petroleum transportation was the key ingredient in control of the entire industry. The major actor in this particular economic drama was John D. Rockefeller. Rockefeller had been born in upstate New York, the son of a talented patent medicine salesman, but he had grown up in Cleveland, Ohio, a growing commercial center (it was a Great Lake port and both a canal and railroad terminus), and had learned accountancy in a local commercial college. His first job was as a bookkeeper for what was then called a commission agent, a business that collected commissions for arranging the shipment of bulk orders of farm products. A commission agent's success depended on getting preferential treatment from railroads and shipping companies. Rockefeller carried this insight with him, first when he went into a partnership as his own commission agent and then, in 1865, when he became the co-owner of an oil refinery in Cleveland.

Rockefeller and his associates were determined to control the then chaotic business of oil refining. They began by arranging for a secret rebate of oil shipments from one of the two railroads then serving Cleveland. Then in the space of less than a month, using the rebate as an incentive, they managed to coerce other Cleveland refiners into selling out and obtained control of the city's refining. Within a year or two, Rockefeller was buying up refineries in other cities as well. He had also convinced the railroads that he was using that they should stop carrying oil to refineries owned by others, so that he was in almost complete control of the price offered to drillers. In the early 1870s, a group of drillers banded together to build pipelines that would take their oil to railroads with which Rockefeller wasn't allied. Rockefeller responded to this challenge by assembling a monopoly on the ownership of tank cars (since the pipelines did not go all the way to the refineries and railroad tank cars were still necessary), and by 1879, he had been so successful in squeezing the finances of the pipeline companies that their stockholders were forced to sell out to him. In that year, as a result of their control both of refineries and pipelines, Rockefeller and his associates controlled 90 percent of the refined oil in the United States.

Having bought up the competing pipelines (having let other people take the risks involved in developing new technologies for building and maintaining those lines), Rockefeller was quick to see their economic value. In 1881, one of his companies completed a six-inch line from the Pennsylvania oil fields to his refinery in Bayonne, New Jersey—the first pipeline that functioned independently of the railroads. By 1900, Rockefeller had built pipelines to Cleveland, Philadelphia, and Baltimore, and Standard Oil (Rockefeller's firm) was moving 24,000 barrels of crude a day (he still used the railroads to move the oil after it had been refined).

By that point, hundreds of civil and mechanical engineers were working for Rockefeller's pipeline companies (which held several patents on pipeline improvements), and several dozen chemists and chemical engineers were working in his refineries (and developing new techniques, such as the Frasch process for taking excess sulfur out of petroleum). In addition, Standard Oil was pioneering financial, management, and legal techniques for operating a business that had to control a huge physical network, spread out over several states. Since the laws dealing with corporations differed in each state and since some of them prevented a corporation in one state from owning property in another, one of Rockefeller's attorneys worked out a corporate arrangement so that Standard Oil had a different corporation in each state in which it operated (Standard Oil of New Jersey, Standard Oil of Ohio, and so forth). The stockholders in each corporation turned their stock over to a group of trustees, who managed the whole enterprise from New York—the famous Standard Oil Trust, of which Rockefeller himself was the single largest stockholder and therefore the major trustee. (The trust, as a way to organize a complex business, was soon picked up in tobacco and sugar refining and other industries involved in large-scale chemical processing, leading Congress, worried about the monopolistic possibilities, to pass the Sherman Anti-Trust Act in 1890.)

By 1900, the Standard Oil Trust (which had successfully battled antitrust proceedings in court) controlled most of the oil produced in Pennsylvania, and it owned most of the new oil fields that had been discovered in Ohio and Indiana. Rockefeller's almost complete stranglehold on the industry wasn't broken until oil was discovered early in the twentieth century in Texas, Oklahoma, Louisiana, and California, outside the reach of the pipelines he controlled and the railroads with which he was associated. Increased competition was accompanied by the continued growth not only of the pipeline network, but also of the industry as a whole: 26 million barrels of petroleum were processed in 1880, 45 million in 1890, 63 million in 1900, 209 million in 1910 (as gasoline was just beginning to edge out kerosene as the most important petroleum product), and 442 million in 1920 (when the Model T had been in production for almost eight years).

Like the telegraph and the railroad (and in combination with the telegraph and the railroad), the oil pipeline network had become a pervasive influence on the American economy and on the daily life of Americans. In the last decades of the nineteenth century, a very large number of Americans, especially those living outside of the major cities, used one of its products, kerosene, for heating and lighting their homes and for cooking. During the same decades, American industry became dependent on other fractions of petroleum to lubricate the machinery with which it was producing everything from luxurious cloth to common nails. Finally, in the early decades of the twentieth century, with the advent first of the internal combustion engine fueled by gasoline and then of automobiles and trucks powered by that engine, Americans discovered that access to petroleum was becoming a necessary condition not only of their working lives but also of their leisure time.

The Telephone System

Technologically the telephone was similar to the telegraph, but socially it was very different. The device patented by Alexander Graham Bell in 1876 was rather like a telegraph line: voices rather than signals could be transmitted by electric current because the transmitter lever and the receiving pencil had been replaced by very sensitive diaphragms. Aware of the difficulties that Morse had encountered in reaping profits from his patents—and aware that he had no head for business—Bell decided to turn over the financial and administrative details of creating a telephone network to someone else.

The businessmen and the attorneys who managed the Bell Telephone Company did their work well. While the railroad, telegraph, and petroleum networks had been integrated by corporate takeovers, the telephone system was integrated, from the very beginning, by corporate design. A crucial decision had been made early on: Bell Telephone would manufacture all the telephone instruments, then lease the instruments to local companies, which would operate telephone exchanges under license to Bell. This meant that for the first sixteen years of telephone network development (sixteen years was then the length of monopoly rights under a patent), the Bell Telephone Company could dictate, under the licensing agreements, common technologies for all the local telephone systems. Bell could also control the costs of telephone services to local consumers.

Because of this close supervision by one company, the telephone system was integrated from the very beginning. Between 1877 and 1893, the Bell Telephone Company, through its affiliated local operating companies, controlled and standardized virtually every telephone, every telephone line, and every telephone exchange in the nation. Indeed in the 1880s, the officers of Bell were confident that they could profitably begin long-distance service (that is, service that would connect one local operating company with another) precisely because all of the operating companies were using its standardized technology. Bell needed to hire physicists and electrical engineers to solve the technical problems involved in maintaining voice clarity over very long wires, but the organizational problems involved in connecting New York with Chicago and Chicago with Cleveland turned out to be minimal.

On the assumption that the telephone system would end up being used very similarly to the telegraph network, the officers of Bell had decided that their most important customers would be other businesses, particularly those in urban areas. They decided, as a marketing strategy, to keep rates fairly high, in return for which they would work to provide the clearest and most reliable service possible. By the end of the company's first year of operation, 3,000 telephones had been leased, 1 for every 10,000 people. By 1880, there were 60,000 (1 per 1,000), and when the Bell patents expired in 1893, there were 260,000 (1 per 250). About two thirds of these phones were located in businesses. Most of the country's business information was still traveling by mail and by telegraph (because businessmen wanted a written record of their transactions), but certain kinds of businesses were starting to find the telephone very handy: in 1891, the New York and New Jersey Telephone Company served 937 physicians and hospitals, 401 pharmacies, 363 liquor stores, 315 stables, 162 metalworking plants, 146 lawyers, 126 contractors, and 100 printing shops.

After the Bell patents expired, independent telephone companies entered the business despite Bell's concerted effort to keep them out. By 1902, there were almost 9,000 such independent companies, companies not part of the Bell system. When the organizers of the Bell system had analogized the telephone to the telegraph, they had made a crucial sociological mistake. They understood that in technological terms the telephone was similar to the telegraph, but they failed to understand that in social terms it was quite different. The telephone provided user-to-user communication (with the telegraph there were always intermediaries). In addition, the telephone was a form of voice communication; it facilitated emotional communication, something that was impossible with a telegraph. In short, what the organizers of the Bell system had failed to understand was that people would use the telephone to socialize with each other.

The independent companies took advantage of Bell's mistake. Some of them offered services that Bell hadn't thought to provide. Dial telephones were one such service, allowing customers to contact each other without having to rely on an operator (who sat at a switchboard, manually connecting telephone lines, one to another, with plugs). Operators were notorious for relieving the boredom of their jobs by listening in on conversations, something many customers wanted to avoid. Party lines were another such service. Anywhere from two to ten residences could share the same telephone line and telephone number, which drastically lowered the costs of residential services. Many lower-income people turned out to be willing to put up with the inconvenience of having to endure the ringing of telephones on calls meant for other parties in exchange for having telephone service at affordable rates.

Yet other independent companies served geographic locales that the Bell companies had ignored. This was particularly the case in rural areas where there were farm households. Bell managers apparently hadn't thought that farmers would want telephones, but it turned out that they were wrong. Farm managers used telephones to get prompt reports on prices and weather. Farm households used telephones to summon doctors in emergencies and to alleviate the loneliness of lives lived far from neighbors and relatives. In 1902, relatively few farm households had telephones, but as the independent companies grew, so did the number of farm-based customers; by 1920, just under 39 percent of all farm households in the United States had telephone service (while only 34 percent of nonfarm households did).

All this competition in telephone service had the net effect that any economist could have predicted: prices for telephone service fell, even in the Bell system. In order to keep the system companies competitive, the central Bell company had to cut the rates that it charged its affiliates for the rental of phones, and these savings were passed on to consumers. In New York City, as just one example, rates fell from $150 for 1,000 calls in 1880 to $51 in 1915 (figures adjusted for inflation).

As a result, in the period between 1894 and 1920, the telephone network expanded profoundly. Middle-class people began to pay for telephone service to their homes. Farm households became part of the telephone network (in record numbers). Retail businesses began to rely on telephones in their relations with their customers. By 1920, there were 13 million telephones in use in the country, 123 for every 1,000 people. Eight million of those 13 million phones belonged to Bell and 4 million to independent companies that connected to Bell lines. In just forty years, the telephone network, which provided point-to-point voice communication, had joined the telegraph, railroad, and petroleum networks as part of the economic and social foundation of industrial society.

The Electric System

Like the telegraph and telephone systems, the electric system was (and still is) quite literally a network of wires. Physicists, who had been experimenting with electricity since the middle of the eighteenth century, knew that under certain conditions electricity could produce light. Unfortunately, the first devices invented for generating a continuous flow of electricity—batteries—did not create a current strong enough for illumination. However, in 1831 the British experimenter Michael Faraday perfected a device that was based on a set of observations that scientists had made a decade earlier: all electric current will make a magnet move and a moving magnet will create an electric current. Faraday built an electric generator (a rotating magnet with a conducting wire wound around it)—a device that could, unlike the battery, create a continuous flow of current strong enough to be used for lighting.

Within a short time, the generator was being used to power arc lamps in which the light (and a lot of heat) was produced by sparking across a gap in the conducting wires. Arc lamps were first used in British and French lighthouses in the 1860s; the generator that created the electricity was powered by a steam engine. A few years later, arc lamps were also being used for street lighting in some American cities. Unfortunately, arc lamps were dangerous; they had to be placed very far away from people and from anything that might be ignited by the sparks. By the mid-1870s, several people in several different countries were racing with each other to find a safer form of electrical lighting, the incandescent lamp. In such a lamp, light would be derived from a glowing, highly resistant filament and not a spark; but the filament had to be kept in a vacuum so that it wouldn't oxidize (and disappear) too fast.

Thomas Alva Edison won the race. In 1878, when Edison started working on electrical lighting, he already had amassed a considerable reputation (and a moderate fortune) as an inventor. His first profitable invention had been the quadruplex telegraph, which could carry four messages at once, and he had also made successful modifications to the stock ticker, the telegraph system for relaying stock prices from the floor of the stock exchange to the offices of investors and brokers. These inventions had enhanced his reputation with Wall Street financiers and attorneys. In 1876, when he decided to become an independent inventor, building and staffing his own laboratory in Menlo Park, New Jersey, and again in 1878, when he decided that he wanted his laboratory to crack the riddle of electric lighting, he had no trouble borrowing money to invest in the enterprise.

Actually, they were enterprises. From the beginning, Edison understood that he wanted to build a technological system *and* a series of businesses to manage that system. The first of these businesses was the Edison Electric Light Company, incorporated for the purpose of financing research and development of electric lighting. Most of the stock was purchased by a group of New York financiers; Edison received stock in return for the rights to whatever lighting patents he might develop. Once Edison had actually invented a workable lightbulb (it had a carbonized thread as its filament), he proceeded to design other devices, and create other companies, that would all be parts of the system. The Edison Electric Illuminating Company of New York, founded in 1880, was created to build and maintain the very first central generating station providing electric service to customers. When this station opened its doors in 1882 (as its site Edison chose the part of Manhattan with the highest concentration of office buildings), it contained several steam-driven generators (built to Edison's design by the Edison Machine Company) and special cables to carry the electricity underground (made by the Edison Electric Tube Company). Customers who signed up for electric service had their usage measured by meters that Edison had

invented; their offices were outfitted with lamp sockets that Edison had designed into which they were to place lightbulbs that another Edison company manufactured.

Information about this new system spread very fast (thanks to publicity generated by the Edison Electric Light Company), and within a few months (not even years), entrepreneurs were applying to Edison for licenses to build electric generating plants all over the country, indeed all over the world. Having been designed as a system, the electrical network grew very fast. There was only one generating plant in the country in 1882, but by 1902, there were 2,250, and by 1920, almost 4,000. These plants had a total generating capacity of 19 million kilowatts. Just over a third of the nation's homes were wired for electricity by 1920, by which time electricity was being used not only for lighting but also for cooling (electric fans), ironing (the electric iron replaced the so-called sad iron quickly), and vacuuming (the vacuum cleaner was being mass-produced by 1915).

The Edison companies (some of which eventually merged with other companies to become the General Electric Company) were not, however, able to remain in control of the electric system for as long (or as completely) as the Bell companies were able to dominate the telephone business or Standard Oil the petroleum business. Part of the reason for this lay in the principles of electromagnetic induction, which can be used to create electric motors as well as electric generators. The same experimenters who were developing electric generators in the middle years of the nineteenth century were also developing electric motors, and one of the first applications of those motors was in a business very different from the lighting business: electric traction for electric intraurban streetcars, often known as trolley cars. The first of these transportation systems was installed in Richmond, Virginia, in 1888 by a company owned by Frank Sprague, an electrical engineer who had briefly worked for Edison.

Sprague had invented an electric motor that, he thought, would be rugged enough to power carriages running day in and day out on city streets. As it turned out, the motor had to be redesigned, and redesigned again, before it worked very well, and Sprague also had to design trolley poles (for conducting the electricity from the overhead wires to the carriage) and a controlling system (so that the speed of the motor could be varied by the person driving the carriage). In the end, however, the electric streetcar was successful, and the days of the horse-pulled carriage were clearly numbered. Fourteen years after Sprague's first system began operating, the nation had 22,576 miles of track devoted to street railways.

Electric motors were also being used in industry. The earliest motors, like the streetcar motors, had been direct current (d.c.) motors, which needed a special and often fragile device (called a commutator) to transform the alternating current (a.c.) produced by generators. In 1888, an a.c. motor was invented by Nikola Tesla, a Serbian physicist who had emigrated to the United States. Tesla's patents were assigned to the Westinghouse Company, which began both to manufacture and to market them. At that point, the use of electric motors in industry accelerated. The very first factory to be completely electrified was a cotton mill, built in 1894. As electric motors replaced steam engines, factory design and location changed; it was no longer necessary to build factories that were several stories high (to facilitate power transmission from a central engine) or to locate them near water sources (to feed the steam boilers). The first decade of the twentieth century was a turning point in the use of electric power in industry as more and more factories converted; by 1901, almost 400,000 motors had been installed in factories, with a total capacity of almost 5 million horsepower.

In short, the electrical system was more complex than the telephone and petroleum systems because it consisted of several different subsystems (lighting, traction, industrial power) with very different social goals and economic strategies; because of its complexity, no single company could dominate it. By 1895, when the first generating plant intended to transmit electricity over a long distance became operational (it was a hydroelectric plant built to take advantage of Niagara Falls, transmitting electricity twenty miles to the city of Buffalo), there were several hundred companies involved in the electric

industry: enormous companies such as Westinghouse and General Electric that made everything from generators to lightbulbs; medium-sized companies, such as the ones that ran streetcar systems or that provided electric service to relatively small geographic areas; and small companies, which made specialized electric motors or parts for electric motors. Despite this diversity, the electric system was unified by the fact that its product, electric energy, had been standardized. By 1910, virtually all the generating companies (which, by now, had come to be called utility companies) were generating alternating current at sixty cycles per second. This meant that all electric appliances were made to uniform specifications and all transmission facilities could potentially be connected to one another. By 1920, electricity had supplanted gas, kerosene, and oils for lighting. In addition, it was being used to power sewing machines in ready-made clothing factories, to separate aluminum from the contaminants in its ores, to run projectors through which motion pictures could be viewed, to carry many thousands of commuters back and forth, and to do dozens of other chores in workplaces and residences. As transmission towers marched across the countryside and yet another set of wire-carrying poles were constructed on every city street, few Americans demonstrated any inclination to decline the conveniences that the youngest technical system—electricity—was carrying in its wake.

The Character of Industrialized Society

As inventors, entrepreneurs, and engineers were building all these multifarious technological systems, Americans were becoming increasingly dependent on them. Each time a person made a choice—to buy a kerosene lamp or continue to use candles, to take a job in an electric lamp factory or continue to be a farmer, to send a telegraph message instead of relying on the mail, to put a telephone in a shop so that customers could order without visiting—that person, whether knowingly or not, was becoming increasingly enmeshed in a technological system. The net effect of all that construction activity and all those choices was that a wholly new social order, and wholly different set of social and economic relationships between people, emerged: industrial society.

In industrial societies, manufactured products play a more important economic role than agricultural products. More money is invested in factories than in farms; more bolts of cloth are produced than bales of hay; more people work on assembly lines than as farm laborers. Just over half (53 percent) of what was produced in the United States was agricultural in 1869 and only a third (33 percent) was manufactured. In 1899 (just thirty years later), those figures were reversed: half the nation's output was in manufactured goods and only a third was agricultural, despite the fact that the nation's total farm acreage had increased rapidly as a result of westward migration. Manufacturing facilities were turning out products that were becoming increasingly important aspects of everyday life: canned corn and lightbulbs, cigarettes and underwear.

In a preindustrial society, the countryside is the base for economic and political power. In such societies, most people live in rural districts. Most goods that are traded are agricultural products; the price of fertile land is relatively high; and wealth is accumulated by those who are able to control that land. Industrialized societies are dominated by their cities. More people live and work in cities than on farms; most goods are manufactured in cities; most trade is accomplished there; wealth is measured in money and not in land. Furthermore, the institutions that control money—banks—are urban institutions.

As the nineteenth century progressed, more and more Americans began living either in the rural towns in which factories were located (which, as a result, started to become small cities) or in the older cities that had traditionally been the center of artisanal production and of commerce. Native-born Americans began moving from the countryside to the city; many newly arrived Americans (and there were millions of newcomers to America in the nineteenth century) settled in cities. Just over half of all Americans (54 percent) were farmers or farm laborers in 1870, but only one in three was by 1910. Some American families underwent the rural–

urban transition slowly: a daughter might move off the farm to a rural town when she married, and then a granddaughter might make her fortune in a big city. Others had less time: a man might be tending olive groves in Italy one day and working in a shoe factory in Philadelphia two months later.

During the 1840s, the population of the eastern cities nearly doubled, and several midwestern cities (St. Louis, Chicago, Pittsburgh, Cincinnati) began to grow. In 1860, there were nine port cities that had populations over 100,000 (Boston, New York, Brooklyn, Philadelphia, Baltimore, New Orleans, Chicago, Cincinnati, and St. Louis)—by 1910, there were fifty. Just as significantly, the country's largest cities were no longer confined to the eastern seaboard or to the Midwest. There were several large cities in the plains states, and half the population of the far west was living not in its fertile valleys or at the feet of its glorious mountains, but in its cities: Los Angeles, Denver, San Francisco, Portland, and Seattle. By 1920, for the first time in the nation's history, just slightly over half of all Americans lived in communities that had more than 10,000 residents.

Money was flowing in the same direction that people were; by 1900, the nation's wealth was located in its cities, not in its countryside. The nation's largest businesses and its wealthiest individuals were in its cities. J. P. Morgan and Cornelius Vanderbilt controlled their railroad empires from New York; Leland Stanford and Charles Crocker ran theirs from San Francisco; John D. Rockefeller operated from Cleveland and New York; Andrew Carnegie, at least initially, from Pittsburgh. Probably by 1880, and certainly by 1890, stock exchanges and investment bankers had become more important to the nation's economic health than cotton wharves and landed gentry.

This transition to an urban society had political consequences because political power tends to follow the trail marked out by wealth (and, in a democracy, to some extent by population). In the early years of the nineteenth century, when the independent political character of the nation was being formed, most Americans still lived on farms and American politics was largely controlled by people who earned their living directly from the land. After the Civil War, city residents (being both more numerous and more wealthy) began to flex their political muscles and to express their political interests more successfully. The first twelve presidents of the United States had all been born into farming communities, but from 1865 until 1912, the Republican party, then the party that most clearly represented the interests of big business and of cities, controlled the White House for all but eight years, and those eight years were the two terms served by Grover Cleveland, who before becoming president had been the mayor of Buffalo, New York.

The transition to an urban society also had economic and technological consequences. In a kind of historical feedback loop, industrialization caused cities to grow and the growth of cities stimulated more industrialization. Nineteenth-century cities were, to use the term favored by urban historians, walking cities. Since most residents could not afford either the cost or the space required to keep a horse and carriage, they had to be able to walk to work or to work in their own homes. Since businesses also had to be within walking distance of each other, this meant that as cities grew they became congested; more and more people had both to live and to work within the same relatively limited space. With congestion came disease; all nineteenth-century American cities were periodically struck by devastating epidemics: cholera, dysentery, typhoid fever.

Even before they understood the causes of these epidemics, city governments became convinced that they had to do something both to relieve the congestion and to control the diseases. Streets had to be paved, running water provided, sewers constructed, new housing encouraged. This meant that reservoirs had to be built, aqueducts and pumping stations constructed, trenches dug, pipes purchased, brickwork laid, new construction techniques explored. All of this municipal activity not only stimulated American industry but also served as a spur to the growth of civil engineering.

In addition, in the years between 1870 and 1920, many American cities actively stimulated industrialization by seeking out manufacturing interests and offering operating incentives to them. Many of the nation's older cities found themselves in economic trouble as railroad depots become more important than ports as nodes in the country's transportation system. In their distress, these cities decided that their futures lay not in commerce but in manufacturing, and they began to seek out manufacturing entrepreneurs to encourage industrial growth. By that time, the steam engine having been perfected and its manufacture made relatively inexpensive, manufacturers had ceased to depend on waterwheels as a power source, which meant that they could easily (and profitably) establish their enterprises in cities rather than in the countryside; the development of the electric motor only served to increase this potential.

Minneapolis became a center of flour milling, Kansas City of meatpacking, Memphis of cotton seed oil production, Rochester of shoe manufacturing, Schenectady of electric equipment, New York of ready-made clothing, Pittsburgh of steel and glass manufacture. Local banks helped manufacturers start up in business and local politicians helped recruit a docile labor force, all in the interests of stabilizing or augmenting a city's economy. Nationwide the net result was a positive impetus to the growth of industry; the processes of industrialization and urbanization are mutually reinforcing.

If American cities grew prodigiously during the second half of the nineteenth century, so, too, did the American population as a whole: between 1860 and 1920, the population of the United States more than tripled (from 31 million to 106 million). Some of the increase was the result of a high natural birthrate; in general, American families were larger than what is needed to keep a population at a stable size from one generation to the next. In addition, as the result of improvements in public health and improvements in the food supply, the death rate was declining and life expectancy was rising. People were living longer and that meant that in any given year a declining proportion of the total population was dying. On top of this, immigrants were arriving in record numbers. The figures are astounding; the total, between the end of the Civil War and the passage of the Immigration

Restriction Acts (1924), came to over 30 million people. Like their native-born contemporaries, immigrants had a high birthrate and a declining death rate and more of their children lived past infancy and then enjoyed a longer life expectancy, all of which further contributed to the mushrooming size of the American population. This startling population increase—almost 20 percent—reflects another crucial difference between societies that have become industrialized and those that have not. In a preindustrialized society the size of the population changes in a more or less cyclical fashion. If the weather cooperates and the crops are bounteous and peace prevails, people remain reasonably healthy and many children live past infancy; over the course of time the population will grow. But eventually the population will grow too large to be supported by the available land or the land itself will become infertile. Droughts may come or heavy rains; locusts may infest the fields or diseases may strike the cattle. Men will be drawn off to battle just when it is time to plow the fields or soldiers engaged in battles will trample the wheat and burn the barns. Then starvation will ensue. People will succumb to disease; fewer children will be born, and more of them will die in infancy. The population will shrink.

Under preindustrial conditions, such population cycles have been possible. Sometimes the cycle will take two generations to recur, sometimes two centuries, but it has recurred as long as there have been agricultural peoples who have been keeping records of themselves. Industrialization breaks this cyclical population pattern. Once a country has industrialized, natural disasters and wars do not seem to have a long-term effect on the size of its population; the rate of increase may slow for a few years or so, but there is still an increase. And the standard of living keeps rising as well. People stay relatively healthy; they live longer lives. Generally speaking, they can have as many (or as few) children as they want, knowing that, also generally speaking, most of their children will live past infancy. This is the salient characteristic that makes underdeveloped countries long for development: industrialized countries seem able to support extraordinarily large populations without any long-term

collapse either in the size of the population or in the standard of living.

Industrialized countries can do this because agriculture industrializes at the same time that manufacturing does. In the transition to industrialization, what is happening on the farm is just as important as what is happening in the factories since, to put it bluntly, people cannot work if they cannot eat. These social processes—sustained growth of the population and the industrialization of agriculture—are interlocked. Both were proceeding rapidly in the United States between the years 1870 and 1920 as American farmers simultaneously pushed west and industrialized, settling new territory and developing more productive farming techniques. As the frontier moved westward, roughly 400 million new acres were put under cultivation: virgin prairies became farms, fertile mountain valleys were planted in orchards, grassy hills became grazing land for sheep and cattle. The total quantity of improved acreage (meaning land that had been cleared or fenced or otherwise made suitable for agricultural use) in the United States multiplied two and a half times between 1860 and 1900.

This alone would have considerably expanded the nation's agricultural output, but newly introduced agricultural implements profoundly altered the work process of farming (particularly grain growing) and increased its productivity. The first of these was the reaper (patented by Cyrus McCormick in 1834 and in limited use even before the Civil War). The reaper, which was pulled by horses, replaced hand labor. Once a reaper had been purchased, a farm owner could quadruple the amount of acreage cut in one day or fire three day laborers who had previously been employed for the harvest or greatly increase the acreage put to plow (since the number of acres planted had always been limited by what could be reaped in the two prime weeks of harvest).

The reaper was followed by the harvester (which made binding the grain easier), followed by the self-binder (which automatically bound the grain into shocks), and—in the far west—followed by the combine, a steam-driven tractor (which cut a swath of over forty feet, then threshed and bagged the grain automatically, sometimes at the rate of three 150-pound bags a minute). In those same years, haymaking was altered by the introduction of automatic cutting and baling machinery, and plowing was made considerably easier by the invention of the steel plow (John Deere, 1837) and the chilled-iron plow (James Oliver, 1868), both of which had the advantage of being nonstick surfaces for the heavy, wet soils of the prairies.

The net result, by 1900, was that American farmers were vastly more productive than they had been in 1860. Productivity has two facets: it is a measure both of the commodities being produced and of the labor being used to produce them. Statistics on wheat production indicate how radically American agriculture was changing in the second half of the nineteenth century. In 1866, there were roughly 15.5 million acres devoted to wheat production in the United States; farmers achieved average yields of 9.9 bushels per acre, resulting in a total national production of about 152 million bushels. By 1898, acreage had roughly trebled (to 44 million), yields had almost doubled (to 15.3 bushels per acre), and the total production was 675 million bushels.

All this was accomplished with a marked saving of labor. By the hand method, 400 people and 200 oxen had to work ten hours a day to produce 20,000 bushels of wheat; by the machine method, only 6 people (and 36 horses) were required. Farms were getting larger, ownership was being restricted to a smaller and smaller number of people and more machinery was required for profitable farming (between 1860 and 1900, the annual value of farm implements manufactured in the United States went from $21 million to $101 million)—at the same time, the firms were becoming more productive.

What this means, put another way, was that a smaller proportion of the nation's people were needed to produce the food required by its ever larger population. Some people left their farms because they hated the farming life, some because they could not afford to buy land as prices began to rise, some because they were forced off the land by the declining profitability of small farms. The farming population (this includes both owners and laborers) began to shrink in relation to the rest of the population.

New transportation facilities and new food-based industries made it easier and cheaper for the residents of cities and towns to eat a more varied diet. The fledgling canning industry was spurred by the need to supply food for troops during the Civil War. After the war, the canners turned to the civilian market, and by the 1880s, urban Americans had become accustomed to eating canned meat, condensed milk (invented by Gail Borden in 1856), canned peas, and canned corn. The Heinz company was already supplying bottled ketchup and factory pickles to a vast population, and the Campbell's company was just about to start marketing soups. By 1900, cheese and butter making had become largely a factory operation, made easier and cheaper by the invention of the centrifugal cream separator in 1879.

After the Civil War, the railroads replaced steamboats and canal barges as the principal carriers of farm products (from wheat to hogs, from apples to tobacco), thus both shortening the time required to bring goods to market and sharply lowering the cost of transportation. After the 1880s, when refrigerated transport of various kinds was introduced, this trend accelerated: even more products could be brought to market (butchered meat, for example, or fresh fish) in an even shorter time. New refrigeration techniques transformed beer making from a home to a factory operation; by 1873, there were some 4,000 breweries in the United States with an output of 10 million barrels a year. Commercial baking had also expanded and Americans were becoming fond of factory-made crackers and cookies. In the end, then, another historical feedback loop had been established, a loop connecting industrialization with agricultural change. Industrialization made farming more productive, which made it possible for the population to increase, which created a larger market for manufactured goods, which increased the rate of industrialization.

Conclusion: Industrialization and Technological Systems

By 1920, a majority of Americans had crossed the great divide between preindustrial and industrial societies. The foods they ate, the conditions under which they worked, the places in which they lived—all had been transformed. The majority of Americans were no longer living on farms. They were eating food that had been carried to them by one technological system (the railroad) after having been processed by machines that were powered by a second (electricity) and lubricated by a third (petroleum). If they wanted to light their domiciles at night or heat their dwelling places during cold weather, they could not avoid interacting with one or another technological system for distributing energy—unless they were willing to manufacture their own candles (even then, they might have ended up buying paraffin from Standard Oil). The social ties that bound individuals and communities together—someone has been elected, someone else has died, young men are about to be drafted, a young woman has given birth—were being carried over, communicated through, and to some extent

controlled by technological networks that were owned by large, monopolistically inclined corporations. More people were living longer lives; fewer babies were dying in infancy; the standard of living for many Americans (albeit not for all) was rising. And at the very same time, because of the very same processes, people were becoming more dependent on each other.

Early in the nineteenth century the process of industrialization had appeared (to those who were paying attention) as a rather discrete undertaking: a spinning factory in a neighboring town, a merchant miller up the river, a railroad station a few miles distant. By the end of the century, virtually all Americans must have been aware that it had become something vastly different: a systematic undertaking that had created interlocking physical and social networks in which all Americans—rich or poor, young or old, urban or rural—were increasingly enmeshed.

I.4   ROSALIND WILLIAMS

History as Technological Change

In this selection from her book *Retooling: A Historian Confronts Technological Change,* MIT's dean of undergraduate education and student affairs reflects on how the idea of historical change has become nearly synonymous with technological change and how the term *technology* has been reduced to meaning only information technology. While acknowledging the important role that technological innovation has played in human history, Williams wants to resist the idea that all historical change can be reduced to or explained by technological change. But she also observes that we are now on the verge of another great transformation of the human habitat, comparable in significance to those brought about by the Agricultural and the Industrial Revolutions. The question is how will this transformation affect our sense of human identity? Where will we be able to find meaning and purpose in a world that is our own creation?

Focus Questions

1. What does Williams mean when she says that "Technological innovation resembles but hollows out the idea of progress"?
2. What are some examples of previous technological revolutions and how have they transformed the human habitat? According to Williams, what kind of transformation of the human habitat appears to be taking place because of the information revolution?

3. What does she mean when she describes the world of the information age as a reflexive or "boomerang" world?
4. Discuss and evaluate her claim that "history and nature are weakening as well-defined external frameworks that give meaning to human life." How would other authors, such as Strong (selection I.12) and Kurzweil, (selection II.8) view this claim?

Keywords

artificial habitats, information technology, innovation, progress, reflexivity, technological revolutions

ONE DOMINANT ASSUMPTION ABOUT the information age is that it represents a "new world" of technological change that relentlessly pushes into retreat an "old world" of culturally driven resistance, much as the soldiers of the Roman Empire pushed the Celts back into the western hills of Britain. Today's conflict, we are told, is between the new economy and the old one, between digital and analog, between systems and life-world, between globalization and identity. The human race is split between dynamic "change agents" and the stagnant non-retooled, between neo-nomadic "symbolic analysts" who work with bits and a "disposable labor force that can be automated and/or hired/fired/offshored. . . ."[1]

Such binary thinking is extended to history itself. The information revolution is leading us into a new phase of history, in which technological change will be the major and constant determinant of human life. History becomes the record of a grand struggle between the irresistible force of technology-driven "change" or "innovation" on the one hand and misguided if understandable culturally driven resistance to change on the other, with "change" and "innovation" inevitably winning.

This is supposedly an age without a sense of history, but the view of history as a struggle between technological change and technological resistance is powerful and pervasive today. Implicit rather than explicit, it is less a theory (which would imply

some conscious awareness of the issues and some effort at logical consistency) than an ideology (ideologies are not especially logical or consistent).[2] It is an ideology of history in which the very word 'history' has been displaced by 'technology'. Instead of being a figure in the ground of history, technology has become the ground—not an element of historical change, but the thing itself. We have come to assume that where technology is going is where history is going, as if they are now one and the same.

The ideology of technological change has become the dominant, if implicit, theory of history in our time, even for those who never pick up a history book. In Karl Mannheim's famous distinction, ideology is a set of "wish-images" intended to evolve the existing order into a better one, while utopia represents a wish to break the bonds of the existing order, to overturn it for a new reality. Mannheim adds: "The utopia of the ascendant bourgeoisie was the idea of 'freedom.'"[3] Innovation has come to define a utopia of freedom, an ideal place running by market and technological laws, where creative minds and free-flowing capital unite to make a new world abundant in possibilities and energy. This is a much more appealing world than the one we actually live in, where innovations become hardened into bureaucracies, where actions have consequences, and where waves of change wash back on shore. The utopian "no place" of market-driven innovation presents an agreeable escape from the complexities and consequences of a crowded, risky world. Mannheim emphasizes that ideology and utopia are ideal types; in practice, it is often difficult to distinguish them within the social order or even

From *Retooling: A Historian Confronts Technological Change,* by Rosalind Williams, 2002, p. 14–26. Reprinted by permission of MIT Press.

within an individual's mind. In the view of history as technological innovation, however, we can often discern a set of "wish-images" that is utopian without being especially progressive.

As an MIT administrator, I rarely heard anyone talk explicitly about history, but I often heard people express the implicit view of history as technological change. They did this through repeated use of a cluster of deceptively simple words: 'technology,' 'change,' 'culture,' 'space,' 'time,' 'community.' These words are highly interdependent, deriving their meaning from the others and forming a closed world of cross-references. They are also highly reflexive, acquiring meaning from the very changes they are supposed to analyze.[4] They also drain meaning away from other, formerly more significant words, such as 'engineering' and 'progress.'

The sun of this linguistic system is 'technology.' In 1861, when MIT was given its name, the word was novel, even daring, and grandly comprehensive. Proclaimed in chiseled stone below the Great Dome, 'technology' still defines, in a lofty way, the Institute's mission. But in everyday meetings below and around the dome 'technology' has little grandeur. It has come to mean *information technology*—a recent, drastic, telling reduction. In committee meetings, when we sketched business processes or organizational models on a flip chart, someone would write 'technology' with a circle around it. We would talk about designing new learning spaces to accommodate "the technology." We would write and review reports saying things like "The primary motivation to revise the policy [is] the recognition that technology has transformed the means by which we collect, manage, and provide access to student information."

At no time, in any of these contexts, did anyone suggest that 'technology' might include more than information technology, nor did anyone challenge its status as an independent entity, 'Technology' once was a grand term, though also a dangerous one, because it was so often used as an abstract, independent historical agent.[5] It is still dangerous in this way, but it is no longer grand. It means information technology and it means change.

While 'technology' expands its rhetorical reach, that of 'engineering' shrinks. Never a glamorous term (though it was a solid one), it is now used more rarely, and mostly in a connection with a specific project or department. Even more conspicuous in its absence is the word 'progress.' Not long ago, discussions of technology were dominated by "progress talk."[6] At MIT today, people talk a lot about scientific progress, referring to the kind of discovery that would win a Nobel Prize, but little about technological progress, except with irony.

Instead, 'technology' is linked with 'change.' Everyone talks about change as relentless and inevitable but also, almost always, as pointless, in the double sense of lacking a purpose and lacking an end. Progress has a story line; change does not. After one meeting about new software systems, a participant told me that a consultant had advised her to use the concept of a "change journey" to help people overcome their resistance to change. When I inquired what was the destination of such a journey, I was told that it might be thought of as arriving at a point of comfort with change. 'Change,' like 'technology,' has been sharply reduced in meaning. Of all the possible types of change—political, intellectual, cultural, social—technological change is all that really matters.[7] The change journey takes us through familiar landscapes of science, engineering, politics, the market, work, family. These too may change, everyone acknowledges, but the assumption is that they will do so only as a consequence of technological change.

Technological innovation resembles but hollows out the idea of progress.[8] Progress is measured in reference to human-defined goals: change and innovation are measured by market success. Market-driven innovation may tend to move in certain directions (Moore's Law, globalism, systems integration), but those directions are defined less by human purposes than by the rules of the market and the inner workings of technology itself. Innovation does not necessarily translate into human progress, any more than biological evolution means progress of the species (as Darwin well understood). Today's ideology of history as technological innovation turns the market, the motor of capitalist acquisition, into the motor of history itself, with technology as its agent.

It is easy to unmask the rhetoric of innovation and change, and to show that it is a cynical management tool justifying any sort of human disruption (moving, working harder or longer, being laid off) as the inevitable downside of the larger good. But then why is this view of history so widely, if semiconsciously, accepted?[9] Management babble is heavily discounted by most of us. In the midst of its ideological torrent, we try to keep living reasonably human lives, trying to figure out who we are, how to connect with others, how to accomplish something meaningful, how to enjoy the time we have. Still, the rhetoric of change management has some ring of truth, because it expresses, however inadequately, everyday experience in a world dominated by technologies we have created.

The rhetoric of change management has the effect, however, of trivializing the whole concept of change. Significant change is much more than a new software system or product. It is historical, in that it involves human relationships, expectations, and meanings. There is no single digital divide that we will step over collectively into the information age, leaving behind the creaky old world of everyday life for a sleek new world of frictionless systems. There are many fault lines in history today, and many of them run right through us. The change agent and the change resister are often the same person.[10] We are living through a transformation of the human habitat that is much more comprehensive than what is usually thought of as "technological change."

The New Human Habitat

Predictions about the information revolution have become the "airport reading" of the world—a substitute for beach reading in a harried age, just as predictable but a lot less engaging, celebrating not the steamy pleasures of physical reality but the disembodied pleasures of virtual reality. Computing will be ubiquitous, our rooms will read our thoughts, the air will hum with messages, the Internet will become an omninet, we will be lifted out of the mud of localism to digital globalism—all on the other side of the great historical divide. Many historians of technology dismiss most of these predictions

as unfounded digital evangelism. Historians are trained to look for continuity, to be wary of revolutionary claims, to spot inconsistencies. On the latter point, Alex Roland, a recent past president of the Society for the History of Technology (SHOT), notes that people who talk about technological revolution are often talking about different things: "Fifteen years ago we were confidently told that we were in a computer revolution. Now it is an information revolution. A more proper label might be a communications revolution. Or it may turn out in hindsight to have been a solid-state-physics revolution, or a digital revolution, or a micro-electronics revolution, or a control revolution. Some people think that the coming revolution in genetic engineering will outweigh all of these."[11]

So what kind of technological change is it that we are living through, and how does it compare with other major transformations in history? Is this another industrial revolution (the productive one of steam engines, cotton mills, and railroads), or is it more like the second industrial revolution (the consumer one of electricity, automobiles, cinema, and chemical industries)? Is the telegraph "the Victorian Internet,"[12] or is the Internet more like electricity? Or should we compare information to energy?

No analogy seems quite right. The industrial revolution of the late eighteenth and the early nineteenth century was defined by an unprecedented leap in human productivity brought about by the exploitation of the vast energy reserves stored in fossil fuels.[13] If you compare the efficiency of the steam-powered thresher in Laurel with the labor of hand threshing, and if you multiply that kind of efficiency millions of times in millions of settings, you begin to grasp the essence of the industrial revolution.

The second industrial revolution (which occurred in the late nineteenth century) also increased productivity, but its distinctive contributions were the distribution of cheap and flexible energy in the form of electricity, the construction of grid upon grid of communication and transportation systems (subways, automobiles, telephone, radio), and what contemporaries called "the democratization of luxury" through the proliferation of cheaper and more varied consumer goods. Collectively these technological innovations made everyday life far more comfortable and interesting than ever before. In the words of another past president of SHOT, Robert Post: "The late nineteenth century was the greatest period of technological change in terms of things that affected huge numbers of people's lives in basic ways—much more so than today."[14]

In all these discussions, historians are trying to develop a sort of historical Richter scale: What are the minor shocks, and what are the major ones? All of us are trying to get a sense of the scale of change in the midst of constant tremors. At one MIT meeting about educational technologies, a participant from the software industry commented: "Education is the building and technology is the earthquake." On the historical Richter scale, however, many historians of technology would say that the so-called information revolution is not so big. They disagree with the hypothesis of fundamental change preached by digital evangelists, in part because historians are used to measuring change by productivity rates and living standards. These measures miss some distinctive features of information technology. At the heart of information technology is the manipulation of symbols, not of matter. It does not simply "impact" culture and society; the technology itself is inherently cultural and social from the start. Directly as well as indirectly, it affects human experiences of space, time, communication, and consciousness.

From this perspective, the most appropriate historical analogy is another communications revolution: the invention of the mass media, or the printing press, or perspective, or numerals and the alphabet, or, behind them all, the invention of language—by far the most complex and sophisticated human invention, and a prerequisite for storing and passing on all other forms of technological knowledge and practice.[15] But this analogy too is inadequate, insofar as information technology has transformed production and consumption as well as consciousness and communications.

If comparisons are hard to find, it is not because technological change is less significant today than in the past but because we are breaking it up into episodes instead of seeing it whole. The digital divide is a major episode, not the whole story. The technological revolution we are living through includes everything Roland names: computers, information, communications, solid-state physics, digital electronics, control, genetics. It also includes the two industrial revolutions, which now may be seen as partial and preparatory. The essential feature of the larger technological revolution is the creation of a new habitat for human existence.[16] On the historical Richter scale, it is The Big One. Elting Morison, a historian who joined the MIT faculty in 1946, described it as follows:

> We are well on the way, in our timeless effort to bring the natural environment under control, to replacing it by an artificial environment of our own contriving. This special environment has a structure, a set of tempos, and a series of dynamic reactions that are not always nicely scaled to human responses. The interesting question seems to be whether man, having succeeded after all these years in bringing so much of the natural environment under his control, can now manage the imposing system he has created for the specific purpose of enabling him to manage his natural environment.[17]

Morison's formulation shows how difficult it is to find adequate and precise (not to mention gender-neutral) language to describe the new human habitat. Calling our environment "artificial" or "special," as Morison does, suggests something unnatural or even abnormal about it. There is nothing more natural, however, than the human creativity and ingenuity that have shaped this new environment. For human beings, the production of technology is as natural as is the production of enzymes for certain bacteria.[18] Nor is an "artificial" environment "replacing" the natural one. Nature has ended not in the sense of going away but only in the sense of being so mixed and mingled with human processes that it can no longer be identified as a separate entity.[19] In the words of the social theorist Ulrich Beck: "Not a hair or a crumb of it is still 'natural,' if 'natural' means nature being left to itself."[20]

Human beings have always tried to control nature so as to make life safer, more predictable, more abundant, and more fulfilling. But since the beginning of recorded history, and back into unrecorded history, non-human nature has been the ground of human life. This relationship between technology and nature, between figure and ground, which had been reversing slowly over centuries, reversed decisively in the past century. The built world has become the ground of human existence, now framing and embedding non-human nature. We have gone from using technology to control and exploit our habitat to using it to detach ourselves from our habitat.[21]

We continue to struggle for words with which to express this new phase of history. As early as the first industrial revolution, Georg W. F. Hegel contrasted "first" or given nature with "second nature" created by humankind. In similar language, the historian of technology Thomas Parke Hughes has referred to the technological world as the "second creation." In the 1960s, Lewis Mumford contrasted "the organic habitat" with "this new megatechnics . . . a uniform, all-enveloping structure, designed for automatic operation."[22] I find myself using the verbal shorthand of referring to a technological world, or, more accurately, a *hybrid* world—a world in which technology and nature are inextricably mixed.

There is a convincing historical precedent for the replacement of one human habitat by another: the Neolithic revolution, usually dated around 10,000 BCE and usually defined by the integrated invention of agriculture, of cities, and indeed of history itself, since the concomitant invention of writing permitted, for the first time, a durable collective memory. Left behind, except in specific settings and in deepest memory, was the pastoral life of hunting and gathering, which had been the human, or humanoid, way of life for hundreds of thousands of years.[23] All the transformative events of the Neolithic revolution—writing, agriculture, settlements—were based in material change, but they also redefined what it meant to be human.[24] As the historian of religion Mircea

Eliade notes, when most of humankind started raising crops "an ancient world, the world of nomadic hunters, with its religions, its myths, its moral conceptions, was ebbing away." Eliade continues: "Thousands and thousands of years were to elapse before the final lamentations of the old world died away, forever doomed by the advent of agriculture. One must also suppose that the profound spiritual crisis aroused by man's decision *to call a halt and bind himself to the soil* must have taken many hundreds of years to become completely integrated."[25]

The technological revolution of our times is the "decision"—collective, unconscious, incremental—to unbind ourselves from the soil. Eliade reminds us how far-reaching are the implications of binding ourselves instead to a self-constructed world. For millennia, the fact of settlement—humans living with other humans in a place over time—has shaped our ideas and practices of work, family, time and space, and society. This fact has also shaped our souls: solace, redemption, transcendence, and meaning have been defined by the twin powers of human community and non-human nature. It may be centuries before the lamentations for a lost world fade away and the human imagination can come to terms with its new habitat.

A technological world is partly natural and intensely human. The new fact of history on a material level is that nature is now so thoroughly intermixed with technology. The new fact of history on a social level is that we keep running into ourselves, as it were, as we build our values and our social order into the world. Sociologists describe this as the transition from modern society to something beyond: post-modernism, or (as Anthony Giddens prefers) post-modernity or radical modernity, or (as Ulrich Beck prefers) a risk society. Such thinkers stress the "reflexivity" of our society, meaning that we live in a world of echoes, a "boomerang" world (Beck's term) where everything that goes out comes back, where everything gets sampled and remixed, where everything has consequences, where social relationships co-evolve with material ones, where technology changes the very institutions producing it.[26]

The reflexivity of the world can be read positively (Giddens: "The reflexivity of modern social life consists in the fact that social practices are constantly examined and reformed in the light of incoming information about those very practices, thus constitutively altering their character"[27]) or less positively (Beck: "The gain in power from techno-economic 'progress' is being increasingly overshadowed by the production of risks"[28]). In any case, the process keeps getting more intensely reflexive. Once the marketplace takes the prime role in directing technological change, as it has since the 1970s, the process feeds back into itself.[29] A leading product of information technology is more information technology, all molded by the imperatives of a capitalist economy.

In terms of technological development, this is a virtuous circle—but it is still a circle, which accounts for the cultural paradox that the digital age engenders both a sense of liberating possibilities and a sense of oppression. Because of its socialized nature, information technology enhances social abilities, arguably our most human trait. But as information technology keeps reinforcing its dominance in terms defined by the market, other forms of sociability get selected out. A business-oriented society becomes more and more so as the system responds to its own feedback. In a world we have largely constructed, we keep encountering ourselves—but the projected "selves" we keep running into represent only a part of capacities, and arguably not the finest part.[30]

In the words of the historian Elting Morison, the historical challenge of our time is to build "a technological firmament that will really fit us" and "to organize a technological world we can live in."[31] History has not ended any more than nature is ended. Inevitably history will reveal itself to be much more powerful and unpredictable than the latest software upgrade. Inevitably nature will remind us of the fragility and impermanence of our control of the organic habitat. But history and nature are weakening as well-defined external frameworks that give meaning to human life. For most of human experience they were much more vast than the scale of individual existence, and their vastness provided solace in the case of nature and hope in the case of history. When nature becomes

so intermingled with humanity, and when historical change becomes defined as an extension of technological change, neither nature nor history provides a self-evident framework for human meaning and identity. The only larger framework left, it seems, is humanity itself.

NOTES

1. See Nicholas Negroponte, *Being Digital* (Knopf, 1995). (Negroponte, the longtime director of MIT's Media Lab, recently stepped down from that position.) The dichotomy of lifeworld and systems is associated with Jürgen Habermas; see Fred R. Dallmayr, "Life-World: Variations on a Theme," in *Life-World and Politics: Between Modernity and Postmodernity,* ed. S. White (University of Notre Dame Press, 1989), pp. 45–46 and notes. The dialectic of globalization and identity is a major theme of Manuel Castells, whose works are referenced throughout this book. The term "symbolic analyst" comes from Robert Reich, *The Work of Nations: Preparing Ourselves for 21st Century Capitalism* (Knopf, 1991). The quote about the disposable labor force is from Manuel Castells, *The Rise of the Network Society*, second edition (Blackwell, 2000 [1995]), p. 295.

2. This discussion is based on a book by Edward T. Layton Jr.: *The Revolt of the Engineers: Social Responsibility and the American Engineering Profession* (Press of Case Western Reserve University, 1971), p. 53. The historian of technology, Susan Douglas, reminds us that "the study of ideology is essential to the study of technology." She defines it as "the entire constellation of images, myths and ideas through which people come to understand the material world and their place in that world." Social groups are engaged in an ongoing struggle about the myths and meanings that will be accepted as the natural and obvious way to interpret social reality. "This," Douglas claims, "is a struggle invariably won by the dominant classes." (Susan J. Douglas, "Jürgen Habermas Meets Mel Kranzberg: What Media Theory Has to Offer the History of Technology and Vice Versa," paper presented at annual meeting of Society of the History of Technology, 1987, p. 2.)

3. Karl Mannheim, *Ideology and Utopia: An Introduction to the Sociology of Knowledge* (Harcourt, Brace, 1936 [1929]), p. 203; see pp. 192–211 passim.

4. In listening for these words, their clustering, and their mutual defining, I am drawing on an honorable tradition in intellectual history—best exemplified by Raymond William's book *Culture and Society, 1780–1950* (Columbia University Press, 1958)—of analyzing the social and cultural implications of the industrial revolution. Williams highlighted the reflexive or circular relationship between key terms of social analysis in the nineteenth century (culture, society, industry, art, etc.) and the changes they supposedly described. In addition, Williams showed how key concepts tended to cluster, so that their meanings shifted in response to alterations in the others. See Marx, "Technology: The Emergence of a Hazardous Concept," *Social Research* 64 (1997), no. 3, p. 967.

5. Leo Marx, who has tracked the use of the word, calls 'technology' a "hazardous concept," unstable and reflexive in meaning, and particularly dangerous when used as the subject of a sentence, implying that it is an independent, autonomous historical agent, as in "the archetypal sentence: 'Technology is changing the way we live.'" Marx argues that the word 'technology' began to be used in the late nineteenth century to fill a "conceptual void" in explaining how the utilitarian, instrumentalist branch of human activity, directed at controlling the physical world, could so powerfully generate social change. (Marx, "Technology: The Emergence of a Hazardous Concept," pp. 968, 974–975, 977.) The naming of MIT in 1862 was one of the first public uses of the term. (The choice probably was influenced by Jacob Bigelow, a Boston botanist and physician, who had used the term in a Harvard lecture in 1828; he later became an MIT trustee.)

6. John Staudenmaier, "Perils of Progress Talk: Some Historical Considerations," in *Science, Technology, and Social Progress*, ed. S. Goldman (Lehigh University Press, 1989).

7. The process by which technological change began to displace historical change began in the seventeenth century with the controversy of the "ancients" and the "moderns." The "moderns" might concede equality or even superiority to the ancients in arts or philosophy, but they felt they clinched their case in arguing for progress when they emphasized that only the moderns possessed the compass, the printing press, gunpowder, and (most important) the experimental method. These arguments from progress in inventiveness were extrapolated to history as a whole; progress in what we now would call technology was cited as irrefutable evidence for historical progress from antiquity to the modern age. When technology entered the study of history, history itself began to be redefined as the study of the record of human progress, See Richard Foster Jones, *Ancients and Moderns: A Study of the Background of The Battle of the Books* (Washington University Studies, New Series in Language and Literature, no. 6, 1936). See also Hannah Arendt, *The Human Condition* (Doubleday Anchor Books, 1959 [1958]), esp. pp. 119–133.

8. Anthony Giddens, *The Consequences of Modernity* (Stanford University Press, 1990), p. 51. Giddens puts "emptying out" in quotes in the text I am paraphrasing.

9. As Douglas reminds us in "Jürgen Habermas Meets Mel Kranzberg," the " 'engineering of consent' is not a one-time event, in which meanings are clamped down and everyone accepts them." Consent is by no means automatic. It is an ongoing process in which people adjust their ideas and beliefs but also protest in a variety of ways. If the ideological framework becomes too much at odds with daily experience and with common sense, then the disparity has to be resolved for the social order to be stable: "The dominant ideology must incorporate certain criticisms and concerns while successfully marginalizing others, and illustrate that such concerns can be resolved best under the existing sociopolitical system."

10. Thomas Friedman makes this point when he uses a Lexus automobile and an olive tree to represent two sides of a technological divide: "Half the world seemed to be emerging from the Cold War intent on building a better Lexus, dedicated to modernizing, stream-lining and privatizing their economies in order to thrive in the system of globalization. And half of the world—sometimes half the same country, sometimes half the same person—was still caught up in the fight over who owns which olive tree." (*The Lexus and the Olive Tree*, Farrar, Straus and Giroux, 1999, p. 27.)

11. Alex Roland, email, March 5, 2000.

12. See Tom Standage, *The Victorian Internet: The Remarkable Story of the Telegraph and the Nineteenth Century's On-Line Pioneers* (Walker, 1998).

13. The concept of revolution migrated physics (the path of the planets around the sun) to history (the overturning of British rule in America in the 1770s, the end of the monarchy in France in 1789), and then, in the early nineteenth century, in a deliberate

analogy with events in France, was applied to machine production in the metaphor of the industrial revolution. When the metaphor of revolution is applied to industry, it implies a suddenness and completeness that might occur in the political arena (the king is executed, Robespierre rules) but does not apply in the arena of production. But to say that the metaphor is misleading is to miss the point. In the words of Leo Marx: "The whole issue becomes irrelevant once we recognize that we are dealing with a metaphor, and that its immense appeal rests, not on its capacity to describe the actual character of industrialization, but rather on its vivid suggestiveness. It evokes the uniqueness of the new way of life, as experienced, and, most important, it is a vivid expression of the affinity between technology and the great political revolution of modern times." (*The Machine in the Garden*, p. 187n)

14. Steve Lohr, "The Future Came Faster in the Old Days," *New York Times,* October 5, 1997.

15. Lewis Mumford calls the invention of language "infinitely more complex and sophisticated . . . than the Egyptian or Mesopotamian kit of tools" ("Technics and the Nature of Man," *Technology and Culture* 7, 1966, no. 3, p. 308).

16. On the term 'habitat,' see Gayle L. Ormiston, "Introduction," in *From Artifact to Habitat: Studies in the Critical Engagement of Technology,* ed. G. Ormiston (Lehigh University Press, 1990), p. 13.

17. Elting Morison, "Introductory Observations," in Morison, *Men, Machines, and Modern Times* (MIT Press, 1966), p. 16. See my discussion of the language and imagery of the artificial environment in *Notes on the Underground: An Essay on Technology, Society, and the Imagination* (MIT Press, 1990), pp. 1–8.

18. Manuel Castells (*The Rise of the Network Society,* p. 15) puts it into one long sentence: "Matter includes nature, human-modified nature, human-produced nature, and human nature itself, the labors of history forcing us to move away from the classic distinction between humankind and nature, since millenniums of human action have incorporated the natural environment into society, making us, materially and symbolically, an inseparable part of this environment."

19. Bill McKibben makes this point in *The End of Nature* (Random House, 1989).

20. Ulrich Beck, *Risk Society: Towards a New Modernity* (Sage, 1992 [1986]), p. 81.

21. Here I am paraphrasing Mumford ("Technics and the Nature of Man," p. 303), who writes: "In terms

of the currently accepted picture of the relation of man to technics, our age is passing from the primeval state of man, marked by his invention of tools and weapons for the purpose of achieving mastery over the forces of nature, to a radically different condition, in which he will not only have conquered nature but detached himself completely from the organic habitat."

22. Mumford, "Technics and the Nature of Man," p. 303.

23. See Stanley H. Ambrose, "Paleolithic Technology and Human Evolution," *Science* 291 (2001), no. 5509, pp. 1748–1752: "Stone tool technology, robust australopithecines, and the genus *Homo* appeared almost simultaneously 2.5 [million years ago]" (p. 1748). The systematic use of fire evidently began between 1 million and 1.5 million years ago, and around 300,000 years ago "technological and cultural evolution accelerated" in a way that suggests "the emergence of true cultural traditions and cultural areas" (p. 1751). The stone tool technologies between 2.5 and 0.3 million years ago "are remarkable for their slow pace of progress . . . and for limited mobility and regional interaction. . . . with the appearance of near-modern brain size, anatomy, and perhaps of grammatical language ~0.3 [million years ago], the pace quickens exponentially" (p. 1752).

24. See Peter F. Drucker, "The First Technological Revolution and Its Lessons," *Technology and Culture* 7 (1966), no. 2, pp. 143–151. This article is Drucker's presidential address to the Society for the History of Technology, presented on December 29, 1965, in San Francisco. He defines "the first technological revolution" as "the irrigation city, which then rapidly became the irrigation empire." (p. 143).

25. Mircea Eliade, *The Forge and the Crucible,* second edition (University of Chicago Press, 1978 [1956]), pp. 177–178. For a discussion of this passage in a different context, see Williams, *Notes on the Underground,* pp. 1–4.

26. The concept of reflexive modernization was articulated most clearly by Beck in *Risk Society.* See also Anthony Giddens's books *The Consequences of Modernity* (cited above) and *Modernity and Self-Identity in the Late Modern Age* (Stanford University Press, 1992).

27. Giddens, *The Consequences of Modernity,* p. 38.

28. Beck, *Risk Society,* pp. 12–13.

29. Under the governing structures of market relationships, the abiding imperative of capitalist accumulation—to increase profits—is accomplished in a

few major ways. The circulation of capital can be maximized through increasing its extension in space (broadening the market) and its intensity over time (accelerating capital turnover). Also, production costs can be lowered, productivity can be raised, and new products can be brought to market. Particularly in the last three decades, all these ways of increasing profit are closely linked to technological innovation, which has become the primary driver of capitalist acquisition. See Castells, *The Rise of the Network Society*, pp. 68–69, 95. Castells comments: "Information processing is focused on improving the technology of information processing as a source of productivity, in a virtuous circle of interaction between the knowledge sources of technology and the application of technology to improve knowledge generation and information processing. . . . Or, more briefly, a prime characteristic of the information age is its circularity, characterized by the immediate application to its own development of technologies it generates . . ." (ibid., p. 32).

30. "Meanwhile man . . . exalts himself to the posture of lord of the earth. In this way the impression comes to prevail that everything man encounters exists only insofar as it is his construct. This illusion gives rise in turn to one final delusion: It seems as though man everywhere and always encounters only himself. Heisenberg has with complete correctness pointed out that the real must present itself to contemporary man in this way. *In truth, however, precisely nowhere does man today any longer encounter himself, i.e. his essence.*" (Martin Heidegger, "The Question Concerning Technology," in *The Question Concerning Technology and Other Essays,* Harper & Row, 1977, p. 27.) Hannah Arendt (*The Human Condition*, p. 237) quotes Heisenberg's observation about "man encountering only himself."

31. The first quote (from Morison, *From Know-How to Nowhere*) is cited by Thomas P. Hughes in "Memorials: Elting Morison, 1909–1995," *Technology and Culture* 37 (1996), no. 4, p. 874. The second quote, also from "Memorials," is cited by Leo Marx (ibid., p. 867).

Social Perspectives

CORLANN GEE BUSH   I.5

Women and the Assessment of Technology

In this reading, author Corlann Gee Bush director of affirmative action, Montana State University, develops a feminist analysis of technology. In doing so, she tries to "unthink" and "rethink" several popular assumptions about technology, particularly ones that suggest that technological fixes can cure social problems that afflict women. She distinguishes the design, user, environmental, and cultural contexts in which technologies operate and provides examples of how technological innovations such as the washing machine have had unexpected impacts on the cultural context of women. She then develops what she calls an equity analysis approach to technology assessment that aims to consider all of the various types of impacts that a technological innovation can have on different groups in society, and she illustrates this analysis with the example of refrigeration technology. She warns against oversimplifying new technologies into "triumphs" or "threats" and suggests a new way of looking at the multifaceted impacts of technology on society.

Focus Questions

1. What does the author mean when she uses the term *valence* to describe a particular property of technologies? What are some examples of the valences of particular technologies?

2. What are the four contexts in which technologies operate?
3. How does Bush's approach to understanding the social and ethical impacts of technology compare with that of Freeman Dyson (selection I.11)?

Keywords

design, feminism, Native Americans, progress, refrigeration, social equality, tech-myth, valence, welfare

"Everything is what it is, what it isn't, and its direct opposite. That technique, so skillfully executed, might help account for the compelling irrationality . . . *double double think is very easy to deal with if we just realize that we have only to double double unthink it*."
—Dworkin 1974, p. 63.

ALTHOUGH ANDREA DWORKIN IS HERE analyzing Pauline Reage's literary style in the *Story of O*, her realization that we can "double double unthink" the mind fetters by which patriarchal thought binds women is an especially useful one. For those of us who want to challenge and change female victimization, it is a compelling concept.

Something Else Again

The great strength of the women's movement has always been its twin abilities to unthink the source of oppression and to use this analysis to create a new and synthesizing vision. Assertiveness is, for example, something else again: a special, learned behavior that does more than merely combine attributes of passivity and aggressiveness. Assertiveness is an unthinking and a transcendence of those common, control-oriented behaviors.[1]

Similarly, in their books *Against Our Will* and *Rape: The Power of Consciousness*, Susan Brownmiller (1974) and Susan Griffin (1979) unthink rape as a

crime of passion and rethink it as a crime of violence—insights which led to the establishment of rape crisis and victim advocacy services. But a good feminist shelter home-crisis service is something else again: it is a place where women are responsible for the safety and security of other women, where women teach self-defense and self-esteem in each other. In like manner, women's spirituality is something else again. Indebted both to Mary Daly for unthinking Christianity in *Beyond God the Father* (1973) and *The Church and the Second Sex* (1968) and to witchcraft for rethinking ritual, women's spirituality is more than a synthesis of those insights, it is a transformation for them.

In other words, feminist scholarship and feminist activism proceed not through a sterile, planar dialectic of thesis, antithesis, synthesis, but through a dynamic process of unthinking, rethinking, energizing, and transforming. At its best, feminism creates new life forms out of experiences as common as seawater and insights as electrifying as lightning.

The purpose of this chapter is to suggest that a feminist analysis of technology would be, like assertiveness, something else again. I will raise some of the questions that feminist technology studies should seek to ask, and I will attempt to answer them. Further, I hope to show how scholars, educators, and activity can work together toward a transformation of technological change in our society.

The endeavor is timely not least because books such as this, journal issues, articles, and conferences are increasingly devoting time and energy to the subject or because technologically related political issues such as the anti-nuclear movement and genetic engineering consume larger and larger amounts of both our news space and our consciousness. The most important reason why feminists must unthink and rethink women's relationship to technology is that the tech-fix (Weinberg 1966, p. 6) and the public policies on which it is based are no longer working. The tech-fix is the belief that technology can be used to solve all types of problems, even social ones. Belief in progress and the tech-fix has long been used to rationalize inequity: it is only a matter of time until technology extends material benefits to all citizens, regardless of race, sex, class, religion, or nationality.

> Technology has expanded our productive capacity so greatly that even though our distribution is still inefficient, and unfair by Marxian precepts, there is more than enough to go around. Technology has provided a "fix"—greatly expanded production of goods—which enables our capitalistic society to achieve many of the aims of the Marxist's social engineer without going through the social revolution Marx viewed as inevitable. Technology has converted the seemingly intractable social problem of *widespread* poverty into a relatively tractable one (Weinberg 1966, p. 7).

While Weinberg himself advocates cooperation among social and technical engineers in order to make a "better society, and thereby, a better life, for all of us who are part of society" (Weinberg 1966, p. 10), less conscientious philosophers and politicians have seen in the tech-fix a justification for laissez-faire economics and discriminatory public policy. Despite its claim to the contrary, the tech-fix has not worked well for most women or for people of color; recent analyses of the feminization of poverty, for example, indicate that jobs, which have always provided men with access to material goods, do not get women out of poverty.

> Social welfare programs based on the old male model of poverty do not consider the special nature of women's poverty. One fact that is little understood and rarely reflected in public welfare policy is that women in poverty are almost invariably productive workers, participating fully in

both the paid and the unpaid work force. The inequities of present public policies molded by the traditional economic role of women cannot continue. Locked into poverty by capricious programs designed by and for male policy makers . . . women who are young and poor today are destined to grow old and poor as the years pass. Society cannot continue persisting with the male model of a job automatically lifting a family out of poverty . . . (McKee 1982, p. 36).

As this example illustrates, the traditional social policies for dealing with inequity—*get a job*—and traditional solutions—*produce more efficiently*—have not worked to make a better society for women. Therefore, it is essential that women begin the unthinking of these traditions and the thinking of new relationships between social and technical engineering.

Unthinking Tech-Myths

In her poem "To An Old House in America," Adrienne Rich describes the attitude that women should take toward the task of unthinking public policy in regard to technology: "I do not want to simplify/Or: I would simplify/By naming the complexity/It has been made o'er simple all along" (Rich 1975, p. 240). Partly because it is in their best interest to do so and partly because they truly see nothing else, most politicians and technocrats paint the canvas of popular opinion about technology with the broadest possible brushstrokes, rendering it, in pure type, as TOOL, as THREAT, or as TRIUMPH.[2] From each of these assumptions proceed argument, legislation, public policy, and, ironically, powerlessness. In order to develop a feminist critique of technology, we must analyze these assumptions and unthink them, making them simpler by naming their complexity.

The belief that technology represents the triumph of human intelligence is one of America's most cherished cultural myths; it is also the easiest to understand, analyze, and disprove. Unfortunately, to discuss it is to resort to cliches: "There's nothing wrong that a little good old American ingenuity can't fix"; "That's progress"; or "Progress is our most important product." From such articles of faith in technology stemmed Manifest Destiny, the mechanization of agriculture, the urbanization of rural and nomadic cultures, the concept of the twentieth as the "American Century," and every World's Fair since 1893. That such faith seems naive to a generation that lives with the arms race, acid rain, hazardous waste, and near disasters at nuclear power plants is not to diminish one *byte* either Western culture's faith in the tech-fix or its belief that technological change equals material progress. And, indeed, like all generalizations, this myth is true—at least partially. Technology *has* decreased hardships and suffering while raising standards of health, living, and literacy throughout the industrialized world.

But, not without problems, as nay-sayers are so quick to point out. Those who perceive technology as the ultimate threat to life on the planet look upon it as an iatrogenic disease, one created, like nausea in chemotherapy patients, by the very techniques with which we treat the disease. In this view, toxic wastes, pollution, urban sprawl, increasing rates of skin cancer, even tasteless tomatoes, are all problems created through our desire to control nature through technology. Characterized by their desire to go cold turkey on the addiction to the tech-fix, contemporary critics of technology participate in a myriad of activities and organizations (Zero Population Growth, Friends of the Earth, Sierra Club, the Greenpeace Foundation) and advocate a variety of goals (peace, arms limitation, appropriate technology, etc.). And, once again, their technology-as-threat generalization is true, or at least as true as its opposite number: in truth, no one, until Rachel Carson (1955), paid much attention to the effects of technology on the natural world it tried to control; indeed, technology has created problems as it has set out to solve others.

Fortunately, the inadequacy of such polarized thinking is obvious: technology is neither wholly good nor wholly bad. "It has both positive and negative effects, and it usually has the two *at the same time and in virtue of each other*" (Mesthene 1970, p. 26). Every innovation has both positive and negative consequences that pulse through the social fabric like waves through water.

Much harder to unthink is the notion that technologies are merely tools: neither good nor bad but neutral, moral only to the extent that their user is moral. This, of course, is the old saw "guns don't kill people, people kill people" writ large enough to include not only guns and nuclear weapons but also cars, televisions, and computer games. And there is truth here, too. Any given person can use any given gun at any given time either to kill another person for revenge or to shoot a grouse for supper. The gun is the tool through which the shooter accomplishes his or her objectives. However, just as morality is a collective concept, so too are guns. As a class of objects, they comprise a technology that is designed for killing in a way that ice picks, hammers, even knives—all tools that have on occasion been used as weapons—are not. To believe that technologies are neutral tools subject only to the motives and morals of the user is to miss completely their collective significance. Tools and technologies have what I can only describe as *valence*, a bias or "charge" analogous to that of atoms that have lost or gained electrons through ionization. A particular technological system, even an individual tool, has a tendency to interact in similar situations in identifiable and predictable ways. In other words, particular tools or technologies tend to be favored in certain situations, tend to perform in a predictable manner in these situations, and tend to bend other interactions to them. Valence tends to seek out or fit in with certain social norms and to ignore or disturb others.

Jacques Ellul (1964) seems to be identifying something like valence when he describes "the specific weight" with which technique is endowed:

> It is not a kind of neutral matter, with no direction, quality, or structure. It is a power endowed with its own peculiar force. It refracts in its own specific sense the wills which make use of it and the ends proposed for it. Indeed, independently of the objectives that man pretends to assign to any given technical means, that means always conceals in itself a finality which cannot be evaded (pp. 140–41).

While this seems to be overstating the case a bit—valence is not the atom, only one of its attributes—tools and techniques do have tendencies to pull or push behavior in definable ways. Guns, for example, are valenced to violence; the presence of a gun in a given situation raises the level of violence by its presence alone. Television, on the other hand, is valenced to individuation; despite the fact that any number of people may be present in the same room at the same time, there will not be much conversation because the presence of the TV itself pulls against interaction and pushes toward isolation. Similarly, automobiles and microwave ovens are individuating technologies while trains and campfires are accretionary ones.

Unthinking tech-myths and understanding valence also requires greater clarity of definition (Winner 1977, pp. 10–12). Several terms, especially *tool, technique,* and *technology,* are often used interchangeably when, in fact, they describe related but distinguishable phenomena. *Tools* are the implements, gadgets, machines, appliances, and instruments themselves. A hammer is, for example, a tool as is a spoon or an automatic washing machine. *Techniques* are the skills, methods, procedures, and processes that people perform in order to use tools. Carpentry is, therefore, a technique that utilizes hammers, baking is a technique that uses spoons, and laundering a technique that employs washing machines. *Technology* refers to the organized systems of interactions that utilize tools and involve techniques for the performance of tasks and the accomplishment of objectives. Hammers and carpentry are some of the tools and techniques of architectural or building technology. Spoons and baking, washing machines and laundering are some of the tools and techniques of domestic or household technology.

A feminist critique of the public policy debate over technology should, thus, unthink the tripartite myth that sees technology in simple categories as tool, triumph, or threat. In unthinking it, we can simplify it by naming its complexity:

- A tool is not a simple isolated thing but is a member of a class of objects designed for specific purposes.
- Any given use of tools, techniques, or technologies can have both beneficial and detrimental effects at the same time.

- Both use and effect are expressions of a valance or propensity for tools to function in certain ways in certain settings.
- Polarizing the rhetoric about technology enables advocates of particular points of view to gain adherents and power while doing nothing to empower citizens to understand, discuss, and control technology on their own.

"Making it o'er simple all along" has proven an excellent technique for maintaining social control. The assertion that technology is beneficial lulls people into believing that there is nothing wrong that can't be fixed, so they do nothing. Likewise, the technophobia that sees technology as evil frightens people into passivity and they do nothing. The argument that technology is value-free either focuses on the human factor in technology in order to obscure its valence or else concentrates on the autonomy of technology in order to obscure its human control. In all cases, the result is that people feel they can do nothing. In addition, by encouraging people to argue with and blame each other, rhetoric wars draw public attention away from more important questions such as: Who is making technological decisions? On what basis? What will the effects be?

Context, Context, Whither Art Thou, Context?

In unthinking the power dynamics of technological decision making, a feminist critique needs to pay special attention to the social messages whispered in women's ears since birth: mother to daughter, "Don't touch that, you'll get dirty"; father to daughter, "Don't worry your pretty little head about it"; teacher to young girl, "It doesn't matter if you can't do math"; woman to woman, "Boy, a man must have designed this."

Each of these statements is talking about a CONTEXT in which technological decisions are made, technical information is conveyed, and technological innovations are adopted. That such social learning is characterized by sex role stereotyping should come as no surprise. What may be surprising is not the depths of women's ignorance—after all, women have, by and large, been encouraged to be ignorant—but the extent to which men in general, inventors, technocrats, even scholars, all share an amazing ignorance about the contexts in which technology operates. There are four:

1. *The design or developmental context* which includes all the decisions, materials, personnel, processes, and systems necessary to create tools and techniques from raw materials.

2. *The user context* which includes all the motivations, intentions, advantages, and adjustments called into play by the use of particular techniques or tools.

3. *The environmental context* that describes non-specific physical surroundings in which a technology or tool is developed and used.

4. *The cultural context* which includes all the norms, values, myths, aspirations, laws, and interactions of the society of which the tool or technique is a part.

Of these, much more is known about the design or developmental context of technology than about the other three put together. Western culture's collective lack of knowledge about all but the developmental context of technology springs in part from what Langdon Winner calls technological orthodoxy: a "philosophy of sorts" that has seldom been "subject to the light of critical scrutiny" (Winner 1979, p. 75). Standard tenets of technological orthodoxy include:

- That men know best what they themselves have made.

- That the things men make are under their firm control.

- That technologies are neutral: they are simply tools that can be used one way or another; the benefit or harm they bring depends on how men use them (Winner 1979, p. 76).

If one accepts these assumptions, then there is very little to do except study processes of design and invent ever-newer gadgets. The user and environmental contexts become obscured if not invisible, an invisibility further confirmed by the fact that,

since the Industrial Revolution, men have been inventors and designers while women have been users and consumers of technology. By and large, men have created, women have accommodated.

The sex role division of labor that characterizes Western societies has ensured that boys and girls have been brought up with different expectations, experiences, and training, a pattern that has undergone remarkably little change since the nineteenth century.

> Games for girls were carefully differentiated from boys' amusement. A girl might play with a hoop or swing gently, but the "ruder and more daring gymnastics of boys" were outlawed. Competitive play was also anathema: A "little girl should never be ambitious to swing higher than her companions." Children's board games afforded another insidious method of inculcating masculinity and femininity. On a boys' game board the player moved in an upward spiral, past temptations, obstacles, and reverses until the winner reached a pinnacle of propriety and prestige. A girl's playful enactment of her course in life moved via circular ever-inward path to the "mansion of happiness," a pastel tableau of mother and child. The dice of popular culture were loaded for both sexes and weighted with domesticity for little women. The doctrine of (separate) spheres was thereby insinuated in the personality of the child early in life and even during the course of play (Ryan 1979, p. 92).

It is difficult to invent a better mousetrap if you're taught to be afraid of mice; it is impossible to dream of becoming an engineer if you're never allowed to get dirty.

As compared to women, men do, indeed, know a great deal about what they would call the "design interface" of technology; they know more about how machines work; they discovered the properties of elements and the principles of science. They know math, they develop cost-benefit risk analyses; they discover, invent, engineer, manufacture, and sell. Collectively, men know almost everything there is to know about the design and development of tools, techniques, and systems; but they understand far less about how their technologies are used—in part because there is less money in understanding than in designing, in part because the burden of adjusting to technological change falls more heavily on women. What is worse, however, is that most men do not know that they do not know anything about women and the user context.

> From the preliminary conceptualization to the final marketing of a product, most decision making about technology is done by men who design, usually subconsciously, a model of the physical world in which they would like to live, using material artifacts which meet the needs of the people—men—they best know. The result is technological development based on particular sets of male conditioning, values, and roles . . . (Zimmerman 1981, p. 2).

Ironically, until very recently, most women did not realize that they possessed information of any great significance. With all the cultural attention focused on the activity in the developmental context, it was hard to see beyond the glare of the spotlights into the living rooms and kitchens and laundries where women were working and living out the answers to dozens of unverbalized questions: How am I spending my time here? How is my work different from what I remember my mother doing? Am I really better off? Why does everything seem so out of control? Rephrased, these are the questions that will comprise a feminist assessment of technology: How have women's roles changed as a result of modern technology? Has women's status in society kept pace with the standard of living? Do women today have more opportunities or merely more expectations? What is the relationship of material possessions to personal freedom?

Think for a moment about washing machines. Almost every family in the United States has access to one; across the country, women spend thousands of hours each day in sorting, washing, drying, folding, and ironing clothes. The automatic washing machine has freed women from the pain and toil described so well by Agnes Smedley (1973) in *Daughter of Earth*. But as washing technology has changed, so too has clothing (it gets dirtier faster) and wardrobes (we own more clothes) and even standards of cleanliness (clothes must be whiter

than white), children change clothes more often, there are more clothes to wash. Joan Vanek (1974, p. 118), in her work on time spent in housework, asserts that women spent as much time in household-related tasks in 1966 as they did in 1926.

More has changed, however, than just standards of cleanliness. Doing laundry used to be a collective enterprise. When I was a child in the late 1940s and early 1950s, my mother and grandmother washed the family's clothes together. My grandmother owned a semiautomatic machine but she lived 45 miles away; my mother had hot water, a large sink, and five children. Every Sunday, we would dump the dirty clothes in a big wicker basket and drive to my grandmother's house where all the womenfolk would spend the afternoon in the basement, talking and laughing as we worked. By evening, the wicker basket would again be full, but this time with neatly folded, clean smelling piles of socks, sheets, towels, and underwear that would have to last us a week. Crisply ironed dresses and slacks, on hangers, waited to be hung, first on those little hooks over the side doors of the car, then in our closets at home.

Nostalgic as these memories are, doing laundry was not romantic. It was exhausting, repetitious work, and neither my mother nor I would trade in our own automatic washers to go back to it (Armitage 1982, pp. 3–6). Yet, during my childhood, laundry was a communal activity, an occasion for gossip, friendship, and bonding. Laundering was hard work, and everyone in the family and in the society knew it and respected us as laborers. Further, having laundry and a day on which to do it was an organizing principle (Monday, wash day; Tuesday, iron; Wednesday . . .) around which women allocated their time and resources. And, finally, there was a closure, a sense of completion and accomplishment impossible to achieve today when my sister washes, dries, folds, and irons her family's clothes every day or when I wash only because I have nothing to wear.

Admittedly, this homey digression into soap opera (One Woman's Wash) is a far cry from the design specification and cost-benefit analyses men use to describe and understand the developmental context of washing machines, but it is equally valid for it describes the user context in the user's terms. Analyzing the user context of technological change is a process of collecting thousands and thousands of such stories and rethinking them into an understanding of the effects of technological change on women's lives.[3] From unthinking the developmental context as such and rethinking the user context, it is only a short step to studying the environmental and cultural contexts of technological change. Of these, our knowledge of the environmental context is the better developed, partly because we have given it more serious attention but mostly because environmental studies has been a legitimate career option for men.

While concern about the effects of technology on the natural environment is an idea that can be traced back to de Crevecoeur (1782) and James Fenimore Cooper (1832), Rachel Carson (1955, 1961, 1962) is the person most responsible for our current level of ecological awareness and for the scientific rather than aesthetic basis on which it rests. As we learn more about the fragile reciprocity within ecosystems, we begin to unthink the arrogance of our assumption that we are separate from and superior to nature. In an ecosystem, it is never possible to do only *one* thing; for every action there are chain reactions of causes and effects. The continued survival of the world depends upon developing more precise models of the environment so we can predict and prevent actual catastrophe without being immobilized by the risking of it.

Perhaps no one could have foreseen that the aerosol sprays we used to apply everything from paint to antiperspirant would degrade the earth's ozone layer, but no one seems to have asked. That drums for burying toxic waste would eventually corrode and leak seems so obvious that millions ought to have been able to predict the risk, yet no one seems to have had the desire or the clout to deal with the problem of hazardous waste before it became a crisis. In pursuit of progress, we have been content to ignore the ecological consequences of our technological decisions because, until it was pointed out to us, we did not realize that there *was* an environmental context surrounding the tools we use.

The environmental impact analysis (EIA) has become the most popular means by which governments and industries attempt to predict and assess the ecological impact of technological change. While most EIAs are long, tedious, and nonconfrontive, the idea behind them and much of the work that has gone into them is sound. In her articles on appropriate technology, Judy Smith (1978, 1981) from the Women and Technology Projection in Missoula, Montana, has suggested that sex-role impact reports could be used to improve our understanding of the cultural context of technology in much the same way that the EIA has improved our knowledge of the environmental context.

And we do need something, for we know next to nothing about the interactions of culture and technology, having always seen these as separate phenomena. Most people welcome technological change because it is *material,* believing that it makes things better, but it doesn't make them different. They resist social change because it is *social* and personal; it is seen as making things different . . . worse. The realization that technological change stimulates social change is not one that most people welcome.

Feminists need to unthink this cultural blindness. Because women are idealized as culture carriers, as havens of serenity in a heartless world (Lasch 1977), women are supposed to remain passive while the rest of the culture is allowed, even encouraged, to move rapidly ahead. Women are like the handles of a slingshot whose relatively motionless support enables the elastic and shot to build up energy and to accelerate past them at incredible speeds. The culture measures its progress by women's status. When women do try to move, when they try to make changes rather than accommodations, they are accused of selfishness, of me-ness, of weakening the family, of being disloyal to civilization (Rich 1979, pp. 275–310).

However, it is crucial that feminists continue to unthink and rethink the cultural contexts of technology for a reason more significant than our systematic exclusion from it: it is dangerous not to. Technology always enters into the present culture, accepting and exacerbating the existing norms and values. In a society characterized by a sex-role division of labor, any tool or technique—it has valence, remember—will have dramatically different effects on men than on women.

Two examples will serve to illustrate this point. Prior to the acquisition of horses between the late sixteenth and mid-seventeenth centuries, women and dogs were the beasts of burden for Native American tribes on the Great Plains. Mobility was limited by both the topography and the speed at which people and dogs could walk. Physical labor was women's province in Plains culture, but since wealth in those societies was determined by how many dogs a person "owned" and since women owned the dogs, the status of women in pre-equestrian tribes was relatively high—they owned what men considered wealth (Roe 1955, p. 29). Women were central to the economic and social life of their tribes in more than the ownership of the dogs. They controlled the technology of travel and food: they were responsible for the foraging, gathering, and preserving of food for the tribe and, in many cases, determined the time and routes of tribal migration. They had access to important women's societies and played a central part in religious and community celebrations (Liberty 1982, p. 14).

Women's roles in Plains Indian societies changed profoundly and rapidly as horses were acquired and domesticated. In less than two centuries—for some tribes in less than a generation—a new culture evolved. The most immediate changes were technological and economic; horses became the technology for transportation and they were owned by men. Women could still own dogs, but this was no longer the measure of wealth it had been.

With their "currency" debased, women's status slipped further as important economic, social, and religious roles were reassigned to men. As the buffalo became a major source of food and shelter, the value of women's foraging activities decreased. Hunting ranges were expanded, causing more frequent moves with women doing more of the packing up and less of the deciding about when and where to go. As each tribe's hunting range increased, competition for land intensified; and warfare,

raiding, and their concomitants for women—rape and slavery—also increased.

Of course, not all the effects were negative. Technologies are substitutes for human labor: horses made women's work easier and more effective. Also, several tribes, including the Blackfeet, allowed a woman to retain ownership of her own horse and saddle. However, a woman was seldom allowed to trade or raid for horses, and her rights to her husband's herd usually ended with his death.

Thus, for Native American women, the horse was a mixed blessing. It eased their burdens and made transportation easier. But it also added new tasks and responsibilities without adding authority over those tasks or increasing autonomy. The opposite was true for men; the horse provided few new tasks and responsibilities—men had always been responsible for hunting, defense, and warfare—but it did enhance these traditional roles, giving men more decision-making authority, more autonomy, and more access to status. Paradoxically, while a woman's absolute status was greatly improved by the changes from dog to horse culture, her status relative to men actually declined. In this manner, horses changed the nature of Native American culture on the high plains, but women and men were affected in profoundly different ways.

A similar phenomenon occurred at the end of the horse farming era in the Palouse region of Idaho and Washington in the United States. During the 1920s, it was common for a farmer to employ fifteen to twenty-five hired men and to use twenty-five to forty-four horses to harvest his crops; farmers and their hands worked back-breaking, twenty-hour days. On the other hand, women also worked long days during harvest, cooking five meals a day for as many as forty people. During the year, women were responsible for a family's food, nutrition, health, safety, and sanitation. Women's work had economic value. Performing their traditional roles as wives, mothers, and homemakers, women were economically crucial to the survival of the labor intensive family farm (Bush 1982). Unfortunately, in the same manner that the horse made a Plains Indian woman's work easier even as it lowered her status relative to men, so too did the conversion from horses to diesel power and electricity ease the farm wife's hardships while it decreased the economic significance of her labor. In both cases, technological innovation had profoundly different consequences for men's and women's work. In both cases, the innovation was coded or valenced in such a way that it loaded the status of men's roles while eroding status for women.

Technology and Equity

Technology is, therefore, an equity issue. Technology has everything to do with who benefits and who suffers, whose opportunities increase and whose decrease, who creates and who accommodates. If women are to transform or "re-valence" technology, we must develop ways to assess the equity implications of technological development and develop strategies for changing social relationships as well as mechanical techniques. To do this, we must have a definition of technology that will allow us to focus on such questions of equity.

Not surprisingly, there are no such empowering definitions in the existing literature. Equity has not been a major concern of either technophobes or technophiles. In fact, most definitions of technology fall short on several counts. The most commonly accessible definitions, those in dictionaries, tell us little: Webster's "the science of the industrial arts" and "science used in a practical way," and the American Heritage Dictionary's "the application of science, especially to industrial and commercial objectives" and "the entire body of methods, and materials used to achieve such objectives" are definitions so abstract as to be meaningless. Other attempts clarify function but lose the crucial connection to science, as in James Burke's (1980, p. 23) "the sum total of all the objects and systems used to produce goods and perform services."

Better definitions connect technology to other categories of human behavior and to human motivation.

A form of cultural activity devoted to the production or transformation of material objects, or

the creation of procedural systems, in order to expand the realm of practical human possibility (Hannay & McGinn 1980, p. 27).

On rare occasions, definitions do raise equity questions as in John McDermott's attempt:

Technology, in its concrete, empirical meaning, refers fundamentally to systems of rationalized control over large groups of men, events, and machines by small groups of technically skilled men operating through organizational hierarchy (McDermott 1969, p. 29).

However, this definition is really defining *technocracy* rather than *technology*. More often, there are romantic definitions that enmesh us in cotton candy:

[Technology's task] is to employ the earth's resources and energy income in such a way as to support all humanity while also enabling all people to enjoy the whole earth, all its historical artifacts and its beautiful places without any man enjoying life around earth at the cost of another (Fuller 1969, p. 348).

While no one could argue with such ideals, Buckminster Fuller leaves us where the boon and bane theorists leave us—confounded by doublethink. It is impossible to ask tough questions of such a definition or to examine closely why technology does not now support all humanity equally.

More distressing is the tendency of scholars to use the generic "he/man" to represent all of humanity. For example, "without one man interfering with the other, without any man enjoying life around earth at the cost of another" is a statement that completely disregards the fact that, around the earth, men enjoy their lives at *women's* cost. Similarly, statements such as "because of the autonomy of technique, man cannot choose his means any more than his ends" (Ellul 1964, p. 40) and "the roots of the machine's genealogical tree is in the brain of this conceptual man . . . after all it was he who made the machine" (Usher 1954, p. 22) grossly mislead us because they obscure the historical and contemporary roles that women have played in technological development. Worse, they reinforce the most disabling myth of all, the assumption that men and women are affected similarly by and benefit equally from technological change.

Therefore, because of the oversimplification of some definitions and the exclusion of women from others, feminists need to rethink a definition of technology that both includes women and facilitates an equity analysis. Such a definition might be:

> Technology is a form of human cultural activity that applies the principles of science and mechanics to the solution of problems. It includes the resources, tools, processes, personnel, and systems developed to perform tasks and create immediate particular, and personal and/or competitive advantages in a given ecological, economic, and social context (Bush in *Taking Hold of Technology* 1981, p. 1).

The chief virtue of this definition is its consideration of advantage; people accept and adopt technology to the extent that they see advantage for themselves and, in competitive situations, disadvantage for others. Thus, an equity analysis of an innovation should focus on benefits and risk within the contexts in which the technology operates. An equity analysis of a technology would examine the following:

The developmental context:

- the principles of science and mechanics applied by the tool or technique
- the resources, tools, processes, and systems employed to develop it
- the tasks to be performed and the specific problems to be solved

The user context:

- the current tool, technique, or system that will be displaced by its use
- the interplay of this innovation with others that are currently in use
- the immediate personal advantage and competitive advantage created by the use of technology
- the second and third level consequences for individuals

The environmental context:

- the ecological impact of accepting the technology versus the impact of continuing current techniques

The cultural context:

- the impact on sex roles
- the social system affected
- the organization of communities
- the economic system involved and the distribution of goods within this system

A specific example will serve to illustrate how an equity analysis might be approached. Refrigeration was "invented" in the 1840s in Apalachicola, Florida, by John Gorrie as a by-product of his work on a cure for malaria (Burke 1980, p. 238). Gorrie's invention was a freezing machine that used a steam-driven piston to compress air in a cylinder that was surrounded by salt water. (As the piston advances, it compresses air in the cylinder; as the piston retracts, the air expands.) An expanding gas draws heat from its surroundings; after several strokes of the piston, the gas has extracted all the heat available from the surrounding brine. If a flow of continuously cold air is then pumped out of the cylinder into the surrounding air, the result is air conditioning; if the air is continuously allowed to cool the brine solution, the brine itself will draw heat from water, causing it to freeze and make ice. If the gas (air) or brine is allowed to circulate in a closed system, heat will be drawn from the surrounding air or matter (food), causing refrigeration.

THE DEVELOPMENTAL CONTEXT

Thus, refrigeration applies the laws of science (especially the properties of gases) and the principles of mechanics (thermodynamics and compression) to perform the tasks of making ice, preserving and freezing food, and cooling air. Refrigeration also solves the problems of retarding food spoilage and coping with heat waves, thereby creating personal advantage. The resources and tools used include a gas, a solution, a source of energy, and a piston-driven compressor.

The developmental context is enormously complex and interconnected; however, a general analysis would include all the supply, manufacture, and distribution systems for the refrigeration units themselves—everything from the engineers who design the appliances, to the factory workers who make, inspect, and pack them, to the truckers who transport them, to the clerk who sells them. A truly expansive analysis of the development context would also include the food production, packing, and distribution systems required to make available even one box of frozen peas as well as the artists, designers, paper producers, and advertisers who package the peas and induce us to buy them.

THE USER CONTEXT

Refrigeration has affected our lives in such a myriad of ways that elaborating on them all would require another paper in itself. Refrigeration has important commercial uses as well as medical ones, and it would not be overstating the case to assert that there is no aspect of modern life that has not been affected by refrigeration. Nonetheless, a more limited analysis of refrigeration as it has affected domestic and family life in the United States is both revealing and instructive.

To the self-sufficient farm family of the early twentieth century, refrigeration meant release from the food production and preservation chores that dominated much of men's and women's lives: canning garden produce to get the family through the winter; butchering, smoking, and drying meat from farm-raised hogs and cattle; milking cows daily and churning butter. The advantages of owning a refrigerator in such a situation were immediate and dramatic: food could be preserved for longer periods of time so there was less spoilage; food could be cooked ahead of serving time allowing women to spend less time in meal preparation; freezing produce and meat was a faster, easier, and more sanitary process than canning or smoking, again, saving women time and improving the family's health. The refrigerator thus generated positive changes for women, freeing them from hard, hot work and improving their absolute status. However, the second and third level effects of refrigeration

technology were not as benign for women as the primary effects.

Since refrigeration kept food fresh for long periods of time, fresh produce could be shipped across country, thus improving nutrition nationwide. Food processing and preservation moved out of the home, and new industries and services paid workers to perform the duties that had once been almost solely women's domestic responsibilities. Within the home, the nature of women's work changed from responsibility for managing food production to responsibility for managing food consumption. Also, farmers stopped growing food for family subsistence and local markets and started growing cash crops for sale on national and international markets. Opportunities for employment shifted from farm labor to industrial labor, and families moved from rural areas to cities and suburbs. Thus, the use of refrigeration changed the work roles of individual women and men and, through them, the economy, the content of work, and the nature of culture and agriculture.

THE ENVIRONMENTAL CONTEXT

An analysis of the environmental context of refrigeration technology would examine the effects of the developmental and user contexts on the environment by asking such questions as: Since refrigeration affects agriculture, what are the ecological effects of cash crop monoculture on, say, soil erosion or the use of pesticides? Since refrigeration retards the growth of bacteria and preserves blood and pharmaceuticals, what are the consequences for disease control? What are the effects of increased transportation of food on energy supplies and air pollution?

THE CULTURAL CONTEXT

Finally, an examination of the sex role impact of refrigeration technology would reveal a disparate effect on men and women. In the United States, men have been largely responsible for food production, women for food preservation and preparation. Refrigerators were a valenced technology that affected women's lives by, generally, removing food preservation from their domestic duties and relocating it in the market economy. Women now buy what they once canned. Women's traditional roles have been eroded, as their lives have been made easier. On the other hand, men, who originally had very little to do with food preservation, canning, or cooking, now control the processes by which food is manufactured and sold. Men's roles and responsibilities have been loaded and their opportunities increased, although their work has not necessarily been made easier. Refrigeration has, thus, been adopted and diffused throughout a sexist society; we should not be surprised to learn that its effects have been dissimilar and disequitable.

The Great Chain of Causation

Of course, not one of us thinks about the effects of refrigeration on soil erosion or women's status when we open the fridge to get a glass of milk. We are gadget-rich and assessment-poor in this society, yet each private act connects us to each other in a great chain of causation. Unfortunately, to think about the consequences of one's actions is to risk becoming immobilized; so the culture teaches us to double think rather than think, and lulls us into believing that individual solutions can work for the collective good.

Of course, we can continue to double think such things only so long as we can foist negative effects and disadvantages off onto someone else: onto women if we are men, onto blacks if we are white, onto youth if we are old, onto the aged if we are young. Equity for others need not concern us as long as *we* are immediately advantaged.

Feminists, above all, must give the lie to this rationale, to unthink it; for if the women's movement teaches anything, it is that there can be no individual solutions to collective problems. A feminist transformation of technological thought must include unthinking the old myths of technology as threat or triumph and rethinking the attendant rhetoric. A feminist unthinking of technology should strive for a holistic understanding of the contexts in which it operates and should present an unflinching analysis of its advantages and disadvantages.

Above all, a feminist assessment of technology must recognize technology as an equity issue. The challenge to feminists is to transform society in order to make technology equitable and to transform technology in order to make society equitable. A feminist technology should, indeed, be something else again.

NOTES

1. I am indebted for this insight to Betsy Brown and the other students in my seminar "The Future of the Female Principle," University of Idaho, Spring 1982.

2. In *Technological Change: Its Impact on Man and Society* (1970), Emmanuel Mesthene identifies "three unhelpful views about technology: technology as blessing, technology as curse, and technology as unworthy of notice." He does not mention the "technology as neutral tool argument," perhaps because he is one of its leading proponents.

3. Obviously, oral history is the only way that scholars can accumulate this data. Oral historians should ask respondents questions about their acquisition of and adaptation to household appliances. Such questions might include: "When did you get electricity?"; "What was the first appliance you bought?"; "What was your first washing machine like?"; "How long did it take you to learn how to use it?"; "What was your next machine like?"; "When did you get running water?"; "Are you usually given appliances for presents or do you buy them yourself?," etc.

REFERENCES

Armitage, Susan. 1982. Wash on Monday: The housework of farm women in transition. *Plainswoman* VI, 2:3–6.

Boulding, Elise. 1976. *The underside of history: A view of women through time.* Boulder, Colo.: Westview Press.

Brownmiller, Susan. 1974. *Against our will: Men, women and rape.* New York: Simon and Schuster.

Burke, James. 1980: *Connections.* Boston: Little, Brown.

Bush, Corlann Gee. 1982. The barn is his; the house is mine: Agricultural technology and sex roles. *Energy and transport.* Eds. George Daniels and Mark Rose, Beverly Hills, Calif.: Sage Publications, 235–59.

Carson, Rachel. 1955. *The edge of the sea.* Boston: Houghton Mifflin.

Carson, Rachel. 1961. *The sea around us.* New York: Oxford University Press.

Carson, Rachel. 1962. *Silent spring.* Boston: Houghton Mifflin.

Cooper, James Fenimore. 1832. *The pioneer.* Philadelphia: Carey & Lea.

Daly, Mary. 1968. *The church and the second sex.* New York: Harper & Row.

Daly, Mary. 1973. *Beyond God the father: Toward a philosophy of women's liberation.* Boston: Beacon Press.

de Crevecoeur, Michel Guillaume St. Jean. 1968. *Letters from an American farmer: Reprint of 1782 edition.* Magnolia, Mass.: Peter Smith.

Draper, Patricia. 1975. Kung women: Contrasts in sexual egalitarianism in foraging and sedentary contexts. *Toward an anthropology of women.* Ed. Rayna Reiter. New York: Monthly Review Press: 77–109.

Dworkin, Andrea. 1974. *Woman hating.* New York: E. P. Dutton.

Ellul, Jacques. 1964. *The technological society.* New York: Knopf.

Fuller, R. Buckminster. 1969. *Utopia or oblivion: The prospects for humanity.* New York: Bantam Books.

Griffin, Susan. 1979. *Rape: The power of consciousness.* New York: Harper & Row.

Hannay, N. Bruce; and McGinn, Robert. 1980. The anatomy of modern technology. *Daedalus* 109, 1:25–53.

Lasch, Christopher. 1977. *Haven in a heartless world: The family besieged.* New York: Basic Books.

Liberty, Margot. 1982. Hell came with horses: Plains Indian women in the equestrian era. *Montana: The Magazine of Western History* 32, 3:10–19.

McDermott, John. 1969. Technology: The opiate of the intellectuals. *New York Review of Books* XVI, 2 (July):25–35.

McKee, Alice. 1982. The feminization of poverty. *Graduate Woman* 76, 4:34–36.

Mesthene, Emmanuel G. 1970. *Technological change: Its impact on man and society.* Cambridge, Mass.: Harvard University Press.

Rich, Adrienne. 1975. *Poems: Selected and new 1950–1974.* New York: W. W. Norton.

Rich, Adrienne. 1979. Disloyal to civilization. *On lies, secrets and silence: Selected prose.* New York: W. W. Norton.

Roe, Frank Gilbert. 1955. *The Indian and the horse.* Norman, Okla.: University of Oklahoma Press.

Ryan, Mary P. 1979. *Womanhood in America: From colonial times to the present.* 2nd ed. New York: Franklin Watts.

Smedley, Agnes. 1973. *Daughter of earth.* Old Westbury, N.Y.: The Feminist Press.

Smith, Judy. 1978. *Something old, something new, something borrowed, something due: Women and appropriate technology.* Butte, Mont.: National Center for Appropriate Technology.

Smith, Judy. 1981. Women and technology: What is at stake? *Graduate Woman* 75, 1:33–35.

Stanley, Autumn. 1984. *Mothers of invention. Women inventors and innovators through the ages.* Metuchen, N.J.: Scarecrow Press.

Taking hold of technology: Topic guide for 1981–83. 1981. Washington, D.C.: American Association of University Women.

Tanner, Nancy; and Zihlman, Adrienne. 1976. Women in evolution: Part I. Innovation and selection in human origins. *Signs* 1 (Spring): 585–608.

Usher, Abbott Payson. 1954. *A history of mechanical inventions.* Cambridge: Harvard University Press.

Vanek, Joann. 1974. Time spent in housework. *Scientific American* 231 (November): 116–20.

Weinberg, Alvin M. 1966. Can technology replace social engineering? *University of Chicago Magazine* 59:6–10.

Winner, Langdon. 1977. *Autonomous technology: Technics-out-of-control as a theme in political thought.* Cambridge: MIT Press.

Winner, Langdon. 1979. The political philosophy of alternative technology. *Technology in Society* 1:75–86.

Zimmerman, Jan. 1981. Introduction. *Future, technology and woman: Proceedings of the conference.* San Diego, Calif.: Women's Studies Department, San Diego State University.

RICHARD SCLOVE   I.6
_____

I'd Hammer Out Freedom: Technology as Politics and Culture

Even though technologies are usually developed to meet a particular need or solve a specific problem, they often have secondary functions or unintended effects on our lives. In this article, Richard Sclove is interested in how technologies exist within, are influenced by, and in turn, exert influence on society. He claims that they often work in subtle ways to both define and set limits on human interaction.

The view of "technology as society" discussed in this article states that although technology influences the social experience, it is not the sole determinant of how society develops. As a technology goes through various evolutionary stages, it assumes a greater role in our lives, and we become less aware of its influence and less likely to seek alternative ways of doing something. It is important, claims Sclove, for societies to look for alternative technologies more in keeping with humane ideals and aspirations.

Focus Questions

1. Identify one modern technology and discuss its development. In what ways has this technology changed the way you live from both a positive and negative perspective, and what future changes might occur that could have even more impact on your life?
2. Identify one environmental and organizational background imperative of a contemporary technology. How might those conditions have influenced that technology's development and its influence on our lives?
3. What are some ways in which Sclove's concept of *polypotency* relates to the issues of "freedom, power, authority, community, and justice" raised in the reading by Langdon Winner (selection I.7)?

Keywords

artifact, citizenship, democracy, primary function, social consequences, social structure

Technological innovations are similar to legislative acts or political foundings that establish a framework for public order that will endure over many generations.
                                                    —Langdon Winner

WHAT IS TECHNOLOGY? People ordinarily think of technology as machinery or gadgetry, as an economic factor of production, as know-how, as what engineers do, or as progress. Often they characterize technologies in terms of a single intended function. What is a hammer? It's what someone uses to pound nails into boards. What is a telephone? It's a device that enables people to converse at a distance. Some technologies, however, have more than one intended function. Hammers, for example, can pound nails into boards but can also extract them. This is the core of the contemporary view of technology. People understand technologies in terms of a primary function—or, occasionally, several functions—that each is intended to accomplish.

Beyond this, our society has in the past few decades come to acknowledge that technologies tend to produce at least two general kinds of "secondary" or "unintended" effects. First, they generate environmental consequences: pollution, resource depletion, and ecosystem modification. Each of these may, in turn, have direct or indirect effects on human life. Second, they promote unintended social consequences—consequences that are generally mediated by economic markets (e.g., the replacement of workers by machines or the emergence of boom-towns). Thus common knowledge has it that technologies perform one or perhaps a few intended functions, while also producing a limited range of unintended social and environmental consequences.

Although this view of technology is straightforward, it is also incomplete and misleading. It diverts attention from many significant aspects of technology, including some of central concern to democracy. By synthesizing recent technological criticism, the alternative view of technology introduced here incorporates the accepted view's sound insights but situates these within a broader perspective that recognizes technologies as a species of social structure.

The phrase "social structure" refers to the background features that help define or regulate patterns of human interaction. Familiar examples include laws, dominant political and economic institutions, and systems of cultural belief. Technologies qualify as social structures because they function politically and culturally in a manner comparable to these other, more commonly recognized kinds of social structures.

Technologies as Social Structures

Ibieca, a Spanish village, found that its indoor plumbing came at the expense of community integration. That is an instance of a technology helping to structure social relations. Upsetting a traditional pattern of water use compromised important means through which the village had previously perpetuated itself as a self-conscious community. In the United States the automobile has played a somewhat similar role in disrupting prior patterns of community life.

These are not isolated cases; technologies designed for such mundane tasks as commuting to work or cooking food also routinely help constitute social systems of cooperation, isolation, or domination.

> Technology often embodies and expresses political value choices that, in their operations and effects, are binding on individuals and groups, whether such choices have been made in political forums or elsewhere. . . . Technological processes in contemporary society have become the equivalent of a form of law—that is, an authoritative or binding expression of social norms and values from which the individual or a group may have no immediate recourse.

COERCIVE COMPLIANCE

Technologies help regulate social behavior in part because they are themselves governed by both physical and political laws. For example, the operation of many technologies—such as automobiles, medical X-ray machines, or guns—is legally regulated. Thus their misuse can entail a socially enforced penalty.

However, whether or not they are governed by legal regulations, technologies generally embody a variety of other kinds of coercive mandates. The penalty for resisting these mandates may range from an informal reprimand ("Don't lick the food off your knife!") to economic loss or systemic failure (e.g., the gears in a conveyor belt jam, or a worker's hand is injured). These latter results are akin to the consequences befalling those who ignore physical laws (e.g., when someone literally walks on thin ice). Thus physical constraints, or accompanying legal and social sanctions, are among the obvious means through which technologies help structure human behavior.

SUBCONSCIOUS COMPLIANCE

Sometimes technologies shape behavior and relationships less through brute compulsion than via subtle, psychological inducement. For example, social scientists have shown that the physical arrangement of chairs and tables strongly influences the kind of social interaction that occurs in schools, nursing homes, and hospitals. Yet the staff in those institutions had previously attributed behavior (including their own) entirely to the mix of personalities and psychological capabilities. They were surprised to learn that simply shifting the furniture could, for instance, help reanimate a seemingly moribund group of mentally impaired hospital inmates.

OPPORTUNITIES AND CONSTRAINTS

Social structures are also ambiguous in that while they can restrict opportunities in some respects, they can—when appropriately designed—enhance them in others. For example, well-crafted laws help protect basic civil rights and, by providing a relatively stable and well-ordered social context, make it easier for people to realize their life plans.

Besides creating novel opportunities and constraints, technologies also reconfigure prior patterns. For instance, within some offices and factories the proliferation of personal computer networks has enhanced lower level workers' chances to contribute to production decisions while simultaneously challenging midlevel managers' former domains of authority and autonomy. Once deployed, technologies can also aid or hinder the use of other technologies. For instance, telephone systems gradually displaced telegraph services but have more recently facilitated development of computer networks and long-distance data processing.

BACKGROUND CONDITIONS
AS IMPERATIVES

In order to function, technologies require various environmental and organizational background conditions. A television set is only useful so long as viewers know how to operate it, it is protected from inclement weather, there is access to electricity, programs are being produced and distributed, and so on.

Frequently when individuals or groups acquire new technologies or technological facilities, they are at best only dimly conscious of the demands that effective operation will impose or require to be developed. Several years ago a town near mine in western Massachusetts approved construction of an industrial research center, hoping thereby to realize tax benefits. But no one asked beforehand the eventual costs (financial, environmental, and emotional) that

the town would one day bear in order to accommodate both new research activities and the concomitant growth in commuting, ancillary employment, and residential population. These costs could include hazards associated with toxic waste disposal, future loss of open space to new housing, and the burden of upgrading roads, sewer lines, snowplowing capabilities, schools, and school bus lines.

To the extent that a given technology plays only a small part in one's life, maintaining the conditions needed for its operation may be of no particular concern. But as a person or society grows dependent on a technology, the necessary conditions of its operation loom as practical imperatives. The need to support these conditions represents a way in which technologies exert a profound structural social influence.

TECHNOLOGY AS STRUCTURAL
FOR NONUSERS

Often technologies exert comparably significant effects on people who neither operate nor use the technology in question. One clear example involves phenomena that economists label "spillover effects" or "externalities." Homeowners hear neighbors' radios, lawn mowers, or air conditioners; whole communities breathe noxious fumes from an industrial facility. Each person lives in an aesthetic landscape that reflects the aggregate technological choices made by other people or organizations. The psychological texture of our everyday life reflects the influence of countless technological choices and practices in which we did not participate.

Moreover, often such spillover effects exert a structural influence that is dynamic and transformative. For instance, someone might choose not to purchase a power lawn mower to avoid its noise. However, after a few neighbors have bought theirs, this person may reconsider, thinking, "Since I'm suffering from the noise anyway, why not buy my own power mower and at least benefit from the convenience?" In this way each mower purchased contributes to a cycle that gradually transforms a neighborhood of quiet into one rent by the sound of churning engines.

Next reconsider the background conditions necessary for a technology to operate. Many of those conditions have a tremendous impact on lives even if individuals do not own the technology or use the technological service that establishes their raison d'être. Suppose, to state the case dramatically, that as a citizen of a modern nation a woman opts for a relatively self-sufficient mode of life: She refuses to own a car, uses solar collectors on the roof of her home, and plants a large vegetable garden in her yard. What has she accomplished? Something, certainly, but the texture of her world still reflects the existence not only of cars and their immediate culture, but of roadways, automobile manufacturing and marketing systems, oil refineries, electric generating facilities, agribusiness, the private or public bureaucracies that manage these things, and their often tumultuous politics. That is part of what it means to say that technologies are social structures. The aggregate result of a society's many technological choices in one way or another affects every member.

COMMUNICATIVE AND CULTURAL SYSTEMS

Apart from materially influencing social experience, technologies also exert symbolic and other cultural influences. This is true not only of technologies explicitly called communications devices (e.g., cellular phones, televisions, and radios), but of all technologies.

For example, modern sofas generally have two or three separate seat cushions. There is no compelling technical or economic rationale for this design (an affordable, seamless sofa is an easily conceived alternative—as seamless mattresses and Japanese futon sofa-beds attest). Rather, separate sofa cushions define distinct personal spaces and thus respect—but also help to perpetuate—modern Western culture's emphasis on individuality and privacy.

Technologies even play transformative roles within psychological development. For example, earlier this century Swiss psychologist Jean Piaget determined that young children distinguish living from nonliving things according to whether or not the things move, and—as the children develop psychologically—then according to whether things move by themselves or are moved by an outside force. However, more recently, social psychologist Sherry Turkle found that children who play with computer toys that appear to "talk" and "think" develop different criteria for distinguishing "alive" from "not alive." Instead of relying on physical criteria (such as motion), they invent psychological criteria and hypotheses ("Computers are alive because they cheat" or "Computers are not alive because they don't have feelings"). Children's developmental trajectories, including their conceptions of self and moral reasoning, are transformed as a result of their interactions with these machines.

The process that Turkle described with respect to computer toys is a specific instance of a much more general phenomenon. As they reconfigure opportunities and constraints for action, and function simultaneously as symbols and latent communicative media, technologies also reconfigure opportunities and constraints for psychological development.

MACROPOLITICS: TECHNOLOGY *AND* SOCIETY VERSUS TECHNOLOGY *AS* SOCIETY

Many scholars have described cases in which technologies exert a macrolevel influence on societies. Consider historians who focus on the social role of just one or two important technologies at a time. Large scale dams and irrigation systems may have played a decisive role in the creation and maintenance of states in antiquity. Lynn White, Jr. told a now-famous story of the role of the stirrup in the development of European feudalism: stirrups made possible mounted shock combat, which led in turn to heavy full-body armor, heraldry, chivalry, stronger horse breeds, more efficient plowing methods, and so forth. In America, railroads helped establish national markets; promoted coal mining, steelmaking, and the widespread adoption of steam power; provided an influential model of geographically dispersed, hierarchically managed corporate organization; contributed to the adoption of standardized timekeeping; and served as a dominant metaphor with which Americans interpreted their entire civilization.

More recently in the United States one role of new technologies has been to provide grounds for the growth of the federal government, through the proliferation of such agencies as the Federal Communications Commission for regulating telecommunications, the Federal Aviation Administration for regulating the airline industry, the Nuclear Regulatory Commission and the Department of Energy for administering aspects of national energy production and nuclear weapons development, and the like.

In each of these instances, technological innovation plays a role in establishing, transforming, or maintaining states or societies at the macrolevel. Langdon Winner has explored the further hypothesis that the entire ensemble of modern technological systems—including the background conditions required to keep them operating—tends to promote centrally coordinated, technocratic social administration.

Hence there are numerous examples in which technologies affect societies or states in ways that have macrostructural implications. However, this formulation—while both true and dramatic—nonetheless misses the force of this chapter's earlier analysis. Technologies function politically and culturally as social structures by coercing physical compliance; prompting subconscious compliance; constituting systems of social relations; establishing opportunities and constraints for action and self-realization; promoting the evolution of background conditions; affecting nonusers; shaping communication, psychological development, and culture generally; and constituting much of the world within which lives unfold.

Considering all of the preceding functions and effects together, it would be fairer to say that technologies do not merely *affect* society or states, they also *constitute* a substantial portion of societies and states. That, too, is part of what it means to be a social structure. Recognizing the many respects in which technologies contribute to defining who people are, what they can and cannot do, and how they understand themselves and their world should dispel the common myth that technologies are morally or politically neutral.

INFLUENTIAL, NOT DETERMINING

Technologies "structure" social relations in that they shape or help constitute—but do not fully determine—social experience. Water pipes and washing machines did not, for example, literally force Ibiecans to stop gathering at their village's central fountain and washbasin, but instead altered the system of inducements and interdependencies that formerly made such gathering occur naturally.

Aside from the possibility of rejecting or retiring a particular technology, there is always a margin of flexibility in how existing technological artifacts may be used or operated, or in what activities may occur in conjunction with them. This margin is finite, and its extent varies from one technology to the next and over time, but it nevertheless exists. For example, while a conventional assembly line provides only highly restricted opportunities to vary work routines at each station, it does not materially prevent workers from rotating jobs among work stations.

CONTEXT-DEPENDENCY

Developing a railroad network helped catapult the United States to global economic preeminence, but Britain developed railroads earlier and yet nonetheless gradually lost its world economic predominance. Thus railroads (or other technologies) are socially consequential, but how and why they matter depends on the precise technologies in question in each particular context of use.

Moreover, just as social context—including, among other things, a society's preexisting technological order—regulates each technology's material functions and effects, it also regulates a technology's communicative functions and cultural meanings. A few decades ago a belching smokestack symbolized progress. Today—in a different historical context—the same smokestack is more likely to evoke distress or even outrage.

Finally, one important influence on a technology's functions and effects is the minds and culture of people. Nineteenth-century high-wheeler bicycles were perceived by athletic young men as virile, high-speed devices. But to some women and elderly men the same devices signified personal danger. Indeed, conflicting perceptions of the high-wheeler proved consequential to its subsequent technological development. Its perception as a "macho machine" prompted new bicycle designs with ever higher front wheels. The competing perception of the high-wheeler as an "unsafe machine" prompted designs with smaller front wheels, different seat placement, or higher rear wheels. Thus to understand the social function, meaning, and evolution of the high-wheeler, it is essential to explore its psychological and cultural context.

Public controversies concerning technology offer another occasion for observing the role of culture and cognition in establishing a technology's context, and hence its social role. For example, during the 1970s nuclear engineers and electric utility executives generally viewed centralized production of electricity as a critical social need and essential to the concept of commercial nuclear power. To them an alternative to nuclear power needed to be another means of performing this critical function. But other energy policy analysts saw the expanded production of electricity as so inessential that a perfectly viable alternative could be a panel of foam wall insulation that did not generate any electricity.

In evidence here are fragments of a social process of contesting or negotiating what is or is not to count as an essential function of a technology and hence as an alternative. Thus, when technological consequences or meanings become controversial, processes through which technologies are culturally constituted may emerge openly.

CONTINGENT SOCIAL PRODUCTS

There is residual variability in the structural effects associated with any deployed technology—*within a particular social context and even more so among different contexts*. However, a technology's greatest flexibility exists before its final deployment, when artifacts and their accompanying social organization are being conceived and designed.

Technologies do not just appear or happen; they are contingent social products. Thus it is possible, both before and after the fact, to imagine alternative designs. The process by which one set of designs rather than another comes to fruition is influenced by prevailing social structures and forces, including the preexisting technological order. However, this process also reflects explicit or tacit social choices, including political negotiations or struggles.

For example, it is hard to imagine a modern home without an electric refrigerator, but had the

accidents of competing corporate resources played out slightly differently, gas-powered refrigerators that would have run more reliably and quietly could have been the norm. Other feasible alternatives in household technology harbored the potential for even more dramatic social effects. Moreover, although today people think of the guiding impulses behind technological development as necessarily being profit, convenience, or military advantage, throughout history religious or aesthetic motivations have often been just as significant.

Thus there are many potential, competing technological pathways, and each is socially developed. But the flexibility associated with a given technology, or with other social structures, tends to diminish with time. After a society has habituated itself to one technology, alternatives tend to become less accessible. Once designed and deployed, a technology, like a law or a political institution tends—if it is going to endure—gradually to become integrated into larger systems of functionally interdependent artifacts and organizations and then to influence the design of subsequent technologies, laws, and institutions such that the latter all tend to depend on the continued existence of the former. Thus, owing to the accompanying evolution of supporting custom, entrenched interest, and various sunk costs, it is often difficult to achieve radical design alterations once an initial decision has been implemented. A further factor reducing the flexibility of technologies is that they exhibit some of the pure physical recalcitrance that comes with material embodiment. Hence, both technologies and other social structures, once they have come into existence, tend to endure. However, technologies exhibit a remaining characteristic that tends to distinguish them from other social structures and to increase their relative political salience: polypotency.

Polypotency

Technologies function as social structures, but often independently of their (nominally) intended purposes. This is one of the phenomena that the conventional view of technology obscures. The same obfuscation is reflected in studies that profess a broad interest in the political effects of technology but that discuss only technologies designed explicitly to function politically (such as telecommunications, military and police technologies, voting machines, or computer databases). Such technologies indeed function politically, but everyone knows that. That is these technologies' announced purpose. Harder to grasp is the truth that all technologies are associated with manifold latent social effects and meanings, and that it is largely in virtue of these that technologies come to function as social structures. In other words, technologies exhibit superfluous efficacy or "polypotency" in their functions, effects, and meanings. (The word *polypotency,* meaning "potent in many ways," is introduced here for want of a better existing term. The unfamiliarity wears off quickly if one contrasts it with omnipotence, meaning, literally, "potent in all ways.")

For example, when a man uses an ordinary hammer to pound nails, he also learns about the texture and structural properties of materials, he exercises and develops his muscles, he improves his hand-eye coordination, and he generates noise, all while stressing and wearing the hammer itself. As his competence at hammering grows, he feels his self-respect affirmed and approved. At another level, his activity resonates with half-conscious memories of primeval myths about Vulcan and Thor. He is also reminded of the blacksmith and the mythology of the American frontier. He thinks of a judge's gavel, the hammer as a symbol of justice, and a song popularized by the folksinging trio Peter, Paul, and Mary.

Where did the hammer come from? Somebody chopped down a tree and fashioned the handle. Others located and extracted iron ore. Some of that ore was refashioned into a hammer head. If a man touches his tongue to the hammer, with the taste of oxidized iron he senses fleetingly a former age when once-independent craftsmen and farmers first found themselves working under strict supervision in a factory. When he was a child, an uncle first taught him to use a hammer. Now when he hefts a hammer, he feels embedded in a historical relationship with this and other hammers and with the development of the concept of hammers and technology in general.

The hammer's immediate social context of use can vary. The man may work alone, on a project with others, or in a room where each person pursues a different project. He may or may not choose his task; he may or may not earn a wage. Depending on the precise social context of its use, the hammer means different things to him, he sees it differently, and it helps disclose the world to him in different ways. Likewise, his style of using the hammer discloses to others much about his character, competence, and mood.

The hammer differs from a partially automated assembly line in that the latter requires and helps coordinate the simultaneous efforts of many workers. But a hammer also establishes certain limiting possibilities on the social conditions of its use. Hammers have only one handle. They are not designed to permit the type of close collaboration that is possible through computer networks or necessary when using a long, two-handled saw.

The material result of the man's activity is likely to include some bent nails, scrap wood, a hearty appetite, maybe a bruised thumb, a few sore but marginally strengthened muscles, some excess exhalation of carbon dioxide, perspiration, and a product that becomes part of the humanly shaped world. So, is the nail entering the board necessarily the most important feature of the activity called "hammering"? Hammers, like all technologies, are polypotent in their social functions, effects, and meanings.

Today's accepted view of technology takes a step toward acknowledging polypotency by speaking of technologies' unintended or secondary consequences. However, the term "polypotency" is helpful in not presuming that one knows automatically which of a technology's many functions or meanings are the most important or even which are intended. Many social historians of technology have, for example, argued that a latent but intended function of some innovations in manufacturing technology has been to substitute low-paid unskilled workers for higher-paid skilled workers, discipline the remaining workforce, and weaken unions.

It is furthermore useful to introduce the term "focal function" to refer to a technology's (ostensibly) intended purpose. "Nonfocal" then denotes its accompanying complex of additional—but often recessive—functions, effects, and meanings. Thus, 19th-century New England schoolhouses' focal function was to provide a space for educational instruction, whereas one of their nonfocal functions was to help generate—in part via the symbolism of churchlike architectures—a relatively docile workforce.

Occasionally technologies function as social structures precisely by virtue of their focal purpose. For instance, weapons function coercively because they are designed to do just that. But more often and more subtly, it is technologies' latent polypotency that accounts for their structural performance. This is illustrated by many previous examples, ranging from sofa cushions (which help to latently reproduce our culture's sense of privacy) to computer toys (which unexpectedly alter children's psychological development). Even technologies focally designed to function structurally are apt to structure nonfocally as well.

For instance, nuclear weapons are designed focally to coerce, deter, or destroy other societies, but they contribute nonfocally to legitimating authoritarian government institutions within the societies that possess them. Marshall McLuhan popularized this truth as it applies specifically to technologies focally designated as communications devices: "The medium *is* the message." In other words, the technical means of focally delivering a message can, owing to polypotency, matter more than the message itself.

Moreover, often groups of focally unrelated technologies interact latently to produce a structural effect that no one of them could accomplish alone. Distinct sofa cushions would not help establish cultural norms of privacy and individualism were they not part of a complex of artifacts and ritual behavior that contribute jointly toward that same result. (Other artifacts in the complex with sofa cushions include individual eating utensils, private bedrooms, telephone receivers designed to accommodate one person at a time, and so forth.) In short, to achieve social insight and efficacy, it is essential to consider all the different artifacts and practices that comprise a society's technological order.

There are important functional equivalences between technologies and nontechnological social structures (e.g., legal statutes, government agencies, and large corporations). All represent enduring social products that shape subsequent social experience. However, there are also differences, revolving around contrasting levels of social understanding with respect to each.

First, laws and political and economic institutions are contingent social products, and at some level everyone knows this truth. Societies evolve these things through formal political or juridical processes, and it is commonly understood that alternative choices are possible. In contrast, people are prone to misperceive a society's technologies as inevitable, that is, as naturally determined rather than socially shaped and chosen.

Second, laws and other formally evolved social structures are commonly understood to function as social structures. That is their explicit purpose. Certainly, they can also be implicated in the production of various unintended social consequences. Prohibition-era laws were enacted to stop alcohol production, not to drive it underground and contribute to the expansion of organized crime. However, people at least expect that legal statutes and institutions will—because that is their intent—in some way shape social interaction and history. In contrast, people ordinarily expect most technologies to prove structurally inconsequential, and—because focally most of them do—this expectation appears confirmed. But here is where appearances deceive, insofar as it is frequently a technology's nonfocal aspects alone that conspire to manifest profound structural consequences.

Hence, although technologies are as consequential as other social structures, people tend to be more blind both to the social origins of technologies and to their social effects. This dual blindness is partly due to certain myths or misconceptions, such as the myth that technologies are autonomous self-contained phenomena and the myth that they are morally neutral. It is also inculcated through modern technologies themselves, via both their style and their social process of design.

These dual misperceptions concerning technologies actually enhance their relative structural significance, because they enable technologies to exert their influence with only limited social awareness of how, or even that, they are doing so. This helps explain why people are prone to resign themselves to social circumstances established through technological artifice and practices that they might well reject if the same results were proposed through a formal political process.

So long as their social origin, effects, and dynamics remain so badly misperceived, technologies will not suffer the same liability as would, say, functionally comparable laws or economic institutions, of being challenged on the grounds that they are politically or culturally unacceptable. Furthermore, societies will fail to develop the capacity to seek other technologies more consonant—both focally and nonfocally—with their members' ideals and aspirations.

LANGDON WINNER   I.7

Artifacts/Ideas and Political Culture

Although technology usually offers us a bright and rosy future, Langdon Winner suggests that we should be considering what type of technological future we want to build and the extent to which it will be kind to human society. As our modern political culture has evolved, it is important to be aware of the ways in which advancing technology has affected our common experiences of "freedom, power, authority, community, and justice." Even though the artifacts and processes associated with technological systems are taken for granted or thought to be politically neutral, this article examines technology as a major force on our lives, changing relationships between people in subtle but significant ways. This is evident in secondary influences from inventions of the Industrial Revolution, which created an entirely new society that continues to evolve today, even though we might not be conscious of the change. Whether these changes are for the better will be determined by our commitment to building a society in which more people share in the benefits.

Focus Questions

1. Describe the seven concepts mentioned by Winner that are present in the structure of contemporary technology, and give an example of two specific technologies utilized today that embody those ideas.
2. Identify a contemporary technology and discuss one probable answer to each of the three questions normally focused on by individuals, groups, and nations. With the benefit of hindsight, how has that particular technology influenced the kind of world that has developed since its inception?

3. Consider the three guiding maxims proposed by Winner to focus discussion about the relationship between technological choice and the future of political culture. How do these concepts relate to the issue of spreading capitalism discussed by Sachs (selection II.2) and Bhagwati (selection II.3)?

Keywords

capitalism, culture, democracy, feudalism, politics, public policy, UTOPIA

THIS IS A TIME OF GREAT EXCITEMENT about the fruitful possibilities of new technology, but also a time of grave concern about what those possibilities mean for the future of our society. Horizons visible in microelectronics and photonics, biotechnology, composite materials, computing, and other fields hold out prospects of sweeping change in our way of life. How should we regard these prospects?

As individuals, groups, and nations anticipate technological change nowadays, they usually focus upon three questions.

First: How will the technology be used? What are its functions and practical benefits?

Second: How will the technology change the economy? What will it contribute to the production, distribution, and consumption of material wealth?

Third: How will the technology affect the environment? What will its consequences be for global climate change, pollution of the biosphere, and other environmental problems?

While these are important issues, another crucial question is seldom mentioned: What kind of world are we building here? As we develop new devices, techniques and technical systems, what qualities of social, moral, and political life do we create in the process? Will this be a world friendly to human sociability or not?

These are questions about the relationship of technological change to the evolution of modern political culture. In what ways do the development, adoption, and use of instrumental things affect our shared experience of freedom, power, authority, community, and justice? How might we respond creatively to the role technology plays in contemporary political life?

In the titles of a great many books, articles, and conferences these days, the topic is often described as "technology and society" or "technology and culture" or "technology and politics." But if one takes a closer look, such distinctions no longer have much validity. In the late twentieth century, technology and society, technology and culture, technology and politics are by no means separate. They are closely woven together in a multiplicity of settings in which many forms of human living are dependent upon and shaped by technological devices and systems of various kinds. Our useful artifacts reflect who we are, what we aspire to be. At the same time, we ourselves mirror the technologies which surround us; to an increasing extent social activities and human consciousness are technically mediated.

In this light, any attempt to understand the matter might well begin from either of two basic starting points: (1) the technological world seen from the point of view of human beings and (2) the same world seen from the point of view of the artifacts. Although it may seem perverse to do so, I shall begin with the second perspective.

Many of the things that we like to think of as mere tools or instruments now function as virtual members of our society. It makes sense to ask: Which roles, responsibilities, and possibilities for action have been delegated to technological things? Which social features are associated with a particular artifact? For example, does a computer in the workplace function as a servant, slave, controller, guard, supervisor, etc.?

The social roles delegated to the phone answering machine provide a good illustration. It used to

From *Whole Earth Review, No. 73* (Winter 1991), pp. 18–24. *Whole Earth Review,* San Rafael, CA 94901. Subscription available: subs@wholeearthmag.com Reprinted by permission.

be that only executives in business and government could afford to keep a full-time secretary answering the phone, screening calls, and taking messages. Now it is possible to buy a small, inexpensive answering machine that does at least some of that work. An alternative would be to answer the phone yourself, have someone else do it for you, or simply miss some calls. The machine serves as a surrogate, a kind of nonhuman agent that has been given certain kinds of work to do.

An interesting fact about these machines is that their initial use often brings some embarrassment. In the little taped message that precedes the beep, there is often something like an apology. "I'm sorry I can't be here to answer your call . . ." or "I'm sorry you have to talk to this machine, but . . . ." What one sees in cases like this is, I believe, quite common in modern life: the uneasy feeling that accompanies the renegotiation of social and moral boundaries around a technological change. But what is sometimes at first a source of discomfort eventually becomes a widely accepted pattern—"second nature," if you will.

It is clear that in decades to come a great many things like telephone answering machines and automatic bank tellers will become, in effect, members of our society. As their use spreads, the tone of embarrassment that surrounds their early introduction will gradually vanish. For better or worse, the renegotiation of boundaries will be complete. When I phoned a friend recently, I heard a recorded message that said simply: "It's 1991. You know what to do!"

One can also consider technological innovations from the alternate viewpoint—noticing the roles, responsibilities, and possibilities for action delegated to human beings within and around technological systems of various kinds. Now one can ask: Is a person's guiding hand required for the system to function? Does the human give orders or receive them? Is the person active or acted upon? What social qualities accompany the human presence?

I will offer some illustrations in a moment. But first I want to call attention to the fact that once one has entered the twofold perspective I've suggested, one has the beginning of a social and political vision of technology quite different from the one that economists, engineers, and technology policy makers usually employ. One recognizes, first and foremost, that technologies are not merely tools that one "picks up and uses." They can be seen as "forms of life" in which humans and inanimate objects are linked in various kinds of relationships. The interesting question becomes: How can we describe and evaluate technologies seen as "forms of life"?

By comparison, in the conventional view of things, the story usually goes that people employ technologies as simple tools for rather specific instrumental purposes, attempting to wrest new advantages over nature and to gain various economic benefits. Once these instrumental advantages and economic benefits have been obtained, other things may happen. There are what are called secondary, tertiary, and other distant consequences of our actions, often called the "impacts" or "unintended" consequences, the broader social, cultural, political, and environmental effects of technological applications of various kinds.

For some purposes, it is perfectly acceptable to view technological change in the conventional manner. However, if you take a longer view of history, an interesting fact soon emerges. In the fullness of time, the so-called "secondary" consequences or impacts of technological change are often far more significant than the results thought to be "primary" at the time. This is certainly true, for example, of the kinds of changes we associate with the Industrial Revolution of the eighteenth and nineteenth centuries. One could list the thousands upon thousands of instrumental advantages and economic benefits obtained during that period—techniques for making textiles, extracting coal, making locomotives run, etc. But that is not what is truly important about the Industrial Revolution. What matters is the fact that a whole new kind of society was created. The truly enduring part of that revolution, the truly significant aspect is the multiplicity of relationships between people and between humans and technology we call Industrial Society, results many of which arose largely as so-called "secondary" consequences of technological change.

If one looks carefully at contemporary technological innovations in their broader human context, one often finds emerging forms of political culture. Several years ago Maevon Garrett, a woman who had worked as a telephone operator in Baltimore for 18 years, was called into her supervisor's office and abruptly fired. She was informed that a computer had been installed to monitor the performance of telephone operators and that data gathered by the computer showed that she was less efficient than the average worker in processing phone calls. At that moment Maevon Garrett became the victim of norms of productivity and efficiency embodied in the workings of a new technological system.

What is interesting, however, is not only the fact of Ms. Garrett's firing, but her response to it. She pointed out that some portion of her time each day was spent talking with people who dial a telephone operator because they are lonely or in distress—elderly people who live alone, or "latchkey children," youngsters who come home after school to an empty house because their parents are still at work. Ms. Garrett argued she would not hang up on such people just to meet the phone company's hourly quota.

It is reasonable to conclude that she was behaving responsibly, serving a role in civic culture, but not a role recognized by the norms of efficiency and productivity in the system that employed her. This is a case in which conditions of technical rationality and cultural rationality meet in flagrant conflict.

The good news is that after a union protest Maevon Garrett's job was restored. The bad news, however, is that the system's design, the technopolitical regime that caused the problem, still exists and looms before us a rapidly spreading form of life. A study released by the Office of Technology Assessment of the U.S. Congress several years ago noted that approximately seven million American workers now live under rapidly spreading systems of computerized surveillance, an unhappy spin-off of office automation. The title of that report is, appropriately, *The Electronic Supervisor*. To an increasing extent in today's workplaces, computers are delegated the role of supervising; human beings have been assigned roles that involve working faster and faster while ending in less social conversation—all in the name of a system called "communications," but one that drastically limits people's ability to communicate in a human sense.

The term "regime" seems perfectly appropriate in such cases. For once they have been designed, built, and put in operation, sociotechnical systems comprise regimes with features that can be described in a political way. It makes perfect sense to talk about freedom or its absence, equality or inequality, justice or injustice, authoritarianism or democracy, and the kinds of power relationships technological instruments and systems contain.

This is true of extremely simple as well as complex technologies. For example, if one visits the agricultural fields of the southwestern U.S.A., one finds workers using a hoe, "el cortito," a tool with a short handle. There's nothing political about the length of a wooden handle, is there? Well, that depends on the broader social relationships and activities in which it plays a part. To use "el cortito" you must bend over or get down on your knees. A casual observer might say: If you're digging in the ground, isn't it sometimes more comfortable to stand up?

Why, then, has the handle been shortened? The reason is, in large part, that the foremen who manage the work can look across a field, even at a great distance, and tell who is working and who is not. Those who are bending over are the ones working; those standing upright are not and the foreman can apply discipline accordingly. In that light, even the length of the handle of a hoe expresses a regime, a regime of power, authority, and control.

Embodied in the tools and instruments of modern technology is a political world. I am suggesting that we use metaphors and rhetorical devices of political speech to unpack the meaning of various technologies for how we live.

Everyone understands that political ideas can be expressed in language. But ideas of this kind present themselves in material objects as well. In this form they might be called artifact/ideas. In their very silence, artifact/ideas have a great deal to say. They tell us who we are, where we are situated in the social order, what is normal, what is possible, what is excluded. The technological world is filled with artifact/ideas of great consequence for modern political culture. Things often speak louder than words. Among the main ideas present in the structure of contemporary technological devices and systems are the following:

- Power is centralized.
- The few talk and the many listen.
- There are barriers between social classes.
- The world is hierarchically structured.
- The good things are distributed unequally.
- Women and men have different kinds of competence.
- One's life is open to continual inspection.

As they are expressed in the shape of material objects, ideas of this kind are covert. They seldom become topics for discussion in the political sphere as it is usually understood. One reason that artifact/ideas tend to be covert is that most people buy the functional account of the meaning of material things. We are inclined to say: "This is a car which enables us to go from point A to point B." "This is a hoe which helps us to dig in the fields."

Another reason why ideologies in things tend to be covert is that they have been implanted there by those who do not wish those ideas to be known or widely discussed. The apparent solidity of useful things sometimes provides a mask for persons and groups who wish to exercise power while avoiding responsibility. Their alibi is usually something like: "This is the most effective way to do things" or "This is most efficient."

But whatever the source of specific beliefs and instrumental conditions, it is often true that ideas embodied in material things are painful or even dangerous to acknowledge. Artifact/ideas can involve astonishing contradictions. In particular, the mapping of the world encountered in the shape of things frequently contradicts the political ideology to which most people in Western societies claim to be committed.

In particular, many of the artifact/ideas prevalent in our time stand in flagrant contradiction to the ideology of modern democracy. That ideology holds that human beings flourish, achieving what is best in their potential, under conditions of freedom, equality, justice, and self-government. In that light, societies ought to create social conditions and political institutions that make it possible for each human being's potential to develop. Both victories and setbacks in this regard are clearly visible in the laws, constitutions, and political practices that prevail in each historical period.

From this vantage point a technological society is unique only in the sense that it presents new and seemingly unlikely domains—domains of instrumentality—in which the ends of democratic freedom, equality, and justice must somehow be recognized and realized. I take it to be the fundamental failure of modern civilization to have ignored again and again how such questions present themselves in the guise of what appear to be "neutral" technologies. To a considerable extent the ideas embodied in the realm of material things and in opposition to the central ideas that we believe describe and guide our political culture.

There is an important way in which freedom and justice depend in human communities upon the existence of suitable material environments—the creation and maintenance of arrangements in which the goal of becoming free, self-determining individuals is nurtured rather than destroyed. As we look at the kinds of sociotechnical innovations being introduced today, it is often beside the point to ask whether or not they are optimally efficient; by someone's definition they are usually very efficient indeed. Instead the crucial questions concern the kinds of cultural environments such technologies present to us. What one finds are far too many instances of developments of the following kind:

1. communications technologies employed in attempts to control people's thoughts, desires and behaviors;
2. computer technologies used to whittle away people's privacy and erode freedom;
3. information technologies that eliminate what were formerly places of community life;
4. energy systems that make people dependent upon, or even hostage to, sources of fuel over which they exercise no control;

5. systems of manufacturing that seek control by eliminating as much human initiative and creativity as possible.

The appropriate moment to examine and debate conditions such as these is the time during which they are designed and first introduced into the fabric of human activity. At present our society persists in designing a great many technical artifacts in ways that make people feel passive, superfluous, stupid, and incapable of initiating action. Such systems bear the cultural embryos of tomorrow's citizenry. For as we invent new technical systems, we also invent the kinds of people who will use them and be affected by them. The structures and textures of future social and political life can be seen in the blueprints of technologies now on the drawing board.

We often hear these days that the world is engaged in a "technology race" in which nations rise or fall according to their ability to use technologies to competitive advantage. Unfortunately, some of the design strategies that look fabulous from the point of view of efficiency, productivity, and global competitiveness involve what amounts to an ingenious synthesis of oriental feudalism and capitalism. Many people in freedom-loving countries like the United States seem eager to embrace repressive models of social integration expressed in automation, electronic surveillance, and pseudo-democratic "quality circles." But must we embrace these merging patterns of technofeudalism as "the wave of the future"? Would it not be a wiser approach to resist, choosing to explore ways of extending our ideas about freedom and a just society into the realm of technology itself?

In fact, one obvious path that may still be open to us is to cultivate ways of democratizing the process of technology policymaking and, indeed, the process of technological innovation. If this is to be done, both citizens and experts will need to become aware of the social, moral, and political dimensions of choices made in technological policy and technological design. They will need to find ways to act directly and democratically within settings in which the important choices are made.

In that light I would offer three guiding maxims as a way to focus discussion about the relationship between technological choices and the future of political culture. These maxims can be raised at times in which unquestioned assumptions about "productivity," "competitiveness," "the need to innovate," or "technology transfer" seem to provide the only language for talking about the choices at hand.

1. *No innovation without representation*. This suggests that all the groups and social interests likely to be affected by a particular kind of technological change ought to be represented at a very early stage in defining what that technology will be. Yes, let us accept the idea that particular technologies are social creations that arise through a complex, multicentered process. But let us see to it that all the relevant parties are included rather than kept in the dark in this process. If we find that we do not have the kinds of social institutions that make this possible, then let's change our institutions to create such opportunities.

2. *No engineering without political deliberation*. Proposed technological projects should be closely examined to reveal the covert political conditions and artifact/ideas their making would entail. This ought to become an interpretive skill of people in all modern societies. It is especially important for engineers and technical professionals whose wonderful creativity is often accompanied by an appalling narrow-mindedness. The education of engineers ought to prepare them to evaluate the kinds of political contexts, political ideas, political arguments, and political consequences involved in their work. Skill in the arts of democratic citizenship ought to become part of the "tool kit" that engineers master in their education.

3. *No means without ends*. Many of the varieties of innovation now pushed on the public these days amount to "tools looking for uses," "means looking for ends." Those who have dealt with the introduction of computers into the schools in recent years can give many colorful examples of this phenomenon. The current promotion of high definition television and renewed efforts to push President Reagan's Star Wars project offer even more stark illustration. For HDTV and SDI bear little relationship to any significant human need. As we study the prospects offered by new technologies, it

is always essential to ask: Why? Why are we doing this? What are the ends we have chosen and how well do they fit the pattern of means available? In many cases of high tech planning, suitable background music would be the theme from *The Twilight Zone.*

If you were to look for examples of places in which something similar to these three maxims are actually being put to work, I would begin by pointing to some recent experiments in the Scandinavian democracies where a positive, creative politics of technology has recently become a focus of research and development. In one such project, workers in the Swedish newspaper industry—printers, typographers, lithographers, and the like—joined with representatives from management and with university computer scientists to design a new system of computerized graphics used in newspaper layout and typesetting. The name of the project was UTOPIA, a Swedish acronym that means "training, technology, and products from a skilled worker's perspective."

UTOPIA's goal was to fashion a system that would be highly advanced technically, but also one designed in ways that would take into account the skills, needs, and perspectives of all those who would eventually be using it. Rather than develop a system under management directives and then impose it on workers, the project included representation of the people concerned. UTOPIA became the focus of a rigorous program of research and development at a government-sponsored laboratory: The Center for Working Life in Stockholm. Here was a case in which the purely instrumental and economic thrust of a technological innovation encountered a legitimate set of political ends and enlightened artifact/ideas. The result was democratization expressed in hardware, software, and human relationships.

The technological world of the twenty-first century beckons. Will it be better than the one we now inhabit or worse? Will it realize the promise of human freedom or curtail it? And whose interest will be decisive?

If ordinary citizens are to be empowered in shaping the world to come, we must become very skillful in areas where we are now profoundly ignorant, using ideas and abilities that enable us to define and realize human freedom and social justice within the realm of technology itself: within things like new machines for the workplace, computerized systems of information management, biotechnologies in agriculture and medicine, communications devices introduced into our homes. If we cannot develop these skills or do not care to, if we fail to confront the world-shaping powers that new technologies present, then human freedom and dignity could well become obsolete remnants of a bygone era.

ANDREW FEENBERG   I.8

Democratic Rationalization

In the reading from his book *Questioning Technology,* Andrew Feenberg defends the idea that social values play a role in shaping the direction of technological development in modern society. He questions the assumptions involved with the idea of technological determinism and argues for a constructivist theory of technological change in which social values affect the final shapes of the technologies that are adopted. He illustrates his theory by means of several examples that show how technological design has responded to social pressures based on moral or ethical considerations.

When we look back on successful technological designs, they seem to have an air of inevitability about them. But in fact, the "fit" that is finally achieved is the product of a process of social negotiation in which technological designs come to embody social values. Given this, Feenberg is hopeful that new forms of energy-efficient, environmentally friendly designs for buildings and vehicles will eventually be seen as representing technological progress.

Focus Questions

1. What does Feenberg mean by the "ambivalence of technology"?
2. What are the two assumptions associated with the view called "technological determinism"? What arguments and examples does Feenberg use to refute these assumptions?
3. What is the alternative explanation of the adoption of new technologies provided by the constructivist theory? How does constructivism support a redefinition of the humanistic study of technology that interprets technologies as possessing meanings?
4. How does Feenberg account for the tendency of technological elites to view their own activities as autonomous and socially neutral? Do you find this explanation convincing?
5. Compare Feenberg's argument in this selection with those of Lovins, Lovins, and Hawken (selection II.19). How does Feenberg's theory of democratic rationalization support the possibility of the kinds of technological innovations that these other authors are recommending?

Keywords

constructivism, democracy, hermeneutics, paradigms, rationalization, regimes, technological determinism

Technology and Democracy

A great deal of 20th century social thought has been based on a pessimistic view of modernity that achieved its classic expression in Max Weber's theory of rationalization. According to Weber, modernity is characterized by the increasing role of calculation and control in social life, a trend leading to what he called the "iron cage" of bureaucracy. This notion of enslavement by a rational order inspires pessimistic philosophies of technology according to which human beings have become mere cogs in the social machinery, objects of technical control in much the same way as raw materials and the natural environment. While this view is overdrawn, it is true that as more and more of social life is structured by technically mediated organizations such as corporations, state agencies, prisons, and medical institutions, the technical hierarchy merges with the social and political hierarchy.

The idea and (for some) ideal of technocracy grows out of this new situation. Technocracy represents a generalization to society as a whole of the type of "neutral" instrumental rationality supposed to characterize the technical sphere. It assumes the existence of technological imperatives that need only be recognized to guide management of society as a system. Whether technocracy is welcomed or abhorred, these deterministic premises leave no

From *Questioning Technology* by Andrew Feenberg, pp. 75–99. Copyright © 1999. Reprinted by permission of Routledge/ Taylor & Francis Books, Inc. (Footnotes and references have been omitted.)

room for democracy. . . . "Democratic" rationalization is a contradiction in Weberian terms. On those terms, once tradition has been defeated by modernity, radical struggle for freedom and individuality degenerates into an affirmation of irrational life forces against the routine and drab predictability of a bureaucratic order. This is not a democratic program but a romantic anti-dystopian one, the sort of thing that is already foreshadowed in Dostoievsky's *Notes from Underground* and various back to nature ideologies. The new left and all its works have been condemned repeatedly on these grounds.

No doubt the new left is rightly criticized for the excesses of its romanticism, but . . . [this is not the whole story]. Modern societies experienced real crises in the late 1960s that marked a turning point in the willingness of the public to leave its affairs in the hands of experts. Out of that period came not just regressive fantasies but a new and more democratic conception of progress. I have attempted in several previous books to articulate that conception in a third position that is neither technocratic nor romantic. The crux of the argument is the claim that technology is ambivalent, that there is no unique correlation between technological advance and the distribution of social power. The ambivalence of technology can be summarized in the following two principles.

1. Conservation of hierarchy: social hierarchy can generally be reserved and reproduced as new technology is introduced. This principle explains the extraordinary continuity of power in advanced capitalist societies over the last several generations, made possible by technocratic strategies of modernization despite enormous technical changes.

2. Democratic rationalization: new technology can also be used to undermine the existing social hierarchy or to force it to meet needs it has ignored. This principle explains the technical initiatives that often accompany the structural reforms pursued by union, environmental, and other social movements.

This second principle implies that there will generally be ways of rationalizing society that democratize rather than centralize control. We need not go underground or native to escape the iron cage. In this chapter . . . I will show that this is in fact the meaning of the emerging social movements to change technology in a variety of areas such as computers, medicine, and the environment.

But does it make sense to call the changes these movements advocate *rationalizations*? Are they not irrational precisely to the extent that they involve citizens in the affairs of experts? The strongest objections to democratizing technology come from those experts, who fear the loss of their hard-won freedom from lay interference. Can we reconcile public participation with the autonomy of professional technical work? Perhaps, as advocates of technocracy argue, we should strive not to politicize technology but to technicize politics in order to overcome the irrationality of public life. The counter-argument in favor of democratization must establish the rationality of informal public involvement in technical change.

From Determinism to Constructivism

DETERMINISM DEFINED

Faith in progress has been supported for generations by two widely held deterministic beliefs: that technical necessity dictates the path of development, and that that path is discovered through the pursuit of efficiency. So persuasive are these beliefs that even critics of progress such as Heidegger and Ellul share them. I will argue here that both beliefs are false, and that, furthermore, they have anti-democratic implications.

Determinism claims that technologies have an autonomous functional logic that can be explained without reference to society. Technology is presumably social only through the purpose it serves, and purposes are in the mind of the beholder. Technology would thus resemble science and mathematics by its intrinsic independence of the social world. Yet unlike science and mathematics, technology has immediate and powerful social impacts. Society's fate seems to be at least partially dependent on a nonsocial factor which influences it without suffering a reciprocal influence.

Determinism is based on two premises which I will call *unilinear progress* and *determination by the base*.

1. Technical progress appears to follow a unilinear course, a fixed track, from less to more advanced configurations. Each stage of technological development enables the next, and there are no branches off the main line. Societies may advance slowly or quickly, but the direction and definition of progress is not in question. Although this conclusion seems obvious from a backward glance at the history of any familiar technical object, in fact it is based on two claims of unequal plausibility: first, that technical progress proceeds from lower to higher levels of development; and second, that that development follows a single sequence of necessary stages. As we will see, the first claim is independent of the second and not necessarily deterministic.

2. Technological determinism also affirms that social institutions must adapt to the "imperatives" of the technological base. This view, which no doubt has its source in a certain reading of Marx, is long since the common sense of the social sciences. Adopting a technology necessarily constrains one to adopt certain practices that are connected with its employment. Railroads require scheduled travel. Once they are introduced people who formerly could live with rather approximate notions of time—the day marked out by church bells and the sun—need watches. So the imperative consequence of railroads is a new organization of social time. Similarly factories are hierarchical institutions and set the tone for social hierarchy throughout modern societies. Again, there is something plausible about this view, namely that devices and practices are congruent, but the stream of influence is not unidirectional.

These two theses of technological determinism present decontextualized, self-generating technology as the foundation of modern life. And since we in the advanced countries stand at the peak of technological development, the rest of the world can only follow our example. Determinism thus implies that our technology and its corresponding institutional structures are universal, indeed, planetary in scope. There may be many forms of tribal society, many feudalisms, even many forms of early capitalism, but there is only one modernity and it is exemplified in our society for good or ill. . . .

UNDERDETERMINATION

The implications of determinism appear so obvious that it is surprising to discover that neither of its two premises withstand close scrutiny. Yet contemporary sociology undermines the idea of unilinear progress while historical procedures are unkind to determination by the base.

Recent constructivist sociology of technology grows out of the new social studies of science. The "strong program" in sociology of knowledge challenges the exemption of scientific theories from the sort of sociological examination to which we submit nonscientific beliefs. The "principle of symmetry" holds that all contending beliefs are subject to the same type of social explanation regardless of their truth or falsity. This view derives from the thesis of underdetermination, the so-called Duhem-Quine principle in philosophy of science, which refers to the inevitable lack of logically compelling reasons for preferring one competing scientific theory to another. Rationality, in other words, does not constitute a separate and self-sufficient domain of human activity.

A similar approach to the study of technology denies that a purely rational criterion such as technical effectiveness suffices to account for the success of some innovations and the failure of others. Of course it remains true that some things really work and others do not: successful design respects technical principles. But there are often several possible designs with which to achieve similar objectives and no decisive technical reason to prefer one to the others. Here, underdetermination means that technical principles alone are insufficient to determine the design of actual devices.

What then does decide the issue? A commonplace reply is "economic efficiency." But the problem is trickier than it seems at first. Before the efficiency of a process can be measured, both the type and quality of output have to be fixed. Thus economic choices are necessarily secondary to clear definitions of both the problems to which technology is addressed and the solutions it provides. But clarity on these matters is often the outcome rather than the presupposition of technical development. For example, MS DOS lost the competition with the Windows graphical interface, but not before the very nature of computing was transformed by a change in the user base and in the types of tasks to which computers were dedicated. A system that was more efficient for programming and accounting tasks proved less than ideal for secretaries and hobbyists interested in ease of use. Thus economics cannot explain but rather follows the trajectory of development.

Constructivism argues, I think correctly, *that the choice between alternatives ultimately depends neither on technical nor economic efficiency, but on the "fit" between devices and the interests and beliefs of the various social groups that influence the design process.* What singles out an artifact is its relationship to the social environment, not some intrinsic property.

Pinch and Bijker illustrate this approach with the early evolution of the bicycle. In the late 19th Century, before the present form of the bicycle was fixed, design was pulled in several different directions. The object we take to be a self-evident "black box" actually started out as two very different devices, a sportsman's racer and a means of transportation. Some customers perceived bicycling as a competitive sport, while others had an essentially utilitarian interest in getting from here to there. Designs corresponding to the first definition had high front wheels that were rejected as unsafe by riders of the second type, who preferred designs with two equal-sized low wheels. The large diameter front wheel of the sportsman's racer was faster, but it was unstable. Equal-sized wheels made for a safer but less exciting ride. These two designs met different needs and were in fact different technologies with many shared elements. Pinch and Bijker call this original ambiguity of the object designated as a "bicycle," "interpretative flexibility."

Eventually the "safety" design won out, and it benefited from subsequent advances in the field. The entire later history of the bicycle down to the present day stems from that line of technical development. In retrospect, it seems as though the high wheelers were a clumsy and less efficient stage in a progressive development leading through the old "safety" bicycle to current designs. In fact the high wheeler and the safety shared the field for years and neither was a stage in the other's development. The high wheeler represented a possible alternative path of bicycle development that addressed different problems.

The bicycle example is reassuringly innocent as are, no doubt, the majority of technical decisions. But what if the various technical solutions to a problem have different effects on the distribution of power and wealth? Then the choice between them is political and the political implications of that choice will be embodied in some sense in the technology. Of course the discovery of this connection did not await constructivism. Langdon Winner offers a particularly telling example of it. Robert Moses' plans for an early New York expressway included overpasses that were a little too low for city buses. Poor people from Manhattan, who depended on bus transportation, were thereby discouraged from visiting the beaches on Long Island. In this case a simple design specification contained a racial and class bias. We could show something similar with many other technologies, the assembly line for example, which exemplifies capitalist notions of control of the work force. Reversing these biases would not return us to pure, neutral technology, but would simply alter its valuative content in a direction more in accord with our own preferences and therefore less visible to us.

Determinism ignores these complications and works with decontextualized temporal cross-sections in the life of its objects. It claims implausibly to be able to get from one such momentary configuration of the object to the next on purely technical terms. But in the real world all sorts of attitudes and desires crystallize around technical objects and influence their development. Differences in the way social groups interpret and use the objects are not merely extrinsic but make a difference in the nature of the objects themselves. Technology cannot be determining because the "different interpretations by social groups of the content of artifacts

Selection Criteria	Partially Substitutable Artifacts	Shared Effects (e.g. uses)	Unique Effects
1	1		
2	2		
3	3		
4	4		

HOW ARTIFACTS HAVE POLITICS

Artifacts 1–4 share certain effects but each also has its own unique effects which distinguish it from the others. Effects in this sense include uses, contextual requirements that must be met to employ the artifacts, and their unintended consequences. Criteria 1–4 all select the shared effects of the artifacts and each also valorizes one or another of the unique effects. Where different unique effects have different political consequences, competing groups will have preferred criteria corresponding to the fit between their goals and the various artifacts. The criteria can also be combined in the course of the evolution of the artifacts through design changes that adapt one of them to also delivering the unique effects of one or several others. In a political context such combinations correspond to alliances.

lead via different chains of problems and solutions to different further developments." *What* the object *is* for the groups that ultimately decide its fate determines what it *becomes* as it is modified. If this is true, then technological development is a social process and can only be understood as such.

Determinism is a species of Whig history which makes it seem as though the end of the story were inevitable from the beginning. It projects the abstract technical logic of the finished object back into it origins as a cause of development, confounding

our understanding of the past and stifling the imagination of a different future. Constructivism can open up that future, although its practitioners have hesitated so far to engage the larger social issues implied in their method.

INDETERMINISM

If the thesis of unilinear progress falls, the collapse of the notion of determination by the technological base cannot be far behind. Yet it is still frequently invoked in contemporary political debates. I shall return to these debates later in this chapter. For now, let us consider the remarkable anticipation of current conservative rhetoric in the struggle over the length of the workday and child labor in mid-19th Century England. Factory owners and economists denounced regulation as inflationary; industrial production supposedly required children and the long workday. One member of parliament declared that regulation is "a false principle of humanity, which in the end is certain to defeat itself." The new rules were so radical, he concluded, as to constitute "in principle an argument to get rid of the whole system of factory labor." Similar protestations are heard today on behalf of industries threatened with what they call environmental "Luddism."

Yet what actually happened once limitations were imposed on the workday and children expelled from the factory? Did the violated imperatives of technology exact a price? Not at all. Regulation led to an intensification of factory labor that was incompatible with the earlier conditions in any case. Children ceased to be workers and were redefined socially as learners and consumers. Consequently, they entered the labor market with higher levels of skill and discipline that were soon presupposed by technological design and work organization. As a result no one is nostalgic for a return to the good old days when inflation was held down by child labor. That is simply not an option.

This case shows the tremendous flexibility of technical systems. They are not rigidly constraining but on the contrary can adapt to a variety of social demands. The responsiveness of technology to social redefinition explains its adaptability. On this account technology is just another dependent social variable, albeit an increasingly important one, and not the key to the riddle of history.

Determinism, I have argued, is characterized by the principles of unilinear progress and determination by the base; if determinism is wrong, then research must be guided by two contrary principles. In the first place, technological development is not unilinear but branches in many directions, and could reach generally higher levels along several different tracks. And, secondly, social development is not determined by technological development but depends on both technical and social factors.

The political significance of this position should also be clear by now. In a society where determinism stands guard on the frontiers of democracy, indeterminism is political. If technology has many unexplored potentialities, no technological imperatives dictate the current social hierarchy. Rather, technology is a site of social struggle, in Latour's phrase, a "parliament of things" on which political alternatives contend.

Critical Constructivism

TECHNOLOGY STUDY

The picture sketched so far requires a significant change in our definition of technology. It can no longer be considered as a collection of devices, nor, more generally, as the sum of rational means. These definitions imply that technology is essentially nonsocial.

Perhaps the prevalence of such tendentious definitions explains why technology is not generally considered an appropriate field of humanistic study; we are assured that its essence lies in a technically explainable function rather than a hermeneutically interpretable meaning. At most, humanistic methods might illuminate extrinsic aspects of technology, such as packaging and advertising, or popular reactions to controversial innovations such as nuclear power or surrogate motherhood. Of course, if one ignores most of its connections to society, it is no wonder technology appears to be self-generating. Technological determinism draws its force from this attitude.

The constructivist position has very different implications for the humanistic study of technology. They can be summarized in the following three points:

1. Technical design is not determined by a general criterion such as efficiency, but by a social process which differentiates technical alternatives according to a variety of case-specific criteria;
2. That social process is not about fulfilling "natural" human needs, but concerns the cultural definition of needs and therefore of the problems to which technology is addressed;

3. Competing definitions reflect conflicting visions of modern society realized in different technical choices.

The first point widens the investigation of social alliances and conflicts to include technical issues which, typically, have been treated as the object of a unique consensus. The other two points imply that culture and ideology enter history as effective forces not only in politics, but also in the technical sphere. These three points thus establish the legitimacy of applying the same methods to technology that are employed to study social institutions, customs, beliefs, and art. With such a hermeneutic approach, the definition of technology expands to embrace its social meaning and its cultural horizon.

FUNCTION OR MEANING

The role of social meaning is clear in the case of the bicycle. The very definition of the object was at stake in a contest of interpretations: was it to be a sportsman's toy or a means of transportation? It might be objected that this is merely a disagreement over function with no hermeneutic significance. Once a function is selected, the engineer has the last word on its implementation and the humanist interpreter is out of luck. This is the view of most engineers and managers; they are at home with "function" but have no place for "meaning."

. . . I . . . propose a very different model of the essence of technology based not on the distinction of the social and the technical, but crosscutting the customary boundaries between them. In this conception, technology's essence is not an abstraction from the contingencies of function, a causal structure that remains the same through the endless uses to which devices are subjected in the various systems that incorporate them. Rather, the essence of technology is abstracted from a larger social context within which functionality plays a specific limited role. Technologies do of course have a causal aspect, but they also have a symbolic aspect that is determining for their use and evolution. From that standpoint, I would like to introduce Bruno Latour's and Jean Baudrillard's quite different but complementary proposals for what I call a *hermeneutics of technology.*

Latour argues that norms are not merely subjective human intentions but that they are also realized in devices. This is an aspect of what he calls the symmetry of humans and nonhumans which he adds to the constructivist symmetry of true or false theories, successful and unsuccessful devices.

According to Latour, technical devices embody norms that serve to enforce obligations. He presents the door closer as a simple example. A notice posted on a door can remind users to close it, or a mechanism can close it automatically. The door closer, in some sense, does the work of the notice but more efficiently. It materializes the moral obligation to close the door too easily ignored by passersby. That obligation is "delegated" to a device in Latour's sense of the term. According to Latour, the "morality" in this case can be allocated either to persons—by a notice—or to things—by a spring. This Latourian equivalent of Hegelian *Sittlichkeit* opens the technical world to investigation not simply as a collection of functioning devices determined by causal principles but also as the objectification of social values, as a cultural system.

Baudrillard suggests a useful approach to the study of the aesthetic and psychological dimensions of this "system of objects." He adapts the linguistic distinction between denotation and connotation to describe the difference between the functions of technical objects and their many other associations. For example, automobiles are means of transportation—a function; but they also signify the owner as more or less respectable, wealthy, and sexy—connotations. The engineer may think these connotations are extrinsic to the device he or she is working on, but they too belong to its social reality.

Baudrillard's approach opens technology to quasi-literary analysis. Indeed, technologies are subject to interpretation in much the same way as texts, works of art, and actions. However, his model still remains caught in the functionalist paradigm insofar as it takes the distinction between denotation and connotation for granted. In reality, that distinction is a product not a premise of technical change. There is often no consensus on the precise function of new technologies. The personal computer is a case in point; it was launched on the market with infinite promise and no applications.

The story of Chinese sea faring in the 15th century offers another marvelous example of prolonged suspense regarding function. The Chinese built the largest fleet composed of the biggest ships the world had ever seen, but could not agree on the purpose of their own naval achievements. Astonishingly, they dismantled the fleet and retreated into their borders, paving the way for the European conquest of Asia.

In the case of well established technologies, the distinction between function and connotation is usually fairly clear. There is a tendency to project this clarity back into the past to imagine that the technical function of a device called it into being. However, as we have seen, technical functions are not pregiven but are discovered in the course of development and use. Gradually they are locked in by the evolution of the social and technical environment, as for example the transportation functions of the automobile have been institutionalized in low-density urban designs that create the demand for transportation automobiles satisfy. So long as no institutional lock-in ties it decisively to one of its several possible functions, these ambiguities in the definition of a new technology pose technical problems which must be resolved through interactions between designers, purchasers and users.

TECHNOLOGICAL HEGEMONY

Technical design responds not only to the social meaning of individual technical objects, but also incorporates broader assumptions about social values. The cultural horizon of technology therefore constitutes a second hermeneutic dimension. It is one of the foundations of modern forms of social hegemony. As I will use the term, hegemony is domination so deeply rooted in social life that it seems natural to those it dominates. One might also define it as that aspect of the distribution of social power which has the force of culture behind it.

The term "horizon" refers to culturally general assumptions that form the unquestioned background to every aspect of life. Some of these support the prevailing hegemony. For example, in feudal societies, the "chain of being" established hierarchy in the fabric of God's universe and protected the caste relations of the society from challenge. Under this horizon, peasants revolted in the name of the King, the only imaginable source of power. Technocratic rationalization plays an equivalent role today, and technological design is the key to its cultural power.

Technological development is constrained by cultural norms originating in economics, ideology, religion, and tradition. I discussed earlier how assumptions about the age composition of the labor force entered into the design of 19th century production technology. Such assumptions seem so natural and obvious they often lie below the threshold of conscious awareness. When one looks at old photos of child factory workers, one is struck by the adaptation of machines to their height. The images disturb us, but were no doubt taken for granted until child labor became controversial. Design specifications simply incorporated the sociological fact of child labor into the structure of devices. The impress of social relations can be traced in the technology.

The assembly line offers another telling instance. Its technologically enforced labor discipline increases productivity and profits by increasing control through deskilling and pacing work. However, the assembly line only appears as technical progress in a specific social context. It would not look like an advance in an economy based on workers' councils in which labor discipline was largely self-imposed by the work group rather than imposed from above by management. In such a society engineers would seek different ways of increasing productivity. Here again design mirrors back the social order. Thus what Marcuse called "technological rationality" and Foucault the "regime of truth" is not merely a belief, an ideology, but is effectively incorporated into the machines themselves.

Technologies are selected by the dominant interests from among many possible configurations. Guiding the selection process are social codes established by the cultural and political struggles that define the horizon under which the technology will fall. Once introduced, technology offers a material validation of that cultural horizon. Apparently neutral technological rationality is enlisted in support of a hegemony through the bias it acquires in the process of technical development. The more technology society employs, the more significant is this support. The legitimating effectiveness of technology depends on unconsciousness of the cultural-political horizon under which it was designed. A critical theory of technology can uncover that horizon, demystify the illusion of technical necessity, and expose the relativity of the prevailing technical choices.

TECHNICAL REGIMES AND CODES

Disputes over the definition of technologies are settled by privileging one among many possible configurations. This process, called closure, yields an "exemplar" for further development in its field. The exemplar reacts back on the technical discipline from which it originated by establishing standard ways of looking at problems and solutions. These are variously described by social scientists as "technological frames" or "technological regimes" or "paradigms." Rip and Kemp, for example, define a regime as:

> The whole complex of scientific knowledge, engineering practices, production process technologies, product characteristics, skills and procedures, and institutions and infrastructures that make up the totality of a technology. A technological regime is thus the technology-specific context of a technology which prestructures the kind of problem-solving activities that engineers are likely to do, a structure that both enables and constrains certain changes.

Such regimes incorporate many social factors expressed by technologists in purely technical language and practices. I call those aspects of technological regimes which can best be interpreted as direct reflections of significant social values the "technical code" of the technology. *Technical codes define the object in strictly technical terms in accordance with the social meaning it has acquired.* These codes are usually invisible because, like culture itself, they appear self-evident. For example, if tools and workplaces are designed today for adult hands and heights, that is only because children were expelled from industry long ago with design consequences we now take for granted. Technological

regimes reflect this social decision unthinkingly, as is normal, and only social scientific investigation can uncover the source of the standards in which it is embodied.

Technical codes include important aspects of the basic definition of many technical objects insofar as these too become universal culturally accepted features of daily life. The telephone, the automobile, the refrigerator and a hundred other everyday devices have clear and unambiguous definitions in the dominant culture: we know exactly what they are insofar as we are acculturated members of our society. Each new instance of these standard technologies must conform to its defining code to be recognizable and acceptable. But there is nothing obvious about this outcome from a historical point of view. Each of these objects was selected from a series of alternatives by a code reflecting specific social values.

The bicycle reached this point in the 1890s. A technical code defining the bicycle as a safe means of transportation required a seat positioned well behind a small front wheel. The bicycle produced according to this code, known at the time as a "safety," became the forebear of all future designs. The safety connoted women and mature riders, trips to the store, and so on, rather than racing and sport. Eventually the safety was able to incorporate the racing connotations of the bicycle in specialized designs and the old high wheeler was laid to rest. Note that in this typical case the choice of the exemplary design reflected the privilege granted the specific code defining for it, i.e., designating objects as "safe" or "unsafe." The high wheelers could only have won out by a similar privileging of "fast" and "slow."

Because technologies have such vast social implications, technical designs are often involved in disputes between ideological visions. The outcome of these disputes, a hegemonic order of some sort, brings technology into conformity with the dominant social forces, insuring the "isomorphism, the formal congruence between the technical logics of the apparatus and the social logics with which it is diffused." These hermeneutic congruencies offer a way to explain the impact of the larger sociocultural environment on the mechanisms of closure, a still relatively undeveloped field of technology studies.

Kuhnian Perspectives on Technical Change

This analysis leads to an obvious question: if all this is true, why aren't we more aware of the public interventions that have shaped technology in the past? Why does it appear apolitical? It is the very success of these interventions that gives rise to this illusion. Success means that technical regimes change to reflect interests excluded at earlier stages in the design process. But the eventual internalization of these interests in design masks their source in public protest. The waves close over forgotten struggles and the technologists return to the comforting belief in their own autonomy which seems to be verified by the conditions of everyday technical work.

The notion of the "neutrality" of technology is a standard defensive reaction on the part of professions and organizations confronted by public protest and attempting to protect their autonomy. But in reality technical professions are never autonomous; in defending their traditions, they actually defend the outcomes of earlier controversies rather than a supposedly pure technical rationality. Informal public intervention is thus already an implicit factor in design whatever technologists and managers may believe.

Lay initiatives usually influence technical rationality without destroying it. In fact, public intervention may actually improve technology by addressing problems ignored by vested interests entrenched in the design process. If the technical professions can be described as autonomous, it is not because they are truly independent of politics but rather because they usually succeed in translating political demands into technically rational terms.

With some modifications, Kuhn's famous distinction between revolutionary and normal science can be reformulated to explain these aspects of the design process. The alternation of professional and public dominance in technical fields is one of several patterns that correspond roughly to the distinction between normal and revolutionary scientific change. There is, however, a significant difference between science and technology. Natural science eventually becomes far more independent of public opinion than technology. As a result, democratic interventions into scientific change are unusual, and revolutions explode around tensions within the disciplines. Of course even mature science is responsive to politics and culture, but their influence is usually felt indirectly through administrative decisions and changes in education. By contrast, ordinary people are constantly involved in technical activity, the more so as technology advances. It is true that they may be objects rather than subjects of the technologies that affect them, but in any case their closeness offers them a unique vantage point. Situated knowledges arising from that vantage point can become the basis for public interventions even in a mature technological system.

These situated knowledges are usually viewed with skepticism by experts guided by the pursuit of efficiency within the framework of the established technical codes. But in Kuhnian terms, efficiency only applies within a paradigm; it cannot judge between paradigms. To the extent that technical cultures are based on efficiency, they constitute the equivalent of Kuhn's normal science and as such they lack the categories with which to comprehend the paradigmatic changes that will transform them in the course of events. And since democratic interventions are often responsible for such changes, they too remain opaque to the dominant technical culture.

. . .

Progress and Rationality

THE TRADEOFF MODEL

The anti-deterministic arguments of the previous sections of this chapter undermine one basis of the technical professions' claims to autonomy. If they have succeeded in incorporating public concerns in the past, why reject participation on principle today? However, even if the democratic position is granted this much, it is still possible to argue that participation has unreasonable costs. Thus the autonomy thesis still has another leg to stand on. This is the notion that technical rationality can supply the most efficient solution to economic problems when it suffers the least interference. On this basis one might argue that there is an inevitable tradeoff between ideology and technology.

. . . The claims of technical purity were denied most vigorously by anti-technocratic movements . . . that challenged the direction of progress. And the environmental debate turns ultimately on whether environmental goals are compatible with technological advance. Is a democratic alternative to technocracy conceivable? Can a technological society pursue environmental goals without sacrificing prosperity? Many would answer these questions in the negative, claiming that public involvement in technology risks slowing progress to a halt, that democratization and environmental reform are tantamount to Luddite reaction. In this section I will address this objection through an analysis of the limits of technical rationality in social policy.

Let me begin by acknowledging that public fear of technology sometimes results in costly changes or even abandonment of controversial innovations. And of course there is the famous NIMBY ("not in my backyard") syndrome that has greeted nuclear power, toxic waste incinerators, genetic engineering facilities, and other harbingers of a future lived on a higher plane of anxiety.

I call the public's response to new and imponderable risks it is not equipped to evaluate "rational dread." Childhood dread of the monster under the bed can usually be stilled by more information—a simple glance may suffice. But the dread of modern technologies such as atomic energy resists information strategies. On the contrary, often more information leads to still greater concern. To make matters worse, the hope that expert advice could unburden the public has long since been disappointed as general skepticism overtakes the authority of knowledge. The problem is occasionally resolved by forcing a return to an already accepted level of risk rather than achieving habituation to the higher level involved in new technologies.

The American nuclear power industry has indeed been the victim of just such a response. The significance of this case cannot be overestimated: the nuclear industry was one of the major technological projects of modern times. Nuclear power promised to free industrial society from dependence on the fragile bottleneck of fossil fuels. But the industry became fixated on unsafe designs in the 1960s and was unable to adapt to the standards of the 1970s and 1980s. In the head on confrontation with public opinion that followed, technology lost, at least in the US. Today conversion initiatives multiply as the owners of old nuclear plants switch back to fossil fuels.

What is the moral of this story? One can conclude with bitter irony that technology is in fact democratically controlled because "the very irrationality that has come to dominate the nuclear debate confirms that the public will is still what counts." But it is a good question where the "irrationality" lay, in the government and utility industries which pushed for impracticable goals or in the public which called them to account out of unverified fears. Clearly, we would be much better off if the many billions of research dollars spent to develop nuclear power had been employed in other ventures, for example, in the fields of solar energy and energy storage.

In any case, this example is not typical. Fear usually does not kill new technology; for the most part, it simply changes the regulatory environment and the orientation of development. Automotive safety and emission is a good example. Regulation gradually effected changes that were well within the technical capabilities of manufacturers. The results are much safer and less polluting vehicles, not the disaster foreseen by the foes of government "interference."

These issues appear with particular force in the environmental movement. Arguably, this is the single most important domain of democratic intervention into technology. Environmentalists want to reduce harmful and costly side effects of technology to protect nature and human health. This program can be implemented in different ways. As Commoner has argued, in a capitalist society there is a tendency to deflect criticism from technological processes to products and people, from a priori prevention to a posteriori cleanup. The preferred strategies are generally costly and reduce efficiency, with unfortunate political consequences.

Restoring the environment after it has been damaged is a form of collective consumption financed by taxes or higher prices. Because this approach to environmentalism dominates public awareness, it is generally perceived as a cost involving tradeoffs, and not as a rationalization with long-term benefits. But in a modern society, obsessed by economic well-being, that perception is damning. Economists and businessmen are fond of explaining the price we must pay in inflation and unemployment for worshiping at Nature's shrine instead of Mammon's. Poverty awaits those who will not adjust their social and political expectations to technological imperatives.

. . .

The tradeoff model confronts us with dilemmas—environmentally sound technology vs. prosperity, workers' control vs. productivity, etc.—where what we need are syntheses. Unless the problems of modern industrialism can be solved in ways that both enhance public welfare and win public support, there is little reason for hope.

But how can technological reform be reconciled with prosperity when it places a variety of new limits on the economy? The child labor case shows how apparent dilemmas arise on the boundaries of cultural change, specifically where major technological regimes are in transition. In such situations, social groups excluded from the original design network articulate their unrepresented interests politically. New values the outsiders believe would enhance their welfare appear as mere ideology to insiders who are adequately represented by the existing designs.

This is a difference of perspective, not of nature. Yet the illusion of essential conflict is renewed whenever social changes affect technology. At first, satisfying the demands of new groups after the fact has visible costs and, if it is done clumsily, will indeed reduce efficiency until better designs are found. But usually better designs can be found and apparent barriers to growth dissolve in the face of technological change.

This situation indicates the essential difference between economic exchange and technique. Exchange is all about tradeoffs: more of A means less of B. But the aim of technical advance is precisely to

avoid such dilemmas by devising what the French philosopher of technology, Gilbert Simondon, called "concrete" designs that optimize several variables at once. A single cleverly conceived mechanism then corresponds to many different social demands, one structure to many functions. . . . [D]esign is not a zero-sum economic game but an ambivalent cultural process that serves a multiplicity of values and social groups without necessarily sacrificing efficiency.

REGULATION OF TECHNOLOGY

That these conflicts over social control of risk are not new can be seen from the interesting case of the "bursting boilers." Steamboat boilers were the first technology the US Government subjected to safety regulation. Over 5000 people were killed or injured in hundreds of steamboat explosions from 1816, when regulation was first proposed, to 1852, when it was actually implemented. Is this many casualties or few? Consumers evidently were not too alarmed to continue traveling by riverboat in ever increasing numbers. Understandably, ship owners interpreted this as a vote of confidence and protested the excessive cost of safer designs. Yet politicians also won votes demanding safety.

The accident rate fell dramatically once technical improvements were mandated. Legislation would hardly have been necessary to achieve this had these improvements been technically determined. But in fact boiler design was relative to a social judgment about safety. That judgment could have been made on market grounds, as the shippers wished, or politically, with differing results. In either case, those results *constitute* a proper boiler. What a boiler "is" was thus defined through a long process of political struggle culminating finally in uniform codes issued by the American Society of Mechanical Engineers.

This example shows how the technical code responds to the changing cultural horizon of the society. Quite down-to-earth technical parameters such as the choice and processing of materials are *socially* specified by the code. The illusion of technical necessity arises from the fact that the code is thus literally "cast in iron" (at least in the case of the boilers.)

Conservative anti-regulatory social philosophies are based on this illusion. They forget that the design process always already incorporates standards of safety and environmental compatibility; similarly, all technologies support some basic level of user or worker initiative and skill. A properly made technical object simply *must* meet these standards to be recognized as such. Conformity is no ideological extravagance but an intrinsic production cost. Raising the standards means altering the definition of the object, not paying a price for an alternative good or value as the tradeoff model holds.

THE FETISHISM OF EFFICIENCY

But what of the much discussed cost/benefit ratio of design changes such as those mandated by environmental or other similar legislation? These calculations have some application to transitional situations, before technical advances responding to new demands fundamentally alter the terms of the problem. But it is important not to overestimate their scientific value simply because they are expressed in numbers. All too often, the results depend on economists' very rough estimates of the monetary value of such things as a day of trout fishing or an asthma attack. If made without prejudice, these estimates may well help to prioritize policy alternatives, but one cannot legitimately generalize from such pragmatic applications to a universal theory of the cost of regulation.

Such fetishism of efficiency ignores our ordinary understanding of the concept which is primarily of relevance to social philosophy. In that everyday sense, efficiency concerns those values with which economic actors are routinely concerned. The plumber may compare plastic to copper pipe as to their efficiency; he may even consider septic tanks vs. sewer hookups. But he is not expected to calculate the value of the night soil modern plumbing wastes. Such unproblematic aspects of technology can be safely ignored.

In theory one can decompose any technical object and account for each of its elements in terms of the costs it imposes and the goals it meets, whether it be safety, speed, reliability, etc., but in practice no one is interested in opening the "black box" to see what is inside. For example, once the boiler code is

established, such things as the thickness of a wall or the design of a safety valve appear as essential to the object. The cost of these features is not broken out as the specific "price" of safety and compared unfavorably with a more "efficient" but less secure design. Violating the code in order to lower costs is a crime, not a tradeoff.

Design is only controversial while it is in flux. Resolved conflicts over technology are quickly forgotten. Their outcomes, a welter of taken-for-granted technical and legal standards, are embodied in a stable code, and form the background against which economic actors manipulate the unstable portions of the environment in the pursuit of efficiency. The code itself is not normally varied in real world economic calculations, and as further advance occurs on the basis of it, movement backward no longer seems technically feasible.

Anticipating the stabilization of a new code, one can often ignore contemporary arguments that will soon be silenced by the emergence of a new horizon of efficiency calculations. This is what happened with boiler design and child labor; presumably, current debates on the environment will have a similar history and we will someday mock those who object to cleaner air and water as a "false principle of humanity" that violates technological imperatives.

There is a larger issue here. Non-economic values intersect the economy in the technical code. The examples we are dealing with illustrate this point clearly. The legal standards that regulate workers' economic activity have a significant impact on every aspect of their lives. In the child labor case, regulation widened educational opportunities with consequences that are not primarily economic in character. In the riverboat case, the choice of high levels of security was no tradeoff of one good for another, but a non-economic decision about the value of human life and the responsibilities of government.

Technology is thus not merely a means to an end; technical design standards define major portions of the social environment, such as urban and built spaces, workplaces, medical activities and expectations, life patterns, and so on. The economic significance of technical change often pales beside its wider human implications in framing a way of life. In such cases, regulation defines the cultural framework *of* the economy; it is not an act *in* the economy.

THE CONCEPT OF POTENTIALITY

The false dilemmas of technical politics arise from a peculiarity of change in the technical sphere. Technical resources can be configured in many different patterns. Any given configuration realizes a certain fraction of the well-being potentially available at the achieved technical level. Unrealized technical potential stands as a measure of the existing system. Where the contrast between what is and what might be becomes a political issue, technical resources are reconfigured in response to public pressure.

Looking back, the new configuration may seem obvious, but looking forward it is often very difficult to imagine radical technical solutions to contemporary problems. Worse still, without a clear idea of a solution, it is difficult even to formulate the problems clearly in their technical aspect. Thus often only after innovations have been introduced does it become entirely clear to what demand they respond.

Not only is it difficult to anticipate future technical arrangements, it is all too easy to think up utopias that cannot be realized under the existing ones. Thoroughgoing social changes are often inspired by such large ideological visions. In such cases, the long-term success of the new vision depends on its ability to deliver a better life over an extended period. That in turn depends on the technical changes necessary for its realization. Once success has been achieved, it is possible to look back and argue that the older way of life obstructed progress. In anticipation, theory may situate itself imaginatively on the boundary of the new civilizational configuration that will give a concrete content to its speculations, judging this society from the standpoint of a possible successor. However, so long as its hopes remain contingent for their realization on still unimagined technical advances, they can only take an ethical or ideological form. Their concrete formulation depends ultimately on the advances that will someday realize them by locking in the sort of irreversible sequence we call progress.

As progress unfolds on the basis of the constrained choices that have shaped technology in the past, lines of development emerge with a clear direction. What were once values posited in the struggle for the future, become facts inherited from the past as the technical and institutional premises of further advance.

In economics the failure to actualize the full potential of a resource is called "suboptimization." Where suboptimizations are rooted in the technical code, we are dealing not with a specific or local failure but with the generalized wastefulness of a whole technological system. In economic terms, unrealized civilizational potentialities appear as systematic underemployment of major resources due to the restrictions the dominant economic culture places on technical and human development. A new culture is needed to shift patterns of investment and consumption and to open up the imagination to technical advances that transform the horizon of economic action.

The speculative claims of morality become ordinary facts of life through such civilizational advances. The child labor example illustrates these points clearly. Reforms based on ethical demands led to social changes so profound that eventually those demands became self-evident facts of life. At the time, businessmen worried about the economic costs of the reforms, but today these costs seem trivial, even irrelevant, in the light of the enormous human gain that results from the modern practices of child rearing and education. Of course time is of the essence in such cases. The point of view of contemporaries is not arbitrary, just subject to radical reinterpretation in a wider historical context. Something similar seems to be occurring today in the movements for environmental reform and for the equality of women and racial minorities.

Where the struggle for new ideals succeeds in restructuring society around a new culture, it will not be perceived as trading off wealth against morality, but as realizing the economic potentialities associated with its ethical claims. The dilemma of virtue and prosperity is not absolute, but can be mediated in the course of technological developments. . . . To some extent this redefinition has actually taken hold. As it sinks down into the structure of technology itself, through advances that adapt technical systems to the natural environment, it will become "obvious" that environmentalism represents progress.

Because economic culture is not fixed once and for all, and because a population's socially relative goals may be served by a variety of technological means, it is possible to link ideals and interests in a progressive process of technical change. In that progress potentialities that appear at first in ethical or ideological form are eventually realized in an effective consciousness of self-interest. This link makes possible a radical democratic politics of technology.

Philosophical Perspectives

I.9   IAN BARBOUR

Philosophy and Human Values

In this selection taken from the author's Gifford Lectures, philosopher Ian Barbour provides a concise primer on modern ethical theory stressing its application to issues involving technology. The two main schools of thought in ethical theory are consequentialist and deontological. He begins by discussing the leading consequentialist theory, utilitarianism, which holds that the production of "the greatest happiness for the greatest number" is the supreme moral principle. However, Barbour notes several important objections to this theory that undermine its plausibility as a sufficient principle for ethical evaluation and decision making. He goes on to contrast it with the deontological approach that emphasizes rights and obligations, noting that many moral philosophers believe that rights and duties can "trump" a generalized obligation to promote the greatest good. Barbour then explores the ideas of justice, equality, and freedom, briefly explaining how moral philosophers understand each of these important ethical concepts. In particular, he explains the Rawlsian idea of justice and how his concept of the "original position" supports a notion of equality under which inequalities may be allowed if they promote the welfare of the least advantaged members of society. Barbour concludes by identifying the positive and negative senses of freedom and argues that the kinds of freedom that are most important in a technological society are those that enable individuals to participate in decisions affecting their own lives.

Focus Questions

1. How does the concept of cost-benefit analysis relate to utilitarianism? What are the advantages of this approach to economics? What in Barbour's view are the disadvantages of cost-benefit analysis to ethical theory?
2. Is it necessary in Barbour's view for rights and obligations to be "absolute"—that is, allowing no exceptions? How can one understand rights and duties as both binding and flexible?
3. What is Rawls's "original position"? Explain how this idea leads him to propose a theory of justice in which social and economic inequalities should be arranged so as to promote the greatest benefit of the least advantaged.

4. How does Barbour define the ideas of positive and negative freedom? What are some examples of freedoms of each of these kinds that he thinks are critical in a technological society? Explain.

5. How can the ethical principles discussed in this selection help us evaluate technological choices involving issues such as increased surveillance, genetic enhancement, or protecting the global commons? Discuss.

Keywords

consequentialism, cost-benefit analysis, deontology, equality, ethics, freedom, justice, rights, utilitarianism

Utilitarianism and Its Critics

Utilitarianism has been not only an important school of thought among philosophers, but also a major influence among social scientists. Cost-benefit analysis and other formal methods used in environmental and technological decisions share the assumptions of utilitarianism. We can present here only the broad outlines of utilitarian philosophy and some of the issues that it raises for technological policy.

The central principle of utilitarianism is *the greatest good for the greatest number*. That action should be chosen which produces the greatest net balance of good over evil consequences. For Jeremy Bentham, the good was identified with pleasure; one should select the alternative that maximizes the balance of pleasure over pain. John Stuart Mill maintained that happiness is a more inclusive and long-lasting good than pleasure.[1] The utilitarian economists in turn sought to maximize total social welfare, aggregated either from individual welfare or from subjective preferences and perceived satisfactions. There are significant differences among these versions, but some observations can be made about their common assumptions.

Most forms of utilitarianism are *anthropocentric*. "The greatest good for the greatest number" has usually been taken to refer exclusively to human beings. Any harm to other creatures is to be considered only insofar as it affects humanity. We will examine in the next chapter a broader rendition of the principle that includes the good of all sentient beings. Although the principle usually is taken to apply only to presently existing persons, it does not actually distinguish present from future generations. But there are difficulties when future persons are included, since at least in principle the largest total good might be achieved by having an enormous population at a low level of well-being. The question of how much weight to attach to future costs and benefits is also problematic, as we shall see.

Utilitarianism faces serious difficulties in attempting to *quantify* "the greatest good." If the good is identified with happiness, can it be measured on a single numerical scale? Utilitarian economists speak of maximizing satisfactions or preferences. But do people really look on diverse kinds of satisfactions as equivalent and substitutable? Can preferences among persons be compared and then aggregated in order to determine whether the total for society has been maximized? Many economists have concluded that the only practical way to measure people's preferences is by their willingness to pay. But the distribution of purchasing power is very uneven, and it is often misleading to assume that everything that is prized can be priced. The concern for quantification has tended to restrict attention to measurable costs and benefits.

Another criticism is that in utilitarianism only the total good, and not its *distribution* among people, is relevant to moral choice. Suppose the extermination of a small minority would make the majority so happy that the total happiness is increased. Suppose total national income can be increased if we accept great poverty for one segment of society. The utilitarian can object to these actions only if it can be demonstrated that there are indirect repercussions that will harm the total welfare, for utilitarianism finds nothing inherently wrong with injustice or inequality as such. In many cases the long-term social costs of setting a precedent by unjust actions might be so serious that they would outweigh any short-term benefits. But such considerations would not always prevent the sacrifice of some individuals for the social good.

Many contemporary philosophers hold that utilitarian principles must be supplemented by a *principle of justice*. If the total good were the only criterion, we could justify a small social gain even if it entailed a gross injustice. But if justice were the only norm, we would have to correct a small injustice even if it resulted in widespread suffering or social harm. It appears, then, that we need to consider both justice and the total good.[2]

I will suggest later that *cost-benefit* and *risk-benefit* analyses, when supplemented by a principle of justice, are often useful techniques if one is comparing a small number of options and there is a narrow range of very specific objectives. But most policy decisions today involve a large number of options and a broad range of impacts, many of which are difficult or impossible to quantify. The trade-offs are multidimensional and cannot be measured in a single unit or aggregated as a numerical total. They involve highly diverse types of value. I will maintain that environmental impact assessment and technology assessment methods allow a broader range of value considerations and thereby escape some of the limitations of utilitarian calculations. I will also argue that policy choices usually entail value judgments among incommensurables, and therefore the basic decisions must be made through political processes, not by technical experts using formal analytic techniques.

A final objection is a broader one. Utilitarianism judges entirely by consequences. But there are some acts, such as murder or experimentation on human subjects without their voluntary consent, which we do not condone even if they have good consequences. An alternative approach to ethics stresses *duty* and *obligation,* the choice of acts that are right in themselves, apart from the calculation of consequences. Theories based on obligations are called *deontological* (from the Greek *deon,* "that which is binding").

Historically there have been many variants of the idea that particular acts can be judged *right* or *wrong* according to universal principles or laws, without attempting to calculate their consequences. The Stoics said that people have a duty to act in accordance with the natural law, the rational and moral order expressed in the structure of the world. Judaism and Christianity stressed obedience to the divine law revealed in scripture. Immanuel Kant held that the right is determined by the unconditional obligation of rational moral law, apart from any consideration of consequences. He maintained that an action is right if the principle it expresses could be universally applied. For Kant, the demand for freedom and justice is based on the equality of persons as autonomous and rational moral agents; individual persons should never be treated merely as means to social ends.[3]

Whereas utilitarianism emphasizes the social good, deontological ethics typically defends *individual rights*. Fundamental rights must not be violated even in the interest of beneficial social consequences. Rights are in general correlated with *duties*. My right to life implies your duty not to violate my life. The language of rights appears to be absolutist and often does lead to inflexible positions. If rights are "inalienable" and "inviolable" and duties are "categorical," there seems to be no room for compromise. However, it is possible to employ a deontological approach with considerable flexibility. For example, one can formulate a universal rule with built-in qualifications that allow for special cases. Moreover, one duty may be outweighed by other duties. When two rights conflict, one of them may be assigned priority. So rights and duties should not be regarded as absolute.[4]

The defense of *individual rights* is indeed important in a technological age in which governments wield vast powers (through electronic surveillance and the control of information, for example), and they frequently defend their actions by pointing to benefits for society. Only a basic respect for persons can lead us to protect a minority from exploitation for the benefit of the majority. But in an ecologically interdependent world, the direct and indirect consequences of our actions are often far-reaching and should not be neglected. Both the protection of the individual and the good of society must be considered in the complex decisions we face today, and there is no simple formula for combining them.

In some cases that we will examine, the social consequences are paramount (for example, nuclear weapons). In other cases individual rights are the main issue (for instance, the confidentiality of computerized personnel records). Sometimes individual rights and the future welfare of society are very difficult to reconcile, as in the debate over population growth. But in general I will use both a broad evaluation of consequences (going beyond utilitarianism and cost-benefit analysis by including nonquantifiable values) and a defense of rights and duties that avoids absolutism.

The Concept of Justice

Most ideas of justice start from an assumption of *the fundamental equality of persons*. For some people this may be based on a religious conviction of the equal worth of every individual in God's sight. For others it may derive from a doctrine of equal intrinsic human rights ("natural rights") or the requirements of a harmonious social order. Some philosophers have argued from the common nature of persons as rational beings or the universality of basic human capacities. Others take respect for human beings and belief in their equal dignity to be unanalyzable ultimate attitudes. Distributive justice, then, starts with the idea that people should be treated equally because they are fundamentally equal.[5]

Unequal treatment can be justified on a variety of grounds. Special provisions for people with special needs and disabilities is in itself unequal, but the goal is an equal opportunity for a good life. Individuals are selected for positions of leadership, but such positions should be open to anyone with appropriate qualifications. Some differences in income may be justified as an incentive to productivity, from which everyone supposedly benefits, but inequalities of the magnitude that exists in industrial societies today are hardly justifiable for this purpose.[6] The radical inequalities between nations could never be justified by the need for work incentives.

Unequal treatment is justified, in short, only if it helps to *correct some other form of inequality* or if it is *essential for the good of all*. Inequalities of authority are necessary for maintaining the social order, but there can be equal access to the positions and offices that carry such authority. But are there limits to the degree of inequality that we will tolerate for the sake of other social benefits? Are inequalities in some goods and services more significant than in others? Questions of inequality assume added urgency if technology tends to increase the gap between rich and poor and if global scarcities limit the resources available for distribution.

I would maintain that equality is a more compelling value in the distribution of resources to meet *basic human needs* (such as food, health, and shelter—the lowest levels in Maslow's hierarchy) than in the distribution of other goods and services. Food to meet minimum protein and calorie requirements is necessary for life itself; justice in the production and distribution of food to meet these requirements should have the highest priority. Access to health care also is crucial since it so strongly affects life prospects. But some margin beyond bare survival is a prerequisite for a minimally decent human life. Estimates of the minimal material levels for human dignity and self-respect are of course historically and culturally relative; there is no sharp line between physical needs and psychological desires influenced by changing expectations. In the United States, a poverty line has been established for entitlement to food stamps and health care benefits; unemployment insurance and social security also were instituted in the name of justice rather than charity. A project sponsored by the United Nations has tried to establish quantitative measures for basic needs and standards on which there is an emerging world consensus.[7]

The most influential recent treatment of the relation between justice and equality is John Rawls's *A Theory of Justice*. Rawls asks us to imagine a hypothetical "original position" in which a group of people are formulating the basic principles for a social order. No one knows what his or her status will be in the society that is to be established. In agreeing on a "social contract," each person acts from rational self-interest, but impartiality in formulating the rules is guaranteed because these contracting individuals do not know what their own social positions will be. Such a hypothetical situation can help us establish principles for the fair distribution of scarce resources. It is similar to a situation in which the child who cuts the cake does not know which piece he or she will get.

Rawls maintains that persons in such an "original position" would accept two basic principles for the social order:

1. Each person is to have an equal right to the most extensive total system of equal basic liberties compatible with a similar system of liberty for all.

2. Social and economic inequalities are to be arranged so that they are both: (a) to the greatest benefit of the least advantaged, and (b) attached to offices and positions open to all under conditions of fair equality of opportunity.[8]

As Rawls develops it, the second principle requires equality in the distribution of all the primary social goods (income, wealth, power, and self-respect), with the exception noted. Inequalities are allowed only if they maximize benefits to the least advantaged and are attached to offices open to all. Attention to the impact on *the least advantaged* is a product not of altruism but of the rational self-interest of people in the "original position," any of whom might end up in that worst-off status. Rawls suggests that if the least advantaged benefit, it is likely that most other social groups will benefit also. But he rejects the utilitarian view that a loss to some people can be justified by greater gains to others.

Rawls holds that rational contractors would insist that, once a minimal level of material well-being had been reached, *liberty* should have priority over *equality*. The first principle is thereafter to be fulfilled before and independently of the second. Liberty—especially liberty of conscience and political liberty (equal participation in government)–is not to be exchanged for any other benefits, including greater equality. Neither freedom nor justice is subject to trade-offs with other benefits. Political rights should not be sacrificed for the sake of economic gains, except under conditions of extreme scarcity.

Not surprisingly, Rawls has been attacked from the right for being *too egalitarian*. Defenders of free enterprise capitalism say that the degree of equality that Rawls seeks would not provide adequate incentives for the most able persons, and it would protect the indolence of the least able. The enforcement of equality, it is claimed, would require coercive measures and would violate property rights and the acquisition of wealth by legitimate means. If one is really dedicated to freedom, one must set strict limits on the powers of the state, including its power to redistribute legitimately acquired property.[9] But Rawls is attacked from the left for *not being egalitarian enough*. Marxist and socialist critics insist that political equality, which the first principle endorses, is jeopardized by the degree of economic inequality that the second principle allows. For economic power becomes political power in capitalist societies, and inequalities perpetuate themselves.[10]

Rawls's hypothetical *"original position"* has also been criticized. If one starts from separate, autonomous individuals, can an adequate concept of community ever emerge? If one starts by abstracting the individual from all political and historical contexts, can one obtain principles relevant to actual choices in the real world? Despite such limitations, I see the "original position" as a useful analytic device for asking what would be a fair distribution of resources. It is one of the few ways of dealing with justice between generations—simply by asking you to imagine what policies you would recommend if you did not know to which generation you would belong . . .

Freedom as Participation

One consideration in the evaluation of any technological policy is the extent to which it restricts or extends individual freedom. But freedom has many forms, which may be affected in diverse ways by a policy decision. According to the philosopher Joel Feinberg, freedom can be expressed as a relation between *an agent, a constraint, and an activity*. Explicitly or implicitly, it has a general structure: x is free from y to do z. People have particular kinds of constraints and activities in mind when they defend freedom. Sometimes they emphasize the absence of a constraint, and sometimes they emphasize the opportunity for and choice of an activity they deem important.[11]

The negative side of freedom is *the absence of external constraints:* freedom from coercion or direct interference imposed by other persons or institutions. Locke and the early British tradition of libertarian political philosophy interpreted freedom primarily as the absence of interference by other individuals or by the state. They wanted to protect the individual against abuses of the power of government; they sought the maximum scope for individual initiative in economic affairs and in the use of private property. This view was influential among the authors of the U. S. Constitution and was reinforced by the American experience of the frontier, abundant resources, and the vision of a land of unlimited opportunities for everyone. It seemed that a person free of human constraints could pursue the mastery of nature without interfering with other persons.

The positive side of freedom is *the presence of opportunities for choice*. Freedom to choose among genuine alternatives requires a range of real options and the power to act to further the alternative chosen. Even in the absence of external constraints, unequal power results in unequal opportunity for choice. Some degree of personal autonomy is an essential component of freedom. Many of the conditions for the exercise of choice are internal. People vary widely in their awareness of alternatives, ability to make deliberate choices, and personal initiative and self-direction. But in dealing with public policy; we are concerned mainly about the external conditions, the social structures within which people can have some control over their own futures.

The *negative* and *positive* sides of freedom are inescapably related in any social order. If we try to minimize external constraints while there are great inequalities of economic power, the weak will have little protection from domination by the strong. In a complex society, the actions of one person can greatly affect the choices open to other people. Limitations on the actions of some persons are necessary if other persons are to be able to exercise choice. Positive freedom to achieve desired outcomes exists only within an orderly society. The state is an instrument of order and law, but it is also an instrument of freedom when it restricts some actions to make other actions possible. Emphasis on the positive side of freedom is also consistent with the social character

of selfhood . . . in contrast to the more individualistic view of freedom as absence of interference.

Political freedom too has both negative and positive aspects. On the negative side are limits to the powers of government, such as censorship and arbitrary arrest. I will suggest, for example, that citizens must be protected from invasion of privacy through electronic surveillance and the misuse of personal information in computerized databanks. On the positive side are institutions of political self-determination and democratic forms of government whereby each citizen can have a voice in decision-making processes. Civil liberties, such as freedom of speech, assembly, and the press, can be defended both as basic human rights and as preconditions of democracy. The moves toward democracy around the world in the early 1990s involved the right of dissent and freedom to organize opposition parties.

In technological societies, *the right of governments to intervene* to protect health, safety, and welfare has been expanding to include ever-wider areas, as the uses of private property have had more far-reaching public consequences. Such common resources as air and water can only be protected by collective action through regulations or economic incentives. In other cases, governmental powers were expanded to protect citizens from the growing power of private institutions such as industrial corporations and labor unions.

The forms of freedom that are most relevant to technological policy can thus be understood positively as opportunities to participate in the decisions that affect our lives.

1. *Participation in the Marketplace*. In a free market economy, decisions are decentralized among many producers and consumers. The recent overthrow of communist governments around the world reflects a wide recognition of the economic inefficiencies and bureaucracy of state ownership and central control, as well as a desire for democracy in place of political repression. In a market economy, however, the goals of economic efficiency and social justice are not easily reconciled. Some loss of efficiency accompanies the use of taxes to mitigate extremes of wealth and poverty and to support health and welfare measures designed to ensure that no one lacks the basic necessities of life.

Some types of *government action* entail much greater intervention in the marketplace than others. For example, the individual farmer and the agribusiness corporation make decisions in response to market forces, but some government subsidies and regulations are acceptable in agriculture because it affects so many other areas of public policy: food prices, farm income, foreign trade, soil erosion, water pollution, land use, the quality of rural life, and so forth. Again, a heavy tax on the discharge of industrial pollutants relies on economic incentives and allows a greater variety of responses than strategies that mandate specific abatement technologies or set absolute standards for emissions. Energy conservation proposals range from voluntary restraint, through economic incentives, to mandatory fuel efficiency standards and fuel rationing. In each of these cases the consequences of insufficient regulation must be weighed against the dangers of excessive bureaucracy and the losses in efficiency and private initiative.

2. *Participation in Political Processes.* Democracy requires a free press, the right to dissent, and provisions for the election of representatives at local and national levels. Officials can be held accountable, and citizen input can take place, through legislative and regulatory hearings and court challenges. But citizens often feel incompetent to deal with complex technological decisions. The risks to human health and safety from nuclear reactors and toxic substances, for instance, are very difficult to evaluate. Yet such decisions should not be left to technical experts alone, since they require the comparison of diverse risks and benefits and the assessment of alternative policies, which are not purely scientific questions. An industry or a government agency that has an interest in promoting a technology usually has far more extensive legal and scientific resources than those opposing it. . . .

3. *Participation in Work-Related Decisions.* The institutions within which work is carried out vary widely, but they should include some provision for the voices of workers to be heard, such as labor unions, labor-management committees, producer cooperatives, small businesses, or owner-operated farms. We will return to these issues in later chapters in discussing particular agricultural and industrial technologies.

All three types of participation are more difficult in *large-scale technologies* than in those of *intermediate scale*. For example, nuclear energy is complex and centralized; it demands huge capital investments and entails unusual risks that require an exceptional degree of government regulation and strict security measures. By contrast, many forms of solar energy are decentralized; equipment can be locally installed and managed. *Decentralization* counteracts the concentration of economic and political power, and it contributes to diversity and local control. Yet in many cases the *centralization* of authority is necessary. Air and water pollution crosses jurisdictional boundaries. Local governments have been ineffective in controlling pollution because they are dependent on industrial growth for new tax revenues. An increasing national role in environmental regulation and resource conservation is unavoidable, but citizen participation is more difficult at the national level.

To sum up: philosophy can help us clarify ethical principles for evaluating technological choices. It can remind us of the importance of taking into account both the good of society and the rights of individuals. It can give more precise meaning to concepts of justice and freedom (and of course many other ethical concepts). I have defended the idea of justice as the greatest equality compatible with the welfare of the least advantaged. I have suggested that in a technological society the most important form of freedom is participation in the decisions that affect our lives.

NOTES

1. J. S. Mill, *Utilitarianism* (1863; reprint New York: E. P. Dutton, 1914); J. J. C. Smart and Bernard Williams, *Utilitarianism: For and Against* (New York: Cambridge University Press, 1973); Amartya Sen and Bernard Williams, eds., *Utilitarianism and Beyond* (New York: Cambridge University Press, 1984).

2. William Frankena, *Ethics*, 2d ed. (Englewood Cliffs, NJ: Prentice-Hall, 1971).

3. See Frankena, *Ethics*, chap 2.

4. W. D. Ross, *The Right and the Good* (Oxford: Clarendon Press, 1930).

5. Nicholas Rescher, *Distributive Justice*, (Indianapolis: Bobbs-Merrill, 1966); Hugo Bedau, ed., *Justice and*

Equality (Englewood Cliffs, NJ: Prentice-Hall, 1971).

6. Arthur Okun, *Equality and Efficiency* (Washington, DC: Brookings Institute, 1975).

7. John McHale and Magda McHale, *Basic Human Needs* (Houston: University of Houston Press, 1977).

8. John Rawls, *A Theory of Justice* (Cambridge, MA: The Belknap Press of Harvard University Press) p. 83.

9. Robert Nozick, *Anarchy, State, and Utopia* (New York: Basic Books, 1974).

10. Brian Barry, *The Liberal Theory of Justice* (Oxford: Oxford University Press, 1973); Norman Daniels, ed., *Reading Rawls: Critical Studies in a Theory of Justice* (New York: Basic Books, 1974). See also Charles R. Beitz, *Political Theory and International Relations* (Princeton: Princeton University Press, 1979).

11. Joel Feinberg, *Social Philosophy* (Englewood Cliffs, NJ: Prentice-Hall, 1973), chap. 1; P. H. Partridge, "Freedom," *Encyclopedia of Philosophy*, ed. Paul Edwards.

HANS JONAS   I.10

Technology and Responsibility: Reflections on the New Task of Ethics

Hans Jonas is one of a relatively small number of twentieth-century philosophers who have reflected carefully on the relationship between technology and ethics. He is also known for his writing on topics in biomedical ethics. He ended his professional career as Alvin Johnson Professor Emeritus of Philosophy at the New School for Social Research.

In this essay that originally appeared in *Social Research* in 1973, Jonas develops the view that traditional ethics is incapable of handling the kinds of ethical problems that are being created by our contemporary global technological civilization. His view is that to adequately evaluate the ethical significance of contemporary science and technology, we need to do so through the lens of a new kind of ethics, what he terms an "ethics of responsibility." He subsequently expanded the ideas presented in this essay in a book published in 1984 entitled *The Imperative of Responsibility: In Search of an Ethics for the Technological Age.*

Focus Questions

1. What are the three characteristics of traditional "neighbor ethics" that Jonas isolates, and in what respects has modern technology made traditional ethics obsolete?

2. How does Jonas's view that "man himself has been added to the objects of technology" compare to the discussion of the ethics of human cloning by Kass (selection II.12) and Sandel (selection II.13)?

3. What do you think Jonas means when he says, "We need wisdom the most when we believe in it the least"?

Keywords

behavior control, environmental ethics, ethics, genetic engineering, morality, utopia

ALL PREVIOUS ETHICS—whether in the form of issuing direct enjoinders to do and not to do certain things, or in the form of defining principles for such enjoinders, or in the form of establishing the ground of obligation for obeying such principles— had these interconnected tacit premises in common: that the human condition, determined by the nature of man and the nature of things, was given once for all; that the human good on that basis was readily determinable; and that the range of human action and therefore responsibility was narrowly circumscribed. It will be the burden of my argument to show that these premises no longer hold, and to reflect on the meaning of this fact for our moral condition. More specifically, it will be my contention that with certain developments of our powers the *nature of human action* has changed, and since ethics is concerned with action, it should follow that the changed nature of human action calls for a change in ethics as well: this not merely in the sense that new objects of action have added to the case material on which received rules of conduct are to be applied, but in the more radical sense that the qualitatively novel nature of certain of our actions has opened up a whole new dimension of ethical relevance for which there is no precedent in the standards and canons of traditional ethics.

I

The novel powers I have in mind are, of course, those of modern *technology*. My first point, accordingly, is to ask how this technology affects the nature of our acting, in what ways it makes acting under its dominion *different* from what it has been through the ages. Since throughout those ages man was never without technology, the question involves the human difference of *modern* from previous technology. Let us start with an ancient voice on man's powers and deeds which in an archetypal sense itself strikes, as it were, a technological note—the famous Chorus from Sophocles' *Antigone.*

Many the wonders but nothing more wondrous
    than man.
This thing crosses the sea in the winter's storm,
making his path through the roaring waves.
And she, the greatest of gods, the Earth—
deathless she is, and unwearied—he wears her away
as the ploughs go up and down from year to year
and his mules turn up the soil.

The tribes of the lighthearted birds he ensnares, and
    the races
of all the wild beasts and the salty brood of the sea,
with the twisted mesh of his nets, he leads captive,
    this clever man.
He controls with craft the beasts of the open air,
who roam the hills. The horse with his shaggy mane
he holds and harnesses, yoked about the neck,
and the strong bull of the mountain.

Speech and thought like the wind
and the feelings that make the town,
he has taught himself, and shelter against the cold,
refuge from rain. Ever resourceful is he.
He faces no future helpless. Only against death
shall he call for aid in vain. But from baffling
    maladies
has he contrived escape.

Clever beyond all dreams
the inventive craft that he has
which may drive him one time or another to well
    or ill.
When he honors the laws of the land the gods'
    sworn right
high indeed in his city; but stateless the man
who dares to do what is shameful.

This awestruck homage to man's powers tells of his violent and violating irruption into the cosmic order, the self-assertive invasion of nature's various domains by his restless cleverness; but also of his building—through the self-taught powers of speech and thought and social sentiment—the home for his very humanity, the artifact of the city. The raping of nature and the civilizing of himself go hand in hand. Both are in defiance of the elements, the one by venturing into them and overpowering their creatures, the other by securing an enclave against them in the shelter of the city and its laws. Man is the maker of his life *qua* human, bending circumstances to his will and needs, and except against death he is never helpless.

Yet there is a subdued and even anxious quality about this appraisal of the marvel that is man, and nobody can mistake it for immodest bragging. With all his boundless resourcefulness, man is still small by the measure of the elements: precisely this makes his sallies into them so daring and allows those elements to tolerate his forwardness. Making free with the denizens of land and sea and air, he yet leaves the encompassing nature of those elements unchanged, and their generative powers undiminished. Them he cannot harm by carving out his little dominion from theirs. They last, while his schemes have their short lived way. Much as he harries Earth, the greatest of gods, year after year with his plough—she is ageless and unwearied; her enduring patience he must and can trust, and he must conform. And just as ageless is the sea. With all his netting of the salty brood, the spawning ocean is inexhaustible. Nor is it hurt by the plying of ships, nor sullied by what is jettisoned into its deeps. And no matter how many illnesses he contrives to cure, mortality does not bow to cunning.

All this holds because man's inroads into nature, as seen by himself, were essentially superficial, and powerless to upset its appointed balance. Nor is there a hint, in the *Antigone* chorus or anywhere else, that this is only a beginning and that greater things of artifice and power are yet to come—that man is embarked on an endless course of conquest. He had gone thus far in reducing necessity, had learned by his wits to wrest that much from it for the humanity of his life, and there he could stop. The room he had thus made was filled by the city of men—meant to enclose and not to expand—and thereby a new balance was struck within the larger balance of the whole. All the well or ill to which man's inventive craft may drive him one time or another is inside the human enclave and does not touch the nature of things.

The immunity of the whole, untroubled in its depth by the importunities of man, that is, the essential immutability of Nature as the cosmic order, was indeed the backdrop to all of mortal man's enterprises, between the abiding and the changing: the abiding was Nature, the changing his own works. The greatest of these works was the city, and on it he could offer some measure of abidingness by the laws he made for it and undertook to honor. But no long-range certainty pertained to this contrived abidingness. As a precarious artifact, it can lapse or go astray. Not even within its artificial space, with all the freedom it gives to man's determination of self, can the arbitrary ever supersede the basic terms of his being. The very inconstancy of human fortunes assures the constancy of the human condition. Chance and luck and folly, the great equalizers in human affairs, act like an entropy of sorts and make all definite designs in the long run revert to the perennial norm. Cities rise and fall, rules come and go, families prosper and decline; no change is there to stay, and in the end, with all the temporary deflections balancing each other out, the state of man is as it always was. So here too, in his very own artifact, man's control is small and his abiding nature prevails.

Still, in this citadel of his own making, clearly set off from the rest of things and entrusted to him, was the whole and sole domain of man's responsible action. Nature was not an object of human responsibility—she taking care of herself and, with some coaxing and worrying, also of man: not ethics, only cleverness applied to her. But in the city, where men deal with men, cleverness must be wedded to morality, for this is the soul of its being. In this intra-human frame dwells all traditional ethics and matches the nature of action delimited by this frame.

II

Let us extract from the preceding those characteristics of human action which are relevant for a comparison with the state of things today.

1. All dealing with the non-human world, i.e., the whole realm of *techne* (with the exception of medicine), was ethically neutral—in respect both of the object and the subject of such action: in respect of the object, because it impinged but little on the self-sustaining nature of things and thus raised no

question of permanent injury to the integrity of its object, the natural order as a whole; and in respect of the subject it was ethically neutral because *techne* as an activity conceived itself as a determinate tribute to necessity and not as an indefinite, self-validating advance to mankind's major goal, claiming in its pursuit man's ultimate effort and concern. The real vocation of man lay elsewhere. In brief, action on non-human things did not constitute a sphere of authentic ethical significance.

2. Ethical significance belonged to the direct dealing of man with man, including the dealing with himself: all traditional ethics is *anthropocentric*.

3. For action in this domain, the entity "man" and his basic condition was considered constant in essence and not itself an object of reshaping *techne*.

4. The good and evil about which action had to care lay close to the act, either in the praxis itself or in its immediate reach, and were not a matter for remote planning. This proximity of ends pertained to time as well as space. The effective range of action was small, the time-span of foresight, goal-setting, and accountability was short, control of circumstances limited. Proper conduct had its immediate criteria and almost immediate consummation. The long run of consequences beyond was left to change, fate, or providence. Ethics accordingly was of the here and now, of occasions as they arise between men, of the recurrent, typical situations of private and public life. The good man was he who met these contingencies with virtue and wisdom, cultivating these powers in himself, and for the rest resigning himself to the unknown.

All enjoinders and maxims of traditional ethics, materially different as they may be, show this confinement to the immediate setting of the action. "Love thy neighbor as thyself"; "Do unto others as you would wish them to do unto you"; "Instruct your child in the way of truth"; "Strive for excellence by developing and actualizing the best potentialities of your being *qua* man"; "Subordinate your individual good to the common good"; "Never treat your fellow man as a means only but always *also* as an end in himself"—and so on. Note that in all those maxims the agent and the "other" of his action are sharers of a common present. It is those alive now and in some commerce with me that have a claim on my conduct as it affects them by deed or omission. The ethical universe is composed of contemporaries, and its horizon to the future is confined by the foreseeable span of their lives. Similarly confined is its horizon of place, within which the agent and the other meet as neighbor, friend or foe, as superior and subordinate, weaker and stronger, and in all the other roles in which humans interact with one another. To this proximate range of action all morality was geared.

III

It follows that the *knowledge* that is required—besides the moral will—to assure the morality of action, fitted these limited terms: it was not the knowledge of the scientist or the expert, but knowledge of a kind readily available to all men of good will. Kant went so far as to say that "human reason can, in matters of morality, be easily brought to a high degree of accuracy and completeness even in the most ordinary intelligence";[1] that "there is no need of science or philosophy for knowing what man has to do in order to be honest and good, and indeed to be wise and virtuous. . . . [Ordinary intelligence] can have as good a hope of hitting the mark as any philosopher can promise himself";[2] and again: "I need no elaborate acuteness to find out what I have to do so that my willing be morally good. Inexperienced regarding the course of the world, unable to anticipate all the contingencies that happen in it," I can yet know how to act in accordance with the moral law.[3]

Not every thinker in ethics, it is true, went so far in discounting the cognitive side of moral action. But even when it received much greater emphasis, as in Aristotle, where the discernment of the situation and what is fitting for it makes considerable demands on experience and judgment, such knowledge has nothing to do with the science of things. It implies, of course, a general conception of the human good as such, a conception predicated on the presumed invariables of man's nature and condition, which may or may not find expression in a theory of its own. But its translation into practice requires a knowledge of the here and now, and this is entirely non-theoretical. This "knowledge" proper to virtue (of the "where, when, to, whom, and how") stays with the immediate issue, in whose defined context the action *as the agent's own* takes its course and within which it terminates. The good or bad of the action is wholly decided within that short-term context. Its moral quality shines forth from it, visible to its witnesses. No one was held responsible for the unintended later affects of his well-intentioned, well-considered, and well-performed act. The short arm of human power did not call for a long arm of predictive knowledge; the shortness of the one is as little culpable as that of the other. Precisely because the human good, known in its generality, is the same for all time, its relation or violation takes place at each time, and its complete locus is always the present.

IV

All this has decisively changed. Modern technology has introduced actions of such novel scale, objects, and consequences that the framework of former ethics can no longer contain them. The *Antigone* chorus on the *deinotes,* the wondrous power, of man would have to read differently now; and its admonition to the individual to honor the laws of the land would no longer be enough. To be sure, the old prescriptions of the "neighbor" ethics—of justice, charity, honesty, and so on—still hold in their intimate immediacy of the nearest, day by day sphere of human interaction. But this sphere is overshadowed by a growing realm of collective action where doer, deed, and effect are no longer the same as they were in the proximate sphere, and which by the enormity of its powers forces upon ethics a new dimension of responsibility never dreamt of before.

Take, for instance, as the first major change in the inherited picture, the critical *vulnerability* of nature to man's technological intervention—unsuspected before it began to show itself in damage already done. This discovery, whose shock led to the concept and nascent science of ecology, alters the very concept of ourselves as a causal agency in the larger scheme of things. It brings to light, through the effects, that the nature of human action has *de facto* changed, and that an object of an entirely new order—no less than the whole biosphere of the planet—has been added to what we must be responsible for because of our power over it. And of what surpassing importance an object, dwarfing all previous objects of active man! Nature as a human responsibility is surely a *novum* to be pondered in ethical theory. What kind of obligation is operative in it? Is it more than a utilitarian concern? Is it just prudence that bids us not to kill the goose that lays the golden eggs, or saw off the branch on which we sit? But the "we" that here sits and may fall into the abyss is all future mankind, and the survival of the species is more than a prudential duty of its present members. Insofar as it is the fate of *man,* as affected by the condition of nature, which makes us care about the preservation of nature, such care admittedly still retains the anthropocentric focus of all classical ethics. Even so, the difference is great. The containment of nearness and contemporaneity is gone, swept away by the spatial spread and time-span of the cause-effect trains which technological practice sets afoot, even when undertaken for proximate ends. Their irreversibility conjoined to their aggregate magnitude injects another novel factor into the moral equation. To this take their cumulative character: their effects add themselves to one another, and the situation for later acting and being becomes increasingly different from what it was for the initial agent. The cumulative self-propagation of the technological change of the world thus constantly overtakes the conditions of its contributing acts and moves through none but unprecedented situations, for which the lessons of experience are powerless. And not even content with changing its beginning to the point of unrecognizability, the cumulation as such may consume the basis of the whole series, the very condition of itself. All this would have to be co-intended in the will of the single action if this is to be a morally responsible one. Ignorance no longer provides it with an alibi.

Knowledge, under these circumstances, becomes a prime duty beyond anything claimed for it heretofore, and the knowledge must be commensurate with the causal scale of our action. The fact that it cannot really be thus commensurate, i.e., that the predictive knowledge falls behind the technical knowledge which nourishes our power to act, itself assumes ethical importance. Recognition of ignorance becomes the obverse of the duty to know and thus part of the ethics which must govern the ever more necessary self-policing of our out-sized might. No previous ethics had to consider the global condition of human life and the far-off future, even existence, of the race. There now being an issue demands, in brief, a new concept of duties and rights, for which previous ethics and metaphysics provide not even the principles, let alone a ready doctrine.

And what if the new kind of human action would mean that more than the interest of man alone is to be considered—that our duty extends farther and the anthropocentric confinement of former ethics no longer holds? It is at least not senseless anymore to ask whether the condition of extra-human nature, the biosphere as a whole and in its parts, now subject to our power, has become a human trust and has something of a more claim on us not only for our ulterior sake but for its own and in its own right. If this were the case it would require quite some rethinking in basic principles of ethics. It would mean to seek not only the human good, but also the good of things extra-human, that is, to extend the recognition of "ends in themselves" beyond the sphere of man and make the human good include the care for them. For such a role of stewardship no previous ethics has prepared us—and the dominant, scientific view of *Nature* even less. Indeed, the latter emphatically denies us all conceptual means to think of Nature as something to be honored, having reduced it to the indifference of necessity and accident, and divested it of any dignity of ends. But still, a silent plea for sparing its integrity seems to issue from the threatened plenitude of the living world. Should we heed this plea, should we grant its claim as sanctioned by the nature of things, or dismiss it as a mere sentiment on our part, which we may indulge as fair as we wish and can afford to do? If the former, it would (if taken seriously in its theoretical implications) push the necessary rethinking beyond the doctrine of action, i.e., ethics, into the doctrine of being, i.e., metaphysics, in which all ethics must ultimately be grounded. On this speculative subject I will here say no more than that we should keep ourselves open to the thought that natural science may not tell the whole story about Nature.

V

Returning to strictly intra-human considerations, there is another ethical aspect to the growth of *techne* as a pursuit beyond the pragmatically limited terms of former times. Then, so we found, *techne* was a measured tribute to necessity, not the road to mankind's chosen goal—a means with a finite measure of adequacy to well-defined proximate ends. Now, *techne* in the form of modern technology has turned into an infinite forward-thrust of the race, its most significant enterprise, in whose permanent, self-transcending advance to ever greater things the vocation of man tends to be seen, and whose success of maximal control over things and himself appears as the consummation of his destiny. Thus the triumph of *Homo faber* over his external object means also his triumph in the internal constitution of *Homo sapiens,* of whom he used to be a subsidiary part. In other words, technology, apart from its objective works, assumes ethical significance by the central place it now occupies in human purpose. Its cumulative creation, the expanding artificial environment, continuously reinforces the particular powers in man that created it, by compelling their unceasing inventive employment in its management and further advance, and by rewarding them with additional success—which only adds to the relentless claim. This positive feedback of functional necessity and reward—in whose dynamics pride of achievement must not be forgotten—assures the growing ascendancy of one side of man's nature over all the others, and inevitably at their expense.

If nothing succeeds like success, nothing also entraps like success. Outshining in prestige and starving in resources whatever else belongs to the fullness of man, the expansion of his power is accompanied by a contraction of his self-conception and being. In the image he entertains of himself—the potent self-formula which determines his actual being as much as it reflects it—man now is ever-more the maker of what he has made and the doer of what he can do, and most of all the preparer of what he will be able to do next. But not you or I: it is the aggregate, not the individual doer or deed that matters here; and the indefinite future, rather than the contemporary context of the action, constitutes the relevant horizon of responsibility. This requires imperatives of a new sort. If the realm of making has invaded the space of essential action, then morality must invade the realm of making, from which it had formerly stayed aloof, and must do so in the form of public policy. With issues of such inclusiveness and such lengths of anticipation public policy has never had to deal before. In fact, the changed nature of human action changes the very nature of politics.

For the boundary between "city" and "nature" has been obliterated: the city of men, once an enclave in the non-human world, spreads over the whole of terrestrial nature and usurps its place. The difference between the artificial and the natural has vanished, the natural is swallowed up in the sphere of the artificial, and at the same time the total artifact, the works of man working on and through himself, generates a "nature" of its own, i.e., a necessity with which human freedom has to cope in an entirely new sense. Once it could be said *Fiat justitia, pereat mundus*, "Let justice be done, and may the world perish"—where "world," of course, meant the renewable enclave in the imperishable whole. Not even rhetorically can the like be said anymore when the perishing of the whole through the doings of man—be they just or unjust—has become a real possibility. Issues never legislated on come into the purview of the laws which the total city must give itself so that there will be a world for the generations of man to come.

That there *ought* to be through all future time such a world fit for human habitation, and that it ought in all future time to be inhabited by a mankind worthy of the human name, will be readily affirmed as a general axiom or a persuasive desirability of speculative imagination (as persuasive and undemonstrable as the proposition that there being a world at all is "better" than there being none): but as a *moral* proposition, namely, a practical *obligation* toward the posterity of a distant future, and a principle of decision in present action, it is quite different from the imperatives of the previous ethics of contemporaneity; and it has entered the moral scene only with our novel powers and range of prescience.

The *presence of man in the world* had been a first and unquestionable given, from which all idea of obligation in human conduct started out. Now it has itself become an *object* of obligation—the obligation namely to ensure the very premise of all obligation, i.e., the *foothold* for a moral universe in the physical world—the existence of mere *candidates* for a moral order. The difference this makes for ethics may be illustrated in one example.

VI

Kant's categorical imperative said: "Act so that you *can* will that the maxim of our action be made the principle of a universal law." The "can" here invoked is that of reason and its consistency with itself: *Given* the existence of a community of human agents (acting rational beings), the action must be such that it can without self-contradiction be imagined as a general practice of that community. Mark that the basic reflection of morals here is not itself a moral but a logical one: The "I *can* will" or "I *cannot* will" expresses logical compatibility or incompatibility, not moral approbation or revulsion. But there is no self-contradiction in the thought that humanity would once come to an end, therefore also none in the thought that the happiness of present and proximate generations would be bought with the unhappiness or even non-existence of later ones—as little as, after all, in the inverse thought that the existence or happiness of later generations would be bought with the unhappiness or even partial extinction of present ones. The sacrifice of the future for the present is *logically* no more open to attack than the sacrifice of the present for the future.

The difference is only that in the one case the series goes on, and in the other it does not. But that it *ought to go on,* regardless of the distribution of happiness or unhappiness, even with a persistent preponderance of unhappiness over happiness, nay, even of immorality over morality+—this cannot be derived from the rule of self-consistency *within* the series, long or short as it happens to be: it is a commandment of a very different kind, lying outside and "prior" to the series as a whole, and its ultimate grounding can only be metaphysical.

An imperative responding to the new type of human action and addressed to the new type of agency that operates it might run thus: "Act so that the effects of your action are compatible with the permanence of genuine human life"; or expressed negatively: "Act so that the effects of your action are not destructive of the future possibility of such life"; or simply: "Do not compromise the conditions for an indefinite continuation of humanity on earth"; or most generally: "In your present choices, include the future wholeness of Man among the objects of your will."

It is immediately obvious that no rational contradiction is involved in the violation of this kind of imperative. I *can* will the present good with sacrifice of the future good. It is also evident that the new imperative addresses itself to public policy rather than private conduct, which is not in the causal dimension to which that imperative applies. Kant's categorical imperative was addressed to the individual, and its criterion was instantaneous. It enjoined each of us to consider what would happen *if* the *maxim* of my present action were made, or at this moment already were, the principle of a universal legislation; the self-consistency or inconsistency of such a *hypothetical* universalization is made the test for my *private* choice. But it was no part of the reasoning that there is any probability of my private choice *in fact* becoming universal law, or that it might contribute to its becoming that. The universalization is a thought-experiment by the private agent not to test the immanent morality of his action. Indeed, real consequences are not considered at all, and the principle is one not of objective responsibility but of the subjective quality of my self-determination. The new imperative invokes a different consistency: not

that of the act with itself, but that of its eventual *effects* with the continuance of human agency in times to come. And the "universalization" it contemplates is by no means hypothetical—i.e., a purely logical transference from the individual "me" to an imaginary, causally unrelated "all" ("*if* everybody acted like that"); on the contrary, the actions subject to the new imperative—actions of the collective whole—have their universal reference in their actual scope of efficacy: they "totalize" themselves in the progress of their momentum and thus are bound to terminate in shaping the universal dispensation of things. This adds a *time* horizon to the moral calculus which is entirely absent from the instantaneous logical operation of the Kantian imperative: whereas the latter extrapolates into an ever-present order of abstract compatibility, our imperative extrapolates into a predictable real *future* as the open-ended dimension of our responsibility.

VII

Similar comparisons could be made with all the other historical forms of the ethics of contemporaneity and immediacy. The new order of human action requires a commensurate ethics of foresight and responsibility, which is as new as are the issues with which it has to deal. We have seen that these are the issues posed by the works of *Homo faber* in the age of technology. But among those novel works we haven't mentioned yet the potentially most ominous class. We have considered *techne* only as applied to the non-human realm. But man himself has been added to the objects of technology. *Homo faber* is turning upon himself and gets ready to make over the maker of all the rest. This consummation of his power, which may well portend the overpowering of man, this final imposition of art on nature, calls upon the utter resources of ethical thought, which never before has been faced with elective alternatives to what were considered the definite terms of the human condition.

a. Take, for instance, the most basic of these "givens," man's mortality. Who ever before had to make up his mind on its desirable and *eligible* measure? There was nothing to choose about the upper limit, the "three score years and ten, or by reason of strength fourscore." Its inexorable rule was the subject of lament, submission, or vain (not to say foolish) wish-dreams about possible exceptions—strangely enough, almost never of affirmation. The intellectual imagination of a George Bernard Shaw and a Jonathan Swift speculated on the privilege of not having to die, or the curse of not being able to die. (Swift with the latter was the more perspicacious of the two.) Myth and legend toyed with such themes against the acknowledged background of the unalterable, which made the earnest man rather pray "teach us to number our days that we may get a heart of wisdom" (Psalm 90). Nothing of this was in the realm of doing, and effective decision. The question was only how to relate to the stubborn fact.

But lately, the dark cloud of inevitability seems to lift. A practical hope is held out by certain advances in cell biology to prolong, perhaps indefinitely extend the span of life by counteracting biochemical processes of aging. Death no longer appears as a necessity belonging to the nature of life, but as an avoidable, at least in principle tractable and long-delayable, organic malfunction. A perennial yearning of mortal man seems to come nearer fulfillment. And for the first time we have in earnest to ask the question "How desirable is this? How desirable for the individual, and how for the species?" These questions involve the very meaning of our finitude, the attitude toward death, and the general biological significance of the balance of death and procreation. Even prior to such ultimate questions are the more pragmatic ones of who should be eligible for the boon: persons of particular quality and merit? of social eminence? those that can pay for it? everybody? The last would seem the only just course. But it would have to be paid for at the opposite end, at the source. For clearly, on a population-wide scale, the price of extended age must be a proportional slowing of replacement, i.e., a diminished access of new life. The result would be a decreasing proportion of youth in an increasingly aged population. How good or bad would that be for the general condition of man? Would the species gain or lose? And how *right* would it be to preempt the place of youth? Having

to die is bound up with having been born: mortality is but the other side of the perennial spring of "a natality" (to use Hannah Arendt's term). This had always been ordained; now its meaning has to be pondered in the sphere of decision.

To take the extreme (not that it will ever be obtained): if we abolish death, we must abolish procreation as well, for the latter is life's answer to the former, and so we would have a world of old age with no youth, and of known individuals with no surprises of such that had never been before. But this perhaps is precisely the wisdom in the harsh dispensation of our mortality: that it grants us the eternally renewed promise of the freshness, immediacy, and eagerness of youth, together with the supply of otherness as such. There is no substitute for this in the greater accumulation of prolonged experience: it can never recapture the unique privilege of seeing the world for the first time and with new eyes, never relive the wonder which, according to Plato, is the beginning of philosophy, never the curiosity of the child, which rarely enough lives on as thirst for knowledge in the adult, until it wanes there too. This ever renewed beginning, which is only to be had at the price of ever repeated ending, may well be mankind's hope, its safeguard against lapsing into boredom and routine, its chance of retaining the spontaneity of life. Also, the role of the *memento mori* in the individual's life must be considered, and what its attenuation to indefiniteness may do to it. Perhaps a non-negotiable limit to our expected time is necessary for each of us as the incentive to number our days and make them count.

So it could be that what by intent is a philanthropic gift of science to man, the partial granting of his oldest wish—to escape the curse of mortality—turns out to be to the detriment of man. I am not indulging in prediction and, in spite of my noticeable bias, not even in valuation. My point is that already the promised gift raises questions that had never to be asked before in terms of practical choice, and that no principle of former ethics, which took the human constants for granted, is competent to deal with them. And yet they must be dealt with ethically and by principle and not merely by the pressure of interest.

b. It is similar with all the other, quasi-utopian powers about to be made available by the advances of biomedical science as they are translated into technology. Of these, *behavior control* is much nearer to practical readiness than the still hypothetical prospect I have just been discussing, and the ethical questions it raises are less profound but have a more direct bearing on the moral conception of man. Here again, the new kind of intervention exceeds the old ethical categories. They have not equipped us to rule, for example, on mental control by chemical means or by direct electrical action of the brain via implanted electrodes—undertaken, let us assume, for defensible and even laudable ends. The mixture of beneficial and dangerous potentials is obvious, but the lines are not easy to draw. Relief of mental patients from distressing and disabling symptoms seems unequivocally beneficial. But from the relief of the *patient,* a goal entirely in the tradition of the medical art, there is an easy passage to the relief of *society* from the inconvenience of difficult individual behavior among its members: that is, the passage from medical to social application; and this opens up an indefinite field with grave potentials. The troublesome problems of rule and unruliness in modern mass society make the extension of such control methods to non-medical categories extremely tempting for social management. Numerous questions of human rights and dignity arise. The difficult question of preemption care versus enabling care insists on concrete answers. Shall we induce learning attitudes in school children by the mass administration of drugs, circumventing the appeal to autonomous motivation? Shall we overcome aggression by electronic pacification of brain areas? Shall we generate sensations of happiness or pleasure or at least contentment through independent stimulation (or tranquilizing) of the appropriate centers—independent, that is, of the objects of happiness, pleasure, or content and their attainment in personal living and achieving? Candidacies could be multiplied. Business firms might become interested in some of these techniques for performance-increase among their employees.

Regardless of the question of compulsion or consent, and regardless also of the question of undesirable side-effects, each time we thus bypass the human way of dealing with human problems, short-circuiting it by an impersonal mechanism, we have taken away something from the dignity of personal selfhood and advanced a further step on the road from responsible subjects to programmed behavior systems. Social functionalism, important as it is, is only one side of the question. Decisive is the question of what kind of individuals the society is composed of to make its existence valuable as a whole. Somewhere along the line of increasing social manageability at the price of individual autonomy, the question of the worthwhileness of the human enterprise must pose itself. Answering it involves the image of man we entertain. We must think it anew in light of the things we can do to it now and could never do before.

c. This holds even more with respect to the last object of a technology applied on man himself—the genetic control of future men. This is too wide a subject for cursory treatment. Here I merely point to this most ambitious dream of *Homo faber,* summed up in the phrase that man will take his own evolution in hand, with the aim of not just preserving the integrity of the species but of modifying it by improvements of his own design. Whether we have the right to do it, whether we are qualified for that creative role, is the most serious question that can be posed to man finding himself suddenly in possession of such failed powers. Who will be the image-makers, by what standards, and on the basis of what knowledge? Also, the question of the moral right to experiment on future human beings must be asked. These and similar questions, which demand an answer before we embark on a journey into the unknown, show most vividly how far our powers to act are pushing us beyond the terms of all former ethics.

VIII

The ethically relevant common feature in all the examples adduced is what I like to call the inherently "utopian" drift of our actions under the conditions of modern technology, whether it works on non-human or on human nature, and whether the "utopia" at the end of the road be planned or unplanned. By the kind and size of its snowballing effects, technological power propels us into goals of a type that was formerly the preserve of Utopias. To put it differently, technological power has turned what used and ought to be tentative, perhaps enlightening, plays of speculative reason into competing blueprints for projects, and in choosing between them we have to choose between extremes of remote effects. The one thing we can really know of them is their extremism as such—that they concern the total condition of nature on our globe and the very kind of creatures that shall, or shall not, populate it. In consequence of the inevitably "utopian" scale of modern technology, the salutary gap between everyday and ultimate issues, between occasions, is closing. Living now constantly in the shadow of unwanted, built-in, automatic utopianism, we are constantly confronted with issues whose positive choice requires supreme wisdom—an impossible, and in particular for contemporary man, who denies the very existence of its object: viz., objective value and truth. We need wisdom most when we believe in it least.

If the new nature of our acting then calls for a new ethics of long-range responsibility, coextensive with the range of our power, it calls in the name of that very responsibility also for a new kind of humility—a humility not like former humility, i.e., owing to the littleness, but owing to the excessive magnitude of our power, which is the excess of our power to act over our power to foresee and our power to evaluate and to judge. In the face of the quasi-eschatological potentials of our technological processes, ignorance of the ultimate implications becomes itself a reason for responsible restraint—as the second best to the possession of wisdom itself.

One other aspect of the required new ethics of responsibility for and to a distant future is worth mentioning: the insufficiency of representative government to meet the new demands on its normal principles and by its normal mechanics. For according to these, only *present* interests make themselves heard and felt and enforce their condition. It is to them that public agencies are accountable, and this is the way in which concretely the respecting of rights comes about (as distinct from their abstract acknowledgement). But the *future* is not represented, it is not a force that can throw its weight into the scales. The non-existent has no lobby, and the unborn are powerless. Thus accountability to them has no political reality behind it yet in present decision-making, and when they

can make their complaint, then we, the culprits, will no longer be there.

This raises to an ultimate pitch the old question of the power of the wise, or the force of ideas not allied to self-interest, in the body politic. What *force* shall represent the future in the present? However, before *this* question can become earnest in practical terms, the new ethics must find its theory, on which dos and don'ts can be based. That is: before the question of what *force,* comes the question of what *insight* or value-knowledge shall represent the future in the present.

IX

And here is where I get stuck, and where we all get stuck. For the very same movement which put us in possession of the powers that have now to be regulated by norms—the movement of modern knowledge called science—has by a necessary complementarity eroded the foundations from which norms could be derived; it has destroyed the very idea of norm as such. Not, fortunately, the feeling for norm and even for particular norms. But this feeling became uncertain of itself when contradicted by alleged knowledge or at least denied all sanction by it. Anyway and always does it have a difficult enough time against the loud clamors of greed and fear. Now it must in addition blush before the frown of superior knowledge, as unfounded and incapable of foundation. First, Nature has been "neutralized" with respect to value, then man himself. Now we shiver in the nakedness of a nihilism in which near-omnipotence is paired with near-emptiness, greatest capacity with knowing least what for. With the apocalyptic pregnancy of our actions, that very knowledge which we lack has become more urgently needed than at any other stage in the adventure of mankind. Alas, urgency is no promise of success. On the contrary, it must be avowed that to seek for wisdom today requires a good measure of unwisdom. The very nature of the age which cries out for an ethical theory makes it suspiciously look like a fool's errand. Yet we have no choice in the matter but to try.

It is a question whether without restoring the category of the sacred, the category most thoroughly destroyed by the scientific enlightenment, we can have an ethics able to cope with the extreme powers which we possess today and constantly increase and are almost compelled to use. Regarding those consequences imminent enough still to hit ourselves, fear can do the job—so often the best substitute for genuine virtue or wisdom. But this means fails us towards the more distant prospects, which here matter the most, especially as the beginnings seem mostly innocent in their smallness. Only awe of the sacred with its unqualified veto is independent to fit computations of mundane fear and the solace of uncertainty about distant consequences. But religion as a soul-determining force is no longer there to be summoned to the aid of ethics. The latter must stand on its worldly feet—that is, on reason and its fitness for philosophy. And while of faith it can be said that it either is there or is not, of ethics it holds that it must be there.

It must be there because men act, and ethics is for the reordering of actions and for regulating the power to act. It must be there all the more, then, the greater the powers of acting that are to be regulated; and with their size, the ordering principle must also fit their kind. Thus, novel powers to act require novel ethical rules and perhaps even a new ethics.

"Thou shalt not kill" was enunciated because man has the power to kill and often the occasion and even inclination for it—in short, because killing is actually done. It is only under the *pressure* of real habits of action, and generally of the fact that always action already takes place, without *this* having to be commanded first, that ethics as the ruling of such acting under the standard of the good or the permitted enters the stage. Such a *pressure* emanates from the novel technological powers of man, whose exercise is given with their existence. *If* they really are as novel in kind as here contended, and if by the kind of their potential consequences they really have abolished the moral neutrality which the technical commerce with matter hitherto enjoyed—then their pressure bids to seek for new prescriptions in ethics which are competent to assume their guidance, but which first of all can hold their own theoretically against that very pressure. To the demonstration of those premises this paper was devoted. If they are accepted, then we who make thinking our business have a task to last us for our time. We must do it in time, for since we act anyway we shall have some ethic or other in any case, and without a supreme effort to determine the right one, we may be left with a wrong one by default.

NOTES

1. Immanuel Kant, *Groundwork of the Metaphysics of Morals,* preface.
2. *Op. cit.,* chapter 1.
3. *Ibid.* (I have followed H. J. Paton's translation with some changes.)
4. On this last point, the biblical God changed his mind to an all-encompassing "yes" after the Flood.

I.11   FREEMAN DYSON

Technology and Social Justice

Freeman Dyson was born in England and educated at Cambridge University. He served in World War II as an operations research specialist for the Royal Air Force. Following the war, he did graduate training in physics and became professor of physics at Cornell University. In 1953, he joined the faculty at the Institute for Advanced Study in Princeton, New Jersey, where he remains. He is a fellow of the Royal Society of London and a member of the National Academy of Sciences.

The text reprinted here was delivered as the fourth Louis Nizer Lecture on Public Policy for the Carnegie Council on Ethics and International Affairs on November 5, 1997. It relates to themes that he has developed more fully in his book *The Sun, the Genome, and the Internet* (1999). In this lecture, Dyson addresses the issue of whether technological innovation tends to increase or decrease social justice and equality.

There are many who believe that technological innovation is a force for increasing social inequality. New technologies tend to benefit those who are already rich enough to afford them or powerful enough to control them, and because technology is a source of power, its control by elites only serves to enhance their dominance over other members of society. On the other side of this argument, there are those who believe that technological progress is the engine of human progress and that technological innovation acts as a great leveler of society by breaking down the barriers erected by privilege and allowing for a more equitable distribution of knowledge and power.

Dyson examines the evidence for each of these general perspectives and ends up endorsing a qualified "techno-optimist" answer—that "ethics must guide technology toward social justice." Dyson supports his conclusion through a combination of historical reflection, personal anecdotes, and the exercise of technological and moral imagination.

Focus Questions

1. Dyson begins his discussion by giving some historical examples of technological innovations that he claims have increased social justice. What are his examples? Can you think of any others?
2. Why does Dyson believe that "The advent of electrical appliances liberated the servants and shackled their mistresses"?
3. Dyson argues that ethical and religious values can and should influence technological change, and he mentions Max Weber's seminal work *The Protestant Ethic and the Spirit of Capitalism* as providing evidence that this is possible. Do you agree?
4. In the concluding section, Dyson presents a vision in which the nascent technologies of solar energy, genetic engineering, and global Internet communications are combined to help billions of poor people all over the earth to attain a higher standard of living. Do you think this vision is attainable? Why or why not?

Keywords

biomass energy, genetic engineering, high-tech medicine, the Human Genome Project, inequality, the Internet, national health care, social justice, solar energy

IT IS EASY TO FIND historical examples illustrating the thesis that technology may have something to contribute to social justice. In the fourteenth century the new technology of printing changed the face of Europe, bringing books and education out of the monasteries and spreading them far and wide among the people. Printing gave power to the Bible and led directly to the Protestant Reformation in Northern Europe. One may question whether Luther's Germany and Shakespeare's England enjoyed social justice, but they were certainly closer to it than the medieval Germany and England out of which they grew. Luther and Shakespeare brought at least the idea of justice—if not the reality—to ordinary citizens outside the nobility and the priesthood. The Protestant ethic, which took root in Germany, England, Holland, and Scandinavia with the help of printed books, carried with it a perpetual striving for social justice, even if the Utopian visions were seldom achieved.

More recent technologies that contributed in a practical way to social justice were those of public health—clean water supplies, sewage treatment, vaccination, and antibiotics. These technologies could only be effective in protecting the rich from contagion and sickness if they were also available to the poor. Even if the rich and powerful receive preferential treatment, as they usually do, the benefits of public health technology are felt to some extent by everybody. In countries where public health technologies are enforced by law, there is no large gap in life expectancy between rich and poor.

The technology of synthetic materials has also helped to erase differences between rich and poor. Throughout history, until the nineteenth century, only the rich could afford to dress in brilliant colors, furs, and silk. Fine clothes were a badge of privilege and wealth. In the nineteenth century the chemical industry produced artificial dyestuffs. The twentieth century added artificial fur and silk and many other synthetic fabrics cheap enough for working-class women to afford. No longer can one tell a woman's social class by her clothes. It is a measure of social justice in modern societies that the children of the rich now dress down, imitating the style of the majority both in clothes and in behavior.

Household appliances are another technology with a tendency towards social justice. When I was a child in England in the 1920s, my mother employed four full-time servants: a cook, a housemaid, a nursemaid, and a gardener. We didn't consider ourselves rich. My father was a schoolteacher. We were an average middle-class family. In those days an average middle-class family needed four servants to do the hard manual work of cooking, cleaning, child care, and gardening. To do all this work a whole class of people existed who spent their lives as domestic servants. The professional and intellectual classes to which we belonged were riding on the backs of the servant class. Because of the servants, my mother had leisure to organize socially useful projects, such as a club for teenage girls and a birth control clinic. The birth control clinic was undoubtedly a godsend to the women who came to it for instruction in the art of not having unwanted babies. But it did not in any way narrow the gulf between her and them. She always spoke of her birth control clientele like a mistress speaking of servants.

My mother was a kind mistress and treated the servants well, according to the standards of the time, but the servants knew their place. They knew that if they disobeyed orders or answered back, they would be out on the street. Now, like the antebellum South, the servant class in England is gone with the wind, and the wind that blew it away was not the ravaging invasion of Sherman's army, but the peaceful invasion of an army of electric stoves, gas heaters, vacuum cleaners, refrigerators, washing machines, drying machines, garbage disposals, freezers, microwave ovens, juicers, choppers, and disposable diapers. The technology of household appliances made servants unnecessary, and, at the same time, the children of the servant class began to go to college and make the transition to the middle class. The transition was not painless, but it was less painful than a civil war. It was a big step on the road to social justice.

I remember with great fondness the nursemaid, Ethel, who cared for me as a young child. She had left school, as girls of the servant class did in those days, at the age of fourteen. When my sister and I were safely in bed in the night nursery, we sometimes heard the "putt, putt, putt" of a motorbike approaching the house, stopping, and then driving away into the night. That was Ethel's young man taking her out for the evening. The motorbike was the first harbinger of the approaching social revolution. The motorbike was the technology of upward mobility. After Ethel left us and married the young man, she had three daughters of her own, and all of them went to college. One of her grandsons is now a university professor.

Those are enough examples to show that technology can be helpful in the struggle for social justice. But in each case, as Edward Tenner tells us in his book *Why Things Bite Back,* a step forward in technology tends to bring with it an unexpected step backward. A step forward for some people frequently brings with it a step backward for others. And it often happens that when an old privileged class of people is dispossessed and the blessings of wealth and power are spread more equally, the burdens of equalization fall disproportionately upon women. When the revolutions accompanying the technology of printing destroyed the wealth and power of the monasteries over much of Europe, both male and female orders were dispossessed, but the nuns lost more than the monks. Nuns in the old convents were in many ways more free than wives in the new Protestant communities. The old monastic society provided a refuge where women of outstanding ability—for example, Hildegard of Bingen—had access to higher education. Sheltered and supported by the monastic orders, women could follow their vocations as scholars and artists. When the monasteries were dissolved, nuns had to find shelter in other people's homes, either as wives or as servants. The new secular society replaced the monasteries with colleges and universities. In the universities men scholars could find shelter and security, but there was no place for women.

The technology of household appliances, likewise, brought a step backward to the stratum of society to which my mother belonged, the women of the middle class. My mother would be considered by the standards of today a thoroughly liberated woman. Trained as a lawyer, she helped to write the Act of Parliament that opened the professions in England to women. With the help of her servants, she could take care of her husband and children without being confined to the home. She was free to pursue her interests outside the home—her girls' club and birth control clinic. But she was by no means the most liberated of the women in our family. I had a collection of aunts who were in various ways more liberated than my mother. All of them had husbands and most of them had children, but this did not stop them from being liberated. All of them were more adventurous than their husbands. My Aunt Margaret was trained as a nurse and rose to become a matron, which meant that she was the managing administrator of a large hospital. My Aunt Ruth was a figure skater of international repute

who kept an Olympic silver medal among her trophies. My Aunt Dulcibella was the first woman in England to receive an airplane pilot's license. She and her husband had an airplane which they used for traveling around in Africa. They loved Africa, and their lifestyle would have fit in very well with the group of adventurers that Michael Ondaatje describes in his novel *The English Patient*. My Aunt Dulcibella was also a professional actress, and if she had only been eighty years younger, she might have had a starring role in *The English Patient* movie. We did not consider these aunts of ours to be unusual. It was normal at that time for middle-class women to do something spectacular. My mother, with her birth control clinic, was the quiet one, the least daring of the four.

Now, consider what happened to the next generation of middle-class women in England and the United States. Thirty years later, in the 1950s, the servants were gone and the electrical appliances were taking their place. For wives and mothers of the middle class, this was a big step backward. Appliances do not cook the dinner, clean the house, do the shopping, and mind the baby. The middle-class women of the 1950s were far less liberated than their mothers. The liberation that my mother's generation achieved had to be fought for all over again. Even now, in the 1990s, women are only partially liberated. To achieve partial liberation, they have replaced the old domestic servants with day care centers, cleaning ladies, and *au pair* girls imported from overseas. Electrical appliances help, but they only do a small part of the job.

The Institute of Advanced Study, where I have spent my working life, is a peculiar institution with a small permanent faculty. The faculty is supposed to be representative of the most distinguished men and women in academic life. Unfortunately, we have always found it difficult to appoint women to the faculty. The original faculty, appointed in the 1930s, contained one woman, the archaeologist Hetty Goldman. I remember her vividly. She was a formidable lady, small in stature and large in spirit, who led excavations of ancient sites in Turkey, ruling over small armies of Turkish laborers with an iron hand. Her colleagues used to say she was the equal of any two male archaeologists. There was never the slightest doubt that she had the "right stuff" to be an Institute professor. She was a natural leader in her own eyes and in ours. She belonged to my mother's generation of liberated women. She grew up, like my mother, in a society of women with servants. When she retired in 1947, she was not replaced. For almost forty years the Institute faculty was entirely male. In 1985, the sociologist Joan Scott became the second woman to join the faculty. And in 1997 the historian Patricia Crone became the third.

The history of our faculty encapsulates in a nutshell the history of women's liberation: a glorious beginning in the 1920s; a great backsliding in the 1950s; a gradual recovery in the 1980s. It is not altogether fanciful to blame the technology of household appliances for the backsliding. The advent of electrical appliances liberated the servants and shackled their mistresses.

High-Tech Medicine and Computers

I have discussed four technologies that led to large expansions of social justice. Although each of them had compensating negative effects, especially on women, the overall effects of all of them were predominantly positive. It will be just as easy to find examples of technologies that had negative effects. One could mention the technologies of gas chambers and nuclear weapons, useful for the convenient extermination of people to whom we do not wish to extend the benefits of social justice. But the more troubling examples are two of the technologies that are making the most rapid progress today: high-tech medicine and high-tech communication.

All of us who live in the United States are familiar with the ugly face that high-tech medicine presents to the patient: the initial telephone call answered by a machine rather than a human voice; the filling out of forms in the office; the repetitive answering of questions; the battery of routine chemical and physical tests carried out by technicians wearing rubber gloves; and finally, the abbreviated contact with the physician. It is all very different from the old-fashioned practice of medicine, when doctors were personal friends and advisers to

patients and sometimes even made house calls. The face of high-tech medicine is ugly even when the patient is rich, and uglier still when the patient is poor. The ugliness results from many factors working together. First, the prevalence of malpractice litigation, which destroys trust, compelling doctors to conform to rigid rules and surrounding them with layers of bureaucratic documentation. Second, the high cost of the equipment that high-tech medicine demands, forcing medical centers to adopt elaborate cost-accounting systems. Third, the size of the staff needed to operate a high-tech center, with many doctors qualified in narrow specialties so that the patient rarely gets to see the same doctor twice. Fourth, the overwhelming cost of hospitalization, allowing patients a bare minimum of days for rest and recuperation after major illness or surgery. These factors, together, led to the situation that confronts the patient today. What the patient needs most, but finds least, is personal attention.

Since personal attention has become the scarcest resource in high-tech medicine, it is inevitable that it should be distributed unequally. The majority of advanced countries have national health services that attempt, with varying degrees of success, to distribute medical attention fairly. In countries with national health services, medical attention is theoretically available to everybody. This is what the ethic of social justice demands. But the escalating cost of medical attention makes social justice more and more difficult to achieve. One way or another, as personal attention becomes scarcer, people of status tend to receive more of it and people without status to receive less. The national health services in countries where they exist make valiant efforts to preserve the ideal of social justice, but the march of medical technology and the concomitant increase of costs constantly erode the ideal. In the United States, which never had a national health service and does not pretend to distribute medical resources equally, the prospects for social justice are far worse. In the United States a medical system based on the ethic of the free market inevitably favors the rich over the poor, and the inequalities grow sharper as the costs increase.

I have seen in my own family a small example of the dilemma that the growth of high-tech medicine presents to physicians. One of my daughters is a cardiologist. For many years she worked in state-supported hospitals taking care of patients as they flowed through the system, working brutally long hours and still having little time for personal contact with her patients. Her patients in the public hospitals were predominantly poor and uninsured. Many of them had AIDS or gunshot wounds in addition to cardiac problems. The public health system, such as it was, was designed to get these patients out of the hospital and back on the streets as fast as possible. Last year my daughter was offered a job in a private cardiology practice with far shorter hours, better pay and working conditions, and an expectation of long, continued care of her patients. She accepted the offer without much hesitation. She is much happier in her new job. Now, for the first time, she knows her patients as individuals and can tailor their treatments to their individual histories and personalities. She feels that she is a better doctor, and her new job gave her the flexibility to take time off to have her first baby last July. From almost every point of view, her jump into private practice was a wise move. Her only problem was a small twinge of conscience for having abandoned the poor to take care of the rich. In the private practice her patients are not all rich, but they are all paying for the personal attention that she is now able to give them. She was forced to make a choice between social justice and professional satisfaction, and social justice lost. I don't blame her. But in a socially just society, physicians would not be forced to make such choices.

Similar dilemmas, not so stark as the dilemmas of medical practice but equally important, exist in the world of high-tech computing and communications. Here, too, there is a clash between the economic forces driving the technology and the needs of poor people. Access to personal computers and the Internet is like medical insurance: almost everybody needs it, but most poor people don't have it. The people who are wired, the people who browse the World Wide Web and conduct their daily lives and businesses on the Net, have tremendous economic and social advantages. Increasingly, jobs and business opportunities are offered through the Internet. Access to the Internet means access to well-paying jobs. People who are not wired in are in danger of becoming the new servant class. The gulf between the wired and the unwired is wide, and growing wider.

The computer and software industries are driven by two contradictory impulses. On the one hand, they sincerely wish to broaden their market by making computers accessible to everybody. On the other hand, they are forced by competitive pressures to upgrade their products constantly, increasing their power and speed and adding new features and new complications. The top end of the market drives the development of new products, and the new products remain out of the reach of the poor. In the tug of war between broadening the market and pampering the top-end customer, the top-end customer usually wins.

The problem of unequal access to computers is only a small part of the problem of inequality in our society. Until the society is willing to attack the larger problems of inequality in housing, education, and health care, attempts to provide equal access to computers cannot be totally successful. Nevertheless, in attacking the general problems of inequality, computer access might be a good place to start. One of the virtues of the new technology of the Internet is that it has an inherent tendency to become global. The Internet easily infiltrates through barriers of language, custom, and culture. No technical barrier stops it from becoming universally accessible. To provide equality of access to the Internet is technically easier than providing equality of access to housing and health care. Universal access to the Internet would not solve all our social problems, but it would be a big step in the right direction. The Internet could then become an important tool for alleviating other kinds of inequality.

The Protestant Ethic and the Spirit of Capitalism

Up to now I have been talking as if technology came first and ethics second. I have been describing historical events in which technological changes occurred first and then increases or decreases of social justice occurred as a consequence. I depicted technological change as the cause of ethical improvement or deterioration. This view of history is opposed to the view propounded by Max Weber in his seminal book *The Protestant Ethic and the Spirit of Capitalism*. Weber argued that the Protestant ethic came first and the rise of capitalism and the technologies associated with it came second. Weber's view has become the prevailing view of modern historians. Weber said that ethics drove technology. I say that technology drives ethics.

I am not trying to prove Weber wrong. His historical vision remains profoundly true. It is true that the religious revolutions of the sixteenth century engendered an ethic of personal responsibility and restless inquiry, an ethic that encouraged the growth of capitalistic enterprise and technological innovation. It was no accident that Isaac Newton, the preeminent architect of modern science, was also a Protestant theologian. He took his theology as seriously as his science. It was no accident King Henry VIII, the man who brought the Protestant revolution to England, also endowed the college where Newton lived and taught. Henry and Isaac were kindred spirits—both were rebels against authority, enemies of the Pope, tyrants, supreme egoists, suspicious to the point of paranoia, believers in the Protestant ethic, and in love with technology. Henry loved to build ships and Isaac loved to build telescopes. It is true that ethics can drive technology. I am only saying that this is not the whole truth, that technology can also drive ethics, that the chain of causation works in both directions. The technology of printing helped to cause the rise of the Protestant ethic just as much as the Protestant ethic helped to cause the rise of navigation and astronomy.

I am not the first to take issue with Weber on this question. The historian Richard Tawney also studied the interrelationships of religion and capitalism and came to conclusions similar to mine. He held Weber in high esteem and contributed a foreword to the English translation of *The Protestant Ethic and the Spirit of Capitalism*. Here are the concluding sentences of Tawney's foreword: "It is instructive to trace with Weber the influence of religious ideas on economic development. It is not less important to grasp the effect of economic arrangements accepted by an age on the opinion which it holds of the province of religion." Tawney's view is that technology influenced religion as strongly as religion influenced technology. Since my view of history is closer to Tawney's than to Weber's, I now ask the question: How can we push new technologies into directions conducive to social justice? How can we make ethics drive technology in such a way that the evil consequences are minimized and the good maximized? I shall hope to persuade you that the situation we are in is not hopeless, that new technologies offer us real opportunities for making the world a happier place.

The Sun, the Genome, and the Internet

Finally, I turn to the positive side of my message. Technology guided by ethics has the power to help the billions of poor people all over the earth. My purpose is to help push technology in a new direction, away from toys for the rich and toward necessities for the poor. The time is ripe for this to happen. Three huge revolutionary forces are being harnessed just in time for the new century: the sun, the genome, and the Internet. These three forces are strong enough to reverse some of the worst evils of our time. The evils I am hoping to reverse are well known to you all. All over the earth, and especially in the poor countries to the south of us, millions of desperate people leave their villages and pour into overcrowded cities. There are now ten megacities in the world with populations twice as large as New York City. Soon there will be more. We all know that the increase of human population is one of the causes of the migration to cities. The other cause is the poverty and lack of jobs in villages. Both the population explosion and the poverty must be reversed if we are to have a decent future. Many experts on population say that if we can mitigate the poverty, the population will stabilize itself, as it has done in Europe and Japan. I am not an expert on population, so I won't say any more about that. I am saying that poverty can be reduced by a combination of solar energy, genetic engineering, and the Internet. Our task in the next century is to put the new technologies to work in the cause of social justice. Social justice means making the new technologies accessible to everyone, to bring wealth to poor countries and hope to poor people.

I have seen with my own eyes what happens to a village when the economic basis of life collapses, and I have seen how the economic basis of village life can be revived. My wife grew up in Westerhausen, a village in East Germany that was under Communist management. The Communist regime took care of the village economy, selling the output of the farms to Russia at fixed prices, which gave the farmers economic security. The village remained beautiful and, on the whole, pleasant to live in. Nothing much had changed in the village since 1910. One thing the Communist regime did was organize a zoo, with a collection of animals maintained by a few professionals with a lot of help from the local school children. The village was justly proud of its zoo. The zoo was subsidized by the regime so it did not need to worry about being unprofitable. I visited the village under the old regime in 1975 and found it very friendly. Then came 1990 and the unification of Germany. Overnight, the economy of the village was wrecked. The farmers could no longer farm because nobody would buy their products. Russia could not buy because the price had to be paid in West German marks. German consumers would not buy because the local produce was not as good as that available in the supermarkets. The village farmers could not compete with the goods pouring in from France and Denmark. So the farmers were out of work. Most of the younger generation moved out of the village to compete for jobs in the cities, and most of the older generation remained. Many of them, both old and young, are still unemployed. The zoo, deprived of its subsidy, collapsed.

The sad exodus that I saw in the village of Westerhausen when I visited there in 1991 is the same exodus that is happening in villages all over the world. Everywhere the international market devalues the work of the village. Without work, the younger and the more enterprising people move out.

In the seven years since the unification, Westerhausen has slowly been recovering. Recovery is possible because of the process of gentrification. Wealthy people from the local towns move in and modernize the homes abandoned by the farmers. Cottages are demolished to make room for two-car garages. Ancient and narrow roads are widened. The village will survive as a community of nature lovers and commuters. Lying on the northern edge of the Harz Mountains, it is close to the big cities of northern Germany and even closer to unspoiled mountain forests. Its permanent asset is natural beauty.

Two months ago my wife and I were back in the village. The change since we had last visited in 1991 was startling. We stayed in the elegant new home of a friend who had been in my wife's class in the village elementary school fifty years earlier. The village now looks well cared for and prosperous. The recovery from the disaster of 1990 has been slow and difficult, but it has been steady. The government did two things to mitigate the harshness of the free market: it allowed every homeowner to borrow money with almost zero interest from the government to modernize houses, and it allowed every farming cooperative to borrow money with almost zero interest to modernize farms. As a result, the houses that were not bought by outsiders are being modernized, and the few farmers who remained as farmers are flourishing. The zoo has been revived. In addition, there are some new enterprises. A Western immigrant has planted a large vineyard on a south-facing hillside and will soon be producing the first Westerhausen wines. My wife's family and many of her friends still live in the village. They gave us a warm and joyful welcome.

The probable future of Westerhausen can be seen in a thousand villages in England. The typical English village today is not primarily engaged in farming. The typical village remains beautiful and prosperous because of gentrification. Wealthy homeowners pay large sums of money for the privilege of living under a thatched roof. The thatching of roofs is one of the few ancient village crafts that still survives. The thatchers are mostly young, highly skilled, and well paid. The farmers who remain are either gentlemen amateurs, who run small farms as a hobby, or well-educated professionals, who run big farms as a business. The old population of peasant farmers, who used to live in the villages in poverty and squalor, disappeared long ago.

Discreetly hidden in many of the villages are offices and factories engaged in high-tech industry. One of the head offices of IBM Europe is in the English village of Hursley not far from where I was born. In the villages of France, at least in the area I know around Paris, the picture is much the same. Wealth came to the villages because they have what wealthy people seek: peace, security, and beauty.

What would it take to reverse the flow of jobs and people from villages to megacities all over the world? I believe the flow can be reversed by the same process of gentrification that is happening in Westerhausen. To make gentrification possible, the villages themselves must become sources of wealth. How can a godforsaken Mexican village become a source of wealth? Three facts can make it possible. First, solar energy is distributed equitably over the earth. Second, genetic engineering can make solar energy usable everywhere for the local creation of wealth. Third, the Internet can provide people in every village with the information and skills they need to develop their talents. The sun, the genome, and the Internet can work together to bring wealth to the villages of Mexico, just as the older technologies—electricity and automobiles—brought wealth to the villages of England. Let me talk briefly about each of the three new technologies, in turn.

Solar energy is most available where it is most needed—in the countryside rather than in cities, and in tropical countries, where most of the world's population lives, rather than in temperate latitudes. The quantity of solar energy is enormous compared with all other energy resources. Each square mile in the tropics receives about 1,000 megawatts averaged over day and night. This quantity of energy would be ample to support a dense population with all modern conveniences. Solar energy has not yet been used on a large scale for one simple reason: it is too expensive. It cannot compete in a free market with imported coal, oil, and natural gas. The country that has used solar energy on the largest scale is Brazil, where sugar was grown as an energy crop to make alcohol as a substitute for gasoline in cars and trucks. Brazil protected and subsidized the local alcohol industry. The experiment was technically successful, but the cost was high. Brazil has now re-

verted to free-market policies, and the experiment is at an end. What the world needs is not high-cost subsidized solar energy, but solar energy cheap enough to compete with oil.

Solar energy is expensive today because it has to be collected from large areas and there is not yet a technology that covers large areas cheaply. One of the virtues of solar energy is the fact that it can be collected in many ways. It is adaptable to local conditions. The two main tools for collecting it are photoelectric panels, which convert sunlight directly into electricity, and energy crops, like the Brazilian sugar plantations, which convert sunlight into fuel. Roughly speaking, photoelectric collection is the method of choice for deserts, and energy crops are the method of choice for farmland and forests. Each method has its advantages and disadvantages. Photoelectric systems have high efficiency, typically between 10 percent and 15 percent, but are expensive to deploy and maintain. Energy crops have low efficiency, typically around 1 percent, and are expensive and messy to harvest. The electricity produced by photoelectric systems is intermittent and cannot be cheaply converted into storable forms of energy. Fuels produced from energy crops are storable and, therefore, more convenient.

To make solar energy cheap, we need a technology that combines the advantages of photovoltaic and biological systems. Two technical advances would make this possible. First, crop plants could be developed that convert sunlight into fuel with efficiency comparable to photovoltaic collectors, in the range of 10 percent rather than 1 percent. This would reduce the costs of land and harvesting by a large factor. Second, crop plants could be developed that do not need to be harvested at all. An energy crop could be a permanent forest with trees that convert sunlight to liquid fuel and deliver the fuel directly through their roots to a network of underground pipelines. If those two advantages could be combined, we would have a supply of solar energy that was cheap, abundant, ubiquitous, and environmentally benign.

The energy supply system of the future might be a large area of forest with species of trees varying from place to place to suit the local climate and topography. We may hope that substantial parts of the forest would be nature reserves closed to human settlement and populated with wildlife so as to preserve the diversity of the natural ecologies. But the greater part could be open to human settlement, with teeming towns and villages under the trees. Landowners outside the nature reserves would be encouraged, but not compelled, to grow trees for energy. If the trees converted sunlight into fuel with 10 percent efficiency, landowners could sell the fuel for $10,000 per acre per year and easily undercut the present price of gasoline. Owners of farmland and city lots alike would have a strong economic incentive to grow trees. The future energy plantation need not be a monotonous expanse of identical trees in regular rows. It could be as varied and as spontaneous as a natural woodland, interspersed with open spaces and houses, villages, towns, factories, and lakes.

To make this dream of a future landscape come true, the essential tool is genetic engineering. At present, large sums of money are being spent on sequencing the human genome. The Human Genome Project is motivated primarily by its medical applications. It will contribute enormously to the understanding and treatment of human diseases. It does not contribute directly to the engineering of trees. But alongside the human genome many other genomes are being sequenced—bacteria, yeast, worms, and fruit flies. For advancing the art of genetic engineering the genomes of simpler organisms are more useful than the human genome. Before long, we shall also have sequenced the genomes of the major crop plants—wheat, maize, and rice—and after that will come trees. Within a few decades, we shall have achieved a deep understanding of the genome, an understanding that will allow us to breed trees that will turn sunlight into fuel and still preserve the diversity that makes natural forests beautiful.

As soon as we can genetically engineer trees to use sunlight efficiently to make fuel, we shall learn to breed trees that convert sunlight into useful chemicals of other kinds, including silicon chips for computers and gasoline for cars. Economic forces will then move industries from cities to the country. Mining and manufacturing could be economically based on locally available solar energy, with geneti-

cally engineered creatures consuming and recycling the waste products. It might even become possible to build roads and buildings biologically, breeding little polyps to lay down durable structures on land in the same way as their cousins build coral reefs in the ocean.

But the third, and most important, of the triad of new technologies is the Internet. The Internet is essential to enable businesses and farms in remote places to function as part of the modern global economy. The Internet will allow people in remote places to make business deals, buy and sell, keep in touch with their friends, continue their education, and follow their hobbies and avocations, with full knowledge of what is going on in the rest of the world.

This will not be the Internet of today, accessible only to computer-literate people in rich countries and to the wealthy elite in poor countries. It will be a truly global Internet, using a network of satellites in space for communication with places that fiber optics cannot reach and connected to local networks in every village. The new Internet will end the cultural isolation of poor countries and poor people.

Two technical problems have to be solved to make the Internet accessible to almost everybody on a global scale: large-scale architecture and the problem of the "last mile." Large-scale architecture means choosing the most efficient combination of landlines and satellite links to cover every corner of the globe. The Teledesic system of satellite communication now under development is intended to be a partial answer to this problem. The Teledesic system has 280 satellites in a dense network of low orbits, allowing any two points on the globe to be connected with minimum delay. If the Teledesic system fails, some other system will be designed to do the job. The problem of the "last mile" is more difficult. This is the problem of connecting homes and families, wherever they happen to be, with the nearest Internet terminal. The problem of the last mile has to be solved piecemeal, with methods depending on the local geography and the local culture. An ingenious method of solving the last-mile problem in urban American neighborhoods has been introduced recently by Paul Baran, the original inventor of the Internet. Baran's system is called Ricochet and consists of a multitude of small, wireless transmitters and receivers. Each user has a modem that communicates by radio with a local network. The feature that makes the system practical is that the transmitters constantly switch their frequencies so as not to interfere with one another. The system is flexible and cheap, avoiding the large expense of laying cable from the Internet terminal to every apartment and every house. It works well in the environment of urban America. It remains to be seen whether it is flexible and cheap enough to work well in the environment of a Mexican village or a Peruvian barrio.

Suppose, then, we can solve the technical problems of cheap solar energy, genetic engineering of industrial crop plants, and universal access to the Internet. What will follow? My thesis is that the solution of those three problems will bring about a worldwide social revolution, similar to the revolution we have seen in the villages of England and Germany. Cheap solar energy and genetic engineering will provide the basis for primary industries in the countryside. After that, the vast variety of secondary and tertiary economic activities that use the Internet for their coordination—food processing, publishing, education, entertainment, and health care—will follow the primary industries as

they move from overgrown cities to country towns and villages. And as soon as the villages become rich, they will attract people and wealth back from the cities.

I am not suggesting that in the brave new world of the future everyone will be compelled to live in villages. Many of us will always prefer to live in large cities or in towns of moderate size. I am suggesting only that people should be free to choose. When wealth has moved back to villages, people who live there will no longer be forced by economic necessity to move out, and people who live in megacities will no longer be compelled by economic necessity to stay there. Many of us who have the freedom to choose, like the successful stockbrokers and business executives in England and Germany, will choose to live in villages.

So this is my dream: Solar energy, genetic engineering, and the Internet will work together to create a socially just world in which every Mexican village is as wealthy as Princeton. Of course, that is only a dream. Inequalities will persist. Poverty will not disappear. But I see a hope that the world will move far and fast in the directions I have been describing. Ethics must guide technology toward social justice. Let us all help to push the world in that direction as hard as we can. It does no harm to hope.

I.12   DAVID STRONG

Technological Subversion

In this reading taken from the author's book *Crazy Mountains: Learning from Wilderness to Weigh Technology,* philosopher David Strong asks us to consider the basic question, "Why do we value technology?"

In his analysis, we value technological devices because they disburden us of toilsome labor, discomfort, and bother. Technological innovations beckon us with the promise of freedom and happiness. We want things to be easy so that we are freer to pursue our ends without having to worry too much about the means we use to do so, and we believe that being "free" in this sense—that is, disburdened—will make us happy.

Using as his examples the replacement of the hearth by the central heating system and television viewing as a primary form of entertainment, Strong argues that this quest for freedom and happiness through technology provides ease and comfort, often alters the nature of human experience in ways that disconnect us from nature and other people, and ironically produces not happiness but alienation. Although some readers may find this philosophical meditation somewhat demanding, those who study it carefully will find that it rewards their effort.

Focus Questions

1. What does the author mean by the term *technological availability*? What specific values does this concept embody?
2. What is the vision of the "good life" that our modern technological society offers us? Why does the author question the goodness of this way of life?
3. What are the main differences between what Strong calls "things" and what he calls "devices"? What values do we sacrifice when we choose the device paradigm over engagement with things?

Keywords

alienation, commodification, environmental ethics, heating systems, television, wilderness

The Underlying Ethic of Technology

Some have argued that we live in an invisible iron cage. Indeed, technological forces are shaping people's lives in ways that they have little or no control over, especially if the basic framework of technology goes unchallenged; but, as Charles Taylor points out, the conquest of nature had a benevolent point to it. It was to serve humanity. So, he finds that, along with other forces, there are moral forces of work here shaping our lives. We live neither in an iron cage nor in an arena of unconstrained choice; we inhabit a possibility space where some moral choices are being made. There is a kind of ethical appeal to not letting our resources go to waste. So what ethical forces might be called upon to reform technology in a deep way? How should we understand the basic choice we face? For developing what I call the vision and underlying ethic of technology, I will draw heavily upon Albert Borgmann's theory of technology, the best account

of the character of the technological culture we have so far. Then we will use this vision of technology to show that the concerns of environmental ethics and people's better concerns for nature generally will be subverted by technology unless we as a culture come to grips with the irony of this vision and begin to make a fundamentally different choice, that is, choose things over consumption.

Making the Appeal of Technology Intelligible: The Promise of Technology

Neither Heidegger nor Thoreau makes clear what it is about technology that is attractive to people. Claiming that we delight in the exercise of power seems correct enough when we think of the enormous amount of power we wield with technology, yet this view does not address our more intelligible motives and, therefore, does not really address many of the proponents of technology without trivializing their concerns. In one way or another, most of us, if not all, see technology as good. What is at the heart of our petty homocentrism? What good is technology?

Typically people articulate what good technology is when they say that something is better or improved and demonstrate that "that's progress." Advertisements are continually pointing out what is better about the product advertised, even if the chief "advantage" is two for the price of one. Although they may well dupe us, these advertisements normally appeal to standards that at least on a deep and general level are already in place and widely shared in consumer culture. We hear everywhere around us, not just in advertisements, what better is. "It means less work." "It's more comfortable." "It's convenient." "It's healthier." "It's faster and more productive." "It's less of a hassle." "Sleeker looks better." "It's lighter." "It doesn't get in your way." "You don't have to wait on anyone else." "It's exciting." When we see the very latest devices, often our expressions are on the order of "Wow!" or "That's great!" or "Look at that, would you?" So, at deeper levels, there seems to be a good deal of like-mindedness about what constitutes better in our culture.

Another approach is to consider what people think of as clear examples of progress. Television today is far different from what it was in the past. In the early 50s, one was lucky to own a television. Reception was poor, the picture rough and in black and white; the screen was small, the set large; the number of programs was very limited. In addition to other obvious improvements, now the sets come on instantly, are controlled from the couch, can be found in all sizes and nearly everywhere, and have access to a vast number and variety of programs, especially with video cassette recorders. Even if they are not willing to pay the price for all of them, most count these changes as improvements, and rarely do we find people watching a black and white set any longer. What are the standards which make these changes count as improvements?

Television as a clear example of technology will play a key role in our understanding of the nature of the fundamental choice we face, but Borgmann uses another paradigmatic example of technology, the central heating system, to disclose most of these standards of technology. We can easily trace the development of central heating systems back to the wood-burning stove or the hearth. The chief advantages of the heating system over these latter two are various. Central heating *is easier*. We do not have to gather, stack, chop, or carry the wood. An automatic thermostat means that we do not have to

trouble ourselves in the morning or evening with setting a thermostat. Central heating is more *instantaneous*. We do not have to wait for the house to warm up. It's *ubiquitous*. Warmth is provided to each corner of the room, to every room, and everywhere equally well. Finally, a central heating system is *safer* than a hearth. My grandmother was born in a newly built chicken coop because three weeks earlier her family's house burnt down from a chimney fire. So the standards by which people judge central heating to be better than a wood-burning stove are ease, instantaneity, ubiquity, and safety or some combination of these, for example, convenience. These four "technological standards" can be collected under the more general notion of technological availability. To be more *available* is to be an improvement, then, in terms of one or more of the four above standards.

Why does it seem to people that this availability is good? From one perspective, this availability relieves people of burdens: less effort, less time, and less learning skills are required. Available anytime and anyplace, they are disburdened of the constraints of time and place. They are disburdened of having to take risks. Historically, modern technology was envisioned as enabling people not just to subjugate nature, but to do so for the purpose of freeing humanity from misery and toil. To be relieved of these burdens then, fulfills this vision of technology. *To the degree people personally share this vision,* they will also see its concrete manifestations, such as central heating, as unquestionably good. Compared to older versions, the latest portable computers exemplify this relief from burdens and are attractive to many for this reason.

By overcoming nature, technology would, as some in the seventeenth century foresaw, not only relieve humans of burdens, but it would make available to them—easier, safer, quicker, and more ubiquitous—all the goods of the Earth. So, technological availability negatively disburdens people of misery and toil, and positively enriches their lives, makes them happy, it seems. So seen, technology has an attractive glow about it.

Technology promises to bring the forces of nature and culture under control, to liberate us from misery and toil, and to enrich our lives . . .

[More accurately], implied in the technological mode of taking up with the world there is a promise that this approach to reality will, by way of the domination of nature, fuel liberation and enrichment.

Borgmann calls this "the promise of technology."

Clearly those below the middle-class of advanced industrialized countries and those outside those countries do not derive the benefits of technology, although many do feel the pull of its promise. The claims of social justice will not likely be met until the more privileged ones, the middle and higher classes of these industrialized countries, come to terms with the questionable character of technology's promise. So, the critique of technology I am developing here does not apply to those in poverty. It applies only to those who have too much.

For these latter, technology has made good on its promise in important ways. My grandmother's father died from what she believes was pneumonia when she was eleven, leaving her and her younger sister to perform heroic feats to save the cattle from starvation in the drought times of an extended winter that followed. Often hitching the team up before dawn and returning hours after dark, especially in winter, her family took an entire day to get to and from town sixteen miles away. For the privileged, then, many past hardships have now been conquered. Although we may have legitimate concerns about whether there is too much medical technology, no one could reasonably refuse every advance of modern medical technology. The weather will never be brought under control, but, via comfortable structures, nature's heat and cold, rain and snow are controlled as well as darkness and drought. Toilsome labor is largely eliminated within the culture of technology.

A reasonable person may reject motorcycles in favor of horses to do ranch work, but that person still rides to town on paved roads in a car, has parts shipped by air, reads a newspaper and books, transacts business over the phone, and owns at least a radio. No thoughtful person will want to turn her back on technology entirely. Thus, technology, by conquering nature, has relieved humans of severe burdens. Today we are still working to overcome those, such as cancer and AIDS, that remain. So, if

technology does not saddle us in the long run with more than it has relieved us from, it will have made good on this aspect of what at first seemed and still does seem promising about it. It could turn out that ozone depletion, global warming, ecosystem destruction, the population explosion, polluted land, air, streams and oceans, and human and mechanical errors will impose burdens far greater than those we were relieved from in the first place. To meet these problems certainly calls for a reform of present practices. We read or hear of these calls for reform nearly every day. More common critiques of technology, such as David Ehrenfeld's *The Arrogance of Humanism,* attempt to show that technology will fail its own standards, bringing disaster upon us.

Much as reform in these areas is needed and much as these pessimistic critiques deserve thoughtful consideration, the present work will turn to a uniquely different task. It grants and, in fact, seeks to have the reader appreciate, the genuine success of modern technology. Technology has relieved, and technology will, I assume for the purposes at hand, continue to relieve, humans of many hardships of the human condition.

So what is wrong with technology for those within the realm of its benefits? Underlying these standards of availability is really a vision of a good life that is free and prosperous. What is at the bottom of concern with technological availability is an aspiration for freedom and happiness. Most people, at least in the Western tradition, are concerned with liberty and prosperity. For Aristotle only the Greek free man was able to have sufficient time and sufficient wherewithal to develop the moral and intellectual virtues he thought to be required for happiness or eudaemonia. The Hebrew people's understanding of the covenant centered on an idea of prosperity. Jesus preached of a free and abundant life. The Enlightenment, as we see its results in "the pursuit of happiness" in our Declaration of Independence, is fully within this tradition. But to find agreement at this high level of abstraction is not to see that the crucial differences lie with the particular versions of freedom and prosperity. For Socrates living well had to do with human excellence and living a just life, not with materialism. The blessed life and the abundant life of the Hebrews and of Jesus was not commodity happiness. So, too, we must look carefully at the particular idea of freedom and prosperity governing people's attraction to technology, for only at this level of particularity will its misleading and harmful features begin to show. In other words, one can criticize the trivialized forms of freedom and prosperity on which the technological society is centered without, at the same time, criticizing freedom and prosperity more generally as a vision of the good life. Quite the contrary, we can call technology into question even more sharply by showing that technology fails to provide the free, prosperous, and good life we want in our waking moments.

Technological society offers a flattened vision of freedom and prosperity. The more disburdened, the better off I am according to this vision. So, the technological idea of freedom is really one of disburdenment. What about prosperity? Cellular phones are currently a status symbol. These devices which disburden people of the constraints of place are taken to be a sign of affluence because, generally, only the more prosperous have them. So, in part, to be prosperous is to have the latest, most refined device. A sign of affluence, too, is to be able to go to an undiscovered exotic place, have the most channels and compact discs, own specially designed clothing, own what no one else has yet. Thus, in part, to be prosperous is to own the most varied, the widest assortment of commodities. Finally, when people buy a product on sale they get both the commodity they purchased and still have money left over. Why is that attractive? Because they can buy something else with the money saved. They are better off that way, they think, because they get more items for the money. Thus people pursue prosperity through the standards of owning the *most numerous, widest variety, and the very latest (most refined)* commodities. The powers that be in the technological society own and control most of these items. Such is the picture of the good life envied by those keeping up with the Joneses. Our culture's vision of the good life is the goods life.

Does this vision really deliver a good life? If we say no merely because it differs from the blessed life according to Abraham, Moses, and the prophets, or from the Greeks' eudaemonia, our analysis would be dogmatic and presumptuous. Technology must be thought through; it will not be met by simply reacting against it. So, if we answer "no," as I will, then we must be able to provide good reasons.

The Technological Means to Freedom and Happiness: The Device

The ironic consequences of this vision of freedom and prosperity can be drawn out through a careful analysis of the peculiar way technology transforms, or more specifically, dominates nature and culture. Technology does not dominate these in the traditional manner of lording it over them; rather, as Albert Borgmann shows, technology follows a pattern, unique to the modern era, in the way it gets everything under control. We can expose this pattern by examining instances of it.

The central heating system dominates warmth; it brings warmth under control in ways that the wood-burning stoves do not. To show its unique form of domination, Borgmann distinguishes between "things" and "devices." A thing in his sense

> is inseparable from its context, namely its world, and from our commerce with the thing and its world, namely, engagement. The experience of a thing is always and also a bodily and social engagement with the thing's world . . . Thus a stove used to furnish more than mere warmth. It was a *focus,* a hearth, a place that gathered the work and leisure of a family and gave the house a center. Its coldness marked the morning, and the spreading of its warmth marked the beginning of the day. It assigned to various family members tasks that defined their place in the household . . . It provided the entire family a regular and bodily engagement with the rhythm of the seasons that was woven together with the threat of cold and the solace of warmth, the smell of wood smoke, the exertion of sawing and carrying, the teaching of skills, and the fidelity to daily tasks . . . Physical engagement is not simply physical contact but the experience of the world through the manifold sensibility of the body. That sensibility is

sharpened and strengthened in skill. Skill is intensive and refined world engagement.

Here, in his retrieval of the thing's world and our engagement with the thing, Borgmann has been influenced by Heidegger's fourfold account of things. Obviously, Earth and sky are woven together with mortals. He points out that in Roman times the hearth was the abode of household gods, though he does not make much of it. Borgmann's account goes beyond Heidegger in emphasizing social and bodily engagement to a degree to which Heidegger seems insensitive. He also steps beyond Heidegger by highlighting the way things focus practices. Practices call for skills and the development of character; the diversity of different characters is joined to each other through participating in a world of practices. In our terms developed earlier, the hearth is the correlational coexistent thing which establishes the world of the household and, correlatively, calls forth its members and calls on their deeper capacities.

Today the hearth, if it exists at all, is no longer the central location in the house although the mantel still remains a place of honor. What has replaced the thing is the "device." The device (the central heating system) provides a commodity, one element of the original thing (warmth alone) and disburdens people of all the elements that compose the world and engaging character of the thing. This world of the thing, its ties to the natural and cultural world and our engagement with that many-dimensional world on bodily, cerebral, and social levels, is taken over by the *machinery* (the central heating plant itself) of the device.

> The machinery makes no demands on our skill, strength, or attention, and it is less demanding the less it makes its presence felt. In the progress of technology, the machinery of the device has therefore a tendency to become concealed or to shrink. Of all the physical properties of a device, those alone are crucial and prominent which constitute the commodity that the device procures.

To make the commodity even more technologically available, the machinery varies radically in the history of technology (wood or coal or oil or electricity or gas). Owing to this radical variability and to

this concealment, the machinery becomes necessarily *unfamiliar.* I probably do not know by what means the water is heated in a building. But the device is not just machinery or even most importantly machinery. The device makes available a commodity—warmth. Warmth is what the central heating system is for. Just the opposite of the machinery, the commodity tends to *expand* (become ubiquitous in the house), to remain relatively *fixed* as the means change (from coal to electricity) and to be *familiar.* It follows that—unlike with things—there is a wide division between what a device provides, the commodity, and how it provides this commodity, the machinery. Hence, and this is Borgmann's central insight we saw illustrated earlier with second homes, devices *split* means and ends into mere means and mere ends.

Even though these claims that a thing makes on people are not always experienced as burdensome (as we see from the above account), this very world of the thing and the engagement it calls for can be felt at times as a burden or hassle. The technological device and its refinement *disburdens* people of all these problems by expanding the commodity, so that the world of the thing no longer determines when, in what way, and where it is available. Thus, it disburdens them of the claims that call for engagement. In short, the technological device disburdens people of the thing's world and its claims upon them. The device is considered the more refined the more it lifts these burdens from them. The ideal device is one where, from an experiential standpoint, a commodity can be enjoyed unencumbered by means. A reliable self-regulating central heating system whose maintenance and energy bill are taken care of by a management agency can be taken as a paradigmatic example.

The peculiar way technology dominates things is not limited, of course, to the central heating system. Considering how household technologies have changed, Witold Rybczynski in *Home: A Short History of An Idea* writes:

> The evolution of domestic technology . . . demonstrates that the history of physical amenities can be divided into two major phases: all the years leading up to 1890, and the three following

decades. If this sounds outlandish, it is worth re-minding ourselves that tall "modern" devices that contribute to our domestic comfort—central heating, indoor plumbing, running hot and cold water, electric light and power and eleva-tors—were unavailable before 1890, and were well known by 1920. We live, like it or not, on the fair side of a great technological divide. As John Lukacs reminds us, although the home of 1930 would be familiar to us, it would have been unrecognizable to the citizen of 1885.

Just as with household technologies, so too with other features of our surroundings and our cultural and natural environment generally. This thing-to-device example is representative of the pattern of the technological transformations of the Earth. Generally then, this transformation is one in which:

> Devices . . . dissolve the coherent and engaging character of the pre-technological world of things. In a device, the relatedness of the world is replaced by a machinery, but the machinery is concealed, and the commodities, which are made available by a device, are enjoyed without the encumbrance of or the engagement with a context [that is, the world of the thing].

Borgmann calls this pattern the *device paradigm*. At times I will call it the separation pattern of technology.

We can understand our age as one in which we reduce everything to resources that we want to control. Now we can see that the device pattern is used to get control of these resources. The purpose of the device is to supply people with unencumbered commodities. So now we can develop this picture of our age further. The fuller vision is one in which everything gets reduced to resources, machinery and commodities.

Ironic Consequences

So far we have developed a theory by which we can interpret what has taken and is taking place with re-gard to the technological transformation in our time. Using this theory we can pass from techno-logical object to technological object, seeing how they more or less fit the pattern. The illustration of the pattern does not commit us as yet to an evalua-tion of the good or bad of what has taken place. Now we are in a position to begin that task. What are the consequences of this change from things to devices?

Don Ihde finds that technologies transform ex-perience in a "non-neutral" manner. A tool always amplifies in some way certain aspects of normal embodied experience while simultaneously reduc-ing other aspects. A dentist's probe shows the hard-ness and cavities in a tooth to a degree fingers miss, while the wetness and warmth of the tooth felt by the fingers go undetected by probe. This change Ihde finds is non-neutral because the amplified fea-tures are heightened, drawing our attention, while the reduced features tend to go unheeded and are overlooked and often forgotten. Asked what a hearth is for, we find it logical, after having experi-enced central heating, to answer that it supplies heat, ignoring or not even seeing its other aspects. Extending Ihde's insight makes it more intelligible why we become fascinated with commodities, heedless of what has been reduced. Yet pointing out that this change is non-neutral is not enough. We now want to comprehend what exactly has been hidden from us. We need a language which ar-ticulates what is overlooked and forgotten, for then we can see in what ways this change is non-neutral. Our language of things retrieves and focuses this loss. It reveals the general pattern that things are transformed into devices, detaching people from things, their world, and each other.

Ihde further argues that these lost features only tend to recede, thus, implying that they are retriev-able. With certain kinds of instruments (not all technological objects are devices, splitting means and ends), this is true. We can easily retrieve the fea-tures missed by the dentist's probe. With devices, however, these features do not just tend to with-draw, so that a change of attitude, perception, or act of will could retrieve them. Notice that mere warmth, no matter how expanded the commod-ity has become, is not a substitute for the thing of the wood-burning stove. Mere warmth could not be the essence of a household; it does not warrant the kind of attention or care, of heeding. Indeed the source itself is concealed and the warmth is suffused throughout the house so that it fails to provide a focus. So warmth is no substitute for the thing because it lacks a world with which to become engaged. More than this, because it is impossible to recover in the mere warmth of the central heating plant, the full-bodied experience of the hearth, the machinery of devices ineluctably withdraws the world from people. A device is necessarily unfamiliar in the ways that the context of the thing was familiar. Thus the transformation of the thing into a device does not merely tend to obscure possibilities of experience, but its very material structure makes the rich experience of the thing impossible.

Another way of putting this is that devices allow the possibility of only slim points of contact with "narrowly defined aspects of what used to be things of depth." Devices force people to take them as commodity bearers; they leave them no choice. So our way of taking commodities is not a psychological matter, but a real matter. Technology is not only a way of seeing (and for this reason characterizing technology as a vision is perhaps misleading), it is more importantly a way of *shaping*. The very material structure of a device is such that it can be experienced only as holding up a commodity calling for consumption and nothing more.

The implication of this change of shape is alienation. What seemed promising at the outset—relieving people of burdens—leads ironically to disengagement, diversion, distraction, and loneliness. In short, we become not-at-home in the universe. But clearly, simply finding ourselves free from the exclusive use of candles and outhouses does not place us in this alienated position. So how can such positive events as electric lighting and indoor plumbing lead to these ironic results?

To be relieved of famine, cold, darkness, confinement, and other genuine adversities of the human condition was an intelligible and urgent demand for the early phase of modern technology. For the middle-classes of advanced industrialized countries, most, not all, of these kinds of challenges have been met for some time. At the stage of mature technology, the challenges can be quite frivolous. Food processors, electric pencil sharpeners, prepared fishing leaders, automatic cameras, elec-

tric knives, and some pain relievers are typical. The basic question here is: Do we need to be relieved of every last and least burden? Aren't some of these burdens actually good in senses that touch our very humanity? When people reflect on these questions they may answer them differently, but when they act, they tend to act in agreement with a vision that seeks to bring everything under control. Ironically, in the wake of such technological success, in the wake of the initial excitement over owning the latest item, the item falls back into the ordinary every day and they become bored. Being bored, they become disengaged and alienated from what may have been a vital practice, such as preparing meals or gardening or photography. Accordingly, they seek diversion. Thus, ironic consequences follow from the disburdenment of every hassle, problem, or felt demand. If we pursue disburdenment in this unchecked and unreflective manner, as people are doing in the stage of mature technology, then these are the results we should expect.

However, it may seem as though we have been just too nostalgic. The disburdenment devices yield "frees us up for other things" as people commonly say. Yet this perspective makes us think that technology is mostly about freedom, as Charles Taylor thinks, when the promise and vision of technology are mostly a promise of happiness. The most unique and devastating critique of technology is not centered on technological freedom, but on the fact that technology *fails most where it succeeds most* at procuring happiness, at procuring the good things of life. As a culture, we think not only that we can use technology to liberate us, but also that we can use it to fill that new possibility space with technologically available goods. In short, what people are freed up for are not other things, but *more commodities*. Then too when people imagine what they are doing as they throw food into the microwave as freeing themselves up for other and more important things, they ignore how pervasive the technological order is. The totality of technological devices is far more consequential than any particular device. The former point can be advanced best by developing the latter first.

Extensively yet unobtrusively this technological way of taking up with the world pervades and informs what people think, say and do. We need an account of technology as *correlational environment*. Organizations, institutions, the ways nature and culture are arranged and accessible all become modeled on the device. As people make more decisions for consumption against engagement, our average, everyday world is stamped more deeply with the pattern of the device. In other words, devices do not simply liberate people from some things and free them for other and better things. We are surrounded. The things enabling correlational coexistence have nearly disappeared. As the totality of our daily environment changes from an environment of things to an environment of devices, from an environment making demands on people to an environment that is more at their fingertips, this change necessarily entails heedlessness and evokes an attitude of cultural petty homocentrism. So it is important to consider not just the appropriateness of this or that device in a particular context, but to consider what the consequences are of the totality of these devices and people's *typical* use of them. We would expect the consumptive ways of life in such surroundings to be disburdened and disengaged.

So what are people finally freed up for? How do they attempt to use technological means to positively enrich their lives? Typically people use devices to procure entertainment commodities. Hence our culture treats tradition, culture, and nature as resources to be mined. Just as ubiquitously available warmth is not a substitute for the hearth, entertainment commodities are at best insubstantial aspects of the original things. Because they use devices here to procure the delights that matter, final things, these entertainment commodities can be thought of as final commodities. In this respect, to consume a final commodity is no different from consuming an instrumental one that disburdens us of a chore.

The Ironic Consequences of Final Consumption

Television is a clear example of a final commodity. Its refinements from the first sets to those of today fit the same pattern as the refinements in central heating and the refinements of devices in accordance with Borgmann's device paradigm in general. So television is an instance of the vision of domination, liberation, and enrichment. It does not make demands on people and is a window of the world, making all the goods of the Earth available, technologically available, to them in their living rooms.

Understandably, television has tremendous appeal to us as a culture. It's where technology comes home to people. The amount of time they spend watching it indicates its power.

> The A.C. Nielsen Company (1989) currently estimates that people in the United States view upwards of 4 hours of television each day. Given the likelihood that such estimates are inflated, let us assume a more conservative estimate of 2 1/2 hours of television viewing per day over the period of a lifetime. Even at this more conservative rate, a typical American would spend more than 7 full years watching television out of the approximately 47 waking years each of us lives by age 70—this assuming an average of 8 hours of sleep per day. Such a figure is even more striking when we consider that Americans have about 5 1/2 hours a day of free time, or approximately 16 years available for leisure of the same 47-year span. From this point of view and based on a conservative estimate, Americans are spending nearly half of their available free time watching television.

Since it is the most popular way people enjoy final consumption, it is worthwhile to examine in detail the *experience* of this form of consumption as we develop the ironic consequences of final consumption. *Television and the Quality of Life* by Robert Kubey and Mihaly Csikszentmihalyi (cited above) do just that, examining systematically the reported experience of television in contrast to the reported experience of other activities people spend time on in their daily life. So we need to look closely at their findings with a view to showing how technology in the form of TV does not fulfill its promise.

Kubey and Csikszentmihalyi find that television is inexpensive and is easily and quickly available for those who have time for it. It helps people to relax and, at times, may help some to retreat before gathering themselves to face a difficulty. People can watch it for prolonged periods without wearing themselves out physically. It tends to bring families together and family members normally do talk with each other while watching. They also feel better than when watching alone. It is used for news programs, for nature shows, and to present dramas such as *Death of a Salesman*. It could be used to present lectures in chemistry and Plato. It helps connect us with our culture and some of its common stories. On the other hand, "viewing is almost always mildly rewarding in that it provides relaxation, distraction, and escape with minimal effort." It gives people something to do with their time and most report they do want to watch it. With so much of our leisure time taken up with television and with so many benefits, one might mistakenly conclude that people choose to watch because it is better than anything else they could be doing. Yet the actual cumulative benefits they receive from television are rather low and often negative.

Ironically, the reported experience of people viewing television often turns out to be one of disappointment. Not only are chemistry courses not aired because few would watch them, not only do most people gravitate toward watching movies with light and escapist content rather than challenging dramas, but, just as important, half the people who watch television do not use television guides to help them decide what to watch. The stories viewers share, then, are not those shown on public television. The shows tend to support existing beliefs. As Stu Silverman told Kubey, "Television reassures us, it's 'nice,' it doesn't offend or challenge an audience. It is designed to do just the opposite of art, to reassure rather than excite. That often is what people want." Although television does help people to relax, it does not do so any more than other activities such as reading. Moreover, it helps people relax only while watching it and not later as sports and other activities do. Although this study found that television is not a completely passive activity, it is comparatively so. It is not usually challenging, requires little mental alertness, and is reported to exact fewer skills than eating. Only idling was reported to be more passive. Unlike activities that gather and restore a person, a "passive spillover effect" tended to follow watching television, making people feel duller,

more passive, and less able to concentrate. Families for which television provides a center also experience this spillover effect carried over into other family activities. Finally, the positive benefits one receives from television tend to be enjoyed less the more one watches. Heavy viewers are not made happy by watching it; they generally feel worse than light viewers both before and after viewing. Even light viewers do not report themselves to be any happier than average while watching.

Aristotle found amusement, like sleep, to be therapeutic as long as life is oriented around exertion. So, too, Kubey and Csikszentmihalyi find that those who stand to benefit most from television use and need it least. More often television is used to disburden people of problems in ways that do not go to the roots of the problems, are only marginally effective, and, hence, are entirely inappropriate. People disburden themselves of the problem of leisure time that their time-saving and labor-saving devices have created by killing time watching television. They disburden themselves of the problem of loneliness when devices leave them isolated by turning on a device, the television set. Heavy use is higher among singles. Such an answer to loneliness is only a diversion from genuine forms of social engagement. On the other hand, television is often used as a way for family members, usually fathers, to avoid talking with other family members and avoid dealing with family problems. Television resolves the problem of independently ordering one's life, of giving shape to the day. It takes care of boredom. Heavy television viewing is likely driven by a wish to escape, to be disburdened of bad days and bad moods, of personal problems and of alienation from self. Diverting one's attention, it tends to mask the deeper and more real problems a person is having and, hence, leaves these problems unintelligently resolved. Does it meet the task of leading a more rewarding and meaningful life? No. "Happiness is a more complex state than relaxation. It requires a more elusive set of conditions, and is therefore more difficult to obtain." Television seems to "encourage a false sense of well-being in some people," distracting them from and becoming an obstacle to the hard work it takes to realize one's potentials.

More indirectly, we can ask what people are missing when they watch television. When viewers are not pleased with the amount of time they watch television, the entire reason is not only that it is a low-grade activity, one that many think best fits the phrase "Am I lazy!" Part of the reason, too, has to do with what television is displacing. Many report that they feel as though they should have been doing something else. College educated viewers felt this way more often than other people because "they should have been doing something more productive." Television rearranges life through decreasing the amount of time spent involved with other activities. It at times provides a center for the household, but such a center seems flimsy at best, especially in comparison with other potential centers or centers of the past. In another context, Kubey and Csikszentmihalyi speak of these kinds of centers of life.

> When people are asked what they enjoy most, and enough time is left for a genuine answer to emerge, we often find that the most enjoyable things involve doing something, and usually something rather complex and demanding. Rarely does watching television get mentioned, or any other passive or consummatory activity . . . The first reflex for many people is to say that one most enjoys going on vacations, going to movies or restaurants—the typical "leisure" responses in our culture. But as people think more deeply about their real feelings they will mention enjoyable times with their families, and then there is often a point when their faces light up and they say something like: "Actually, the best times in my life have been . . ." and start talking with great enthusiasm about designing and sewing quilts, rock climbing, playing music, working on a basement lathe, or about other activities that require concentrated skill, that do not separate the individual from the end result of his or her effort, and that provide the kind of exhilaration and high focused attention of flow. So . . . we are still able to keep in sight those *vivid signposts* that show what it is that makes life worth living . . . [On] reflecting on such occasions, people often say that not only was the experience enjoyable at

the time, but that it helped them grow and become more than they had been. Compared to such optimal experiences, much television watching could be deemed a waste of time . . . wasting it amounts to wasting life.

Casting television in terms of the symmetrical relationship of correlational coexistence developed earlier, we can see that the medium is just not enough for humans to make the center of their lives. It does not call forth their humanity in any depth. Hence, Kubey and Csikszentmihalyi worry that by spending so much time viewing television "one may well lose opportunities to grow as a human being."

Kubey and Csikszentmihalyi find that a mistaken cultural assumption underlies much of the appeal of television. For them the mistaken cultural assumption is narrowly one of thinking that physical and mental exertion are bad, and that they are unrelated to human growth and living a worthwhile life. In contrast, for us, the more comprehensive mistaken assumption is that technology generally can fulfill our aspirations for freedom and enrichment. Considered from the standpoint of the vision of technology, television is a paradigmatic example of and not an exception to the unimpeded development of technological culture. As for liberation, it is a commodity which does not make demands—in dress, transportation, or manners, or even having to be at home when a program is aired. Following the device's split between means and ends, people exert themselves in labor and expect to relax completely in leisure. They want amusement, not challenge or disturbance. In terms of prosperity, with video cassette players and hundreds of channels, the most, the most varied, and the latest programs can be watched. Advertisements, too, and the settings of the programs themselves celebrate this prosperity of technology. In short, the incredible attraction of television is that it is the homeplace of the vision people are still spellbound by. It confirms them in that vision and tells them what's what in the universe. Its glamour binds and soothes while simultaneously disappointing them with the flatness and shallowness of its nourishment, its ironic unfulfillment. Television as an exemplar of a final commodity represents the ultimate appeal of the promise of technology. It is, then, the success story of the technology. Television is the vision of technological culture.

So while technology is successful on its own terms when it make goods available, its success is merely a Pyrrhic victory. What makes good things rich and involving has been lost. We have been seduced by a shallow semblance. Thus, technology fails to deliver happiness, not because it fails to make goods available, but because such goods as it does make available turn out to be merely ironic goods. What seemed promising in the appearance is disappointing in the reality. Our aspirations for freedom and happiness go awry when we attempt to procure them with devices.

So does technology deliver the goods? Does technology help people live more rewarding and meaningful lives? As people make the things that count in their lives technologically available, they empty them of depth and they lose them. It is a lesson our culture has yet to learn when we let television turn us into something less than members of the animal kingdom.

Part II

Contemporary Technology and the Future

- Globalization, Economics, and Human Rights

- Computers, Robotics, and Information Technology

- Biotechnology and Genetic Engineering

- Population, Energy, and the Environment

Globalization, Economics, and Human Rights

II.1   THOMAS FRIEDMAN

The New System

In this selection from his book *The Lexus and the Olive Tree,* Thomas Friedman, the Pulitzer Prize–winning foreign affairs columnist of *The New York Times,* discusses the phenomenon of globalization. While it may seem odd to include the topic of globalization in a book dealing with the social and ethical issues arising from technological innovation, Friedman's description makes it clear that "Globalization has its own defining technologies: computerization, miniaturization, digitization, satellite communications, fiber optics and the Internet, which reinforce its defining perspective of integration." These technologies are more than just metaphors: They are the critical technologies, along with rapid transportation by container ships and jet-powered air freight, that make possible the globalized financial markets, mass production, and trade that are the defining economic features of the current age. Instantaneous communication and rapid transportation produce global interconnectedness, and this has shifted the rules of the game for corporations as well as governments by placing a premium on innovation and the ability to adapt to change. The technologies of the globalization system have also shifted the balance of power away from national states and toward multinational corporations, global markets, and to "Super-empowered individuals" who know how to leverage these new technologies to produce systemwide effects on international affairs. This dynamic new system contains both threats and opportunities, and we need to understand how it works to navigate a path to the future.

Focus Questions

1. How does Friedman define globalization? What is the dominant culture of globalization and how might this be perceived as a threat by some groups of people?
2. How is the globalization system different from the Cold War system that preceded it? What are the defining characteristics of each of these systems of international relations?
3. Friedman claims that globalization has its own defining structure of power. What are the main elements of this new structure of power and how have new technologies produced these new kinds of power balances?
4. Compare Friedman's view of globalization to those discussed by Bhagwati (selection II.3) and the United Nations (selection II.5). Who are the "winners" and "losers" in today's globalization system?

Keywords

Cold War, competition, creative destruction, free-market capitalism, globalization, homogenization, innovation

WHAT WAS IT THAT FORREST GUMP'S MAMA LIKED to say? Life is like a box of chocolates: you never know what you're going to get inside. For me, an inveterate traveler and foreign correspondent, life is like room service—you never know what you're going to find outside your door.

Take for instance the evening of December 31, 1994, when I began my assignment as the foreign affairs columnist for *The New York Times*. I started the column by writing from Tokyo, and when I arrived at the Okura Hotel after a long transpacific flight, I called room service with one simple request: "Could you please send me up four oranges." I am addicted to citrus and I needed a fix. It seemed to me a simple enough order when I telephoned it in, and the person on the other end seemed to understand. About twenty minutes later there was a knock at my door. A room service waiter was standing there in his perfectly creased uniform. In front of him was a cart covered by a starched white tablecloth. On the tablecloth were four tall glasses of fresh-squeezed orange juice, each glass set regally in a small silver bowl of ice.

"No, no," I said to the waiter, "I want oranges, oranges—not orange juice." I then pretended to bite into something like an orange.

"Ahhhh," the waiter said, nodding his head. "O-ranges, o-ranges."

I retreated into my room and went back to work. Twenty minutes later there was another knock at my door. Same waiter. Same linen-covered room service trolley. But this time, on it were four plates and on each plate was an orange that had been peeled and diced into perfect little sections that were fanned out on a plate like sushi, as only the Japanese can do.

"No, no," I said, shaking my head again. "I want the whole orange." I made a ball shape with my hands. "I want to keep them in my room and eat them for snacks. I can't eat four oranges all cut up like that. I can't store them in my mini-bar. I want the whole orange."

Again, I did my best exaggerated imitation of someone eating an orange.

"Ahhhh," the waiter said, nodding his head. "O-range, o-range. You want whole o-range."

Another twenty minutes went by. Again there was a knock on my door. Same waiter. Same trolley, only this time he had four bright oranges, each one on its own dinner plate, with a fork, knife and linen napkin next to it. That was progress.

"That's right," I said, signing the bill. "That's just what I wanted."

As he left the room, I looked down at the room service bill. The four oranges were $22. How am I going to explain that to my publisher?

But my citrus adventures were not over. Two weeks later I was in Hanoi, having dinner by myself in the dining room of the Metropole Hotel. It was the tangerine season in Vietnam, and vendors were selling pyramids of the most delicious, bright orange tangerines on every street corner. Each morning I had a few tangerines for breakfast. When the waiter came to get my dessert order I told him all I wanted was a tangerine.

He went away and came back a few minutes later.

"Sorry," he said, "no tangerines."

"But how can that be?" I asked in exasperation. "You have a table full of them at breakfast every morning! Surely there must be a tangerine somewhere back in the kitchen?"

"Sorry." He shook his head. "Maybe you like watermelon?"

"O.K.," I said, "bring me some watermelon."

Five minutes later the waiter returned with a plate bearing three peeled tangerines on it.

"I found the tangerines," he said. "No watermelon."

Had I known then what I know now I would have taken it all as a harbinger. For I too would find a lot of things on my plate and outside my door that I wasn't planning to find as I traveled the globe for the *Times*.

Being the foreign affairs columnist for *The New York Times* is actually the best job in the world. I mean, someone has to have the best job, right? Well, I've got it. The reason it is such a great job is that I get to be a tourist with an attitude. I get to go anywhere, anytime, and have attitudes about what I see and hear. But the question for me as I embarked on this odyssey was: Which attitudes? What would be the lens, the perspective, the organizing system—the superstory—through which I would look at the world, make sense of events, prioritize them, opine upon them and help readers understand them?

In some ways my predecessors had it a little easier. They each had a very obvious superstory and international system in place when they were writing. I am the fifth foreign affairs columnist in the history of the *Times*. "Foreign Affairs" is actually the paper's oldest column. It was begun in 1937 by a remarkable woman, Anne O'Hare McCormick, and was originally called "In Europe," because in those days, "in Europe" was foreign affairs for most Americans, and it seemed perfectly natural that the paper's one overseas columnist would be located on the European continent. Mrs. McCormick's 1954 obituary in the *Times* said she got her start in foreign reporting "as the wife of Mr. McCormick, a Dayton engineer whom she accompanied on frequent buying trips to Europe." (*New York Times* obits have become considerably more politically correct since then.) The international system which she covered was the disintegration of balance-of-power Versailles Europe and the beginnings of World War II.

As America emerged from World War II, standing astride the world as the preeminent superpower, with global responsibilities and engaged in a global power struggle with the Soviet Union, the title of the column changed in 1954 to "Foreign Affairs." Suddenly the whole world was America's playing field and the whole world mattered, because every corner was being contested with the Soviet Union. The Cold War international system, with its competition for influence and supremacy between the capitalist West and the communist East, between Washington, Moscow and Beijing, became the superstory within which the next three foreign affairs columnists organized their opinions.

By the time I started the column at the beginning of 1995, though, the Cold War was over. The Berlin Wall had crumbled and the Soviet Union was history. I had the good fortune to witness, in the Kremlin, one of the last gasps of the Soviet Union. The day was December 16, 1991. Secretary of State James A. Baker III was visiting Moscow, just as Boris Yeltsin was easing Mikhail Gorbachev out of power. Whenever Baker had met Gorbachev previously, they had held their talks in the Kremlin's gold-gilded St. Catherine Hall. There was always a very orchestrated entry scene for the press. Mr. Baker and his entourage would wait behind two huge wooden double doors on one end of the long Kremlin hall, with Gorbachev and his team behind the doors on the other end. And then, by some signal, the doors would simultaneously open and each man would stride out and they would shake hands in front of the cameras in the middle of the room. Well, on this day Baker arrived for his meeting at the appointed hour, the doors swung open and Boris Yeltsin walked out, instead of Gorbachev. Guess who's coming to dinner! "Welcome to Russian soil and this Russian building," Yeltsin said to Baker. Baker did meet Gorbachev later in the day, but it was clear that power had shifted. We State Department reporters who were there to chronicle the event ended up spending that whole day in the Kremlin. It snowed heavily while we were inside, and when we finally walked out after sunset we found the Kremlin grounds covered in a white snow blanket. As we trudged to the Kremlin's Spassky Gate, our shoes crunching fresh tracks in the snow, I noticed that the red Soviet hammer and sickle was still flying atop the Kremlin flagpole, illuminated by a spotlight as it had been for some seventy years. I said to myself, "That is probably the last time I'll ever see that flag flying there." In a few weeks it was indeed gone, and with it went the Cold War system and superstory.

But what wasn't clear to me as I embarked upon my column assignment a few years later was what had replaced the Cold War system as the dominant organizing framework for international affairs. So I actually began my column as a tourist without an attitude—just an open mind. For several years, I, like everyone else, just referred to "the post–Cold War world." We knew some new system was aborning that constituted a different framework for international relations, but we couldn't define what it was, so we defined it by what it wasn't. It wasn't the Cold War. So we called it the post–Cold War world.

The more I traveled, though, the more it became apparent to me that we were not just in some messy, incoherent, indefinable post–Cold War world. Rather, we were in a new international system. This new system had its own unique logic, rules, pressures and incentives and it deserved its own name: "globalization." Globalization is not just some economic fad, and it is not just a passing trend. It is an international system—the dominant international system that replaced the Cold War system after the fall of the Berlin Wall. We need to understand it as such. If there can be a statute of limitations on crimes, then surely there must be a statute of limitations on foreign policy clichés. With that in mind, the "post-Cold War world" should be declared over. We are now in the new international system of globalization.

When I say that globalization has replaced the Cold War as the defining international system, what exactly do I mean?

I mean that, as an international system, the Cold War had its own structure of power: the balance between the United States and the U.S.S.R. The Cold War had its own rules: in foreign affairs, neither superpower would encroach on the other's sphere of influence; in economics, less developed countries would focus on nurturing their own national industries, developing countries on export-led growth, communist countries on autarky and Western economies on regulated trade. The Cold War had its own dominant ideas: the clash between communism and capitalism, as well as détente, nonalignment and perestroika. The Cold War had its own demographic trends: the movement of people from east to west was largely frozen by the Iron Curtain, but the movement from south to north was a more steady flow. The Cold War had its own perspective on the globe: the world was a space divided into the communist camp, the Western camp, and the neutral camp, and everyone's country was in one of them. The Cold War had its own defining technologies: nuclear weapons and the second Industrial Revolution were dominant, but for many people in developing countries the hammer and sickle were still relevant tools. The Cold War had its own defining measurement: the throw weight of nuclear missiles. And lastly, the Cold War had its own defining anxiety: nuclear annihilation. When taken all together the elements of this Cold War

system influenced the domestic politics, commerce and foreign relations of virtually every country in the world. The Cold War system didn't shape everything, but it shaped many things.

Today's era of globalization is a similar international system, with its own unique attributes, which contrast sharply with those of the Cold War. To begin with the Cold War system was characterized by one over-arching feature–division. The world was a divided-up, chopped-up place and both your threats and opportunities in the Cold War system tended to grow out of who you were divided from. Appropriately, this Cold War system was symbolized by a single word: the *wall*—the Berlin Wall. One of my favorite descriptions of that world was provided by Jack Nicholson in the movie *A Few Good Men*. Nicholson plays a Marine colonel who is the commander of the U.S. base in Cuba, at Guantánamo Bay. In the climactic scene of the movie, Nicholson is pressed by Tom Cruise to explain how a certain weak soldier under Nicholson's command, Santiago, was beaten to death by his own fellow Marines: "You want answers?" shouts Nicholson. "You want answers?" I want the truth, retorts Cruise. "You can't handle the truth," says Nicholson. "Son, we live in a world that has walls and those walls have to be guarded by men with guns. Who's gonna do it? You? You, Lieutenant Weinberg? I have a greater responsibility than you can possibly fathom. You weep for Santiago and you curse the Marines. You have that luxury. You have the luxury of not knowing what I know—that Santiago's death, while tragic, probably saved lives. And my existence, while grotesque and incomprehensible to you, saves lives. You don't want the truth because deep down in places you don't talk about at parties, you want me on that wall. You need me on that wall."

The globalization system is a bit different. It also has one overarching feature—integration. The world has become an increasingly interwoven place, and today, whether you are a company or a country, your threats and opportunities increasingly derive from who you are connected to. This globalization system is also characterized by a single word: the Web. So in the broadest sense we have gone from a system built around division and walls to a system increasingly built around integration and webs. In the Cold War we reached for the 'hot-line," which was a symbol that we were all divided but at least two people were in charge—the United States and the Soviet Union—and in the globalization system we reach for the Internet, which is a symbol that we are all increasingly connected and nobody is quite in charge.

This leads to many other differences between the globalization system and the Cold War system. The globalization system, unlike the Cold War system, is not frozen, but a dynamic ongoing process. That's why I define globalization this way: it is the inexorable integration of markets, nation-states and technologies to a degree never witnessed before—in a way that is enabling individuals, corporations and nation-states to reach around the world farther, faster, deeper and cheaper than ever before, and in a way that is enabling the world to reach into individuals, corporations and nation-states farther, faster, deeper, cheaper than ever before. This process of globalization is also producing a powerful backlash from those brutalized or left behind by this new system.

The driving idea behind globalization is free-market capitalism—the more you let market forces rule and the more you open your economy to free trade and competition, the more efficient and flourishing your economy will be. Globalization means the spread of free-market capitalism to virtually every country in the world. Therefore, globalization also has its own set of economic rules—rules that revolve around opening, deregulating and privatizing your economy, in order to make it more competitive and attractive to foreign investment. In 1975, at the height of the Cold War, only 8 percent of countries worldwide had liberal, free-market capital regimes, and foreign direct investment at the time totaled only $23 billion, according to the World Bank. By 1997, the number of countries with liberal economic regimes constituted 28 percent, and foreign investment totaled $644 billion.

Unlike the Cold War system, globalization has its own dominant culture, which is why it tends to be homogenizing to a certain degree. In previous eras this sort of cultural homogenization happened on a regional scale—the Romanization of Western Europe and the Mediterranean world, the Islamification of Central Asia, North Africa, Europe and the Middle East by the Arabs and later the Ottomans, or the Russification of Eastern and Central Europe and parts of Eurasia under the Soviets. Culturally speaking, globalization has tended to involve the spread (for better and for worse) of Americanization—from Big Macs to iMacs to Mickey-Mouse.

Globalization has its own defining technologies: computerization, miniaturization, digitization, satellite communications, fiber optics and the Internet, which reinforce its defining perspective of integration. Once a country makes the leap into the system of globalization, its elites begin to internalize this perspective of integration, and always try to locate themselves in a global context. I was visiting Amman, Jordan, in the summer of 1998 and having coffee at the Inter-Continental Hotel with my friend Rami Khouri, the leading political columnist in Jordan. We sat down and I asked him what was new. The first thing he said to me was: "Jordan was just added to CNN's world-wide weather highlights." What Rami was saying was that it is important for Jordan to know that those institutions which think globally believe it is now worth knowing what the weather is like in Amman. It makes Jordanians feel more important and holds out the hope that they will be enriched by having more tourists or global investors visiting. The day after seeing Rami I happened to go to Israel and meet with Jacob Frenkel, governor of Israel's Central Bank and a University of Chicago–trained economist. Frenkel remarked that he too was going through a perspective change: "Before, when we talked about macroeconomics, we started by looking at the local markets, local financial systems and the interrelationship between them, and then, as an afterthought, we looked at the international economy. There was a feeling that what we do is primarily our own business and then there are some outlets where we will sell abroad. Now we reverse the perspective. Let's not ask what markets we should export to, after having decided what to produce; rather let's first study the global framework within which we operate and then decide what to produce. It changes your whole perspective."

While the defining measurement of the Cold War was weight—particularly the throw weight of missiles—the defining measurement of the globalization system is speed—speed of commerce, travel, communication and innovation. The Cold War was about Einstein's mass-energy equation, $e = mc^2$. Globalization tends to revolve around Moore's Law, which states that the computing power of silicon chips will double every eighteen to twenty-four months, while the price will halve. In the Cold War, the most frequently asked question was: "Whose side are you on?" In globalization, the most frequently asked question is: "To what extent are you connected to everyone?" In the Cold War, the second most frequently asked question was: "How big is your missile?" In globalization, the second most frequently asked question is: "How fast is your modem?" The defining document of the Cold War system was "The Treaty." The defining document of globalization is "The Deal." The Cold War system even had its own style. In 1961, according to *Foreign Policy* magazine, Cuban President Fidel Castro, wearing his usual olive drab military uniform, made his famous declaration "I shall be a Marxist-Leninist for the rest of my life." In January 1999, Castro put on a business suit for a conference on globalization in Havana, to which financier George Soros and free-market economist Milton Friedman were both invited.

If the defining economists of the Cold War system were Karl Marx and John Maynard Keynes, who each in his own way wanted to tame capitalism, the defining economists of the globalization system are Joseph Schumpeter and Intel chairman Andy Grove, who prefer to unleash capitalism. Schumpeter, a former Austrian Minister of Finance and Harvard Business School professor, expressed the view in his classic work *Capitalism, Socialism and Democracy* that the essence of capitalism is the process of "creative destruction"—the perpetual cycle of destroying the old and less efficient product or service and replacing it with new, more efficient ones. Andy Grove took Schumpeter's insight that "only the paranoid survive" for the title of his book on life in Silicon Valley, and made it in many ways the business model of globalization capitalism. Grove helped to popularize the view that dramatic, industry-transforming innovations are taking place today faster and faster. Thanks to these technological breakthroughs, the speed by which your latest invention can be made obsolete or turned into a commodity is now lightning quick. Therefore, only the paranoid, only those who are constantly looking over their shoulders to see who is creating something new that will destroy them and then staying just one step ahead of them, will survive. Those countries that are most willing to let capitalism quickly destroy inefficient companies, so that money can be freed up and directed to more innovative ones, will thrive in the era of globalization. Those which rely on their governments to protect them from such creative destruction will fall behind in this era.

James Surowiecki, the business columnist for *Slate* magazine, reviewing Grove's book, neatly summarized what Schumpeter and Grove have in common, which is the essence of globalization economics. It is the notion that: "Innovation replaces tradition. The present—or perhaps the future—replaces the past. Nothing matters so much as what will come next, and what will come next can only arrive if what is here now gets overturned. While this makes the system a terrific place for innovation, it makes it a difficult place to live, since most people prefer some measure of security about the future to a life lived in almost constant uncertainty . . . We are not forced to re-create our relationships with those closest to us on a regular basis. And yet that's precisely what Schumpeter, and Grove after him, suggest is necessary to prosper [today]."

Indeed, if the Cold War were a sport, it would be sumo wrestling, says Johns Hopkins University foreign affairs professor Michael Mandelbaum. "It would be two big fat guys in a ring, with all sorts of posturing and rituals and stomping of feet, but actually very little contact, until the end of the match, when there is a brief moment of shoving and the loser gets pushed out of the ring, but nobody gets killed."

By contrast, if globalization were a sport, it would be the 100-meter dash, over and over and over. And no matter how many times you win, you have to race again the next day. And if you lose by just one-hundredth of a second it can be as if you lost by an hour. (Just ask French multinationals. In 1999, French labor laws were changed, requiring— *requiring*—every employer to implement a four-hour reduction in the legal workweek, from 39 hours to 35 hours, with no cut in pay: Many French firms were fighting the move because of the impact it would have on their productivity in a global market. Henri Thierry, human resources director for Thomson–CSF Communications, a high-tech firm in the suburbs of Paris, told *The Washington Post:* "We are in a worldwide competition. If we lose one point of productivity, we lose orders. If we're obliged to go to 35 hours it would be like requiring French athletes to run the 100 meters wearing flippers. They wouldn't have much of a chance winning a medal.")

To paraphrase German political theorist Carl Schmitt, the Cold War was a world of "friends" and "enemies." The globalization world, by contrast, tends to turn all friends and enemies into "competitors."

If the defining anxiety of the Cold War was fear of annihilation from an enemy you knew all too well in a world struggle that was fixed and stable, the defining anxiety in globalization is fear of rapid change from an enemy you can't see, touch or feel—a sense that your job, community or workplace can be changed at any moment by anonymous economic and technological forces that are anything but stable. The defining defense system of the Cold War was radar—to expose the threats coming from the other side of the wall. The defining defense system of the globalization era is the X-ray machine—to expose the threats coming from within.

Globalization also has its own demographic pattern—a rapid acceleration of the movement of people from rural areas and agricultural lifestyles to urban areas and urban lifestyles more intimately linked with global fashion, food, markets and entertainment trends.

Last, and most important, globalization has its own defining structure of power, which is much more complex than the Cold War structure. The Cold War system was built exclusively around nation-states. You acted on the world in that system through your state. The Cold War was primarily a drama of states confronting states, balancing states and aligning with states. And, as a system, the Cold War was balanced at the center by two superstates: the United States and the Soviet Union.

The globalization system, by contrast, is built around three balances, which overlap and affect one another. The first is the traditional balance between nation-states. In the globalization system, the United States is now the sole and dominant superpower and all other nations are subordinate to it to one degree or another. The balance of power between the United States and the other states, though, still matters for the stability of this system. And it can still explain a lot of the news you read on the front page of the papers, whether it is the containment of Iraq in the Middle East or the expansion of NATO against Russia in Central Europe.

The second balance in the globalization system is between nation-states and global markets. These global markets are made up of millions of investors moving money around the world with the click of a mouse. I call them "the Electronic Herd," and this herd gathers in key global financial centers, such as Wall Street, Hong Kong, London and Frankfurt, which I call "the Supermarkets." The attitudes and actions of the Electronic Herd and the Supermarkets can have a huge impact on nation-states today, even to the point of triggering the downfall of governments. Who ousted Suharto in Indonesia in 1998? It wasn't another state, it was the Supermarkets, by withdrawing their support for, and confidence in, the Indonesian economy. You will not understand the front page of newspapers today unless you bring the Supermarkets into your analysis. Because the United States can destroy you by dropping bombs and the Supermarkets can destroy you by downgrading your bonds. In other words, the United States is the dominant player in maintaining the globalization gameboard, but it is not alone in influencing the moves on that gameboard. This globalization gameboard today is a lot like a Ouija board—sometimes pieces are moved around by the obvious hand of the superpower, and sometimes they are moved around by hidden hands of the Supermarkets.

The third balance that you have to pay attention to in the globalization system—the one that is really the newest of all—is the balance between individuals and nation-states. Because globalization has brought down many of the walls that limited the movement and reach of people, and because it has simultaneously wired the world into networks, it gives more power to individuals to influence both markets and nation-states than at any time in history. Individuals can increasingly act on the world stage directly—unmediated by a state. So you have today not only a superpower, not only Supermarkets, but, as will be demonstrated later in the book, you now have Super-empowered individuals. Some of these Super-empowered individuals are quite angry, some of them quite wonderful—but all of them are now able to act directly on the world stage.

Without the knowledge of the U.S. government, Long-Term Capital Management—a few guys with a hedge fund in Greenwich, Connecticut—amassed more financial bets around the world than all the foreign reserves of China. Osama bin Laden, a Saudi millionaire with his own global network, declared war on the United States in the late 1990s, and the U.S. Air Force retaliated with a cruise missile attack on him (where he resided in Afghanistan) as though he were another nation-state. Think about that. The United States fired 75 cruise missiles, at $1 million apiece, at a person! That was a superpower against a Super-empowered angry man. Jody Williams won the Nobel Peace Prize in 1997 for her contribution to the international ban on landmines. She achieved that ban not only without much government help, but in the face of opposition from all the major powers. And what did she say was her secret weapon for organizing 1,000 different human rights and arms control groups on six continents? "E-mail."

Nation-states, and the American superpower in particular, are still hugely important today, but so too now are Supermarkets and Super-empowered individuals. You will never understand the globalization system, or the front page of the morning paper, unless you see it as a complex interaction between all three of these actors: states bumping up against states, states bumping up against Supermarkets, and Supermarkets and states bumping up against Super-empowered individuals.

Unfortunately, for reasons I will explain later, the system of globalization has come upon us far faster than our ability to retrain ourselves to see and comprehend it. Think about just this one fact: Most people had never even heard of the Internet in 1990, and very few people had an E-mail address then. That was just ten years ago! But today the Internet, cell phones and E-mail have become essential tools that many people, and not only in developed countries, cannot imagine living without. It was no different, I am sure, at the start of the Cold War, with the first appearance of nuclear arsenals and deterrence theories. It took a long time for leaders and analysts of that era to fully grasp the real nature and dimensions of the Cold War system. They emerged from World War II thinking that this great war had produced a certain kind of world, but they soon discovered it had laid the foundations for a world very different from the one they anticipated. Much of what came to be seen as great Cold War architecture and strategizing were responses on the fly to changing events and evolving threats. Bit by bit, these Cold War strategists built the institutions, the perceptions and the reflexes that came to be known as the Cold War system.

It will be no different with the globalization system, except that it may take us even longer to get our minds around it, because it requires so much retraining just to see this new system and because it is built not just around superpowers but also around Supermarkets and Super-empowered individuals. I would say that in 2000 we understand as much about how today's system of globalization is going to work as we understood about how the Cold War system was going to work in 1946—the year Winston Churchill gave his speech warning that an "Iron Curtain" was coming down, cutting off the Soviet zone of influence from Western Europe. We barely understood how the Cold War system was going to play out thirty years after Churchill's speech! That was when Routledge published a collection of essays by some of the top Sovietologists, entitled *Soviet Economy Towards the Year 2000*. It was a good seller when it came out. It never occurred at that time to any of the authors that there wouldn't be a Soviet economy in the year 2000.

If you want to appreciate how few people under-stand exactly how this system works, think about one amusing fact. The two key economists who were advising Long-Term Capital Management, Robert C. Merton and Myron S. Scholes, shared the Nobel Prize for economics in 1997, roughly one year before LTCM so misunderstood the nature of risk in today's highly integrated global marketplace that it racked up the biggest losses in hedge fund history. And what did LTCM's two economists win their Nobel Prize for? For their studies on how complex financial instruments, known as deriva-tives, can be used by global investors to offset risk! In 1997 they won the Nobel Prize for managing risk. In 1998 they won the booby prize for creating risk. Same guys, same market—new world.

II.2   JEFFREY SACHS

International Economics: Unlocking the Mysteries of Globalization

Although there have been previous economic cycles of boom and bust, today's generally improving global economy is built on new relationships that create an interdependent structure in which we all, to a certain extent, depend on each other. Jeffrey Sachs, Director of the Earth Institute at Columbia University, looks at the many ways in which countries at various levels of technological development have joined forces to improve their eco-nomic well-being. The recent shifts in the economic policies of many countries and rapid technological advances are, claims Sachs, bringing changes that are not predictable and only dimly understood today. One critical issue is how decisions will be made in our new world where multinational corporations exercise greater and greater influence. What will be the future roles of citizens and governments in deciding whether a particular economic policy will be beneficial or not and in exercising control over their portion of the global marketplace?

Focus Questions

1. What are the four major issues related to globalization's impact on both developed and developing countries raised by Sachs in this reading?
2. In what ways does this article suggest it is possible that the "increasingly dense net-work of economic interactions" between countries could prove to be problematic?
3. What might be some long-range impacts on employment and the environment if globalization continues at its present rate?

Keywords

division of labor, G-7 countries, GDP, globalization, imperialism, income inequity, International Monetary Fund, macroeconomics, World Trade Organization

INTERNATIONAL ECONOMICS IS CONCERNED with the trade and financial relations of national economies, and the effects of international trade and finance on the distribution of production, income, and wealth around the world and within nations. In recent years, international economics has been increasingly taken up with one central question: How will national economies perform now that nearly all of the world is joined in a single marketplace? As a result of changes in economic *policy* and technology, economies that were once separated by high transport costs and artificial barriers to trade and finance are now linked in an increasingly dense network of economic interactions. This veritable economic revolution over the last 15 years has come upon us so suddenly that its fundamental ramifications for economic growth, the distribution of income and wealth, and patterns of trade and finance in the world economy are only dimly understood.

The most notable features of the new world economy are the increasing links between the high- and low-income countries. After all, the advanced income economies of Europe, Japan, and the United States have been linked significantly through trade flows at least since the 1960s. The great novelty of the current era is the extent to which the poorer nations of the world have been incorporated in the global system of trade, finance, and production as partners and market participants rather than colonial dependencies. For *globalization* enthusiasts, this development promises increased gains from trade and faster growth for both sides of the worldwide income divide. For skeptics, the integration of rich and poor nations promises increasing inequality in the former and greater dislocation in the latter.

National economies are becoming more integrated in four fundamental ways—through trade, finance, production, and a growing web of treaties and institutions. The increased trade linkages are clear: In almost every year since World War II, international trade has grown more rapidly than global production, resulting in a rising share of

Reprinted with permission from *Foreign Policy* 110 (Spring 1998), pp. 97–112. www.foreignpolicy.com.

exports and imports in the GDP of virtually every country. In the past 15 years, cross-border financial flows have grown even more rapidly than trade flows. Foreign direct investment (in which foreign capital gains a controlling interest in a cross-border enterprise), in particular, has grown even more rapidly than overall capital flows.

The sharp rise in foreign direct investment underscores the enormous and increasing role of multinational corporations in global trade, and especially in global production. As scholars such as Peter Dicken have shown, with falling transport and communications costs, it is possible to "divide up the value chain" of production. Different stages of the production process of a single output can be carried out in different parts of the world, depending on the comparative advantages of alternative production sites. Semiconductor chips might be designed in the United States, where the basic wafers are also produced; these are then cut and assembled in Malaysia; and the final products are tested in and shipped from Singapore. These cross-border flows often occur within the same multinational firm. One stunning fact about current trade flows is that an estimated one-third of merchandise trade is actually composed of shipments among the affiliates of a single company, as opposed to arms-length transactions among separate exporters and importers.

The fourth major aspect of globalization is the increased harmonization of economic institutions. Part of this is a matter of imitation. Most of the developing world chose nonmarket, economic strategies of development upon independence after World War II. These state-led models of development came crashing down in the 1980s, followed by a massive shift toward market-based, private sector-led growth. Beyond mere imitation, however, has come a significant rise in international treaty obligations regarding trade, investment policy, tax policy, intellectual property rights, banking supervision, currency convertibility, foreign investment policy, and even the control of bribery. A growing web of treaties ties nations together through multilateral obligations (such as the G-7 group, with 132 member countries), regional obligations (the European Union and other trade blocs), and bilateral obligations (for example, binational tax treaties between the United States and dozens of other governments).

The Implications of Globalization

The implications of globalization for both the developed and developing countries are currently the subject of intensive research and heated policy debates. Four main sets of issues are now under investigation. First, will globalization promote faster economic growth, especially among the four-fifths of the world's population (4.5 billion people) still living in developing countries? Second, will globalization promote or undermine macroeconomic stability? Are the sudden and unexpected collapses of emerging market economies in recent years (such as Mexico in 1994 and East Asia in 1997) the result of deep flaws in the globalization process, or are they manageable, perhaps avoidable bumps in the road to greater prosperity? Third, will globalization promote growing income inequality, and, if so, is the problem limited to low-skilled workers in the advanced economies, or is this inequality a deeper result of intensifying market forces in all parts of the world? Fourth, how should governmental institutions at all levels—regional, national, and international—adjust their powers and responsibilities in view of the emergence of a global market?

Economic Growth

Adam Smith famously declared in the *Wealth of Nations* that "the discovery of America, and that of a passage to the East Indies by the Cape of Good Hope are the two greatest and most important events recorded in the history of mankind." He reasoned that by "uniting, in some measure, the most distant parts of the world, by enabling them to relieve one another's wants, to increase one another's enjoyments, and to encourage one another's industry, their general tendency would seem to be beneficial." The discoveries, of course, were not enough to guarantee these benefits. Smith himself recognized that the depredations of imperialism had deprived the native inhabitants of the New World and the

East Indies of most of the benefits of globalization in his day. In our century, two world wars, the Great Depression, and 40 years of post–World War II protectionism in most of the developing world again frustrated Smith's vision of mutual gains from trade. Now, finally, can we envision the Smithian mechanism operating to worldwide advantage?

Much current theorizing on economic growth, such as the research by Gene Grossman and Elhanan Helpman, offers reasons for cheer. Smith's conjectures of dynamic gains to trade are at the core of many new mathematical models of "endogenous growth." These models stress that long-term growth depends on increased productivity and innovation, and that the incentives for both depend (as Smith conjectured) on the scope of the market. If innovators are selling into an expanded world market, they will generally have more incentive to innovate. If productivity is raised by refining the production process among a larger number of specialized subunits, and if each subunit faces fixed costs of production, then a larger market will allow these fixed costs to be spread over a larger production run.

One part of the argument has found strong empirical support in recent years. The fastest-growing developing countries in the past two decades have been those that succeeded in generating new export growth, especially in manufactured goods. Andrew Warner and I have demonstrated that economies that tried to go it alone by protecting their economies from imports through high trade barriers grew much less rapidly than more open export-oriented economies. Moreover, the manufactured exports of the developing countries have themselves exemplified the Smithian principle of division of labor. Steven Radelet and I found that in almost all cases of developing-country, export-led growth, the exports themselves have been part of a highly refined division of labor, in which final goods (e.g. automobiles, avionics, electronic machinery) are produced in multisite operations, with the labor-intensive parts of the production process reserved for the developing countries.

This kind of "new division of labor" in manufacturers was inconceivable to early postwar development economists such as Raul Prebisch, who counseled protectionism as the preferred path for industrialization in poor countries. These economists simply could not conceive of the production process being a complementary relationship between advanced and developing countries. In the standard theory, then, both sides of the great income divide stand to benefit from globalization: the developed countries by reaching a larger market for new innovations and the developing economies by enjoying the fruits of those innovations while sharing in global production via multinational enterprises.

Modern theorizing still stresses, however, that the gains in growth might not in fact be shared by all. Two major theoretical exceptions that do find some supporting empirical evidence are most often discussed. The first exception is based on geography. The gains from trade depend on the transport costs between a national economy and the rest of the world being low enough to permit an extensive interaction between the economy and world markets. If the economy is geographically isolated—for example, landlocked in the high Andes or the Himalayas or Central Africa, as in the cases of Bolivia, Nepal, and Rwanda—the chances for extensive trade are extremely limited. Also, as MIT economist Paul Krugman has shown, the combination of increasing returns to scale and high transport costs may cause economic activity to concentrate somewhat accidentally in some areas at the expense of others. Climate may also have serious adverse effects. Generally speaking, the tropics impose additional burdens of infectious disease and often poor agricultural conditions (involving soil, water, and pests) not found in the temperate zones. For these reasons, a significant portion of the world's population may face severe geographical obstacles to development, despite the overall beneficial effects of globalization.

The second major theoretical exception, recognized in development thinking at least since Alexander Hamilton's call for protection of nascent U.S. industry, is the risk that producers of natural resources might get "trapped" into an unsatisfactory specialization of trade, thereby delaying or blocking the improvements in industry necessary for economic development. Kiminori Matsuyama was among the first to formulate a mathematical model to test this idea. Early evidence, derived from studies Warner and I conducted, gives some support to the "dynamic Dutch Disease" effect. Dutch Disease occurs when a boom in the natural resources that a country exports causes a national currency to strengthen, thereby undermining the profitability of nonresource-based industries. (The name comes from the de-industrialization that allegedly followed Holland's development of North Sea gas fields in the 1960s.) The "dynamic" effect is the supposed long-term loss of growth coming from the specialization in primary goods (e.g. gas exports) rather than manufactured products, which supposedly offer better opportunities for long-term productivity growth.

The findings suggest that countries with large natural resource bases, such as the Persian Gulf oil exporters, find themselves uncompetitive in most manufacturing sectors. This condition, in turn, seems to be consistent with lower long-term growth, possibly because manufacturing rather than primary production (agriculture and mining) offers better possibilities for innovation, learning by doing, and productivity improvement in the long term. Economic theory suggests that some form of nonmarket intervention—ranging from the protection of nascent industries to the subsidization of manufacturing—could have beneficial effects in these circumstances. The practicalities of such real-world interventions, however, are heatedly debated and open to question.

Macroeconomic Stability

In a famous cry of despair in the middle of the Great Depression, John Maynard Keynes, in his essay "National Self-Sufficiency," argued that economic entanglements through trade and finance added to global destabilization. He went so far as to declare "let goods be homespun whenever it is reasonably and conveniently possible; and, above all, let finance be primarily national."

After the depression, Keynes changed his mind and championed a postwar return to open trade based on convertible currencies. In his design of the new IMF, however, he kept to his view that financial flows ought to remain restricted so as to minimize the chance that international financial disturbances would create global macroeconomic instabilities. For this reason, the Articles of Agreement of the IMF call on member countries to maintain currencies that are convertible for current transactions (essentially trade and the repatriation of profits and interest) but not necessarily for capital flows.

As globalization has taken off in the past two decades, many forms of international capital flows have risen dramatically. Foreign direct investment, portfolio investment through country funds, bank loans, bond lending, derivatives (swaps, options, forward transactions), reinsurance, and other financial instruments, have all grown enormously. Both developed and developing countries have increasingly opened their capital markets to foreign participation. In 1997, the IMF endorsed a move toward amending the Articles of Agreement to call for open capital flows. The Organization for Economic Cooperation and Development, World Trade Organization (WTO), and Bank for International Settlements have also increasingly sought international standards for the liberalization and supervision of international investment flows.

Economic theory generally asserts that trade in financial assets will benefit individual countries in ways analogous to trade in goods. Financial transactions, in theory, allow two kinds of gains from trade: increased diversification of risk and intertemporal gains (a better ability to borrow and lend over time, more consistent with desired patterns of investment and consumption). The theory, however, also hints at some limits to this optimistic view, and the experience of international financial liberalization gives real reason for pause. Perhaps Keynes' skepticism should still apply, despite our supposedly much enhanced capability to identify and manage financial risks.

The real meaning of the Mexican crash and the East Asian financial crisis is still far from clear, but both experiences have shown that unfettered financial flows from advanced to emerging markets can create profound destabilization. The problem, it seems, is that financial markets are subject to certain key "market failures" that are exacerbated, rather than limited, by globalization. One kind of

failure is the tendency of underregulated and undercapitalized banks to gamble recklessly with depositor funds, since from the owner/management point of view, bank profits accrue to themselves, while bank losses get stuck with the government. Thus, international financial liberalization of a poorly capitalized banking system is an invitation to overborrowing and eventual financial crisis.

The second kind of failure is financial panic, which comes when a group of creditors suddenly decides to withdraw loans from a borrower, out of fear that the other creditors are doing the same thing. Each lender flees for the exit because the last one out will lose his claims, assuming that the borrower does not have the liquid assets to cover a sudden withdrawal of loans. This kind of panic was once familiar in the form of bank runs, which used to afflict U.S. banks before the introduction of federal deposit insurance in 1934. It seems to be prevalent in international lending, especially in international bank loans to emerging markets. Both in Mexico in late 1994 and several East Asian economies in 1997 (Indonesia, Malaysia, the Philippines, and South Korea), once enthusiastic international bankers suddenly pulled the plug on new credits and the rollover of old credits. This withdrawal of funding sent the emerging markets into a tailspin, with falling production and the risk of outright international default. Emergency bailout loans led by the IMF aimed to block the defaults, but did not address the core causes of the crises.

These dramatic experiences are giving second thoughts in many quarters to the pressures for rapid liberalization of international capital flows. While the official Washington community still presses for liberalization of the capital market, voices are being raised for putting a "spanner in the works" to slow capital movements with an aim toward preventing financial market panics. Ideas include the taxation of international transactions (such as the famous proposal of James Tobin to tax foreign exchange transactions to deter short-term currency speculation, or Chile's taxation of capital inflows); the direct limitation of short-term bank borrowing from abroad as a banking supervisory standard; and increased disclosure rules. Both the theory and practice of capital market liberalization are therefore in limbo.

Income Distribution

Perhaps no aspect of globalization has been more controversial than the alleged effects of increased trade on income distribution. A series of claims are made that it is a major factor in increasing inequality, both in advanced and developing countries. Of course, within the United States, the main focus of debate is on advanced countries, especially the United States itself.

Over the past 25 years, international economics theory has mostly focused on two kinds of trade: intra-industry and inter-industry. The first kind, in which the United States sells cars to Europe while also importing European cars, is ostensibly based on gains from specialization under conditions of increasing returns to scale. The United States could itself produce "European style" cars, so the argument goes, but chooses not to because it is less costly to have longer production runs of U.S. models, selling some of them to Europe to finance imports of the European models. Intra-industry trade, the theory holds, is a win-win situation for all. Consumers in both Europe and the United States enjoy an expanded range of products, and nobody suffers a loss of income, either absolute or relative.

Inter-industry trade involves the U.S. export of high technology goods to Asia, in return for inexpensive labor-intensive goods imported from Asia. In this case, trade is motivated by differing factor proportions. The United States produces goods that are intensive in physical capital and skills—advanced telecommunications equipment, for example—and imports goods that are intensive in labor, such as footwear and apparel. The theory suggests that both regions can gain overall from this kind of trade, though workers within each country may well lose. In the United States, for example, workers in the footwear and apparel sectors may lose their jobs in the face of increased low-wage competition, while skilled workers in Asia could conceivably lose out when skill-intensive goods are imported from the United States. More generally, according to basic Heckscher-Ohlin-Samuelson trade theory, unskilled U.S. workers may suffer relative and even absolute income declines, while skilled workers in the developing countries could similarly suffer a loss of relative and/or absolute income.

Since intra-industry trade is generally strongest among similar-income countries (e.g. U.S./European trade), while inter-industry trade is strongest among dissimilar countries (e.g. U.S./developing Asia), the income-distributional ramifications of trade between rich and poor countries are ostensibly more threatening to particular social groups, a point stressed early on by Krugman. It is therefore the increasing linkages of rich and poor countries that have become the cornerstone of political challenges to globalization.

Despite the hard work of researchers, there is still no consensus on the effects of the globalized economy on income distribution within the advanced and emerging markets. Clearly, the period of dramatic globalization (especially during the 1980s and 1990s) has also been one of rising income inequality within the United States, and especially of a loss of relative income for low-skilled workers, consistent with basic trade theory. However, as with many important economic phenomena, the cause of this widening income inequality is almost surely multifaceted. While trade might be one culprit, changes in technology such as the computer revolution might also favor skilled workers over unskilled ones, thereby contributing to the rising inequality. Most researchers agree that a combination of factors has played a role in the widening inequality, and the majority of them, including Krugman and Robert Lawrence, put the preponderant weight on technology rather than trade. They do this for one main reason: The share of U.S. workers that are in direct competition with low-skilled workers in the emerging markets seems to be too small to explain the dramatic widening of inequalities since the end of the 1970s. Less than 5 percent of the U.S. labor market—in apparel, footwear, toys, assembly operations, and the like—appears to be in the "direct line of fire" of low-wage goods from Asia. If the United States is already out of the low-skill industries, then increased globalization in such goods cannot widen inequalities in the United States, and, in fact, would tend to benefit all households by offering less expensive consumer goods.

One problem with such estimates, however, is that they tend to be based on rather simple theoretical models of international trade. Conventional trade measures may not pick up the additional channels through which globalization affects income distribution. Some researchers argue, for example, that increased globalization limits the ability of union workers to achieve a "union wage premium" in collective bargaining because of the risk that firms will simply move overseas in response to higher union wages. Thus, the opening of international trade may have changed the bargaining power of workers vis-à-vis capital in ways not measured by trade flows. More generally, the export of capital to low-wage countries can exacerbate inequalities caused by increased trade. Researchers have not yet uncovered large effects on wages and income distribution through these additional channels, but the scholarship devoted to these topics is still rather sparse.

Some sporadic evidence suggests that growing inequalities are not simply a problem of developed economies but also of developing economies. If the salary premium of skilled workers is rising in both developing and developed economies, something more than inter-industry trade effects are at work. Part of the story could be technological change. Another possible factor (suggested recently by Robert Frank and Philip Cook) is that globalization is supporting a new "winner-take-all" approach in labor markets. The argument holds that skilled workers of all kinds, whether in sports, industry, science, or entertainment, find an expanding world market for their skills, while unskilled workers see no particular gains in an expanding market. Therefore, the scale of the world market would affect skilled workers differently from unskilled ones, leading to a worldwide rise in the market premium for skills. This hypothesis remains as yet almost completely unexamined empirically.

Economic Governance

Without question, globalization is having a deep effect on politics at many levels. Most important, the national marketplace is losing its salience relative to international markets. This is causing a sea change in the role of the nation-state, relative to both local and regional governments on the one side, and multinational political institutions on the other.

In Smith's day, part of the market revolution was the removal of barriers to trade within nations and proto-nations. The freeing of trade among the German states in the Zollverein of 1834, and then the full unification of the German market with the establishment of the German Reich in 1871, exemplify the historical process. In most cases, nineteenth-century market capitalism and the importance of the national marketplace rose hand in hand, even as international trade was itself expanding. Generally speaking, the spread of capitalism within Europe, Japan, and North America gave impetus to the increasing importance of the national economy and thereby of the national government.

At the end of the twentieth century, the national market is being increasingly displaced by the international marketplace. After decades of experimentation, almost all countries have realized that the national market is simply too small to permit an efficient level of production in most areas of industry and even in many areas of services. Efficient production must be geared instead toward world markets. Moreover, globalization has proved a catalyst for internationally agreed-upon rules of behavior in trade, finance, taxation, and many other areas, thus prompting the rise of the WTO and other international institutions as the new bulwarks of the emerging international system. At the same time, communities, local governments, and regions within nations are increasingly asserting their claims to cultural and political autonomy. The nation is no longer their economic protector, and in peaceful regions of the world, the national government is no longer seen as a critical instrument of security. Consequently, regions as far-flung as Catalonia, Northern Italy, Quebec, and Scotland, as well as oblasts in Russia, provinces in China, and states in India, have taken globalization as their cue to pursue greater autonomy within the nation-state.

We are therefore in the midst of a startling, yet early, tug of war between polities at all levels. Where will the future of decision making, tax powers, and regulatory authorities reside: with localities, subnational regions, nation-states, or multilateral institutions (both within geographic regions such as the European Union and at the international level)? To the extent that increased regulatory, tax, and even judicial powers shift to the international setting, how should and will international institutions be governed in the future? Will there be a democracy deficit, as is now charged about decision making in the European Union? What will be the balance of political power between the developed and developing countries, especially as population and economic balances shift over time in favor of the new developing world? And crucially, what will be the balance of power between democratic and nondemocratic polities at the world level? All of these issues are fresh, urgent, and likely to loom large on the research radar screens.

JAGDISH BHAGWATI   II.3

In Defense of Globalization

Even though the process of globalization through the integration of the world economy began with technological developments in transportation and communications, Jagdish Bhagwati, an economist at Columbia University, claims that today's version of this phenomenon is markedly different from what had existed for a number of reasons. Instead of having technology as the change agent today, the author builds the case that recent governmental policy shifts have made the changes we see today possible. The author considers various factors that contributed to the negative view of capitalism and its ability to contribute to solving issues of social injustice held by some, including not only young skeptics but also some intellectuals as well as a few very successful capitalists. The increasing power and influence of multinational organizations are examined, and the views of various groups are considered in an attempt to determine the extent to which social groups feel they are benefiting from or being disadvantaged in this changing world. The author's generally positive view of globalization is tempered somewhat when he acknowledges that unbridled capitalism and globalization might negatively impact communitarian values. Viewing the world through economic lenses, Bhagwati extols the virtues of efficiency in the marketplace even though he appears to be somewhat uneasy with the type of world that might be created if the forces of global capitalism remain unchecked.

Focus Questions

1. What are Bhagwati's key arguments against those who attempt to portray the current stage of globalization as anti-democratic and anti-egalitarian? Why are you either inclined to accept or reject his view of the overall benefits of unbridled capitalism and free trade? Discuss.
2. Contrast the generally positive opinions expressed in this article with the concerns over the privatization of the commons raised by the International Forum on Globalization article (selection II.4). With which point of view are you more inclined to agree and why?
3. How does Bhagwati justify his overwhelmingly positive view of globalization and capitalism? Are you as convinced as he is that the society is not sacrificing "communitarian values" for the apparent self-interest of capitalism? What do you feel might eventually happen to our society if his optimistic view is proven wrong?

4. Discuss both the positive and negative views of globalization presented in this article with the points made in the Friedman article (selection II.1) and the United Nations report (selection II.5).

Keywords

commodification, communitarianism, deconstructionism, economic integration, fair trade, free trade, global integration, imperialism, invisible hand, mercantilism, monopolies, multinationals, usury, xenophobia

Globalization Today: Different from Yesterday

If globalization's perils tend to be exaggerated [by some] . . ., they are also understated by many who say, "Well, we have always had globalization, and it is no big deal." True, rapid integration of the world economy occurred in the late nineteenth and early twentieth centuries. We can go back to the end of the nineteenth century, for instance, and find that trade, capital flows, and migrations were no less then than they are today. If multinationals bother you, then just think of the great East India Company, which virtually paved the way for the British conquest of India, and the Dutch East Indies Company, which dominated Indonesia. Trade grew rapidly along with European outward expansion, as did settlements in the new areas opened up by exploration and conquest. Capital flowed profusely, financing the building of railways in Africa and the extraction of minerals worldwide. Many historians have noticed that the years spanning the two world wars were an interruption of the upward trends in the expansion of world trade and investment, and that it is possible to interpret the postwar liberalization of trade and investment flows as leading to a resumption of the trends set into motion prior to World War I. But all this misses the fact that there are fundamental differences that give globalization today a special, and at times sharp, edge.

From *In Defense of Globalization* by Jagdish Bhagwati, pp. 10–27, a Council on Foreign Relations Book. Copyright © 2004 by Jagdish Bhagwati. Reprinted by permission of Oxford University Press, Inc.

First, the earlier integration of the world economy was driven more by technological developments in transportation and communications than by policy changes. It's true that British prime minister Robert Peel repealed the Corn Laws in 1846, bringing free trade unilaterally to England in the first dramatic move away from mercantilism. We also know that in various ways many European nations, notably France, followed suit with some trade liberalizations of their own, though historians have not yet decided whether their actions were induced by the example of Britain's success with free trade, as expressly predicted by Peel.

But none of these policy changes did as much to integrate the world economy in the latter half of the century as did emerging technological revolutions in transportation by railways and in the oceans. Technological advances in these sectors rapidly reduced costs of transport and communication continually through the nineteenth century. Martin Wolf, the *Financial Times* columnist, has observed: "The first transatlantic telegraph was laid in 1866. By the turn of the century, the entire world was connected by telegraph, and communication times fell from months to minutes."[1]

Of course, the rate of technological change in moving goods and services and knowledge cheaply and rapidly across nations has continued unabated, even accelerating according to some observers. Thus, Wolf writes: "The cost of a three-minute telephone call from New York to London in current prices dropped from about $250 in 1930 to a few cents today. In more recent years, the number of voice paths across the Atlantic has skyrocketed from 100,000 in 1986 to more than 2 million today. The number of Internet hosts has risen from 5,000 in 1986 to more than 30 million now."[2]

But today's most dramatic change is in the degree to which governments have intervened to reduce obstacles to the flow of trade and investments worldwide. The story of globalization today must be written in two inks: one colored by technical change and the other by state action. In fact, even the early postwar hostility toward global integration in many of the poor countries has, as already remarked upon, yielded steadily to the progressive embrace of globalization. But this fact forces upon our attention a disturbing observation: governments that can accelerate globalization can also reverse it. Herein lies a vulnerability that cannot be dismissed complacently. The earlier globalization, in the end, was interrupted for almost a half century with rising trade barriers epitomized by the infamous 1934 Smoot-Hawley Tariff of the United States and declining trade flows and investments after World War I through to the Great Crash of 1929 and World War II.

Second, the new information technologies have created a landscape where movements of services and capital are faster by several orders of magnitude. The rapidity with which huge amounts of funds moved out of East Asia within less than a week in 1998, the precipitous outflows from Mexico in November 1994, and many other instances of substantial and rapid-fire outflows of capital have created immense management problems that elude the grasp of countries that face difficult developmental weaknesses and challenges but want to embrace financial globalization or are forced to do so. Financial panics, crashes, and manias are nothing new, as the renowned economist Charles Kindleberger has reminded us; but their magnitudes and the speed at which they arrive are indeed qualitatively a different, and potentially more dangerous, phenomenon.

Third, the sense of vulnerability, or economic insecurity, is arguably greater today than in earlier periods because the growing integration of nations worldwide into the international economy has intensified competitive pressures from actual and potential rivals elsewhere. In Adam Smith's time, over two centuries ago, orange producers in the tropics

had little worry about competition from Glasgow even though oranges could be grown in glass houses: the cost difference would be so high that the tropical farmers felt secure behind a solid buffer of competitive advantage. England's producers of manufactures also enjoyed easy dominance in many cases because England was ahead of all on industrialization. But today, in most commodities and activities, technology matters and has diffused greatly, both because many have access to similar pools of knowledge and because multinationals can take scarce knowledge almost everywhere if they choose, as they often do, and they do produce globally. The buffer has therefore shrunk dramatically in most activities, and international competition is fierce and feared.

The inevitable effect has been to prompt firms everywhere to worry about "fair trade." Each looks over his foreign rival's shoulder to see if any difference in domestic policy or institutions gives this competitor an "unfair" advantage. The result has been a growing demand for ironing out any such differences, including in labor and environmental standards, as firms seek "level playing fields," ignoring the fact that it is differences, whether of climate and skills or of domestic institutions and policies reflecting local conditions, that lead to beneficial trade among nations.

While these demands, familiar in the rich countries for the most part, have transformed the debate on globalization, and their many ramifications will be subjected to critical examination at different places in this book . . . the other important implication of intensified world competition is that it has exposed producers in the poor countries to increased risks as a result of shifting to world markets in search of greater prosperity. Thus farmers who shift from traditional staples to cash crops because of higher returns at current prices face the prospect that this shift will lead them into ruination if rivals elsewhere with lower prices suddenly move into the market: a phenomenon that is more likely in a world with many potential suppliers with small margins of difference in competitiveness. Since few farmers in the poor countries are likely to take these downside possibilities into account, sudden misery is a possibility that has at times resulted from the shift to global markets. The absence of institutional support to handle these downsides . . . has become a major source of worry.

Finally, fears that globalization intensifies interdependence among nation-states and increasingly constrains their ability to provide for the welfare of their citizens have a salience that did not quite obtain in the earlier period. The growth of the welfare state in the twentieth century—even though we had elements of it starting earlier, as with social security, whose origins go back to Bismarck in Germany—has created a mind-set, an ethos, where the state is expected to be responsible for the welfare of its citizens. The novel fear today is that globalization places limits on the freedom to discharge this critical responsibility.

And so the complacent view that there is nothing new about globalization is simply wrong. We do need to look at the phenomenon closely, seeking to analyze and address the fears that are novel and indeed appear to be plausible at first blush.

A Trilogy of Discontents

ANTI-CAPITALISM

As the twentieth century ended, capitalism seemed to have vanquished its rivals. Francis Fukuyama's triumphalism in his celebrated work *The End of History and The Last Man* (1990) was like a primeval scream of joy by a warrior with a foot astride his fallen prey.[3] It was not just the collapse of communism in Europe and China's decisive turn away from it. As the energetic anti-globalization NGO Fifty Years Is Enough laments, even the Swedish model (with its enhanced Social Democratic commitment to the welfare state, backed by a markedly progressive and redistributive tax system) had lost its appeal. The much-advertised model of "alternative development" in the Indian state of Kerala, with its major emphasis on education and health and only minor attention to growth, had also run into difficulties, much as President Julius Nyerere's celebrated socialist experiment in Tanzania had run the country's economy into the ground. This vanishing of different possibilities has led to what I have called the tyranny of the missing alternative, provoking a

sense of anguished anti-capitalist reactions from both the old and the young.

The old among the disenchanted are few, and so they perhaps matter less than the young, who are many. They are among the anti-capitalists of the postwar years, ranging from socialists to revolutionaries. The communists and Marxists are captive to a nostalgia for their vanished dreams.

When the World Economic Forum met in Davos, Switzerland, in February 2001, there was an anti-Davos meeting in Brazil at the same time.[4] The rhetoric in Brazil was one of revolution. I recall George Soros, who properly considers himself to be a progressive financier, going into a debate from Davos on the video monitor with some of the anti-Davos participants. I recall his frustration, indeed astonishment, when he realized that he was seen as the enemy, not a friend, much as U.S. Democrats were chagrined that Ralph Nader thought during the last presidential election that they were no different from the Republicans.

Soros, who had not previously interacted with these groups, just did not get it: as far as these anti-capitalist revolutionaries are concerned, anyone who is into stocks and bonds should be put *in* stocks and bonds. Indeed, these groups, who were memorializing Che Guevara and listening to Ben Bella, were the exact antitheses of the Arthur Koestlers of the world, who wrote of the god that failed. They were working from a script about the god that died but will come again, much like born-again Christians. They only had to keep the faith.

But we who favor globalization must also confront the young. And if you have watched the streets of Seattle, Washington, Prague, Montreal, and Genoa, where the anti-globalizers have congregated with increasing militancy, or if you see their impassioned protests on the campuses, as I have watched the Anti-Sweatshop Coalition's activities at my own university (Columbia), there can be no doubt that we have here a phenomenon that is truly important in the public space and also more potent: the nostalgia of the fading generation cannot compete with the passions of the rising generation.

So how is the discontent of the young to be explained? Of course, a rare few among them share their predecessor's revolutionary bent. Consider

Global Exchange, an NGO that describes itself as a "human rights group"—this is the in term, much as "socialism" was three decades ago, and its moral resonance immediately gets you onto higher ground and gives you a free pass with the media and the public. It professes radical politics and gets endorsement from the great linguist and activist Noam Chomsky, among other left intellectuals. Its pronouncements on the World Trade Organization are dramatic and drastic: "the WTO only serves the interests of multinational corporations" and "the WTO is killing people.[5]

But Global Exchange and its radical chic are really a fringe phenomenon. There are several explanations, other than strong socialist convictions, of what animates the young in particular. Each may explain part of the reality, while collectively they provide a more complete explanation.

1. Far too many among the young see capitalism as a system that cannot address meaningfully questions of social justice. To my generation, and that of the British left-learning intellectuals such as George Bernard Shaw that preceded it, the Soviet model was a beguiling alternative. Indeed, my much-translated 1966 book *The Economics of Underdeveloped Countries* contains a distinct nod toward the Soviet Union: "The imagination of many . . . nations has been fired, perhaps most of all, by the remarkable way in which the Soviet Union has raised itself to the status of a Great Power by its own bootstraps and in a short span of time."[6] How appalling a misjudgment this view of the Soviet alternative seems today, and how commonplace it was then!

That capitalism may be viewed instead as a system that can paradoxically destroy privilege and open up economic opportunity to the many is a thought that is still uncommon. I often wonder, for example, how many of the young skeptics of capitalism are aware that socialist planning in countries such as India, by replacing markets systemwide with bureaucratically determined rations of goods and services, worsened rather than improved unequal access because socialism meant queues that the well-connected and the well-endowed could jump, whereas markets allowed a larger number to make it to the check-out counter. I have always been astonished at the number of well-meaning socialists,

whose aspirations I admire, who continue to fall for the erroneous view that controls and direct allocations are an appropriate answer to inequality.

2. But the anti-capitalist sentiments are particularly virulent among the young who arrive at their social awakening on campuses in fields other than economics. English, comparative literature, and sociology are fertile breeding grounds.

Thus, deconstructionism, espoused by the French philosopher Jacques Derrida, has left the typical student of literature without anchor because of its advocacy of what amounts to an endless horizon of meanings. Terry Eagleton, the sympathetic chronicler of modern literary theory, has written: "Derrida is clearly out to do more than develop new techniques of reading: deconstruction is for him an ultimately political practice, an attempt to dismantle the logic by which a particular system of thought, and behind that a whole system of political structures and social institutions, maintains its force.[7]

True, Derrida's technique will deconstruct any political ideology, including Marxism. Typically, however, it is focused on deconstructing and devaluing capitalism rather than Marxism, often with nihilistic overtones, which creates the paradox that many now turn to anarchy not from Bakunin but from Derrida.

The near-nihilist influence of the deconstructionism of Derrida in feeding anti-capitalism has been matched by the equally profound influence of Michel Foucault: these have amounted to a double whammy, courtesy of Paris, Foucault's emphasis on discourses as instruments of power and dominance has also led to what is often described as an "anti-rational" approach that challenges the legitimacy of academic disciplines, including economics, and their ability to get at the "truth." There is little doubt that the language of power, and the focus on it, feeds in turn the notion, discussed later, that corporations will dominate and exploit the workers under the liberal rules that define capitalism, and by extension, globalization.[8]

The heavy influence of Marxist texts on students of literature, on the other hand, has been beautifully captured by V. S. Naipaul in his compelling portrait in *Beyond Belief* of the Pakistani guerrilla Shabaz, who went from studying literature in England to starting a revolution in Baluchistan that failed:

> There were close Pakistani friends at the university. Many of them were doing English literature, like Shabaz; it was one of the lighter courses, possibly the lightest, and at this time it was very political and restricted. It was encouraging Marxism and revolution rather than wide reading. So Shabaz and his Pakistani friends in their Marxist study group read the standard (and short) revolutionary texts, Frantz Fanon, Che Guevara. And while they read certain approved Russian writers, they didn't read or get to know about the Turgenev novels, *Fathers and Sons* (1862) and *Virgin Soil* (1877), which dealt with conditions not unlike those in feudal Pakistan, but questioned the simplicities of revolution.[9]

Feeding the anti-globalization movement are also the post-colonial (poco) theorists, who, following Edward Said's pathbreaking writings, have a profound suspicion of Western scholarship as an objective source of interpretation and conceptualization of the colonial societies that were part of the global polity that European expansion created. That suspicion breeds hostility both to Western disciplines such as economics and to the threat that they see from them to the cultures of the communities and nations that have succeeded the colonial rule.

Thus the post-colonial theorists become natural allies of the deconstructionists, the diverse postmodernists (pomos), the Foucault cultists, and the Marxists, in their anti-globalization sentiments in the literature departments. The cauldron draws its boiling waters from many spigots.

As for sociology, many of its students are influenced equally by the new literary theory and the old Marxism. They stand in contempt of economic argumentation that would refute their rejectionist beliefs about capitalism by asserting that economics is about value whereas sociology is about values. But they are wrong today on both counts.

Economists will retort that as citizens they choose ends, but as economists they choose the (best) means. Moreover, accused of indulging the profit motive, they respond with the Cambridge economist Sir Dennis Robertson that economics is

addressed heroically to showing how "man's basest instincts," not his noblest, can be harnessed through appropriate institutional design to produce public good. Adam Smith would surely have died an unsung hero if he had peddled the pedestrian argument that altruism led to public good.

The presumption that sociology is a better guide to virtue than economics is also misplaced. Certainly its related discipline, social anthropology, has traditionally leaned toward preserving cultures, whereas economics in our hands is a tool for change.[10] When I studied in England I was fascinated by social anthropology and deeply buried in the writings of the legendary A. R. Radcliffe-Brown and many others, but I still wound up preferring economics for my vocation. What other choice could really have been made by a young student from a country afflicted by economic misery? Indeed, if reducing poverty by using economic analysis to accelerate growth and therewith pull people up into gainful employment and dignified sustenance is not a compelling moral imperative, what *is*?

But I should add that many of these students are also susceptible to the bitingly critical view of economics as an apologia for capitalism that was brilliantly propounded by Rosa Luxemburg in her classic essay "What Is Economics?"—the first chapter of a proposed ten-chapter work, only six chapters of which were found in her apartment after her murder. She had argued that "the new science of economics," which had reached the status of an academic discipline in Germany, was tantamount to an attempted legitimation of the "anarchy of capitalist production" and was essentially "one of the most important ideological weapons of the bourgeoisie as it struggles with the medieval state and for a modern capitalist state." The "invisible hand," with its rationalization of markets, had a hidden agenda, hence it lacked plausibility. This analysis attracts many.

3. But I also think that an altogether new factor on the scene that propels the young into anti-capitalist attitudes comes from a different, technological source in a rather curious fashion. This is the dissonance that now exists between empathy for others elsewhere for their misery and the inadequate intellectual grasp of what can be done to ameliorate

that distress. The resulting tension spills over into unhappiness with the capitalist system (in varying forms) within which they live and hence anger at it for its apparent callousness.

Today, thanks to television, we have what I call the paradox of inversion of the philosopher David Hume's concentric circles of reducing loyalty and empathy. Each of us feels diminishing empathy as we go from our nuclear family to the extended family, to our local community, to our state or county (say, Lancashire or Louisiana), to our nation, to our geographical region (say, Europe or the Americas), and then to the world. This idea of concentric circles of empathy can be traced back to the Stoics' doctrine of *oikeiosis*—that human affection radiates outward from oneself, diminishing as distance grows from oneself and increasing as proximity increases to oneself. In the same vein, Hume famously argued that "it is not contrary to reason to prefer the destruction of the whole world to the scratching of my finger" and that "sympathy with persons remote from us is much fainter than with persons near and contiguous.[11]

Similarly, his contemporary Adam Smith wrote in 1760 in *The Theory of Moral Sentiments,* which is as celebrated among moral philosophers as *The Wealth of Nations* is among economists:

Let us suppose that the great empire of China, with all its myriads of inhabitants, was suddenly swallowed up by an earthquake and let us consider how a man of humanity in Europe, who had no sort of connexion with that part of the world, would be affected upon receiving intelligence of this dreadful calamity. He would, I imagine, first of all express very strongly his sorrow for the misfortune of that unhappy people, he would make many melancholy reflections upon the precariousness of human life and the vanity of all the labors of man which could thus be annihilated in a moment. He would too, perhaps, if he was a man of speculation, enter into many reasonings concerning the effects which this disaster might produce upon the commerce of Europe and the trade and business of the world in general. And when all this fine philosophy was over, when all these humane sentiments

had been once fairly expressed, he would pursue his business or pleasure, take his repose or his diversion, with the same ease and tranquility as if no such accident had occurred.

The most frivolous disaster which could befall himself would occasion a more real disturbance. If he was to lose his little finger tomorrow, he would not sleep to-night; but, provided he never saw them, he would snore with the most profound security over the ruin of a hundred million of his brethren. The destruction of that immense multitude seems plainly an object less interesting to him than this paltry misfortune of his own. To prevent, therefore, this paltry misfortune to himself would a man of humanity be willing to sacrifice the lives of a hundred million of his brethren, provided he had never seen them?[12]

What the Internet and CNN have done is to take Hume's outermost circle and turn it into the innermost. No longer can we snore while the other half of humanity suffers plague and pestilence and the continuing misery of extreme poverty. Television has disturbed our sleep, perhaps short of a fitful fever but certainly arousing our finest instincts.[13] Indeed, this is what the Stoics, chiefly Hierocles, having observed the concentric circles of vanishing empathy, had urged by way of morality: that "it is the task of a well tempered man, in his proper treatment of each group, to draw circles together somehow towards the centre, and to keep zealously transferring those from the enclosing circles into the enclosed ones."[14]

At the same time, the technology of the Internet and CNN, as Robert Putnam has told us, has accelerated our move to "bowling alone," gluing us to our TV sets and shifting us steadily out of civic participation, so that the innermost circle has become the outermost one.

So the young see and are anguished by the poverty and the civil wars and the famines in remote areas of the world but often have no intellectual training to cope with their anguish and follow it through rationally in terms of appropriate action. Thus, as I watched the kids dressed as turtles at Seattle, during the riotous 1999 WTO ministerial meeting, protesting against the WTO and the Appellate Body's decision in the shrimpturtle case, I wondered how many knew that the environmentalists had really won that decision, not lost it. The ability to unilaterally impose requirements on foreign shrimpers on the high oceans to use turtle-excluding devices (nets with narrow necks), failing which imports of shrimp would be disallowed, was upheld, not denied. When I asked, of course, no one knew the facts, and so they did not really understand what they were protesting. When I mischievously asked some if they had read Roald Dahl's famous story "The Boy Who Talked with Animals," about a boy who freed a giant turtle and sailed away on it into the far ocean, they shook their turtle heads.[15] It has become fashionable to assert that the demonstrating youth know much about the policies they protest; but that is only a sentiment of solidarity with little basis in fact. True, there are several serious NGOs with real knowledge and serious policy critiques, such as the World Wildlife Fund, and I shall presently consider their phenomenal growth and the opportunity they present for making economic and social well-being a shared success between the agents of economic globalization and the civil society—the two great phenomena as we enter the twenty-first century. But they are not the tumultuous many who are agitating in the streets.

4. Overlaying the entire scene, of course, is the general presumption that defines many recent assertions by intellectuals that somehow the proponents of capitalism, and of its recent manifestations in regard to economic reforms such as the moves to privatization and to market liberalization (including trade liberalization), are engaged, as Edward Said claims, in a "dominant discourse [whose goal] is to fashion the merciless logic of corporate profit-making and political power into a normal state of affairs." Following Pierre Bourdieu, Said endorses the view that "Clinton-Blair neoliberalism, which built on the conservative dismantling of the great social achievements in health, education, labor and security of the welfare state during the Thatcher-Reagan period, has constructed a paradoxical *doxa*, a symbolic counterrevolution."[16] In Bourdieu's own words, this is "conservative but presents itself as progressive; it seeks the restoration of the past order in some of its most archaic aspects (especially as regards economic relations), yet it passes off regressions, reversals, surrenders, as forward-looking reforms or revolutions leading to a whole new age of abundance and liberty).[17]

But, frankly, this view stands reality on its head. Of course, we have known since Orwell that words do matter, and the smart duelists in the controversies over public policy will often seize the high ground by appropriating to themselves and their own causes, before their adversaries do, beguiling words such as *progressive*. Thus, believe it or not, protectionists in trade have been known to ask for "tariff reform"; today, they ask for "fair trade," which no one can deny except for the informed few who see that it is used to justify unfair trade practices. Phrases such as "corporate profit making" and 'trickle-down' do the same for the friends of Bourdieu, creating and fostering a pejorative perception of the market-using policy changes that they reject.

It is therefore not surprising that today's critics turn to the same linguistic weapons as the anti-capitalist forces of yesterday. But let us ask: is it "conservative" or "radical" to seek to correct, in light of decades of experience and in the teeth of entrenched forces, the mistakes and the excesses of past policies, no matter how well motivated? In fact, as reformers know only too well, it takes courage and élan to challenge orthodoxies, especially those that are conventionally associated with "progressive" forces.

As for the policies themselves, the fierce binary contrast drawn by Bourdieu is an abstraction that misses the central issues today. The debate is really not about conservative counterrevolution and the enlightened past order. It is rather about shifting the center of gravity in public action more toward the use of markets and less toward dirigisme. It is not about "whether markets"; it is about where the "limits to markets" must be drawn. This is a question that, as will be discussed, provokes spirited complaints from the recent communitarians who wish the limits to markets to be drawn more tightly.

The present-day turn toward reforms in the developing countries is also prompted by excessive and knee-jerk dirigisme. As I often say, the problem with many of these countries was that Adam Smith's invisible hand was nowhere to be seen. Their turn to economic reforms is to be attributed not to the rise of "conservatism" but to a pragmatic reaction of many to the failure of what a number of us once considered to be "progressive" policies that would lift us out of poverty, illiteracy, and many other ills. As John Kenneth Galbraith once said about Milton Friedman—and here I take only the witticism and not sides—"Milton's misfortune is that his policies have been tried."

Anti-Globalization

Anti-capitalism has turned into anti-globalization among left-wing students for reasons that are easy to see. After all, Lenin wrote extensively about imperialism and its essential links to capitalism, and present-day writers such as Immanuel Wallerstein have seen the growing integration of the world economy in related ways as the organic extension of national capitalism.[18]

Lenin's views on imperialism provide an insight into a principal reason why anti-globalization is seen by those on the left so readily as following from anti-capitalism. In his famous work *Imperialism: The Highest Stage of Capitalism*, Lenin stated that the distinctive characteristics of capitalism in the form of monopolies, oligarchy, and the exploitation of the weak by the strong nations compel us to define it as "parasitic, decaying capitalism."[19] Nikolai Bukharin, for whose work *Imperialism and the World Economy* Lenin wrote a preface, considered that imperialism with its attendant globalization of the world economy is little more than capitalism's "[attempt] to tame the working class and to subdue social contradictions by decreasing the steam pressure through the aid of a colonial valve"; that "having eliminated [through monopolies] competition within the state, [capitalism has] let loose all the devils of a world scuffle."[20]

The notion that globalization is merely an external attenuation of the internal struggles that doom capitalism, and that globalization is also in essence capitalist exploitation of the weak nations, provides not only an inherent link between capitalism and globalization but also makes globalization an instrument for the exploitation of the weak nations. And this certainly has resonance again among the idealist young on the left. Capitalism seeks globalization to benefit itself but harms others abroad. The Lenin-Bukharin argument then leads, as certainly as a heat-seeking missile reaching its target, to anti-capitalist sentiments.

ANTI-CORPORATION ATTITUDES

But central to that perspective is the notion, of course, that it is the "monopolies" (for that is indeed how the multinationals are often described even today in much of the anti-globalization literature) that are at the heart of the problem: they do not benefit the people abroad; they exploit them instead. Indeed, this notion of globalization as an exploitative force that delays the doomsday for capitalism at home and harms those abroad has captured some of the more militant among the naive youth today.

The anti-corporation attitudes come to many others who are not aficionados of left-wing literature, also from the obvious sense that multinationals are the principal agents and beneficiaries of capitalism and of globalization.[21] Yet others find it plausible that multinationals must necessarily be bad in a global economy because global integration without globally shared regulations must surely amount to an advantageous playing field for multinationals. These corporations would then be able to seek profits by searching for the most likely locations to exploit workers and nations, thereby putting intolerable pressure on their home states to abandon their gains in social legislation. This is what is known as a race to the bottom. Indeed, this view is so credible that even a shrewd and perceptive intellectual such as Alan Wolfe, who sees through cant better than most, has recently written disapprovingly and casually of the "policies of increasingly rapacious global corporations."[22]

These anti-corporation arguments are not supported by the facts. But many believe them. And they zero in with a "gotcha" mentality, seizing on every venal misdeed of a multinational they can find, seeking to validate through these specific examples their general anti-corporation biases. This surely accounts for the return of Ralph Nader, the great scourge of manifest misdeeds by corporations. It has also magically transformed Julia Roberts, whose triumph in *Pretty Woman* reflected chiefly her marvelous good looks, into an acclaimed actress in *Erin Brockovich* and introduced the gifted actor Russell Crowe to celebrity on the screen in *The Insider*, both movies where a David takes on the Goliath in shape of a truly venal corporation.

The anti-corporation militancy that is on the rise among the young anti-globalizers is also strategic. We have witnessed the brilliant way in which the anti-globalizers managed to use the meetings of the international agencies such as the World Bank, the IMF, and particularly the WTO (originally the GATT), the pride of progressive architectural design regarding the management of the world economy and the permanent legacy of legendary men of vision, to protest and to profess their anti-globalization sentiments. After all, these meetings were where the world's media gathered. What better place to create mayhem and get attention from the vast multitude of reporters looking for a story? So while the old guerrillas struck where you least expected them, these new guerrillas have struck where you most expected them: at these meetings.

The same strategic sense has been displayed in going after the corporations as well. Nike and Gap, two fine multinationals, now have a permanent set of critics, with newsletters and websites worldwide. With Nike and Gap having overseas operations in numerous locations, it is not possible to avoid lapses altogether from whatever is defined as good behavior: the host governments often force the hiring of domestic managers who are regrettably part of cultures that are not as egalitarian and mindful of the dignity of others working below them as the West would like them to be. When lapses occur, these firms become obvious targets in a propaganda war that is stacked against them. Naomi Klein, the Canadian writer, admits frankly that, faced with the amorphous but overwhelming phenomenon of globalization, the only way to get at it is to latch on to something concrete and targetable.[23]

The same strategic thought recurs in the writings of other anti-capitalist activists. Thus the Nicaragua Solidarity Network of Greater New York

reported that in Brazil "[o]n Mar. 8 [2001], International Women's Day, women linked to landless rural worker movements in Rio Grande do Sul state gathered in front of a McDonald's restaurant in Porto Alegre, the state capital, to protest. . . . Nina Tonin, a member of the National Board of Directors of the Movement of Landless Rural Workers (MST), said the group chose McDonald's because it is *'a symbol of the intervention politics of the big monopolies operating in Brazil.'*"[24]

So they go after the corporations that spread and constitute the globalization that is reprehensible. We then also see teenagers carrying placards outside Staples, the office products chain that has succeeded immensely throughout the United States, and demonstrating in front of Starbucks while their more militant adult friends threw stones through the coffee chain's windows in Seattle. I talk with them at every opportunity; I find enthusiasm, even idealism, but never any ability to engage concretely on the issues they take a stand on. But then the Kleins of the anti-globalization movement are not fazed; it is all strategic, it is in a good cause.

Indeed, it is hard to understand the deep and unyielding hostility to multinational corporations, manifest on the streets and on campuses, except by analogy to earlier times. Perhaps the classic parallel is with the stigma attached to usury in medieval times: interest and moneylenders then, as profits and corporations now, invited implacable hostility. The exaction of interest was forbidden by ecclesiastical and civil laws, its practice turned into a crime. Even as trade and globalization increased with mercantile expansion and laws began to change (with occasional relapses), usury remained beyond the pale, contrary to conventional and persistent norms.

By 37 *Henry VIII, cap. ix,* the old laws against usury are, indeed, abolished, and a rate of ten percent is indirectly legalized by the fixing of severe penalties for any rate higher; but the practice is condemned, and classed with corrupt bargains. . . . In 1552, however, by *6 Edward VI, cap. xx,* the act of Henry VIII is annulled . . . and severe penalties are enacted against any usury what ever, "forasmuch as Usurie is by the word of God utterly prohibited, as a vyce most odious and detestable . . ." In 1570, by 13 *Elizabeth, cap. viii, 6 Edward VI* is annulled and 37 *Henry VIII re-enacted, but* "forasmuch as all Usurie, being forbidden by the Law of God is synne and detestable . . ." It is expressly provided that all offenders shall "also be punished and corrected according to the ecclesiastical laws heretofore made against usury."[25]

Other Ideological and Intellectual Sources of Anti-Globalization

While the sources of anti-globalization rooted in anti-capitalism in the diverse ways set out so far are dominant in the current discourse, there are others, not quite so influential, that cannot be ignored.

THE RIGHT

In this variegated landscape, complementing those who lean on the left are forces on the right. Thus for every Ralph Nader there is a Pat Buchanan. But the Buchanans are instead knee-deep in xenophobia and crude assertions of national identity and sovereignty. These beliefs lead directly to proposals to isolate America from commerce by building tariff walls. Thus in the 1990s Buchanan called for tariffs against the Japanese, asking for a 10 percent tariff on every Japanese import, and has argued recently against letting Chinese imports freely into the United States.[26] Interestingly, the right-wing extremists in India's ruling Bharatiya Janata Party are also fanatically for self-reliance in trade and incoming foreign investment.

The anti-globalization sentiments on the right extend easily to anti-immigration attitudes, whereas the left's fascination with anti-globalization rarely extends to a fortress mentality on immigration. While some liberal environmental groups slide into anti-immigration rhetoric when they argue that immigration adds to environmental problems, the general posture of the liberal anti-globalization groups is one of benign neglect. Surprisingly, however, there are a rare few progressive segments of the anti-globalization movement that are for free immigration. The anthropologist David Graeber has drawn attention to the Italian group Ya Basta!, whose platform includes guaranteed free movement of people across borders: an objective that has simply no political salience or social resonance, to be brutally frank.

COMMUNITARIANISM AND LIMITS TO MARKETS

The "liberal international economic order," as the spread of capitalism and markets worldwide is sometimes described, has also been challenged by political philosophers of influence, these coming from the Anglo-Saxon campuses rather than from the banks of the Seine. Thus, communitarians in the United States such as Michael Sandel of Harvard and Michael Walzer of Princeton's Institute for Advanced Study have tried to define limits on the use of markets.

To illustrate, Sandel has objected to the use of global-efficiency-enhancing international trade in permits for carbon dioxide emissions among members of the Kyoto treaty on global warming. With such trade, Brazil would be able to reduce its emissions but effectively sell the reduction achieved as a tradable permit to the United States, which would then credit it as a contribution toward the fulfillment of its own target of emission reductions, thus reducing by the traded amount the emission reduction it had to achieve. This trade would mean that a country where the real cost of reducing carbon dioxide emissions is higher would be able to buy the tradable permits from one where the real cost was lower: the world cost of reducing emissions would obviously fall with such trade. But Sandel once argued in a *New York Times* op-ed article why it was "immoral" to buy the rights to pollute: we expect everyone in a community to make a shared effort toward such goals.[27] A good example would be that our community would be offended if the rich boys could buy their way out of fighting a war (though one must admit that the substitution of a professional army for conscription is precisely a case where that communitarian sense has given way to the notion of efficiency). Sandel himself produces the example of parking spaces for handicapped people. The community would be offended if the rich could buy permits to use such spaces. But here again, the rich can always park their BMWs in these spaces and pay the fines if caught. To my knowledge, no one threatens that the luxury cars illegally parked in these spaces will be destroyed and the violators will be incarcerated, thus raising the effective price paid for such spaces by the rich to levels that really do amount to prohibition. In short, while communitarian principles do intrude frequently to place limits on markets, and hence on the principle of efficiency that markets help to implement, the communitarian spirit itself is subject to limits in practice.

It is likely that the extent of communitarian limits on markets will erode with capitalism taking hold. This is what Marx had in mind as he observed what he called the "commodification" process—what economists call increased commercialization. Thus, the balance between altruism, love, duty, and the other virtues, on one hand, and pursuit of self-interest, on the other hand, may shift away from those virtues as capitalism progresses. For instance, love may become sex, with reverence and mystique yielding to gratification. It is hard to see this in one's own culture, but during O. J. Simpson's trial I was struck by the fact that when newspapers described how he had been looking through the window as Nicole made love to her boyfriend, they all said that she and her friend had had dinner, come home, had coffee, and then "had sex." Mind you, none said they had "made love." So making love was reduced to having sex, the way they had dinner and then coffee. And, just as you might remark that the coffee was an espresso, the reports added that the sex was oral!

But the communitarians surely exaggerate the commodification that markets wreak. There is movement the other way too, and often it comes about because of the rapid pace of technical change, which has accelerated both the pace of economic globalization and that of globalized civil society. The cloning debate shows how societies will seek to place limits on what will be left to markets.

In the world as we know it, therefore, both communitarian and liberal principles coexist in varying forms. The important question is not whether we should have one or the other but whether capitalism and globalization are such an inexorable force that they propel society into a headlong rush away from traditional communitarian values and ways. The evidence for such an alarmist conclusion is not compelling.

ANTI-AMERICANISM

Yet another source of anti-globalization sentiments is the resentment that comes from the rise of the United States to a military and economic hegemony so unprecedented that the French call America, with which they have a notorious love-hate relationship, a hyperpower, as if being called a superpower is no longer the highest accolade.

Since this hegemony is exercised in the global context, the resentment of the United States follows worldwide. The loss of the Soviet Union as a countervailing superpower is mourned, even as the collapse of the scourge of communism is celebrated. The anti-Americanism that American power and its exercise—no matter how benign and invited—creates is then an important source of anti-globalization sentiment. Throwing sand into the gears of globalization is seen as a way to spit on American hegemony, if not to limit the exercise of it in the political, cultural, and economic domains.

So we then face a motley crew, a mélange of anti-globalizers animated by different ideas and passions and yet appearing to be an undifferentiated mass. Nonetheless, those of us who favor globalization cannot retreat from the task of meeting their concerns head-on. In the end, despite the chaotic nature of the anti-globalization movement, we can impose some commonalities and order before we offer a response. That is just what I propose now to do.

NOTES

1. Martin Wolf, "Will the Nation-State Survive Globalization?" *Foreign Affairs* 80, 1 (2001), 181–82.
2. Ibid., 182.
3. Francis Fukuyama, *The End of History and the Last Man* (New York: Free Press, 1992).
4. This meeting in Porto Alegre has now become an annual, parallel affair and describes itself as the World Social Forum, in contrast to the World Economic Forum of Davos. The contrasting choice of terminology is clearly intended to suggest that they are for social outcomes and for humanity, whereas their opponents are for profits and against humanity.
5. See http://www.globalexchange.org/campaigns/rulemakers/topTenReasons.html.

6. Jagdish Bhagwati, *The Economics of Underdeveloped Countries* (London: Weidenfeld and Nicolson, 1966), Chapter 1. I must add two vignettes about this first book of mine. First, its Chapter 1 is titled "Poverty and Income Distribution." Second, I had the curious satisfaction of getting back at a social-democratic critic, Dr. Louis Emmerij, when I gave a keynote speech at Antwerp many years ago. When I had talked about poverty and how to address it, he got up and said that it was good to see that Professor Bhagwati was "finally" turning to poverty. So I retorted, "As it happens, I was rereading my 1966 book on underdeveloped countries last week to write my speech today, and I am sorry to have to tell you that the first chapter was concerned precisely with poverty."

Besides, I must say that the book contained a moving photograph of a malnourished, starving child in Africa. At a time when it was fashionable to equate developmental analysis with esoteric questions such as the optimal choice of techniques, where the modeling was used to arrive at the disastrous conclusion that capital-intensive techniques were appropriate in poor countries, as they would raise savings and lead to faster growth, it seemed like heresy and a betrayal of economics to focus directly on poverty and pestilence and to concretize them with telling pictorial evidence. In fact, John Chipman, a world-class economist at the University of Minnesota and a fine friend, wrote to me at the time that he had heard a colleague exclaim: "Bhagwati has gone bananas; he has published a book with a picture of a starving child in it!"

7. Terry Eagleton, *Literary Theory: An Introduction,* 2nd. ed. (Minneapolis: University of Minnesota Press, 2001), 128.

8. See also the quote from Edward Said further below. Blair Hoxby has reminded me that, earlier than Foucault, these antirational views may be traced to Theodor Adorno and Max Horkheimer's *Dialectic of Enlightenment,* first published in German in 1944.

9. V. S. Naipaul, *Beyond Belief: Islamic Excursions Among Converted Peoples* (New York: Vintage, 1999), 276.

10. Today social anthropology has moved into a more liberal stance, under the influence of postcolonial and postmodern theorists. Nonetheless, it is not free from its status quo bias on culture, which seeks to value rather than vanquish the old, and to be skeptical and suspicious of change. The influence on policy of this discipline has revived as social anthropologists have found their way into foundations, the World Bank, and several NGOs.

11. David Hume, *A Treatise of Human Nature* (London: J. M. Dent, 1911), 2:128. See also David Hume, *An Enquiry Concerning the Principles of Morals,* ed. J. B. Schneewind (Indianapolis: Hackett, 1983): "Sympathy, we shall allow, is much fainter than our concern for ourselves, and sympathy with persons remote from us, much fainter than with persons near and contiguous" (49); and "It is wisely ordained by nature, that private connexions should commonly prevail over universal views and considerations; otherwise our affections and actions would be dissipated and lost, for want of a proper limited object. Thus a small benefit done to ourselves, and our near friends, excites more lively sentiments of love and approbation than a great benefit done to a distant commonwealth" (49).

12. Adam Smith, *The Theory of Moral Sentiments,* ed. D. Raphael and A. L. Macfie (Oxford: Clarendon, 1976), 136–37.

13. This new consciousness of ills elsewhere, and the aroused conscience that often goes with it, does not imply that remedial action will necessarily follow. Famines, pestilence, war crimes, and much else that plagues humanity has continued to our great embarrassment and sorrow.

14. Hierocles, in A. A. Long and D. N. Sedley, eds., *The Hellenistic Philosophers* (Cambridge: Cambridge University Press, 1987). The quote from Hierocles is from Fonna Forman-Barzilai, "Adam Smith as Globalization Theorist," available at http://www.ciaonet.org/olj/cr/cr_v14_4_fof01.pdf, 4.

15. This delightful story has been reprinted as the lead story in Roald Dahl's collection *The Wonderful Story of Henry Sugar* (New York: Puffin, 1988).

16. Edward W. Said, "The Public Role of Writers and Intellectuals," *The Nation,* September 17, 2001, no. 8, vol. 273, 27.

17. Ibid.

18. Immanuel Wallerstein, "Development: Lodestar or Illusion?" in Leslie Sklair, ed., *Capitalism and Development* (London: Routledge, 1994).

19. V. I. Lenin, *Imperialism: The Highest Stage of Capitalism* (Moscow, USSR: Progress Publishers, 1982; 18th printing) chapter 8, titled "Parasitism and Decay of Capitalism," 96.

20. Nikolai Bukharin, *Imperialism and World Economy* (New York: Howard Fertig, 1966), 169.

21. Chapter 12 offers a comprehensive analysis of corporations and their role in today's globalized economy.

Arguments such as effects on local culture are addressed in Chapter 9.

22. Alan Wolfe, "The Snake: Globalization, America, and the Wretched Earth," *The New Republic*, October 1, 2001, 31.

23. Naomi Klein, *No Logo: No Space, No Choice, No Jobs* (New York: Picador, 2002).

24. Nicaragua Solidarity Network.

25. Elmer Edgar Stoll, "Shylock," *Shakespeare Studies* (New York: Stechert, 1927). Quoted in *The Merchant of Venice*, ed. Kenneth Myrick (New York: Signet Classic, 1987), 165.

26. See my op-ed article "What Buchanan Owes Clinton," *New York Times*, February 22, 1996. The melodramatic title, chosen (as always) by the newspaper, reflected the fact that I was pointing to some parallels between Buchanan's demands and the Clinton administration's Japan-bashing attitudes and the proposals of some of the administration's supporters who had in fact asked for even higher tariffs against the Japanese. The situation was ironic, in my view; a liberal administration sharing the views of a xenophobe!

27. Michael Sandel, "It's Immoral to Buy the Right to Pollute," *New York Times*, December 15, 1997.

II.4   INTERNATIONAL FORUM ON GLOBALIZATION

What Should Be Off-Limits to Globalization?

Since Garrett Hardin published his seminal essay "The Tragedy of the Commons" in 1968 (selection II.16), much has changed in the world. Even though Hardin's article emphasized the potentially negative impact of population growth on our planet, his basic concern was the urgent need to address the ethics of unrestrained self-interest in a shrinking and increasingly interdependent world. Changes in the international system such as those described by Friedman (selection II.1) and Sachs (selection II.2) suggest that since the end of the Cold War, multinational corporations have become increasingly powerful and influential actors in international affairs. In the continual search for increased profits, companies, both large and small, have attempted to commodify natural resources, such as water and seeds for food crops, which until recently had been either free or available at very low cost. This article, published by the International Forum on Globalization, a group of economists, scholars, activists, and others concerned with the long-range impact of economic globalization, argues that the value of preserving the commons is being ignored in the rapidly accelerating search for financial gain. If this trend is allowed to continue unchecked, it could have irreversible negative consequences for our planet. The future of humanity could be at stake if human rights and democratic local control are not respected in decisions over what is and is not for sale in the global marketplace.

Focus Questions

1. How do the authors of this article define the notion of the "commons"? What are some examples of the kinds of things that traditionally have been thought to belong to the commons? What are some examples of the kinds of things the authors believe should belong to the "modern commons"?

2. Which of the current threats to a commons discussed in this article do you feel is the most serious? Explain why. To what extent do you think citizens of the developed world are aware of these threats? Would you be willing to take action and what price might you be willing to pay to protect people in the less developed nations and indigenous peoples from these threats?

3. Critically evaluate the specific proposals to protect the commons made at the end of this article. What could motivate different interest groups either to welcome or oppose such changes, and on what might they base their rationale for their positions? Explain.

4. Compare the position on globalization taken in this reading to that found in Bhagwati (selection II.3) and also the United Nations (selection II.5). Where do you stand on the debate over the limits of globalization? Discuss.

Keywords

biodiversity, biopiracy, commodification, the commons, enclosure, human rights, indigenous people, NAFTA, subsidiarity, sustainability, TRIPS

AS RECENTLY AS TWO DECADES AGO, large parts of the world were not part of economic globalization. The majority of people in the world still lived off the land, many with little dependence on outside markets. In many rural areas, seeds were exchanged as the collective property of the community, not the private property of Monsanto or Cargill. Many of the three hundred million indigenous people in the world lived in complete isolation from global trade activity. Most municipal water systems were under local government or community control. Much of the economic activity in the Soviet Union, Eastern Europe, and China was not linked to global markets. Most developing countries restricted foreign investment in their banking, insurance, and other critical economic sectors. Most stock markets were national, closed to global investors. Even though global corporations clamored to enter each of these domains, national and local governments and communities maintained strong barriers.

All of that has changed. Under two decades of market fundamentalism, introduced by Ronald Reagan, Margaret Thatcher, Helmut Kohl, and their counterparts elsewhere, the boundaries came crashing down. Some of this was seen in dramatic fashion on CNN in living rooms around the world, such as the destruction of the Berlin Wall. Some happened in the face of remarkable citizen opposition, such as the passage of NAFTA in 1993 and the WTO in 1994. Other battles over the global spread of corporate control occurred on the local stage, such as the determined fight by Bolivian workers and peasants to keep the municipal water system in Cochabamba out of the hands of Bechtel and the struggles of Indian peasants against the Cargill and Monsanto assertions of property rights over their seeds. During these two decades, global corporations—with the strong support of many national governments—forcefully asserted their right to any market anywhere. And today their reach has extended into virtually every domain of even remote rural communities around the world.

One of the most critical points of unity among the authors of this document is that this encroachment of corporate globalization into every aspect of life and the environment must stop. We seek to shift the framework of the overall debate on globalization in this sense: we believe that many aspects of social and economic life around the world should be off-limits to the processes of economic globalization. In this chapter, we offer the beginnings of a framework for choosing which arenas should be off-limits to which aspects of economic globalization.

From "The Commons: What Should be Off-Limits to Globalization?" in *Alternatives to Economic Globalization: A Better World is Possible,* by the International Forum on Globalization, pp. 79–104. Copyright © 2002 by International Forum on Globalization. Reprinted by permission of Berrett-Koehler Publishers, Inc.

On one level, there is already agreement across the spectrum of the globalization debate that certain goods and services should be kept out of trade. For example, governments around the world have created a global convention to ban trade in hazardous wastes. Likewise, there is a global convention against the trafficking of endangered species. And there is growing global action against the trafficking across borders of women sold into sexual bondage.

Now, the International Forum on Globalization would like to expand the debate beyond the "pernicious" goods mentioned above to include the rights of peoples and obligations of nations concerning what has traditionally been called *the commons*.

In this chapter, we offer an overview of the many notions of the commons around the world and spell out the current threats of economic globalization to commons such as freshwater, the genetic commons, communal lands, and others. We then introduce the concept of the modern commons— that is, the role of governments in carrying out a sacred public trust to perform certain key services that were once the province of communities and families but have been captured by and subsumed into the nation-state. We argue that selling off these services to global corporations—which operate on an entirely different set of priorities than the public interest—is a grave violation of these modern commons, many of which should never be commodified. We argue that they are also obligations of governments as trustees of the common rights and services of people. Finally, we offer a few ideas on how the commons might be protected from the worst aspects of economic globalization.

We offer these suggestions in the spirit of opening up a complex discussion. We do not pretend to present the final answers.

Understanding the Commons

Much of the thrust of economic globalization over these decades has been driven by global corporations pushing to develop and market every type of natural resource. In a world where natural resources were already seriously overexploited, corporations have attempted to convert every remaining nook and cranny of the natural world and human experience into commodified form.

Now, areas of life traditionally considered out of bounds are being considered for monetized activity, private ownership, or global trade. These are aspects of life that had been accepted since time immemorial as collective property, or the common heritage of all peoples and communities, existing for everyone to share as they have for millennia. These are what have been known as the commons.

Obvious among them are the air we breath, the freshwater we drink, the oceans and the diverse wildlife and plant biodiversity of the world, the genes all creatures pass to following generations, the stores of human knowledge and wisdom, the informal support systems of the community, the seeds that communities use for replanting, the public square, shared languages and culture, and among indigenous peoples, communal lands that have been worked cooperatively for thousands of years.

Some commons are gifts from the bounty of nature and are crucial to the survival of people and the earth. Most cultures have innumerable rituals to celebrate these gifts and rules or taboos against harming them. Other commons are new, including, for example, the broadcast spectrum or the Internet. Still others are ancient, such as the common grazing meadows of Africa, Europe, and Asia, folklore, and cultural artifacts.

Some commons may be thought of as global, such as the atmosphere, the oceans, outer space, and because they have no territorial claimants, Antarctica and the moon. Others may be thought of as community commons: public spaces, common lands, forests, the gene pool, local innovative knowledge with respect to medicinal plants, and seeds that communities have developed over centuries.

Author Jonathan Rowe of California's Tomales Bay Institute points out that the key characteristic of all aspects of the commons is that they belong to everyone. No one has traditionally had exclusive rights to them. We have inherited them jointly; they are our common heritage. They "are more basic to our lives than the state or the market," says Rowe. He goes on to say, "One cannot imagine a life without air fit to breathe, oceans rich with life, free clean water, a vibrant biodiversity. These are things we have always taken for granted. The commons have the quality of always having been there, one generation after another, available forever to all."

Later in this chapter, we will advocate for yet another category—the "modern commons" of public services like health, water purification and distribution, education, information, each of which was once achieved informally within small local and indigenous communities that have since been absorbed by the state and are also now on tap for privatization.

The modern nation-state has also taken onto itself the collective security of its citizens, which in a less technologically oriented and mobile world was once the province of communities. In that context, we need to discuss the varieties of security protection that a modern state is obliged to offer in addition to its obvious military roles. Since adopting the Universal Declaration of Human Rights in 1948, the United Nations has helped governments define basic human rights. Governments are obligated to protect human rights, as well as food security, as fundamental to life. Protection of cultural diversity is also a basic duty and right. Nothing in the global trading system should ever be permitted to reduce these fundamental priorities. (At present, many elements of the WTO and other trade agreements work directly against countries that try to protect these fundamental rights, which we now propose as part of the modern commons.)

Precise categorization of each type of commons is difficult to achieve because many cross several categories—for example, river water (which may pass through several regions and countries), biodiversity (which may be local or national), the broadcast spectrum (which may be local, national, or international), and the genetic structures of life. Similarly, protections against trade that destroys the commons—toxins, armaments, and so on—must be national and international.

Nonetheless, the purpose of this discussion is to lay on the table one central principle:

> Any global trading system needs to recognize and yield to the primary notion that not every aspect of experience should be subject to its centralized rules, and many aspects should never be included in global trade or investment of any kind or in the rules that govern trade and investment.

Such complex questions are usually omitted from discussions about global trading systems, which usually keep their focus on new resources, expansion, and profit. But these questions must be addressed if any kind of social or environmental sustainability is to be obtained. How can communal spaces be effectively protected? Do any effective instruments now exist? What new ones can be proposed? How do we define the areas of the commons, common heritage, or government services that should *never* be subject to trade—or at least never be subject to the authority of global agreements that impinge on local or national sovereignty? What are the obligations of nation-states in the modern world? What goods are too dangerous—toxins, weapons, and drugs, for example—to be allowed into the global trade system at all? Should we establish taboos for certain kinds of trade?

Current Threats to the Commons

The conversion of the commons into commodified, privatized, "enclosed" form has been under way for centuries . . . In the current context, the main engines of this conversion are the global corporations and the global bureaucracies that increasingly have served these corporations. With the help of the new global trade and finance bureaucracies, corporations are finding opportunities in some virgin territory that most humans never thought could possibly be fodder for corporate enterprise. Here are a few examples.

THREATS TO THE FRESHWATER COMMONS

Unthinkable as it may seem, freshwater—a common heritage basic to the survival of all human beings—is being opened up to private ownership, commodification, export, and trade. It's as if water were an ordinary commodity, like new computer parts or car tires, rather than a shared, irreplaceable, and limited resource needed by all creatures of the earth.

In many parts of the world, the rights to freshwater in rivers, streams, and lakes are being sold to giant transnational corporations like Bechtel, Vivendi, and others. (Before its collapse, Enron was also a main player in water deals.) These firms have started charging users for every drink of water or liter of irrigation. For people who cannot pay the fees—and many cannot—they, their families, and their fields go thirsty.

Private corporations around the world have identified freshwater as the last great untapped natural resource to be exploited for profit. They are quickly taking control of water and water services to kick-start trade in what authors Maude Barlow and Tony Clarke have labeled *blue gold*. Indeed, water is becoming just as important as a prior era's black gold—oil.

Companies have been able to proceed aggressively because water has been defined as a tradable commodity by both NAFTA and the WTO. Once the tap is turned on—that is, once any deals are made by *any* state or municipality in a country to privatize water or water services—the tap cannot be turned back off without violating corporate rights. The WTO contains specific provisions prohibiting the use of export controls to prevent the export of water, and NAFTA contains a clause (chapter 11 of NAFTA) that gives companies the right to sue governments for lost *future* profits. This applies, for example, in cases where governments try to stop water export. Water services are also among those slated to be labeled as a commodity in the new General Agreement on Trade in Services (GATS), under a new category called "Environmental Services."

Once water is privatized, commodified, and put on the open market, it is not available to everyone who needs it but only to those who pay. Right now, contrary to popular understanding, most of the world's freshwater is used by corporate industrial agriculture and in manufacturing, such as in the computer industry for manufacture of computer chips. Relatively little is left for drinking or small-scale farming.

Already, the privatization of water has been the subject of enormous angry protests in many countries, notably Bolivia, South Africa, Canada, and elsewhere. In Cochabamba, Bolivia, for example, hundreds of thousands of people rose up against the fees being charged by Bechtel Corporation after it gained control of the municipality's water distribution system and immediately raised prices. On the brink of a revolution, the Bolivian government finally cancelled its agreement with Bechtel, which responded by suing the government under investment rules of a Bolivia-Netherlands trade agreement that mirror the NAFTA rules. As we go to press, the case is still pending.

THREATS TO THE GENETIC COMMONS

Another commons that few people ever thought could be subject to privatization and development is the genetic commons—the vast building blocks of all life on earth. Yet this too is now subject to reinvention through genetic engineering and transformed into patentable commodities.

The late David Brower of Earth Island Institute once called the genetic commons "the last untapped wilderness on earth," but that is no longer true. Like our great forests, the genetic commons are on the verge of rampant commercial intervention. In some areas, like agriculture, the process is well under way. Third World agriculture activists call it *biopiracy*.

According to Andrew Kimbrell of the International Center for Technology Assessment, "Corporations are now scouring the globe seeking valuable plant, animal, and human genes that they can claim as their own private property, as if they invented them. Thousands of gene patents have already been given to corporations, which are now able to patent whole life forms and own them."

Most of this activity falls within the life science industries. Corporations like Monsanto, Novartis, DuPont, Pioneer, and others have benefited enormously from the WTO's TRIPs [trade-related aspects of intellectual property rights] agreement, which confirms their ability to patent plant and seed varieties according to their genetic makeup. Even though these varieties were developed over centuries by indigenous farming communities that shared them with one another freely in a process that is at the core of these cultures, now fees must be paid to use them.

Global corporations insist that this valuable genetic material should not be locked up by small communities but that the whole world should have access to it. Indeed, corporations use the language of the global commons until such time as they confirm their monopoly patents on the material. At that point, all arguments in defense of the commons are abandoned. Instead, the corporations then argue that *they* should be permitted to lock up these genetic materials through patents in order to have a chance of recouping their research investment—for the benefit of all humanity.

Pharmaceutical corporations are especially eager for access and the rights to patent genetic materials. Their representatives travel the globe, exploring traditional native remedies in jungles and fields. They also extract blood and scrape "buccal mucosa" from the skin of native peoples wherever they can, hoping to find genes that contain natural resistance to certain maladies. Usually they accomplish this without disclosing why they are doing it or how much profit they stand to make from their findings and their patents. Among indigenous peoples, the right of "free and prior informed consent" has now become a major international demand before governments can bring in development projects and before companies are permitted to enter.

The cynicism of such practices became especially clear when global pharmaceutical corporations refused to set aside the rules of the WTO's TRIPs agreement in South Africa to permit low-cost, locally developed AIDS drugs to be substituted for the expensive patented varieties they controlled. Only after intense global protest did the patent holders agree to lower prices for AIDS victims there. But the TRIPs rules remain in force for all other instances.

The authors of this document believe that seeds, medicines, and other genetic materials that have been developed in communities for centuries or millennia should always be subject to community control. Any agreement with outsiders to use these materials must be on the basis of fair and equal negotiations on a case-by-case basis, after full discussion of all the relevant facts.

THREATS TO COMMUNAL LANDS

In hundreds of cultures around the world, the notion of private, individual land ownership is anathema. Communal land ownership—or no land ownership—is traditional practice and belief among indigenous and farming communities on every continent. This worldview is fundamental to these millions of people, their cultures, their agriculture, and their economic, political, and spiritual practices. In peasant farming communities of South America and Asia and in indigenous communities everywhere, the notion that an individual or corporation could legally gather under its own authority large fruitful tracts of land—thus depriving the people who shared it for millennia—is outrageous beyond all understanding.

Native American activist Winona La Duke has described the land ownership issue among indigenous peoples by pointing out that in her own Ojibway culture, the term *nishnabe akin* means "the land to which the people belong." It is a notion that is the exact opposite of Western ideas about land ownership. It is also at the heart of many teachings about humans and land being in *relationship* with each other, with reciprocal obligations.

In contrast, the new trade agreements and policies of international banks and corporations are designed to delegitimize the authority of any such reciprocal arrangements and to solidify private ownership so that land can be more easily bought and exploited. For example, one of the United States' specific demands in NAFTA negotiations with Mexico was that Mexico break up the traditional *ejidos* of the Mayan corn farmers, the system of communal land ownership that began with the successful Zapatista revolution of the early 1900s.

The history of the "enclosure" of the commons is largely devoted to the privatization of communal lands throughout the planet. In most places, the process is so far along that it is rarely publicly argued. However, this has begun to change as mass movements like Brazil's landless peasant movement (Movement of Landless Rural Workers) and other such movements around the world have demanded dramatic land reforms and redistribution under the principle that land, like water, is basic for sustenance.

APPROPRIATION OF THE GLOBAL COMMONS FOR WASTE SINKS

Ownership and privatization are not the only threats to the commons. There is also the effective appropriation of particular global commons as free dumping grounds and waste sinks for the activity of global corporations.

The atmosphere, oceans, and even outer space have become dangerously polluted, freely appropriated by oil, energy, shipping, and toxic industries as convenient sites to dump effluents and wastes. In the case of automobiles, ships, and the fossil fuel industry, it is an intrinsic result of the technologies that effluents rise to the atmosphere.

When similar pollution takes place in a local commons or inside national borders—say, local smokestack emissions or runoff into rivers—government agencies exist specifically to try to do something about it. This is not to say these agencies do a good job of regulating such activity—often they do not—but at least they offer an authority to address the matter and a place where citizens may focus their complaints.

When it comes to the global commons, however, few such agencies exist. There have been some efforts over the last half-century to apply some pollution regulations. The Kyoto Protocol on Global Warming, the Montreal Protocol on Substances That Deplete the Ozone Layer, the United Nations Convention on the Law of the Sea, the Stockholm Convention on Persistent Organic Pollutants agreement, among other multilateral environment agreements (MEAs), are efforts to control impacts on global commons. But all have suffered from tremendous political resistance, weak regulatory regimes, and poor enforcement ability. Still, MEAs remain one hope for rational international recognition, on a case-by-case basis, of the collective rights to maintain the commons in a condition that serves all people and the planet's other species.

An important problem, however, is that when such agreements do begin to make progress in limiting corporate activity, the World Trade Organization can threaten to negate them by asserting its own superior authority on behalf of the primacy of global trade activity. For example, at the November 2001 WTO ministerial meeting in Doha, Qatar, the WTO made explicit its intentions to codify its superiority to MEAs, potentially wiping out generations of effort.

Other solutions to the problem have also been proposed. They include a variety of trust agreements where certain commons would be held as the explicit property of all people in trust for the future. Any encroachments would have to go through very complex permission procedures, thus at least slowing and making visible the problems before they occur.

Sadly, there are hundreds of examples of threats to the commons of the kind we have given here. All reflect increased global pressure on remaining pristine areas. Fortunately, however, there is also increased popular resistance to these encroachments. New methods and instruments must be found or created to prevent continued destruction.

The Tradition of the Commons

In most parts of the world, the tradition of the commons is ages old, though it varies from place to place and culture to culture. These are a few examples.

EUROPE

In Europe, the concept of the commons dates back at least fifteen hundred years. It referred to commonly shared areas of land and resources enjoyed by all members of village communities, including pasture for the grazing of animals, water from streams and lakes, and all the products of field and forest that people used to sustain their lives. The notion that any of these could be enclosed or turned into the private property of individuals or institutions like corporations was, at first, unthinkable.

The commons deteriorated over time in feudal Europe. There were struggles over definitions of the commons, and large parts of them were appropriated through military force by feudal lords and kings. Still, vast areas remained available for village use as traditional common areas.

As trade developed between regions, and especially with the rise of a large European-wide market for wool, lords and merchants increasingly sought to ensure and expand their own supply by privatizing more and more of the common areas, most importantly land. As they succeeded in enclosing ever larger areas, peasant communities began to lose access to resources they had previously taken for granted. Self-sustainability became more difficult.

Rather than remaining as subsistence farmers who also traded in local markets, peasants increasingly became "cottagers"—small artisanal producers—or sought day-labor jobs with the large landowners on lands they had formerly shared. With the coming of the Industrial Revolution, cottage industries declined, and people were entirely removed from their land and sources of sustenance. They became factory workers with no connection to the land. The peasants thus evolved into the proletariat.

Some mainstream economists have justified and praised this conversion of the commons to private property as a way of establishing clear ownership and therefore the ability to protect resources from exploitation. But this justification for what was essentially robbery of shared common resources ignores two important facts. First, the people whose lives depended on the commons were almost always excellent caretakers of it and remained so over many centuries. In fact, it was basic to the survival and success of the commons that the entire community shared its values as well as its sustaining virtues and helped protect and preserve it. Second, the people who enclosed the commons, appropriating it for private use, were nearly always outsiders, absentee owners with little personal dedication to nurturing, conserving, or taking care of these resources for the future. The reason they sought private ownership was to exploit the resources as fast as possible. They did not try to own it in order to save it, the assertion of mainstream economists notwithstanding. Rather, they usually pillaged and polluted it.

With the advent of corporate ownership and rights of private property, ownership was made still more abstract or removed from resources, which were increasingly understood only in quantifiable, objective terms. Forests, for example, were no longer appreciated for their community sustainability, the biodiversity they fostered, or their spiritual contexts. Instead, they became "board-feet," ripe for exploitation. That is certainly the situation we face today, in its most amplified form.

INDIGENOUS COMMUNITIES

In other parts of the world, terms like *commons* were not well-known, but the concepts of shared community use and protection of common resources were basic, endemic, understood and respected by entire societies.

Among indigenous peoples around the world, virtually all political, social, and spiritual values have traditionally been so deeply intertwined with the values and teachings of the natural world that these societies say they are inseparable. It is not really a question of a community commons, as understood by the Europeans. It is more that all creatures—human as well as plant and animal—are directly related, equal, and with equal rights to exist in a fulfilling manner. All economic, political, and spiritual teachings are rooted in that primary relationship.

It is little wonder, therefore, that invading societies—at least those that did not actually slaughter the native populations—made enormous efforts to undermine and destroy their commitment to their traditional relationships to land and nature. That was the only way they could succeed in getting their hands on the resources they desired.

Native peoples were pushed to separate from their lands in hundreds of different ways. Primary among these efforts was the aggressive attempt to undermine traditional religious values and cosmologies as well as traditional native stories and teachings about the need to live in harmony with, and as part of, nature. The actions of missionaries throughout the Americas, the Pacific Islands, and Africa are well-known in this context. They actively helped shift the traditional value system toward a new and more hierarchical view of humans and nature and toward the individualistic notion of private property. In the United States, Australia, and elsewhere, "reeducation" also played an important role—that is, young people were forcibly removed from their traditional communities and placed into boarding schools that did not allow native languages or teachings. The result was a kind of self-loathing that undermined native cultures and their traditional collective economic values.

Equally important were legal maneuvers, such as requiring adjudicatory land title. Since native societies did not traditionally conceive of themselves as "owners" of land but as part of it as a community, "title" and "ownership" of land were an absurdity, but one which they were required to address. The histories of the relationships between invading and native societies are replete with stories of how legalistic maneuvering succeeded in separating Indians from millions of acres of land they formerly enjoyed in a collective manner. These acts of removal and separation continue to this day, notably in the United States.

One particularly appalling recent example is the U.S. Congress's creation of the Alaska Native Claims Settlement Act (ANCSA), purported to be a guarantor of native land rights in Alaska, where these rights had never been abrogated. In fact, ANCSA was the final step in extinguishing the native relationship and rights to enjoy the lands in the traditional manner. Rather than native Alaskans being granted title, or simply granted recognition of "aboriginal rights of ownership" as requested, the Alaskan lands were divided and made into native corporations, managed by native boards of directors, who were given ownership of the lands. But in order to survive, these corporations needed to cut down their forests or exploit their minerals just as any corporation would. These corporate acts, albeit carried out by natives, were contrary to their prior indigenous values. So for the larger society, the desired outcome was achieved; the communal relationship to nature was removed and replaced by an exploitative one, thus providing new fodder for global corporations.

The global invasion of communally held native lands—which has happened on every continent and continues today—has had terrible outcomes, from destruction of the traditional reciprocal relationship between humans and nature to major social breakdowns.

The conflict of values endemic to these pressures over ownership of common lands and resources was very well described in the book *A Basic Call to Consciousness,* published in 1977 by the Iroquois Nation, in a submission to the United Nations Conference on Indigenous Peoples. Here are some short excerpts:

> The majority of the world does not find its roots in Western culture or tradition. The majority of the world finds its roots in the natural world, and it is the natural world, and the tradition of the natural world, which must prevail.
>
>   . . .

> The original instructions direct that we are to express a great respect, an affection, and gratitude toward all the spirits which create and support life. When people cease to respect and express gratitude for these many things, then all life will be destroyed.
>
>   . . .

> To this day the territories we still hold are filled with trees, animals, and the other gifts from the Creation. In these places we still receive our nourishment from our Mother Earth. Many thousands of years ago, all the people of the world believed in the same way of life, that of harmony with the universe. [But] the way of life known as Western Civilization is on a death path on which their own culture has no viable answers.
>
>   . . .

> The Indo-European people who have colonized our lands have shown very little respect for the things that create and support life. We believe that these people ceased their respect for the world a long time ago. The air is foul, the waters poisoned, the trees dying, the animals disappearing. Even the systems of weather are changing. Our ancient teachings warned us that if Man interfered with the natural laws, these things would come to be.
>
>   . . .

> The traditional native people hold the key to the reversal of the processes in Western Civilization. Our culture is among the most ancient continuously existing cultures in the world. We are the spiritual guardians of this place. We are here to impart this message.

ASIA

Traditional societies everywhere on the planet share values similar to the ones expressed by the North American Iroquois leadership. Concepts like Mother Earth combined with belief in nonhierarchical, nonownership-based, communal relationships to field and forest can be found among all peoples who still live in a direct relationship with the earth.

Most people in India today still derive their livelihoods and meet their survival needs from the biological resources of the country, as forest dwellers, farmers, fisherfolk, healers, and livestock owners.

Indigenous knowledge systems in medicine, agriculture, and fisheries are the primary basis for meeting their food, health, and cultural needs. In these traditional communities, the biodiversity of the forests and fields and the historic innovations of plant life for food and medicinal purposes have never been seen as the individual property of any person or family but as community resources available to all people. None can be excluded, and neither the state nor any other economically powerful entity can monopolize use of any aspect of the commons, biologically or intellectually.

There is a vibrant struggle in India today over the commons—not only the biological commons (land, forests, water) that have been the basis of sustainability for a great majority of India's population to the present time but also the *intellectual commons*. This refers to the cumulative knowledge that agricultural communities have collected and freely shared for centuries, as well as the innovations they have achieved in developing plant varieties for food and medicine. Global biotech and pharmaceutical companies have been aggressively patenting these examples of the intellectual commons, preventing their common use, and privatizing them for their own purposes. This invasion has led to a level of outrage on the part of India's farmers, indigenous people, and peasant communities that has brought literally millions of people onto the streets in protest against the World Trade Organization's TRIPs agreement, which protects the rights of corporations to engage in these practices.

Community rights to control the biological and intellectual commons are recognized in law as sui generis rights—equivalent to a patent, but recognizing roots in a community rather than an individual. This system is based in part on usufruct rights, which entitle farmers and laborers access to resources needed for their own sustenance, such as common pastures, water, and biodiversity. Sustainability and justice are inherent in such a system of usufruct rights because there are physical limits on how much any one person can labor; hence there are limited returns for labor, unlike capital and private property.

The battle over the biological and intellectual rights of farmers in India, and against the WTO's

TRIPs agreement, comes at the end of a long and painful history of prior enclosures of the commons in India. The policy of deforestation and enclosure of the commons in India began in 1865, when the Indian Forest Act authorized the government to declare forests as "unmeasured" lands or "reserves" for state use. This began what was called the scientific management of forests, but it was really the first step in a long series of moves to remove forests from people and convert them to commodities available for private ownership. Peasant communities that had formerly sustained themselves based on the forests' resources were forced to produce indigo instead of food and pay taxes for salt. They experienced the rapid erosion of their usufruct rights to food, fuel, and livestock pastures, as well as forests and sacred sites. This was a primary cause of their later impoverishment, which led directly to their resistance to further erosion of their common rights by global biotech corporations.

Threats to the "Modern Commons"

In most developed countries, it is hard to remember the time when the central political and economic unit was the local community or when resources were commonly shared. Over the past several centuries, political, economic, and technological evolution in much of the world has conspired to bring far more specialization and industrialization of economic activity, far less economic and social self-reliance, and far greater dependence on dominant centralized political units—cities, states, provinces, and national governments—to provide for the common fundamental needs and services that people require, such as education, transportation, health care, environmental protection, security, and the certainty that there will be sufficient food, housing, and work.

All governments now acknowledge their responsibility in these matters, though they perform them with varying levels of success. Canadians and Danes tend to believe their governments have performed well, at least until recently, whereas Russians and Burmese may not feel this way. Most governments get mixed grades on these matters—good in some ways, bad in others. The United States, for example, has kept its economic and sanitation performance generally high but has been very poor in matters of health care and transportation, and its delivery of these services is marked by extreme inequality. Maude Barlow's forthcoming book, *Profit Is Not the Cure,* details the impact of the World Bank, the IMF, the WTO, and their market-opening policies on the erosion of health care services all over the world, and she chronicles the private sector firms that have benefited. Two decades of these policies have left a legacy of unequal access and health crises for the poor worldwide.

The United Nations Universal Declaration of Human Rights asserts that in addition to the services that nations are expected to perform, governments are also expected to ensure certain basic human rights, religious and political freedoms, and the right to *meaningful* work at fair wages with human dignity. In fact, the U.N. declaration asserts that every person on the planet has an "inherited right to citizenship," which includes health care, education, and work. Moreover, every government has the duty to *defend* the fundamental human rights of every one of its citizens, even beyond its borders. Such assertions also imply that governments have the duty to protect their own ability to perform these services and ensure these fundamental rights against attempts to weaken them.

The authors of this report believe that these services and protections qualify as a kind of "modern commons," in which the state has assumed the responsibility for the common good that once resided in local communities. Even as more power devolves back toward the local—an outcome most of us support—we believe that states have a vital role to play in protecting the community stewardship of both traditional and modern commons. The performance of these responsibilities, however, is now under tremendous threat from global economic institutions.

Great pressure is being applied to national governments by corporations and global bureaucracies to privatize and commodify most public services. Global corporations seek to put them in the same category of commercial activity as toothpaste, cars, real estate services, or movies, provided by private industry at market rates.

Yet there are profound differences between the sacred trust arrangement of governments to provide for basic needs and rights and the private, contracted provision of products, entertainment, and commercial services. Corporations operate from a hierarchy of values that requires profit and growth. Yet as corporations make inroads as providers of health, education, water, or food security, the delivery of these services will go only to people who can pay the market rate. The many who cannot will essentially fall out of the system. *Hence, we would argue that any acts that separate governments from their obligation to provide for all people regardless of economic status are to be prevented.*

Similarly, any efforts by global bureaucracies to *require* that governments privatize such services should be resisted by governments and activists alike—and ultimately banned. At this moment, the current WTO negotiations in Geneva over the expansion of the General Agreement on Trade in Services (GATS) are a case in point.

If the GATS agreement is finalized, then most of the services we have listed here as fundamental rights of citizens and obligations of governments will be subsumed under the new rules of GATS. In other words, corporations will have the right to establish a commercial presence and operate what have until now been domestic services inside countries. These include health care, elder care, child care, water purification and delivery, education, prisons, domestic rail and air transportation, public broadcasting, parks, museums and cultural institutions, social security and welfare programs, and public works of all kinds. As mentioned in Chapter 1, the United States or Canada might find ExxonMobil running public broadcasting while Mitsubishi runs social security; France might have Disney operating the Louvre; Enron or WorldCom could be running the German health care system; and Shell Oil could be in charge of the Japanese railroads and perhaps child rearing as well. Such outcomes are not unrealistic: as we already mentioned, U.S. giant Bechtel was on the verge of running a significant piece of Bolivia's water delivery system until recently, nearly causing a revolution because of its prices to the poor.

The U.N. Covenant on Economic, Social, and Cultural Rights includes the right to education and health. Of all services, these are shaping up as the most potentially lucrative for the global corporations pushing the GATS agreement. Global expenditures on education now exceed $2 trillion, and global expenditures on health care exceed $3.5 trillion. Global corporations are aiming at nothing less than the dismantling of public education and health care systems. Already they have succeeded in lobbying over forty countries, including all of Europe, to be listed in the GATS.

The obligation of governments to provide services for their citizens may soon be reduced to whether some distant corporation will or will not charge an affordable rate for people to send their children to school or to a doctor.

In our view, no global agreement should have the power to forcibly intervene in the trust agreement between governments and citizens.

Of course, there are many other threats to basic social programs and services and basic rights to food and health, aside from the upcoming GATS agreement. In chapter 1, we discussed the structural adjustment programs of the World Bank and the International Monetary Fund. To be eligible for development loans or debt relief, dozens of developing countries were forced to abandon a multitude of social programs and allow for-profit foreign corporations to enter, commercialize, and privatize these operations to the detriment of local people.

We have also discussed the WTO's TRIPs agreement, which enables global corporations to claim intellectual property rights over the genetic heritage of people and communities and to redefine the role and form of agriculture. Farming and the community way of life it has sustained are becoming dominated by global corporations who have rendered farmers dependent on them for seeds, fertilizers, pesticides, and herbicides. Structural adjustment programs have also played a big role in this shift in agriculture, requiring nations to convert their farms to export-oriented, specialized production and permit entry of global corporations that accelerate the process. This has driven farmers off lands where they formerly grew food for their communities and has increased hunger and migration.

Because food security is one of the most fundamental human rights, every government has an interest in ensuring it as an essential foundation for social stability and public health. We believe this means that no development banks or trade agreements should be given the right to *require* that any country revamp its agricultural production systems, allow foreign entry and investment, or open itself to cheaper food from abroad to its own detriment. Of course, any country may choose to allow such entry if conditions warrant, but it should not to be *forced* to do so.

Cultural diversity and integrity is another area that can be seen as part of the commons and is arguably a fundamental right that should be protected by nations. It too is now threatened in many ways by global trade agreements. The right of social, religious, cultural, and indigenous groups to preserve their practices, beliefs, artifacts, and artistic expressions is crucial to maintaining diversity within and among nations and in the world. This also applies to the efforts of nation-states to prevent foreign domination of their own national cultural expressions, through media and artistic creations. Many countries, notably Canada and France—both deeply concerned about retaining film and television industries in domestic hands—have been fighting strenuously to retain their rights to protect their own cultures.

Current WTO trade law subjects culture to the disciplines of the agreement, including "national treatment," "most favored nation," and the prohibition against quantitative restrictions. (All of these WTO rules open up countries to foreign media and other cultural products, often to the detriment of local cultural expressions, which can be overpowered.) There have been several complaints over culture at the WTO since its inception. All have had the effect of limiting the right of a state to protect its cultural industries. The most significant was a 1997 ruling in which the United States successfully forced Canada to abandon protections of its magazine industry, even though American magazines already made up 85 percent of all of those available at Canadian newsstands. Then—U.S. trade representative Charlene Barshefsky said the decision would serve as a useful weapon against Canada's and other countries' protection of their film, books, and broadcasting industries.

The United States is taking such a hard line because any exemption for Canada would set a negative precedent for other countries, especially in the developing world, where cultural protection is an emerging issue. The fact that the effort to undermine these protections failed at the Seattle WTO ministerial meetings does not mean the problems are over. Both the GATS and the TRIPs agreement will have a direct impact on the telecommunications sector, including the Internet, digital and e-commerce spheres, public broadcasting, patents, trademarks, and copyright law. All are now on the table. They should be taken off.

In sum, we argue that in all of the preceding issues, nation-states and communities should not be subjected to the rules of global trade agreements or multilateral institutions like the WTO or the IMF. Trade in these areas should be subject to national and local decision-making processes alone. Only in this way will it be possible for nations to act on behalf of the common interests of their citizens and to fulfill their own obligations to them.

Proposals

At the start of this chapter, we said that the issues raised here—the preservation outside of the global trading system of the remaining nonmonetized, nonprivatized commons and the governmental trust in preserving fundamental services and rights (the modern commons)—would be nuanced and complex. We proceeded from the principle that not every aspect of human experience or nature should be commodified or subjected to the rules of global trade regimes that require adherence to the global free trade model. However, defining exactly which aspects to exclude, and precisely when, is not simple and needs to be the subject of continuing discussion and debate. Stimulating that discussion has been our main purpose in this chapter.

To further the process, we end the chapter with a short list of broad policies consistent with the ten principles for sustainable societies.

The Authority of Trade Agreements Must Be Narrowly Defined Global trade bureaucracies and international financial agencies should not have authority over state or national decision making when it comes to the commons, natural heritage resources, the preservation of national choice in domestic services, or fundamental human rights. Trade and investment agreements should not be allowed to require a national or state government to privatize or commercialize remaining areas of the commons or public services, or to force countries to open up these areas to foreign investment and competition, either by imposing rules requiring governments to conform or penalizing them for not doing so.

Decisions on Common Property Resources and Public Services Should Be Local or National Decisions about common property resources and public services should be reserved to the localities and nations involved, consistent with the principle of subsidiarity. Local commons are the province of local communities. National commons should be subject to national democratic decision-making processes. Global commons should be addressed by multilateral agreements on issues of sustainability and equitable access. No commons—whether local, national, or global—are the proper subject of a multilateral trade agreement. Decisions about the ownership, control, and operation of fundamental public services—including health care and hospitals, water management and delivery, natural resource use, education, transportation, public broadcasting, agriculture and food security, culture, social security, welfare, military, police, and jails—should be specifically excluded from multilateral trade and investment agreements.

Some nations and communities may determine that it is in their public interest to contract for private operation of some of these resources and public services. Indeed, there is sometimes a role for private ownership and markets to play in the management, allocation, and delivery of certain common heritage resources—including land, seeds, and water—but only in a framework of effective, democratically accountable public regulation that guarantees fair pricing, equitable access, quality, and public stewardship. However, decisions in these matters are properly local or national and have no place being prescribed by global trade and investment regimes concerned only with advancing private commercial interests. Nor is it acceptable for any international agreement to dictate actions by local or national jurisdictions that would result in excluding individuals or communities from equitable access to services and resources, such as clean water, that are essential to life and health.

Things Fundamental to Life and Human Survival Should Not Be Privatized or Monopolized Certain aspects of the commons that are basic to survival should not be privatized or subject to trade agreements. These include the atmosphere, bulk freshwater, and the genetic and molecular building blocks of life (including the human genome). It may be permissible to patent truly distinctive seed varieties created by privately funded research, for a limited period of time, but the patenting of naturally occurring seeds or seed varieties developed by farming communities or by publicly funded research should not be allowed.

Some Aspects of Life Should Not Be Patented or Otherwise Monopolized Here we include some areas of life that *are* now partly privatized and traded but should never be subject to corporate *patent* rights or monopoly ownership as offered by TRIPs. At present, these include genes, seeds, plant varieties, and animal breeds—with the possible exception of temporary rights to the exclusive production and sale of distinctive plant and animal varieties created through privately funded breeding programs. The general principle is this: No patents on life. There is also a need to rethink

patent rules on life-sustaining pharmaceuticals—for example, AIDS drugs—to ensure fair pricing and access by all who need them, without regard to financial means.

The Right of Countries to Choose Not to Import or Export Goods They Deem Harmful and Pernicious Should Be Protected; Trade in Certain Pernicious Goods May Properly Be Prohibited by International Agreement A country properly has the right to ban the import or export of certain goods that it considers to present a threat to health and safety, including GMOs, toxins, weapons, and addictive drugs, as well as tobacco and alcohol, for which existing trade agreements now prohibit exclusions. Some currently traded goods are so harmful to the environment, public health, safety, peace, and the global commons that it may be appropriate to create an international agreement to ban them entirely. Candidates would include toxic and nuclear wastes, endangered species, land mines, and sex workers. Such issues, however, are appropriately addressed by international forums and agreements devoted specifically to these topics, not by specialized trade bodies or trade and investment agreements.

International Agreements Are Needed to Protect Global and Transnational Commons Because certain activities in one country can have serious consequences for common resources in other countries, a system is needed to regulate them. For conditions like acid rain, air pollution, ozone depletion, ocean pollution or overexploitation, climate change, and so on, or where common resources such as rivers serve multiple jurisdictions, negotiations are needed on a bilateral or multilateral basis to protect the threatened commons and secure a just and equitable allocation of benefits. These negotiations should take place in forums dedicated to dealing with such issues and should be placed outside the jurisdiction and authority of trade bodies.

II.5   UNITED NATIONS

Globalization and Its Impact on the Full Enjoyment of All Human Rights

This report, prepared for the United Nations General Assembly in August 2000, discusses the effects of advances in communications and transportation technologies on the global economy. It warns that because the benefits of globalization are not being distributed equitably among the world's peoples, the continued development of a technologically advanced economy may have adverse consequences for the enjoyment of human rights.

The editors thought it important to include this selection in the reader to draw attention to the interdependence between technology and the rules of international trading and financial systems and to highlight the role of multinational corporations in the global economy. The report highlights the wide disparities in the access to advanced communications technologies between people in the richer, more developed countries and those in poor countries—the so-called digital divide. It also contains data showing that trade liberalization and financial deregulation do not necessarily result in a fairer distribution of the benefits of economic growth and are sometimes accompanied by illegal trade, such as black market weapons, drugs, and even human beings.

In conclusion, the authors argue that although technological innovation and globalization have the potential to lift millions of people out of dire poverty, this promise will not be realized unless human rights are factored into our economic policies.

Focus Questions

1. The report discusses trade-related aspects of intellectual property rights (TRIPS) under the World Trade Organization (WTO) agreements. Do the authors of this report believe that the current trading rules strike the appropriate balance between the rights of corporations and those of people? Explain.
2. What are some facts cited in the report that indicate that the benefits of technological innovation and international trade are not being distributed equitably among the world's peoples? To what extent should we be concerned about the disparities mentioned in this report?
3. What is the Global Compact initiative about? Do you think it is sensible to ask multinational corporations to assume some responsibility for protecting human rights, labor rights, and the environment? Discuss the idea of corporate social responsibility in light of globalization.
4. Do you believe technological innovation and economic growth can be organized to benefit everyone? Discuss.

Keywords

development, direct foreign investment, globalization, human rights, multinational corporations, structural adjustment, trade liberalization, trafficking, TRIPS, UN Global Compact, WTO

Globalization—Issues and Challenges

Globalization is a term often used without any formal definition. The United Nations Development Programme *Human Development Report 1999* noted that globalization is not new, but that the present era of globalization has distinctive features. Shrinking space, shrinking time and disappearing borders are linking people's lives more deeply, more intensely, more immediately than ever before.[1] The present report assumes that globalization is multidimensional. It can be broken down into numerous complex and interrelated processes that have a dynamism of their own, resulting in both varied and often unpredictable effects. While there have been previous eras that have experienced globalization, the present era has certain distinctive features, including, although not limited to, advances in new technology, in particular information and communications technology, cheaper and quicker transport, trade liberalization, the increase in financial flows and the growth in the size and power of corporations. In order to advance a constructive exchange of views on globalization, States might consider conveying to the Secretary-General their views on how globalization might best be defined and approached from the perspective of human rights.

While many people are benefiting from new opportunities for travel and from new communications technology, new levels of wealth through increased trade, investment and capital flows, others are being left behind, in poverty, effectively marginalized from the hopes that globalization holds out.

Globalization therefore presents an important challenge to the international community. Over 50 years ago, the international community agreed, within the framework of the Universal Declaration of Human Rights, that, "Everyone is entitled to a social and international order in which the rights and freedoms set forth in this Declaration can be fully realized." According to the norms and standards of international human rights law, such an international and social order is one that promotes the inherent dignity of the human person, respects the right of people to self-determination and seeks social progress through participatory development and by promoting equality and non-discrimination in a peaceful, interdependent and accountable world.[2]

The norms and standards of international human rights law have an important role in providing principles for globalization. At the same time, the international rules established under the General Agreement on Tariffs and Trade (GATT) and the World Trade Organization (WTO), and the macroeconomic policies of the International Monetary Fund (IMF) and the World Bank play a significant role in shaping and directing globalization. While the norms and standards of international human rights law stress participation, non-discrimination, empowerment and accountability, the global economy stresses economic objectives of free trade, growth, employment and sustainable development. The challenge facing the international community is to ensure that these two sets of objectives can be brought together to meet the commitment to a social and international order conducive to the enjoyment of all human rights. "The Global Compact" with business proposed by the Secretary-General in 1999 is an example of a strategy designed to address issues such as these.

The present report begins with an examination of the framework of international economic rules and policies from the perspective of the principles and goals of human rights law. This examination is followed by an overview of the principal effects of globalization as they have so far been identified by the reports of United Nations organizations, programmes and agencies, specifically as a result of trade liberalization, the increase in international financial flows, the advances in information and communications technology and the growth in the size and power of transnational corporations. The report concludes that the norms and standards of human rights are crucial to a full assessment of the cultural, political, social, environmental and economic dimensions of globalization.

From "Globalization and Its Impact on the Full Enjoyment of All Human Rights," preliminary report of the Secretary-General, United Nations, *General Assembly 31 August 2000*, pp. 2–12. Reprinted by permission of the United Nations.

The Global Economy and Human Rights

While various national, regional as well as international rules and policies drive many of the processes of globalization, in particular liberalization, deregulation and privatization, the trade rules established within the framework of the World Trade Organization (WTO) Agreement (the WTO agreements) and the macroeconomic policies of international financial institutions have a particularly strong influence in shaping the workings of the global economy. A review of the global economy as it functions within the framework of the policies of the international financial institutions and the rules of WTO will assist in establishing the extent to which an enabling environment supportive of the enjoyment of human rights exists.

The global economy is of course only one aspect in the creation of a social and international order conducive to the enjoyment of human rights. A just, efficient and equitable social order must also exist at the national level. Good governance at the national level is therefore an essential element. Good governance is important, not only from the perspective of ensuring respect for human rights at the national level, but as a means of incorporating and implementing international norms faithfully. The following issues are raised to solicit responses from States on the diverse effects of globalization at the national, regional and international levels, as a means of developing understanding for a constructive exchange of views on globalization.

THE WORLD TRADE ORGANIZATION AGREEMENTS

On 15 April 1995, the Members of the General Agreement on Tariffs and Trade (GATT) signed the Final Act of the Uruguay Round of Multilateral Trade Negotiations, a document including the various agreements setting rules relevant to trade in goods, services and intellectual property. The various agreements set the principles for trade liberalization, as well as the permitted exceptions, and established a procedure for settling disputes. As a result of the Uruguay Round, WTO, the organization responsible for strengthening the rule of law governing international trade, was created.

There is an unavoidable link between the international trading regime and the enjoyment of human rights. Economic growth through free trade can increase the resources available for the realization of human rights. However, economic growth does not automatically lead to greater promotion and protection of human rights. From a human rights perspective, questions are raised: does economic growth entail more equitable distribution of income, more and better jobs, rising wages, more gender equality and greater inclusiveness? From a human rights perspective, the challenge posed is how to channel economic growth equitably to ensure the implementation of the right to development and fair and equal promotion of human well-being.

There are points of potential convergence between trade principles and objectives and the norms and standards of international human rights law. Looking at the WTO agreements themselves, the guiding principles can be said to mirror, to some extent, the principles of human rights law and, as such, to provide an opening for a human rights approach to the international trade regime.

The WTO agreements seek to create a liberal and rules-based multilateral trading system under which enterprises from Member States can trade with each other under conditions of fair competition. The goals of WTO itself link the objectives of increasing living standards, full employment, the expansion of demand, production and trade in goods and services with the optimal use of the world's resources, in accordance with the objective of sustainable development. The agreements seek to achieve these ends by establishing rules geared towards reducing barriers to trade and ensuring respect for the principle of non-discrimination among Member States. The WTO agreements also encourage preferential treatment in favour of developing countries and least developed countries in the form of special assistance and longer implementation periods, the non-prohibition on export subsidies and the obligation to consider constructive remedies in anti-dumping actions against imports from developing countries.

The goals and principles of the WTO agreements and those of human rights law do, therefore, share much in common. Goals of economic growth, increasing living standards, full employment and the optimal use of the world's resources are conducive to the promotion of human rights, in particular the right to development.[3] Parallels can also be drawn between the principles of fair competition and non-discrimination under trade law and equality and non-discrimination under human rights law. Furthermore, the special and differential treatment offered to developing countries under the WTO rules reflects notions of affirmative action under human rights law.

These parallels can even be traced to the origins of GATT. It will be recalled that, in 1945, the United Nations was established to uphold peace on the foundations of respect for human rights and economic and social progress and development. The International Trade Organization, which was envisaged in the Havana Charter for an International Trade Organization of 1947, included the International Bank for Reconstruction and Development (IBRD) and IMF as part of that vision. Article XX of the original GATT recognized non-trade public interest values in particular cases where values and rules conflict. Article XX provided that nothing in the Agreement should be construed to prevent the adoption or enforcement by any contracting party of measures necessary to protect public morals, necessary to protect human, animal or plant life or health, relating to the products of prison labour, relating to the conservation of exhaustible natural resources if such measures were made effective in conjunction with restrictions on domestic production or consumption or essential to the acquisition or distribution of products in general or local short supply. The exceptions referred to call to mind the protection of the right to life, the right to a clean environment, the right to food and to health, the right to self-determination over the use of natural resources and the right to development and freedom from slavery, to mention a few. The exceptions under GATT give rise to the question: to what extent does article XX indicate a point of convergence between trade rules and international human rights law? The challenge ahead is to develop the human rights aspects incorporated in international trade law, in particular as a result of the inclusion of article XX, so that the development and implementation of trade rules

promote the social and international order envisaged under article 28 of the Universal Declaration of Human Rights.

While the goals and principles of the WTO agreements and international human rights law converge to some extent, the rules which have been adopted to achieve the goals of the former do not always produce results that are consistent with human rights imperatives. To take a case in point, specific issues arise in relation to the standards set concerning intellectual property rights.

First, the minimum standards for the protection and enforcement of intellectual property rights included under the Agreement on Trade-Related Aspects of Intellectual Property Rights (the TRIPS agreement) have led to the expression of concerns of balance and fairness.[4] Issues have been raised in relation to the protection of the intellectual property of indigenous peoples and local communities. It has been said that, while some of the standards in the TRIPS agreement are relevant to the protection of the knowledge and technology of these groups, the question arises whether the standards established under the TRIPS agreement are sufficient to provide comprehensive protection to the intellectual property of indigenous peoples and local communities. It has been pointed out, for example, that, in spite of the relevance of intellectual property of indigenous peoples to the development of modern technology, including biotechnology and technology relevant to the protection of the environment, universities and companies have taken and developed traditional medicines and other knowledge, protecting the resulting technology with intellectual property rights, without the equitable sharing of the benefits and profits with the original holders of that knowledge. It has also been contended that the TRIPS agreement, in its present form, has not been effective in preventing such uses of culture and technology. One question that has been raised from a human rights perspective is: how can international rules be adapted to protect and promote the cultural rights of indigenous peoples and other groups?[5]

Similarly, questions have been raised over the adequacy of the TRIPS agreement in addressing the needs of developing countries, generally technology users, to access needed technology for development and the protection of the environment.[6] Figures related to patent applications demonstrate an overwhelming presence of technology holders in developed countries.[7] Furthermore, an examination of the flow of royalty fees indicates that the overwhelming proportion of payments and receipts of royalties and licence fees flow between countries with high incomes. For example, in 1998, while sub-Saharan Africa paid US$ 273 million in royalty and licensing fees, and Europe and Central Asia paid US$ 723 million, high-income countries paid US$ 53,723 million. To put this in perspective, high-income countries dwarf the rest of the world in royalty and licencing fee receipts, with high-income countries receiving US$ 63,051 million and the rest of the world only US$ 1,283 million.[8]

While there are many complex reasons explaining the concentration of technology holders and technology transfer in and among developed countries, the figures are significant. Given the importance of technology to development, the TRIPS agreement has implications for the enjoyment of human rights, in particular the right to development, which need to be explored further.

The Committee on Economic, Social and Cultural Rights issued a statement to the Third Ministerial Conference of WTO noting that human rights norms must shape the process of international economic policy formulation so that the benefits for human development of the evolving international trading regime will be shared equitably by all, in particular the most vulnerable sectors.[9] The Committee stated its willingness to collaborate with WTO in the realization of economic, social and cultural rights.

THE POLICIES OF INTERNATIONAL FINANCIAL INSTITUTIONS

The implementation of macroeconomic policies, in particular through the projects and programmes of the international financial institutions, has also played a significant role in shaping globalization. The design and implementation of structural adjustment programmes have heightened concerns that macroeconomic policies do not sufficiently accommodate the need to promote and protect human rights. The special rapporteur of the working group on structural adjustment programmes established by the Economic and Social Council has noted that, while such programmes might be necessary and in fact beneficial for economic growth and social development, their design has generally been motivated by the objective of ensuring repayment of interest on debts owed to international creditor institutions and not by the promotion and protection of human rights.[10] The Committee on Economic and Social Rights has underlined the importance of including the promotion and protection of human rights within the framework of structural adjustment programmes.[11]

The Effects of Globalization: Preliminary Remarks

While the rules and policies of the global economy are important in shaping an international and social order conducive to the protection of human rights, the active features of globalization, the growth in trade and financial flows, the new information and communication technology and the growth in size and power of corporations, have a dynamism of their own which affect human rights in ways beyond the rules and policies referred to above. The following section identifies issues needing further research concerning some of the possible impacts of these processes on the enjoyment of human rights. The summary of issues is built on recognition of the many positive effects that the processes of globalization have on the enjoyment of human rights for many. However, from a human rights perspective, the principles of equality and non-discrimination underline the importance of promoting the human rights of all. This concern forms the basis for the identification of the issues that follow. The issues are identified in order to assist States in identifying factors relevant for a continuing dialogue on globalization.

ADVANCES IN COMMUNICATIONS AND INFORMATION TECHNOLOGY

One of the most influential elements in the globalization process has been the explosion of information and communications technology. The Internet has enabled people from different regions and cultures to communicate rapidly and across great distances and to access information quickly. Indeed, the Internet is the fastest growing communications tool, with more than 140 million users as at mid-1998, and the number of users expected to pass 700 million by 2001.[12]

In addition, communications networks can foster advances in health and education. The Internet has enabled the interconnection of civil society, which has had a direct impact on the promotion and protection of human rights. The successful organization of civil society has been assisted by the interconnection of individuals and interested groups made possible through modern telecommunication and information technology.

In spite of the benefits flowing from information and communications technology, the uneven spread of new technology can also result in the marginalization of people. World Bank figures indicate that while in high-income countries there are 607 Internet hosts per 10,000 people, in sub-Saharan Africa and in South Asia there are, respectively, only 2 and 0.17 hosts per 10,000 people. Similarly, while in high-income countries, there are, on average, 311 people per 1,000 with personal computers, in Latin America and the Caribbean, there are only 34, and in South Asia there are only 2.9 per 1,000.[13] In the *Human Development Report, 1999,* it has been noted that, in spite of the positive effects of the new technology, it also introduces problems of marginalization. The report characterizes marginalization in the form of divisions by geographical location (countries of the Organisation for Economic Cooperation and Development (OECD) have 91 per cent of connections), education (30 per cent of users have at least one university degree), income (only wealthy people and countries can afford Internet connections) and language (80 per cent of web sites are in English).[14]

The new technology can also be used to abuse human rights, in particular through the spread of hate speech. The Internet, in particular, has been used for the propagation of racism, child pornography and religious intolerance through the spread of violent, sexist, pornographic, anti-minority and anti-religious hate speech and images. The technical difficulty of regulating the content of messages broadcast through the Internet makes it a particularly effective means of misusing the freedom of expression and inciting discrimination and other abuses of human rights. This aspect of the Internet poses particular problems for Governments as protectors of human rights. It will be one of the key issues at the World Conference against Racism, Racial Discrimination, Xenophobia and Related Intolerance, which is to be held in Durban, South Africa, in 2001.

LIBERALIZATION OF TRADE AND FINANCIAL FLOWS

In recent years, many countries, spurred on by liberalizing international and regional trade policies, have based their development strategies on increasing integration into the global financial and trading systems. This has led to a dramatic increase in world exports of goods and services, from $4.7 trillion in 1990 to $7.5 trillion in 1998.[15] Today, nearly one fifth of all goods and services produced are being traded internationally.[16] The results have generally been an increase in capital inflows and outflows and a growth in the share of external trade relative to national income.

Increased trade and investment have brought significant benefits to many nations and people. There is evidence to suggest that increased trade and investment are related to higher rates of economic growth and productivity.[17] A recent WTO study suggests that trade provides an important contribution to the economic growth of nations and may ultimately lead to the alleviation of poverty.[18]

However, dismantling trade barriers and the growth of international trade do not always have a positive impact on human rights.[19]

For example, while some nations have benefited from impressive increases in trade and financial flows over the past decade, other countries have not fared so well.[20] The *Human Development Report 2000* noted that, in 1998, least developed countries, with 10 per cent of the world population, accounted for only 0.4 per cent of global exports, representing a consistent fall from 0.6 per cent in 1980 and 0.5 per cent in 1990. Sub-Saharan Africa's share declined to 1.4 per cent, down from 2.3 per cent in 1980 and 1.6 per cent in 1990.[21] Similarly, capital flows tended to remain highly concentrated between developed countries, or to a limited number of developing countries. For example, in 1998, the 10 top developing country recipients accounted for 70 per cent of foreign direct investment (FDI) flows.[22] In 1998, the 48 least developed countries received only $3 billion of the total FDI flow of $600 billion that year.

These figures raise several questions for further consideration: to what extent are the figures connected to trade and financial liberalization? To what extent are they related to a failure to liberalize trade and finance effectively? What other factors cause the low rates of foreign direct investment? To what extent do they identify the benefits of globalization being shared unevenly or at different rates? Finally, how could a human rights approach to trade liberalization correct perceived inequalities in international trade and investment?

It should be recognized that the trade protectionism, which the liberalization of trade is now replacing, can have a negative impact on the promotion and protection of human rights. The uneven distribution of trade and finance is not helped by the significant restrictions on trade that often face developing countries. Indeed, as developing countries open up their economies, they are often faced with significant trade barriers or restricted access in their areas of natural comparative advantage, such as agriculture or textiles.[23] For example, a report of the Department of Economic and Social Affairs notes that, in the agricultural sector, the total level of support in the form of subsidies for agriculture in OECD countries averaged $350 billion during the period from 1996 to 1998, a figure that represents double the agricultural exports from developing countries over the same period. This makes it difficult for developing countries to compete, which is particularly harmful, given the importance of the agricultural sector as a source of income and employment. Ironically, sub-Saharan Africa has one of the most liberal agricultural sectors in the world, in spite of its small share of the global market.[24]

While dismantling barriers to trade and investment opens up markets to new opportunities, a recent study on the social impact of globalization carried out by the International Labour Organization (ILO) found that it can also leave countries vulnerable to global economic changes in exchange rates, wages and commodity prices.[25] This vulnerability to external shocks is exacerbated by a lack of sophisticated economic and social structures in many developing countries.

Ultimately, trade liberalization and financial deregulation have diverse impacts that are often difficult to assess. Country studies undertaken by ILO also indicate that, while it has the potential to improve people's welfare, globalization occurs in a context of rising inequalities.[26] For example, the final ILO report on country studies states that there is a trend towards wider income inequalities, not only in most of the countries under study, but also in other member States. The report goes on to state that there is little evidence that trade is the main direct factor at work.[27] Further research is needed to clarify any linkages between the processes of globalization, trade liberalization and inequality.

While globalization has led to the dismantling of barriers to the trade in goods and services, labour is increasingly restricted inside national and ethnic boundaries. The increasing barriers to trade in labour, and migration in general, have been coupled with a resistance to promote and protect the human rights of migrants. Although the General Assembly adopted the International Convention on the Protection of the Rights of All Migrant Workers and Their Families in 1990, 10 years ago, it still lacks the sufficient number of ratifications by States for it to come into force.

The effect of the growth in trade on workers rights is difficult to assess. A study of nine countries undertaken by the Department of Economic and Social Affairs noted that trade liberalization was accompanied by reduced wages, underemployment, informalization of labour and adverse impacts on unskilled labour, particularly in the manufacturing sector.[28] In relation to women's workers' rights, globalization seems to have had the effect of repeating existing patterns of discrimination against women, but on an international scale. The *World Survey on the Role of Women in Development* indicates that, on the positive side, the orientation of manufacturing production towards exports has led to a significant increase in the share of female workers in export industries. In the international financial services sector, women enjoy high rates of employment, increasingly even at higher levels. However, the report also shows that, in the export manufacturing sector, women workers are generally confined to low skill wage occupations, and it appears that, as jobs and wages improve in quality, women tend to be excluded from them.[29] In the informal sector, it appears that women suffer as a result of the growth of trade with imports displacing women, as workers and as small entrepreneurs, disproportionately to men.[30] This is occurring, in spite of the significant role that women play in the globalization process. As the survey states, "it is now a well-known fact that industrialization in the context of globalization is as much female led as it is export led."[31]

It is also important to highlight certain negative aspects of international trade in a globalizing world. In doing so, a distinction is made between the rules and policies of the international community concerning trade liberalization and particular international trade practices in a globalizing world. While the globalization of trade has been accompanied by the growth in particular types of trade that lead to human rights abuses, these should not be confused with international rules and policies that are intended to produce trade liberalization. Nonetheless, a report of the Subcommission on the Promotion and Protection of Human Rights notes that, in some instances, and particularly in impoverished and undemocratic societies, globalization has facilitated trade in the form of international arms transfers, which, in turn, provide the necessary tools for armed conflict.[32] The same report links globalization with an increase in the dumping of environmental waste near the homes of low income or minority groups and notes significant dumping in developing countries. Globalization has also been accompanied by the rise in the international trafficking of drugs, diamonds and even human beings, including children. Such aspects of international trade raise issues of the right to life, the right to a clean environment, and the right to development. Further research is needed into the links between the processes of globalization and negative aspects of international trade and the ways in which policies may be formulated to promote and protect human rights in this regard.

The growth of trafficking in women and girls and the sex industry are causes of major concern. Each year, millions of individuals, the vast majority of them women and children, are tricked, sold or coerced into situations of exploitation from which they cannot escape.[33] The causes and effects of trafficking are complex, however several observations are relevant to the discussion of trafficking. First, trafficking in women and girls reflects global inequalities, as it invariably involves movement from a poorer country to a wealthier one.[34] Secondly, trafficking, in particular for prostitution, is becoming more widespread. Crime cartels, operating transnationally, are often the mediator for trafficking, and trafficking for prostitution can be traced to the demand caused by the rapidly expanding global sex industry.[35] As a result, trafficked people suffer abuses of their human rights, in particular freedom from slavery, freedom of movement, freedom from fear, discrimination and injustice.

GROWTH OF CORPORATIONS

The need to compete in new and often distant markets has led to a wave of mergers and acquisitions, which have enabled companies to specialize in core competencies that ensure international competitive advantages in particular areas. This, in turn, has led to the phenomenon of the mega-corporation, with cross-border mergers and acquisitions exceeding the value of $1,100 billion in 1999. As a result, some transnational corporations have greater economic wealth than States. A report by the United Nations Research Institute for Social Development (UNRISD) noted that the annual sales of one transnational corporation exceeds the combined gross domestic product of Chile, Costa Rica and Ecuador.[36]

The comparative size and power of transnational corporations raises issues that need to be considered. In a worst case scenario, transnational corporations may be able to use their position of comparative power over States to play nations and communities off against each other in an effort to receive the most advantageous benefits.[37] The relative power of transnational corporations must not detract from the enjoyment of human rights.

Questions have been raised about the social costs of schemes to attract foreign investment such as economic processing zones. Questions have also been raised about the employment practices of transnational corporations and their effects on the human rights of their employees. Greater attention is needed in order to devise strategies that link investment policy with the protection of workers' rights. In this regard, ILO has been active in developing strategies for the protection of workers rights, in particular through the development and implementation of the Declaration on Fundamental Principles and Rights at Work, as well as the ILO Convention (No. 182) concerning the Prohibition and Immediate Action for the Elimination of the Worst Forms of Child Labour. In the outcome document of the World Summit for Social Development of July 2000, States committed themselves to improving the quality of work in the context of globalization, including through the promotion of these and other ILO initiatives.[38]

Concerns about the impact of the operations of transnational corporations in relation to the protection of cultural diversity were also expressed in the *Human Development Report 1999*.[39] Some commentators fear that failure to give appropriate attention and support to the cultures of local and indigenous peoples, as a counterbalance to foreign influence, could result in pressures on local cultures.[40] Moreover, media control in the hands of a limited number of transnational media corporations can also have implications for the freedom of expression. Highly concentrated media ownership vests powers of censorship in the hands of media owners to determine where and what they publish.[41]

At the same time, transnational corporations can play an important role in promoting and protecting human rights. The Global Compact initiative of the Secretary-General was first proposed in 1999 to challenge business leaders to promote and apply, within their own domains, nine principles derived from international instruments, including the Universal Declaration of Human Rights, to advance human rights, labour and environmental standards.[42] At a meeting held at United Nations Headquarters on 26 July 2000, global leaders from business, labour and civil society met with the Secretary-General to formally launch this initiative. They agreed to work together within the common framework of the Global Compact to strengthen responsible corporate citizenship and the social pillars of globalization through dialogue and operational activities. While the Global Compact is not a substitute for effective action by Governments, or for the implementation of existing or future international agreements, it is a significant step in the direction of voluntary cooperation between the United Nations and the private sector in order to ensure that corporations have a positive impact on the enjoyment of human rights.

Conclusions

POVERTY

The above preliminary overview of globalization identifies evidence to suggest that while globalization provides potential for the promotion and protection of human rights through economic growth, increased wealth, greater interconnection between peoples and cultures and new opportunities for development, its benefits are not being enjoyed evenly at the current stage. Indeed, many people are still living in poverty. On the positive side, World Bank figures indicate that the number of people living on less than $1 a day has been relatively stable in the past decade, in spite of an increase in the world's population, and, as a percentage rate, the percentage of people living in extreme poverty decreased from 29 per cent to 24 per cent between 1990 and 1998. Nonetheless, poverty alleviation is uneven. While East Asia and the Pacific, the Middle East and North Africa have had significant reductions in poverty, poverty rates in South Asia, Latin America and the Caribbean and sub-Saharan Africa have remained relatively stable, while Europe and Central Asia have experienced significant increases in poverty.[43] Statistics also reveal that 790 million people suffer from malnutrition, 880 million have no access to basic health services, 900 million adults are illiterate and 20 per cent of the world's population lacks access to safe drinking water. In sub-Saharan Africa, 51 per cent of the population lives in absolute poverty. The majority of people living in poverty are women.[44]

Poverty is both a cause and effect of human rights abuses. The Vienna Declaration and Programme of Action, adopted at the World Conference on Human Rights in 1993, affirmed that extreme poverty and social exclusion constitute a violation of human dignity. It is difficult to assess the extent to which the various agents of globalization, trade liberalization, deregulation of finance and the growth of corporations and new technology, lead to or alleviate poverty. A study commissioned by WTO indicates that domestic policy in areas such as education and health has a greater impact on poverty than trade does, and concludes that trade liberalization is generally a positive contributor to poverty alleviation.[45] Nonetheless, it is clear that poverty is still a part of the present era of globalization. Given the potential for growth that is offered by globalization, there is a need for more effective strategies to harness this potential as a means of alleviating poverty for all nations and regions.

A SOCIAL AND INTERNATIONAL ORDER

The challenge of article 28 of the Universal Declaration of Human Rights, to ensure the entitlement of everyone to a social and international order supportive of the realization of human rights, remains. At the heart of the challenge is the need to examine the social, political, cultural and economic, dimensions of globalization, and the impact they have on the rights of every human being. As the Secretary-General said in his report to the Millennium Assembly:

> "The economic sphere cannot be separated from the more complex fabric of social and political life, and sent shooting off on its own trajectory. To survive and thrive, a global economy must have a more solid foundation in shared values and institutional practices—it must advance broader, and more inclusive, social purposes."[46]

The keys to achieving these goals exist. The world conferences of the 1990's set out commitments and programmes for the promotion and protection of human rights, the advancement of women and social development. In June 2000, States agreed on new initiatives to achieve social development during the present era of globalization, including through the constant monitoring of the social impacts of economic policies, the reduction of negative impacts of international financial turbulence on social and economic development, the strengthening of the capacities of developing countries, in particular through the strengthening of capacities for trade as it relates to health, and the integration of social as well as economic aspects in the design of structural adjustment and reform programmes.[47]

The goals and programmes are already formulated. The strategy to achieve them lies in acknowledging that the principles and standards of human rights should be adopted as an indispensable framework for globalization. Human rights embody universal shared values and are the common standard of achievement for all peoples and all nations.[48] By adopting a human rights approach, globalization can be examined in its civil, cultural, political, social and economic contexts so that the international community can meet its commitment to an international and social order conducive to respect for human rights. This must be the strategy of governance at all levels—to secure respect of all human rights for everyone.

NOTES

1. United Nations Development Programme (UNDP), *Human Development Report 1999,* Oxford University Press, New York, 1999, p. 1. The report goes on to note that globalization is not a new phenomenon in historical terms, but that it is different today. Some of the characteristics are new markets—foreign exchange and capital markets linked globally, operating 24 hours a day, with dealings at a distance in real time; new tools—Internet links, cellular phones, media networks; new actors—the World Trade Organization (WTO) with authority over national Governments, the multinational corporations with more economic power than many States, the global network of non-governmental organizations (NGOs) and other groups that transcend national boundaries; new rules—multilateral agreements on trade, services and intellectual property, backed by strong enforcement mechanisms and more binding for national governments reducing the scope for national policy.

2. See articles 1, 2 and 28 of the Universal Declaration of Human Rights, parts I and II of the International Covenant on Economic, Social and Cultural Rights and the International Covenant on Civil and Political Rights and article 1 of the United Nations Declaration on the Right to Development.

3. See also articles 3 (Right to life), 23 (Right to work) and 25 (Right to an adequate standard of living) of the Universal Declaration of Human Rights.

4. It should be noted that the protection of intellectual property is a human right under article 27 of the Universal Declaration of Human Rights and article 15 of the International Covenant on Economic, Social and Cultural Rights. In particular, article 15 (1) (c) notes that "The States Parties to the present Covenant recognize the right of everyone . . . to benefit from the protection of the moral and material interests resulting from any scientific, literary or artistic production of which he is the author." Intellectual property rights themselves, as for example those established according to the minimum standards contained in the TRIPS agreement, are not themselves human rights. However they could be a means of promoting and protecting the human right to intellectual property, so long as the granting of such intellectual property rights achieves the balance and fairness required by article 27 of the Universal Declaration and article 15 of the Covenant.

5. There is of course nothing in the TRIPS agreement that prevents States taking individual action to protect the technology and knowledge of indigenous peoples and local communities.

6. While article 7 of the TRIPS agreement states that the protection and enforcement of intellectual property rights should contribute to the transfer and dissemination of technology, the agreement does not develop any mechanism to achieve this.

7. For example: in 1997, patent applications numbered 2,785,420 in high-income countries, while in East Asia and the Pacific they numbered 290,630; in the Middle East and North Africa there were only 1,716 applications; and in sub-Saharan Africa, 392,959, with only 38 of those being filed by residents. See World Bank, *World Development Indicators 2000*, World Bank, Washington, D.C., 2000, table 5.12.

8. World Bank, op. cit., table 5.12.

9. See E/CN.12/1999/9, para. 5.

10. See E/CN.4/1999/47.

11. See E/1999/22, paras. 378-393. See also, E/C.12/1/Add.7/Rev.1, para. 21.

12. UNDP, op. cit., p. 5.

13. World Bank, op. cit., table 5.12.

14. UNDP, 1999, op. cit., p. 6.

15. UNDP, *Human Development Report 2000*, Oxford University Press, New York, 2000, p. 82.

16. UNDP, 1999, op. cit., p. 1.

17. International Labour Office, *Country studies on the social impact of globalization: final report*, ILO, Governing Body, 276th Session, GB. 276/ WP/SDL/1, para. 30.

18. Ben-David, D. and L. Alan Winters, "Trade, Income Disparity and Poverty," *Special Studies No. 5*, World Trade Organization, WTO Publications, Geneva, 1999.

19. See E/CN.4/Sub.2/1999/11, para. 3.

20. Even those countries that have experienced impressive increases in trade and financial flows have suffered downturns and reversals in fortune as a result of financial crises, such as the Asian financial crisis of 1997.

21. UNDP, 2000, op. cit., p. 82.

22. A/AC.253/25, para. 41.

23. See the comments of Joseph Stiglitz, former World Bank chief economist, quoted in E/CN.4/Sub.2/2000/13, para. 14.

24. A/AC.253/25, para. 21.

25. International Labour Office, op. cit., para. 68 (f).

26. Ibid., para. 3.

27. Ibid.

28. See Janine Berg and Lance Taylor, "External liberalization, economic performance and social policy," New School for Social Research, Working Paper Series: Globalization, Labour Markets and Social Policy, February 2000. Cited in A/AC.253/25, para. 9.

29. See E/1999/44, para. 52.

30. Ibid., para. 55.

31. Ibid., para. 50.

32. E/CN.4/Sub.2/1999/8, para. 16.

33. E/ECE/RW.2/2000/3, para. 1.

34. Ibid., para. 11.

35. Ibid., para. 17.

36. United Nations Research Institute for Social Development, *States of Disarray: The Social Effects of Globalization*, report on the World Summit for Social Development, Geneva, March 1995, p. 153. Similarly, according to the *Human Development*

Report 1999, the assets of the top three billionaires are more than the combined gross national product of all least developed countries.

37. See E/CN.4/Sub.2/1995/11, para. 53.

38. A/S-24/8/Rev.1, para. 38.

39. UNDP, 1999, op. cit., para. 4 (f).

40. E/CN.4/Sub.2/1999/8, para. 19. Also, UNDP 1999, op.

41. Ghai, Y., "Rights, Markets and Globalization: East Asian Experience," *Report of the Symposium on Human Development and Human Rights,* UNDP and the Office of the United Nations High Commissioner for Human Rights, Royal Ministry of Foreign Affairs, Oslo, Norway, 2–3 October 1998, p. 130.

42. See Mary Robinson, United Nations High Commissioner for Human Rights, *Putting principles into practice: creating a Global Compact with the business sector, 2000.*

43. World Bank, 2000, op. cit., p. 4.

44. See UNDP, 1999, op. cit.; *United Nations Action Strategy for Halving Poverty* (25 May 2000); and *United Nations Bulletin on the Eradication of Poverty* (Nos. 1–5).

45. Ben-David, D. and L. Alan Winters, op. cit.

46. A/54/2000, para. 25.

47. See A/S-24/2/Add.2 (Parts I and III), paras. 6 bis, 10, 82, 82 bis and 103 ter.

48. See *Universal Declaration of Human Rights,* preamble.

Computers, Robotics, and Information Technology

HANS MORAVEC　　　　　　　　　　　　　　　　　　II.6

Universal Robots

Humans have long dreamt of a time when machines would take over the more mundane and onerous tasks of life. In this piece, Hans Moravec, principal research scientist at the Robotics Institute of Carnegie Mellon University, discusses how he envisions the future of powerful computer-controlled machines.

These yet-to-be-developed universal robots, claims Moravec, will be able to perceive their environs as they become more powerful and ultimately be able to modify their behavior and actions in the most appropriate way. The completion of remedial activities will be driven by the robot's "desire" to achieve the desired objective. By improving their performance, future robots will become more humanlike in that they will be able to teach themselves and learn.

As Darwin proposed more than 100 years ago, life forms undergo constant change, and the new organisms that are better adapted to their environment thrive and may displace older life forms. Similarly, Moravec suggests that the ability of computers will develop in the future as a result of newer technology because they will develop the ability to "learn." This will occur because they will be able to save and modify "conditioning suites," which have proven to be particularly effective and efficient.

Focus Questions

1. How does Moravec see universal robots evolving from today's powerful, affordable computers, and in what ways will these future machines differ from robots presently used in industrial and other applications?

2. Compare Moravec's theory of universal robots and how they might serve us with the technologies described by Kurzweil (selection II.8). Do you believe that increasingly humanlike robots of the future might prove to be more a curse than a blessing? Why?

3. If machines continue to become more powerful and intelligent as suggested by this article, do you think we have the foresight to plan for that possible occurrence and the will to ensure that the inevitable changes are beneficial?

Keywords

artificial intelligence, automation, conditioning, evolution, learning, MIPS, robotics, spatial awareness, Turing test

AFFORDABLE COMPUTERS RACED PAST 1 MIPS* in the 1990s, but the benefits have been slow to reach commercial robots. There are hundreds of millions of computers, but only a few hundred thousand robots, many over a decade old. The perceived potential of robotics is limited, and the engineering investment it receives consequently modest. Advanced industrial robots are controlled by last generation's 1- to 10-MIPS computers, less intelligent than an insect. High-speed robot arms use the processing power to precisely plan, measure, and adjust joint motions about one hundred times per second. Mobile robot computers are kept busy tracking a few special navigational features, calculating the robot's position, checking for obstacles and planning and adjusting travel about ten times per second. As with insects, success depends on special properties of the environment: precise location and timing of workspace components for factory arms, correct placement and programming of the navigational features, and absence of too much obscuring clutter for mobile machines. Insects behave more interestingly than present robots because evolutionary competition has drawn them into wickedly risky behavior. Insect survival relies as much on mass reproduction as on individual success; only a tiny, lucky fraction of each generation lives long enough to

produce offspring. Even so, similar limitations surface in both domains. A single misplaced beacon draws a Stanford Hospital robot down a stairwell, and a moth spirals to its death, navigation system fixated on a streetlight rather than the moon. To reduce such risks, $100,000 machines are designed to be plodding dullards, restricted to carefully mapped and marked surroundings.

Robot systems are now installed, debugged, and updated by trained specialists, who measure and prepare the workspace and tailor job- and site-specific control programs. Few jobs are large and static enough to warrant such time-consuming and expensive preparations. If mobile robots for delivery, cleaning, and inspection could be unpacked anywhere and simply trained by leading them once through their task, they would find thousands of times as many buyers. The performance of this decade's experimental robots strongly suggests that 10 MIPS is inadequate to do this sufficiently well. Insectlike 100-MIPS machines, with programs that build coarse 2D maps of their surroundings, or track hundreds of points in 3D, might, just possibly, free-navigate tolerably in some circumstances. One thousand MIPS computers, mental matches for the tiniest lizards, can manage multi-million cell 3D grid maps and probably *are* adequate to guide free-roving robots. The basic idea would be to align current maps to old maps stored during training: the more content in the maps, the less chance of error. One thousand MIPS is just about to appear in personal computers, and thus in research robots. It may show up in commercial robots early in the

*Millions of instructions per second

next decade, multiplying their numbers along with their usefulness.

Utility robots for the home could then follow, maybe around 2005, drawn by an assured mass market for affordable machines that could effectively keep a house clean. Early entrants will probably be very specialized, like the conceptual autonomous robot vacuum cleaner. This design senses its world with a triangle of tiny video cameras on each of four sides, is controlled by a 1,000-MIPS computer, and moves in any direction (and scrubs) using three individually steered and driven wheels. About once a second, it stereoscopically measures the range of several thousand points in its vicinity and merges them into a three-dimensional "evidence grid" map. The grid gives the robot a spatial intelligence comparable to a tiny lizard's, but more precise. Taken out of its box and activated in a new home, the robot memorizes its surroundings in 3D. Then, perhaps, it asks "when and how often should I clean this room, and what about the one beyond the door?" Its spatial comprehension would keep it doing its job and out of trouble for years at a stretch. Perhaps it maintains a "web page" by wireless connection, where its maps and schedules can be examined and altered.

Universality

Commercially successful robots will engender a growing industry and more capable successors. The simple vacuum cleaner may be followed by larger utility robots with dusting arms. Arms may become stronger and more sensitive, to clean other surfaces. Mobile robots with dexterous arms, vision and touch sensors, and several thousand MIPS of processing will be able to do various tasks. With proper programming and minor accessories, such machines could pick up clutter, retrieve and deliver articles, take inventory, guard homes, open doors, mow lawns, or play games. New applications will spur further advancements when existing robots fall short in acuity, precision, strength, reach, dexterity, or processing power. Capability, numbers sold, engineering and manufacturing quality, and cost effectiveness will increase in a mutually reinforcing spiral.

Rossum's Universal Robots was the title of an influential internationally performed play written in 1921 by a Czech playwright, Karel Čapek. At his brother's suggestion, Čapek coined the term "robot" from the Czech word for hard, menial labor. In the play, a universal robot was an artificial human being built to do drudge work of any sort, especially in factories.

In 1935 Alan Turing instantiated David Hilbert's concept of mechanizing mathematics. He designed conceptual machines that moved along a tape, reading and writing discrete symbols according to simple fixed rules, and showed they could do any finite mathematical operation. He also demonstrated that there exist particular machines that interpret the initial contents of their tape as a description of any other machine and proceed, slowly, to simulate this other machine. Such *Universal Turing Machines* inspired some of the first electronic computers and still serve as mathematical tools for studying computation.

Computers are the physical realization of Turing's universal machines, but they are universal only in symbol manipulation—paperwork. A universal *robot* extends the idea into the realm of physical perception and action. Because there is a far greater variety and quantity of physical work to do in the world than paperwork, universal robots are likely to become far more numerous than plain universal computers as soon as their capabilities and costs warrant. Advanced utility robots reprogrammed for various tasks will be a partial step in that direction. Call them the accidental, zeroth generation of universal robot. Subsequent generations will be designed from the start for universality.

First-Generation Universal Robots

Estimated time of arrival: 2010

Processing power: 3,000 MIPS (lizard-scale)

Distinguishing feature: General-purpose perception, manipulation, and mobility

A robot's activities are assembled from its fundamental perception and action repertoire. First-generation robots will exist in a world built for humans, and that repertoire most usefully would resemble a human's. The general size, shape, and strength of the machine should be humanlike, to allow passage through and reach into the same spaces. Its mobility should be efficient on flat ground, where most tasks will happen, but it should somehow be able to traverse stairs and rough ground, lest the robot be trapped on single-floor "islands." It should be able to manipulate most everyday objects, and to find them in the nearby world.

Two-, four-, and six-legged robots of all sizes, able to cross many types of terrain, are becoming common in research. Many, however, are powered externally via wires, and those that carry their own power move slowly and only for short distances on internal power. The mechanics are complex and heavy, with many parts and linkages and at least three motors per leg. Developments in materials, design, motors, power sources, and automated manufacture may ultimately change the economics, but, for the immediate future, legged locomotion cannot compete in performance, cost, or reliability with wheeled vehicles in mostly flat work areas. Typically, a wheeled robot can travel for a day on a battery charge, while a walker, going more slowly, expires in an hour. Yet simple wheels cannot negotiate stairs—a decades-old dilemma for inventors of powered wheelchairs. Among the patented stair-climbing solutions are pivoted tracks, three-spoked wheels ending in smaller wheels, and specialized mechanical feet of many varieties. All have significant costs in weight, efficiency, or maneuverability over plain wheeled vehicles. Robots needed as "frequent climbers" may be configured with such mechanics, but the majority probably will simply roll.

Elevators and ramps mandated for wheelchairs will also provide access to nonclimbing robots. Where such conveniences are lacking, universal robots may be able to lay their own ramps, temporarily dock with stair-climbing mechanisms, or even winch themselves up and down on cables. They have the advantage over humans of being exactly as patient as their control programs specify.

Robots that simply travel have uses, but many jobs call for grasping, transporting, and rearranging ingredients, parts, and tools. Fixed industrial arms, with about six rotary or sliding joints, have good reach and agility but are too large and heavy for mobile robots. NASA, the U.S. space agency, has supported research on lightweight robot arms made of materials like graphite composites, with compact high-torque motors and controls that compensate for flexing in the thin limbs. Cheaper derivatives of these designs could make excellent arms for universal robots. Since many jobs require bringing pairs of objects into contact, robots will probably be able to have several arms, of various sizes.

Human hands are much more complicated than arms, and harder to imitate in robots. Most industrial robot grippers work like miniature vices, others use fixtures shaped for specific jobs, and a few change their "end effectors" from task to task. Inventors worldwide have devised many clever hands that mold themselves to odd objects, but lacking the ability to control their detailed forces, they fail in some grips, and none are used in practice. More elaborate hands, humanlike and otherwise, with multiple individually controlled fingers, have been demonstrated by robotics researchers. With their many segments, linkages, and motors, they tend to be heavy and expensive, and controlling them to sensitively grasp, grip, orient, and fit objects is a difficult area of ongoing research. Because they operate only occasionally, and exert modest forces over short distances, hands can afford to be less energy efficient than mobility systems or arms and so can use types of "muscle" chosen to be more compact than efficient. Particularly compact are "shape-memory" alloys, metals which, easily bent at room temperature, return with great force to their original shape when heated. Given the difficulties, the first generations of universal robot will probably make do with simple, imprecise hands, leaving fine dexterity for the future.

The navigational needs of universal and house-cleaning robots are similar. A robot will perceive its surroundings with sensors, probably video cameras configured for stereoscopic vision, and construct a 3D mental map. From the map it will recognize locations, plan trajectories, and detect objects by shape, color, and location. This latter ability will be more important, and thus better developed, in universal robots than in housecleaners. Universal robot maps may be higher resolution, giving them a sharper sense of general spatial awareness. They will probably need an especially fine map of the volume around their hands to precisely locate work objects and visually monitor manipulation. An interesting technique, used successfully in research projects and becoming more practical as cameras shrink, is to put video cameras on the hands themselves, in the palms or on the fingers.

A few thousand MIPS is just enough computing power for a moving robot to maintain a coarse map of its surroundings and use it for locating itself relative to trained itineraries and to plan and control driving. When not traveling, there is power enough to construct a fine map of a manipulator workspace, to locate particular objects, and to plan and control arm motions. Speech and text recognition is advanced enough today that robots of 2010 will surely be able to converse and read. They will also be linked with the Internet, giving them a kind of telepathy. Using it, they will be able to report and take instructions remotely and to download new programs for new kinds of work. Information security will be even more important then than now, because carelessly or maliciously programmed robots will be physically dangerous.

Universal robots may find their very first uses in factories, warehouses, and offices, where they will be more versatile than the older generation of robots they replace. Because of their breadth of applicability, their numbers should grow rapidly and their costs decline. When they become cheap enough for households, they will extend the utility of personal computers from a few tasks in the data world to many in the physical world. Perhaps a program for basic housecleaning will be included with each robot, as word processors were shipped with early personal computers.

As with computers, some applications of robots will surprise their manufacturers. Robot programs may be developed to do light mechanical work (e.g., assembling other robots), deliver warehoused inventories, prepare specific gourmet meals, tune up certain types of cars, hook patterned rugs, weed lawns, run races, play games, arrange earth, stone, and brick, or sculpt. Some tasks will need specialized hardware attachments like tools and chemical sensors. Each application will require its own

original software, very complex by today's computer program standards. The programs will contain modules for recognizing, grasping, manipulating, transporting, and assembling particular items, perhaps modules developed via learning programs on supercomputers. In time, a growing library of subtask modules may ease the construction of new programs.

A first-generation robot will have the brain power of a reptile, but most application programs will be so hard pressed to accomplish their primary functions that they will endow the robot with the personality of a washing machine.

Second-Generation Universal Robots

Estimated time of arrival: 2020

Processing power: 100,000 MIPS (mouse-scale)

Distinguishing feature: Accommodation learning

First-generation robots will be rigid slaves to inflexible programs, relentless in pursuing their tasks—or repeating their errors. Their programs will contain the frozen results of learning done on bigger computers under human supervision. Except for specialized episodes like recording a new cleaning route or the location of work objects, they will be incapable of learning new skills or adapting to unanticipated circumstances. Even modest alterations of behavior will require new programming, probably from the original software suppliers.

Second-generation robots, with thirty times the processing power, will learn some of their tricks on the job. Their big advantage is adaptive learning, which "closes the loop" on behavior. Each robot action is repeatedly adjusted in response to measurements of the action's past effectiveness. In the simplest technique, programs will be provided with alternative ways, both in the large and the small, to accomplish steps in a task. Alternatives that succeed become more likely to be invoked in similar circumstances, while alternatives that fail become less probable. "Statistical learning" is another approach, in which a large number of behavior-modifying parameters (e.g., weights in simulated neural nets) are repeatedly tweaked to nudge actual behavior closer to an ideal. Programs for second-generation robots will use many such learning techniques, creating new abilities—and new pitfalls.

Some programs may learn with human assistance. To teach a robot to recognize shoes, its owner might assemble some shoes in a cluttered room, and point them out. The robot, running an object-learning program, will note the shape and color of both the shoes, and of other objects, to train a statistical classifier to distinguish shoes from non-shoes. If the robot later meets a still-ambiguous object, say a gravy boat, it may ask the owner's opinion, to further tune the classifier. Similar programs might learn minor motor skills by first recording movements as the robot is led by hand through the motions, then optimizing the details in practice playbacks. Learned modules, though tedious to create, will probably be easy to package and employ. A general tidying-up program, for instance, could be modified to gather shoes by grafting in a shoe-recognizing module.

Second-generation robots will occasionally be trained by humans, but more often will simply learn from their experiences. The behavior loop is closed in the latter case by a collection of constantly running *conditioning* programs, or modules, that watch out for generally desirable or undesirable situations and generate signals that act on the task-oriented programs that actually control the robot. Each major and minor step in a second-generation application program will have a variety of alternatives: a grasp can be underhand or overhand, harder or softer, an arm movement can be faster or slower, lifting can be done with one arm or two, an object can be sought with one of several recognition modules, two objects can be assembled in a number of locations, and so on. Each alternative will have associated with it a relative probability of being chosen. Whenever a conditioning module issues a signal, the probabilities of recently executed alternatives are altered. Conditioning signals come in two broad categories: positive, which raise the probabilities, and negative, which lower them. What situations the conditioning modules respond to, and what type and strength of signal they send, is entirely up to the robot's

programmers. Some choices seem sensible. Strong negative signals should result from collisions, from objects dropped or crushed, when a task fails or when the robot's batteries are nearly discharged. A near miss, a task completed unusually slowly, or an excessive acceleration might trigger weak negative signals. A rapidly completed task, charged batteries, or an absence of negative signals could produce positive signals. Some conditioning modules may be tied to the robot's speech recognition, generating positive signals for words of praise and negative ones for criticism. Speech recognizers in the 1990s struggle merely to identify the words being spoken. By 2010 they should be able to identify speakers and emotional overtones as well. A second-generation robot with a "general-behavior" program having options for almost any action at every step could probably be slowly trained for new tasks purely through Skinnerian conditioning, like a circus bear. More practical "user-trainable" programs will probably allow the key steps to be directly specified by voice instruction and leading by hand, with the conditioning saved for fine-tuning.

If a first-generation robot working in your kitchen runs into trouble, say, fumbling a key step because a portion of the workspace is awkwardly small, you have the option of abandoning the task, changing its environment, or somehow obtaining altered software that accomplishes the problematic step in a different way. A second-generation robot will make a number of false starts, but most probably will find its own solution. It will adjust to its home in thousands of subtle ways and gradually improve its performance. While a first-generation robot's personality is determined entirely by the sequence of operations in the application program it runs at the moment, a second-generation robot's character is more a product of the suite of conditioning modules it hosts. The conditioning system might, in time, censor an entire application program, if it gave consistently negative results.

Learning is dangerous because it leaps from a few experiences to general rules of behavior. If the experiences happen to be untypical, or the conditioning system misidentifies the relevant conditions, future behavior may be permanently warped. An important element in the ALVINN automatic driving system, which learns to follow a particular type of road by imitating human driving, is a carefully contrived augmentation of the actual camera scenes. Dean Pomerleau's program transforms each real training image and its associated steering command into thirty different ones by geometrically altering them in a way that approximates shifting the truck up to a half lane-width in either direction. Without this stratagem, learned steering is dangerously erratic away from the center of the lane. The program adds other artifacts to teach the system to ignore areas beyond the road edge and distant traffic. Other flexible learning programs, including those in my own research, behave similarly: they are prone to learn dangerous irrelevancies and miss important features if their training experiences are not properly structured. Occasionally, as in the transition from ALVINN to RALPH, enough is known in advance to hardwire in reasonable restraints. More often, though, the necessary information is unavailable at programming time.

Even animals and humans, veterans of tens of millions of years of evolutionary honing, are vulnerable to inappropriate learning. A friend's dog, struck by a car while crossing a road, continued wantonly to cross roads. It would, however, under all circumstances, avoid the region of the sidewalk from which it had set out before the accident. People and animals can be victims of self-reinforcing phobias or obsessions, instilled by a few traumatic experiences or abusive treatment in formative years. A first-generation robot, "trained" off-line under careful factory supervision, will suffer no permanent ill effects from events that interfere with its work but leave it physically undamaged. A second-generation robot, though, could be badly warped by accidents or practical jokes. It might remain impaired until its conditioned memory is cleared, restoring it to naive infancy. Or perhaps, sometimes, robot psychologists could slowly undo the damage. Devising conditioning suites that teach quickly, but resist aberrations, will be among the greatest challenges for programmers of second-generation robots. There is probably no perfect solution, but there are ways to approach the problem.

Second-generation robots of 2020 will have onboard computers as powerful as the supercomputers that learned for first-generation machines a decade before. But by 2020 supercomputers will be proportionally more powerful and will themselves play a background role. The many individual programs of a conditioning suite, each responding to some specific stimulus, interact with one another and with the robot's control programs and environment in ways that will be far too entangled to anticipate accurately. It would be possible to evaluate particular suites by trying them out in robots, the acid test in any case, but that would be a slow and dangerous way to sift a large number of rough candidates. Some would certainly behave in unexpected ways that could damage the robot or even endanger the testers.

Faster and safer initial screenings might be done in factory supercomputer simulations of robots in action. To be of value, simulations would have to be good models, predicting accurately such things as the probability that a given grip can lift a particular object, or that a vision module can find a given something in a particular clutter. Simulating the everyday world in full physical detail will still be beyond computer capacity in 2020, but it should be possible to approximate the results by generalizing data collected from actual robots, essentially to learn from the working experience of real robots how everyday things behave. A large systematic collection effort under human supervision will probably be necessary lest there be too many gaps or distortions. A proper simulator would contain thousands of learned models for various basic interactions (call them *interaction models*), in what amounts to a robotic version of common-sense physics. It would be a perceptual/motor counterpart to the purely verbal framework being collected by the Cyc effort to endow reasoning programs with common sense.

The simulators could be used to automatically find effective conditioning suites, in effect, to learn how to learn. A suite might be evaluated on a simulated robot running a few favorite application programs in a simulated household for a few simulated days. Repeatedly, suites that produced particularly effective and safe work would be saved, modified slightly, and tried again, while those that did poorly would be discarded. This kind of process, called a genetic algorithm, is a computerized version of Darwinian evolution. It is sometimes the most effective way to optimize when the relation between the adjustments (the choice and settings of conditioning modules, in this case) and the quantity to be optimized (robot performance) has no simple model.

Third-Generation Universal Robots

Estimated time of arrival: 2030

Processing power: 3,000,000 MIPS (monkey-scale)

Distinguishing feature: World modeling

Adaptive second-generation robots will find jobs everywhere and may become the largest industry on earth. But teaching them new skills, whether by writing programs or through training, will be very tedious. A third generation of universal robots will have on-board computers as powerful as the supercomputers that optimized second-generation robots. They will learn much faster because they do much trial and error in fast simulation rather than slow and dangerous physicality. Once again, a process done by human-supervised supercomputers at the factory in one robot generation will be improved and installed directly on the next generation, and once again new opportunities and new problems will arise.

With a fast-enough simulator, it will be possible for a robot to maintain a running account of the actual events going on around it—to simulate its world in real time. Doing so requires that almost everything the robot senses be recognized for the kind of object it is, so that the proper interaction models can be called up. Recognizing arbitrary objects by sight is as difficult as knowing how they will interact. It will require modules specially trained for each kind of thing (call them *perception models*). Some perception models may already have been developed for second-generation factory simulators to help automate the tedious job of creating simulations of robot workspaces. An additional effort to fill gaps and systematize the factory repertoire will surely be necessary to prepare it for fully automatic use in the third generation. Perception models will allow a robot's three-dimensional map of a room to be transformed into a working model where each object is identified and linked with its proper interaction models.

A continuously updated simulation of self and surroundings gives a robot interesting abilities. By running the simulation slightly faster than real time, the robot can preview what it is about to do, in time to alter its intent if the simulation predicts it will turn out badly—a kind of consciousness. On a larger scale, before undertaking a new task, the robot can simulate it many times, with conditioning system engaged, learning from the simulated experiences as it would from physical ones. Consequently well trained for the task, it would likely succeed the first time it attempted it physically— unlike a second-generation machine, which makes all its mistakes out in real life.

When it has some spare time, the robot can replay previous experiences, and try variations on them, perhaps learning ways to improve future performance. A sufficiently advanced third-generation robot, whose simulation extends to other agents— robots and people—would be able to observe a task being done by someone else and formulate a program for doing the task itself. It could imitate.

A third-generation robot might also be induced to invent its own simple programs in response to a specialized conditioning module whose rewards are proportional to how nearly a sequence of robot actions achieves a desired end. Repeated simulations of a general-behavior program with such a "teacher" might gradually shape the program into one that accomplishes the specified result. The teacher can be quite simple compared to the sequence of actions it induces, and could be constructed via voiced commands. The statement *"Put the glass on the table"* might create a conditioning module whose reward is proportional to the distance of the glass bottom from the tabletop. Steered by this, and by standard modules such as ones that generate negative signals if the glass spills or drops, repeated simulations may devise a sequence of arm motions that does the job.

There are complications. A simulator will be dangerously misleading unless it accurately models objects and events. A newly delivered robot is unlikely to have good representations of the personalized knickknacks it freshly encounters and will need some way of learning, perhaps by assigning to new object perception and interaction models from a set of generic classes. Then it would tune the interaction models of particular objects whenever a real event and its simulation differed. Since it would be dangerous to start a robot on a complex task before it had good models of the items involved, third-generation robots will require noncritical "play" periods wherein things are handled, spaces explored, and minor activities attempted, simply to tune up the simulation.

Although they will be able to adapt, imitate, and create simple programs of their own, third-generation robots will still rely on externally supplied programs to do complicated jobs. Since their motor and perceptual functions will be quite sophisticated, and their memories and potential skills large, it will be possible to write wonderfully elaborate control programs for them, accomplishing large jobs, with nuances within nuances. It will be increasingly difficult for human programmers to keep track of the many details and interactions. Fortunately, the task can be largely automated. Shakey, the first computer-controlled mobile robot, had at its heart a reasoning program called STRIPS (Standard Research Institute Problem Solver) that expressed the robot's situation and capabilities as sentences of symbolic logic. STRIPS solved for the sequence of actions that achieved a requested result as a proof of a mathematical theorem. On Shakey's 0.3 MIPS computer, neither the theorem prover nor the sensory processing that fed it could handle the complexity of realistic situations, and Shakey was limited to maneuvering around a few blocks.

Despite Shakey's limitations in 1969, the idea of planning robot actions with a theorem prover was sound. Given a correct description of the initial and desired state of the world, and the robot's abilities, along with enough time and space to work, a theorem prover will find an absolutely correct solution, of arbitrary generality, subtlety, and deviousness, if one exists. By the time of the third universal-robot generation, supercomputers will provide 100,000,000 MIPS, and (thanks to continuing progress in the top-down Artificial Intelligence industry) programs will exist that will be able to perform STRIPS-like reasoning with real-world richness. So factory supercomputers in 2030 will accept complex goals (find a sequence of robot actions that assembles the robot described in the following design database), and compile them via theorem provers into wonderfully intricate control programs for third-generation robots which will, in the field, adapt them to their actual circumstances.

Fourth-Generation Universal Robots

Estimated time of arrival: 2040
Processing power: 100,000,000 MIPS (human-scale)
Distinguishing feature: Reasoning

In the decades while the "bottom-up" evolution of robots is slowly transferring the perceptual and motor faculties of human beings into machinery, the conventional Artificial Intelligence industry will be perfecting the mechanization of reasoning. Since today's programs already match human beings in some areas, those of forty years from now, running on computers a million times as fast as today's, should be quite superhuman. Today's reasoning programs work from small amounts of unambiguous information prepared by human beings. Data from robot sensors such as cameras is much too voluminous and noisy for them to use. But a good robot simulator will contain neatly organized and labeled descriptions of the robot and its world, ready to feed a reasoning program. It could state, for instance, if a knife is on a countertop, or if the robot is holding a cup, or even if a human is angry.

Fourth-generation universal robots will have computers powerful enough to simultaneously simulate the world and reason about the simulation. Like the factory supercomputers of the third generation, fourth-generation robots will be able to devise ultrasophisticated robot programs, for other robots or for themselves. Because of another gift from the Artificial Intelligence industry, they will also be able to understand natural languages. Disembodied language understanders may use a verbal common-sense database similar to the one being developed by the Cyc project, where the meaning of words is defined in reference only to other words. Fourth-generation robots will understand concepts and statements more deeply, through the action of their simulators. When someone tells a robot *"The water is running in the bathtub,"* the robot can update its simulation of the world to include flow into the unseen tub, where a simulated extrapolation would indicate an undesirable overflow later and so motivate the robot to go to turn off the tap. A purely verbal representation might accomplish the same thing if it included the statements such as "A filling bathtub will overflow if its water is not shut off." However, a few general principles in a simulator, interacting in combinations, can substitute for an indefinite number of sentences.

Similarly, a reasoning program, making inferences about physical things, might be enhanced by a simulator. Candidate inferences would be rejected if they failed in a parallel simulation of a typical case, and, conversely, persistent coincidences in the simulation could suggest statements that can be proved or assumed. The robot would be visualizing as it listened, spoke, and reasoned. A modest but very successful version of such an approach was used in one of the earliest Artificial Intelligence programs, a geometry theorem prover by Herbert Gelernter in 1959. Starting with the postulates and rules of inference in Euclid's "Elements," Gelernter's program proved some of the theorems, using

algebraic "diagrams" to eliminate false directions in the proofs. Before attempting to prove two triangles congruent in a certain construction, for instance, the program would generate an example of the construction, using random numbers for the unspecified quantities, and measure the resulting triangles. If the specific diagramed triangles did not match within the precision of the arithmetic, the program abandoned the attempt to prove them congruent in general.

Simulator-augmented language understanding and reasoning may be so effective in robots that it will be adopted for use in plain computer programs, "grounding" them in the physical world via the experiences of the robots that tuned the simulators. In time the distinction between robot controllers and disembodied reasoners will diminish, and reasoning programs will sometimes link to robot bodies to interact physically with the world, and robot minds will sometimes retire into large computers to do some intense thinking off-line.

A fourth-generation robot will be able to accept statements of purpose from humans and "compile" them into detailed programs that accomplish the task. With a database about the world at large, the statements could become quite general—things like "earn a living," "make more robots," or "make a smarter robot." In fact, fourth-generation robots will have the general competence of human beings and resemble us in some ways, but in others will be like nothing the world has seen. As they design their own successors, the world will become ever stranger.

II.7   BILL JOY

Why the Future Doesn't Need Us

When this article by the chief scientist and cofounder of Sun Microsystems was published in *Wired Magazine* in April 2000, it created quite a buzz. Joy is clearly no Luddite, but in this reading, he issues a stern warning about the dangers that lie ahead for humanity if we continue down the current technological path toward creating superintelligent, self-replicating machines. The idea that our machines might one day destroy us has been a staple of science fiction books and movies, but the prospect of a race of superintelligent robots actually displacing human beings as the dominant life form on the planet has long been dismissed as overheated fantasy.

In the autobiographical section of his discussion, Joy recounts how he became a technophile and how his own work and that of colleagues have opened up the realistic possibility of creating robots with human-level intelligence by the year 2030. When the potentials of contemporary biotechnology and nanotechnology are examined, Joy thinks we face the prospect of enabling the creation of weapons of mass destruction that could threaten the very existence of life on Earth. While contemplating these dangers, Joy recommends that we approach these twenty-first century technological possibilities with a degree of humility and that we learn from the experience of the twentieth century, particularly with respect to nuclear energy, how difficult it is to control the technological genie once it gets out of the bottle. In a personal and almost confessional style, Joy struggles with the question of what kind of future we humans want for ourselves. After having devoted a career to the pursuit of material progress through science and technology, he is now having second thoughts about whether this is the path that we should be taking.

Focus Questions

1. What is surprising about the long quote that Joy discusses at the beginning of this reading? Is this dystopian vision wholly unrealistic?
2. What is GNR? Why are these technologies different from the NBC technologies of the twentieth century? Explain.
3. What are the important ethical values and principles that Joy believes we need to remember as we contemplate the technological future? Does he believe that "ethical humans" will be able to control the forces that "technological humans" unleash?
4. Compare this selection with those by Jonas (I.10), Kurzweil (II.8), Kass (II.12), and Sandel (II.13). What are the common themes and issues running through these readings?

Keywords

biotechnology, chaos theory, extinction, genetic engineering, Luddites, nanotechnology, nuclear weapons, robotics, self-replication, terrorism, weapons of mass destruction

---

FROM THE MOMENT I BECAME INVOLVED in the creation of new technologies, their ethical dimensions have concerned me, but it was only in the autumn of 1998 that I became anxiously aware of how great are the dangers facing us in the 21st century. I

can date the onset of my unease to the day I met Ray Kurzweil, the deservedly famous inventor of the first reading machine for the blind and many other amazing things.

Ray and I were both speakers at George Gilder's Telecosm conference, and I encountered him by chance in the bar of the hotel after both our sessions were over. I was sitting with John Searle, a Berkeley philosopher who studies consciousness.

While we were talking, Ray approached and a conversation began, the subject of which haunts me to this day.

I had missed Ray's talk and the subsequent panel that Ray and John had been on, and they now picked right up where they'd left off, with Ray saying that the rate of improvement of technology was going to accelerate and that we were going to become robots or fuse with robots or something like that, and John countering that this couldn't happen, because the robots couldn't be conscious.

While I had heard such talk before, I had always felt sentient robots were in the realm of science fiction. But now, from someone I respected, I was hearing a strong argument that they were a near-term possibility. I was taken aback, especially given Ray's proven ability to imagine and create the future. I already knew that new technologies like genetic engineering and nanotechnology were giving us the power to remake the world, but a realistic and imminent scenario for intelligent robots surprised me.

It's easy to get jaded about such breakthroughs. We hear in the news almost every day of some kind of technological or scientific advance. Yet this was no ordinary prediction. In the hotel bar, Ray gave me a partial preprint of his then-forthcoming book *The Age of Spiritual Machines,* which outlined a utopia he foresaw—one in which humans gained near immortality by becoming one with robotic technology. On reading it, my sense of unease only intensified; I felt sure he had to be understating the dangers, understating the probability of a bad outcome along this path.

I found myself most troubled by a passage detailing a *dys*topian scenario:

The New Luddite Challenge

First let us postulate that the computer scientists succeed in developing intelligent machines that can do all things better than human beings can do them. In that case presumably all work will be done by vast, highly organized systems of machines and no human effort will be necessary. Either of two cases might occur. The machines might be permitted to make all of their own decisions without human oversight, or else human control over the machines might be retained.

If the machines are permitted to make all their own decisions, we can't make any conjectures as to the results, because it is impossible to guess how such machines might behave. We only point out that the fate of the human race would be at the mercy of the machines. It might be argued that the human race would never be foolish enough to hand over all the power to the machines. But we are suggesting neither that the human race would voluntarily turn power over to the machines nor that the machines would willfully seize power. What we do suggest is that the human race might easily permit itself to drift into a position of such dependence on the machines that it would have no practical choice but to accept all of the machines' decisions. As society and the problems that face it become more and more complex and machines become more and more intelligent, people will let machines make more of their decisions for them, simply because machine-made decisions will bring better results than man-made ones. Eventually a stage may be reached at which the decisions necessary to keep the system running will be so complex that human beings will be incapable of making them intelligently. At that stage the machines will be in effective control. People won't be able to just turn the machines off, because they will be so dependent on them that turning them off would amount to suicide.

On the other hand it is possible that human control over the machines may be retained. In that case the average man may have control over certain private machines of his own, such as his car or his personal computer, but control over large systems of machines will be in the hands of a tiny elite—just as it is today, but with two differences. Due to improved techniques the elite will have greater control over the masses; and because human work will no longer be necessary the masses will be superfluous, a useless burden on the system. If the elite is ruthless they may simply decide to exterminate the mass of humanity. If they are humane they may use propaganda or other psychological or biological techniques to reduce the birth rate until the mass of humanity becomes extinct, leaving the world to the elite. Or, if the elite consists of soft-hearted liberals, they may decide to play the role of good shepherds to the rest of the human race. They will see to it that everyone's physical needs are satisfied, that all children are raised under psychologically hygienic conditions, that everyone has a wholesome hobby to keep him busy, and that anyone who may become dissatisfied undergoes "treatment" to cure his "problem." Of course, life will be so purposeless that people will have to be biologically or psychologically engineered either to remove their need for the power process or make them "sublimate" their drive for power into some harmless hobby. These engineered human beings may be happy in such a society, but they will most certainly not be free. They will have been reduced to the status of domestic animals.[1]

In the book, you don't discover until you turn the page that the author of this passage is Theodore Kaczynski—the Unabomber. I am no apologist for Kaczynski. His bombs killed three people during a 17-year terror campaign and wounded many others. One of his bombs gravely injured my friend David Gelernter, one of the most brilliant and visionary computer scientists of our time. Like many of my colleagues, I felt that I could easily have been the Unabomber's next target.

Kaczynski's actions were murderous and, in my view, criminally insane. He is clearly a Luddite, but simply saying this does not dismiss his argument; as difficult as it is for me to acknowledge, I saw some merit in the reasoning in this single passage. I felt compelled to confront it.

Kaczynski's dystopian vision describes unintended consequences, a well-known problem with the design and use of technology, and one that is clearly related to Murphy's law—"Anything that can go wrong, will." (Actually, this is Finagle's law, which in itself shows that Finagle was right.) Our overuse of antibiotics has led to what may be the biggest such problem so far: the emergence of antibiotic-resistant and much more dangerous bacteria. Similar things happened when attempts to eliminate malarial mosquitoes using DDT caused them to acquire DDT resistance; malarial parasites likewise acquired multi-drug-resistant genes.[2]

The cause of many such surprises seems clear: The systems involved are complex, involving interaction among and feedback between many parts. Any changes to such a system will cascade in ways that are difficult to predict; this is especially true when human actions are involved.

I started showing friends the Kaczynski quote from *The Age of Spiritual Machines*; I would hand them Kurzweil's book, let them read the quote, and then watch their reaction as they discovered who had written it. At around the same time, I found Hans Moravec's book *Robot: Mere Machine to Transcendent Mind*. Moravec is one of the leaders in robotics research, and was a founder of the world's largest robotics research program, at Carnegie Mellon University. *Robot* gave me more material to try out on my friends—material surprisingly supportive of Kaczynski's argument. For example:

The Short Run (Early 2000s)

Biological species almost never survive encounters with superior competitors. Ten million years ago, South and North America were separated by a sunken Panama isthmus. South America, like Australia today, was populated by marsupial mammals, including pouched equivalents of rats, deers, and tigers. When the isthmus connecting North and South America rose, it took only a few thousand years for the northern placental species, with slightly more effective metabolisms and reproductive and nervous systems, to displace and eliminate almost all the southern marsupials.

In a completely free marketplace, superior robots would surely affect humans as North American placentals affected South American marsupials (and as humans have affected countless species). Robotic industries would compete vigorously among themselves for matter, energy, and space, incidentally driving their price beyond human reach. Unable to afford the necessities of life, biological humans would be squeezed out of existence.

There is probably some breathing room, because we do not live in a completely free marketplace. Government coerces nonmarket behavior, especially by collecting taxes. Judiciously applied, governmental coercion could support human populations in high style on the fruits of robot labor, perhaps for a long while.

A textbook dystopia—and Moravec is just getting wound up. He goes on to discuss how our main job in the 21st century will be "ensuring continued cooperation from the robot industries" by passing laws decreeing that they be "nice,"[3] and to describe how seriously dangerous a human can be "once transformed into an unbounded superintelligent robot." Moravec's view is that the robots will eventually succeed us—that humans clearly face extinction.

I decided it was time to talk to my friend Danny Hillis. Danny became famous as the cofounder of Thinking Machines Corporation, which built a very powerful parallel supercomputer. Despite my current job title of Chief Scientist at Sun Microsystems, I am more a computer architect than a scientist, and I respect Danny's knowledge of the information and physical sciences more than that of any other single person I know. Danny is also a highly regarded futurist who thinks long-term—four years ago he started the Long Now Foundation, which is building a clock designed to last 10,000 years, in an attempt to draw attention to the pitifully short attention span of our society. . . .

So I flew to Los Angeles for the express purpose of having dinner with Danny and his wife, Pati. I went through my now-familiar routine, trotting out the ideas and passages that I found so disturbing. Danny's answer—directed specifically at Kurzweil's scenario of humans merging with robots—came swiftly, and quite surprised me. He said, simply, that the changes would come gradually, and that we would get used to them.

But I guess I wasn't totally surprised. I had seen a quote from Danny in Kurzweil's book in which he said, "I'm as fond of my body as anyone, but if I can be 200 with a body of silicon, I'll take it." It seemed that he was at peace with this process and its attendant risks, while I was not.

While talking and thinking about Kurzweil, Kaczynski, and Moravec, I suddenly remembered a novel I had read almost 20 years ago—*The White Plague,* by Frank Herbert—in which a molecular biologist is driven insane by the senseless murder of his family. To seek revenge he constructs and disseminates a new and highly contagious plague that kills widely but selectively. (We're lucky Kaczynski was a mathematician, not a molecular biologist.) I was also reminded of the Borg of *Star Trek,* a hive of partly biological, partly robotic creatures with a strong destructive streak. Borg-like disasters are a staple of science fiction, so why hadn't I been more concerned about such robotic dystopias earlier? Why weren't other people more concerned about these nightmarish scenarios?

Part of the answer certainly lies in our attitude toward the new—in our bias toward instant familiarity and unquestioning acceptance. Accustomed to living with almost routine scientific breakthroughs, we have yet to come to terms with the fact that the most compelling 21st-century technologies—robotics, genetic engineering, and nanotechnology—pose a different threat than the technologies that have come before. Specifically, robots, engineered organisms, and nanobots share a dangerous amplifying factor: They can self-replicate. A bomb is blown up only once—but one bot can become many, and quickly get out of control.

Much of my work over the past 25 years has been on computer networking, where the sending and receiving of messages creates the opportunity for out-of-control replication. But while replication in a computer or a computer network can be a nuisance, at worst it disables a machine or takes down a network or network service. Uncontrolled self-replication in these newer technologies runs a much greater risk: a risk of substantial damage in the physical world.

Each of these technologies also offers untold promise: The vision of near immortality that Kurzweil sees in his robot dreams drives us forward; genetic engineering may soon provide treatments, if not outright cures, for most diseases; and nanotechnology and nanomedicine can address yet more ills. Together they could significantly extend our average life span and improve the quality of our lives. Yet, with each of these technologies, a sequence of small, individually sensible advances leads to an accumulation of great power and, concomitantly, great danger.

What was different in the 20th century? Certainly, the technologies underlying the weapons of mass destruction (WMD)—nuclear, biological, and chemical (NBC)—were powerful, and the weapons an enormous threat. But building nuclear weapons required, at least for a time, access to both rare—indeed, effectively unavailable—raw materials and highly protected information; biological and chemical weapons programs also tended to require large-scale activities.

The 21st-century technologies—genetics, nanotechnology, and robotics (GNR)—are so powerful that they can spawn whole new classes of accidents and abuses. Most dangerously, for the first time, these accidents and abuses are widely within the reach of individuals or small groups. They will not require large facilities or rare raw materials. Knowledge alone will enable the use of them.

Thus we have the possibility not just of weapons of mass destruction but of knowledge-enabled mass destruction (KMD), this destructiveness hugely amplified by the power of self-replication.

I think it is no exaggeration to say we are on the cusp of the further perfection of extreme evil, an evil whose possibility spreads well beyond that which weapons of mass destruction bequeathed to the nation-states, on to a surprising and terrible empowerment of extreme individuals.

Nothing about the way I got involved with computers suggested to me that I was going to be facing these kinds of issues.

My life has been driven by a deep need to ask questions and find answers. When I was 3, I was already reading, so my father took me to the elementary school, where I sat on the principal's lap and read him a story. I started school early, later skipped a grade, and escaped into books—I was incredibly motivated to learn. I asked lots of questions, often driving adults to distraction.

As a teenager I was very interested in science and technology. I wanted to be a ham radio operator but didn't have the money to buy the equipment.

Ham radio was the Internet of its time: very addictive, and quite solitary. Money issues aside, my mother put her foot down—I was not to be a ham; I was antisocial enough already.

I may not have had many close friends, but I was awash in ideas. By high school, I had discovered the great science fiction writers. I remember especially Heinlein's *Have Spacesuit Will Travel* and Asimov's *I, Robot,* with its Three Laws of Robotics. I was enchanted by the descriptions of space travel, and wanted to have a telescope to look at the stars; since I had no money to buy or make one, I checked books on telescope-making out of the library and read about making them instead. I soared in my imagination.

Thursday nights my parents went bowling, and we kids stayed home alone. It was the night of Gene Roddenberry's original *Star Trek,* and the program made a big impression on me. I came to accept its notion that humans had a future in space, Western-style, with big heroes and adventures. Roddenberry's vision of the centuries to come was one with strong moral values, embodied in codes like the Prime Directive: to not interfere in the development of less technologically advanced civilizations. This had an incredible appeal to me; ethical humans, not robots, dominated this future, and I took Roddenberry's dream as part of my own.

I excelled in mathematics in high school, and when I went to the University of Michigan as an undergraduate engineering student I took the advanced curriculum of the mathematics majors. Solving math problems was an exciting challenge, but when I discovered computers I found something much more interesting: a machine into which you could put a program that attempted to solve a problem, after which the machine quickly checked the solution. The computer had a clear notion of correct and incorrect, true and false. Were my ideas correct? The machine could tell me. This was very seductive.

I was lucky enough to get a job programming early supercomputers and discovered the amazing power of large machines to numerically simulate advanced designs. When I went to graduate school at UC Berkeley in the mid-1970s, I started staying up late, often all night, inventing new worlds inside the machines. Solving problems. Writing the code that argued so strongly to be written.

In *The Agony and the Ecstasy,* Irving Stone's biographical novel of Michelangelo, Stone described vividly how Michelangelo released the statues from the stone, "breaking the marble spell," carving from the images in his mind.[4] In my most ecstatic moments, the software in the computer emerged in the same way. Once I had imagined it in my mind I felt that it was already there in the machine, waiting to be released. Staying up all night seemed a small price to pay to free it—to give the ideas concrete form.

After a few years at Berkeley I started to send out some of the software I had written—an instructional Pascal system, Unix utilities, and a text editor called vi (which is still, to my surprise, widely used more than 20 years later)—to others who had similar small PDP-11 and VAX minicomputers. These adventures in software eventually turned into the Berkeley version of the Unix operating system, which became a personal "success disaster"—so many people wanted it that I never finished my PhD. Instead I got a job working for Darpa putting Berkeley Unix on the Internet and fixing it to be reliable and to run large research applications well. This was all great fun and very rewarding. And, frankly, I saw no robots here, or anywhere near.

Still, by the early 1980s, I was drowning. The Unix releases were very successful, and my little project of one soon had money and some staff, but the problem at Berkeley was always office space rather than money—there wasn't room for the help the project needed, so when the other founders of Sun Microsystems showed up I jumped at the chance to join them. At Sun, the long hours continued into the early days of workstations and personal computers, and I have enjoyed participating in the creation of advanced microprocessor technologies and Internet technologies such as Java and Jini.

From all this, I trust it is clear that I am not a Luddite. I have always, rather, had a strong belief in the value of the scientific search for truth and in the ability of great engineering to bring material progress. The Industrial Revolution has immeasurably improved everyone's life over the last couple hundred years, and I always expected my career to involve the building of worthwhile solutions to real problems, one problem at a time.

I have not been disappointed. My work has had more impact than I had ever hoped for and has been more widely used than I could have reasonably expected. I have spent the last 20 years still trying to figure out how to make computers as reliable as I want them to be (they are not nearly there yet) and how to make them simple to use (a goal that has met with even less relative success). Despite some progress, the problems that remain seem even more daunting.

But while I was aware of the moral dilemmas surrounding technology's consequences in fields like weapons research, I did not expect that I would confront such issues in my own field, or at least not so soon.

Perhaps it is always hard to see the bigger impact while you are in the vortex of a change. Failing to understand the consequences of our inventions while we are in the rapture of discovery and innovation seems to be a common fault of scientists and technologists; we have long been driven by the overarching desire to know that is the nature of science's quest, not stopping to notice that the progress to newer and more powerful technologies can take on a life of its own.

I have long realized that the big advances in information technology come not from the work of computer scientists, computer architects, or electrical engineers, but from that of physical scientists. The physicists Stephen Wolfram and Brosl Hasslacher introduced me, in the early 1980s, to chaos theory and nonlinear systems. In the 1990s, I learned about complex systems from conversations with Danny Hillis, the biologist Stuart Kauffman, the Nobel-laureate physicist Murray Gell-Mann, and others. Most recently, Hasslacher and the electrical engineer and device physicist Mark Reed have been giving me insight into the incredible possibilities of molecular electronics.

In my own work, as codesigner of three microprocessor architectures—SPARC, picoJava, and MAJC—and as the designer of several implementations thereof, I've been afforded a deep and first-hand acquaintance with Moore's law. For decades, Moore's law has correctly predicted the exponential rate of improvement of semiconductor technology.

Until last year I believed that the rate of advances predicted by Moore's law might continue only until roughly 2010, when some physical limits would begin to be reached. It was not obvious to me that a new technology would arrive in time to keep performance advancing smoothly.

But because of the recent rapid and radical progress in molecular electronics—where individual atoms and molecules replace lithographically drawn transistors—and related nanoscale technologies, we should be able to meet or exceed the Moore's law rate of progress for another 30 years. By 2030, we are likely to be able to build machines, in quantity, a million times as powerful as the personal computers of today—sufficient to implement the dreams of Kurzweil and Moravec.

As this enormous computing power is combined with the manipulative advances of the physical sciences and the new, deep understandings in genetics, enormous transformative power is being unleashed. These combinations open up the opportunity to completely redesign the world, for better or worse: The replicating and evolving processes that have been confined to the natural world are about to become realms of human endeavor.

In designing software and microprocessors, I have never had the feeling that I was designing an intelligent machine. The software and hardware is so fragile and the capabilities of the machine to "think" so clearly absent that, even as a possibility, this has always seemed very far in the future.

But now, with the prospect of human-level computing power in about 30 years, a new idea suggests itself: that I may be working to create tools which will enable the construction of the technology that may replace our species. How do I feel about this? Very uncomfortable. Having struggled my entire career to build reliable software systems, it seems to me more than likely that this future will not work out as well as some people may imagine. My personal experience suggests we tend to overestimate our design abilities.

Given the incredible power of these new technologies, shouldn't we be asking how we can best coexist with them? And if our own extinction is a likely, or even possible, outcome of our technological development, shouldn't we proceed with great caution?

The dream of robotics is, first, that intelligent machines can do our work for us, allowing us lives of leisure, restoring us to Eden. Yet in his history of such ideas, *Darwin Among the Machines,* George Dyson warns: "In the game of life and evolution there are three players at the table: human beings, nature, and machines. I am firmly on the side of nature. But nature, I suspect, is on the side of the machines." As we have seen, Moravec agrees, believing we may well not survive the encounter with the superior robot species.

How soon could such an intelligent robot be built? The coming advances in computing power seem to make it possible by 2030. And once an intelligent robot exists, it is only a small step to a robot species—to an intelligent robot that can make evolved copies of itself.

A second dream of robotics is that we will gradually replace ourselves with our robotic technology, achieving near immortality by downloading our consciousnesses; it is this process that Danny Hillis thinks we will gradually get used to and that Ray Kurzweil elegantly details in *The Age of Spiritual Machines.* . . .

But if we are downloaded into our technology, what are the chances that we will thereafter be ourselves or even human? It seems to me far more likely that a robotic existence would not be like a human one in any sense that we understand, that the robots would in no sense be our children, that on this path our humanity may well be lost.

Genetic engineering promises to revolutionize agriculture by increasing crop yields while reducing the use of pesticides; to create tens of thousands of novel species of bacteria, plants, viruses, and animals; to replace reproduction, or supplement it, with cloning; to create cures for many diseases, increasing our life span and our quality of life; and much, much more. We now know with certainty that these profound changes in the biological sciences are imminent and will challenge all our notions of what life is.

Technologies such as human cloning have in particular raised our awareness of the profound ethical and moral issues we face. If, for example, we were to reengineer ourselves into several separate and unequal species using the power of genetic engineering, then we would threaten the notion of equality that is the very cornerstone of our democracy.

Given the incredible power of genetic engineering, it's no surprise that there are significant safety issues in its use. My friend Amory Lovins recently cowrote, along with Hunter Lovins, an editorial that provides an ecological view of some of these dangers. Among their concerns: that "the new botany aligns the development of plants with their economic, not evolutionary, success." . . . Amory's long career has been focused on energy and resource efficiency by taking a whole-system view of human-made systems; such a whole-system view often finds simple, smart solutions to otherwise seemingly difficult problems, and is usefully applied here as well.

After reading the Lovins' editorial, I saw an op-ed by Gregg Easterbrook in *The New York Times* (November 19, 1999) about genetically engineered crops, under the headline: "Food for the Future: Someday, rice will have built-in vitamin A. Unless the Luddites win."

Are Amory and Hunter Lovins Luddites? Certainly not. I believe we all would agree that golden rice, with its built-in vitamin A, is probably a good thing, if developed with proper care and respect for the likely dangers in moving genes across species boundaries.

Awareness of the dangers inherent in genetic engineering is beginning to grow, as reflected in the Lovins' editorial. The general public is aware of, and uneasy about, genetically modified foods, and seems to be rejecting the notion that such foods should be permitted to be unlabeled.

But genetic engineering technology is already very far along. As the Lovins note, the USDA has already approved about 50 genetically engineered crops for unlimited release; more than half of the world's soybeans and a third of its corn now contain genes spliced in from other forms of life.

While there are many important issues here, my own major concern with genetic engineering is narrower: that it gives the power—whether militarily, accidentally, or in a deliberate terrorist act—to create a White Plague.

The many wonders of nanotechnology were first imagined by the Nobel-laureate physicist Richard Feynman in a speech he gave in 1959, subsequently published under the title "There's Plenty of Room at the Bottom." The book that made a big impression on me, in the mid-'80s, was Eric Drexler's *Engines of Creation,* in which he described beautifully how manipulation of matter at the atomic level could create a utopian future of abundance, where just about everything could be made cheaply, and almost any imaginable disease or physical problem could be solved using nanotechnology and artificial intelligences.

A subsequent book, *Unbounding the Future: The Nanotechnology Revolution,* which Drexler cowrote, imagines some of the changes that might take place in a world where we had molecular-level "assemblers." Assemblers could make possible incredibly low-cost solar power, cures for cancer and the common cold by augmentation of the human immune system, essentially complete cleanup of the environment, incredibly inexpensive pocket supercomputers—in fact, any product would be manufacturable by assemblers at a cost no greater than that of wood—spaceflight more accessible than transoceanic travel today, and restoration of extinct species.

I remember feeling good about nanotechnology after reading *Engines of Creation.* As a technologist, it gave me a sense of calm—that is, nanotechnology showed us that incredible progress was possible, and indeed perhaps inevitable. If nanotechnology was our future, then I didn't feel pressed to solve so many problems in the present. I would get to Drexler's utopian future in due time; I might as well enjoy life more in the here and now. It didn't make sense, given his vision, to stay up all night, all the time.

Drexler's vision also led to a lot of good fun. I would occasionally get to describe the wonders of nanotechnology to others who had not heard of it. After teasing them with all the things Drexler described I would give a homework assignment of my own: "Use nanotechnology to create a vampire; for extra credit create an antidote."

With these wonders came clear dangers, of which I was acutely aware. As I said at a nanotechnology conference in 1989, "We can't simply do our science and not worry about these ethical issues."[5] But my subsequent conversations with physicists convinced me that nanotechnology might not even work—or, at least, it wouldn't work anytime soon. Shortly thereafter I moved to Colorado, to a skunk works I had set up, and the focus of my work shifted to software for the Internet, specifically on ideas that became Java and Jini.

Then, last summer, Brosl Hasslacher told me that nanoscale molecular electronics was now practical. This was *new* news, at least to me, and I think to many people—and it radically changed my opinion about nanotechnology. It sent me back to *Engines of Creation*. Rereading Drexler's work after more than 10 years, I was dismayed to realize how little I had remembered of its lengthy section called "Dangers and Hopes," including a discussion of how nanotechnologies can become "engines of destruction." Indeed, in my rereading of this cautionary material today, I am struck by how naive some of Drexler's safeguard proposals seem, and how much greater I judge the dangers to be now than even he seemed to then. (Having anticipated and described many technical and political problems with nanotechnology, Drexler started the Foresight Institute in the late 1980s "to help prepare society for anticipated advanced technologies"—most important, nanotechnology.)

The enabling breakthrough to assemblers seems quite likely within the next 20 years. Molecular electronics—the new subfield of nanotechnology where individual molecules are circuit elements—should mature quickly and become enormously lucrative within this decade, causing a large incremental investment in all nanotechnologies.

Unfortunately, as with nuclear technology, it is far easier to create destructive uses for nanotechnology than constructive ones. Nanotechnology has clear military and terrorist uses, and you need not be suicidal to release a massively destructive nanotechnological device—such devices can be built to be selectively destructive, affecting, for example, only a certain geographical area or a group of people who are genetically distinct.

An immediate consequence of the Faustian bargain in obtaining the great power of nanotechnology is that we run a grave risk—the risk that we might destroy the biosphere on which all life depends.

As Drexler explained:

"Plants" with "leaves" no more efficient than today's solar cells could out-compete real plants, crowding the biosphere with an inedible foliage. Tough omnivorous "bacteria" could out-compete real bacteria: They could spread like blowing pollen, replicate swiftly, and reduce the biosphere to dust in a matter of days. Dangerous replicators could easily be too tough, small, and rapidly spreading to stop—at least if we make no preparation. We have trouble enough controlling viruses and fruit flies.

Among the cognoscenti of nanotechnology, this threat has become known as the "gray goo problem." Though masses of uncontrolled replicators need not be gray or gooey, the term "gray goo" emphasizes that replicators able to obliterate life might be less inspiring than a single species of crabgrass. They might be superior in an evolutionary sense, but this need not make them valuable.

The gray goo threat makes one thing perfectly clear: We cannot afford certain kinds of accidents with replicating assemblers.

Gray goo would surely be a depressing ending to our human adventure on Earth, far worse than mere fire or ice, and one that could stem from a simple laboratory accident.[6] Oops.

It is most of all the power of destructive self-replication in genetics, nanotechnology, and robotics (GNR) that should give us pause. Self-replication is the modus operandi of genetic engineering, which uses the machinery of the cell to replicate its designs, and the prime danger underlying gray goo in nanotechnology. Stories of runamok robots like the Borg, replicating or mutating to escape from the ethical constraints imposed on them by their creators, are well established in our science fiction books and movies. It is even possible that self-replication may be more fundamental than we thought, and hence harder—or even impossible—to control. A recent article by Stuart Kauffman in *Nature* titled "Self-Replication: Even Peptides Do It" discusses the discovery that a 32-amino-acid peptide can "autocatalyse its own synthesis." We don't know how widespread this ability is, but Kauffman notes that it may hint at "a route to self-reproducing molecular systems on a basis far wider than Watson-Crick base-pairing."[7]

In truth, we have had in hand for years clear warnings of the dangers inherent in widespread knowledge of GNR technologies—of the possibility of knowledge alone enabling mass destruction. But these warnings haven't been widely publicized; the public discussions have been clearly inadequate. There is no profit in publicizing the dangers.

The nuclear, biological, and chemical (NBC) technologies used in 20th-century weapons of mass destruction were and are largely military, developed in government laboratories. In sharp contrast, the 21st-century GNR technologies have clear commercial uses and are being developed almost exclusively by corporate enterprises. In this age of triumphant commercialism, technology—with science as its handmaiden—is delivering a series of almost magical inventions that are the most phenomenally lucrative ever seen. We are aggressively pursuing the promises of these new technologies within the now-unchallenged system of global capitalism and its manifold financial incentives and competitive pressures.

This is the first moment in the history of our planet when any species, by its own voluntary actions, has become a danger to itself—as well as to vast numbers of others.

It might be a familiar progression, transpiring on many worlds—a planet, newly formed, placidly revolves around its star; life slowly forms; a kaleidoscopic procession of creatures evolves; intelligence emerges which, at least up to a point, confers enormous survival value; and then technology is invented. It dawns on them that there are such things as laws of Nature, that these laws can be revealed by experiment, and that knowledge of these laws can be made both to save and to take lives, both on unprecedented scales. Science, they recognize, grants immense powers. In a flash, they create world-altering contrivances. Some planetary civilizations see their way through, place limits on what may and what must not be done, and safely pass through the time of perils. Others, not so lucky or so prudent, perish.

That is Carl Sagan, writing in 1994, in *Pale Blue Dot,* a book describing his vision of the human future in space. I am only now realizing how deep his insight was, and how sorely I miss, and will miss, his voice. For all its eloquence, Sagan's contribution was not least that of simple common sense—an attribute that, along with humility, many of the leading advocates of the 21st-century technologies seem to lack.

I remember from my childhood that my grandmother was strongly against the overuse of antibiotics. She had worked since before the first World War as a nurse and had a commonsense attitude that taking antibiotics, unless they were absolutely necessary, was bad for you.

It is not that she was an enemy of progress. She saw much progress in an almost 70-year nursing career; my grandfather, a diabetic, benefited greatly from the improved treatments that became available in his lifetime. But she, like many levelheaded people, would probably think it greatly arrogant for us, now, to be designing a robotic "replacement species," when we obviously have so much trouble making relatively simple things work, and so much trouble managing—or even understanding—ourselves.

I realize now that she had an awareness of the nature of the order of life, and of the necessity of living with and respecting that order. With this respect comes a necessary humility that we, with our early-21st-century chutzpah, lack at our peril. The commonsense view, grounded in this respect, is often right, in advance of the scientific evidence. The clear fragility and inefficiencies of the human-made systems we have built should give us all pause; the fragility of the systems I have worked on certainly humbles me.

We should have learned a lesson from the making of the first atomic bomb and the resulting arms race. We didn't do well then, and the parallels to our current situation are troubling.

The effort to build the first atomic bomb was led by the brilliant physicist J. Robert Oppenheimer. Oppenheimer was not naturally interested in politics but became painfully aware of what he perceived as the grave threat to Western civilization from the Third Reich, a threat surely grave because of the possibility that Hitler might obtain nuclear weapons. Energized by this concern, he brought his strong intellect, passion for physics, and charismatic leadership skills to Los Alamos and led a rapid and successful effort by an incredible collection of great minds to quickly invent the bomb.

What is striking is how this effort continued so naturally after the initial impetus was removed. In a meeting shortly after V-E Day with some physicists who felt that perhaps the effort should stop, Oppenheimer argued to continue. His stated reason seems a bit strange: not because of the fear of large casualties from an invasion of Japan, but because the United Nations, which was soon to be formed, should have foreknowledge of atomic weapons. A more likely reason the project continued is the momentum that had built up—the first atomic test, Trinity, was nearly at hand.

We know that in preparing this first atomic test the physicists proceeded despite a large number of possible dangers. They were initially worried, based on a calculation by Edward Teller, that an atomic explosion might set fire to the atmosphere. A revised calculation reduced the danger of destroying the world to a three-in-a-million chance. (Teller says he was later able to dismiss the prospect of atmospheric ignition entirely.) Oppenheimer, though, was sufficiently concerned about the result of Trinity that he arranged for a possible evacuation of the southwest part of the state of New Mexico. And, of course, there was the clear danger of starting a nuclear arms race.

Within a month of that first, successful test, two atomic bombs destroyed Hiroshima and Nagasaki. Some scientists had suggested that the bomb simply be demonstrated, rather than dropped on Japanese cities—saying that this would greatly improve the chances for arms control after the war—but to no avail. With the tragedy of Pearl Harbor still fresh in Americans' minds, it would have been very difficult for President Truman to order a demonstration of the weapons rather than use them as he did—the desire to quickly end the war and save the lives that would have been lost in any invasion of Japan was very strong. Yet the overriding truth was probably very simple: As the physicist Freeman

Dyson later said, "The reason that it was dropped was just that nobody had the courage or the foresight to say no."

It's important to realize how shocked the physicists were in the aftermath of the bombing of Hiroshima, on August 6, 1945. They describe a series of waves of emotion: first, a sense of fulfillment that the bomb worked, then horror at all the people that had been killed, and then a convincing feeling that on no account should another bomb be dropped. Yet of course another bomb was dropped, on Nagasaki, only three days after the bombing of Hiroshima.

In November 1945, three months after the atomic bombings, Oppenheimer stood firmly behind the scientific attitude, saying, "It is not possible to be a scientist unless you believe that the knowledge of the world, and the power which this gives, is a thing which is of intrinsic value to humanity, and that you are using it to help in the spread of knowledge and are willing to take the consequences."

Oppenheimer went on to work, with others, on the Acheson-Lilienthal report, which, as Richard Rhodes says in his recent book *Visions of Technology,* "found a way to prevent a clandestine nuclear arms race without resorting to armed world government"; their suggestion was a form of relinquishment of nuclear weapons work by nation-states to an international agency.

This proposal led to the Baruch Plan, which was submitted to the United Nations in June 1946 but never adopted (perhaps because, as Rhodes suggests, Bernard Baruch had "insisted on burdening the plan with conventional sanctions," thereby inevitably dooming it, even though it would "almost certainly have been rejected by Stalinist Russia anyway"). Other efforts to promote sensible steps toward internationalizing nuclear power to prevent an arms race ran afoul either of US politics and internal distrust, or distrust by the Soviets. The opportunity to avoid the arms race was lost, and very quickly.

Two years later, in 1948, Oppenheimer seemed to have reached another stage in his thinking, saying, "In some sort of crude sense which no vulgarity, no humor, no overstatement can quite extinguish, the physicists have known sin; and this is a knowl-edge they cannot lose."

In 1949, the Soviets exploded an atom bomb. By 1955, both the US and the Soviet Union had tested hydrogen bombs suitable for delivery by aircraft. And so the nuclear arms race began.

Nearly 20 years ago, in the documentary *The Day After Trinity,* Freeman Dyson summarized the scientific attitudes that brought us to the nuclear precipice:

> "I have felt it myself. The glitter of nuclear weapons. It is irresistible if you come to them as a scientist. To feel it's there in your hands, to re-lease this energy that fuels the stars, to let it do your bidding. To perform these miracles, to lift a million tons of rock into the sky. It is something that gives people an illusion of illimitable power, and it is, in some ways, responsible for all our troubles—this, what you might call technical ar-rogance, that overcomes people when they see what they can do with their minds."[8]

Now, as then, we are creators of new technologies and stars of the imagined future, driven—this time by great financial rewards and global competi-tion—despite the clear dangers, hardly evaluating what it may be like to try to live in a world that is the realistic outcome of what we are creating and imagining.

In 1947, *The Bulletin of the Atomic Scientists* began putting a Doomsday Clock on its cover. For more than 50 years, it has shown an estimate of the rela-tive nuclear danger we have faced, reflecting the changing international conditions. The hands on the clock have moved 15 times and today, standing at nine minutes to midnight, reflect continuing and real danger from nuclear weapons. The recent addi-tion of India and Pakistan to the list of nuclear powers has increased the threat of failure of the nonproliferation goal, and this danger was reflected by moving the hands closer to midnight in 1998.

In our time, how much danger do we face, not just from nuclear weapons, but from all of these technologies? How high are the extinction risks?

The philosopher John Leslie has studied this question and concluded that the risk of human ex-tinction is at least 30 percent,[9] while Ray Kurzweil believes we have "a better than even chance of mak-ing it through," with the caveat that he has "always been accused of being an optimist." Not only are these estimates not encouraging, but they do not include the probability of many horrid outcomes that lie short of extinction.

Faced with such assessments, some serious peo-ple are already suggesting that we simply move be-yond Earth as quickly as possible. We would colo-nize the galaxy using von Neumann probes, which hop from star system to star system, replicating as they go. This step will almost certainly be necessary 5 billion years from now (or sooner if our solar sys-tem is disastrously impacted by the impending col-lision of our galaxy with the Andromeda galaxy within the next 3 billion years), but if we take Kurzweil and Moravec at their word it might be necessary by the middle of this century.

What are the moral implications here? If we must move beyond Earth this quickly in order for the species to survive, who accepts the responsibil-ity for the fate of those (most of us, after all) who are left behind? And even if we scatter to the stars, isn't it likely that we may take our problems with us or find, later, that they have followed us? The fate of our species on Earth and our fate in the galaxy seem inextricably linked.

Another idea is to erect a series of shields to de-fend against each of the dangerous technologies. The Strategic Defense Initiative, proposed by the Reagan administration, was an attempt to design such a shield against the threat of a nuclear attack from the Soviet Union. But as Arthur C. Clarke, who was privy to discussions about the project, ob-served: "Though it might be possible, at vast ex-pense, to construct local defense systems that would 'only' let through a few percent of ballistic missiles, the much touted idea of a national um-brella was nonsense. Luis Alvarez, perhaps the greatest experimental physicist of this century, re-marked to me that the advocates of such schemes were 'very bright guys with no common sense.'"

Clarke continued: "Looking into my often cloudy crystal ball, I suspect that a total defense might indeed be possible in a century or so. But the technology involved would produce, as a by-product, weapons so terrible that no one would bother with anything as primitive as ballistic missiles."[10]

In *Engines of Creation,* Eric Drexler proposed that we build an active nanotechnological shield—a form of immune system for the biosphere—to defend against dangerous replicators of all kinds that might escape from laboratories or otherwise be maliciously created. But the shield he proposed would itself be extremely dangerous—nothing could prevent it from developing autoimmune problems and attacking the biosphere itself.[11]

Similar difficulties apply to the construction of shields against robotics and genetic engineering. These technologies are too powerful to be shielded against in the time frame of interest; even if it were possible to implement defensive shields, the side effects of their development would be at least as dangerous as the technologies we are trying to protect against.

These possibilities are all thus either undesirable or unachievable or both. The only realistic alternative I see is relinquishment: to limit development of the technologies that are too dangerous, by limiting our pursuit of certain kinds of knowledge.

Yes, I know, knowledge is good, as is the search for new truths. We have been seeking knowledge since ancient times. Aristotle opened his Metaphysics with the simple statement: "All men by nature desire to know." We have, as a bedrock value in our society, long agreed on the value of open access to information, and recognize the problems that arise with attempts to restrict access to and development of knowledge. In recent times, we have come to revere scientific knowledge.

But despite the strong historical precedents, if open access to and unlimited development of knowledge henceforth puts us all in clear danger of extinction, then common sense demands that we reexamine even these basic, long-held beliefs.

It was Nietzsche who warned us, at the end of the 19th century, not only that God is dead but that "faith in science, which after all exists undeniably, cannot owe its origin to a calculus of utility; it must have originated *in spite of* the fact that the disutility and dangerousness of the 'will to truth,' of 'truth at any price' is proved to it constantly." It is this further danger that we now fully face—the consequences of

our truth-seeking. The truth that science seeks can certainly be considered a dangerous substitute for God if it is likely to lead to our extinction.

If we could agree, as a species, what we wanted, where we were headed, and why, then we would make our future much less dangerous—then we might understand what we can and should relinquish. Otherwise, we can easily imagine an arms race developing over GNR technologies, as it did with the NBC technologies in the 20th century. This is perhaps the greatest risk, for once such a race begins, it's very hard to end it. This time—unlike during the Manhattan Project—we aren't in a war, facing an implacable enemy that is threatening our civilization; we are driven, instead, by our habits, our desires, our economic system, and our competitive need to know.

I believe that we all wish our course could be determined by our collective values, ethics, and morals. If we had gained more collective wisdom over the past few thousand years, then a dialogue to this end would be more practical, and the incredible powers we are about to unleash would not be nearly so troubling.

One would think we might be driven to such a dialogue by our instinct for self-preservation. Individuals clearly have this desire, yet as a species our behavior seems to be not in our favor. In dealing with the nuclear threat, we often spoke dishonestly to ourselves and to each other, thereby greatly increasing the risks. Whether this was politically motivated, or because we chose not to think ahead, or because when faced with such grave threats we acted irrationally out of fear, I do not know, but it does not bode well.

The new Pandora's boxes of genetics, nanotechnology, and robotics are almost open, yet we seem hardly to have noticed. Ideas can't be put back in a box; unlike uranium or plutonium, they don't need to be mined and refined, and they can be freely copied. Once they are out, they are out. Churchill remarked, in a famous left-handed compliment, that the American people and their leaders "invariably do the right thing, after they have examined every other alternative." In this case, however, we must act more presciently, as to do the right thing only at last may be to lose the chance to do it at all.

As Thoreau said, "We do not ride on the railroad; it rides upon us"; and this is what we must fight, in our time. The question is, indeed, Which is to be master? Will we survive our technologies?

We are being propelled into this new century with no plan, no control, no brakes. Have we already gone too far down the path to alter course? I don't believe so, but we aren't trying yet, and the last chance to assert control—the fail-safe point—is rapidly approaching. We have our first pet robots, as well as commercially available genetic engineering techniques, and our nanoscale techniques are advancing rapidly. While the development of these technologies proceeds through a number of steps, it isn't necessarily the case—as happened in the Manhattan Project and the Trinity test—that the last step in proving a technology is large and hard. The breakthrough to wild self-replication in robotics, genetic engineering, or nanotechnology could come suddenly, reprising the surprise we felt when we learned of the cloning of a mammal.

And yet I believe we do have a strong and solid basis for hope. Our attempts to deal with weapons of mass destruction in the last century provide a shining example of relinquishment for us to consider: the unilateral US abandonment, without preconditions, of the development of biological weapons. This relinquishment stemmed from the realization that while it would take an enormous effort to create these terrible weapons, they could from then on easily be duplicated and fall into the hands of rogue nations or terrorist groups.

The clear conclusion was that we would create additional threats to ourselves by pursuing these weapons, and that we would be more secure if we did not pursue them. We have embodied our relinquishment of biological and chemical weapons in the 1972 Biological Weapons Convention (BWC) and the 1993 Chemical Weapons Convention (CWC).[12]

As for the continuing sizable threat from nuclear weapons, which we have lived with now for more than 50 years, the US Senate's recent rejection of the Comprehensive Test Ban Treaty makes it clear relinquishing nuclear weapons will not be politically easy. But we have a unique opportunity, with the end of the Cold War, to avert a multipolar arms race. Building on the BWC and CWC relinquishments, successful abolition of nuclear weapons could help us build toward a habit of relinquishing dangerous technologies. (Actually, by getting rid of all but 100 nuclear weapons worldwide—roughly the total destructive power of World War II and a considerably easier task—we could eliminate this extinction threat.[13])

Verifying relinquishment will be a difficult problem, but not an unsolvable one. We are fortunate to have already done a lot of relevant work in the context of the BWC and other treaties. Our major task will be to apply this to technologies that are naturally much more commercial than military. The substantial need here is for transparency, as difficulty of verification is directly proportional to the difficulty of distinguishing relinquished from legitimate activities.

I frankly believe that the situation in 1945 was simpler than the one we now face: The nuclear technologies were reasonably separable into commercial and military uses, and monitoring was aided by the nature of atomic tests and the ease with which radioactivity could be measured. Research on military applications could be performed at national laboratories such as Los Alamos, with the results kept secret as long as possible.

The GNR technologies do not divide clearly into commercial and military uses; given their potential in the market, it's hard to imagine pursuing them only in national laboratories. With their widespread commercial pursuit, enforcing relinquishment will require a verification regime similar to that for biological weapons, but on an unprecedented scale. This, inevitably, will raise tensions between our individual privacy and desire for proprietary information, and the need for verification to protect us all. We will undoubtedly encounter strong resistance to this loss of privacy and freedom of action.

Verifying the relinquishment of certain GNR technologies will have to occur in cyberspace as well as at physical facilities. The critical issue will be to make the necessary transparency acceptable in a world of proprietary information, presumably by providing new forms of protection for intellectual property.

Verifying compliance will also require that scientists and engineers adopt a strong code of ethical conduct, resembling the Hippocratic oath, and that they have the courage to whistleblow as necessary, even at high personal cost. This would answer the call—50 years after Hiroshima—by the Nobel laureate Hans Bethe, one of the most senior of the surviving members of the Manhattan Project, that all scientists "cease and desist from work creating, developing, improving, and manufacturing nuclear weapons and other weapons of potential mass destruction."[14] In the 21st century, this requires vigilance and personal responsibility by those who would work on both NBC and GNR technologies to avoid implementing weapons of mass destruction and knowledge-enabled mass destruction.

Thoreau also said that we will be "rich in proportion to the number of things which we can afford to let alone." We each seek to be happy, but it would seem worthwhile to question whether we need to take such a high risk of total destruction to gain yet more knowledge and yet more things; common sense says that there is a limit to our material needs—and that certain knowledge is too dangerous and is best forgone.

Neither should we pursue near immortality without considering the costs, without considering the commensurate increase in the risk of extinction. Immortality, while perhaps the original, is certainly not the only possible utopian dream.

I recently had the good fortune to meet the distinguished author and scholar Jacques Attali, whose book *Lignes d'horizons* (*Millennium,* in the English translation) helped inspire the Java and Jini approach to the coming age of pervasive computing. . . . In his new book *Fraternités,* Attali describes how our dreams of utopia have changed over time:

> At the dawn of societies, men saw their passage on Earth as nothing more than a labyrinth of pain, at the end of which stood a door leading, via their death, to the company of gods and to *Eternity.* With the Hebrews and then the Greeks, some men dared free themselves from theological demands and dream of an ideal City where *Liberty* would flourish. Others, noting the evolution

of the market society, understood that the liberty of some would entail the alienation of others, and they sought *Equality.*

Jacques helped me understand how these three different utopian goals exist in tension in our society today. He goes on to describe a fourth utopia, *Fraternity,* whose foundation is altruism. Fraternity alone associates individual happiness with the happiness of others, affording the promise of self-sustainment.

This crystallized for me my problem with Kurzweil's dream. A technological approach to Eternity—near immortality through robotics—may not be the most desirable utopia, and its pursuit brings clear dangers. Maybe we should rethink our utopian choices.

Where can we look for a new ethical basis to set our course? I have found the ideas in the book *Ethics for the New Millennium,* by the Dalai Lama, to be very helpful. As is perhaps well known but little heeded, the Dalai Lama argues that the most important thing is for us to conduct our lives with love and compassion for others, and that our societies need to develop a stronger notion of universal responsibility and of our interdependency; he proposes a standard of positive ethical conduct for individuals and societies that seems consonant with Attali's Fraternity utopia.

The Dalai Lama further argues that we must understand what it is that makes people happy, and acknowledge the strong evidence that neither material progress nor the pursuit of the power of knowledge is the key—that there are limits to what science and the scientific pursuit alone can do.

Our Western notion of happiness seems to come from the Greeks, who defined it as "the exercise of vital powers along lines of excellence in a life affording them scope."[15]

Clearly, we need to find meaningful challenges and sufficient scope in our lives if we are to be happy in whatever is to come. But I believe we must find alternative outlets for our creative forces, beyond the culture of perpetual economic growth; this growth has largely been a blessing for several hundred years, but it has not brought us unalloyed happiness, and we must now choose between the pursuit of unrestricted and undirected growth through science and technology and the clear accompanying dangers.

It is now more than a year since my first encounter with Ray Kurzweil and John Searle. I see around me cause for hope in the voices for caution and relinquishment and in those people I have discovered who are as concerned as I am about our current predicament. I feel, too, a deepened sense of personal responsibility—not for the work I have already done, but for the work that I might yet do, at the confluence of the sciences.

But many other people who know about the dangers still seem strangely silent. When pressed, they trot out the "this is nothing new" riposte—as if awareness of what could happen is response enough. They tell me, There are universities filled with bioethicists who study this stuff all day long. They say, All this has been written about before, and by experts. They complain, Your worries and your arguments are already old hat.

I don't know where these people hide their fear. As an architect of complex systems I enter this arena as a generalist. But should this diminish my concerns? I am aware of how much has been written about, talked about, and lectured about so authoritatively. But does this mean it has reached people? Does this mean we can discount the dangers before us?

Knowing is not a rationale for not acting. Can we doubt that knowledge has become a weapon we wield against ourselves?

The experiences of the atomic scientists clearly show the need to take personal responsibility, the danger that things will move too fast, and the way in which a process can take on a life of its own. We can, as they did, create insurmountable problems in almost no time flat. We must do more thinking up front if we are not to be similarly surprised and shocked by the consequences of our inventions.

My continuing professional work is on improving the reliability of software. Software is a tool, and as a toolbuilder I must struggle with the uses to which the tools I make are put. I have always believed that making software more reliable, given its many uses, will make the world a safer and better

place; if I were to come to believe the opposite, then I would be morally obligated to stop this work. I can now imagine such a day may come.

This all leaves me not angry but at least a bit melancholic. Henceforth, for me, progress will be somewhat bittersweet.

NOTES

1. The passage Kurzweil quotes is from Kaczynski's Unabomber Manifesto, which was published jointly, under duress, by *The New York Times* and *The Washington Post* to attempt to bring his campaign of terror to an end. I agree with David Gelernter, who said about their decision:

   "It was a tough call for the newspapers. To say yes would be giving in to terrorism, and for all they knew he was lying anyway. On the other hand, to say yes might stop the killing. There was also a chance that someone would read the tract and get a hunch about the author; and that is exactly what happened. The suspect's brother read it, and it rang a bell.

   "I would have told them not to publish. I'm glad they didn't ask me. I guess."

   (*Drawing Life: Surviving the Unabomber.* Free Press, 1997: 120.)

2. Garrett, Laurie. *The Coming Plague: Newly Emerging Diseases in a World Out of Balance.* Penguin, 1994: 47–52, 414, 419, 452.

3. Isaac Asimov described what became the most famous view of ethical rules for robot behavior in his book *I, Robot* in 1950, in his Three Laws of Robotics: 1. A robot may not injure a human being, or, through inaction, allow a human being to come to harm. 2. A robot must obey the orders given it by human beings, except where such orders would conflict with the First Law. 3. A robot must protect its own existence, as long as such protection does not conflict with the First or Second Law.

4. Michelangelo wrote a sonnet that begins:

   Non ha l' ottimo artista alcun concetto
   Ch' un marmo solo in sè non circonscriva
   Col suo soverchio; e solo a quello arriva
   La man che ubbidisce all' intelletto.

   Stone translates this as:

   The best of artists hath no thought to show
   which the rough stone in its superfluous shell

*doth not include; to break the marble spell
is all the hand that serves the brain can do.*

Stone describes the process: "He was not working from his drawings or clay models; they had all been put away. He was carving from the images in his mind. His eyes and hands knew where every line, curve, mass must emerge, and at what depth in the heart of the stone to create the low relief."

(*The Agony and the Ecstasy.*
Doubleday, 1961: 6, 144.)

5. First Foresight Conference on Nanotechnology in October 1989, a talk titled "The Future of Computation." Published in Crandall, B. C. and James Lewis, editors. *Nanotechnology: Research and Perspectives.* MIT Press, 1992: 269. See also *www. foresight.org/Conferences/MNT01/Nano1.html.*

6. In his 1963 novel *Cat's Cradle,* Kurt Vonnegut imagined a gray-goo-like accident where a form of ice called ice-nine, which becomes solid at a much higher temperature, freezes the oceans.

7. Kauffman, Stuart. "Self-replication: Even Peptides Do It." *Nature,* 382, August 8, 1996: 496. See *www. santafe.edu/sfi/People/kauffman/sak-peptides.html.*

8. Else, Jon. *The Day After Trinity: J. Robert Oppenheimer and the Atomic Bomb* (available at *www. pyramiddirect.com*).

9. This estimate is in Leslie's book *The End of the World: The Science and Ethics of Human Extinction,* where he notes that the probability of extinction is substantially higher if we accept Brandon Carter's Doomsday Argument, which is, briefly, that "we ought to have some reluctance to believe that we are very exceptionally early, for instance in the earliest 0.001 percent, among all humans who will ever have lived. This would be some reason for thinking that humankind will not survive for many more centuries, let alone colonize the galaxy. Carter's doomsday argument doesn't generate any risk estimates just by itself. It is an argument for *revising* the estimates which we generate when we consider various possible dangers." (Routledge, 1996: 1, 3, 145.)

10. Clarke, Arthur C. "Presidents, Experts, and Asteroids." *Science,* June 5, 1998. Reprinted as "Science and Society" in *Greetings, Carbon-Based Bipeds! Collected Essays, 1934–1998.* St. Martin's Press, 1999: 526.

11. And, as David Forrest suggests in his paper "Regulating Nanotechnology Development," available at *www.foresight.org/NanoRev/Forrest1989.html,* "If we used strict liability as an alternative to regulation it would be impossible for any developer to internalize the cost of the risk (destruction of the biosphere), so theoretically the activity of developing nanotechnology should never be undertaken." Forrest's analysis leaves us with only government regulation to protect us—not a comforting thought.

12. Meselson, Matthew. "The Problem of Biological Weapons." Presentation to the 1,818th Stated Meeting of the American Academy of Arts and Sciences, January 13, 1999. (*minerva.amacad.org/ archive/bulletin4.htm*)

13. Doty, Paul. "The Forgotten Menace: Nuclear Weapons Stockpiles Still Represent the Biggest Threat to Civilization." *Nature,* 402, December 9, 1999: 583.

14. See also Hans Bethe's 1997 letter to President Clinton, at *www.fas.org/bethecr.htm.*

15. Hamilton, Edith. *The Greek Way.* W. W. Norton & Co., 1942: 35.

RAY KURZWEIL   II.8

Promise and Peril

As an inventor who developed the first print-to-speech reading machine in 1976, the music synthesizer in 1982, and a speech-recognition system in 1987, as well as an entrepreneur, author, and artificial intelligence guru, Ray Kurzweil is uniquely qualified to comment on the rate of technological change, especially if computers are involved. In this piece from *Interactive Week,* he expresses concern that many do not appreciate the fact that the pace of change is increasing at a rate far faster than is commonly thought. The "law of accelerating returns," as he calls this phenomenon, is evident in many areas such as computers, medical care, communication, and biology.

Unlike some other technologists, Kurzweil does not feel it would be appropriate to limit technological development in a particular area because an advance might be used in a way that would ultimately be harmful to humans or the planet. Although getting rid of the bad aspects of a technology might be highly desirable, he feels that it is not possible because of the interdependence of all parts of our technological systems.

However, Kurzweil believes it is necessary that we systematically evaluate the possible future impacts of a technology. Only through such a process can we ensure that the maximum benefit of a technology is obtained while its risks are minimized; and there might be some cases where this is only possible through some level of "relinquishment." Our shared human values and ethics will ultimately decide how we deal with emerging high-risk technologies, which will determine how we live in the future.

Focus Questions

1. What evidence does Kurzweil offer for the increasing rate of technological change?
2. In considering the possible future impact of technology, what three stages does Kurzweil suggest humans go through?
3. Describe some of the future technologies mentioned in this article that pose potential threats. In what ways might those same technologies prove beneficial to humans?
4. How does the author feel technology might be controlled, and why does he feel this will be very difficult to do?

Keywords

democratization, encryption "trap door," historical exponential view, intuitive linear view, law of accelerating returns, nanobots, nanotechnology, paradigm shift, pathogen, relinquishment, self-replicating technologies

BILL JOY, COFOUNDER OF SUN MICROSYSTEMS and principal developer of the Java programming language, has recently taken up a personal mission to warn us of the impending dangers from the emergence of self-replicating technologies in the fields of genetics, nanotechnology and robotics, which he aggregates under the label "GNR." Although his

From *Interactive Week*, 10/23/00, Vol. 7, Issue 43, "Promise & Peril: Genetics, Nanotechnology and Robotics in the 21st Century," by Ray Kurzweil. Copyright © 2000 by Ray Kurzweil. Reprinted by permission of the author.

warnings are not entirely new, they have attracted considerable attention because of Joy's credibility as one of our leading technologists. It reminds me of the attention that George Soros, the currency arbitrager and arch capitalist, received when he made vaguely critical comments about the excesses of unrestrained capitalism.

According to Joy, the day is close at hand when it will be feasible to create genetically altered designer pathogens in college laboratories.

Then, at a later date, we'll have to contend with self-replicating entities created through nanotechnology, the field devoted to manipulating matter on the scale of individual atoms. Although nano-engineered "self-replicators" are at least one decade, and probably more than two decades, away, the specter that concerns Joy can be described as an unstoppable, nonbiological cancer.

Finally, if we manage to survive these first two perils, we'll encounter robots whose intelligence will rival and ultimately exceed our own. Such robots may make great assistants, but who's to say that we can count on them to remain reliably friendly to mere humans?

Although I am often cast as the technology optimist who counters Joy's pessimism, I do share his concerns regarding self-replicating technologies; indeed, I played a role in bringing these dangers to Bill's attention. In many of the dialogues and forums in which I have participated on this subject, I end up defending Joy's position with regard to the feasibility of these technologies and scenarios when they come under attack by commentators who I believe are being quite shortsighted in their skepticism. Even so, I do find fault with Joy's prescription—halting the advance of technology and the pursuit of knowledge in broad fields such as nanotechnology.

Before addressing our differences, let me first discuss the salient issue of feasibility. Many long-range forecasts of technical feasibility dramatically underestimate the power of future technology for one simple reason: They are based on what I call the "intuitive linear" view of technological progress rather than the "historical exponential view." When people think of a future period, they intuitively assume that the current rate of progress will continue for the period being considered. In fact, the rate of technological progress is not constant, but since it is human nature to adapt to the changing pace, the intuitive view is that the pace will continue at the current rate. It is typical, therefore, that even sophisticated commentators, when considering the future, extrapolate the current pace of change over the next 10 years or 100 years to determine their expectations—the "intuitive linear" view.

But any serious examination of the history of technology reveals that technological change is at least exponential. There are a great many examples of this, including constantly accelerating developments in computation, communication, brain scanning, multiple aspects of biotechnology and miniaturization. One can examine these data in many different ways, on many different time scales and for a wide variety of phenomena. Whatever the approach, we find—at least—double exponential growth.

This phenomenon, which I call the "law of accelerating returns," does not rely on a mere assumption of the continuation of Moore's Law, which predicts, in effect, the quadrupling of computer power every 24 months. Rather, it is based on a rich model of diverse technological processes, a model I have been developing over the past couple of decades.

What it clearly shows is that technology, particularly the pace of technological change, has been advancing at least exponentially since the advent of technology. Thus, while people often overestimate what can be achieved in the short term because there is a tendency to leave out necessary details, we typically underestimate what can be achieved in the long term because exponential growth is ignored.

This observation also applies to rates of paradigm shifts, which are currently doubling approximately every decade. At that rate, the technological progress in the 21st century will be equivalent to changes that in the linear view would require on the order of 20,000 years.

This exponential progress in computation and communication technologies is greatly empowering the individual. That's good news in many ways, because those technologies are largely responsible for the pervasive trend toward democratization and the reshaping of power relations at all levels of society. But these technologies are also empowering and amplifying our destructive impulses. It's not necessary to anticipate all the ultimate uses of a technology to see danger in, for example, every college biotechnology lab's having the ability to create self-replicating biological pathogens.

Nevertheless, I do reject Joy's call for relinquishing broad areas of technology—for example, nanotechnology. Technology has always been a double-edged sword. We don't need to look any further than today's technology to see this. Take biotechnology. We have already seen substantial benefits:

more effective AIDS treatments, human insulin and many others. In the years ahead, we will see enormous gains in overcoming cancer and many other diseases, as well as in greatly extending human longevity, all presumably positive developments—although even these are controversial. On the other hand, the means will soon exist in a routine biotechnology laboratory to create a pathogen that could be more destructive to humans or other living organisms than an atomic bomb.

If we imagine describing the dangers that exist today—enough nuclear explosive power to destroy all mammalian life, just for starters—to people who lived a couple of hundred years ago, they would think it mad to take such risks. On the other hand, how many people in the year 2000 would really want to go back to the short, disease-filled, poverty-stricken, disaster-prone lives that 99 percent of the human race struggled through a couple of centuries ago? We may romanticize the past, but until fairly recently, most of humanity lived extremely fragile lives, in which a single common misfortune could spell disaster. Substantial portions of our species still live this precarious existence, which is at least one reason to continue technological progress and the social and economic enhancements that accompany it.

Cautiously Enriching Life

People often go through three stages in examining the impact of future technology: awe and wonderment at its potential to overcome age-old problems, a sense of dread at a new set of grave dangers that accompany these new technologies, followed, finally and hopefully, by the realization that the only viable and responsible path is to set a careful course that can realize the promise while managing the peril.

Joy eloquently describes the plagues of centuries past and how new, self-replicating technologies, such as mutant bioengineered pathogens or "nanobots" (molecule-sized robots), run amok may bring back the fading notion of pestilence. As I stated earlier, these are real dangers. It is also the case, which Joy acknowledges, that it has been

technological advances, such as antibiotics and improved sanitation, that have freed us from the prevalence of such plagues. Human suffering continues and demands our steadfast attention. Should we tell the millions of people afflicted with cancer and other devastating conditions that we are canceling the development of all bioengineered treatments because there is a risk that these same technologies might one day be used for malevolent purposes? That should be a rhetorical question. Yet, there is a movement to do exactly that. Most people, I believe, would agree that such broad-based relinquishment of research and development is not the answer.

In addition to the continued opportunity to alleviate human distress, another important motivation for continuing technological advancement is economic gain. The continued acceleration of many intertwined technologies are roads paved with gold. (I use the plural here because technology is clearly not a single path.) In a competitive environment, it is an economic imperative to go down these roads. Relinquishing technological advancement would be economic suicide for individuals, companies and nations.

Which brings us to the issue of relinquishment—the wholesale abandonment of certain fields of research—which is Joy's most controversial recommendation and personal commitment. I do feel that relinquishment at the right level is part of a responsible and constructive response to genuine perils. The issue, however, is exactly this: At what level are we to relinquish technology?

Ted Kaczynski, the infamous Unabomber, would have us renounce all of it. This, in my view, is neither desirable nor feasible, and the futility of such a position is only underscored by the senselessness of Kaczynski's deplorable tactics.

Another level would be to forgo certain fields—nanotechnology, for example—that might be regarded as too dangerous. But even these slightly less sweeping strokes of relinquishment are also untenable. Nanotechnology is simply the inevitable result of a persistent trend toward miniaturization that pervades all of technology. It is far from a single, centralized effort, but rather is being pursued by myriad projects with diverse goals.

One observer wrote:

"A further reason why industrial society cannot be reformed . . . is that modern technology is a unified system in which all parts are dependent on one another. You can't get rid of the 'bad' parts of technology and retain only the 'good' parts. Take modern medicine, for example. Progress in medical science depends on progress in chemistry, physics, biology, computer science and other fields. Advanced medical treatments require expensive, high-tech equipment that can be made available only by a technologically progressive, economically rich society. Clearly you can't have much progress in medicine without the whole technological system and everything that goes with it."

The observer I am quoting is Kaczynski. Although one might properly resist him as an authority, I believe he is correct on the deeply entangled nature of the benefits and risks of technology. Where Kaczynski and I clearly part company is in our overall assessment of the relative balance between the two. Joy and I have engaged in dialogues on this issue both publicly and privately, and we concur that technology will and should progress and that we need to be actively concerned with its dark side. If Bill and I disagree, it's on the granularity of relinquishment that is both feasible and desirable.

Abandonment of broad areas of technology will only push these technologies underground where development would continue unimpeded by ethics or regulation. In such a situation, less stable, less responsible practitioners—for example, terrorists—would have a monopoly on deadly expertise.

I do think that relinquishment at the right level needs to be part of our ethical response to the dangers of 21st century technologies. One salient and constructive example of this is the proposed ethical guideline by the Foresight Institute, founded by nanotechnology pioneer Eric Drexler. This guideline would call on nanotechnologists to relinquish the development of physical entities that can self-replicate in a natural environment. Another example is a ban on self-replicating physical entities that contain their own codes for self-replication.

In a design that nanotechnologist Ralph Merkle calls the "Broadcast Architecture," such entities would have to obtain such codes from a centralized secure server, which would guard against undesirable replication.

The Broadcast Architecture is impossible in the biological world, which represents at least one way in which nanotechnology can be made safer than biotechnology. In other ways, nanotech is potentially more dangerous because nanobots can be physically stronger than protein-based entities and more intelligent. But it will eventually be possible to combine the two by having nanotechnology provide the codes within biological entities (replacing DNA), in which case we can use the much safer Broadcast Architecture.

Parsing Perils

As responsible technologists, our ethics should include such "fine-grained" relinquishment, among other professional ethical guidelines. Other protections will need to include oversight by regulatory bodies, the development of technology-specific "immune" responses, as well as computer-assisted surveillance by law enforcement organizations. Many people are not aware that our intelligence agencies already use advanced technologies such as automated word spotting to monitor a substantial flow of telephone conversations. As we go forward, balancing our cherished rights of privacy with our need to be protected from the malicious use of powerful 21st century technologies will be one of many profound challenges. This is the reason recent issues of an encryption "trap door," in which law enforcement authorities would have access to otherwise secure information, and the FBI's Carnivore e-mail snooping system have been so contentious.

As a test case, we can take a small measure of comfort from how we have dealt with one recent technological challenge. There exists today a new form of fully nonbiological, self-replicating entity that didn't exist just a few decades ago: the computer virus. When this form of destructive intruder first appeared, strong concerns were voiced that as such viruses became more sophisticated, software pathogens had the potential to destroy the computer network medium in which they live. Yet the "immune system" that has evolved in response to this challenge has been largely effective. Although destructive, self-replicating software entities do cause damage from time to time, the injury is but a small fraction—much less than one-tenth of 1 percent—of the benefit we receive from the computers and communication links that harbor them.

One might counter that computer viruses lack the lethal potential of biological viruses or of destructive nanotechnology. Although true, this strengthens my observation. The fact that computer viruses are not usually deadly to humans only encourages more people to create and release them.

It also means that our response to the danger is relatively relaxed. Conversely, when it comes to self-replicating entities that are potentially lethal on a large scale, our response on all levels will be vastly more intense.

Technology will remain a double-edged sword, and the story of the 21st century has not yet been written. So, while we must acknowledge and deal with the dangers, we must also recognize that technology represents vast power to be used for all humankind's purposes. We have no choice but to work hard to apply these quickening technologies to advance our human values, despite what often appears to be a lack of consensus on what those values should be.

II.9   MAX MORE

Embrace, Don't Relinquish, the Future

Responding to Bill Joy's essay "Why the Future Doesn't Need Us" (selection II.7), Max More, a transhumanist and chairman of the Extropy Institute, argues that a policy of relinquishing new technologies is both impossible and unethical. The term *transhumanism* was coined by author Julian Huxley in a 1957 essay in which he opined that the evolutionary trajectory of the human species pointed toward transcendence: "The human species can, if it wishes, transcend itself—not just sporadically, an individual here in one way, an individual there in another way, but in its entirety, as humanity. We need a name for this new belief. Perhaps *transhumanism* will serve: man remaining man, but transcending himself, by realizing new possibilities of and for his human nature." Contemporary transhumanists such as More believe that the possibility for human transcendence lies in twenty-first century GNR technologies—genetic engineering, molecular nanotechnology, and robotics and artificial intelligence. He portrays Joy's fears about these emerging technologies as misleading and his prescription for abandoning the unlimited pursuit of new knowledge as unworkable. For More, "we cannot prevent the rise of non-biological intelligence," so instead, we should "embrace it and extend ourselves to incorporate it." Moreover, if we deny ourselves access to new knowledge, we also give up the hope of improving the human condition by eliminating genetic and other diseases and, one day, perhaps even understanding how to slow down the aging process itself. Finding philosophical support for the philosophy of transhumanism in the writings of Friedrich Nietzsche, particularly in his view of the Overman, whose will to power leads him to seek self-overcoming, More proposes that humankind should be preparing for a "grand evolutionary leap."

Focus Questions

1. Why does More believe that a policy of relinquishment is unworkable? Why does he think it is unethical? Do you agree with his arguments for these conclusions?
2. How does More describe the difference between Moravec's vision of the future of robotics and artificial intelligence and the vision that he and Kurzweil share? Which of these visions do you think is more plausible? Which is more desirable?
3. More's criticism of Joy often sounds harsh. What assumptions and values do he and Joy seem to share? How do their views differ? Is there some middle ground that can be found between them?
4. Compare the position taken by More in this essay with the positions taken by Silver (selection II.11) and Kass (selection II.12) regarding human genetic engineering and human cloning. What is your position on the question of relinquishment of GNR technologies?

Keywords

cyborgs, extropy, intelligent design, nanotechnology, Nietzsche, relinquishment, transhumanism

WHEN A SCIENTIST PUBLISHES A PAPER, her peers expect to see evidence that she has read prior work relevant to her topic. They expect the scientist to have studied the field thoroughly before contributing a paper, especially in a controversial field. Bill Joy, as former Chief Scientist at Sun Microsystems, should understand this. In reading his essay "Why the Future Doesn't Need Us" I was struck less by his message than by what his words revealed: weak research into existing thinking about the implications of future technologies. Compounding this error of omission were his unrealistic thoughts about "relinquishment," and his slighting of those who have deeply considered these issues as lacking in common sense. At the same time, I appreciated his courage in publicly laying out his fears and stimulating wider discussion.

Joy's pessimistic assessment of the dangers of advanced technologies differs greatly from my own. Some threats are real, and the balance of benefits over harms clearly depends greatly on the choices we make, but I see the most likely outcomes

as being more benign. That disagreement, though significant in itself, stands independently of my present concern. Even if I agreed with Joy's apocalyptic vision of technology run amok, I would *still* feel compelled to challenge his call for the relinquishment of the "GNR" technologies of genetic engineering, molecular manotechnology, and robotics (and all associated fields).

Having pondered these issues for many years, from technical, economic, political, and philosophical perspectives, I reject Joy's relinquishment policy on three grounds: First, it is unworkable. Second, it is ignoble. Third, it would result in authoritarian control while still failing to achieve its purpose. I will leave the last objection to others and focus on the first two.

Shoot Off First, Ask Questions Later

Joy says that a conversation between inventor-entrepreneur Ray Kurzweil and philosopher John Searle ignited his apocalyptic thinking. Apart from attending a Foresight Institute conference back in 1989, Joy shows no sign of having read any of the writings or listening to any of the talks of those who have devoted themselves to the issues he raises. Despite the clarity of Kurzweil's writing, Joy

"Embrace, Don't Relinquish, the Future" by Max More. Originally published May 7, 2000 at Extropy.org. Reprinted by permission.

still isn't clear whether we are supposed to "become robots or fuse with robots or something like that."

Someone in Joy's influential position has a responsibility to delve into prior thinking on these issues before scaring a public already unreasonably (but selectively) afraid of advanced technologies, including one of his targets: genetic engineering. However, he fails to match the obvious gravity of his concern with adequate seriousness of research. He gives no credit to the years of work by the Foresight Institute, not only in promoting the idea of nanotechnology, but in developing technical solutions and policy measures to address its potential dangers. Certainly, Extropy Institute—a multi-disciplinary think tank and educational organization devoted to "Incubating Better Futures"—would have welcomed a chance to provide input to Joy before he released his missive to the masses.

Joy doesn't stop at racing to judgment before doing adequate research. He seems to go out of his way to paint a distorted picture of those who disagree with his views as lacking both common sense and humility. I was disappointed to see him cite Carl Sagan, one of my intellectual inspirations, in the course of criticizing "leading advocates of the 21st-century technologies" as lacking in simple common sense, along with humility. Balanced discussion of this difficult topic is not helped when one side makes accusations about common sense while advocating policies such as global relinquishment, which practically all expert commentators recognize as hopelessly unrealistic. I can't help being darkly amused by an interview with Joy in which he draws a parallel between his essay and Einstein's 1939 letter to President Roosevelt.

What disturbs me most about Joy's mischaracterizations is not the offense they cause, nor the hypocrisy that lies beneath them. It is that Joy's approach increases the polarization of views. Rather than seriously engaging with those of us who have thought carefully about these matters, his grandstanding threatens to set us at odds. This kind of unproductive conflict would be expected from a consistently technophobic activist. From an accomplished technologist like Joy, we should expect better.

While acknowledging the tremendously beneficial possibilities of emerging technologies, Bill Joy

judges them as being too dangerous for us to handle. The only acceptable course in his view is relinquishment. He wants everyone in the world "to limit development of the technologies that are too dangerous, by limiting our pursuit of certain kinds of knowledge." Joy joins the centuries-old procession of theocrats, autocrats, and technocrats in attacking our pursuit of unlimited knowledge. He mentions the myth of Pandora's box. He might have thrown in the anti-humanistic and anti-transhumanistic myths of the Garden of Eden, the Tower of Babel, and the demise of Icarus. Moving from myth to reality, he should have been explicit in describing the necessary means deployed throughout history: burning books, proscribing the reading of dangerous ideas, and state control of science.

Relinquishment Cannot Work

The first of my objections to relinquishment has already been well made by Ray Kurzweil. Joy's fantasies about relinquishment ride on the assumption that "we could agree, as a species" to hold back from developing the GNR technologies and presumably any enabling or related technologies. Perhaps Joy's experience in having a staff of engineers to do his bidding has blinded him to a fact too obvious to state without embarrassment: the six billion humans on this planet do not and will not agree to relinquish technologies that offer massive benefits as well as defensive and offensive military capabilities.

We have failed to prevent the spread of nuclear weapons technology, despite its terrifying nature and relative ease in detection. How are we to prevent all companies, all governments, all hidden groups in the world from working on these technologies? Mr. Joy, please note: all six billion of these people—many desperately in need of the material and medical benefits offered by these technologies—will not read the Dalai Lama and go along with your master plan. Relinquishment is a utopian fantasy worthy of the most blinkered hippies of the '60s. Adding coercive enforcement to the mix moves the idea from utopian fantasy to frightening dystopia.

Ray Kurzweil points to a fine-grained relinquishment that can at least reduce the dangers of runaway technologies among those willing to play this game. Nanotechnology pioneer Eric Drexler has long recommended designing nanomachines that will quickly cease functioning if not fed some essential and naturally uncommon ingredient. Ralph Merkle's 'broadcast architecture' offers another way to develop nanomachines under control. These and other proposals can reduce the hazards of accidental nanotechnological disasters.

However, we can pursue intelligent design, ethical guidelines, and oversight only piecemeal, not universally. Less cautious or less benevolent developers will refuse even this fine-grained relinquishment. That fact makes it imperative to *accelerate* the development of advanced technologies in open societies. Only by possessing the most advanced technological knowledge can we hope to defend ourselves against the attacks and accidents from outside our sphere of influence. We should be pushing for better understanding of nanotech defenses, accelerated decoding and deactivation of genetically-engineered pathogens, and putting more thought into means of limiting runaway independent superintelligent AI.

Stewart Brand, co-founder of the *Whole Earth Catalog,* recently showed that he understands this far better than Joy when he wrote in *Technology Review:* "The best way for doubters to control a questionable new technology is to embrace it, lest it remain wholly in the hands of enthusiasts who don't see what's questionable about it."

I will not address genetic engineering since I regard this as an insignificant danger compared to those of nanotechnology and runaway artificial intelligence (AI). The dangers of runaway artificial superintelligence have received less attention than those of nanotechnology. Perhaps that is because the prospect of AI seems to move further away every time we take a step forward. Bill Joy cites only Hans Moravec on this issue, perhaps because Moravec's view is the most frightening available (with the possible exception of Hugo De Garis). In Moravec's view of the future, superintelligent machines, initially harnessed for human benefit, soon leave us behind. In the most pessimistic *Terminator*-like scenario, they might remove us from the scene as an annoyance.

Oddly, despite having read Kurzweil's book, Joy never discusses Ray's thoroughly different (and more plausible) scenario. In Ray's future projections, we gradually augment ourselves with computer and robotic technology, becoming superhumanly intelligent. Moravec's apartheid of human and machine is replaced with the integration of biology and technology.

While a little research would have shown Joy that futurists, especially transhumanist thinkers, have indeed addressed the danger of explosively evolving, unfriendly AI, I grant that we must *continue* to address this issue. Again, global relinquishment is not an option. Rather than a futile effort to prevent AI development, we should concentrate on warding off dangers within our circle of influence and developing preventative measures against rogue AIs.

Human beings are the dominant species on this planet. Joy wants to protect our dominance by blocking the development of smarter and more powerful beings. I find it odd that Joy, working at a company like Sun Microsystems, can think only of the old corporate strategy where dominant companies attempted to suppress disruptive innovations. Perhaps he should take a look at Cisco Systems, or Microsoft, both of which have adopted a different strategy: Embrace and extend. Humanity would do well to borrow from the new business strategists' approach.

Realistically, we cannot prevent the rise of non-biological intelligence. We can embrace it and extend ourselves to incorporate it. The more quickly and continuously we absorb computational advances, the easier it will be and the less risk of a technology runaway. Absorption and integration will include economic interweaving of these emerging technologies with our organizations as well as directly interfacing our biology with sensors, displays, computers, and other devices. This way we avoid an us-vs.-them situation. *They* become part of *us.*

Relinquishment is Ignoble

Some people reach moral conclusions by consulting an ultimate authority. Their authority gives them answers that are received and applied without questioning. For those of us who prefer a more rational approach to ethical thought, reaching a conclusion involves consulting our basic values then carefully deciding which of the available paths ahead will best reflect those values. Our factual beliefs about how the world works will therefore profoundly affect our moral reasoning.

Two individuals may share values but reach differing conclusions due to divergent factual beliefs. Referring to some person or practice as "unethical" obscures the interplay of factual and normative differences. That is why I say that "relinquishment is ignoble" rather than "relinquishment is unethical." I suspect that my moral and philosophical disagreement with Joy over relinquishment results both from differing beliefs about the facts and differing basic values.

Joy assigns a high probability to the extinction of humanity if we do not relinquish certain emerging technologies. Joy's implicit calculus reminds me of Pascal's Wager. Finding no rational basis for accepting or rejecting belief in a God, Pascal claimed that belief was the best bet. Choosing not to believe had minimal benefits and the possibility of an infinitely high cost (eternal damnation). Choosing to believe carried small costs and offered potentially infinite rewards (eternity in Heaven). Now, the extinction of the human race is not as bad as eternity in Hell, but most of us would agree that it's an utterly rotten result. If relinquishment can drastically reduce the odds of such a large loss, while costing us little, then relinquishment is the rational and moral choice. A clear, simple, easy answer. Alas, Joy, like Pascal, loads the dice to produce his desired result.

I view the chances of success for global relinquishment as practically zero. Worse, I believe that partial relinquishment will frighteningly increase the chances of disaster by disarming the responsible while leaving powerful abilities in the hands of those full of authoritarian ambition, resentment, and hatred. We may find a place for the fine-grained voluntary relinquishment of inherently dangerous means, where safer technological paths are available. But unilateral relinquishment means unilateral disarmament. I can only hope that Bill Joy never becomes a successful Neville Chamberlain of 21st century technologies. In place of relinquishment, we would do better to accelerate our

development of these technologies, while focusing on developing protections against and responses to their destructive uses.

My assessment of the costs of relinquishment differ from Joy's for another reason. Billions of people continue to suffer illness, damage, starvation, and all the plethora of woes humanity has had to endure through the ages. The emerging technologies of genetic engineering, molecular nanotechnology, and biological-technological interfaces offer solutions to these problems. Joy would stop progress in robotics, artificial intelligence, genetics, and related fields. Too bad for those now regaining hearing and sight thanks to implants. Too bad for the billions who will continue to die of numerous diseases that could be dispatched through genetic and nanotechnological solutions. I cannot reconcile the deliberate indulgence of continued suffering with any plausible moral perspective.

Like Joy, I too worry about the extinction of human beings. I see it happening everyday, one by one. We call this serial extinction of humanity "aging and death." Because aging and death have always been with us and have seemed inevitable, we often rationalize this serial extinction as natural and even desirable. We cry out against the sudden death of large numbers of humans. But, unless it touches someone close, we rarely concern ourselves with the constant drip, drip, drip of individual lives decaying and disintegrating into nothingness. Some day, not too far in the future, people will look back on our complacency and rationalizations with horror and disgust. They will wonder why people gathered in crowds to protest genetic modification of crops, yet never demonstrated in favor of accelerating anti-aging research. Holding back from developing the technologies targeted by Joy will not only shift power into the hands of the destroyers, it will mean an unforgivable lassitude and complicity in the face of entropy and death.

Joy's concerns about technological dangers may seem responsible. But his unbalanced obsession with his fears and lack of emphasis on the enormous benefits, can only put a drag on progress. We are already seeing fear, ignorance, and various hidden agendas spurring resistance to genetic research and biotechnology. Of course we must take care in how we develop these technologies. But we must also recognize how they can tackle cancer, heart disease, birth defects, crippling accidents, Parkinson's disease, schizophrenia, depression, chronic pain, aging, and death, not to mention various environmental challenges including pollution and species extinction.

On the basis of Joy's recent writing and speaking, I have to assume that we disagree not only about the facts, but also in our basic values. Joy seems to value safety, stability, and caution above all. I value challenge, relief of humanity's historical ills, and the drive to transcend our existing limitations, whether biological, intellectual, emotional, or spiritual. Joy appears to be a philosophical cousin of those who wield the "precautionary principle" to block technological progress. I have proposed an alternative "Proactionary Principle" to pursue advances while responsibly searching for and mitigating unwanted side-effects.

Joy quotes the fragmented yet brilliant figure of Friedrich Nietzsche to support his call for an abandonment of the unfettered pursuit of knowledge. Nietzsche is telling the reader that our trust in science "cannot owe its origin to a calculus of utility; it must have originated *in spite of* the fact that the disutility and dangerousness of the 'will to truth,' or 'truth at any price' is proved to it constantly," Joy has understood Nietzsche so poorly that he thinks Nietzsche here is supporting his call for relinquishing the unchained quest for knowledge in favor of safety and comfort. Nietzsche was no friend to "utility." He despised the English Utilitarian philosophers because they elevated pleasure (or happiness) to the position of ultimate value. Even a cursory reading of Nietzsche should make it obvious that he valued not comfort, ease, or certainty. Nietzsche *liked* the dangerousness of the will to truth. He liked that the search for knowledge endangered dogma and its comforts and delusions.

Nietzsche's Zarathustra says: "The most cautious people ask today: 'How may man still be preserved?'" He might have been talking of Bill Joy when he continues: "Zarathustra, however, asks as the sole and first one to do so: 'How shall man be *overcome*?'" . . . "Overcome for me these masters of the present, O my brothers—these petty people: *they* are the overman's greatest danger!" If we interpret Nietzsche's inchoate notion of the overman as

the transhumans who will emerge from the integration of biology and the technologies feared by Joy, we can see with whom Nietzsche would likely side. I will limit myself to one more quotation from Nietzsche:

> And life itself confided this secret to me: "Behold," it said, "I am *that which must always overcome itself*. Indeed, you call it a will to procreate or a drive to an end, to something higher, farther, more manifold: but all this is one . . . Rather would I perish than forswear this; and verily, where there is perishing . . . there life sacrifices itself—for [more] power . . . Whatever I create and however much I live it—soon I must oppose it and my life; . . . 'will to existence': that will does not exist . . . not will to life but . . . will to power. There is much that life esteems more highly than life itself.
> *Zarathustra* II 12 (K: 248)

Like Nietzsche, I find mere survival normatively and spiritually inadequate. Even if, contrary to my view, relinquishment improved our odds of survival, that would not make it the most noble or inspiring choice if we value the unfettered search for knowledge and intellectual, emotional, and spiritual progress. Does that mean doing nothing while technology surges ahead? No. We can minimize the dangers, ease the cultural transition, and accelerate the arrival of benefits in three ways: We can develop a sophisticated philosophical perspective on the issues. We can seek to use new technologies to enhance emotional and psychological health, freeing ourselves from the irrationalities and destructiveness built into the genes of our species. And we can integrate those approaches using a sophisticated, balanced decision making procedure such as I have set out in the form of the Proactionary Principle.

We should be spurring research to understand emotions and the neural basis of feeling and motivation. I've seen some good work in this area (such as Joseph LeDoux's *The Emotional Brain*), but until very recently cognitive science has ignored emotions. If we are to flourish in the presence of incredible new technological abilities, we would do well to focus on using them to debug human nature. Power can corrupt, but knowledge that brings the power to self-modify so as to refine our psychology can ward off corruption and destruction. It is vital that we advance our abilities to refine our own emotions.

Improving philosophical understanding will speed the absorption and integration of new technologies. If we continue to approach rapid and profound technological change with philosophical worldviews rooted in old myths and pre-scientific story-making, we will needlessly fear change, miss out on potential advances, and be caught unprepared. When the announcement came from Scotland proclaiming the first successful mammalian cloning, the Pope issued a statement opposing cloning on grounds that made no sense. (His vague objection would apply equally to identical twins.) President Clinton and other leaders also automatically moved to ban human cloning, with no indication of clear thinking based in science and philosophy.

Transhumanists at Extropy Institute and elsewhere have been developing philosophical thinking fitting to these powerful emerging technologies. In our books, essays, talks, and email forums, we have explored a vast range of emerging philosophical issues in depth. In August 1999, I chaired Extropy Institute's fourth conference: Biotech Futures: Challenges and Choices of Life Extension and Genetic Engineering. The conference laid out the likely path of emerging technologies and dissected issues raised. In my own talk, I analyzed implicit

philosophical mistakes that engender fear and resistance to the changes we anticipate. I summarized our own goals in a Letter to Mother Nature, and have laid out some guiding values in The Extropian Principles. More recently (since the first version of this response to Joy), I have developed a comprehensive, balanced decision procedure, set out in the Proactionary Principle.

Bill Joy's essay and subsequent talks may feed the public's fear and misunderstanding of our potential future. On the other hand, perhaps his thoughts will raise interest in the philosophical, normative, and policy issues in a productive way. As a strategic philosopher committed to incubating better futures, I, along with my colleagues in Extropy Institute, welcome constructive input from Joy in this continuing learning process. Humanity is on the edge of a grand evolutionary leap. Let's not pull back from the edge, but by all means let's check our flight equipment as we prepare for takeoff.

The Extropian Principles: http://www.maxmore.com/extprn3.htm

Letter to Mother Nature: http://www.maxmore.com/mother.htm

Technological Self-Transformation: http://www.maxmore.com/selftrns.htm

The Proactionary Principle: http://www.extropy.org/proactionaryprinciple.htm

---

II.10   JAY STANLEY AND BARRY STEINHARDT

Bigger Monster, Weaker Chains

George Orwell's chilling novel *1984* depicts a society ruled by a totalitarian government bent on total manipulation and control of what people think and where every person is being constantly watched by Big Brother. When Orwell published his novel in 1949, the technologies that made such a dystopia possible were still in the realm of science fiction. But since that time, technological advances in digital cameras, computers, global positioning satellites, "data-mining," and other surveillance technologies have made "total information awareness" a real possibility. In addition, in response to the terrorist attacks of September 11, 2001, the government of the United States has increased its surveillance activities in the name of national security while at the same time keeping the details of what they have been doing secret from the general public. Civil libertarians, such as the authors of this report prepared for the American Civil Liberties Union in 2003, are alarmed at the erosion of personal privacy that these technological and political developments portend. Americans, they argue, are being increasingly watched, tracked, and recorded, both by private corporations and by a security-obsessed government. They fear that "privacy, while not dead, is on life support" and argue that the best way to prevent the emergence of a "surveillance society" is to enact strong new privacy laws based on the constitutional principle of the Fourth Amendment, laws which do not leave the right to privacy at the mercy of advancing technology.

Focus Questions

1. What are some ways in which private corporations are increasingly using data surveillance to track and record our daily activities? Are you at all troubled by this trend toward the consolidation and commodification of personal information? Why or why not?
2. The authors claim that the post-9/11 legislation such as the USA Patriot Act expanded the government's authority to spy on its own citizens while weakening the system of judicial checks and balances on those powers. Explain why the authors think this is the case.
3. Why are the authors concerned about the possibility of a national ID card linked to a national database containing personal information about every citizen? Do you share their concerns, or do you believe that such a step would help the government protect us from criminals and terrorists? Where does the proper balance lie between personal privacy and national security?
4. Discuss this reading in light of the readings by Winner (selection I.7) and Cummings (selection II.14). Whose political values are embedded in the new surveillance technologies?

Keywords

biometrics, Carnivore, data profiling, data surveillance, digitization, Echelon, genetic information, GPS, PATRIOT Act, privacy, RFID chips, TIPS, video surveillance

The Growing Surveillance Monster

In the film *Minority Report,* which takes place in the United States in the year 2050, people called "Precogs" can supposedly predict future crimes, and the

From *Bigger Monster, Weaker Chains: The Growth of an American Surveillance Society* by Jay Stanley and Barry Steinhardt, January 2003. American Civil Liberties Union Technology and Liberty Program. Reprinted by permission of the American Civil Liberties Union.

nation has become a perfect surveillance society. The frightening thing is that except for the psychic Pre-cogs, the technologies of surveillance portrayed in the film already exist or are in the pipeline. Replace the Pre-cogs with "brain fingerprinting"—the supposed ability to ferret out dangerous tendencies by reading brain waves—and the film's entire vision no longer lies far in the future. Other new privacy invasions are coming at us from all directions, from video and data surveillance to DNA scanning to new data-gathering gadgets.

VIDEO SURVEILLANCE

Surveillance video cameras are rapidly spreading throughout the public arena. A survey of surveillance cameras in Manhattan, for example, found that it is impossible to walk around the city without being recorded nearly every step of the way. And since September 11 the pace has quickened, with new cameras being placed not only in some of our most sacred public spaces, such as the National Mall in Washington and the Statue of Liberty in New York harbor, but on ordinary public streets all over America.

As common as video cameras have become, there are strong signs that, without public action, video surveillance may be on the verge of a revolutionary expansion in American life. There are three factors propelling this revolution:

1. **Improved technology.** Advances such as the digitization of video mean cheaper cameras, cheaper transmission of far-flung video feeds, and cheaper storage and retrieval of images.

2. **Centralized surveillance.** A new centralized surveillance center in Washington, DC is an early indicator of what technology may bring. It allows officers to view images from video cameras across the city—public buildings and streets, neighborhoods, Metro stations, and even schools. With the flip of a switch, officers can zoom in on people from cameras a half-mile away.[1]

3. **Unexamined assumptions that cameras provide security.** In the wake of the September 11 attacks, many embraced surveillance as the way to prevent future attacks and prevent crime. But it is far from clear how cameras will increase security. U.S. government experts on security technology, noting that "monitoring video screens is both boring and mesmerizing," have found in experiments that after only 20 minutes of watching video monitors, "the attention of most individuals has degenerated to well below acceptable levels."[2] In addition, studies of cameras' effect on crime in Britain, where they have been extensively deployed, have found no conclusive evidence that they have reduced crime.[3]

These developments are creating powerful momentum toward pervasive video surveillance of our public spaces. If centralized video facilities are permitted in Washington and around the nation, it is inevitable that they will be expanded—not only in the number of cameras but also in their power and ability. It is easy to foresee inexpensive, one-dollar cameras being distributed throughout our cities and tied via wireless technology into a centralized police facility where the life of the city can be monitored. Those video signals could be stored indefinitely in digital form in giant but inexpensive databases, and called up with the click of a mouse at any time. With face recognition, the video records could even be indexed and searched based on who the systems identify—correctly, or all too often, incorrectly.

Several airports around the nation, a handful of cities, and even the National Park Service at the Statue of Liberty have installed face recognition. While not nearly reliable enough to be effective as a security application,[4] such a system could still violate the privacy of a significant percentage of the citizens who appeared before it (as well as the privacy of those who do not appear before it but are falsely identified as having done so). Unlike, say, an iris scan, face recognition doesn't require the knowledge, consent, or participation of the subject; modern cameras can easily view faces from over 100 yards away.

Further possibilities for the expansion of video surveillance lie with unmanned aircraft, or drones, which have been used by the military and the CIA overseas for reconnaissance, surveillance, and targeting. Controlled from the ground, they can stay airborne for days at a time. Now there is talk of deploying them domestically. Senate Armed Services Committee Chairman John Warner (R, VA) said in December 2002 that he wants to explore their use in Homeland Security, and a number of domestic government agencies have expressed interest in deploying them. Drones are likely to be just one of many ways in which improving robotics technology will be applied to surveillance.[5]

The bottom line is that surveillance systems, once installed, rarely remain confined to their original purpose. Once the nation decides to go down the path of seeking security through video surveillance, the imperative to make it work will become overwhelming, and the monitoring of citizens in public places will quickly become pervasive.

DATA SURVEILLANCE

An insidious new type of surveillance is becoming possible that is just as intrusive as video surveillance—what we might call "data surveillance." Data surveillance is *the collection of information about an identifiable individual, often from multiple sources, that can be assembled into a portrait of that person's activities.*[6] Most computers are programmed to automatically store and track usage data, and the spread of computer chips in our daily lives means that more and more of our activities leave behind "data trails." It will soon be possible to combine information from different sources to recreate an individual's activities with such detail that it becomes no different from being followed around all day by a detective with a video camera.

Some think comprehensive public tracking will make no difference, since life in public places is not "private" in the same way as life inside the home. This is wrong; such tracking would represent a radical change in American life. A woman who leaves her house, drives to a store, meets a friend for coffee, visits a museum, and then returns home may be in public all day, but her life is still private in that she is the only one who has an overall view of how she spent her day. In America, she does not expect that her activities are being watched or tracked in any systematic way—she expects to be left alone. But if current trends continue, it will be impossible to have any contact with the outside world that is not watched and recorded.

The Commodification of Information   A major factor driving the trend toward data surveillance forward is the commodification of personal information by corporations. As computer technology exploded in recent decades, making it much easier to collect information about what Americans buy and do, companies came to realize that such data is often very valuable. The expense of marketing efforts gives businesses a strong incentive to know as much about consumers as possible so they can focus on the most likely new customers. Surveys,

sweepstakes questionnaires, loyalty programs and detailed product registration forms have proliferated in American life—all aimed at gathering information about consumers. Today, any consumer activity that is *not* being tracked and recorded is increasingly being viewed by businesses as money left on the table.

On the Internet, where every mouse click can be recorded, the tracking and profiling of consumers is even more prevalent. Web sites can not only track what consumers buy, but what they *look at*—and for how long, and in what order. With the end of the Dot Com era, personal information has become an even more precious source of hard cash for those Internet ventures that survive. And of course Americans use the Internet not just as a shopping mall, but to research topics of interest, debate political issues, seek support for personal problems, and many other purposes that can generate deeply private information about their thoughts, interests, lifestyles, habits, and activities.

Genetic Privacy   The relentless commercialization of information has also led to the breakdown of some longstanding traditions, such as doctor-patient confidentiality. Citizens share some of their most intimate and embarrassing secrets with their doctors on the old-fashioned assumption that their conversations are confidential. Yet those details are routinely shared with insurance companies, researchers, marketers, and employers. An insurance trade organization called the Medical Information Bureau even keeps a centralized medical database with records on millions of patients. Weak new medical privacy rules will do little to stop this behavior.

An even greater threat to medical privacy is looming: genetic information. The increase in DNA analysis for medical testing, research, and other purposes will accelerate sharply in coming years, and will increasingly be incorporated into routine health care.

Unlike other medical information, genetic data is a unique combination: both difficult to keep confidential and extremely revealing about us. DNA is very easy to acquire because we constantly slough off hair, saliva, skin cells and other samples of our

DNA (household dust, for example, is made up primarily of dead human skin cells). That means that no matter how hard we strive to keep our genetic code private, we are always vulnerable to other parties' secretly testing samples of our DNA. The issue will be intensified by the development of cheap and efficient DNA chips capable of reading parts of our genetic sequences.

Already, it is possible to send away a DNA sample for analysis. A testing company called Genelex reports that it has amassed 50,000 DNA samples, many gathered surreptitiously for paternity testing. "You'd be amazed," the company's CEO told *U.S. News & World Report*. "Siblings have sent in mom's discarded Kleenex and wax from her hearing aid to resolve the family rumors."[7]

Not only is DNA easier to acquire than other medical information, revealing it can also have more profound consequences. Genetic markers are rapidly being identified for all sorts of genetic diseases, risk factors, and other characteristics. None of us knows what time bombs are lurking in our genomes.

The consequences of increased genetic transparency will likely include:

- **Discrimination by insurers.** Health and life insurance companies could collect DNA for use in deciding who to insure and what to charge them, with the result that a certain proportion of the population could become uninsurable. The insurance industry has already vigorously opposed efforts in Congress to pass meaningful genetic privacy and discrimination bills.

- **Employment discrimination.** Genetic workplace testing is already on the rise, and the courts have heard many cases. Employers desiring healthy, capable workers will always have an incentive to discriminate based on DNA—an incentive that will be even stronger as long as health insurance is provided through the workplace.

- **Genetic spying.** Cheap technology could allow everyone from schoolchildren to dating couples to nosy neighbors to routinely check out each other's genetic codes. A likely high-profile example: online posting of the genetic profiles of celebrities or politicians.

Financial Privacy   Like doctor-patient confidentiality, the tradition of privacy and discretion by financial institutions has also collapsed; financial companies today routinely put the details of their customers' financial lives up for sale.

A big part of the problem is the Gramm-Leach-Bliley Act passed by Congress in 1999. Although Gramm-Leach is sometimes described as a "financial privacy law," it created a very weak privacy standard—so weak, in fact, that far from protecting Americans' financial privacy, the law has had the effect of ratifying the increasing abandonment of customer privacy by financial companies.

Gramm-Leach effectively gives financial institutions permission to sell their customers' financial data to anyone they choose. That includes the date, amount, and recipient of credit card charges or checks a customer has written; account balances; and information about the flow of deposits and withdrawals through an account. Consumers provide a tremendous amount of information about themselves when they fill out applications to get a loan, buy insurance, or purchase securities, and companies can also share that information. In fact, the only information a financial company may NOT give out about you is your account number.

Under Gramm-Leach, you get no privacy unless you file complex paperwork, following a financial institution's precise instructions before a deadline they set, and repeating the process for each and every financial service provider who may have data about you. And it is a process that many companies intentionally make difficult and cumbersome; few let consumers "opt out" of data sharing through a Web site or phone number, or even provide a self-addressed envelope.

Gramm-Leach is an excellent example of the ways that privacy protections are being weakened even as the potential for privacy invasion grows.

New Data-Gathering Technologies   The discovery by businesses of the monetary value of personal information and the vast new project of tracking the habits of consumers has been made possible by advances in computers, databases and the Internet. In the near future, other new technologies will continue to fill out the mosaic of information it is possible to collect on every individual. Examples include:

- **Cell phone location data.** The government has mandated that manufacturers make cell phones capable of automatically reporting their location when an owner dials 911. Of course, those phones are capable of tracking their location at other times as well. And in applying the rules that protect the privacy of telephone records to this location data, the government is weakening those rules in a way that allows phone companies to collect and share data about the location and movements of their customers.

- **Biometrics.** Technologies that identify us by unique bodily attributes such as our fingerprints, faces, iris patterns, or DNA are already being proposed for inclusion on national ID cards and to identify airline passengers. Face recognition is spreading. Fingerprint scanners have been introduced as security or payment mechanisms in office buildings, college campuses, grocery stores and even fast-food restaurants. And several companies are working on DNA chips that will be able to instantly identify individuals by the DNA we leave behind everywhere we go.

- **Black boxes.** All cars built today contain computers, and some of those computers are being programmed in ways that are not necessarily in the interest of owners. An increasing number of cars contain devices akin to the "black boxes" on aircraft that record details about a vehicle's operation and movement. Those devices can "tattle" on car owners to the police or insurance investigators. Already, one car rental agency tried to charge a customer for speeding after a GPS device in the car reported the transgression back to the company. And cars are just one example of how products and possessions can be programmed to spy and inform on their owners.

- **RFID chips.** RFID chips, which are already used in such applications as toll-booth speed passes, emit a short-range radio signal containing a unique code that identifies each chip. Once the cost of these chips falls to a few pennies each, plans are underway to affix them to products in stores, down to every can of soup and tube of toothpaste. They will allow everyday objects to "talk" to each other—or to anyone else who is listening. For example, they could let market researchers scan the contents of your purse or car from five feet away, or let police officers scan your identification when they pass you on the street.

- **Implantable GPS chips.** Computer chips that can record and broadcast their location have also been developed. In addition to practical uses such as building them into shipping containers, they can also serve as location "bugs" when, for example, hidden by a suspicious husband in a wife's purse. And they can be implanted under the skin (as can RFID chips).

If we do not act to reverse the current trend, data surveillance—like video surveillance—will allow corporations or the government to constantly monitor what individual Americans do every day. Data surveillance would cover *everyone,* with records of every transaction and activity squirreled away until they are sucked up by powerful search engines, whether as part of routine security checks, a general sweep for suspects in an unsolved crime, or a program of harassment against some future Martin Luther King.

GOVERNMENT SURVEILLANCE

Data surveillance is made possible by the growing ocean of privately collected personal data. But who would conduct that surveillance? There are certainly business incentives for doing so; companies called data aggregators (such as Acxiom and ChoicePoint) are in the business of compiling detailed databases on individuals and then selling that information to others. Although these companies are invisible to the average person, data aggregation is an enormous, multi-billion-dollar industry. Some databases are even "co-ops" where participants agree to contribute data about their customers in return for the ability to pull out cross-merchant profiles of customers' activities.

The biggest threat to privacy, however, comes from the government. Many Americans are naturally concerned about corporate surveillance, but only the government has the power to take away liberty—as has been demonstrated starkly by the post-September 11 detention of suspects without trial as "enemy combatants."

In addition, the government has unmatched power to centralize all the private sector data that is being generated. In fact, the distinction between government and private-sector privacy invasions is fading quickly. The Justice Department, for example, reportedly has an $8 million contract with data aggregator ChoicePoint that allows government agents to tap into the company's vast database of personal information on individuals.[8] Although the Privacy Act of 1974 banned the government from maintaining information on citizens who are not the targets of investigations, the FBI can now evade that requirement by simply purchasing information that has been collected by the private sector. Other proposals—such as the Pentagon's "Total Information Awareness" project and airline passenger profiling programs—would institutionalize government access to consumer data in even more far-reaching ways.

Government Databases   The government's access to personal information begins with the thousands of databases it maintains on the lives of Americans and others. For instance:

- The FBI maintains a giant database that contains millions of records covering everything from criminal records to stolen boats and databases with millions of computerized fingerprints and DNA records.
- The Treasury Department runs a database that collects financial information reported to the government by thousands of banks and other financial institutions.
- A "new hires" database maintained by the Department of Health and Human Services, which contains the name, address, social security number, and quarterly wages of every working person in the U.S.

- The federal Department of Education maintains an enormous information bank holding years worth of educational records on individuals stretching from their primary school years through higher education. After September 11, Congress gave the FBI permission to access the database without probable cause.
- State departments of motor vehicles of course possess millions of up-to-date files containing a variety of personal data, including photographs of most adults living in the United States.

Communications Surveillance   The government also performs an increasing amount of eavesdropping on electronic communications. While technologies like telephone wiretapping have been around for decades, today's technologies cast a far broader net. The FBI's controversial "Carnivore" program, for example, is supposed to be used to tap into the e-mail traffic of a particular individual. Unlike a telephone wiretap, however, it doesn't cover just one device but (because of how the Internet is built) filters through *all* the traffic on the Internet Service Provider to which it has been attached. The only thing keeping the government from trolling through all this traffic is software instructions that are written by the government itself. (Despite that clear conflict of interest, the FBI has refused to allow independent inspection and oversight of the device's operation.)

Another example is the international eavesdropping program codenamed Echelon. Operated by a partnership consisting of the United States, Britain, Canada, Australia, and New Zealand, Echelon reportedly grabs e-mail, phone calls, and other electronic communications from its far-flung listening posts across most of the earth. (U.S. eavesdroppers are not supposed to listen in on the conversations of Americans, but the question about Echelon has always been whether the intelligence agencies of participating nations can set up reciprocal, back-scratching arrangements to spy on each others' citizens.) Like Carnivore, Echelon may be used against particular targets, but to do so its operators must sort through massive amounts of information about potentially millions of people. That is worlds away from the popular conception of the old wiretap where an FBI agent listens to one line. Not only the volume of intercepts but the potential for abuse is now exponentially higher.

The "Patriot" Act   The potential for the abuse of surveillance powers has also risen sharply due to a dramatic post-9/11 erosion of legal protections against government surveillance of citizens. Just six weeks after the September 11 attacks, a panicked Congress passed the "USA PATRIOT Act," an overnight revision of the nation's surveillance laws that vastly expanded the government's authority to spy on its own citizens and reduced checks and balances on those powers, such as judicial oversight. The government never demonstrated that restraints on surveillance had contributed to the attack, and indeed much of the new legislation had nothing to do with fighting terrorism. Rather, the bill represented a successful use of the terrorist attacks by the FBI to roll back unwanted checks on its power. The most powerful provisions of the law allow for:

• **Easy access to records.** Under the PATRIOT Act, the FBI can force anyone to turn over records on their customers or clients, giving the government unchecked power to rifle through individuals' financial records, medical histories, Internet usage, travel patterns, or any other records. Some of the most invasive and disturbing uses permitted by the Act involve government access to citizens' reading habits from libraries and bookstores. The FBI does not have to show suspicion of a crime, can gag the recipient of a search order from disclosing the search to anyone, and is subject to no meaningful judicial oversight.

• **Expansion of the "pen register" exception in wiretap law.** The PATRIOT Act expands exceptions to the normal requirement for probable cause in wiretap law.[9] As with its new power to search records, the FBI need not show probable cause or even reasonable suspicion of criminal activity, and judicial oversight is essentially nil.

• **Expansion of the intelligence exception in wiretap law.** The PATRIOT Act also loosens the

evidence needed by the government to justify an intelligence wiretap or physical search. Previously the law allowed exceptions to the Fourth Amendment for these kinds of searches only if "the purpose" of the search was to gather foreign intelligence. But the Act changes "the purpose" to "a significant purpose," which lets the government circumvent the Constitution's probable cause requirement even when its main goal is ordinary law enforcement.[10]

• **More secret searches.** Except in rare cases, the law has always required that the subject of a search be notified that a search is taking place. Such notice is a crucial check on the government's power because it forces the authorities to operate in the open and allows the subject of searches to challenge their validity in court. But the PATRIOT Act allows the government to conduct searches without notifying the subjects until long after the search has been executed.

Under these changes and other authorities asserted by the Bush Administration, U.S. intelligence agents could conduct a secret search of an American citizen's home, use evidence found there to declare him an "enemy combatant," and imprison him without trial. The courts would have no chance to review these decisions—indeed, they might never even find out about them.[11]

The "TIPS" Program   In the name of fighting terrorism, the Bush Administration has also proposed a program that would encourage citizens to spy on each other. The Administration initially planned to recruit people such as letter carriers and utility technicians, who, the White House said, are "well-positioned to recognize unusual events." In the face of fierce public criticism, the Administration scaled back the program, but continued to enlist workers involved in certain key industries. In November 2002 Congress included a provision in the Homeland Security Act prohibiting the Bush Administration from moving forward with TIPS.

Although Congress killed TIPS, the fact that the Administration would pursue such a program reveals a disturbing disconnect with American values and a disturbing lack of awareness of the history of governmental abuses of power. Dividing citizen from citizen by encouraging mutual suspicion and reporting to the government would dramatically increase the government's power by extending surveillance into every nook and cranny of American society. Such a strategy was central to the Soviet Union and other totalitarian regimes.

Loosened Domestic Spying Regulations   In May 2002, Attorney General John Ashcroft issued new guidelines on domestic spying that significantly increase the freedom of federal agents to conduct surveillance on American individuals and organizations. Under the new guidelines, FBI agents can infiltrate "any event that is open to the public," from public meetings and demonstrations to political conventions to church services to 12-step programs. This was the same basis upon which abuses were carried out by the FBI in the 1950s and 1960s, including surveillance of political groups that disagreed with the government, anonymous letters sent to the spouses of targets to try to ruin their marriages, and the infamous campaign against Martin Luther King, who was investigated and harassed for decades. The new guidelines are purely for spying on Americans; there is a separate set of Foreign Guidelines that cover investigations inside the U.S. of foreign powers and terrorist organizations such as Al Qaeda.

Like the TIPS program, Ashcroft's guidelines sow suspicion among citizens and extend the government's surveillance power into the capillaries of American life. It is not just the reality of government surveillance that chills free expression and the freedom that Americans enjoy. The same negative effects come when we are constantly forced to wonder whether we *might* be under observation— whether the person sitting next to us is secretly informing the government that we are "suspicious."

The Synergies of Surveillance

Multiple surveillance techniques added together are greater than the sum of their parts. One example is face recognition, which combines the power of computerized software analysis, cameras, and databases to seek matches between facial images. But the real synergies of surveillance come into play with data collection.

The growing piles of data being collected on Americans represent an enormous invasion of privacy, but our privacy has actually been protected by the fact that all this information still remains scattered across many different databases. As a result, there exists a pent-up capacity for surveillance in American life today—a capacity that will be fully realized if the government, landlords, employers, or other powerful forces gain the ability to *draw together* all this information. A particular piece of data about you—such as the fact that you entered your office at 10:29 AM on July 5, 2001—is normally innocuous. But when enough pieces of that kind of data are assembled together, they add up to an extremely detailed and intrusive picture of an individual's life and habits.

DATA PROFILING AND "TOTAL INFORMATION AWARENESS"

Just how real this scenario is has been demonstrated by another ominous surveillance plan to emerge from the effort against terrorism: the Pentagon's "Total Information Awareness" program. The aim of this program is to give officials easy, unified access to every possible government and commercial database in the world.[12] According to program director John Poindexter, the program's goal is to develop "ultra-large-scale" database technologies with the goal of "treating the world-wide, distributed, legacy databases as if they were one centralized database." The program envisions a "full-coverage database containing all information relevant to identifying" potential terrorists and their supporters. As we have seen, the amount of available information is mushrooming by the day, and will soon be rich enough to reveal much of our lives.

The TIA program, which is run by the Defense Advanced Research Projects Agency (DARPA), not only seeks to bring together the oceans of data that are already being collected on people, but would be designed to afford what DARPA calls "easy future scaling" to embrace new sources of data as they become available. It would also incorporate other work being done by the military, such as their "Human Identification at a Distance" program, which seeks to allow identification and tracking of people from a distance, and therefore without their permission or knowledge.[13]

Although it has not received nearly as much media attention, a close cousin of TIA is also being created in the context of airline security. This plan involves the creation of a system for conducting background checks on individuals who wish to fly and then separating out either those who appear to be the most trustworthy passengers (proposals known as "trusted traveler") or flagging the least trustworthy (a proposal known as CAPS II, for Computer Assisted Passenger Screening) for special attention.

The *Washington Post* has reported that work is being done on CAPS II with the goal of creating a "vast air security screening system designed to instantly pull together every passenger's travel history and living arrangements, plus a wealth of other personal and demographic information" in the hopes that the authorities will be able to "profile passenger activity and intuit obscure clues about potential threats." The government program would reportedly draw on enormous stores of personal information from data aggregators and other sources, including travel records, real estate histories, personal associations, credit card records, and telephone records. Plans call for using complex computer algorithms, including highly experimental technologies such as "neural networks," to sort through the reams of new personal information and identify "suspicious" people.[14]

The dubious premise of programs like TIA and CAPS II—that "terrorist patterns" can be ferreted out from the enormous mass of American lives, many of which will inevitably be quirky, eccentric, or riddled with suspicious coincidences—probably dooms them to failure. But failure is not likely to lead these programs to be shut down—instead, the government will begin feeding its computers more and more personal information in a vain effort to make the concept work. We will then have the worst of both worlds: poor security and a super-charged surveillance tool that would destroy Americans' privacy and threaten our freedom.

It is easy to imagine these systems being expanded in the future to share their risk assessments with other security systems. For example, CAPS could be linked to a photographic database and surveillance cameras equipped with face recognition software. Such a system might sound an alarm when a subject who has been designated as "suspicious" appears in public. The Suspicious Citizen could then be watched from a centralized video monitoring facility as he moves around the city.

In short, the government is working furiously to bring disparate sources of information about us together into one view, just as privacy advocates have been warning about for years. That would represent a radical branching off from the centuries-old Anglo-American tradition that the police conduct surveillance only where there is evidence of involvement in wrongdoing. It would seek to protect us by monitoring *everyone* for signs of wrongdoing—in short, by instituting a giant dragnet capable of sifting through the personal lives of Americans in search of "suspicious" patterns. The potential for abuse of such a system is staggering.

The massive defense research capabilities of the United States have always involved the search for ways of outwardly defending our nation. Programs like TIA[15] involve turning those capabilities inward and applying them to the American people—something that should be done, if at all, only with extreme caution and plenty of public input, political debate, checks and balances, and Congressional oversight. So far, none of those things have been present with TIA or CAPS II.

NATIONAL ID CARDS

If Americans allow it, another convergence of surveillance technologies will probably center around a national ID card. A national ID would immediately combine new technologies such as biometrics and RFID chips along with an enormously powerful database (possibly distributed among the 50 states). Before long, it would become an overarching means of facilitating surveillance by allowing far-flung pools of information to be pulled together into a single, incredibly rich dossier or profile of our lives. Before long, office buildings, doctors' offices, gas stations, highway tolls, subways and buses would incorporate the ID card into their security or payment systems for greater efficiency, and data that is currently scattered and disconnected will get organized around the ID and lead to the creation of what amounts to a national database of sensitive information about American citizens.

History has shown that databases created for one purpose are almost inevitably expanded to other uses; Social Security, which was prohibited by federal law from being used as an identifier when it was first created, is a prime example. Over time, a national ID database would inevitably contain a wider and wider range of information and become accessible to more and more people for more and more purposes that are further and further removed from its original justification.

The most likely route to a national ID is through our driver's licenses. Since September 11, the American Association of Motor Vehicle Administrators has been forcefully lobbying Congress for funds to establish nationwide uniformity in the design and content of driver's licenses—and more importantly, for tightly interconnecting the databases that lie behind the physical licenses themselves.

An attempt to retrofit driver's licenses into national ID cards will launch a predictable series of events bringing us toward a surveillance society:

- Proponents will promise that the IDs will be implemented in limited ways that won't devastate privacy and other liberties.

- Once a limited version of the proposals is put in place, its limits as an anti-terrorism measure will quickly become apparent. Like a dam built halfway across a river, the IDs cannot possibly be effective unless their coverage is total.

- The scheme's ineffectiveness—starkly demonstrated, perhaps, by a new terrorist attack—will create an overwhelming imperative to "fix" and "complete" it, which will turn it into the totalitarian tool that proponents promised it would never become.

A perfect example of that dynamic is the requirement that travelers present driver's licenses when boarding airplanes, instituted after the explosion (now believed to have been mechanical in cause) that brought down TWA Flight 800 in 1996. On its own, the requirement was meaningless as a security measure, but after September 11 its existence quickly led to calls to begin tracking and identifying citizens

on the theory that "we already have to show ID, we might as well make it mean something."

Once in place, it is easy to imagine how national IDs could be combined with an RFID chip to allow for convenient, at-a-distance verification of ID. The IDs could then be tied to access control points around our public places, so that the unauthorized could be kept out of office buildings, apartments, public transit, and secure public buildings. Citizens with criminal records, poor CAPS ratings or low incomes could be barred from accessing airports, sports arenas, stores, or other facilities. Retailers might add RFID readers to find out exactly who is browsing their aisles, gawking at their window displays from the sidewalk or passing by without looking. A network of automated RFID listening posts on the sidewalks and roads could even reveal the location of all citizens at all times. Pocket ID readers could be used by FBI agents to sweep up the identities of everyone at a political meeting, protest march, or Islamic prayer service.

Conclusion

If we do not take steps to control and regulate surveillance to bring it into conformity with our values, we will find ourselves being tracked, analyzed, profiled, and flagged in our daily lives to a degree we can scarcely imagine today. We will be forced into an impossible struggle to conform to the letter of every rule, law, and guideline, lest we create ammunition for enemies in the government or elsewhere. Our transgressions will become permanent Scarlet Letters that follow us throughout our lives, visible to all and used by the government, landlords, employers, insurance companies and other powerful parties to increase their leverage over average people. Americans will not be able to engage in political protest or go about their daily lives without the constant awareness that we are—or could be—under surveillance. We will be forced to constantly ask of even the smallest action taken in public, "Will this make me look suspicious? Will this hurt my chances for future employment? Will this reduce my ability to get insurance?" The exercise of free speech will be chilled as Americans become conscious that their every word may be reported to the government by FBI infiltrators, suspicious fellow citizens or an Internet Service Provider.

Many well-known commentators like Sun Microsystems CEO Scott McNealy have already pronounced privacy dead. The truth is that a surveillance society does loom over us, and privacy, while not yet dead, is on life support.

Heroic measures are required to save it.

Four main goals need to be attained to prevent this dark potential from being realized: a change in the terms of the debate, passage of comprehensive privacy laws, passage of new laws to regulate the powerful and invasive new technologies that have and will continue to appear, and a revival of the Fourth Amendment to the U.S. Constitution.

1. CHANGING THE TERMS OF THE DEBATE

In the public debates over every new surveillance technology, the forest too often gets lost for the trees, and we lose sight of the larger trend: the seemingly inexorable movement toward a surveillance society. It will always be important to understand and publicly debate every new technology and every new technique for spying on people. But unless each new development is also understood as just one piece of the larger surveillance mosaic that is rapidly being constructed around us, Americans are not likely to get excited about a given incremental loss of privacy like the tracking of cars through toll booths or the growing practice of tracking consumers' supermarket purchases.

We are being confronted with fundamental choices about what sort of society we want to live in. But unless the terms of the debate are changed to focus on the forest instead of individual trees, too many Americans will never even recognize the choice we face, and a decision against preserving privacy will be made by default.

2. COMPREHENSIVE PRIVACY LAWS

Although broad-based protections against government surveillance, such as the wiretap laws, are being weakened, at least they exist. But surveillance is increasingly being carried out by the private sector— frequently at the behest of government—and the laws protecting Americans against non-governmental privacy invasions are pitifully weak.

In contrast to the rest of the developed world, the U.S. has no strong, comprehensive law protecting privacy—only a patchwork of largely inadequate protections. For example, as a result of many legislators' discomfort over the disclosure of Judge Robert Bork's video rental choices during his Supreme Court confirmation battle, video records are now protected by a strong privacy law. Medical records are governed by a separate, far weaker law that allows for wide-spread access to extremely personal information. Financial data is governed by yet another "privacy" law—Gramm-Leach—which as we have seen really amounts to a license to share financial information. Another law protects only the privacy of children under age 13 on the Internet. And layered on top of this sectoral approach to privacy by the federal government is a geographical patchwork of constitutional and statutory privacy protections in the states.

The patchwork approach to privacy is grossly inadequate. As invasive practices grow, Americans will face constant uncertainty about when and how these complex laws protect them, contributing to a pervasive sense of insecurity. With the glaring exception of the United States, every advanced industrialized nation in the world has enacted overarching privacy laws that protect citizens against private-sector abuses. When it comes to this fundamental human value, the U.S. is an outlaw nation. For example, the European Union bars companies from evading privacy rules by transferring personal information to other nations whose data-protection policies are "inadequate." That is the kind of law that is usually applied to Third World countries, but the EU counts the United States in this category.

We need to develop a baseline of simple and clear privacy protections that crosses all sectors of our lives and give it the force of law. Only then can Americans act with a confident knowledge of when they can and cannot be monitored.

3. NEW TECHNOLOGIES AND NEW LAWS

The technologies of surveillance are developing at the speed of light, but the body of law that protects us is stuck back in the Stone Age. In the past, new technologies that threatened our privacy, such as telephone wiretapping, were assimilated over time into our society. The legal system had time to adapt and reinterpret existing laws, the political system had time to consider and enact new laws or regulations, and the culture had time to absorb the implications of the new technology for daily life. Today, however, change is happening so fast that none of this adaptation has time to take place—a problem that is being intensified by the scramble to enact unexamined anti-terrorism measures. The result is a significant danger that surveillance practices will become entrenched in American life that would never be accepted if we had more time to digest them.

Since a comprehensive privacy law may never be passed in the U.S.—and certainly not in the near future—law and legal principles must be developed or adapted to rein in particular new technologies such as surveillance cameras, location-tracking devices, and biometrics. Surveillance cameras, for example, must be subject to force-of-law rules covering important details like when they will be used, how long images will be stored, and when and with whom they will be shared.

4. REVIVING THE FOURTH AMENDMENT

The right of the people to be secure in their persons, houses, papers, and effects, against unreasonable searches and seizures, shall not be violated, and no warrants shall issue, but upon probable cause, supported by oath or affirmation, and particularly describing the place to be searched, and the persons or things to be seized.

—Fourth Amendment to the U.S. Constitution

The Fourth Amendment, the primary Constitutional bulwark against Government invasion of our privacy, was a direct response to the British authorities' use of "general warrants" to conduct broad searches of the rebellious colonists.

Historically, the courts have been slow to adapt the Fourth Amendment to the realities of developing technologies. It took almost 40 years for the U.S. Supreme Court to recognize that the Constitution applies to the wiretapping of telephone conversations.[16]

In recent years—in no small part as the result of the failed "war on drugs"—Fourth Amendment principles have been steadily eroding. The circumstances under which police and other government officials may conduct warrantless searches has been rapidly expanding. The courts have allowed for increased surveillance and searches on the nation's highways and at our "borders" (the legal definition of which actually extends hundreds of miles inland from the actual border). And despite the Constitution's plain language covering "persons" and "effects," the courts have increasingly allowed for warrantless searches when we are outside of our homes and "in public." Here the courts have increasingly found we have no "reasonable expectation" of privacy and that therefore the Fourth Amendment does not apply.

But like other Constitutional provisions, the Fourth Amendment needs to be understood in contemporary terms. New technologies are endowing the government with the 21st Century equivalent of Superman's X-ray vision. Using everything from powerful video technologies that can literally see in the dark, to biometric identification techniques like face recognition, to "brain fingerprinting" that can purportedly read our thoughts, the government is now capable of conducting broad searches of our "persons and effects" while we are going about our daily lives—even while we are in "public."

The Fourth Amendment is in desperate need of a revival. The reasonable expectation of privacy cannot be defined by the power that technology affords the government to spy on us. Since that power is increasingly limitless, the "reasonable expectation" standard will leave our privacy dead indeed.

But all is not yet lost. There is some reason for hope. In an important pre-9/11 case, *Kyllo vs. U.S.*,[17] the Supreme Court held that the reasonable expectation of privacy could not be determined by the power of new technologies. In a remarkable opinion written by conservative Justice Antonin Scalia, the Court held that without a warrant the police could not use a new thermal imaging device that searches for heat sources to conduct what was the functional equivalent of a warrantless search for marijuana cultivation in Danny Kyllo's home.

The Court specifically declined to leave Kyllo "at the mercy of advancing technology." While Kyllo involved a search of a home, it enunciates an important principle: the Fourth Amendment must adapt to new technologies. That principle can and should be expanded to general use. The Framers never expected the Constitution to be read exclusively in terms of the circumstances of 1791.

NOTES

1. Jess Bravin, "Washington Police to Play 'I Spy' with Cameras, Raising Concerns," *Wall Street Journal*, Feb. 13, 2002.

2. See http://www.ncjrs.org/school/ch2a 5.html.

3. See http://www.scotcrim.u-net.com/researchc2.htm.

4. The success rate of face recognition technology has been dismal. The many independent findings to that effect include a trial conducted by the U.S. military in 2002, which found that with a reasonably low false-positive rate, the technology had less than a 20% chance of successfully identifying a person in its database who appeared before the camera. See http://www.aclu.org/issues/privacy/FINAL 1 Final Steve King.pdf, 17th slide.

5. Richard H. P. Sia, "Pilotless Aircraft Makers Seek Role for Domestic Uses," *CongressDaily*, Dec. 17, 2002.

6. Data surveillance is often loosely referred to as "data mining." Strictly speaking, however, data mining refers to the search for hidden patterns in large, pre-existing collections of data (such as the finding that sales of both beer and diapers rise on Friday nights). Data mining need not involve personally identifiable information. Data surveillance, on the other hand, involves the collection of information about an identifiable individual. Note, however, that when data surveillance is carried out on a mass scale, a search for patterns in people's activities—data mining—can then be conducted as well. This is what appears to be contemplated in the Total Information Awareness and CAPS II programs (see below).

7. Dana Hawkins, "As DNA Banks Quietly Multiply, Who Is Guarding the Safe?" *U.S. News & World Report*, Dec. 2, 2002.

8. Glenn R. Simpson, "Big Brother-in-Law: If the FBI Hopes to Get the Goods on You, It May Ask ChoicePoint," *Wall St. Journal*, Apr. 13, 2001.

9. The expanded exception involves what are called "pen register/trap & trace" warrants that collect "addressing information" but not the content of a communication. Those searches are named after devices that were used on telephones to show a list of telephone numbers dialed and received (as opposed to tapping into actual conversations). The PATRIOT Act expands the pen register exception onto the Internet in ways that will probably be used by the government to collect the actual content of communications and that allow nonspecific "nationwide" warrants in violation of the Fourth Amendment's explicit requirement that warrants "must specify the place to be searched."

10. In August, the secret "FISA" court that oversees domestic intelligence spying released an opinion rejecting a Bush Administration attempt to allow criminal prosecutors to use intelligence warrants to evade the Fourth Amendment entirely. The court noted that agents applying for warrants had regularly filed false and misleading information. In November 2002, however, the FISA appeals court (three judges chosen by Supreme Court Chief Justice William Rehnquist), meeting for the first time ever, ruled in favor of the government.

11. See Charles Lane, "In Terror War, 2nd Track for Suspects," *Washington Post*, Dec. 1, 2002. Online at http://www.washingtonpost.com/wp-dyn/articles/A58308-2002Nov30.html.

12. See "Pentagon Plans a Computer System That Would Peek at Personal Data of Americans," *New York Times*, Nov. 9, 2002; "US Hopes to Check Computers Globally," *Washington Post*, Nov. 12, 2002; "The Poindexter Plan," *National Journal*, Sept. 7, 2002.

13. Quotes are from the TIA homepage at http://www.darpa.mil/iao/index.htm and from public 8/2/02 remarks by Poindexter, online at http://www.fas.org/irp/agency/dod/poindexter.html.

14. Robert O'Harrow Jr., "Intricate Screening of Fliers in Works," *Washington Post*, Feb. 1, 2002, p. A1.

15. The TIA is just one part of a larger post-9/11 expansion of federal research and development efforts. The budget for military R&D spending alone has been increased by 18% in the current fiscal year to a record $58.8 billion. Bob Davis, "Massive Federal R&D Initiative to Fight Terror Is Under Way," *Wall Street Journal*, Nov. 25, 2002.

16. In 1967 the Supreme Court finally recognized the right to privacy in telephone conversations in the case *Katz v. U.S.* (389 US 347), reversing the 1928 opinion *Olmstead v. U.S.* (277 US 438).

17. 190 F.3d 1041, 2001.

Biotechnology and Genetic Engineering

II.11   LEE M. SILVER

A Glimpse of Things to Come

Princeton University molecular biologist Lee Silver opened his 1997 book *Remaking Eden: Cloning and Beyond in a Brave New World* with this provocative discussion of what human reproduction might look like in 2010, 2050, and 2350. He predicts that reproductive genetic engineering technology will make it possible for lesbian couples to have children that are genetically related to both "parents," that genetic resistance to diseases such as AIDS will be woven into an embryo's DNA, that human cloning will become widely accepted, and that, in the further future, the human race will divide into two classes: the Naturals and the Gene-enriched, or GenRich. The Naturals and the GenRich will grow up in separate worlds, and eventually, the genetic gulf between them will become so wide that they will become separate species. But Silver's vision differs from the dystopia imagined by Aldous Huxley in his 1932 novel *Brave New World*. In Silver's vision, it is not a totalitarian government that controls people's personal reproductive decisions; rather, it is the free market. Affluent parents will choose to give their children genetic advantages that science and biotechnology make available, just as they now choose to pay for private schools and tutors to prepare them to get into the elite colleges. Such a "free-market eugenics" is consistent with the American values of individual liberty and free markets, and if parentally selected genetic enhancement does not cause harm to the child being enhanced, what reason can there be not to embrace this libertarian version of a brave new world?

Focus Questions

1. What arguments does Silver give for thinking that human genetic enhancement should be regarded as morally permissible? What are the arguments used by opponents of genetic enhancement?
2. Compare Silver's position with that in the reading by Leon Kass (selection II.12). How does Kass attempt to argue against Silver's position regarding human reproductive cloning? Which of these arguments do you find more persuasive?
3. In the reading by Michael Sandel (selection II.13), several arguments against the prospect of genetic enhancement are discussed. How do Sandel's arguments stack up against Silver's? Which of these authors does a better job dealing with the "unfairness" objection?
4. Compare the debate over human reproductive genetic engineering with the debate over robotics and artificial intelligence and the possibility of creating transhuman cyborgs. What similarities are there between these two debates? Is your personal position on these issues the same or is it different? Explain.

Keywords

cloning, disease resistance, genetic enhancement, individual freedom, reproductive technology, reprogenetics

Dateline Boston: June 1, 2010

Sometime in the not-so-distant future, you may visit the maternity ward at a major university hospital to see the newborn child or grandchild of a close friend. The new mother, let's call her Barbara, seems very much at peace with the world, sitting in a chair quietly nursing her baby, Max. Her labor was—in the parlance of her doctor—"uneventful," and she is looking forward to raising her first child. You decide to make pleasant conversation by asking Barbara whether she knew in advance that her baby was going to be a boy. In your mind, it seems like a perfectly reasonable question since doctors have long given prospective parents the option of learning the sex of their child-to-be many months before the predicted date of birth. But Barbara seems taken aback by the question. "Of course I knew that Max would be a boy," she tells you. "My husband Dan and I chose him from our embryo pool. And when I'm ready to go through this again, I'll choose a girl to be my second child. An older son and a younger daughter—a perfect family."

Now, it's your turn to be taken aback. "You made a conscious choice to have a boy rather than a girl?" you ask.

"Absolutely!" Barbara answers. "And while I was at it, I made sure that Max wouldn't turn out to be fat like my brother Tom or addicted to alcohol like Dan's sister Karen. It's not that I'm personally biased or anything," Barbara continues defensively. "I just wanted to make sure that Max would have the greatest chance for achieving success. Being overweight or alcoholic would clearly be a handicap."

You look down in wonderment at the little baby boy destined to be moderate in both size and drinking habits.

Max has fallen asleep in Barbara's arms, and she places him gently in his bassinet. He wears a contented smile, which evokes a similar smile from his mother. Barbara feels the urge to stretch her legs and asks whether you'd like to meet some of the new friends she's made during her brief stay at the hospital. You nod, and the two of you walk into the

From *Remaking Eden: Cloning and Beyond in a Brave New World* by Lee M. Silver, pp. 1–11. Reprinted by permission of HarperCollins Publishers, Inc.

room next door where a thirty-five-year old woman named Cheryl is resting after giving birth to a nine-pound baby girl named Rebecca.

Barbara introduces you to Cheryl as well as a second woman named Madelaine, who stands by the bed holding Cheryl's hand. Little Rebecca is lying under the gaze of both Cheryl and Madelaine. "She really does look like both of her mothers, doesn't she?" Barbara asks you.

Now you're really confused. You glance at Barbara and whisper, "Both mothers?"

Barbara takes you aside to explain. "Yes. You see Cheryl and Madelaine have been living together for eight years. They got married in Hawaii soon after it became legal there, and like most married couples, they wanted to bring a child into the world with a combination of both of their bloodlines. With the reproductive technologies available today, they were able to fulfill their dreams."

You look across the room at the happy little nuclear family—Cheryl, Madelaine, and baby Rebecca— and wonder how the hospital plans to fill out the birth certificate.

Dateline Seattle: March 15, 2050

You are now forty years older and much wiser to the ways of the modern world. Once again, you journey forth to the maternity ward. This time, it's your own granddaughter Melissa who is in labor. Melissa is determined to experience natural childbirth and has refused all offers of anesthetics or painkillers. But she needs something to lift her spirits so that she can continue on through the waves of pain. "Let me see her pictures again," she implores her husband Curtis as the latest contraction sweeps through her body. Curtis picks the photo album off the table and opens it to face his wife. She looks up at the computer-generated picture of a five-year-old girl with wavy brown hair, hazel eyes, and a round face. Curtis turns the page, and Melissa gazes at an older version of the same child: a smiling sixteen-year-old who is 5 feet, 5 inches tall with a pretty face. Melissa smiles back at the future picture of her yet-to-be-born child and braces for another contraction.

There is something unseen in the picture of their child-to-be that provides even greater comfort to

Melissa and Curtis. It is the submicroscopic piece of DNA—an extra gene—that will be present in every cell of her body. This special gene will provide her with lifelong resistance to infection by the virus that causes AIDS, a virus that has evolved to be ever more virulent since its explosion across the landscape of humanity seventy years earlier. After years of research by thousands of scientists, no cure for the awful disease has been found, and the only absolute protection comes from the insertion of a resistance gene into the single-cell embryo within twenty-four hours after conception. Ensconced in its chromosomal home, the AIDS resistance gene will be copied over and over again into every one of the trillions of cells that make up the human body, each of which will have its own personal barrier to infection by the AIDS-causing virus HIV. Melissa and Curtis feel lucky indeed to have the financial wherewithal needed to endow all of their children with this protective agent. Other, less well-off American families cannot afford this luxury.

Outside Melissa's room, Jennifer, another expectant mother, is anxiously pacing the hall. She has just arrived at the hospital and her contractions are still far apart. But, unlike Melissa, Jennifer has no need for a computer printout to show her what her child-to-be will look like as a young girl or teenager. She already has thousands of pictures that show her future daughter's likeness, and they're all real, not virtual. For the fetus inside Jennifer is her identical twin sister—her clone—who will be born thirty-six years after she and Jennifer were both conceived within the same single-cell embryo. As Jennifer's daughter grows up, she will constantly behold a glimpse of the future simply by looking at her mother's photo album and her mother.

Dateline U.S.A.: May 15, 2350

It is now three hundred years later and although you are long since gone, a number of your great-great-great-great-great-great-great-great-great-great-grandchildren are now alive, mostly unbeknownst to one another. The United States of America still exists, but it is a different place from the one familiar to you. The most striking difference is that the extreme polarization of society that began during the 1980s has now reached its logical conclusion, with all people belonging to one of two classes. The people of one class are referred to as *Naturals,* while those in the second class are called the *Gene-enriched* or simply the *GenRich.*

These new classes of society cut across what used to be traditional racial and ethnic lines. In fact, so much mixing has occurred during the last three hundred years that sharp divisions according to race—black versus white versus Asian—no longer exist. Instead, the American populace has finally become the racial melting pot that earlier leaders had long hoped for. The skin color of Americans comes in all shades from African brown to Scandinavian pink, and traditional Asian facial features are present to a greater or lesser extent in a large percentage of Americans as well.

But while racial differences have mostly disappeared, another difference has emerged that is sharp and easily defined. It is the difference between those who are genetically enhanced and those who are not. The GenRich—who account for 10 percent of the American population—all carry synthetic genes. Genes that were created in the laboratory and did not exist within the human species until twenty-first century reproductive geneticists began to put them there. The GenRich are a modern-day hereditary class of genetic aristocrats.

Some of the synthetic genes carried by present-day members of the GenRich class were already carried by their parents. These genes were transmitted to today's GenRich the old-fashioned way, from parent to child through sperm or egg. But other synthetic genes are new to the present generation. These were placed into GenRich embryos through the application of genetic engineering techniques shortly after conception.

The GenRich class is anything but homogeneous. There are many types of GenRich families, and many subtypes within each type. For example, there are GenRich athletes who can trace their descent back to professional sports players from the twenty-first century. One subtype of GenRich athlete is the GenRich football player, and a sub-subtype is the GenRich running back. Embryo selection techniques have been used to make sure that a GenRich running back has received all of the natural genes that made his unenhanced foundation ancestor excel at the position. But in addition, at each generation beyond the foundation ancestor, sophisticated genetic enhancements have accumulated so that the modern-day GenRich running back can perform in a way not conceivable for any unenhanced Natural. Of course, all professional baseball, football, and basketball players are special GenRich subtypes. After three hundred years of selection and enhancement, these GenRich individuals all have athletic skills that are clearly "nonhuman" in the traditional sense. It would be impossible for any Natural to compete.

Another GenRich type is the GenRich scientist. Many of the synthetic genes carried by the GenRich scientist are the same as those carried by all other members of the GenRich class, including some that enhance a variety of physical and mental attributes, as well as others that provide resistance to all known forms of human disease. But in addition, the present-day GenRich scientist has accumulated a set of particular synthetic genes that work together with his "natural" heritage to produce an enhanced scientific mind. Although the GenRich scientist may appear to be different from the GenRich athlete, both GenRich types have evolved by a similar process. The foundation ancestor for the modern GenRich scientist was a bright twenty-first-century scientist whose children were the first to be selected and enhanced to increase their chances of becoming even brighter scientists who could produce even more brilliant children. There are numerous other GenRich types including GenRich businessmen, GenRich musicians, GenRich artists, and even GenRich intellectual generalists who all evolved in the same way.

Not all present-day GenRich individuals can trace their foundation ancestors back to the twenty-first century, when genetic enhancement was first perfected. During the twenty-second and even the twenty-third centuries, some Natural families garnered the financial wherewithal required to place their children into the GenRich class. But with the passage of time, the genetic distance between Naturals and the GenRich has become greater and greater, and now there is little movement up from the Natural to GenRich class. It seems fair to say

that society is on the verge of reaching the final point of complete polarization.

All aspects of the economy, the media, the entertainment industry, and the knowledge industry are controlled by members of the GenRich class. GenRich parents can afford to send their children to private schools rich in the resources required for them to take advantage of their enhanced genetic potential. In contrast, Naturals work as low-paid service providers or as laborers, and their children go to public schools. But twenty-fourth-century public schools have little in common with their predecessors from the twentieth century. Funds for public education have declined steadily since the beginning of the twenty-first century, and now Natural children are only taught the basic skills they need to perform the kinds of tasks they'll encounter in the jobs available to members of their class.

There is still some intermarriage as well as sexual intermingling between a few GenRich individuals and Naturals. But, as one might imagine, GenRich parents put intense pressure on their children not to dilute their expensive genetic endowment in this way. And as time passes, the mixing of the classes will become less and less frequent for reasons of both environment and genetics.

The environmental reason is clear enough: GenRich and Natural children grow up and live in segregated social worlds where there is little chance for contact between them. The genetic reason, however, was unanticipated.

It is obvious to everyone that with each generation of enhancement, the genetic distance separating the GenRich and Naturals is growing larger and larger. But a startling consequence of the expanding genetic distance has just come to light. In a nationwide survey of the few interclass GenRich-Natural couples that could be identified, sociologists have discovered an astounding 90 percent level of infertility. Reproductive geneticists have examined these couples and come to the conclusion that the infertility is caused primarily by an incompatibility between the genetic makeup of each member.

Evolutionary biologists have long observed instances in which otherwise fertile individuals taken from two separate populations prove infertile when mated to each other. And they tell the sociologists and the reproductive geneticists what is going on: the process of species separation between the Gen-Rich and Naturals has already begun. Together, the sociologists, the reproductive geneticists, and the evolutionary biologists are willing to make the following prediction: If the accumulation of genetic knowledge and advances in genetic enhancement technology continue at the present rate, then by the end of the third millennium, the GenRich class and the Natural class will become the GenRich humans and the Natural humans—entirely separate species with no ability to cross-breed, and with as much romantic interest in each other as a current human would have for a chimpanzee.

Dateline Princeton, New Jersey: The Present

Are these outrageous scenarios the stuff of science fiction? Did they spring from the minds of Hollywood screenwriters hoping to create blockbuster movies without regard to real world constraints? No. The scenarios described under the first two datelines emerge directly from scientific understanding and technologies that are already available today. The scientific framework for the last scenario is based on straightforward extrapolations from our current knowledge base. Furthermore, if biomedical advances continue to occur at the same rate as they do now, the practices described are likely to be feasible long before we reach my conservatively chosen datelines.

It's time to take stock of the current state of science and technology in the fields of reproduction and genetics and to ask, in the broadest terms possible, what the future may hold. Most people are aware of the impact that reproductive technology has already had in the area of fertility treatment. The first "test tube baby"—Louise Brown—is already eighteen years old, and the acronym for in vitro fertilization—IVF—is commonly used by laypeople. The cloning of human beings has become a real possibility as well, although many are still confused about what the technology can and cannot do. Advances in genetic research have also been in the limelight, with the almost weekly identification of

new genes implicated in diseases like cystic fibrosis and breast cancer, or personality traits like novelty-seeking and anxiety.

What has yet to catch the attention of the public at large, however, is the incredible power that emerges when current technologies in reproductive biology and genetics are brought together in the form of *reprogenetics*. With reprogenetics, parents can gain complete control over their genetic destiny, with the ability to guide and enhance the characteristics of their children, and their children's children as well. But even as reprogenetics makes dreams come true, like all of the most powerful technologies invented by humankind, it may also generate nightmares of a kind not previously imagined.

Of course, just because a technology becomes feasible does not mean that it will be used. Or does it? Society, acting through government intervention, could outlaw any one or all of the reprogenetic practices that I have described. Isn't the *non*use of nuclear weapons for the purpose of mass destruction over the last half century an example of how governments can control technology?

There are two big differences between the use of nuclear technology and reprogenetic technology. These differences lie in the resources and money needed to practice each. The most crucial resources required to build a nuclear weapon—large reactors and enriched sources of uranium or plutonium—are tightly controlled by the government itself. The resources required to practice reprogenetics—precision medical tools, small laboratory equipment, and simple chemicals—are all available for sale, without restriction, to anyone with the money to pay for them. The cost of developing a nuclear weapon is billions of dollars. In contrast, a reprogenetics clinic could easily be run on the scale of a small business anywhere in the world. Thus, even if restrictions on the use of reprogenetics are imposed in one country or another, those intent on delivering and receiving these services will not be restrained. But on what grounds can we argue that they should be restrained?

In response to this question, many people point to the chilling novel *Brave New World* written by Aldous Huxley in 1931. It is the story of a future worldwide political state that exerts complete control over human reproduction and human nature as well. In this brave new world, the state uses fetal hatcheries to breed each child into a predetermined intellectual class that ranges from alpha at the top to epsilon at the bottom. Individual members of each class are predestined to fit into specific roles in a soulless utopia where marriage and parenthood are prevented and promiscuous sexual activity is strongly encouraged, where universal immunity to diseases has been achieved, and where an all-enveloping state propaganda machine and mood-altering drugs make all content with their positions in life.

While Huxley guessed right about the power we would gain over the process of reproduction, I think he was dead wrong when it came to predicting *who* would use the power and for what purposes. What Huxley failed to understand, or refused to accept, was the driving force behind babymaking. It is individuals and couples who want to reproduce themselves in their own images. It is individuals and couples who want their children to be happy and successful. And it is individuals and couples—like Barbara and Dan and Cheryl and Madelaine and Melissa and Curtis and Jennifer, *not governments*—who will seize control of these new technologies. They will use some to reach otherwise unattainable reproductive goals and others to help their children achieve health, happiness, and success. And it is in pursuit of this last goal that the combined actions of many individuals, operating over many generations, could perhaps give rise to a polarized humanity more horrific than Huxley's imagined Brave New World.

There are those who will argue that parents don't have the right to control the characteristics of their children-to-be in the way I describe. But American society, in particular, accepts the rights of parents to control every other aspect of their children's lives from the time they are born until they reach adulthood. If one accepts the parental prerogative after birth, it is hard to argue against it before birth, if no harm is caused to the children who emerge.

Many think that it is inherently unfair for some people to have access to technologies that can provide advantages while others, less well-off, are forced to depend on chance alone. I would agree. It is inherently unfair. But once again, American society adheres to the principle that personal liberty and personal fortune are the primary determinants of what individuals are allowed and able to do. Anyone who accepts the right of affluent parents to provide their children with an expensive private school education cannot use "unfairness" as a reason for rejecting the use of reprogenetic technologies.

Indeed, in a society that values individual freedom above all else, it is hard to find any legitimate basis for restricting the use of reprogenetics. And therein lies the dilemma. For while each individual use of the technology can be viewed in the light of personal reproductive choice—with no ability to change society at large—together they could have dramatic, unintended, long-term consequences.

As the technologies of reproduction and genetics have become ever more powerful over the last decade, most practicing scientists and physicians have been loathe to speculate about where it may all lead. One reason for reluctance is the fear of getting it wrong. It really is impossible to predict with certainty which future technological advances will proceed on time and which will encounter unexpected roadblocks. This means that like Huxley's vision of a fetal hatchery, some of the ideas proposed here may ultimately be technically impossible or exceedingly difficult to implement. On the other hand, there are sure to be technological breakthroughs that no one can imagine now, just as Huxley was unable to imagine genetic engineering, or cloning from adult cells, in 1931.

There is a second reason why fertility specialists, in particular, are reluctant to speculate about the kinds of future scenarios that I describe here. It's called politics. In a climate where abortion clinics are on the alert for terrorist attacks, and where the religious right rails against any interference with the "natural process" of conception, IVF providers see no reason to call attention to themselves through descriptions of reproductive and genetic manipulations that are sure to provoke outrage.

The British journal *Nature* is one of the two most important science journals in the world (the other being the American journal *Science*). It is published weekly and is read by all types of scientists from biologists to physicists to medical researchers. No one would ever consider it to be radical or sensationalist in any way. On March 7, 1996, *Nature* published an article that described a method for cloning unlimited numbers of sheep from a single fertilized egg, with further implications for improving methods of genetic engineering. It took another week before the ramifications of this isolated breakthrough sank in for the editors. On March 14, 1996, they wrote an impassioned editorial saying in part: "That the growing power of molecular genetics confronts us with future prospects of being able to *change the nature of our species* [my emphasis] is a fact that seldom appears to be addressed in depth. Scientific knowledge may not yet permit detailed understanding, but the possibilities are clear enough. This gives rise to issues that in the end will have to be related to people within the social and ethical environments in which they live. . . . And the agenda is set by mankind as a whole, not by the subset involved in the science."

They are right that the agenda will not be set by scientists. But they are wrong to think that "mankind as a whole"—unable to reach consensus on so many other societal issues—will have any effect whatsoever. The agenda is sure to be set by individuals and couples who will act on behalf of themselves and their children. . . . The use of reprogenetic technologies is inevitable. It will not be controlled by governments or societies or even the scientists who create it.

There is no doubt about it. For better *and* worse, a new age is upon us. And whether we like it or not, the global marketplace will reign supreme.

II.12   LEON KASS

Preventing a Brave New World

In this article, Leon Kass, Addie Clark Harding Professor at the Committee on Social Thought at the University of Chicago and chairman of the President's Commission on Bioethics, argues that modern medical science is poised to cross an ethical boundary that will have momentous consequences for the future of humanity. Harking back to the dystopian vision of Aldous Huxley's classic *Brave New World* (1932), Kass argues that "the technological imperative, liberal democratic society, compassionate humanitarianism, moral pluralism, and free markets" are leading us down a path that places us at risk of losing our humanity. Kass argues that we should enact a worldwide ban on human cloning as a means of deterring "renegade scientists" from engaging in the practice. His proposed ban would apply to both reproductive and therapeutic cloning of human embryos because he believes that banning only reproductive cloning would prove impossible to enforce. Kass believes that we have the power to exercise control over the technological project but can only do so if we muster the political will to just say "no" to human cloning.

Focus Questions

1. What are the three main factors that Kass identifies as limiting our ability to control the onward march of the biomedical project? What other factors contribute to our inability to avoid the dangers Kass is concerned about?

2. What reasons does Kass give for "drawing the line" at human reproductive cloning by prohibiting the practice? Are these reasons convincing? Do the same arguments apply with equal force to therapeutic cloning?
3. Why does Kass believe that employing cloning or genetic engineering techniques to produce human children is "profoundly dehumanizing, no matter how good the product"?
4. Compare Kass's arguments to those offered by Cummings (selection II.14) and Sagoff (selection II.15). Is there a moral difference between applying genetic engineering techniques to humans and to plants and nonhuman animals? Explain.

Keywords

dehumanization, genetic determinism, infertility, reproductive cloning, reproductive freedom, somatic cell nuclear transfer

I.

The urgency of the great political struggles of the twentieth century, successfully waged against totalitarianisms first right and then left, seems to have blinded many people to a deeper and ultimately darker truth about the present age: all contemporary societies are travelling briskly in the same utopian direction. All are wedded to the modern technological project; all march eagerly to the drums of progress and fly proudly the banner of modern science; all sing loudly the Baconian anthem, "Conquer nature, relieve man's estate." Leading the triumphal procession is modern medicine, which is daily becoming ever more powerful in its battle against disease, decay, and death, thanks especially to astonishing achievements in biomedical science and technology—achievements for which we must surely be grateful.

Yet contemplating present and projected advances in genetic and reproductive technologies, in neuroscience and psychopharmacology, and in the development of artificial organs and computer-chip implants for human brains, we now clearly recognize new uses for biotechnical power that soar beyond the traditional medical goals of healing disease and relieving suffering. Human nature itself lies on the operating table, ready for alteration, for eugenic and psychic "enhancement," for wholesale re-design. In leading laboratories, academic and industrial, new creators are confidently amassing their powers and quietly honing their skills, while on the street their evangelists are zealously prophesying a post-human future. For anyone who cares about preserving our humanity, the time has come to pay attention.

Some transforming powers are already here. The Pill. In vitro fertilization. Bottled embryos. Surrogate wombs. Cloning. Genetic screening. Genetic manipulation. Organ harvesting. Mechanical spare parts. Chimeras. Brain implants. Ritalin for the young, Viagra for the old, Prozac for everyone. And, to leave this vale of tears, a little extra morphine accompanied by Muzak.

Years ago Aldous Huxley saw it coming. In his charming but disturbing novel, *Brave New World* (it appeared in 1932 and is more powerful on each re-reading), he made its meaning strikingly visible for all to see. Unlike other frightening futuristic novels of the past century, such as Orwell's already dated *Nineteen Eighty-Four*, Huxley shows us a dystopia that goes with, rather than against, the human grain. Indeed, it is animated by our own most humane and progressive aspirations. Following those aspirations to their ultimate realization, Huxley enables us to recognize those less obvious but often more pernicious evils that are inextricably linked to the successful attainment of partial goods.

Huxley depicts human life seven centuries hence, living under the gentle hand of humanitarianism rendered fully competent by genetic manipulation, psychoactive drugs, hypnopaedia, and high-tech amusements. At long last, mankind has succeeded in eliminating disease, aggression, war, anxiety, suffering, guilt, envy, and grief. But this victory comes at the heavy price of homogenization, mediocrity, trivial pursuits, shallow attachments, debased tastes, spurious contentment, and souls without loves or longings. The Brave New World has achieved prosperity, community, stability, and nigh-universal contentment, only to be peopled by creatures of human shape but stunted humanity. They consume, fornicate, take "soma," enjoy "centrifugal bumble-puppy," and operate the machinery that makes it all possible. They do not read, write, think, love, or govern themselves. Art and science, virtue and religion, family and friendship are all passe. What matters most is bodily health and immediate gratification: "Never put off till tomorrow the fun you can have today." Brave New Man is so dehumanized that he does not even recognize what has been lost.

Huxley's novel, of course, is science fiction. Prozac is not yet Huxley's "soma"; cloning by nuclear transfer or splitting embryos is not exactly "Bokanovskification"; MTV and virtual-reality parlors are not quite the "feelies"; and our current safe and consequenceless sexual practices are not universally as loveless or as empty as those in the novel. But the kinships are disquieting, all the more so since our technologies of bio-psycho-engineering are still in their infancy, and in ways that make all too clear what they might look like in their full maturity. Moreover, the cultural changes that technology has already wrought among us should make us even more worried than Huxley would have us be.

In Huxley's novel, everything proceeds under the direction of an omnipotent—albeit benevolent—world state. Yet the dehumanization that he portrays does not really require despotism or external control. To the contrary, precisely because the society of the future will deliver exactly what we most want—health, safety, comfort, plenty, pleasure, peace of mind and length of days—we can reach the same humanly debased condition solely on the basis of free human choice. No need for World Controllers. Just give us the technological imperative, liberal democratic society, compassionate humanitarianism, moral pluralism, and free markets, and we can take ourselves to a Brave New World all by ourselves—and without even deliberately deciding to go. In case you had not noticed, the train has already left the station and is gathering speed, but no one seems to be in charge.

Some among us are delighted, of course, by this state of affairs: some scientists and biotechnologists, their entrepreneurial backers, and a cheering claque of sci-fi enthusiasts, futurologists, and libertarians. There are dreams to be realized, powers to be exercised, honors to be won, and money—big money—to be made. But many of us are worried, and not, as the proponents of the revolution self-servingly claim, because we are either ignorant of science or afraid of the unknown. To the contrary, we can see all too clearly where the train is headed, and we do not like the destination. We can distinguish cleverness about means from wisdom about ends, and we are loath to entrust the future of the race to those who cannot tell the difference. No friend of humanity cheers for a post-human future.

Yet for all our disquiet, we have until now done nothing to prevent it. We hide our heads in the sand because we enjoy the blessings that medicine keeps supplying, or we rationalize our inaction by declaring that human engineering is inevitable and we can do nothing about it. In either case, we are complicit in preparing for our own degradation, in some respects more to blame than the bio-zealots who, however misguided, are putting their money where their mouth is. Denial and despair, unattractive outlooks in any situation, become morally reprehensible when circumstances summon us to keep the world safe for human flourishing. Our immediate ancestors, taking up the challenge of their time, rose to the occasion and rescued the human future from the cruel dehumanizations of Nazi and Soviet tyranny. It is our more difficult task to find ways to preserve it from the soft dehumanizations of well-meaning but hubristic biotechnical "re-creationism"—and to do it without undermining biomedical science or rejecting its genuine contributions to human welfare.

Truth be told, it will not be easy for us to do so, and we know it. But rising to the challenge requires recognizing the difficulties. For there are indeed many features of modern life that will conspire to frustrate efforts aimed at the human control of the biomedical project. First, we Americans believe in technological automatism: where we do not foolishly believe that all innovation is progress, we fatalistically believe that it is inevitable ("If it can be done, it will be done, like it or not"). Second, we believe in freedom: the freedom of scientists to inquire, the freedom of technologists to develop, the freedom of entrepreneurs to invest and to profit, the freedom of private citizens to make use of existing technologies to satisfy any and all personal desires, including the desire to reproduce by whatever means. Third, the biomedical enterprise occupies the moral high ground of compassionate humanitarianism, upholding the supreme values of modern life—cure disease, prolong life, relieve suffering—in competition with which other moral goods rarely stand a chance. ("What the public wants is not to be sick," says James Watson, "and if we help them not to be sick, they'll be on our side.")

There are still other obstacles. Our cultural pluralism and easygoing relativism make it difficult to reach consensus on what we should embrace and what we should oppose; and moral objections to this or that biomedical practice are often facilely dismissed as religious or sectarian. Many people are unwilling to pronounce judgments about what is good or bad, right and wrong, even in matters of great importance, even for themselves—never mind for others or for society as a whole. It does not help that the biomedical project is now deeply entangled with commerce: there are increasingly powerful economic interests in favor of going full steam ahead, and no economic interests in favor of going slow. Since we live in a democracy, moreover, we face political difficulties in gaining a consensus to direct our future, and we have almost no political experience in trying to curtail the development of any new biomedical technology. Finally, and perhaps most troubling, our views of the meaning of our humanity have been so transformed by the scientific-technological approach to the world that we are in danger of forgetting what we have to lose, humanly speaking.

But though the difficulties are real, our situation is far from hopeless. Regarding each of the aforementioned impediments, there is another side to the story. Though we love our gadgets and believe in progress, we have lost our innocence regarding technology. The environmental movement especially has alerted us to the unintended damage caused by unregulated technological advance, and has taught us how certain dangerous practices can be curbed. Though we favor freedom of inquiry, we recognize that experiments are deeds and not speeches, and we prohibit experimentation on human subjects without their consent, even when cures from disease might be had by unfettered research; and we limit so-called reproductive freedom by proscribing incest, polygamy, and the buying and selling of babies.

Although we esteem medical progress, biomedical institutions have ethics committees that judge research proposals on moral grounds, and, when necessary, uphold the primacy of human freedom and human dignity even over scientific discovery. Our moral pluralism notwithstanding, national commissions and review bodies have sometimes reached moral consensus to recommend limits on permissible scientific research and technological application. On the economic front, the patenting of genes and life forms and the rapid rise of genomic commerce have elicited strong concerns and criticisms, leading even former enthusiasts of the new biology to recoil from the impending commodification of human life. Though we lack political institutions experienced in setting limits on biomedical innovation, federal agencies years ago rejected the development of the plutonium-powered artificial heart, and we have nationally prohibited commercial traffic in organs for transplantation, even though a market would increase the needed supply. In recent years, several American states and many foreign countries have successfully taken political action, making certain practices illegal and placing others under moratoriums (the creation of human embryos solely for research; human germ-line genetic alteration). Most importantly, the majority of Americans are not yet so degraded or so cynical as to fail to be revolted by the society depicted in Huxley's novel. Though the obstacles to effective action are significant, they offer no excuse for resignation. Besides, it would be disgraceful to concede defeat even before we enter the fray.

Not the least of our difficulties in trying to exercise control over where biology is taking us is the fact that we do not get to decide, once and for all, for or against the destination of a post-human world. The scientific discoveries and the technical powers that will take us there come to us piecemeal, one at a time and seemingly independent from one another, each often attractively introduced as a measure that will "help [us] not to be sick." But sometimes we come to a clear fork in the road where decision is possible, and where we know that our decision will make a world of difference—indeed, it will make a permanently different world. Fortunately, we stand now at the point of such a momentous decision. Events have conspired to provide us with a perfect opportunity to seize the initiative and to gain some control of the biotechnical project. I refer to the prospect of human cloning, a practice absolutely central to Huxley's fictional world. Indeed, creating and manipulating life in the laboratory is the gateway to a Brave New World, not only in fiction but also in fact.

"To clone or not to clone a human being" is no longer a fanciful question. Success in cloning sheep, and also cows, mice, pigs, and goats, makes it perfectly clear that a fateful decision is now at hand: whether we should welcome or even tolerate the cloning of human beings. If recent newspaper reports are to be believed, reputable scientists and physicians have announced their intention to produce the first human clone in the coming year. Their efforts may already be under way.

The media, gawking and titillating as is their wont, have been softening us up for this possibility by turning the bizarre into the familiar. In the four years since the birth of Dolly the cloned sheep, the tone of discussing the prospect of human cloning has gone from "Yuck" to "Oh?" to "Gee whiz" to "Why not?" The sentimentalizers, aided by leading bioethicists, have downplayed talk about eugenically cloning the beautiful and the brawny or the best and the brightest. They have taken instead to defending clonal reproduction for humanitarian or compassionate reasons: to treat infertility in people who are said to "have no other choice," to avoid the risk of severe genetic disease, to "replace" a child who has died. For the sake of these rare benefits, they would have us countenance the entire practice of human cloning, the consequences be damned.

But we dare not be complacent about what is at issue, for the stakes are very high. Human cloning, though partly continuous with previous reproductive technologies, is also something radically new in itself and in its easily foreseeable consequences—especially when coupled with powers for genetic "enhancement" and germline genetic modification that may soon become available, owing to the recently completed Human Genome Project. I exaggerate somewhat, but in the direction of the truth: we are compelled to decide nothing less than whether human procreation is going to remain human, whether children are going to be made to order rather than begotten, and whether we wish to say yes in principle to the road that leads to the dehumanized hell of *Brave New World*.

. . .

For we have here a golden opportunity to exercise some control over where biology is taking us. The technology of cloning is discrete and well defined, and it requires considerable technical know-how and dexterity; we can therefore know by name many of the likely practitioners. The public demand for cloning is extremely low, and most people are decidedly against it. Nothing scientifically or medically important would be lost by banning clonal reproduction; alternative and nonobjectionable means are available to obtain some of the most important medical benefits claimed for (nonreproductive) human cloning. The commercial interests in human cloning are, for now, quite limited; and the nations of the world are actively seeking to prevent it. Now may be as good a chance as we will ever have to get our hands on the wheel of the runaway train now headed for a post-human world and to steer it toward a more dignified human future.

II.

What is cloning? Cloning, or asexual reproduction, is the production of individuals who are genetically identical to an already existing individual. The procedure's name is fancy—"somatic cell nuclear transfer"—but its concept is simple. Take a mature but unfertilized egg; remove or deactivate its nucleus; introduce a nucleus obtained from a specialized (somatic) cell of an adult organism. Once the egg begins to divide, transfer the little embryo to a woman's uterus to initiate a pregnancy. Since almost all the hereditary material of a cell is contained within its nucleus, the re-nucleated egg and the individual into which it develops are genetically identical to the organism that was the source of the transferred nucleus.

An unlimited number of genetically identical individuals—the group, as well as each of its members, is called "a clone"—could be produced by nuclear transfer. In principle, any person, male or female, newborn or adult, could be cloned, and in any quantity; and because stored cells can outlive their sources, one may even clone the dead. Since cloning requires no personal involvement on the part of the person whose genetic material is used, it could easily be used to reproduce living or deceased persons without their consent—a threat to reproductive freedom that has received relatively little attention.

Some possible misconceptions need to be avoided. Cloning is not Xeroxing: the clone of Bill Clinton, though his genetic double, would enter the world hairless, toothless, and peeing in his diapers, like any other human infant. But neither is cloning just like natural twinning: the cloned twin will be identical to an older, existing adult; and it will arise not by chance but by deliberate design; and its entire genetic makeup will be preselected by its parents and/or scientists. Moreover, the success rate of cloning, at least at first, will probably not be very high: the Scots transferred two hundred seventy-seven adult nuclei into sheep eggs, implanted twenty-nine clonal embryos, and achieved the birth of only one live lamb clone.

For this reason, among others, it is unlikely that, at least for now, the practice would be very popular; and there is little immediate worry of mass-scale production of multicopies. Still, for the tens of thousands of people who sustain more than three hundred assisted-reproduction clinics in the United States and already avail themselves of in vitro fertilization and other techniques, cloning would be an option with virtually no added fuss. Panos Zavos, the Kentucky reproduction specialist who has announced his plans to clone a child, claims that he has already received thousands of e-mailed requests from people eager to clone, despite the known risks of failure and damaged offspring. Should commercial interests develop in "nucleus-banking," as they have in sperm-banking and egg-harvesting; should famous athletes or other celebrities decide to market their DNA the way they now market their autographs and nearly everything else; should techniques of embryo and germline genetic testing and manipulation arrive as anticipated, increasing the use of laboratory assistance in order to obtain "better" babies—should all this come to pass, cloning, if it is permitted, could become more than a marginal practice simply on the basis of free reproductive choice.

What are we to think about this prospect? Nothing good. Indeed, most people are repelled by nearly all aspects of human cloning: the possibility of mass production of human beings, with large clones of look-alikes, compromised in their individuality; the idea of father-son or mother-daughter "twins"; the bizarre prospect of a woman bearing and rearing a genetic copy of herself, her spouse, or even her deceased father or mother; the grotesqueness of conceiving a child as an exact "replacement" for another who has died; the utilitarian creation of embryonic duplicates of oneself, to be frozen away or created when needed to provide homologous tissues or organs for transplantation; the narcissism of those who would clone themselves, and the arrogance of others who think they know who deserves to be cloned; the Frankensteinian hubris to create a human life and increasingly to control its destiny; men playing at being God. Almost no one finds any of the suggested reasons for human cloning compelling, and almost everyone anticipates its possible misuses and abuses. And the popular belief that human cloning cannot be prevented makes the prospect all the more revolting.

Revulsion is not an argument; and some of yesterday's repugnances are today calmly accepted—not always for the better. In some crucial cases, however, repugnance is the emotional expression of deep wisdom, beyond reason's power completely to articulate it. Can anyone really give an argument fully adequate to the horror that is father–daughter incest (even with consent), or bestiality, or the mutilation of a corpse, or the eating of human flesh, or the rape or murder of another human being? Would anybody's failure to give full rational justification for his revulsion at those practices make that revulsion ethically suspect?

I suggest that our repugnance at human cloning belongs in this category. We are repelled by the prospect of cloning human beings not because of the strangeness or the novelty of the undertaking, but because we intuit and we feel, immediately and without argument, the violation of things that we rightfully hold dear. We sense that cloning represents a profound defilement of our given nature as procreative beings, and of the social relations built on this natural ground. We also sense that cloning is a radical form of child abuse. In this age in which everything is held to be permissible so long as it is freely done, and in which our bodies are regarded as mere instruments of our autonomous rational will, repugnance may be the only voice left that speaks up to defend the central core of our humanity. Shallow are the souls that have forgotten how to shudder.

III.

Yet repugnance need not stand naked before the bar of reason. The wisdom of our horror at human cloning can be at least partially articulated, even if this is finally one of those instances about which the heart has its reasons that reason cannot entirely know. I offer four objections to human cloning: that it constitutes unethical experimentation; that it threatens identity and individuality; that it turns procreation into manufacture (especially when understood as the harbinger of manipulations to come); and that it means despotism over children

and perversion of parenthood. Please note: I speak only about so-called reproductive cloning, not about the creation of cloned embryos for research. The objections that may be raised against creating (or using) embryos for research are entirely independent of whether the research embryos are produced by cloning. What is radically distinct and radically new is reproductive cloning.

Any attempt to clone a human being would constitute an unethical experiment upon the resulting child-to-be. In all the animal experiments, fewer than two to three percent of all cloning attempts succeeded. Not only are there fetal deaths and stillborn infants, but many of the so-called "successes" are in fact failures. As has only recently become clear, there is a very high incidence of major disabilities and deformities in cloned animals that attain live birth. Cloned cows often have heart and lung problems; cloned mice later develop pathological obesity; other live-born cloned animals fail to reach normal developmental milestones.

The problem, scientists suggest, may lie in the fact that an egg with a new somatic nucleus must re-program itself in a matter of minutes or hours (whereas the nucleus of an unaltered egg has been prepared over months and years). There is thus a greatly increased likelihood of error in translating the genetic instructions, leading to developmental defects some of which will show themselves only much later. (Note also that these induced abnormalities may also affect the stem cells that scientists hope to harvest from cloned embryos. Lousy embryos, lousy stem cells.) Nearly all scientists now agree that attempts to clone human beings carry massive risks of producing unhealthy, abnormal, and malformed children. What are we to do with them? Shall we just discard the ones that fall short of expectations? Considered opinion is today nearly unanimous, even among scientists: attempts at human cloning are irresponsible and unethical. We cannot ethically even get to know whether or not human cloning is feasible.

If it were successful, cloning would create serious issues of identity and individuality. The clone may experience concerns about his distinctive identity not only because he will be, in genotype and in appearance, identical to another human being, but because he may also be twin to the person who is his "father" or his "mother"—if one can still call them that. Unaccountably, people treat as innocent the homey case of intra-familial cloning—the cloning of husband or wife (or single mother). They forget about the unique dangers of mixing the twin relation with the parent-child relation. (For this situation, the relation of contemporaneous twins is no precedent; yet even this less problematic situation teaches us how difficult it is to wrest independence from the being for whom one has the most powerful affinity.) Virtually no parent is going to be able to treat a clone of himself or herself as one treats a child generated by the lottery of sex. What will happen when the adolescent clone of Mommy becomes the spitting image of the woman with whom Daddy once fell in love? In case of divorce, will Mommy still love the clone of Daddy, even though she can no longer stand the sight of Daddy himself?

Most people think about cloning from the point of view of adults choosing to clone. Almost nobody thinks about what it would be like to be the cloned child. Surely his or her new life would constantly be scrutinized in relation to that of the older version. Even in the absence of unusual parental expectations for the clone—say, to live the same life, only without its errors—the child is likely to be ever a curiosity, ever a potential source of déjà vu. Unlike "normal" identical twins, a cloned individual—copied from whomever—will be saddled with a genotype that has already lived. He will not be fully a surprise to the world: people are likely always to compare his doings in life with those of his alter ego, especially if he is a clone of someone gifted or famous. True, his nurture and his circumstance will be different; genotype is not exactly destiny. But one must also expect parental efforts to shape this new life after the original—or at least to view the child with the original version always firmly in mind. For why else did they clone from the star basketball player, the mathematician, or the beauty queen—or even dear old Dad—in the first place?

Human cloning would also represent a giant step toward the transformation of begetting into making, of procreation into manufacture (literally, "handmade"), a process that has already begun with in vitro fertilization and genetic testing of embryos. With cloning, not only is the process in hand, but the total genetic blueprint of the cloned individual is selected and determined by the human artisans. To be sure, subsequent development is still according to natural processes; and the resulting children will be recognizably human. But we would be taking a major step into making man himself simply another one of the man-made things.

How does begetting differ from making? In natural procreation, human beings come together to give existence to another being that is formed exactly as we were, by what we are—living, hence perishable, hence aspiringly erotic, hence procreative human beings. But in clonal reproduction, and in the more advanced forms of manufacture to which it will lead, we give existence to a being not by what we are but by what we intend and design.

Let me be clear. The problem is not the mere intervention of technique, and the point is not that "nature knows best." The problem is that any child whose being, character, and capacities exist owing to human design does not stand on the same plane as its makers. As with any product of our making, no matter how excellent, the artificer stands above it, not as an equal but as a superior, transcending it by his will and creative prowess. In human cloning, scientists and prospective "parents" adopt a technocratic attitude toward human children: human children become their artifacts. Such an arrangement is profoundly dehumanizing, no matter how good the product.

Procreation dehumanized into manufacture is further degraded by commodification, a virtually inescapable result of allowing baby-making to proceed under the banner of commerce. Genetic and reproductive biotechnology companies are already growth industries, but they will soon go into commercial orbit now that the Human Genome Project has been completed. "Human eggs for sale" is already a big business, masquerading under the pretense of "donation." Newspaper advertisements on elite college campuses offer up to $50,000 for an egg "donor" tall enough to play women's basketball and with SAT scores high enough for admission to Stanford; and to nobody's surprise, at such prices there are many young coeds eager to help shoppers obtain the finest babies money can buy. (The egg and womb-renting entrepreneurs shamelessly proceed on the ancient, disgusting, misogynist premise that most women will give you access to their bodies, if the price is right.) Even before the capacity for human cloning is perfected, established companies will have invested in the harvesting of eggs from ovaries obtained at autopsy or through ovarian surgery, practiced embryonic genetic alteration, and initiated the stockpiling of prospective donor tissues. Through the rental of surrogate-womb services, and through the buying and selling of tissues and embryos priced according to the merit of the donor, the commodification of nascent human life will be unstoppable.

Finally, the practice of human cloning by nuclear transfer—like other anticipated forms of genetically engineering the next generation—would enshrine and aggravate a profound misunderstanding of the meaning of having children and of the parent-child relationship. When a couple normally chooses to procreate, the partners are saying yes to the emergence of new life in its novelty—are saying yes not only to having a child, but also to having whatever child this child turns out to be. In accepting our finitude, in opening ourselves to our replacement, we tacitly confess the limits of our control.

Embracing the future by procreating means precisely that we are relinquishing our grip in the very activity of taking up our own share in what we hope will be the immortality of human life and the human species. This means that our children are not our children: they are not our property, they are not our possessions. Neither are they supposed to live our lives for us, or to live anyone's life but their own. Their genetic distinctiveness and independence are the natural foreshadowing of the deep truth that they have their own, never-before-enacted life to live. Though sprung from a past, they take an uncharted course into the future.

Much mischief is already done by parents who try to live vicariously through their children. Children are sometimes compelled to fulfill the broken dreams of unhappy parents. But whereas most parents normally have hopes for their children, cloning parents will have expectations. In cloning, such overbearing parents will have taken at the start a decisive step that contradicts the entire meaning of the open and forward-looking nature of parent-child relations. The child is given a genotype that has already lived, with full expectation that this blueprint of a past life ought to be controlling the life that is to come. A wanted child now means a child who exists precisely to fulfill parental wants. Like all the more precise eugenic manipulations that will follow in its wake, cloning is thus inherently despotic, for it seeks to make one's children after one's own image (or an image of one's choosing) and their future according to one's will.

Is this hyperbolic? Consider concretely the new realities of responsibility and guilt in the households of the cloned. No longer only the sins of the parents, but also the genetic choices of the parents, will be visited on the children—and beyond the third and fourth generation; and everyone will know who is responsible. No parent will be able to blame nature or the lottery of sex for an unhappy adolescent's big nose, dull wit, musical ineptitude, nervous disposition, or anything else that he hates about himself. Fairly or not, children will hold their cloners responsible for everything, for nature as well as for nurture. And parents, especially the better ones, will be limitlessly liable to guilt. Only the truly despotic souls will sleep the sleep of the innocent.

IV.

The defenders of cloning are not wittingly friends of despotism. Quite the contrary. Deaf to most other considerations, they regard themselves mainly as friends of freedom: the freedom of individuals to reproduce, the freedom of scientists and inventors to discover and to devise and to foster "progress" in genetic knowledge and technique, the freedom of entrepreneurs to profit in the market. They want large-scale cloning only for animals, but they wish to preserve cloning as a human option for exercising our "right to reproduce"—our right to have children, and children with "desirable genes." As some point out, under our "right to reproduce" we already practice early forms of unnatural, artificial, and extra-marital reproduction, and we already practice early forms of eugenic choice. For that reason, they argue, cloning is no big deal.

We have here a perfect example of the logic of the slippery slope. The principle of reproductive freedom currently enunciated by the proponents of cloning logically embraces the ethical acceptability of sliding all the way down: to producing children wholly in the laboratory from sperm to term (should it become feasible), and to producing children whose entire genetic makeup will be the product of parental eugenic planning and choice. If reproductive freedom means the right to have a child of one's own choosing by whatever means, then reproductive freedom knows and accepts no limits.

Proponents want us to believe that there are legitimate uses of cloning that can be distinguished from illegitimate uses, but by their own principles no such limits can be found. (Nor could any such limits be enforced in practice: once cloning is permitted, no one ever need discover whom one is cloning and why.) Reproductive freedom, as they understand it, is governed solely by the subjective wishes of the parents-to-be. The sentimentally appealing case of the childless married couple is, on these grounds, indistinguishable from the case of an individual (married or not) who would like to clone someone famous or talented, living or dead. And the principle here endorsed justifies not only cloning but also all future artificial attempts to create (manufacture) "better" or "perfect" babies.

The "perfect baby," of course, is the project not of the infertility doctors, but of the eugenic scientists and their supporters, who, for the time being, are content to hide behind the skirts of the partisans of reproductive freedom and compassion for the infertile. For them, the paramount right is not the so-called right to reproduce, it is what the biologist Bentley Glass called, a quarter of a century ago, "the right of every child to be born with a sound physical and mental constitution, based on a sound genotype . . . the inalienable right to a sound heritage." But to secure this right, and to achieve the requisite quality control over new human life, human conception and gestation will need to be brought fully into the bright light of the laboratory, beneath which the child-to-be can be fertilized, nourished, pruned, weeded, watched, inspected, prodded, pinched, cajoled, injected, tested, rated, graded, approved, stamped, wrapped, sealed, and delivered. There is no other way to produce the perfect baby.

If you think that such scenarios require outside coercion or governmental tyranny, you are mistaken. Once it becomes possible, with the aid of human genomics, to produce or to select for what some regard as "better babies"—smarter, prettier, healthier, more athletic—parents will leap at the opportunity to "improve" their offspring. Indeed, not to do so will be socially regarded as a form of child neglect. Those who would ordinarily be opposed to such tinkering will be under enormous pressure to compete on behalf of their as yet unborn children—just as some now plan almost from their children's birth how to get them into Harvard. Never mind that, lacking a standard of "good" or "better," no one can really know whether any such changes will truly be improvements.

Proponents of cloning urge us to forget about the science-fiction scenarios of laboratory manufacture or multiple-copy clones, and to focus only on the sympathetic cases of infertile couples exercising their reproductive rights. But why, if the single cases are so innocent, should multiplying their performance be so off-putting? (Similarly, why do others object to people's making money from that practice if the practice itself is perfectly acceptable?) The so-called science-fiction cases—say, Brave New World—make vivid the meaning of what looks to us, mistakenly, to be benign. They reveal that what looks like compassionate humanitarianism is, in the end, crushing dehumanization.

V.

Whether or not they share my reasons, most people, I think, share my conclusion: that human cloning is unethical in itself and dangerous in its likely consequences, which include the precedent that it will establish for designing our children. Some reach this conclusion for their own good reasons, different from my own: concerns about distributive justice in access to eugenic cloning; worries about the genetic effects of asexual "inbreeding";

aversion to the implicit premise of genetic deter-minism; objections to the embryonic and fetal wastage that must necessarily accompany the efforts; religious opposition to "man playing God." But never mind why: the overwhelming majority of our fellow Americans remain firmly opposed to cloning human beings.

For us, then, the real questions are: What should we do about it? How can we best succeed? These questions should concern everyone eager to secure deliberate human control over the powers that could re-design our humanity, even if cloning is not the issue over which they would choose to make their stand. And the answer to the first question seems pretty plain. What we should do is work to prevent human cloning by making it illegal.

We should aim for a global legal ban, if possible, and for a unilateral national ban at a minimum—and soon, before the fact is upon us. To be sure, le-gal bans can be violated; but we certainly curtail much mischief by outlawing incest, voluntary servi-tude, and the buying and selling of organs and ba-bies. To be sure, renegade scientists may secretly undertake to violate such a law, but we can deter them by both criminal sanctions and monetary penalties, as well as by removing any incentive they have to proudly claim credit for their technological bravado.

Such a ban on clonal baby-making will not harm the progress of basic genetic science and tech-nology. On the contrary, it will reassure the public that scientists are happy to proceed without violat-ing the deep ethical norms and intuitions of the hu-man community. It will also protect honorable sci-entists from a public backlash against the brazen misconduct of the rogues. As many scientists have publicly confessed, free and worthy science proba-bly has much more to fear from a strong public re-action to a cloning fiasco than it does from a cloning ban, provided that the ban is judiciously crafted and vigorously enforced against those who would violate it.

. . .

. . . I now believe that what we need is an all-out ban on human cloning, including the creation of embryonic clones. I am convinced that all halfway measures will prove to be morally, legally, and strategically flawed, and—most important—that they will not be effective in obtaining the desired result. Anyone truly serious about preventing hu-man reproductive cloning must seek to stop the process from the beginning. Our changed circum-stances, and the now evident defects of the less re-strictive alternatives, make an all-out ban by far the most attractive and effective option.

Here's why. Creating cloned human children ("reproductive cloning") necessarily begins by pro-ducing cloned human embryos. Preventing the lat-ter would prevent the former, and prudence alone might counsel building such a "fence around the law." Yet some scientists favor embryo cloning as a way of obtaining embryos for research or as sources of cells and tissues for the possible benefit of others. (This practice they misleadingly call "therapeutic cloning" rather than the more accurate "cloning for research" or "experimental cloning," so as to ob-scure the fact that the clone will be "treated" only to exploitation and destruction, and that any potential future beneficiaries and any future "therapies" are at this point purely hypothetical.)

The prospect of creating new human life solely to be exploited in this way has been condemned on moral grounds by many people—including The Washington Post, President Clinton, and many other supporters of a woman's right to abortion—as displaying a profound disrespect for life. Even those who are willing to scavenge so-called "spare embryos"—those products of in vitro fertilization made in excess of people's reproductive needs, and otherwise likely to be discarded—draw back from creating human embryos explicitly and solely for research purposes. They reject outright what they regard as the exploitation and the instrumentaliza-tion of nascent human life. In addition, others who are agnostic about the moral status of the embryo see the wisdom of not needlessly offending the sen-sibilities of their fellow citizens who are opposed to such practices.

But even setting aside these obvious moral first impressions, a few moments of reflection show why an anti-cloning law that permitted the cloning of embryos but criminalized their transfer to pro-duce a child would be a moral blunder. This would be a law that was not merely permissively "pro-choice" but emphatically and prescriptively "anti-life." While permitting the creation of an embryonic life, it would make it a federal offense to try to keep it alive and bring it to birth. Whatever one thinks of the moral status or the ontological status of the human embryo, moral sense and practical wisdom recoil from having the government of the United States on record as requiring the destruction of nascent life and, what is worse, demanding the punishment of those who would act to preserve it by (feloniously!) giving it birth.

But the problem with the approach that targets only reproductive cloning (that is, the transfer of the embryo to a woman's uterus) is not only moral but also legal and strategic. A ban only on reproductive cloning would turn out to be unenforceable. Once cloned embryos were produced and available in laboratories and assisted-reproduction centers, it would be virtually impossible to control what was done with them. Biotechnical experiments take place in laboratories, hidden from public view, and, given the rise of high-stakes commerce in biotechnology, these experiments are concealed from the competition. Huge stockpiles of cloned human embryos could thus be produced and bought and sold without anyone knowing it. As we have seen with in vitro embryos created to treat infertility, embryos produced for one reason can be used for another reason: today "spare embryos" once created to begin a pregnancy are now used in research, and tomorrow clones created for research will be used to begin a pregnancy.

Assisted reproduction takes place within the privacy of the doctor-patient relationship, making outside scrutiny extremely difficult. Many infertility experts probably would obey the law, but others could and would defy it with impunity, their doings covered by the veil of secrecy that is the principle of medical confidentiality. Moreover, the transfer of embryos to begin a pregnancy is a simple procedure (especially compared with manufacturing the embryo in the first place), simple enough that its final steps could be self-administered by the woman, who would thus absolve the doctor of blame for having "caused" the illegal transfer. (I have in mind something analogous to Kevorkian's suicide machine,

which was designed to enable the patient to push the plunger and the good "doctor" to evade criminal liability.)

Even should the deed become known, governmental attempts to enforce the reproductive ban would run into a swarm of moral and legal challenges, both to efforts aimed at preventing transfer to a woman and—even worse—to efforts seeking to prevent birth after transfer has occurred. A woman who wished to receive the embryo clone would no doubt seek a judicial restraining order, suing to have the law overturned in the name of a constitutionally protected interest in her own reproductive choice to clone. (The cloned child would be born before the legal proceedings were complete.) And should an "illicit clonal pregnancy" be discovered, no governmental agency would compel a woman to abort the clone, and there would be an understandable storm of protest should she be fined or jailed after she gives birth. Once the baby is born, there would even be sentimental opposition to punishing the doctor for violating the law—unless, of course, the clone turned out to be severely abnormal.

For all these reasons, the only practically effective and legally sound approach is to block human cloning at the start, at the production of the embryo clone. Such a ban can be rightly characterized not as interference with reproductive freedom, nor even as interference with scientific inquiry, but as an attempt to prevent the unhealthy, unsavory, and unwelcome manufacture of and traffic in human clones.

. . .

I appreciate that a federal legislative ban on human cloning is without American precedent, at least in matters technological. Perhaps such a ban will prove ineffective; perhaps it will eventually be shown to have been a mistake. (If so, it could later be reversed.) If enacted, however, it will have achieved one overwhelmingly important result, in addition to its contribution to thwarting cloning: it will place the burden of practical proof where it belongs. It will require the proponents to show very clearly what great social or medical good can be had only by the cloning of human beings. Surely it is only for such a compelling case, yet to be made or even imagined, that we should wish to risk this major departure—or any other major departure—in human procreation.

Americans have lived by and prospered under a rosy optimism about scientific and technological progress. The technological imperative has probably served us well, though we should admit that there is no accurate method for weighing benefits and harms. And even when we recognize the unwelcome outcomes of technological advance, we remain confident in our ability to fix all the "bad" consequences—by regulation or by means of still newer and better technologies. Yet there is very good reason for shifting the American paradigm, at least regarding those technological interventions into the human body and mind that would surely effect fundamental (and likely irreversible) changes in human nature, basic human relationships, and what it means to be a human being. Here we should not be willing to risk everything in the naive hope that, should things go wrong, we can later set them right again.

Some have argued that cloning is almost certainly going to remain a marginal practice, and that we should therefore permit people to practice it. Such a view is shortsighted. Even if cloning is rarely undertaken, a society in which it is tolerated is no longer the same society—any more than is a society that permits (even small-scale) incest or cannibalism or slavery. A society that allows cloning, whether it knows it or not, has tacitly assented to the conversion of procreation into manufacture and to the treatment of children as purely the projects of our will. Willy-nilly, it has acquiesced in the eugenic redesign of future generations. The humanitarian superhighway to a Brave New World lies open before this society.

But the present danger posed by human cloning is, paradoxically, also a golden opportunity. In a truly unprecedented way, we can strike a blow for the human control of the technological project, for wisdom, for prudence, for human dignity. The prospect of human cloning, so repulsive to contemplate, is the occasion for deciding whether we shall be slaves of unregulated innovation, and ultimately its artifacts, or whether we shall remain free human beings who guide our powers toward the enhancement of human dignity. The humanity of the human future is now in our hands.

II.13   MICHAEL J. SANDEL

The Case against Perfection

In this reading, Michael Sandel, professor of political philosophy at Harvard University and also a member of the President's Council on Bioethics, develops an answer to some of the hardest ethical questions raised by genetic engineering, particularly the use of this technology for human genetic enhancement. It is one thing, he argues, to employ genetic technologies to prevent or cure diseases or repair injuries but quite another to use them to produce children who are genetically advantaged by parental choice. Many people have moral qualms about performance-enhancing drugs in sports, but it is difficult to isolate exactly the ethical basis of these intuitions. Sandel examines and dismisses several plausible explanations for such qualms but finds each of these arguments insufficient. Instead, he argues that what is problematic about drug or genetic enhancement is that it represents "a Promethean aspiration to remake nature, including human nature, to serve our purposes and satisfy our desires." This desire to remake ourselves coexists with a countervailing value in the "giftedness of life"—that is, the appreciation that "our talents and powers are not wholly our own doing." The "ethic of giftedness" provides a moral basis for rejecting the vision of "free-market eugenics" that has been advocated by many bioethicists. Instead, Sandel argues for constraining our drive to mastery with a humility born of the recognition that our individual genetic endowments should remain "gifts" rather than become products of deliberate design.

Focus Questions

1. Why does Sandel think that the objection to human cloning from autonomy or the value of an "open future" is unconvincing? What about the argument from unfairness? How can these objections be answered?
2. What does Sandel mean by the "ethic of willfulness"? How is this ethic manifest, for instance, in the use of performance-enhancing drugs by athletes?
3. What three key features of the moral landscape would be undermined, in Sandel's view, by the use of genetic enhancement technologies? Do you agree that these values should be protected and preserved?
4. Compare Sandel's view to those of More (selection II.9) and Silver (selection II.11). Is there any way to reconcile or balance their respective positions?

Keywords

eugenics, gene therapy, genetic enhancement, human growth hormone, performance-enhancing drugs, sex selection, sperm donation

BREAKTHROUGHS IN GENETICS PRESENT us with a promise and a predicament. The promise is that we may soon be able to treat and prevent a host of debilitating diseases. The predicament is that our newfound genetic knowledge may also enable us to manipulate our own nature—to enhance our muscles, memories, and moods; to choose the sex, height, and other genetic traits of our children; to make ourselves "better than well." When science moves faster than moral understanding, as it does today, men and women struggle to articulate their unease. In liberal societies they reach first for the language of autonomy, fairness, and individual rights. But this part of our moral vocabulary is ill equipped to address the hardest questions posed by genetic engineering. The genomic revolution has induced a kind of moral vertigo.

Consider cloning. The birth of Dolly the cloned sheep, in 1997, brought a torrent of concern about the prospect of cloned human beings. There are good medical reasons to worry. Most scientists agree that cloning is unsafe, likely to produce offspring with serious abnormalities. (Dolly recently died a premature death.) But suppose technology improved to the point where clones were at no greater risk than naturally conceived offspring. Would human cloning still be objectionable? Should our hesitation be moral as well as medical? What, exactly, is wrong with creating a child who is a genetic twin of one parent, or of an older sibling who has tragically died—or, for that matter, of an admired scientist, sports star, or celebrity?

Some say cloning is wrong because it violates the right to autonomy: by choosing a child's genetic makeup in advance, parents deny the child's right to an open future. A similar objection can be raised against any form of bioengineering that allows parents to select or reject genetic characteristics.

From "The Case Against Perfection" by Michael J. Sandel, *The Atlantic Monthly,* April 2004, pp. 51–62. Reprinted by permission.

According to this argument, genetic enhancements for musical talent, say, or athletic prowess, would point children toward particular choices, and so designer children would never be fully free.

At first glance the autonomy argument seems to capture what is troubling about human cloning and other forms of genetic engineering. It is not persuasive, for two reasons. First, it wrongly implies that absent a designing parent, children are free to choose their characteristics for themselves. But none of us chooses his genetic inheritance. The alternative to a cloned or genetically enhanced child is not one whose future is unbound by particular talents but one at the mercy of the genetic lottery.

Second, even if a concern for autonomy explains some of our worries about made-to-order children, it cannot explain our moral hesitation about people who seek genetic remedies or enhancements for themselves. Gene therapy on somatic (that is, non-reproductive) cells, such as muscle cells and brain cells, repairs or replaces defective genes. The moral quandary arises when people use such therapy not to cure a disease but to reach beyond health, to enhance their physical or cognitive capacities, to lift themselves above the norm.

Like cosmetic surgery, genetic enhancement employs medical means for nonmedical ends—ends unrelated to curing or preventing disease or repairing injury. But unlike cosmetic surgery, genetic enhancement is more than skin-deep. If we are ambivalent about surgery or Botox injections for sagging chins and furrowed brows, we are all the more troubled by genetic engineering for stronger bodies, sharper memories, greater intelligence, and happier moods. The question is whether we are right to be troubled, and if so, on what grounds.

In order to grapple with the ethics of enhancement, we need to confront questions largely lost from view—questions about the moral status of nature, and about the proper stance of human beings toward the given world. Since these questions verge on theology, modern philosophers and political theorists tend to shrink from them. But our new powers of biotechnology make them unavoidable. To see why this is so, consider four examples already on the horizon: muscle enhancement, memory enhancement, growth-hormone treatment, and reproductive technologies that enable parents to choose the sex and some genetic traits of their children. In each case what began as an attempt to treat a disease or prevent a genetic disorder now beckons as an instrument of improvement and consumer choice.

Muscles

Everyone would welcome a gene therapy to alleviate muscular dystrophy and to reverse the debilitating muscle loss that comes with old age. But what if the same therapy were used to improve athletic performance? Researchers have developed a synthetic gene that, when injected into the muscle cells of mice, prevents and even reverses natural muscle deterioration. The gene not only repairs wasted or injured muscles but also strengthens healthy ones. This success bodes well for human applications. H. Lee Sweeney, of the University of Pennsylvania, who leads the research, hopes his discovery will cure the immobility that afflicts the elderly. But Sweeney's bulked-up mice have already attracted the attention of athletes seeking a competitive edge. Although the therapy is not yet approved for human use, the prospect of genetically enhanced weight lifters, home-run sluggers, linebackers, and sprinters is easy to imagine. The widespread use of steroids and other performance-improving drugs in professional sports suggests that many athletes will be eager to avail themselves of genetic enhancement.

Suppose for the sake of argument that muscle-enhancing gene therapy, unlike steroids, turned out to be safe—or at least no riskier than a rigorous weight-training regimen. Would there be a reason to ban its use in sports? There is something unsettling about the image of genetically altered athletes lifting SUVs or hitting 650-foot home runs or running a three-minute mile. But what, exactly, is troubling about it? Is it simply that we find such superhuman spectacles too bizarre to contemplate? Or does our unease point to something of ethical significance?

It might be argued that a genetically enhanced athlete, like a drug-enhanced athlete, would have an unfair advantage over his unenhanced competitors. But the fairness argument against enhancement has a fatal flaw: it has always been the case that some athletes are better endowed genetically than others, and yet we do not consider this to undermine the fairness of competitive sports. From the standpoint of fairness, enhanced genetic differences would be no worse than natural ones, assuming they were safe and made available to all. If genetic enhancement in sports is morally objectionable, it must be for reasons other than fairness.

Memory

Genetic enhancement is possible for brains as well as brawn. In the mid-1990s scientists managed to manipulate a memory-linked gene in fruit flies, creating flies with photographic memories. More recently researchers have produced smart mice by inserting extra copies of a memory-related gene into mouse embryos. The altered mice learn more quickly and remember things longer than normal mice. The extra copies were programmed to remain active even in old age, and the improvement was passed on to offspring.

Human memory is more complicated, but biotech companies, including Memory Pharmaceuticals, are in hot pursuit of memory-enhancing drugs, or "cognition enhancers," for human beings. The obvious market for such drugs consists of those who suffer from Alzheimer's and other serious memory disorders. The companies also have their sights on a bigger market: the 81 million Americans over fifty who are beginning to encounter the memory loss that comes naturally with age. A drug that reversed age-related memory loss would be a bonanza for the pharmaceutical industry: a Viagra for the brain. Such use would straddle the line between remedy and enhancement. Unlike a treatment for Alzheimer's, it would cure no disease; but insofar as it restored capacities a person once possessed, it would have a remedial aspect. It could also have purely nonmedical uses: for example, by a lawyer cramming to memorize facts for an upcoming trial, or by a business executive eager to learn Mandarin on the eve of his departure for Shanghai.

Some who worry about the ethics of cognitive enhancement point to the danger of creating two classes of human beings: those with access to enhancement technologies, and those who must make

do with their natural capacities. And if the enhancements could be passed down the generations, the two classes might eventually become subspecies—the enhanced and the merely natural. But worry about access ignores the moral status of enhancement itself. Is the scenario troubling because the unenhanced poor would be denied the benefits of bioengineering, or because the enhanced affluent would somehow be dehumanized? As with muscles, so with memory: the fundamental question is not how to ensure equal access to enhancement but whether we should aspire to it in the first place.

Height

Pediatricians already struggle with the ethics of enhancement when confronted by parents who want to make their children taller. Since the 1980s human growth hormone has been approved for children with a hormone deficiency that makes them much shorter than average. But the treatment also increases the height of healthy children. Some parents of healthy children who are unhappy with their stature (typically boys) ask why it should make a difference whether a child is short because of a hormone deficiency or because his parents happen to be short. Whatever the cause, the social consequences are the same.

In the face of this argument some doctors began prescribing hormone treatments for children whose short stature was unrelated to any medical problem. By 1996 such "off-label" use accounted for 40 percent of human-growth-hormone prescriptions. Although it is legal to prescribe drugs for purposes not approved by the Food and Drug Administration, pharmaceutical companies cannot promote such use. Seeking to expand its market, Eli Lilly & Co. recently persuaded the FDA to approve its human growth hormone for healthy children whose projected adult height is in the bottom one percentile—under five feet three inches for boys and four feet eleven inches for girls. This concession raises a large question about the ethics of enhancement: If hormone treatments need not be limited to those with hormone deficiencies, why should they be available only to very short children? Why shouldn't all shorter-than-average children be able to seek treatment? And what about a child of average height who wants to be taller so that he can make the basketball team?

Some oppose height enhancement on the grounds that it is collectively self-defeating; as some become taller, others become shorter relative to the norm. Except in Lake Wobegon, not every child can be above average. As the unenhanced began to feel shorter, they, too, might seek treatment, leading to a hormonal arms race that left everyone worse off, especially those who couldn't afford to buy their way up from shortness.

But the arms-race objection is not decisive on its own. Like the fairness objection to bioengineered muscles and memory, it leaves unexamined the attitudes and dispositions that prompt the drive for enhancement. If we were bothered only by the injustice of adding shortness to the problems of the poor, we could remedy that unfairness by publicly subsidizing height enhancements. As for the relative height deprivation suffered by innocent bystanders, we could compensate them by taxing those who buy their way to greater height. The real question is whether we want to live in a society where parents feel compelled to spend a fortune to make perfectly healthy kids a few inches taller.

Sex Selection

Perhaps the most inevitable nonmedical use of bioengineering is sex selection. For centuries parents have been trying to choose the sex of their children. Today biotech succeeds where folk remedies failed.

One technique for sex selection arose with prenatal tests using amniocentesis and ultrasound. These medical technologies were developed to detect genetic abnormalities such as spina bifida and Down syndrome. But they can also reveal the sex of the fetus—allowing for the abortion of a fetus of an undesired sex. Even among those who favor abortion rights, few advocate abortion simply because the parents do not want a girl. Nevertheless, in traditional societies with a powerful cultural preference for boys, this practice has become widespread.

Sex selection need not involve abortion, however. For couples undergoing *in vitro* fertilization (IVF), it is possible to choose the sex of the child before the fertilized egg is implanted in the womb.

One method makes use of preimplantation genetic diagnosis (PGD), a procedure developed to screen for genetic diseases. Several eggs are fertilized in a petri dish and grown to the eight-cell stage (about three days). At that point the embryos are tested to determine their sex. Those of the desired sex are implanted: the others are typically discarded. Although few couples are likely to undergo the difficulty and expense of IVF simply to choose the sex of their child, embryo screening is a highly reliable means of sex selection. And as our genetic knowledge increases, it may be possible to use PGD to cull embryos carrying undesired genes, such as those associated with obesity, height, and skin color. The science-fiction movie *Gattaca* depicts a future in which parents routinely screen embryos for sex, height, immunity to disease, and even IQ. There is something troubling about the *Gattaca* scenario, but it is not easy to identify what exactly is wrong with screening embryos to choose the sex of our children.

One line of objection draws on arguments familiar from the abortion debate. Those who believe that an embryo is a person reject embryo screening for the same reasons they reject abortion. If an eight-cell embryo growing in a petri dish is morally equivalent to a fully developed human being, then discarding it is no better than aborting a fetus, and both practices are equivalent to infanticide. Whatever its merits, however, this "pro-life" objection is not an argument against sex selection as such.

The latest technology poses the question of sex selection unclouded by the matter of an embryo's moral status. The Genetics & IVF Institute, a for-profit infertility clinic in Fairfax, Virginia, now offers a sperm-sorting technique that makes it possible to choose the sex of one's child before it is conceived. X-bearing sperm, which produce girls, carry more DNA than Y-bearing sperm, which produce boys; a device called a flow cytometer can separate them. The process, called MicroSort, has a high rate of success.

If sex selection by sperm sorting is objectionable, it must be for reasons that go beyond the debate about the moral status of the embryo. One such reason is that sex selection is an instrument of sex discrimination—typically against girls, as illustrated by the chilling sex ratios in India and China. Some speculate that societies with substantially more men than women will be less stable, more violent, and more prone to crime or war. These are legitimate worries—but the sperm-sorting company has a clever way of addressing them. It offers MicroSort only to couples who want to choose the sex of a child for purposes of "family balancing." Those with more sons than daughters may choose a girl, and vice versa. But customers may not use the technology to stock up on children of the same sex, or even to choose the sex of their firstborn child. (So far the majority of MicroSort clients have chosen girls.) Under restrictions of this kind, do any ethical issues remain that should give us pause?

The case of MicroSort helps us isolate the moral objections that would persist if muscle-enhancement, memory-enhancement, and height-enhancement technologies were safe and available to all.

It is commonly said that genetic enhancements undermine our humanity by threatening our capacity to act freely, to succeed by our own efforts, and to consider ourselves responsible—worthy of praise or blame—for the things we do and for the way we are. It is one thing to hit seventy home runs as the result of disciplined training and effort, and something else, something less, to hit them with the help of steroids or genetically enhanced muscles. Of course, the roles of effort and enhancement will be a matter of degree. But as the role of enhancement increases, our admiration for the achievement fades—or, rather, our admiration for the achievements shifts from the player to his pharmacist. This suggests that our moral response to enhancement is a response to the diminished agency of the person whose achievement is enhanced.

Though there is much to be said for this argument, I do not think the main problem with enhancement and genetic engineering is that they undermine effort and erode human agency. The deeper danger is that they represent a kind of hyperagency—a Promethean aspiration to remake nature, including human nature, to serve our purposes and satisfy our desires. The problem is not the drift to mechanism but the drive to mastery. And what the drive to mastery misses and may even

destroy is an appreciation of the gifted character of human powers and achievements.

To acknowledge the giftedness of life is to recognize that our talents and powers are not wholly our own doing, despite the effort we expend to develop and to exercise them. It is also to recognize that not everything in the world is open to whatever use we may desire or devise. Appreciating the gifted quality of life constrains the Promethean project and conduces to a certain humility. It is in part a religious sensibility. But its resonance reaches beyond religion.

It is difficult to account for what we admire about human activity and achievement without drawing upon some version of this idea. Consider two types of athletic achievement. We appreciate players like Pete Rose, who are not blessed with great natural gifts but who manage, through striving, grit, and determination, to excel in their sport. But we also admire players like Joe DiMaggio, who display natural gifts with grace and effortlessness. Now, suppose we learned that both players took performance-enhancing drugs. Whose turn to drugs would we find more deeply disillusioning? Which aspect of the athletic ideal—effort or gift—would be more deeply offended?

Some might say effort: the problem with drugs is that they provide a shortcut, a way to win without striving. But striving is not the point of sports; excellence is. And excellence consists at least partly in the display of natural talents and gifts that are no doing of the athlete who possesses them. This is an uncomfortable fact for democratic societies. We want to believe that success, in sports and in life, is something we earn, not something we inherit. Natural gifts, and the admiration they inspire, embarrass the meritocratic faith; they cast doubt on the conviction that praise and rewards flow from effort alone. In the face of this embarrassment we inflate the moral significance of striving, and depreciate giftedness. This distortion can be seen, for example, in network-television coverage of the Olympics, which focuses less on the feats the athletes perform than on heartrending stories of the hardships they have over-come and the struggles they have waged to triumph over an injury or a difficult upbringing or political turmoil in their native land.

But effort isn't everything. No one believes that a mediocre basketball player who works and trains even harder than Michael Jordan deserves greater acclaim or a bigger contract. The real problem with genetically altered athletes is that they corrupt athletic competition as a human activity that honors the cultivation and display of natural talents. From this standpoint, enhancement can be seen as the ultimate expression of the ethic of effort and willfulness—a kind of high-tech striving. The ethic of willfulness and the biotechnological powers it now enlists are arrayed against the claims of giftedness.

The ethic of giftedness, under siege in sports, persists in the practice of parenting. But here, too, bioengineering and genetic enhancement threaten to dislodge it. To appreciate children as gifts is to accept them as they come, not as objects of our design or products of our will or instruments of our ambition. Parental love is not contingent on the talents and attributes a child happens to have. We choose our friends and spouses at least partly on the basis of qualities we find attractive. But we do not choose our children. Their qualities are unpredictable, and even the most conscientious parents cannot be held wholly responsible for the kind of children they have. That is why parenthood, more than other human relationships, teaches what the theologian William F. May calls an "openness to the unbidden."

May's resonant phrase helps us see that the deepest moral objection to enhancement lies less in the perfection it seeks than in the human disposition it expresses and promotes. The problem is not that parents usurp the autonomy of a child they design. The problem lies in the hubris of the designing parents, in their drive to master the mystery of birth. Even if this disposition did not make parents tyrants to their children, it would disfigure the relation between parent and child, and deprive the parent of the humility and enlarged human sympathies that an openness to the unbidden can cultivate.

To appreciate children as gifts or blessings is not, of course, to be passive in the face of illness or disease. Medical intervention to cure or prevent illness or restore the injured to health does not desecrate nature but honors it. Healing sickness or injury does not override a child's natural capacities but permits them to flourish.

Nor does the sense of life as a gift mean that parents must shrink from shaping and directing the development of their child. Just as athletes and artists have an obligation to cultivate their talents, so parents have an obligation to cultivate their children, to help them discover and develop their talents and gifts. As May points out, parents give their children two kinds of love: accepting love and transforming love. Accepting love affirms the being of the child, whereas transforming love seeks the well-being of the child. Each aspect corrects the excesses of the other, he writes: "Attachment becomes too quietistic if it slackens into mere acceptance of the child as he is." Parents have a duty to promote their children's excellence.

These days, however, overly ambitious parents are prone to get carried away with transforming love—promoting and demanding all manner of accomplishments from their children, seeking perfection. "Parents find it difficult to maintain an equilibrium between the two sides of love," May observes. "Accepting love, without transforming love, slides into indulgence and finally neglect. Transforming love, without accepting love, badgers and finally rejects." May finds in these competing impulses a parallel with modern science: it, too, engages us in beholding the given world, studying and savoring it, and also in molding the world, transforming and perfecting it.

The mandate to mold our children, to cultivate and improve them, complicates the case against enhancement. We usually admire parents who seek the best for their children, who spare no effort to help them achieve happiness and success. Some parents confer advantages on their children by enrolling them in expensive schools, hiring private tutors, sending them to tennis camp, providing them with piano lessons, ballet lessons, swimming lessons, SAT-prep courses, and so on. If it is permissible and even admirable for parents to help their children in these ways, why isn't it equally admirable for parents to use whatever genetic technologies may emerge (provided they are safe) to enhance their children's intelligence, musical ability, or athletic prowess?

The defenders of enhancement are right to this extent: improving children through genetic engineering is similar in spirit to the heavily managed, high-pressure child-rearing that is now common. But this similarity does not vindicate genetic enhancement. On the contrary, it highlights a problem with the trend toward hyperparenting. One conspicuous example of this trend is sports-crazed parents bent on making champions of their children. Another is the frenzied drive of overbearing parents to mold and manage their children's academic careers.

As the pressure for performance increases, so does the need to help distractible children concentrate on the task at hand. This may be why diagnoses of attention deficit and hyperactivity disorder have increased so sharply. Lawrence Diller, a pediatrician and the author of *Running on Ritalin,* estimates that five to six percent of American children under eighteen (a total of four to five million kids) are currently prescribed Ritalin, Adderall, and other stimulants, the treatment of choice for ADHD. (Stimulants counteract hyperactivity by making it easier to focus and sustain attention.) The number of Ritalin prescriptions for children and adolescents has tripled over the past decade, but not all users suffer from attention disorders or hyperactivity. High school and college students have learned that prescription stimulants improve concentration for those with normal attention spans, and some buy or borrow their classmates' drugs to enhance their performance on the SAT or other exams. Since stimulants work for both medical and nonmedical purposes, they raise the same moral questions posed by other technologies of enhancement.

However those questions are resolved, the debate reveals the cultural distance we have traveled since the debate over marijuana, LSD, and other drugs a generation ago. Unlike the drugs of the 1960s and 1970s Ritalin and Adderall are not for checking out but for buckling down, not for beholding the world and taking it in but for molding the world and fitting in. We used to speak of nonmedical drug use as "recreational." That term no longer applies. The steroids and stimulants that figure in the enhancement debate are not a source of recreation but a bid for compliance—a way of answering a competitive society's demand to improve our performance and perfect our nature. This demand for performance and perfection animates the impulse to rail against the given. It is the deepest source of the moral trouble with enhancement.

Some see a clear line between genetic enhancement and other ways that people seek improvement in their children and themselves. Genetic manipulation seems somehow worse—more intrusive, more sinister—than other ways of enhancing performance and seeking success. But morally speaking, the difference is less significant than it seems. Bioengineering gives us reason to question the low-tech, high-pressure child-rearing practices we commonly accept. The hyperparenting familiar in our time represents an anxious excess of mastery and dominion that misses the sense of life as a gift. This draws it disturbingly close to eugenics.

The shadow of eugenics hangs over today's debates about genetic engineering and enhancement. Critics of genetic engineering argue that human cloning, enhancement, and the quest for designer children are nothing more than "privatized" or "free-market" eugenics. Defenders of enhancement reply that genetic choices freely made are not really eugenic—at least not in the pejorative sense. To remove the coercion, they argue, is to remove the very thing that makes eugenic policies repugnant.

Sorting out the lesson of eugenics is another way of wrestling with the ethics of enhancement. The Nazis gave eugenics a bad name. But what, precisely, was wrong with it? Was the old eugenics objectionable only insofar as it was coercive? Or is there something inherently wrong with the resolve to deliberately design our progeny's traits?

James Watson, the biologist who, with Francis Crick, discovered the structure of DNA, sees nothing wrong with genetic engineering and enhancement, provided they are freely chosen rather than state-imposed. And yet Watson's language contains more than a whiff of the old eugenic sensibility. "If you really are stupid, I would call that a disease," he recently told *The Times* of London. "The lower 10 percent who really have difficulty, even in elementary school, what's the cause of it? A lot of people would like to say, 'Well, poverty, things like that.'"

It probably isn't. So I'd like to get rid of that, to help the lower 10 percent." A few years ago Watson stirred controversy by saying that if a gene for homosexuality were discovered, a woman should be free to abort a fetus that carried it. When his remark provoked an uproar, he replied that he was not singling out gays but asserting a principle: women should be free to abort fetuses for any reason of genetic preference—for example, if the child would be dyslexic, or lacking musical talent, or too short to play basketball.

Watson's scenarios are clearly objectionable to those for whom all abortion is an unspeakable crime. But for those who do not subscribe to the pro-life position, these scenarios raise a hard question: If it is morally troubling to contemplate abortion to avoid a gay child or a dyslexic one, doesn't this suggest that something is wrong with acting on any eugenic preference, even when no state coercion is involved?

Consider the market in eggs and sperm. The advent of artificial insemination allows prospective parents to shop for gametes with the genetic traits they desire in their off-spring. It is a less predictable way to design children than cloning or pre-implantation genetic screening, but it offers a good example of a procreative practice in which the old eugenics meets the new consumerism. A few years ago some Ivy League newspapers ran an ad seeking an egg from a woman who was at least five feet ten inches tall and athletic, had no major family medical problems, and had a combined SAT score of 1400 or above. The ad offered $50,000 for an egg from a donor with these traits. More recently a Web site was launched claiming to auction eggs from fashion models whose photos appeared on the site, at starting bids of $15,000 to $150,000.

On what grounds, if any, is the egg market morally objectionable? Since no one is forced to buy or sell, it cannot be wrong for reasons of coercion. Some might worry that hefty prices would exploit poor women by presenting them with an offer they couldn't refuse. But the designer eggs that fetch the highest prices are likely to be sought from the privileged, not the poor. If the market for premium eggs gives us moral qualms, this, too, shows

that concerns about eugenics are not put to rest by freedom of choice.

A tale of two sperm banks helps explain why. The Repository for Germinal Choice, one of America's first sperm banks, was not a commercial enterprise. It was opened in 1980 by Robert Graham, a philanthropist dedicated to improving the world's "germ plasm" and counteracting the rise of "retrograde humans." His plan was to collect the sperm of Nobel Prize-winning scientists and make it available to women of high intelligence, in hopes of breeding super-smart babies. But Graham had trouble persuading Nobel laureates to donate their sperm for his bizarre scheme, and so settled for sperm from young scientists of high promise. His sperm bank closed in 1999.

In contrast, California Cryobank, one of the world's leading sperm banks, is a for-profit company with no overt eugenic mission. Cappy Rothman, M.D., a co-founder of the firm, has nothing but disdain for Graham's eugenics, although the standards Cryobank imposes on the sperm it recruits are exacting. Cryobank has offices in Cambridge. Massachusetts, between Harvard and MIT, and in Palo Alto, California, near Stanford. It advertises for donors in campus newspapers (compensation up to $900 a month), and accepts less than five percent of the men who apply. Cryobank's marketing materials play up the prestigious source of its sperm. Its catalogue provides detailed information about the physical characteristics of each donor, along with his ethnic origin and college major. For an extra fee prospective customers can buy the results of a test that assesses the donor's temperament and character type. Rothman reports that Cryobank's ideal sperm donor is six feet tall, with brown eyes, blond hair, and dimples, and has a college degree—not because the company wants to propagate those traits, but because those are the traits his customers want: "If our customers wanted high school dropouts, we would give them high school dropouts."

Not everyone objects to marketing sperm. But anyone who is troubled by the eugenic aspect of the Nobel Prize sperm bank should be equally troubled by Cryobank, consumer-driven though it be. What, after all, is the moral difference between designing children according to an explicit eugenic purpose and designing children according to the dictates of the market? Whether the aim is to improve humanity's "germ plasm" or to cater to consumer preferences, both practices are eugenic insofar as both make children into products of deliberate design.

A number of political philosophers call for a new "liberal eugenics." They argue that a moral distinction can be drawn between the old eugenic policies and genetic enhancements that do not restrict the autonomy of the child. "While old-fashioned authoritarian eugenicists sought to produce citizens out of a single centrally designed mould," writes Nicholas Agar, "the distinguishing mark of the new liberal eugenics is state neutrality." Government may not tell parents what sort of children to design, and parents may engineer in their children only those traits that improve their capacities without biasing their choice of life plans. A recent text on genetics and justice, written by the bioethicists Allen Buchanan, Dan W. Brock, Norman Daniels, and Daniel Wikler, offers a similar view. The "bad reputation of eugenics," they write, is due to practices that "might be avoidable in a future eugenic program." The problem with the old eugenics was that its burdens fell disproportionately on the weak and the poor, who were unjustly sterilized and segregated. But provided that the benefits and burdens of genetic improvement are fairly distributed, these bioethicists argue, eugenic measures are unobjectionable and may even be morally required.

The libertarian philosopher Robert Nozick proposed a "genetic supermarket" that would enable parents to order children by design without imposing a single design on the society as a whole: "This supermarket system has the great virtue that it involves no centralized decision fixing the future human type(s)."

Even the leading philosopher of American liberalism, John Rawls, in his classic *A Theory of Justice* (1971), offered a brief endorsement of noncoercive eugenics. Even in a society that agrees to share the benefits and burdens of the genetic lottery, it is "in the interest of each to have greater natural assets," Rawls wrote. "This enables him to pursue a preferred plan of life." The parties to the social contract "want to insure for their descendants the best genetic endowment (assuming their own to be fixed)." Eugenic policies are therefore not only permissible but required as a matter of justice. "Thus over time a society is to take steps at least to preserve the general level of natural abilities and to prevent the diffusion of serious defects."

But removing the coercion does not vindicate eugenics. The problem with eugenics and genetic engineering is that they represent the one-sided triumph of willfulness over giftedness, of dominion over reverence, of molding over beholding. Why, we may wonder, should we worry about this triumph? Why not shake off our unease about genetic enhancement as so much superstition? What would be lost if biotechnology dissolved our sense of giftedness?

From a religious standpoint the answer is clear. To believe that our talents and powers are wholly our own doing is to misunderstand our place in creation, to confuse our role with God's. Religion is not the only source of reasons to care about giftedness, however. The moral stakes can also be described in secular terms. If bioengineering made the myth of the "self-made man" come true, it would be difficult to view our talents as gifts for which we are indebted, rather than as achievements for which we are responsible. This would transform three key features of our moral landscape: humility, responsibility, and solidarity.

In a social world that prizes mastery and control, parenthood is a school for humility. That we care deeply about our children and yet cannot choose the kind we want teaches parents to be open to the unbidden. Such openness is a disposition worth affirming, not only within families but in the wider world as well. It invites us to abide the unexpected, to live with dissonance, to rein in the impulse to control. A *Gattaca*-like world in which parents became accustomed to specifying the sex and genetic traits of their children would be a world inhospitable to the unbidden, a gated community writ large. The awareness that our talents and abilities are not wholly our own doing restrains our tendency toward hubris.

Though some maintain that genetic enhancement erodes human agency by overriding effort, the real problem is the explosion, not the erosion, of responsibility. As humility gives way, responsibility expands to daunting proportions. We attribute less to chance and more to choice. Parents become responsible for choosing, or failing to choose, the right traits for their children. Athletes become responsible for acquiring, or failing to acquire, the talents that will help their teams win.

One of the blessings of seeing ourselves as creatures of nature, God, or fortune is that we are not wholly responsible for the way we are. The more we become masters of our genetic endowments, the greater the burden we bear for the talents we have and the way we perform. Today when a basketball player misses a rebound, his coach can blame him for being out of position. Tomorrow the coach may blame him for being too short. Even now the use of performance-enhancing drugs in professional sports is subtly transforming the expectations players have for one another; on some teams players who take the field free from amphetamines or other stimulants are criticized for "playing naked."

The more alive we are to the chanced nature of our lot, the more reason we have to share our fate with others. Consider insurance. Since people do not know whether or when various ills will befall them, they pool their risk by buying health insurance and life insurance. As life plays itself out, the healthy wind up subsidizing the unhealthy, and those who live to a ripe old age wind up subsidizing the families of those who die before their time. Even without a sense of mutual obligation, people pool their risks and resources and share one another's fate.

But insurance markets mimic solidarity only insofar as people do not know or control their own risk factors. Suppose genetic testing advanced to the point where it could reliably predict each person's medical future and life expectancy. Those confident of good health and long life would opt out of the pool, causing other people's premiums to skyrocket. The solidarity of insurance would disappear as those with good genes fled the actuarial company of those with bad ones.

The fear that insurance companies would use genetic data to assess risks and set premiums recently led the Senate to vote to prohibit genetic discrimination in health insurance. But the bigger danger, admittedly more speculative, is that genetic enhancement, if routinely practiced, would make it harder to foster the moral sentiments that social solidarity requires.

Why, after all, do the successful owe anything to the least-advantaged members of society? The best answer to this question leans heavily on the notion of giftedness. The natural talents that enable the successful to flourish are not their own doing but, rather, their good fortune—a result of the genetic lottery. If our genetic endowments are gifts, rather than achievements for which we can claim credit, it is a mistake and a conceit to assume that we are entitled to the full measure of the bounty they reap in a market economy. We therefore have an obligation to share this bounty with those who, through no fault of their own, lack comparable gifts.

A lively sense of the contingency of our gifts—a consciousness that none of us is wholly responsible for his or her success—saves a meritocratic society from sliding into the smug assumption that the rich are rich because they are more deserving than the poor. Without this, the successful would become even more likely than they are now to view themselves as self-made and self-sufficient, and hence wholly responsible for their success. Those at the bottom of society would be viewed not as disadvantaged, and thus worthy of a measure of compensation, but as simply unfit, and thus worthy of eugenic repair. The meritocracy, less chastened by chance, would become harder, less forgiving. As perfect genetic knowledge would end the simulacrum of solidarity in insurance markets, so perfect genetic control would erode the actual solidarity that arises when men and women reflect on the contingency of their talents and fortunes.

Thirty-five years ago Robert L. Sinsheimer, a molecular biologist at the California Institute of Technology, glimpsed the shape of things to come. In an article titled "The Prospect of Designed Genetic Change" he argued that freedom of choice would vindicate the new genetics, and set it apart from the discredited eugenics of old.

To implement the older eugenics would have required a massive social programme carried out over many generations. Such a programme could not have been initiated without the consent and co-operation of a major fraction of the population, and would have been continuously subject to social control. In contrast, the new eugenics could, at least in principle, he implemented on a quite individual basis, in one generation, and subject to no existing restrictions.

According to Sinsheimer, the new eugenics would be voluntary rather than coerced, and also more humane. Rather than segregating and eliminating the unfit, it would improve them. "The old eugenics would have required a continual selection for breeding of the fit, and a culling of the unfit," he wrote. "The new eugenics would permit in principle the conversion of all the unfit to the highest genetic level."

Sinsheimer's paean to genetic engineering caught the heady, Promethean self-image of the age. He wrote hopefully of rescuing "the losers in that chromosomal lottery that so firmly channels our human destinies," including not only those born with genetic defects but also "the 50,000,000 'normal' Americans with an IQ of less than 90." But he also saw that something bigger than improving on nature's "mindless, age-old throw of dice" was at stake. Implicit in technologies of genetic intervention was a more exalted place for human beings in the cosmos. "As we enlarge man's freedom, we diminish his constraints and that which he must accept as given," he wrote, Copernicus and Darwin had "demoted man from his bright glory at the focal point of the universe," but the new biology would restore his central role. In the mirror of our genetic knowledge we would see ourselves as more than a link in the chain of evolution: "We can be the agent of transition to a whole new pitch of evolution. This is a cosmic event."

There is something appealing, even intoxicating, about a vision of human freedom unfettered by the given. It may even be the case that the allure of that vision played a part in summoning the genomic age into being. It is often assumed that the powers of enhancement we now possess arose as an inadvertent by-product of biomedical progress—the genetic revolution came, so to speak, to cure disease, and stayed to tempt us with the prospect of enhancing our performance, designing our children, and perfecting our nature. That may have the story backwards. It is more plausible to view genetic engineering as the ultimate expression of our resolve to see ourselves astride the world, the masters of our nature. But that promise of mastery is flawed. It threatens to banish our appreciation of life as a gift, and to leave us with nothing to affirm or behold outside our own will.

CLAIRE HOPE CUMMINGS

II.14

Trespass

A great deal of attention has been given to the prospect of human genetic engineering, but comparatively little notice has been paid to the growing use of genetic engineering technologies on plants and animals. For more than a decade, food products made from genetically modified organisms (GMOs) have been on American supermarket shelves, and millions of people have eaten them with no apparent ill effects. So what is the fuss about when environmentalists and some others warn the public about the dangers of so-called "Frankenfoods"? Are these fears merely the concerns of overwrought Luddites, or might there be some good reasons to be concerned about the genetic manipulation of nonhuman organisms? Lawyer and environmental journalist Claire Hope Cummings describes the history of the development of genetically modified foods, paying particular attention to the lack of regulatory oversight by the U.S. government prior to their release into the general food supply. The rapid introduction into the market of GMOs was made possible by "regulatory capture" of the government by agribusiness interests coupled with the increasing trend toward privately funded research at our nation's leading universities. In the process, scant attention was paid to the risk of genetic contamination of non-GMO plant species by genetic materials from their bioengineered cousins. Cummings thinks that GMO foods have been literally forced down our throats by big business, with little or no way for the public to opt out of this uncontrolled experiment whose ultimate effects on human health and the environment remain unknown.

Focus Questions

1. What does Cummings describe as "the central dogma" of modern molecular biology? Is there evidence to suggest that this belief might turn out to be false?
2. What is the significance of the "revolving door" between government and agribusiness? How does this help explain why the federal government decided not to require labels on food products containing GMOs?
3. Does the fact that private corporations fund much of the academic research concerning the safety of GMOs concern you? Why or why not?
4. Evaluate Cummings' thesis that genetic contamination represents a "trespass" on the commons in light of the view of the commons articulated by the International Forum on Globalization (selection II.4). Are you troubled by the trend toward privatizing what was formerly regarded as the common inheritance of all humans? Explain why or why not.

Keywords

academic freedom, agribusiness, genetic contamination, genetically modified organisms (GMOs), molecular biology, regulatory oversight, substantial equivalence, transgenic instability

---

HIDDEN INSIDE HILGARD HALL, one of the oldest buildings on the campus of the University of California at Berkeley, is a photograph that no one is supposed to see. It's a picture of a crippled and contorted corncob that was not created by nature, or even by agriculture, but by genetic engineering.[1] The cob is kept in a plastic bin called "the monster box," a collection of biological curiosities put together by someone who works in a secure biotechnology research facility.

What the photo shows is a cob that apparently started growing normally, then turned into another part of the corn plant, then returned to forming kernels, then went back to another form—twisting back and forth as if it could not make up its mind about what it was. It was produced by the same recombinant DNA technology that is used to create the genetically modified organisms (GMOs) that

From "Trespass" by Claire Hope Cummings from *World Watch* magazine, January/February 2005. Copyright © 2004 Worldwatch Institute. Reprinted by permission.

are in our everyday foods. When I saw this photo, I knew it was saying something very important about genetic engineering. I thought it should be published. But the person who owns it is frankly afraid of how the biotechnology industry might react, and would not agree. In order to get permission even to describe the photo for this article, I had to promise not to reveal its owner's identity.

What the distorted corncob represents is a mute challenge to the industry's claim that this technology is precise, predictable, and safe. But that this challenge should be kept hidden, and that a scientist who works at a public university should feel too intimidated to discuss it openly, told me that something more than just a scientific question was being raised. After all, if the new agricultural biotech were really safe and effective, why would the industry work so hard—as indeed it does—to keep its critics cowed and the public uninformed? Was there something about the way genetic engineering was developed, about how it works, that was inviting a closer look—a look that the industry would rather we not take? I had gone to Berkeley to see for myself what was going on behind biotechnology.

The University of California at Berkeley ("Cal") is the stage on which much of the story of genetic engineering has played out over the last 25 years. The biotechnology industry was born here in the San Francisco Bay area, and nurtured by scientists who worked at Berkeley and nearby universities. Critical controversies over the role genetic engineering and related research should have in society have erupted here. Even the architecture of the campus reflects the major scientific and policy divisions that plague this technology. Two buildings, in particular, mirror the two very different versions of biology that emerged in the last half of the twentieth century, and reflect two very different visions for agriculture in the future.

Hilgard Hall was built in 1918, at a time when mastering the classical form and celebrating beauty were important, perhaps even integral, to the accepted function of a building. Hilgard's facade is exquisitely decorated with friezes depicting sheaves of wheat, beehives, bunches of grapes, cornucopias, and bas relief sculptures of cow heads surrounded with wreaths of fruit. Above the entrance, carved in

huge capital letters are the words, "TO RESCUE FOR HUMAN SOCIETY THE NATIVE VALUES OF RURAL LIFE." The massive front door opens to a grand two-story hall graced with granite, marble, and carved brass. But behind that elegant entrance is a building left in disrepair. Getting around inside Hilgard means navigating worn marble staircases and dark corridors laced with exposed pipes and heating ducts. The room where the monster box photograph is kept is small and dank. This building is home to the "old" biology—the careful observation of life, living systems, and their complex interactions. Being inside Hilgard is a visceral lesson in how Cal is neglecting the classic study of the intimate inter-relationships among agriculture, the environment, and human society.

Nearby, and standing in stark contrast to Hilgard's faded splendor, is a newer, modern office building, Koshland Hall. Koshland is not unattractive, with its pitched blue tile roof lines and bright white walls lined with blue steel windows, but it was built in the mid-1990s in a functional style that, like most new campus buildings, has all the charm and poetry of an ice cube. The interior is clean and well lit. Next to office doors hang plaques that name the corporations or foundations that fund the activities inside. This is the home of the "new biology"—the utilitarian view that life is centered in DNA and molecules can be manipulated at will. Molecular biology is clearly doing well at Cal.

Koshland Hall was named after a distinguished member of the faculty, Daniel Koshland, former editor of the journal *Science* and chair of Berkeley's Department of Biochemistry, now a professor emeritus. He has the unique distinction of having been present at the two most important scientific revolutions of our time: he participated both in the Manhattan Project, which developed nuclear weapons, and in the early development of molecular biology. He is credited with "transforming" the biological sciences at Berkeley.

The New Biology

One hundred years ago, no one had heard of a "gene." The word was not recognized until 1909, and even after that it remained an abstraction for decades.

At the time, scientists and others were making an effort to find a material basis for life, particularly heritability, the fundamental function of life. The story of genetic engineering in the United States begins with the decision to identify genes as the basis of life. But the ideological roots of this story go even deeper, into the nation's earlier history and attachment to the ideas of manifest destiny, eugenics, and social engineering.

Early in the twentieth century, the new "science" of sociology made its appearance—along with the highly appealing belief that social problems were amenable to scientific solutions. In time, sociology began to combine with genetic science, giving strong impetus to technocratic forms of social control, and particularly to eugenics—the belief that the human race could be improved by selective breeding. Until the 1930s, the science of genetics had not developed much beyond Mendelian principles of heredity, but eugenics was already being promoted as the solution to social problems. As the idea that genes determined traits in people took hold, eugenics twisted it to foster the concept that there were "good" genes and "bad" genes, good and bad traits. Eugenics eventually gained a powerful foothold both in the popular imagination and in the U.S. government, as well as in Nazi Germany. Even today, these notions underlie the decisions biotechnologists make about what genes and traits are beneficial, what organisms are engineered, and who gets to decide how this technology will be used.

According to Lily Kay, an assistant professor of the history of science at Massachusetts Institute of Technology, genetic engineering came about as the result of the concerted effort of a few scientists, who, along with their academic and philanthropic sponsors, had a shared vision about how they could use genetics to reshape science and society. In her book *The Molecular Vision of Life: Caltech, the Rockefeller Foundation, and the Rise of the New Biology,* Kay writes that this vision was not so much about underlying biological principles as it was about social values. The new biology that evolved from this thinking was founded on a strong belief in "industrial capitalism" and its perceived mandate for "science-based social intervention." The potential

for this idea, and the intentional strategy to use it for social purposes was clearly understood from the outset, says Kay. The developers of "molecular biology" (a term coined by the Rockefeller Foundation) were confident that it would offer them a previously unimagined power and control over both nature and society.

Science was molded to this agenda in 1945, when Vannevar Bush, the head of President Franklin D. Roosevelt's wartime Office of Scientific Research and Development, wrote "Science, The Endless Frontier"—a landmark report that outlined how science could better serve the private sector. As Kay tells the story, at that point the search for a science-based social agenda began in earnest. It was funded and directed by business corporations and foundations acting together as "quasi-public entities" using both private and public funds to harness "the expertise of the human sciences to stem what was perceived as the nation's social and biological decay and help realize the vision of America's destiny." Eventually, the combined efforts of corporate, academic, and government interests began to bear fruit and "the boundary between individual and corporate self-interest, between private and public control, would be increasingly blurred."[2]

The story of how James Watson and Francis Crick described the structure of the DNA helix in 1953 is well known. Less known, but of considerable consequence, is what followed. With little hesitation, they announced that DNA is "the secret of life"—and began to promote what was to become known as "the central dogma"—the notion that genetic information flows in only one direction, from DNA to RNA to a protein, and that this process directly determines an organism's characteristics. This dogma was, as described by geneticist Mae-Wan Ho, author of *Living with the Fluid Genome,* "just another way of saying that organisms are hardwired in their genetic makeup and the environment has little influence on the structure and function of the genes." In her book, Dr. Ho argues that the central dogma is too simplistic. She observes that not all DNA "codes for proteins" and that the genome is fluid and interactive. Similarly, in a 1992 *Harper's Magazine* article, "Unraveling the DNA Myth: The Spurious Foundation of Genetic Engineering,"

Queens College biologist Barry Commoner writes that "the central dogma is the premise that an organism's genome—its total complement of DNA genes—should fully account for its characteristic assemblage of inherited traits. The premise, unhappily, is false."

Still, the singular view of "life as DNA" dominated biology in the late twentieth century, in part because its very simplicity provided the biological rationale for engineering DNA. Technological advances in other fields—the study of enzymes that cut DNA, and bacteria that recombine it—were teamed up with high speed computers that provided the computational muscle needed. And yet, even as the old biology became the "new and improved" molecular biology, it was promoted with a social pedigree about how it would serve the public. Its mandate was the same one that was used to colonize the "new world" and to settle the Wild West—the promise that *this* progress would provide everyone a better life.

Judging by his comments, if James Watson had had his way, research would have proceeded undeterred by any concerns over the hazards that genetic engineering posed. He said he'd always felt that the "certain promise" of this revolutionary new technology far outweighed its "uncertain peril." But others, such as Paul Berg of Stanford University, were calling for a more measured approach. In 1975 Berg joined other scientists concerned about the risks of genetic engineering in a meeting held at the Asilomar conference center, near Monterey, California. It was a rare collective action, with participants coming from a spectrum of universities, government agencies, and research institutes.

In his introductory remarks, David Baltimore of MIT noted that the participants were there to discuss "a new technique of molecular biology," one that "appears to allow us to outdo the standard events of evolution by making combinations of genes which could be unique in natural history." He went on to say that they should design a strategy to go forward that would "maximize the benefits and minimize the hazards." They produced a 35-page report that detailed their concerns about creating new pathogens and toxins, the emergence of allergens and disease vectors that could cause cancer or immune disorders, as well as "unpredictable adverse consequences" and the specter of "wide ecological damages."

Then, in the last hours of the meeting, on the very last night, a couple of the participants pointed out that the public had the right to assess and limit this technology. What happened next was pivotal. These scientists believed they were entitled to benefit from the extraordinary potential of genetic engineering and they argued that they could find technological fixes for any problems that might emerge. Susan Wright, author of *Molecular Politics,* a history of biotech regulatory policy, recalls that there was virtual unanimity for the idea that scientists would create a central role for themselves in policymaking—to the exclusion of society in general. From then on, Wright says, this "reductionist discourse" became doctrine. Asilomar defined the boundaries of public discourse, and the questions about potential hazards that were raised there went unanswered.

Public Policy: The Endless Frontier

The inoculation that Asilomar gave biotechnology against the ravages of government control was given a booster shot a few years later when executives from the Monsanto Corporation visited the Reagan White House. The industry sought and obtained assurance that they would not be blindsided by regulation. After all, these early developers of GMOs were agrochemical companies like Dow Chemical, DuPont, Novartis, and Monsanto, who were the sources of pervasive chemical pollution that resulted in the environmental laws that were passed in the 1960s. This time, they were intent on getting to the lawmakers before the public did.

The resulting "regulatory reform" was announced in 1992, by then Vice President Dan Quayle, at a press conference in the Indian Treaty Room near his office. It was custom-made for the industry. The new policy left just enough oversight in place to give the industry political cover, so that they could offer assurances to the public that the government was watching out for the public interest when in fact it was not. The regulatory system that was adopted, which is essentially what is still in place today, is basically voluntary and passive. It's a "don't look, don't tell" arrangement whereby the industry doesn't tell the government about problems with its products and the government doesn't look for them.

Quayle said that government "will ensure that biotech products will receive the same oversight as other products, instead of being hampered by unnecessary regulation." The rationale for this policy was a concept called "substantial equivalence," which means that GMOs are not substantially different than conventional crops and foods. The science journal *Nature* dubbed substantial equivalence a "pseudo-scientific concept . . . created primarily to provide an excuse for not requiring biochemical and toxicological tests." Nevertheless, it was adopted by all three agencies responsible for food and agriculture—the United States Department of Agriculture, the Environmental Protection Agency, and the Food and Drug Administration—and it is the reason there have been no safety studies of GMO foods, no post-market monitoring, no labels, no new laws, no agency coordination, and no independent review.

Henry Miller, head of biotechnology at FDA from 1979 to 1994, told the *New York Times* in 2001 that government agencies did "exactly what big agribusiness had asked them to do and told them to do." During Miller's tenure at the FDA, staff scientists were writing memos that called for further testing and warning that there were concerns about food safety. But the man in charge of policy development at FDA was Michael Taylor, a former lawyer for Monsanto. And, according to Steven Druker, a public-interest lawyer who obtained three of these internal FDA memos, under Taylor "references to the unintended negative effects of bioengineering were progressively deleted from drafts of the policy statement."

Taylor went on to become an administrator at the USDA in charge of food safety and biotechnology, and then became a vice-president at Monsanto. All three agencies continue to employ people who are either associated with biotech companies or who formerly worked for them. At least 22 cases of this "revolving door" between government and industry have been documented. Biotech lawyers

and lobbyists serve in policy-making positions, leave government for high paying jobs with industry, and in some cases return to government to defend industry interests again. Still, dismantling regulatory oversight was only part of industry's overall strategy to commercialize GMOs.

Breaking the Biological Barriers

All the big agrochemical seed companies—DuPont, Monsanto, Pioneer Hi-Bred, and Dekalb—were betting the farm on genetic technologies in the 1980s. But just one crop, corn, stood in their way. Corn was becoming the "Holy Grail" of agricultural biotechnology because these companies knew that if this idea was ever going to be commercially viable, it had to work with corn—which is of central importance to American agriculture. As they raced to find a way to genetically engineer corn, they perfected the complicated steps required to transform plants into transgenic crops. It all came together in June 1988, when Pioneer Hi-Bred patented the first viable and replicable transgenic corn plant.

In the end, the secret of recombining DNA was found not so much through a process of tedious, repetitive experimentation as of that traditional, Wild-West way of getting what you want—using stealth and brute force. The primary problem genetic engineers faced was how to get engineered DNA into target cells without destroying them. For some plants, like tobacco and soybeans, the problem was solved by the use of stealth. A soil microbe that produces cancer-like growths in plants was recruited to "infect" cells with new modified DNA. This *agrobacterium* formed a non-lethal hole in the wall of a plant cell that allowed the new DNA to sneak in. But that method did not work with corn. For corn, a more forceful cell invasion technique was called for, one that resulted in the invention of the gene gun.

One day in December 1983, during the Christmas break at Cornell University, three men put on booties, gowns, and hair coverings, picked up a gun, and entered the university's National Submicron Facility. John Sanford, a plant breeder at Cornell, and his colleagues, the head of the facility and a member of his staff, were about to shoot a bunch of onions to smithereens. For years, they had been looking for ways to speed up the conventional plant breeding process using genetic transformation techniques. Like other researchers, they had had difficulty forcing DNA fragments through the relatively thick walls of plant cells. They'd tried using lasers to drill mini-holes in cell walls and everything from ion beams to microscopic needles to electric shocks, but these methods either failed to deliver the payload or destroyed the cells in the process.

Then one day, while waging a backyard battle with some pesky squirrels, Sanford got the idea of using a gun. He figured out how to load the gun with specially coated microscopic beads, and then he and his friends tried the idea out on the onions. Soon, pieces of onion were splattered everywhere and the smell of onions and gun powder permeated the air. They kept up this odorous massacre until they figured out how to make it work. It seemed implausible, even laughable, at the time. But the gene gun, which uses .22-caliber ballistics to shoot DNA into cells, is now found in biotechnology laboratories all over the world.

Although it is clearly a "hit or miss" technique, transferring DNA is actually straightforward. The tricky part is getting the target plant to accept the new genes. That requires overcoming billions of years of evolutionary resistance that was specifically designed to keep foreign DNA out. You simply can't get a fish and a strawberry to mate, no matter how hard you try—or at least you couldn't until now. Genetic engineers are now able to take a gene that produces a natural anti-freeze from an arctic flounder and put it into a strawberry plant so that its fruit is frost resistant. But this feat can only be accomplished through the use of specially designed genes that facilitate the process. Along with the trait gene, every GMO also contains genetically engineered vectors and markers, antibiotic resistance genes, viral promoters made from the cauliflower mosaic virus, genetic switches and other constructs that enable the "transformation" process.

Once all these genes are inserted, where they end up and what they may do are unknown. The only precise part of this technique is the identification and extraction of the trait DNA from the donor organism. After that, it's a biological free-for-all. In genetic engineering, failure is the rule. The way you get GMO crops to look and act like normal crops is to do thousands and thousands of insertions, grow the ones that survive out, and then see what you get. What you finally select for further testing and release are those "happy accidents" that appear to work. The rest of the millions of plants, animals and other organisms that are subjected to this process are sacrificed or thrown out—or end up in some lab technician's monster box.

Process, Not Product

The public controversy over GMOs has focused largely on the products, on how they are marketed, and on what is planted where. But it now appears that the process used to make them, and the novel genetic constructs used in the process, may constitute greater threats to human and environmental health than the products themselves. There are documented reports of allergenic reactions to GMO foods. According to a report in *Nature Biotechnology,* for example, the commonly used cauliflower mosaic virus contains a "recombination hotspot" that makes it unstable and prone to causing mutations, cancer, and new pathogens. The British Medical Association and the U.S. Consumer's Union have both warned about new allergies and/or adverse impacts on the immune system from GMO foods. And public health officials in Europe are concerned that anti-bacterial resistance marker genes in GMOs could render antibiotics ineffective. There have been only about 10 studies done on human health and GMOs, and half of them indicate reasons for concern, including malformed organs, tumors, and early death in rats.

There are also increasing reports of a phenomenon previously thought to be rare, "horizontal gene transfer," which happens when genes travel not just "vertically" through the normal processes of digestion and reproduction, but laterally, between organs in the body or between organisms—sort of like Casper the Ghost floating through a wall. Geneticist Mae-Wan Ho, who has been documenting this phenomenon, says it's happening because the new technology "breaks all the rules of evolution; it short-circuits evolution altogether. It bypasses reproduction, creates new genes and gene combinations that have never existed, and is not restricted by the usual barriers between species."

In 2001, the world's most widely grown GMO, Monsanto's Round-up Ready soybean, was found to contain some mysterious DNA. Monsanto claimed it was native to the plant. When it was shown instead to be the result of the transformation process, Monsanto couldn't explain how it got there. And it has been shown that the nutritional profile of the transgenic soybean is different than that of the conventional variety.

A new report, based on peer-reviewed scientific literature and USDA documents,[3] has found that significant genetic damage to the integrity of a plant occurs when it is modified, including rearrangement of genes at the site of the insertion and thousands of mutations and random modifications throughout the transgenic plant. Another study, by David Schubert of the Salk Institute for Biological Studies in La Jolla, California, found that just one transgenic insertion can disrupt 5 percent of the genes in a single-cell bacterium. Translated into plant terms, that means 15,000 to 300,000 genes get scrambled. Industry was given a blank check by government allowing it to commercialize the technology prematurely, before science could validate the techniques being used to evaluate the safety of the products being developed.

Strategic Contamination

Even before GMOs were released in the mid-1990s, they were thought by some scientists to be promiscuous. Now that GMO contamination is running rampant, it's hard to believe that the biotech industry wasn't aware of that risk. The industry would have had to ignore early warnings such as a study done at the University of Chicago which found one transgenic plant that was 20 times more likely to interbreed with related plants than its natural variety. But now, because herbicide-tolerant genes are getting into all sorts of plants, farmers have to contend with "super-weeds" that cannot be controlled with common chemicals, and American agriculture is riddled with fragments of transgenic material. The Union of Concerned Scientists recently reported that the seeds of conventional crops—traditional varieties of corn, soybeans, and canola—are now

"pervasively contaminated with low levels of DNA originating from engineered varieties of these crops." One laboratory found transgenic DNA in 83 percent of the corn, soy, and canola varieties tested.

GMO contamination is causing mounting economic losses, as farmers lose their markets, organic producers lose their certification, and processors have to recall food products. The contamination is even beginning to affect property values. Consumers are eating GMOs, whether they know it or not, and even GMOs not approved for human consumption have shown up in our taco shells. New "biopharmaceutical" crops used to grow drugs have leaked into the human food supply. And across the nation, hundreds of open field plots are growing transgenic corn, rice, and soybeans that contain drugs, human genes, animal vaccines, and industrial chemicals, without sufficient safeguards to protect nearby food crops.

It's not only food and farming that are affected. Part of what makes GMOs such an environmental threat is that, unlike chemical contamination, GMOs are living organisms, capable of reproducing and recombining, and once they get out, they can't be recalled. Now that there are genetically engineered fish, trees, insects, and other organisms, there's no limit to the kind of environmental surprises that can occur. The widespread ecological damage discussed at Asilomar is now a reality. In just one example of what can happen, a study found that when just 60 transgenic fish were released into a wild population of tens of thousands of fish, all the wild fish were wiped out in just 40 generations. And what will happen when there are plantations of transgenic trees, which can disperse GMO pollen for up to 40 miles and over several decades? Without physical or regulatory restraints, GMOs pose a very real threat to the biological integrity of the planet. As GMO activists say, it gives "pollution a life of its own."

The unasked question that lingers behind all the stories of GMO contamination is: what is the role of industry? How do the manufacturers of GMOs benefit from gene pollution? The fact is, the industry has never lifted a finger to prevent it and the biological and political system they have designed for it encourage its spread. The industry calls contamination an "adventitious presence," as if it were a benign but unavoidable consequence of modern life, like background radiation from nuclear testing.

In the United States, there are no legal safeguards in place to protect the public—not even labels. Labels would at least provide the consumer with a means for tracing the source of any problems that occur. Plus, without liability laws, the industry avoids accountability for any health or environmental damage it causes. It opposes independent testing and then takes advantage of the lack of data to make false assurances about its products' safety. The *Wall Street Journal* reported in 2003 that "makers of genetically modified crops have avoided answering questions and submitted erroneous data" on the safety of their products to the federal government. They have spent hundreds of millions of dollars on massive public relations campaigns that use sophisticated "perception management" techniques all aimed at falsely assuring the public, and government agencies, that their products are useful and safe.

Beyond their not having to label and segregate GMOs, biotech companies can manufacture, sell, and distribute them without having to take expensive precautions against contamination. They do not have to monitor field practices or do any post-market studies. When farms or factories are contaminated with GMOs, the industry is not held responsible for clean-up costs, as would be the case with chemical contamination. Instead, massive GMO food and crop recalls have been subsidized by taxpayers. Industry not only doesn't pay for a farmer's losses; it often sues the farmer for patent infringement and makes money on the deal. Monsanto, in particular, has profited richly by extorting patent infringement fines from farmers whose crops were inadvertently contaminated.

In September 2004, a study reported that herbicide-resistant genes from Monsanto's new bioengineered creeping bentgrass were found as far away as measurements were made—13 miles downwind. Monsanto's response was that there was nothing to worry about; it had proprietary herbicides that could take care of the problem, assuring more the sale of its products than a limit to the contamination. By assiduously avoiding any responsibility for the proliferation of GMOs, and by defeating attempts by the public to contain them, the agricultural biotechnology industry has thus

virtually ensured that GMO contamination will continue unabated. A biotech industry consultant with Promar International, Don West-fall, put it this way: "the hope of industry is that over time the market is so flooded that there's nothing you can do about it. You just sort of surrender."

The most alarming case of GMO contamination is the discovery of transgenes in corn at the center of the origin of corn in Mexico. From the time GMO corn was first planted in the U.S. Midwest, it took only six years to make its way back home in the remote mountainous regions of Puebla and Oaxaca, Mexico. Ignacio Chapela, a Mexican-born microbial biologist, was the scientist who first reported this contamination in 2001. Early in 2002, I visited the area with Dr. Chapela to investigate the cultural and economic implications of his findings. While I was there I got a first-hand look at the complicity of government and industry in the spread of GMO contamination.

The genetic diversity of corn, the world's most important food crop after rice, has been fostered for thousands of years by Zapotec and hundreds of other indigenous farming communities who have lived in these mountainous areas since before the Spanish arrived. Now their traditional land-based ways of life, the sacred center of their culture, and the source of their economic livelihood, corn, has been imperiled by this new form of colonization. The farmers I talked to there were well informed, but worried about their cultural and economic survival. What they did not understand was how transgenic corn got into their fields.[+]

Early press reports blamed the farmers themselves, based on the observation that in order to help support their families and communities, some of them travel to the U.S. to work as migrant workers. But in fact, it turned out that the cause of the contamination was the Mexican government and "free trade" rules. Although Mexico had banned the commercial planting of transgenic corn, under pressure of NAFTA and the biotech industry it was importing corn from the U.S. that it knew was contaminated. It then distributed this whole-kernel corn to poor communities as food aid, without labels or warnings to rural farmers that it should not be used for seed. This highly subsidized corn, which is being dumped on third world farmers at prices that are lower than the cost of production, undermines local corn markets. But instead of taking steps to stop the spread of this contamination, or to protect its farming communities, or even to guard its fragile biodiversity, the Mexican government, the international seed banks, and the biotech industry all deflected public and media attention to a convenient scapegoat—Dr. Chapela.

The Suppression of Science

Chapela and his graduate student, David Quist, had published their findings in the peer-reviewed journal *Nature*.[5] They had actually made two findings: first, that GMOs had contaminated Mexico's local varieties of corn—in technical terms, that "introgression" had occurred. And second, they found that once transgenes had introgressed into other plants, the genes did not behave as expected. This is evidence of transgenic instability, which scientists now regard with growing concern. But allegations of such instability can be dangerous to make because they undermine the central dogma's basic article of faith: that transgenes are stable and behave predictably. Not surprisingly, the industry attacked the first finding, but was foiled when the Mexican government's own studies found even higher levels and more widespread GMO contamination than the *Nature* article had reported. The industry then focused its attack to the finding of transgenic instability.

For over a year, the industry relentlessly assailed Quist and Chapela's work, both in the press and on the Internet. As the debate raged on, scientists argued both sides, fueled, Chapela says, by a well developed and generously funded industry public relations strategy that did not hesitate to make the attacks personal. Monsanto even retained a public relations firm to have employees pose as independent critics. The outcome was unprecedented. The editor of *Nature* published a letter saying that "in light of the criticisms . . . the evidence available is not sufficient to justify" the publication of the original paper. This "retraction" made reference to the work of two relatively unknown biologists, Matthew Metz and Nick Kaplinsky. At the time, Kaplinsky was still a graduate student in the Department of

Plant and Microbial Biology at UC Berkeley. Metz had finished his work at Berkeley and was a postdoctoral fellow at the University of Washington. What few knew was that their role in the *Nature* controversy was linked to another dispute that they, Quist, and Chapela, had been involved in. That earlier dispute, too, was about the integrity of science. And in that case, Chapela had led the faculty opposition—and Quist had been a part of the student opposition—to private funding of biotechnology research at UC Berkeley.

The Pie on the Wall

The University of California at Berkeley is a "land grant" institution, meaning that it was created to support California's rich agricultural productivity. But by the late 1990s, Cal had all but abandoned its original mission. Berkeley had become the national leader in collecting royalty payments on its patents, many of which related to the development of genetic engineering. This development was facilitated by the passage of the Bayh-Dole Act of 1980, which allowed universities to patent their research, even if it was publicly funded. By the fall of 1998, the private funding of research at Berkeley was in its full glory. That year, the dean of the College of Natural Resources, Gordon Rausser, announced that he had brokered an unprecedented research deal with the Novartis Corporation, then a multinational Swiss agrochemical and pharmaceutical giant.

Novartis was giving just one department of the College, the Department of Plant and Microbial Biology, $25 million over a 5-year period. The deal was fraught with conflicts of interest, not the least of which was that Novartis employees served on academic committees and got first license rights to the Department's research products. Novartis proudly announced that "the ultimate goal" of the agreement was "to achieve commercialization of products." This took private intrusion into the public sector to a new level, allowing private investors to profit directly from public investment in research, and arousing concerns about the increasing privatization of public research institutions across the country.

In true Berkeley fashion, the controversy erupted into protests. When the deal was announced in November 1998, I covered the press conference. It was held in a packed room upstairs in Koshland Hall, home of the Department of Plant and Microbial Biology. Novartis executives stood shoulder to shoulder with UC Berkeley administrators and leading faculty. They all looked on benevolently while the agreement was formally signed. Then the speeches started. Steven Briggs, president of Novartis Agricultural Discovery Institute, the foundation that funnels corporate money to the university and gets government research and tax credits for Novartis, signed the deal on behalf of Novartis. Briggs, who is an expert on the corn genome, called the agreement—without the least suggestion of irony—"the final statement in academic freedom."

The person most responsible for the Novartis deal, Dean Rausser, was proud of his considerable connections in the private sector. While he was dean, he built a consulting company worth millions. During the press conference, he stood at the front of the room with the other key participants. The press and other guests were seated in folding chairs facing them, and students sat on the floor along the walls. Hefty security men in blue blazers with wires dangling from their ears were lined up along the back wall. I was in the front row. Suddenly I felt a commotion erupting behind me. Something rushed past my head, missed its intended target, and splattered on the wall behind the front table. Then another object followed, grazed Dean Rausser, and landed on the floor at his feet. It all happened fast, but I soon realized that I was in the middle of a pie-throwing protest. In their hallmark style, which is humorous political theater, the "Biotic Baking Brigade" had tossed two vegan pumpkin pies (it was Thanksgiving week, after all) at the signers of the Novartis agreement.

As campus security guards wrestled the protesters to the floor and then pulled them out of the room, the AP reporter who was sitting next to me jumped up and ran out to call in her story. I stayed and watched Dean Rausser, who had been speaking at the time. He just looked down, brushed some pie off his suit, then smiled and shrugged. I got the distinct feeling he was enjoying the moment. He went on with his presentation, and for the rest of the time he was speaking, pie filling drooled down the wall behind him.

As a child of the '60s and a member of the UC Berkeley class of 1965, I was reminded of the winter of 1964, when Mario Savio gave his famous "rage against the machine" speech[6] on the steps of the campus administration building. When it began, the Free Speech Movement was about academic freedom but it enlarged into demonstrations against the war in Vietnam and support for the civil rights and women's movements. A lot was achieved, especially in terms of environmental protection. But it was always about who controls the levers of "the machine," as Savio called it. By 1998, however, the conservative backlash that was provoked by these protests was in full bloom. Private interests had successfully dismantled the regulatory system, invaded the ivy tower, and taken over the intellectual commons. The corporate executives and their academic beneficiaries who were there to celebrate the Novartis agreement clearly had nothing to fear—a fact that was neatly affirmed by Dean Rausser's shrug.

The Novartis funding ended in 2003. By then, faculty and graduate students who were on both sides of the debate had gone their separate ways. Dr. Chapela stayed, and continued to teach at Berkeley. As 2003 drew to a close, he was up for a tenure appointment. Even though he'd garnered extraordinary support from faculty, students, and the public, his role in opposing corporate funding on campus apparently cost him his teaching career. After an unusually protracted process, the University denied him tenure. In 2004, a 10-person team at Michigan State University that had spent two years evaluating the Novartis-Berkeley agreement concluded that the deal was indeed "outside the mainstream for research contracts with industry" and that Berkeley's relationship with Novartis created a conflict of interest in the administration that affected their tenure decision against Dr. Chapela.

Instead of applauding and bravery of scientists who question biotechnology, or at least encouraging further scientific inquiry, the industry and its cronies in the academic world denounce their critics. Dr. Chapela has now joined a growing number of scientists who have paid a high price for their integrity. Others have lost jobs, been discredited in the press, told to change research results or to repudiate their findings.[7] And for each victim whose story is told publicly, there are others who have been silenced and cannot come forward. The implications of the trend toward the privatization of research and the repression of academic freedom go far beyond the question of where the funds come from and who decides what gets studied. It's a trend that deeply undermines the public's faith in science, and the result is that society will lose the means to adequately evaluate new technologies. It may also mean that we adopt a view of the natural world so mechanistic that we will not even recognize the threats we face.

If science were free to operate in the public interest, it could provide the intellectual framework for innovations that work with nature, instead of against it. There already are technologists that use natural solutions to heal the wounds of the industrial age, formulate sustainable food production and energy solutions, create new economic opportunities through the imaginative use of ecological design, and build local self-reliant communities that foster both cultural and biological survival. So we do have a choice of technologies, and nature remains abundantly generous with us. What we do not have, given the perilous environmental state of the planet, is a lot of time left to sort this out. And as long as the critics are silenced, we can be lulled by the "certain promises" of genetic engineering, that it will provide magic answers to those age old problems of hunger and disease, and in doing so, be diverted from attending to its "uncertain perils."

The Nature of Trespass

Trespass, in legal parlance, means "an unlawful act that causes injury to person or property." It connotes an act of intrusion, usually by means of stealth, force, or violence. It also implies the right to allow or to refuse an intrusion. A trespass occurs when that right has been violated. Genetic engineering technology is a trespass on the public commons. This is because of the way transgenics are designed and the way "the molecular vision" has been pursued. This vision required that science be compromised to the point where it would overlook the complex boundary conditions that form the very foundation of life. It had to have the hubris to break the species barriers and place itself directly in the path of evolution, severing organisms from their hereditary lineage. And it requires the use of stealth and violence to invade the cell wall, and the implanting of transgenic life forms into an involuntary participant with organisms that are especially designed to overcome all resistance to this rude intrusion.

This trespass continues when ownership is forced on the newly created organisms in the form of a patent. The patenting of a life form was widely considered immoral, and until the U.S. Supreme Court approved the patenting of life in 1980, it was illegal. With that one decision, private interests were given the right to own every non-human life form on earth. We clearly are, as President Bush recently declared, "the ownership society." Now, when GMOs enter the borderless world of free trade and permeate every part of the web of life, they carry within them their owner's mark and effectively privatize every organism they infiltrate. This is made all the more unacceptable because this expensive technology is so unnecessary. Most of what agricultural biotechnology sells, such as insect-resistant plants and weed-control strategies, is already available by other means. Traditional plant breeding can produce all these advances and more—including increased yield, drought or salt resistance, and even nutritional enhancements. The whole point of the commercial use of the genetic engineering technology is the patents, and the social control they facilitate. The reason GMOs were inserted into crops is so that agbiochemical companies could own the seed supply and control the means and methods of food production, and profit at each link in the food chain.

Genetic engineering is a manifestation—perhaps the ultimate manifestation—of the term "full spectrum dominance." In this case, the dominance is achieved on multiple levels, first by exerting biological control over the organism itself, then by achieving economic control over the marketplace and then through "perceptual" control over public opinion. GMOs are disguised to look just like their natural counterparts, and then are released into the environment and the human food chain through a matrix of control that identifies and disables every political, legal, educational, and economic barrier that could thwart their owners' purpose. Arguably, this description suggests a more sinister level of intention than really exists. But the fact remains that denial of choice has been accomplished and it is crucial to this strategy's success. As a Canadian GMO seed industry spokesperson, Dale Adolphe, put it: "It's a hell of a thing to say that the way we win is don't give the consumer a choice, but that might be it."

Agricultural genetic engineering is dismantling our once deeply held common vision about how we feed ourselves, how we care for the land, water, and seeds that support us, and how we participate in decisions that affect us on the most intimate personal and most essential community level. The ultimate irony of our ecological crisis, says David Loy, a professor and author of works on modern Western thought, is that "our collective project to secure ourselves is what threatens to destroy us." But still, there are problems with making moral arguments like these. One is that we lack a practical system of public ethics—some set of common standards we can turn to for guidance. Another is that it does not address the most serious threat to our security, which is that no amount of science, fact, or even moral suasion is of any consequence when we are left with no options.

At the end of my inquiry I came to the conclusion that genetic engineering, at least as it is being used in agriculture is, by design, inherently invasive and unstable. It has been imposed on the American public in a way that has left us with no choice and no way to opt out, biologically or socially. Thus, the reality is that the evolutionary legacy of our lives, whether as human beings, bees, fish, or trees, has been disrupted. We are in danger of being severed from our own ancestral lines and diverted into another world altogether, the physical and social dimensions of which are still unknown and yet to be described.

NOTES

1. Although I use the terms "biotechnology" and "genetic engineering" interchangeably, along with references to "transgenes" and "genetically modified organisms," I am, in all cases, referring to recombinant DNA technology used to cross species boundaries. I am not using the term "biotechnology" in its general sense, which can include natural processes. This analysis of genetic engineering will focus *only* on its agricultural applications. It does not address issues that might apply to medical or other uses.

2. Kay, Lily E. *The Molecular Vision of Life. Caltech, the Rockefeller Foundation, and the Rise of the New Biology,* Oxford University Press, 1993, p. 23.

3. "Genome Scrambling—Myth or Reality? Transformation-induced Mutations in Transgenic Crop Plants" by Drs. Wilson, Latham, and Steinbrecher is available at www.econexus.info.

4. The full story of how GMOs got into native corn in Mexico is told in "Risking Corn, Risking Culture," by this author, Claire Hope Cummings, *World Watch,* November/December 2002.

5. Quist, D. and Chapela, I., "Transgenic DNA Introgressed into Traditional Maize Landraces in Oaxaca. Mexico." *Nature,* 414:541–543, November 29, 2001.

6. In that speech Savio said that there comes a time when "the operation of the machine becomes so odious, makes you so sick at heart, that you can't take part. You can't even passively take part and you've got to put your bodies upon the gears and upon the wheels, upon the levers, upon all the apparatus, and you got to make it stop. . . ."

7. The stories of four such scientists and their reflections on their experiences can be heard on a recording of a remarkable conversation among them called "The Pulse of Scientific Freedom in the Age of the Biotech Industry" held on the UC Berkeley campus in December, 2003. A link to the web archive is available at http://nature.berkeley.edu/pulseofscience/plx/conv.txt1.html.

II.15   MARK SAGOFF

Genetic Engineering and the Concept of the Natural

In the past several years, there has been a furor generated over the use of genetically modified organisms (GMOs) in the world food supply. Particularly in Europe, but also in several other countries, there are active consumer movements whose goal is to rid the supermarket shelves of any trace of GMO ingredients. The controversy has ignited a trade war between the United States, which has a rather laissez-faire attitude toward GMO crops, and its European trading partners, whose consumers are demanding GMO labeling, if not a complete ban, on GMO foods.

In this selection, philosopher Mark Sagoff takes a look at food labeling in general; he argues that the consumer's preference for "all-natural" foods has been stimulated in large part by the food industry itself, which has decided to sell its products along with the fantasy that our food is produced without technological intervention. Sagoff distinguishes four senses in which something may be said to be "natural" and argues that part of the problem with the food industry is that it equivocates on the meaning of this term and tries to have it both ways. Illustrating the different senses of "natural" with passages from Shakespeare's *The Winter's Tale,* Sagoff artfully reminds us that there are moral, aesthetic, and cultural value aspects to the debate over genetically engineered foods and that trade-offs between these values and those of convenience and consumerism can be papered over but not avoided by advertising claims made by corporate agribusiness.

Focus Questions

1. Why does Sagoff think that the current practice of advertising foods as "natural" is an example of consumer constructivism?
2. What are the four senses of "natural" that Sagoff distinguishes? Which of these senses correctly apply to genetically engineered foods? Which don't? Explain.
3. Is it possible to give consumers what they want with no trade-offs, as industry spokespersons suggest? Why or why not?
4. Compare this reading to those of Strong (selection I.12) and Lovins, Lovins, and Hawken (selection II.19). In what sense has modern technology subverted the concept of nature?

Keywords

agribusiness, consumerism, genetic engineering, GMOs, labeling, multinational corporations, nature

WHY DO MANY CONSUMERS view genetically engineered foods with suspicion? I want to suggest that it is largely because the food industry has taught them to do so. Consumers learn from advertisements and labels that the foods they buy are all natural—even more natural than a baby's smile. "The emphasis in recent years," *Food Processing* magazine concludes, "has been on natural or nature-identical ingredients." According to *Food Product Design,* "the desire for an all natural label extends even to pet food."

The food industry, I shall argue, wishes to embrace the efficiencies offered by advances in genetic engineering. This technology, both in name and in concept, however, belies the image of nature or of the natural to which the food industry constantly and conspicuously appeals. It should be no surprise that consumers who believe genetically modified foods are not "natural" should for that reason regard them as risky or as undesirable. If they knew how much technology contributes to other foods they eat, they might be suspicious of them as well.

All-Natural Technology

Recently, I skimmed through issues of trade magazines, such as *Food Technology* and *Food Processing,* that serve the food industry. In full-page advertisements, manufacturers insist the ingredients they market come direct from primordial Creation or, at least, that their products are identical to nature's own. For example, Roche Food Colours runs in these trade magazines a full-page ad that displays a bright pink banana over the statement: "When nature changes her colours, so will we." The ad continues:

> Today more and more people are rejecting the idea of artificial colours being used in food and drink. . . .

From "Genetic Engineering and the Concept of the Natural" by Mark Sagoff, *Philosophy and Public Policy Quarterly, Spring/Summer 2001,* Vol. 21 (2/3), pp 2–10. Copyright © 2001 Institute for Philosophy and Public Policy. Reprinted by permission.

> Our own food colours are, and always have been, strictly identical to those produced by nature.

> We make pure carotenoids which either singly or in combination achieve a whole host of different shades in the range of yellow though orange to red.

> And time and time again they produce appetising natural colours, reliably, economically, and safely.

> Just like nature herself.

Advertisement after advertisement presents the same message: food comes directly from nature or, at least, can be sold as if it did. Consider, for example, a full-page advertisement that McCormick and Wild, a flavor manufacturer, runs regularly in *Food Processing.* The words "BACK TO NATURE" appear under a kiwi fruit dripping with juice. "Today's consumer wants it all," the advertisement purrs, "great taste, natural ingredients, and new ideas. . . . Let us show you how we can put the world's most advanced technology in natural flavors at your disposal. . . ."

This advertisement clearly states the mantra of the food industry: "Today's consumer wants it all." Great taste. Natural ingredients. New ideas. The world's most advanced technology. One can prepare the chemical basis of a flavor, for example, benzaldehyde—almond—artificially with just a little chemical know-how, in this instance, by mixing oil of clove and amyl acetate. To get exactly the same compound as a "natural" flavor, one must employ far more sophisticated technology to extract and isolate benzaldehyde from peach and apricot pits. The "natural" flavor, an extract, contains traces of hydrogen cyanide, a deadly poison evolved by plants to protect their seeds from insects. Even so, consumers strongly prefer all-natural to artificial flavors, which sell therefore at a far lower price.

In its advertisements, the Haarmann & Reimer Corporation (H&R) describes its flavor enhancers as "HypR Clean Naturally." With "H&R as your partner, you'll discover the latest advances in flavor technology" that assure "the cleanest label possible." A "clean" label is one that includes only natural ingredients and no reference to technology. In a competing advertisement, Chr. Hansen's Laboratory announces itself as the pioneer in "culture and enzyme technologies. . . . And because our flavors are completely natural, you can enjoy the benefits of 'all-natural' labeling." Flavor manufacturers tout their stealth technology—i.e., technology so advanced it disappears from the consumer's radar screen. The consumer can be told he or she is directly in touch with nature itself.

The world's largest flavor company, International Flavors & Fragrances (IFF) operates manufacturing facilities in places like Dayton, New Jersey, an industrial corridor of refineries and chemical plants. Under a picture of plowed, fertile soil, the IFF Laboratory, in a full-page display, states, "Where Nature is at work, IFF is at work." The text describes "IFF's natural flavor systems." The slogan follows: "IFF technology. In partnership with Nature." Likewise, MEER Corporation of Bergen, New Jersey, pictures a rainforest under the caption, "It's A Jungle Out There!" The ad states that "true-to-nature" flavorings "do not just happen. It takes . . . manufacturing and technical expertise and a national distribution network . . . for the creation of natural, clean label flavors."

Food colors are similarly sold as both all natural and high tech. "VegetoneH colors your foods *naturally* for a healthy bottom line," declares Kalsec, Inc., of Kalamazoo, Michigan. Its ad shows a technician standing before a computer and measuring chemicals into a test tube. The ad extols the company's "patented natural color systems." The terms "natural" and "patented" fit seamlessly together in a conceptual scheme in which there are no trade-offs and no compromises. The natural is patentable. If you think any of this is contradictory, you will not get far in the food industry.

Organic TV Dinners

As a typical American suburbanite, I can buy not just groceries but "Whole Foods" at Fresh Fields and other upscale supermarkets. I am particularly impressed by the number of convenience foods that are advertised as "organic." Of course, one might think that any food may be whole and that all foods are organic. Terms like "whole" and "organic," however, appeal to and support my belief that the products that carry these labels are less processed and more natural—closer to the family farm—than are those that are produced by multinational megacorporations, such as Pillsbury or General Foods.

My perusal of advertisements in trade magazines helped disabuse me of my belief that all-natural, organic, and whole foods are closer to nature in a substantive sense than other manufactured products. If I had any residual credulity, it was removed by an excellent cover story, "Behind the Organic-Industrial Complex," that appeared in a recent issue of the *New York Times Magazine*. The author, Michael Pollan, is shocked, shocked to find that the prepackaged microwavable all-natural organic TV dinners at his local Whole Foods outlet are not gathered from the wild by red-cheeked peasants in native garb. They are highly-processed products manufactured by multinational corporations. Contrary to the impression created by advertisements, organic and other all-natural foods are often fabricated by the same companies—using comparable technologies—as those that produce Velveeta and Miracle Whip. And the ingredients come from as far away as megafarms in Chile—not from local farmers' markets.

Reformers who led the organic food movement in the 1960s wished to provide an alternative to agribusiness and to industrial food production, but some of these reformers bent to the inevitable. As Pollan points out, they became multimillionaire executives of Pillsbury and General Mills in charge of organic food production systems. This makes sense. A lot of advanced technology is needed to produce and market an all-natural or an organic ready-to-eat meal. Consumers inspect food labels to ward off artificial ingredients; yet they also want the convenience of a low-priced, pre-prepared, all-natural dinner.

At General Mills, as one senior vice president, Danny Strickland, told Pollan, "Our corporate philosophy is to give consumers what they want with no trade-offs." Pollan interprets the meaning of this statement as follows. "At General Mills," Pollan explains, "the whole notion of objective truth has been replaced by a value-neutral consumer constructivism, in which each sovereign shopper constructs his own reality."

Mass-marketed organic TV dinners do not compromise; they combine convenience with a commitment to the all-natural, eco-friendly, organic ideology. The most popular of these dinners are sold by General Mills through its subsidiary, Cascadian Farms. The advertising slogan of Cascadian Farms, "Taste You Can Believe In," as Pollan observes, makes no factual claims of any sort. It "allows the consumer to bring his or her personal beliefs into it," as the Vice President for Marketing, R. Brooks Gekler, told Pollan. The absence of any factual claim is essential to selling a product, since each consumer buys an object that reflects his or her particular belief system.

What is true of marketing food is true of virtually every product. A product will sell if it is all-natural and eco-friendly and, at the same time, offers the consumer the utmost in style and convenience. A recent *New York Times* article, under the title, "Fashionistas, Ecofriendly and All-Natural," points out that the sales of organic food in the United States topped $6.4 billion in 1999 with a projected annual increase of 20 percent. Manufacturers of clothes and fashion accessories, such as solar-powered watches, are cashing in on the trend. Maria Rodale, who helps direct a publishing empire covering "natural" products, founded the women's lifestyle magazine *Organic Style*. Rodale told the *Times* that women want to do the right thing for "the environment but not at the cost of living well." Advances in technology give personal items and household wares an all-natural eco-friendly look that is also the last word in fashion. Consumers "don't want to sacrifice anything," Ms. Rodale told a reporter. Why should there be a trade-off between a commitment to nature and a commitment to the good life? "Increasingly there are options that don't compromise on either front."

The food industry does not sell food any more than the fashion industry sells clothes or the automobile industry sells automobiles. They sell imagery. The slogan, "Everything the consumer wants with no trade-offs," covers all aspects of our dream-world. Sex without zippers, children without zits, lawns without weeds, wars without casualties, and food without technology. Reality involves trade-offs and rather substantial ones. For this reason, if you tried to sell reality, your competitor would drive you out of business by avoiding factual claims and selling fantasy—whatever consumers believe in—instead. Consumers should not be confused or disillusioned by facts. They are encouraged to assume that they buy products of Nature or Creation. In view of this fantasy, how could consumers view genetic engineering with anything but suspicion?

Nature's Own Methods

Genetic engineering, with its stupendous capacity for increasing the efficiencies of food production in all departments, including flavors and colorings, raises a problem. How can genetic recombination be presented to the consumer as completely natural—as part of nature's spontaneous course—as have other aspects of food technology? A clean label would tell consumers there is nothing unnatural or inauthentic about genetically engineered products. Industry has responded in two complementary ways to this problem.

First, the food industry has resisted calls to label bioengineered products. Gene Grabowski of the Grocery Manufacturers Association, for example, worries that labeling "would imply that there's something wrong with food, and there isn't." Michael J. Phillips, an economist with the Biotechnology Industry Organization, adds that labeling "would only confuse consumers by suggesting that the process of biotechnology might in and of itself have an impact on the safety of food. This is not the case."

Second, manufacturers point out that today's genetic technologies do not differ, except in being more precise, from industrial processes that result in the emulsifiers, stabilizers, enzymes, proteins, cultures, and other ingredients that do enjoy the benefits of a clean label. Virtually every plant consumed by human beings—canola, for example—is the product of so much breeding, hybridization, and modification that it hardly resembles its wild ancestors. This is a good thing, too, since these wild ancestors were barely edible if not downright poisonous. Manufacturers argue that genetic engineering differs from conventional breeding only because it is more accurate and therefore changes nature less.

For example, Monsanto Corporation, in a recent full-page ad, pictures a bucolic landscape reminiscent of a painting by Constable. The headline reads, "FARMING: A picture of the Future." The ad then represents genetic engineering as all natural—or at least as natural as are conventional biotechnologies that have enabled humanity to engage successfully in agriculture. "The products of biotechnology will be based on nature's own methods," the ad assures the industry. "Monsanto scientists are working with nature to develop innovative products for farmers of today, and of the future."

In this advertisement, Monsanto applies the tried-and-true formula to which the food industry has long been committed—presenting a technology as revolutionary, innovative, highly advanced, and as "based on nature's own methods." *Everything* is natural. Why not? As long as there are no distinctions, there are no trade-offs. Consumers can buy what they believe in. A thing is natural if the public believes it is. "There is something in this more than natural," as Hamlet once said, "if philosophy could find it out."

Four Concepts of the Natural

If consumers reject bioengineered food as "unnatural," what does this mean? In what way are foods that result from conventional methods of genetic mutation and selection, which have vastly altered crops and livestock, more "natural" than those that depend in some way on gene splicing? Indeed, is anything in an organic TV dinner "natural" other than, say, the rodent droppings that may be found in it? Since I am a philosopher, not a scientist, I am particularly interested in the moral, aesthetic, and cultural—as distinct from the chemical, biological, or physical—aspects of the natural world. I recognize that many of us depend in our moral, aesthetic, and spiritual lives on distinguishing those things

for which humans are responsible from those that occur as part of nature's spontaneous course.

Philosophers have long pondered the question whether the concept of the natural can be used in a normative sense—that is, whether to say that a practice or a product is "natural" is somehow to imply that it is better to that extent than one that is not. Why should anyone assume that a product that is "natural" is safer, more healthful, or more aesthetically or ethically attractive than one that is not? And why is technology thought to be intrinsically risky when few of us would survive without quite a lot of it?

Among the philosophers who have questioned the "naturalistic fallacy"—the assumption that what is natural is for that reason good—the nineteenth-century British philosopher John Stuart Mill has been particularly influential. In his "Essay on Nature," Mill argues that the term "nature" can refer either to the totality of things ("the sum of all phenomena, together with the causes which produce them") or to those phenomena that take place "without the agency . . . of man." Plainly, everything in the world—including every technology—is natural and belongs equally to nature in the first sense of the term. Mill comments:

> To bid people to conform to the laws of nature when they have no power but what the laws of nature give them—when it is a physical impossibility for them to do the smallest thing otherwise than through some law of nature—is an absurdity. The thing they need to be told is, what particular law of nature they should make use of in a particular case.

Of nature in the second sense—that which takes place without the agency of man—Mill has a dour view. "Nearly all the things which men are hanged or imprisoned for doing to one another, are nature's every day performances," Mill wrote. Nature may have cared for us in the days of the Garden of Eden. In more recent years, however, humanity has had to alter Creation to survive. Mill concludes, "For while human action cannot help conforming to nature in one meaning of the term, the very aim and object of action is to alter and improve nature in the other meaning."

Following Mill, it is possible to distinguish four different conceptions of nature to understand the extent to which bioengineered food may or may not be natural. These four senses of the term include:

1. *Everything in the universe.* The significant opposite of the "natural" in this sense is the "supernatural." Everything technology produces has to be completely natural because it conforms to all of nature's laws and principles.

2. *Creation in the sense of what God has made.* The distinction here lies between what is sacred because of its pedigree (God's handiwork) and what is profane (what humans produce for pleasure or profit).

3. *That which is independent of human influence or contrivance.* The concept of "nature" or the "natural" in this sense, e.g., the "pristine," is understood as a privative notion defined in terms of the absence of the effects of human activity. The opposite of the "natural" in this sense is the "artificial."

4. *That which is authentic or true to itself.* The opposite of the "natural" in this sense is the specious, illusory, or superficial. The "natural" is trustworthy and honest, while the sophisticated, worldly, or contrived is deceptive and risky.

These four conceptions of nature are logically independent. To say that an item or a process—genetic engineering, for example—is "natural" because it obeys the laws of nature, is by no means to imply it is "natural" in any other sense. That genetically manipulated foods can be found within (1) the totality of phenomena does not show that they are "natural" in the sense that they are (2) part of primordial Creation; (3) free of human contrivance; or (4) authentic and expressive of the virtues of rustic or peasant life.

The problem of consumer acceptance of biotechnology arises in part because the food industry sells its products as natural in the last three senses. The industry wishes to be regulated, however, only in the context of the first conception of nature, which does not distinguish among phenomena on the basis of their histories, sources, or provenance.

The industry argues that only the biochemical properties of its products should matter to regulation; the process (including genetic engineering) is irrelevant to food safety and should not be considered.

The food industry downplays the biochemical properties of its products, however, when it advertises them to consumers. The industry—at least if the approach taken by General Mills is typical—tries to give the consumer whatever he believes in. If the consumer believes in a process by which rugged farmers on the slopes of the Cascades raise organic TV dinners from the soil by sheer force of personality, so be it. You will see the farm pictured on the package to suggest the product is close to Creation, free of contrivance, and authentic or expressive of rural virtues. What you will not see on any label—if the industry has its way—is a reference to genetic engineering. The industry believes regulators should concern themselves only with the first concept of nature—the scientific concept—and thus with the properties of the product. Concepts related to the process are used to evoke images that "give consumers what they want with no trade-offs."

Shakespeare on Biotechnology

I confess that, as a consumer, I find organic foods appealing and I insist on "all-natural" ingredients. Am I just foolish? You might think that I would see through labels like "all natural" and "organic"—not to mention "whole" foods—and that I would reject them as marketing ploys of a cynical industry. Yet like many consumers, I want to believe that the "natural" is somewhat better than the artificial. Is this just a fallacy?

Although I am a professional philosopher (or perhaps because of this), I would not look first to the literature of philosophy to understand what may be an irrational—or at least an unscientific—commitment to buying "all natural" products. My instinct would be to look in Shakespeare to understand what may be contradictory attitudes or inexplicable sentiments.

Shakespeare provides his most extensive discussion of biotechnology in *The Winter's Tale,* one of his comedies. In Act IV, Polixenes, King of Bohemia, disguises himself to spy upon his son, Florizel, who has fallen in love with Perdita, whom all believe to be a shepherd's daughter. In fact, though raised as a shepherdess, Perdita is the castaway daughter of the King of Sicily, a close but now estranged friend of Polixenes. Perdita welcomes the disguised Polixenes and an attendant lord to a sheep shearing feast in late autumn, offering them dried flowers "that keep/ Seeming and savour all winter long." Polixenes merrily chides her: "well you fit our ages/ With flowers of winter."

She replies that only man-made hybrids flourish so late in the fall:

. . . carnations, and streak'd gillyvors,
Which some call nature's bastards. Of that kind
Our rustic garden's barren; and I care not
To get slips of them.

Polixenes asks why she rejects cold-hardy flowers such as gillyvors, a dianthus. She answers that they come from human contrivance, not from "great creating nature." She complains there is "art" in their "piedness," or variegation. Polixenes replies: "Say there be;

Yet nature is made better by no mean
But nature makes that mean; so over that art
Which you say adds to nature, is an art
That nature makes. . . . This is an art
Which does mend nature—change it rather; but
The art itself is nature.

The statement, "The art itself is nature" anticipates the claim made by Monsanto that "The products of biotechnology will be based on nature's own methods." Polixenes, Mill, and Monsanto remind us that everything in the universe conforms to nature's own principles, and relies wholly on nature's powers. From a scientific perspective, in other words, all nature is one. The mechanism of a lever, for example, may occur in the physiology of a wild animal or in the structure of a machine. Either way, it is natural. One might be forced to agree, then, that genetic engineering applies nature's own methods and principles; in other words, "the art itself is nature."

The exchange between Perdita and Polixenes weaves together the four conceptions of nature I identified earlier in relation to John Stuart Mill. When Polixenes states, "The art itself is nature," he uses the term "nature" to comprise everything in the Universe, that is, everything that conforms to physical law. Second, Perdita refers to "great creating nature," that is, to Creation, i.e., the primordial origin and condition of life before the advent of human society. Third, she contrasts nature to art or artifice by complaining that hybrids do not arise spontaneously but show "art" in their "piedness." Finally, Perdita refers to her "rustic garden," which, albeit cultivated, is "natural" in the sense of simple or unadorned, in contrast to the ornate horticulture that would grace a royal garden. The comparison between the court and the country correlates, of course, with the division that exists in Perdita herself—royal in carriage and character by her birth, yet possessed of rural virtues by her upbringing.

Shakespeare elaborates this last conception of "nature" as the banter continues between Perdita and the disguised Polixenes. To his assertion, "The art itself is nature," Perdita concedes, "So it is." Polixenes then drives home his point: "Then make your garden rich in gillyvors,/ And do not call them bastards."

To which Perdita responds:

I'll not put
The dibble in earth to set one slip of them;
No more than were I painted I would wish
This youth should say 'twere well, and only therefore
Desire to breed by me.

Besides comparing herself to breeding stock—amusing in the context, since she speaks to her future father-in-law in the presence of his son—Perdita reiterates a fourth and crucial sense of the "natural." In this sense, what is "natural" is true to itself; it is honest, authentic, and genuine. This conception reflects Aristotle's theory of the "nature" of things, which refers to qualities that are spontaneous because they are inherent or innate.

Perdita stands by her insistence on natural products—from flowers she raises to cosmetics she uses—in spite of Polixenes' cynical but scientific reproofs. Does this suggest Perdita is merely a good candidate for Ms. Rodale's organic chic? Should she receive a free introductory copy of *Organic Style*? Certainly not. There is something about Perdita's rejection of biotechnology that withstands this sort of criticism. Why have Perdita's actions a moral authority or authenticity that the choices consumers make today may lack?

Having It Both Ways

Perdita possesses moral authority because she is willing to live with the consequences of her convictions and of the distinctions on which they are based. By refusing to paint herself to appear more attractive, for example, Perdita contrasts her qualities, which are innate, to those of the "streak'd gillyvor," which owe themselves to technological meddling. This comparison effectively gives her the last word because she suits the action to it: she does not and would not paint herself to attract a lover. Similarly, Perdita does not raise hybrids, though she admits, "I would I had some flow'rs" that might become the "time of day" of the youthful guests at the feast, such as Florizel.

Perdita does not try to have it both ways—to reject hybrids but also to grow cold-hardy flowers. She ridicules those who match lofty ideals with ordinary actions—whose practice belies their professed principles. For example, Camillo, the Sicilian lord who attends Polixenes, compliments Perdita on her beauty. He says, "I should leave grazing, were I of your flock,/ And only live by gazing." She laughs at him and smartly replies, "You'd be so lean that blasts of January/ Would blow you through and through."

Many people today share Perdita's affection for nature and her distaste for technology. Indeed, it is commonplace to celebrate Nature's spontaneous course and to condemn the fabrications of biotechnology. Jeremy Rifkin speaks of "Playing Ecological Roulette with Mother Nature's Designs"; Ralph Nader has written the foreword to a book titled, *Genetically Engineered Food: Changing the Nature of Nature*. The Prince of Wales, in a tirade against biotechnology, said, "I have always believed that agriculture should proceed in harmony with nature, recognising that there are natural limits to our ambitions. We need to rediscover a reverence for

the natural world to become more aware of the relationship between God, man, and creation."

While consumers today share Perdita's preference for the natural in the sense of the authentic and unadorned and spurn technological meddling, they do not share her willingness to live with the consequences of their commitment. They expect to enjoy year round fruits and vegetables of unblemished appearance, and consistent taste and nutritional quality. Gardeners wish to plant lawns and yards with species that are native and indigenous, and they support commissions and fund campaigns to throw back the "invasions" of exotic and alien species. Yet they also want lawns that resist drought, blight, and weeds, and—to quote Perdita again—to enjoy flowers that "come before the swallow dares, and take/The winds of March with beauty." In other words, the consumer wants it both ways. Today's consumers, as Ms. Rodale knows, "don't want to sacrifice anything." Today's consumers insist, as did Perdita, on the local, the native, the spontaneous. Yet they lack her moral authority because they are unwilling to live with the consequences of their principles or preferences. Consumers today refuse to compromise; they expect fruits and flowers that survive "the birth/ Of trembling winter" and are plentiful and perfect all year round.

Naked Lunch

Those who defend genetic engineering in agriculture are likely to regard as irrational consumer concerns about the safety of genetically manipulated crops. The oil and other products of Roundup Ready soybeans, according to this position, pose no more risks to the consumer than do products from conventional soybeans. Indeed, soybean oil, *qua* oil, contains neither DNA nor protein and so will be the same whether or not the roots of the plant are herbicide resistant. Even when protein or DNA differs, no clear argument can be given to suppose that this difference—e.g., the order of a few nucleotides—involves any danger. Crops are the outcome of centuries or millennia of genetic crossing, selection, mutation, breeding, and so on. Genetic engineering adds but a wrinkle to the vast mountains of technology that separate the foods we eat from wild plants and animals.

The same kind of argument may undermine consumer beliefs that "natural" colors and flavors are safer or more edible than artificial ones. In fact, chemical compounds that provide "natural" and "artificial" flavors can be identical and may be manufactured at the same factories. The difference may lie only in the processes by which they are produced or derived. An almond flavor that is produced artificially, as I have mentioned, may be purer and therefore safer than one extracted from peach or apricot pits. Distinctions between the natural and the artificial, then, need not correspond with differences in safety, quality, or taste—at least from the perspective of science.

Distinctions consumers draw between the natural and the artificial—and preferences for the organic over the engineered—reflect differences that remain important nonetheless to our cultural, social, and aesthetic lives. We owe nature a respect that we do not owe technology. The rise of objective, neutral, physical and chemical science invites us, however, to disregard all such moral, aesthetic, and cultural distinctions and act only on facts that can be scientifically analyzed and proven. Indeed, the food industry, when it is speaking to regulators rather than advertising to consumers, insists on this rational, objective approach.

In an essay titled, "Environments at Risk," Mary Douglas characterizes the allure of objective, rational, value-neutral, science:

> This is the invitation to full self-consciousness that is offered in our time. We must accept it. But we should do so knowing that the price is William Burroughs' *Naked Lunch*. The day when everyone can see exactly what it is on the end of everyone's fork, on that day there is no pollution and no purity and nothing edible or inedible, credible or incredible, because the classifications of social life are gone. There is no more meaning.

Advances in genetic engineering invite us to the full self-consciousness that Douglas describes and aptly analogizes to the prison life depicted in *Naked Lunch*. It is the classifications of social life—not those of biological science—that clothe food and everything else with meaning. Genetic engineering poses a problem principally because it crosses moral, aesthetic, or cultural—not biological—boundaries. The fact that the technology exists and is successful shows, indeed, that the relevant biological boundaries (i.e., between species) that might have held in the past now no longer exist.

Given advances in science and technology, how can we maintain the classifications of social life—for example, distinctions between natural and artificial flavors and between organic and engineered ingredients? How may we, like Perdita, respect the difference between the products of "great creating nature" and those of human contrivance? Perdita honors this distinction by living with its consequences. Her severest test comes when Polixenes removes his disguise and threatens to condemn her to death if she ever sees Florizel again. Florizel asks her to elope, but she resigns herself to the accident of their origins—his high, hers (she believes) low—that separates them forever. Dressed up as a queen for the festivities, Perdita tells Florizel: "I will queen it no further. Leave me, sir; I will go milk my ewes and weep."

Perdita, of course, both renounced her cake and ate it, too. In Act IV, she gives up Florizel and his kingdom, but in Act V she gets them. Her true identity as a princess is eventually discovered, and so the marriage happily takes place. If you or I tried to live as fully by our beliefs and convictions—if we insisted on eating only those foods that come from great creating nature rather than from industry—we would not be so fortunate. "You'd be so lean that blasts of January/Would blow you through and through."

Perdita is protected by a playwright who places her in a comedy. Shakespeare allows her to live up to her convictions without compromising her lifestyle. This is exactly what the food industry promises to do—"to give consumers what they want with no trade-offs." It is exactly what Ms. Rodale offers—to protect the environment "but not at the cost of living well." The food, fashion, and other industries work off stage to arrange matters so that consumers can renounce genetic engineering, artificial flavors, industrial agriculture, and multinational corporations. At the same time, consumers can enjoy an inexpensive, all-natural, organic, TV dinner from Creation via Cascadian Farms.

Perdita lives in the moral order of a comedy. In that moral order, no compromises and no trade-offs are necessary. You and I are not so fortunately situated. Indeed, we must acknowledge the tragic aspect of life —the truth that good things are often not compatible and that we have to trade off one for the sake of obtaining the other. The food industry, by suggesting that we can have everything we believe in, keeps us from recognizing that tragic truth. The industry makes all the compromises and hides them from the consumer.

This article is based on a presentation made at the National Agricultural Biotechnology Council's annual meeting, "High Anxiety and Biotechnology: Who's Buying, Who's Not, and Why?," held May 22–24, 2001. A version of this article is forthcoming in NABC Report 13 symposium proceedings.

The author acknowledges the support of the National Human Genome Research Institute program on Ethical, Legal, and Social Implications of Human Genetics, Grant R01HG02363; also the National Science Foundation, Grant 9729295.

Sources: *Food Processing,* February 1988. Lucy Saunders, "Selecting an Enzyme," *Food Product Design* (May 1995), online at: http://www.foodproductdesign.com/archive/1995/0595AP.html; Michael Pollan, "Behind the Organic-Industrial Complex," *New York Times Magazine* (May 13, 2001); Ruth La Ferla, "Fashionistas, Ecofriendly and All-Natural," *New York Times* (July 15, 2001); Bill Lambrecht, "Up To 50%+ of Crops Now Genetically Modified," *St. Louis Post-Dispatch,* Washington Bureau (August 22, 1999), and available on-line at http://www.healthresearchbooks.com/articles/labels2.htm; Jim Wilson, "Scientific Food Fight," in *Popular Mechanics* on-line, which is available at http://popularmechanics.com/popmech/sci/0002STRSM.html; John Stuart Mill, "Nature" in *Three Essays on Religion* (New York, Greenwood Press, 1969), reprint of the 1874 ed.; Jeremy Rifkin, "The Biotech Century: Playing Ecological Roulette with Mother Nature's Designs," in *E Magazine* (May/June 1998); Martin Teitel and Kimberly A. Wilson, *Genetically Engineered Food: Changing the Nature of Nature: What You Need to Know to Protect Yourself, Your Family, and Our Planet* (Vermont: Inner Traditions, Int'l, Ltd., 1999); "Seeds of Disaster: An Article by The Prince of Wales," *Daily Telegraph* (June 8, 1998); Mary Douglas, "Environments at Risk," in *Implicit Meanings: Essays in Anthropology* (London: Routledge & Kegan Paul, 1975).

Population, Energy, and the Environment

GARRETT HARDIN   II.16

The Tragedy of the Commons

This article addresses the question of how to deal with the expected growth of the human population in the twenty-first century. Garrett Hardin argues that the problem of controlling human population growth has no technical solution. This is true, he argues, because of a general class of problems that arise from allowing individuals the freedom to act so as to maximize their individual self-interests by exploiting resources held in common. Problems of this kind can produce tragic results because they have the paradoxical effect of eventually bringing ruin to all those who are seeking to maximize their own interests in the belief that doing so will produce "the greatest happiness for the greatest number." The solution to such problems, he suggests, can only be one that sets limits on the individual pursuit of self-interest or on the freedom of the commons.

Focus Questions

1. What does Hardin mean by "the tragedy of the commons"? How does this problem arise?

2. What are some examples of how "Freedom in a commons brings ruin to all"? Can you think of other examples of this general phenomenon?

3. How does the perspective of this reading relate to those developed by the International Forum on Globalization (selection II.4) and Robert Kates (selection II.20)? If the population problem has no technical solution, what kind of solutions, if any, does it have?

Keywords

commons, ethical egoism, game theory, National Parks, over-fishing, population control, rational self-interest, utilitarianism

AT THE END OF A THOUGHTFUL article on the future of nuclear war, J. B. Wiesner and H. F. York concluded that: "both sides in the arms race are . . . confronted by the dilemma of steadily increasing military power and steadily decreasing national security. *It is our considered professional judgment that this dilemma has no technical solution.* If the great powers continue to look for solutions in the area of science and technology only, the result will be to worsen the situation."[1]

I would like to focus your attention not on the subject of the article (national security in a nuclear world) but on the kind of conclusion they reached, namely that there is no technical solution to the problem. An implicit and almost universal assumption of discussions published in professional and semi-popular scientific journals is that the problem under discussion has a technical solution. A technical solution may be defined as one that requires a change only in the techniques of the natural sciences, demanding little or nothing in the way of change in human values or ideas of morality.

In our day (though not in earlier times) technical solutions are always welcome. Because of previous failures in prophecy, it takes courage to assert that a desired technical solution is not possible. Wiesner and York exhibited this courage; publishing in a science journal, they insisted that the solution to the problem was not to be found in the natural sciences. They cautiously qualified their statement with the phrase, "It is our considered

professional judgment. . . ." Whether they were right or not is not the concern of the present article. Rather, the concern here is with the important concept of a class of human problems which can be called "no technical solution problems," and more specifically, with the identification and discussion of one of these.

It is easy to show that the class is not a null class. Recall the game of tick-tack-toe. Consider the problem, "How can I win the game of tick-tack-toe?" It is well known that I cannot, if I assume (in keeping with the conventions of game theory) that my opponent understands the game perfectly. Put another way, there is no "technical solution" to the problem. I can win only by giving a radical meaning to the word "win"; I can hit my opponent over the head; or I can falsify the records. Every way in which I "win" involves, in some sense, an abandonment of the game, as we intuitively understand it. (I can also, of course, openly abandon the game and refuse to play it. This is what most adults do.)

The class of "no technical solution problems" has members. My thesis is that the "population problem," as conventionally conceived, is a member of this class. How it is conventionally conceived needs some comment. It is fair to say that most people who anguish over the population problem are trying to find a way to avoid the evils of overpopulation without relinquishing any of the privileges they now enjoy. They think that farming the seas or developing new strains of wheat will solve the problem—technologically. I try to show here that the solution they seek cannot be found. The population problem cannot be solved in a technical way, any more than can the problem of winning the game of tick-tack-toe.

What Shall We Maximize?

Population, as Malthus said, naturally tends to grow "geometrically," or, as we would now say, exponentially. In a finite world this means that the per-capita share of the world's goods must decrease. Is ours a finite world?

A fair defense can be put forward for the view that the world is infinite; or that we do not know that it is not. But, in terms of the practical problems that we must face in the next few generations with the foreseeable technology, it is clear that we will greatly increase human misery if we do not, during the immediate future, assume that the world available to the terrestrial human population is finite. "Space" is no escape.[2]

A finite world can support only a finite population; therefore, population growth must eventually equal zero. (The case of perpetual wide fluctuations above and below zero is a trivial variant that need not be discussed.) When this condition is met, what will be the situation of mankind? Specifically, can Bentham's goal of "the greatest good for the greatest number" be realized?

No—for two reasons, each sufficient by itself. The first is a theoretical one. It is not mathematically possible to maximize for two (or more) variables at the same time. This was clearly stated by von Neumann and Morgenstern,[3] but the principle is implicit in the theory of partial differential equations, dating back at least to D'Alembert (1717–1783).

The second reason springs directly from biological facts. To live, any organism must have a source of energy (for example, food). This energy is utilized for two purposes: mere maintenance and work. For man, maintenance of life requires about 1600 kilocalories a day ("maintenance calories"). Anything that he does over and above merely staying alive will be defined as work, and is supported by "work calories" which he takes in. Work calories are used not only for what we call work in common speech; they are also required for all forms of enjoyment, from swimming and automobile racing to playing music and writing poetry. If our goal is to maximize population it is obvious what we must do: We must make the work calories per person

approach as close to zero as possible. No gourmet meals, no vacations, no sports, no music, no literature, no art.

. . . I think that everyone will grant, without argument or proof, that maximizing population does not maximize goods. Bentham's goal is impossible.

In reaching this conclusion I have made the usual assumption that it is the acquisition of energy that is the problem. The appearance of atomic energy has led some to question this assumption. However, given an infinite source of energy, population growth still produces an inescapable problem. The problem of the acquisition of energy is replaced by the problem of its dissipation, as J. H. Fremlin has so wittily shown.[4] The arithmetic signs in the analysis are, as it were, reversed; but Bentham's goal is unobtainable.

The optimum population is, then, less than the maximum. The difficulty of defining the optimum is enormous; so far as I know, no one has seriously tackled this problem. Reaching an acceptable and stable solution will surely require more than one generation of hard analytical work—and much persuasion.

We want the maximum good per person; but what is good? To one person it is wilderness, to another it is ski lodges for thousands. To one it is estuaries to nourish ducks for hunters to shoot; to another it is factory land. Comparing one good with another is, we usually say, impossible because goods are incommensurable. Incommensurables cannot be compared.

Theoretically this may be true; but in real life incommensurables are commensurable. Only a criterion of judgment and a system of weighting are needed. In nature the criterion is survival. Is it better for a species to be small and hideable, or large and powerful? Natural selection commensurates the incommensurables. The compromise achieved depends on a natural weighting of the values of the variables.

Man must imitate this process. There is no doubt that in fact he already does, but unconsciously. It is when the hidden decisions are made explicit that the arguments begin. The problem for the years ahead is to work out an acceptable theory of weighting. Synergistic effects, nonlinear variation, and difficulties in discounting the future make the intellectual problem difficult, but not (in principle) insoluble.

Has any cultural group solved this practical problem at the present time, even on an intuitive level? One simple fact proves that none has: there is no prosperous population in the world today that has, and has had for some time, a growth rate of zero. Any people that has intuitively identified its optimum point will soon reach it, after which its growth rate becomes and remains zero.

Of course, a positive growth rate might be taken as evidence that a population is below its optimum. However, by any reasonable standards, the most rapidly growing populations on earth today are (in general) the most miserable. This association (which need not be invariable) casts doubt on the optimistic assumption that the positive growth rate of a population is evidence that it has yet to reach its optimum.

We can make little progress in working toward optimum population size until we explicitly exorcise the spirit of Adam Smith in the field of practical demography. In economic affairs, *The Wealth of Nations* (1776) popularized the "invisible hand," the idea that an individual who "intends only his own gain," is, as it were, "led by an invisible hand to promote . . . the public interest."[5] Adam Smith did not assert that this was invariably true, and perhaps neither did any of his followers. But he contributed to a dominant tendency of thought that has ever since interfered with positive action based on rational analysis, namely, the tendency to assume that decisions reached individually will, in fact, be the best decisions for an entire society. If this assumption is correct it justifies the continuance of our present policy of laissez faire in reproduction. If it is correct we can assume that men will control their individual fecundity so as to produce the optimum population. If the assumption is not correct, we need to reexamine our individual freedoms to see which ones are defensible.

Tragedy of Freedom in a Commons

The rebuttal to the "invisible hand" in population control is to be found in a scenario first sketched in a little-known pamphlet in 1833 by a mathematical amateur named William Forster Lloyd (1794–1852).[6] We may well call it "the tragedy of the commons," using the word "tragedy" as the philosopher Whitehead[7] used it. "The essence of dramatic tragedy is not unhappiness. It resides in the solemnity of the remorseless working of things." He then goes on to say, "This inevitableness of destiny can only be illustrated in terms of human life by incidents which in fact involve unhappiness. For it is only by them that the futility of escape can be made evident in the drama."

The tragedy of the commons develops in this way. Picture a pasture open to all. It is to be expected that each herdsman will try to keep as many cattle as possible on the commons. Such an arrangement may work reasonably satisfactorily for centuries because tribal wars, poaching, and disease keep the numbers of both man and beast well below the carrying capacity of the land. Finally, however, comes the day of reckoning, that is, the day when the long-desired goal of social stability becomes a reality. At this point, the inherent logic of the commons remorselessly generates tragedy.

As a rational being, each herdsman seeks to maximize his gain. Explicitly or implicitly, more or less consciously, he asks, "What is the utility to me of adding one more animal to my herd?" This utility has one negative and one positive component.

1. The positive component is a function of the increment of one animal. Since the herdsman receives all the proceeds from the sale of the additional animal, the positive utility is nearly +1.
2. The negative component is a function of the additional overgrazing created by one more animal. Since, however, the effects of overgrazing are shared by all the herdsmen, the negative utility for any particular decision-making herdsman is only a fraction of −1.

Adding together the component partial utilities, the rational herdsman concludes that the only sensible course for him to pursue is to add another animal to his herd. And another. . . . But this is the conclusion reached by each and every rational herdsman sharing a commons. Therein is the tragedy. Each man is locked into a system that compels him to increase his herd without limit in a world that is limited. Ruin is the destination toward which all men rush, each pursuing his own best interest in a society that believes in the freedom of the commons. Freedom in a commons brings ruin to all.

Some would say that this is a platitude. Would that it were! In a sense, it was learned thousands of years ago, but natural selection favors the forces of psychological denial.[8] The individual benefits as an individual from his ability to deny the truth even though society as a whole, of which he is a part, suffers. Education can counteract the natural tendency to do the wrong thing, but the inexorable succession of generations requires that the basis for this knowledge be constantly refreshed.

A simple incident that occurred a few years ago in Leominster, Massachusetts, shows how perishable the knowledge is. During the Christmas shopping season the parking meters downtown were covered with plastic bags that bore tags reading: "Do not open until after Christmas. Free parking courtesy of the mayor and city council." In other words, facing the prospect of an increased demand for already scarce space, the city fathers reinstituted the system of the commons. (Cynically, we suspect that they gained more votes than they lost by this retrogressive act.)

In an approximate way, the logic of the commons has been understood for a long time, perhaps since the discovery of agriculture or the invention of private property in real estate. But it is understood mostly only in special cases which are not sufficiently generalized. Even at this late date, cattlemen leasing national land on the Western ranges demonstrate no more than an ambivalent understanding, in constantly pressuring federal authorities to increase the head count to the point where overgrazing produces erosion and weed-dominance. Likewise, the oceans of the world continue to suffer from the survival of the philosophy of the commons. Maritime nations still respond automatically to the shibboleth of the "freedom of the seas." Professing to believe in the "inexhaustible resources of the oceans," they bring species after species of fish and whales closer to extinction.[9]

The National Parks present another instance of the working out of the tragedy of the commons. At present, they are open to all, without limit. The parks themselves are limited in extent—there is only one Yosemite Valley—whereas population seems to grow without limit. The values that visitors seek in the parks are steadily eroded. Plainly, we must soon cease to treat the parks as commons or they will be of no value to anyone.

What shall we do? We have several options. We might sell them off as private property. We might keep them as public property, but allocate the right to enter them. The allocation might be on the basis of wealth, by the use of an auction system. It might be on the basis of merit, as defined by some agreed-upon standards. It might be by lottery. Or it might be on a first-come, first-served basis, administered to long queues. These, I think, are all objectionable. But we must choose—or acquiesce in the destruction of the commons that we call our National Parks.

Pollution

In a reverse way, the tragedy of the commons reappears in problems of pollution. Here it is not a question of taking something out of the commons, but of putting something in—sewage, or chemical, radioactive, and heat wastes into water; noxious and dangerous fumes into the air; and distracting and unpleasant advertising signs into the line of sight. The calculations of utility are much the same as before. The rational man finds that his share of the cost of the wastes he discharges into the commons is less than the cost of purifying his wastes before releasing them. Since this is true for everyone, we are locked into a system of "fouling our own nest," so long as we behave as independent, rational, free-enterprisers.

The tragedy of the commons as a food basket is averted by private property, or something formally like it. But the air and waters surrounding us cannot readily be fenced, and so the tragedy of the commons as a cesspool must be prevented by different means, by coercive laws or taxing devices that make it cheaper for the polluter to treat his pollutants than to discharge them untreated. We have not progressed as far with the solution of this problem as we have with the first. Indeed, our particular concept of private property, which deters us from exhausting the positive resources of the earth, favors pollution. The owner of a factory on the bank of a stream—whose property extends to the middle of the stream—often has difficulty seeing why it is not his natural right to muddy the waters flowing past his door. The law, always behind the times, requires elaborate stitching and fitting to adapt it to this newly perceived aspect of the commons.

The pollution problem is a consequence of population. It did not much matter how a lonely American frontiersman disposed of his waste. "Flowing water purifies itself every ten miles," my grandfather used to say, and the myth was near enough to the truth when he was a boy, for there were not too many people. But as population became denser, the natural chemical and biological recycling processes became overloaded, calling for a redefinition of property rights.

How to Legislate Temperance

Analysis of the pollution problem as a function of population density uncovers a not generally recognized principle of morality, namely: *the morality of an act is a function of the state of the system at the time it is performed.*[10] Using the commons as a cesspool does not harm the general public under frontier conditions, because there is no public; the same behavior in a metropolis is unbearable. One hundred fifty years ago a plainsman could kill an American bison, cut out only the tongue for his dinner, and discard the rest of the animal. He was not in any important sense being wasteful. Today, with only a few thousand bison left, we would be appalled at such behavior.

In passing, it is worth noting that the morality of an act cannot be determined from a photograph. One does not know whether a man killing an elephant or setting fire to the grassland is harming others until one knows the total system in which his act appears. "One picture is worth a thousand words," said an ancient Chinese, but it may take ten thousand words to validate it. It is as tempting to ecologists as it is to reformers in general to try to persuade others by way of the photographic short-cut. But the essence of an argument cannot be photographed: it must be presented rationally—in words.

That morality is system-sensitive escaped the attention of most codifiers of ethics in the past. "Thou shalt not . . ." is the form of traditional ethical directives which make no allowance for particular circumstances. The laws of our society follow the pattern of ancient ethics, and therefore are poorly suited to governing a complex, crowded, changeable world. Our epicyclic solution is to augment statutory law with administrative law. Since it is practically impossible to spell out all the conditions under which it is safe to burn trash in the back yard or to run an automobile without smog-control, by law we delegate the details to bureaus. The result is administrative law, which is rightly feared for an ancient reason—*Quis custodiet ipsos custodes?*—Who shall watch the watchers themselves? John Adams said that we must have a "government of laws and not men." Bureau administrators, trying to evaluate the morality of acts in the total system, are singularly liable to corruption, producing a government by men, not laws.

Prohibition is easy to legislate (though not necessarily easy to enforce); but how do we legislate temperance? Experience indicates that it can be accomplished best through the mediation of administrative law. We limit possibilities unnecessarily if we suppose that the sentiment of *Quis custodiet* denies us the use of administrative law. We should rather retain the phrase as a perpetual reminder of fearful dangers we cannot avoid. The great challenge facing us now is to invent the corrective feedbacks that are needed to keep custodians honest. We must find ways to legitimate the needed authority of both the custodians and the corrective feedbacks.

Freedom to Breed Is Intolerable

The tragedy of the commons is involved in population problems in another way. In a world governed solely by the principle "dog eat dog"—if indeed there ever was such a world—how many children a family had would not be a matter of public concern. Parents who bred too exuberantly would leave fewer descendants, not more, because they would be unable to care adequately for their children.

David Lack and others have found that such a negative feedback demonstrably controls the fecundity of birds.[11] But men are not birds, and have not acted like them for millenniums, at least.

If each human family were dependent only on its own resources; *if* the children of improvident parents starved to death; *if,* thus, overbreeding brought its own "punishment" to the germ line— *then* there would be no public interest in controlling the breeding of families. But our society is deeply committed to the welfare state,[12] and hence is confronted with another aspect of the tragedy of the commons.

In a welfare state, how shall we deal with the family, the religion, the race, or the class (of indeed any distinguishable and cohesive group) that adopts overbreeding as a policy to secure its own aggrandizement?[13] To couple the concept of freedom to breed with the belief that everyone born has an equal right to the commons is to lock the world into a tragic course of action.

Unfortunately this is just the course of action that is being pursued by the United Nations. In late 1967, some thirty nations agreed to the following: "The Universal Declaration of Human Rights describes the family as the natural and fundamental unit of society. It follows that any choice and decision with regard to the size of the family must irrevocably rest with the family itself, and cannot be made by anyone else."[14]

It is painful to have to deny categorically the validity of this right; denying it, one feels as uncomfortable as a resident of Salem, Massachusetts, who denied the reality of witches in the seventeenth century. At the present time, in liberal quarters, something like a taboo acts to inhibit criticism of the United Nations. There is a feeling that the United Nations is "our last and best hope," that we shouldn't find fault with it; we shouldn't play into the hands of the arch conservatives. However, let us not forget what Robert Louis Stevenson said: "The truth that is suppressed by friends is the readiest weapon of the enemy." If we love the truth we must openly deny the validity of the Universal Declaration of Human Rights, even though it is promoted by the United Nations. We should also join with Kingsley Davis[15] in attempting to get Planned Parenthood–World Population to see the error of its ways in embracing the same tragic ideal.

Conscience Is Self-Eliminating

It is a mistake to think that we can control the breeding of mankind in the long run by an appeal to conscience. Charles Galton Darwin made this point when he spoke on the centennial of the publication of his grandfather's great book. The argument is straightforward and Darwinian.

People vary. Confronted with appeals to limit breeding, some people will undoubtedly respond to the plea more than others. Those who have more children will produce a larger fraction of the next generation than those with more susceptible consciences. The differences will be accentuated, generation by generation.

In C. G. Darwin's words: "It may well be that it would take hundreds of generations for the progenitive instinct to develop in this way, but if it should do so, nature would have taken her revenge, and the variety *Homo contracipiens* would become extinct and would be replaced by the variety *Homo progenitivus*."[16]

The argument assumes that conscience or the desire for children (no matter which) is hereditary—but hereditary only in the most general formal sense. The result will be the same whether the attitude is transmitted through germ cells, or exosomatically, to use A. J. Lotka's term. (If one denies the latter possibility as well as the former, then what's the point of education?) The argument has here been stated in the context of the population problem, but it applies equally well to any instance in which society appeals to an individual exploiting a commons to restrain himself for the general good—by means of his conscience. To make such an appeal is to set up a selective system that works toward the elimination of conscience from the race.

Pathogenic Effects of Conscience

The long-term disadvantage of an appeal to conscience should be enough to condemn it; but it has serious short-term disadvantages as well. If we ask a man who is exploiting a commons to desist "in the name of conscience," what are we saying to him? What does he hear?—not only at the moment but also in the wee small hours of the night when, half asleep, he remembers not merely the words we used but also the nonverbal communication cues we gave him unawares? Sooner or later, consciously or subconsciously, he senses that he has received two communications, and that they are contradictory: 1. (intended communication) "If you don't do as we ask, we will openly condemn you for not acting like a responsible citizen"; 2. (unintended communication) "If you *do* behave as we ask, we will secretly condemn you for a simpleton who can be shamed into standing aside while the rest of us exploit the commons."

Everyman then is caught in what Bateson has called a "double bind." Bateson and his co-workers have made a plausible case for viewing the double bind as an important causative factor in the genesis of schizophrenia.[17] The double bind may not always be so damaging, but it always endangers the mental health of anyone to whom it is applied. "A bad conscience," said Nietzsche, "is a kind of illness."

To conjure up a conscience in others is tempting to anyone who wishes to extend his control beyond the legal limits. Leaders at the highest level succumb to this temptation. Has any president during the past generation failed to call on labor unions to moderate voluntarily their demands for higher wages, or to steel companies to honor voluntary guidelines on prices? I can recall none. The rhetoric used on such occasions is designed to produce feelings of guilt in noncooperators.

For centuries it was assumed without proof that guilt was a valuable, perhaps even an indispensable, ingredient of the civilized life. Now, in this post-Freudian world, we doubt it.

Paul Goodman speaks from the modern point of view when he says: "No good has ever come from feeling guilty, neither intelligence, policy, nor compassion. The guilty do not pay attention to the object but only to themselves, and not even to their own interests, which might make sense, but to their anxieties."[18]

One does not have to be a professional psychiatrist to see the consequences of anxiety. We in the Western world are just emerging from a dreadful two-centuries-long Dark Ages of Eros that was sustained partly by prohibition laws, but perhaps more effectively by the anxiety-generating mechanisms of education. Alex Comfort has told the story well in *The Anxiety Makers;*[19] it is not a pretty one.

Since proof is difficult, we may even concede that the results of anxiety may sometimes, from certain points of view, be desirable. The larger question we should ask is whether, as a matter of policy, we should ever encourage the use of a technique, the tendency (if not the intention) of which, is psychologically pathogenic. We hear much talk these days of responsible parenthood; the coupled words are incorporated into the titles of some organizations devoted to birth control. Some people have proposed massive propaganda campaigns to instill responsibility into the nation's (or the world's) breeders. But what is the meaning of the word conscience? When we use the word *responsibility* in the absence of substantial sanctions are we not trying to browbeat a free man in a commons into acting against his own interest? Responsibility is a verbal counterfeit for a substantial quid pro quo. It is an attempt to get something for nothing.

If the word responsibility is to be used at all, I suggest that it be in the sense Charles Frankel uses it.[20] "Responsibility," says this philosopher, "is the product of definite social arrangements." Notice that Frankel calls for social arrangements—not propaganda.

Mutual Coercion Mutually Agreed Upon

The social arrangements that produce responsibility are arrangements that create coercion, of some sort. Consider bank robbing. The man who takes money from a bank acts as if the bank were a commons. How do we prevent such action? Certainly not by trying to control his behavior solely by a verbal appeal to his sense of responsibility. Rather than rely on propaganda we follow Frankel's lead and insist that a bank is not a commons; we seek the definite social arrangements that will keep it from becoming a commons. That we thereby infringe on the freedom of would-be robbers we neither deny nor regret.

The morality of bank robbing is particularly easy to understand because we accept complete prohibition of this activity. We are willing to say "Thou shalt not rob banks," without providing for exceptions. But temperance also can be created by coercion. Taxing is a good coercive device. To keep downtown shoppers temperate in their use of parking spaces we introduce parking meters for short periods, and traffic fines for longer ones. We need not actually forbid a citizen to park as long as he wants to; we need merely make it increasingly expensive for him to do so. Not prohibition, but carefully biased options are what we offer him. A Madison Avenue man might call this persuasion; I prefer the greater candor of the word *coercion.*

Coercion is a dirty word to most liberals now, but it need not forever be so. As with the four-letter words, its dirtiness can be cleansed away by exposure to the light, by saying it over and over without apology or embarrassment. To many, the word *coercion* implies arbitrary decisions of distant and irresponsible bureaucrats; but this is not a necessary part of its meaning. The only kind of coercion I recommend is mutual coercion, mutually agreed upon by the majority of the people affected.

To say that we mutually agree to coercion is not to say that we are required to enjoy it, or even to pretend we enjoy it. Who enjoys taxes? We all grumble about them. But we accept compulsory taxes because we recognize that voluntary taxes would favor the conscienceless. We institute and (grumblingly) support taxes and other coercive devices to escape the horror of the commons.

An alternative to the commons need not be perfectly just to be preferable. With real estate and other material goods, the alternative we have chosen is the institution of private property coupled with legal inheritance. Is this system perfectly just? As a genetically trained biologist I deny that it is. It seems to me that, if there are to be differences in individual inheritance, legal possession should be perfectly correlated with biological inheritance—that those who are biologically more fit to be the custodians of property and power should legally

inherit more. But genetic recombination continually makes a mockery of the doctrine "like father, like son" implicit in our laws of legal inheritance. An idiot can inherit millions, and a trust fund can keep his estate intact. We must admit that our legal system of private property plus inheritance is unjust—but we put up with it because we are not convinced, at the moment, that anyone has invented a better system. The alternative of the commons is too horrifying to contemplate. Injustice is preferable to total ruin.

It is one of the peculiarities of the warfare between reform and the status quo that is thoughtlessly governed by a double standard. Whenever a reform measure is proposed it is often defeated when its opponents triumphantly discover a flaw in it. As Kingsley Davis has pointed out,[21] worshipers of the staus quo sometimes imply that no reform is possible without unanimous agreement, an implication contrary to historical fact. As nearly as I can make out, automatic rejection of proposed reforms is based on one of two unconscious assumptions: (1) that the status quo is perfect; or (2) that the choice we face is between reform and no action; if the proposed reform is imperfect, we presumably should take no action at all, while we wait for a perfect proposal.

But we can never do nothing. That which we have done for thousands of years is also action. It also produces evils. Once we are aware that the status quo is action, we can then compare its discoverable advantages and disadvantages with the predicted advantages and disadvantages of the proposed reform, discounting as best we can for our lack of experience. On the basis of such a comparison, we can make a rational decision which will not involve the unworkable assumption that only perfect systems are tolerable.

Recognition of Necessity

Perhaps the simplest summary of this analysis of man's population problems is this: the commons, if justifiable at all, is justifiable only under conditions of low-population density. As the human population has increased, the commons has had to be abandoned in one aspect after another.

First we abandoned the commons in food gathering, enclosing farm land and restricting pastures and hunting and fishing areas. These restrictions are still not complete throughout the world.

Somewhat later we saw that the commons as a place for waste disposal would also have to be abandoned. Restrictions on the disposal of domestic sewage are widely accepted in the Western world; we are still struggling to close the commons to pollution by automobiles, factories, insecticide sprayers, fertilizing operations, and atomic energy installations.

In a still more embryonic state is our recognition of the evils of the commons in matters of pleasure. There is almost no restriction on the propagation of sound waves in the public medium. The shopping public is assaulted with mindless music, without its consent. Our government has paid out billions of dollars to create a supersonic transport which would disturb 50,000 people for every one person whisked from coast to coast 3 hours faster. Advertisers muddy the airwaves of radio and television and pollute the view of travelers. We are a long way from outlawing the commons in matters of pleasure. Is this because our Puritan inheritance makes us view pleasure as something of a sin, and pain (that is, the pollution of advertising) as the sign of virtue?

Every new enclosure of the commons involves the infringement of somebody's personal liberty. Infringements made in the distant past are accepted because no contemporary complains of a loss. It is the newly proposed infringements that we vigorously oppose; cries of "rights" and "freedom" fill the air. But what does "freedom" mean? When men mutually agreed to pass laws against robbing, mankind became more free, not less so. Individuals locked into the logic of the commons are free only to bring on universal ruin; once they see the necessity of mutual coercion, they become free to pursue other goals. I believe it was Hegel who said, "Freedom is the recognition of necessity."

The most important aspect of necessity that we must now recognize is the necessity of abandoning the commons in breeding. No technical solution can rescue us from the misery of overpopulation. Freedom to breed will bring ruin to all. At the moment, to avoid hard decisions many of us are tempted to propagandize for conscience and responsible parenthood. The temptation must be resisted, because an appeal to independently acting consciences selects for the disappearance of all conscience in the long run, and an increase in anxiety in the short.

The only way we can preserve and nurture other and more precious freedoms is by relinquishing the freedom to breed, and that very soon. "Freedom is the recognition of necessity"—and it is the role of education to reveal to all the necessity of abandoning the freedom to breed. Only so, can we put an end to this aspect of the tragedy of the commons.

NOTES

1. J. B. Wiesner and H. F. York, *Scientific American* 211 (No. 4), 27 (1964).
2. G. Hardin, *Journal of Heredity* 50, 68 (1959); S. von Hoernor, *Science* 137, 18 (1962).
3. J. von Neumann and O. Morgenstern, *Theory of Games and Economic Behavior* (Princeton University Press, Princeton, N.J., 1947), p. 11.
4. J. H. Fremlin, *New Scientist,* No. 415 (1964), p. 285.
5. A. Smith, *The Wealth of Nations* (Modern Library, New York, 1937), p. 423.
6. W. F. Lloyd, *Two Lectures on the Checks to Population* (Oxford University Press, Oxford, England, 1833).
7. A. N. Whitehead, *Science and the Modern World* (Mentor, New York, 1948), p. 17.
8. G. Hardin, Ed., *Population, Evolution, and Birth Control* (Freeman, San Francisco, 1964), p. 56.
9. S. McVay, *Scientific American* 216 (No. 8), 13 (1966).
10. J. Fletcher, *Situation Ethics* (Westminster, Philadelphia, 1966).
11. D. Lack, *The Natural Regulation of Animal Numbers* (Clarendon Press, Oxford, England, 1954).
12. H. Girvetz, *From Wealth to Welfare* (Stanford University Press, Stanford, Calif., 1950).
13. G. Hardin, *Perspectives in Biology and Medicine* 6, 366 (1963).
14. U. Thant, *International Planned Parenthood News,* No. 168 (February 1968), p. 3.
15. K. Davis, *Science* 158, 730 (1967).
16. S. Tax, Ed., *Evolution After Darwin* (University of Chicago Press, Chicago, 1960), vol. 2, p. 469.

17. G. Bateson, D. D. Jackson, J. Haley, J. Weakland, *Behavioral Science* 1, 251 (1956).

18. P. Goodman, *New York Review of Books* 10 (8), 22 (23 May 1968).

19. A. Comfort, *The Anxiety Makers* (Nelson, London, 1967).

20. C. Frankel, *The Case for Modern Man* (Harper & Row, New York, 1955), p. 203.

21. J. D. Roslansky, *Genetics and the Future of Man* (Appleton-Century-Crofts, New York, 1966), p. 177.

KEVIN E. TRENBERTH   II.17

Stronger Evidence of Human Influence on Climate—The 2001 IPCC Assessment

It is not surprising to hear talk about the "crazy" or "strange" weather and how it seems to be so different from the past. Even though most people have not done extensive research into the history of our planet's weather patterns, there seems to be general agreement that the weather is different from before. Although there is ample evidence that fluctuations in many factors related to weather have changed over the years, there is little agreement about whether those changes have been random or induced by humans.

There is no disagreement, however, about the fact that humans have always had an impact on their environment—beginning with our distant relatives fighting to survive in a hostile world to the present-day high levels of consumption of fossil fuels in many developed, affluent countries. Based on recent research, even the myth of the "noble savage" living in harmony with nature has come into question. Although there were certainly far fewer early humans in the ancient world than today, and their technological capabilities were limited, they left behind indicators of their negative impact on their surroundings, even though it was minimal compared to modern humans. Human environmental impact cannot be denied, and there is now a scientific concensus that global climate changes are due in part to human activity.

Although the debate over what to do about global warming is not likely to be resolved soon, many scientists are discussing a variety of issues related to that topic. The author of this article, Kevin Trenberth, head of the Climate Analysis Section, National Center for Atmospheric Research, believes that, given the level of technological power at our disposal today, it is critical that we carefully consider ways in which to responsibly deal with the mounting evidence that we have influenced the global climate. According to Trenberth, sophisticated analytical models indicate that the projected rates of climate change "exceed anything seen in nature for the past 10,000 years," a fact that should be of concern not only to scientists but to all who call this planet home.

Focus Questions

1. What are some of the major factors and their sources that appear to influence climate change?

2. What climate conditions are mentioned by Trenberth, and how have they shifted over time?

3. Discuss the "greater climate system" and the various factors influencing it.
4. What role do "feedbacks" play in climate modification related to heating and cooling changes?

Keywords

CFCs, climate change, El Niño, feedbacks, global warming, greenhouse gases, hydrological cycle, IPCC, Kyoto Protocol, mean climate, natural climate variability, paleo-climate records, solar radiation

THE INTERGOVERNMENTAL PANEL ON CLIMATE Change (IPCC) reports on the evolving science of global climate change, focusing special attention on the ways in which human activities affect the climate.[1] IPCC reviews the evidence for climate change and the possible causes and considers how the climate system responds to various agents of change. Because our climate models are simplified versions of the real world and are still being improved upon, IPCC evaluates the ability of models to describe the processes involved in the climate system and the functioning of the system as a whole. The panel seeks to attribute recent observed changes to possible causes, especially the human influences, and then, using climate models, projects future change from those causes.

Climate changes have occurred in the past naturally for various reasons, over periods ranging from decades to millennia. Fluctuations in the sun's energy output and other factors that influence the amount and fate of the energy that reaches the Earth's surface have caused natural climate change. And now, by greatly changing the composition of the atmosphere, humankind is performing an enormous geophysical experiment.[2] Human actions alter the Earth's environment in ways that cause climate change.[3] Legitimate debates go on about the extent and rate of change and what, if anything, can

be done about it, but that the experiment is underway is not in doubt.

Land use (e.g., farming and building cities), storage and use of water (e.g., dams, reservoirs, and irrigation), generation of heat (e.g., furnaces), and the use of fossil fuels are the human-induced environmental changes that most influence the climate. The use of fossil fuels introduces visible particulate pollution (called aerosols) and gases such as carbon dioxide (CO_2) into the atmosphere, both of which alter the balance of radiation on Earth. These gases are relatively transparent to incoming solar radiation, yet they absorb and reemit outgoing infrared radiation. The resulting blanketing effect is known as the greenhouse effect, and the gases involved are called greenhouse gases. Not all greenhouse gases are the result of human activities. There is a large natural greenhouse effect that makes the Earth habitable. The increase in CO_2 levels over the last century or two from human activities, as well as the introduction of other greenhouse gases more recently, mean that more energy stays in the system. Global warming and the associated climate change are the expected results.

Observed Climate Change

Records of surface temperature show that a global mean warming of about 0.7°C has occurred over the past 100 years. [Editor's note: The formula for converting Celsius to Fahrenheit is F = C × 1.8 + 32] IPCC reports this change as 0.6 ±0.2°C, but this is a linear fit to what is obviously not a linear trend. . . . Temperatures increased most noticeably from the 1920s to the 1940s; they then leveled off

From "Stronger Evidence of Human Influence on Climate," by Kevin E. Trenberth, *Environment Magazine, Vol. 43* (May, 2001), pp. 10–19. Reprinted with permission of the Helen Dwight Reid Educational Foundation. Published by Heldref Publications, 1319 Eighteenth St., N.W., Washington, D.C. 20036-1802. Copyright © 2001.

from the 1950s to the 1970s and took off again in the late 1970s. The 1990s mark the warmest decade on record, and 1998 is by far the warmest year on record, exceeding the previous record held by 1997. Preliminary annual global mean temperatures in the year 2000 were about the same as for 1999. Synthesis of information from tree rings, corals, ice cores, and historical data further indicates that the 1990s are the warmest decade in at least the past 1,000 years for the Northern Hemisphere, which is as far back as annual-resolution hemispheric estimates of temperatures can be made.[4] The melting of glaciers over most of the world and rising sea levels confirm the reality of the global temperature increases.

There is good evidence from measurements of sea level pressure, wind, and temperature over the twentieth century for decadal changes in the atmospheric circulation and some evidence for similar ocean changes. For instance, these include changes in winds over the North Atlantic and Europe related to the phenomenon known as the North Atlantic Oscillation and changes in El Niño.[5] Such observations signal that increases in temperature are not uniform or monotonic. For example, some places warm more than the average, while other places cool. Changes in precipitation and other components of the hydrological cycle also vary considerably geographically. For instance, it is likely that precipitation has increased by perhaps 1 percent per decade during the twentieth century over most mid- and high-latitude continents of the Northern Hemisphere. Changes in climate variability are also being seen and changes in extremes are beginning to emerge. Perhaps of greatest note are the observed increases in the heat index (which measures humidity and temperature effects on comfort) and the observed trend toward more intense precipitation events.

One persistent controversy in climate change science has been the discrepancy between the trend seen in the so-called satellite temperature record and that seen in the temperature record from the Earth's surface. The controversy stems in part from the fact that the two data sets do not measure the same phenomenon. The satellite record, which

begins in 1979, measures microwave radiation from the lowest 8 kilometers of the Earth's atmosphere and thus depicts temperatures in that part of the atmosphere, which are quite different from those at the surface. Climate models that assess the scenario of increasing greenhouse gases suggest that warming in the lower atmosphere should be greater than that at the surface. But here is the point of contention for skeptics: The observed satellite record shows less warming from 1979–1999. Consequently, doubt has been cast on the veracity of both the surface temperature record and the models. However, when the observed stratospheric ozone depletion is included in the models, the models predict that the surface and tropospheric temperatures increase at about the same rate. In fact, this is what has happened from about 1960 to the present based on balloon observations, which replicate the satellite record after 1979. Because the satellite record includes only two decades, the influence of El Niño and the eruption of Mt. Pinatubo in 1991 leads to a disproportionate relative downward trend in temperatures observed in the lower atmosphere. Other effects, such as changes in cloud cover, have not been accounted for by the models and may also affect the two records differently. Accordingly, the different short-term trend in the satellite record is not at odds with the warming in the surface record.

The Climate System and Its Driving Forces

Because we humans live in and breathe the atmosphere, it is natural for us to focus on the atmospheric changes. But the atmosphere is only one element of a greater climate system that involves interactions among various internal components and external forcings. The internal, interactive components include the atmosphere, the oceans, sea ice, the land and its features (including the vegetation, albedo, biomass, and ecosystems), snow cover, land ice, and the hydrology of the land (including rivers, lakes, and surface and subsurface water). The factors that are normally regarded as external to the system include the sun and its output, the Earth's rotation, sun-Earth geometry and the slowly changing orbit, the physical components of the Earth system such as the distribution of land and ocean, the topographic features on the land, the ocean-bottom topography and basin configurations, and the mass and basic composition of the atmosphere and the oceans. These factors determine the mean climate, which may vary from natural causes. Climate variations arise naturally when the atmosphere is influenced by and interacts with other internal components of the system and "external" forcings.

The continual flow of radiation from the sun provides the energy that drives the Earth's climate. About 31 percent of that radiation gets reflected back into space by molecules, tiny airborne particles (aerosols), clouds, or by the Earth's surface and thus plays no part in the climate. The sun's massive energy input leads to warming. To maintain a balance, the Earth radiates back into space, in the form of "long-wave" or infrared radiation, roughly the same amount of energy that it receives. The amount of radiation lost from the top of the atmosphere to space corresponds to a global mean surface temperature of about −19°C, much colder than the annual average global mean temperature of about 14°C. The higher mean temperature of the Earth, given the amount of energy radiated from its surface, can be explained by the existence of the atmosphere. The Earth's atmosphere intercepts the bulk of energy emitted at the surface and, in turn, reemits energy both toward space and back to the Earth. The energy that escapes into space is emitted from the tops of clouds at various atmospheric levels (which are almost always colder than the surface) or by atmospheric gases that absorb and emit infrared radiation. These greenhouse gases, notably water vapor and CO_2, produce a blanketing effect known as the natural greenhouse effect. Water vapor gives rise to about 60 percent of the current greenhouse effect and CO_2 accounts for about 26 percent.[6] Clouds also absorb and emit infrared radiation and have a blanketing effect similar to that of the greenhouse gases. But because clouds also reflect solar radiation, they act to cool the surface. Though on average the two opposing effects offset one another to a large degree, the net global effect of clouds in our current climate, as determined by space-based measurements, is a small cooling of the surface.

Human Influences

The amount of CO_2 in the atmosphere has increased by about 31 percent since the beginning of the Industrial Revolution, from 280 parts per million (ppm) by volume to 367 ppm. This increase is due mainly to combustion of fossil fuels and the removal of forests. Projections of future CO_2 concentrations suggest that, in the absence of controls, the rate of increase may accelerate and thus double the concentrations of CO_2 from pre-industrial levels within the next 50 to 100 years. Human activities (especially biomass burning; agriculture; animal husbandry; fossil fuel extraction, distillation, and use; and the creation of landfills and rice paddies) have increased the atmospheric concentrations of several other greenhouse gases (methane, nitrous oxide, chlorofluorocarbons [CFCs]) and tropospheric ozone. These other greenhouse gases tend to reinforce the changes caused by increased CO_2 levels. However, the observed decreases in lower stratospheric ozone since the 1970s, caused principally by human-introduced CFCs and halocarbons, contribute a small cooling effect.

Aerosols enter the atmosphere naturally when they are blown off the surface of deserts or dry regions, blasted into the atmosphere during volcanic eruptions, or released during forest fires. They impact climate in various ways. For instance, the aerosols introduced into the atmosphere during the eruption of Mt. Pinatubo in the Philippines in June 1991 blocked enough radiation for two years to cause observable cooling. Human activities contribute to aerosol particle formation mainly through emissions of sulfur dioxide (SO_2) (a major source of acid rain), particularly from coal-burning power stations and through biomass burning. Sulfate aerosols, visible as a milky, whitish haze from airplane windows, reflect a fraction of solar radiation back to space and hence work to cool the Earth's surface. Some aerosols, like soot, absorb solar radiation and lead to local warming of the atmosphere. Other aerosols absorb and reemit infrared radiation. Aerosols play still another role. By acting as the nuclei on which cloud droplets condense, they affect the number and size of droplets in a cloud and thereby alter the reflective and absorptive properties of clouds.[7] Aerosols from human activities are mostly introduced near the Earth's surface and are often washed out of the atmosphere by rain. They typically remain aloft for only a few days near their sources. Aerosols therefore have a very strong regional affect on the climate, usually producing cooling.

The determination of the climatic response to the changes in heating and cooling is complicated by feedbacks. Some of these feedbacks amplify the original warming (positive feedback) and others serve to reduce warming (negative feedback). If, for instance, the amount of CO_2 in the atmosphere were suddenly doubled while all other factors remained constant, the amount of energy absorbed by the atmosphere would increase. With additional energy trapped in the system, a new balance would have to be reached. To accomplish this balance the atmosphere would have to warm up. In the absence of other changes, the warming at the surface and throughout the troposphere would be about 1.2°C.[8] In reality, many other factors could change as a result of doubled CO_2 concentrations, and various feedbacks would come into play. When the positive and negative feedbacks are considered, the best IPCC estimate of the average global warming for doubled CO_2 is 2.5°C. The net effect of the feedbacks is positive and, in fact, roughly doubles the global mean temperature increase otherwise expected. Increases in water vapor that accompany warming contribute the strongest positive feedback.

Modeling of Climate Change

To quantify the response of the climate system to changes in forcing, the complex interactions and feedbacks among the components must be accounted for. . . . Numerical models of the climate system based upon sound, well-established physical principles are the tools used to estimate climate change. Experiments can be run with climate models in which concentrations of greenhouse gases or other influences, like aerosols, are varied. The best

models capture the current understanding of the physical processes involved in the climate system, the interactions among the processes, and the performance of the system as a whole. The predictive powers of a model can be tested by running the model with known forcings from the past through it and then comparing the results to actual climate records. Though models are exceedingly useful tools for carrying out numerical climate experiments, they do have limitations and must be used carefully.[9] The latest models have been able to reproduce the climate of the past century or so with increasing accuracy. . . . Thus the global mean temperature record is well replicated within limits imposed by natural fluctuations merely by specifying the changes in atmospheric composition and changes in the sun.

Detection and Attribution

Two main issues must be settled before politicians are likely to take action: First, it must be discerned whether the recent climate has changed more than expected from natural variability; second, observed climate changes must be attributed to various causes, including human influences. Several key points that emerged from the recent IPCC assessment address these issues:

- The magnitude and rate of change of mean surface temperature globally, or at least in the Northern Hemisphere, over the past few decades is outside the range of anything deduced from paleo-climate records of the last 1,000 years. Data are inadequate before that.
- Estimates of internal climate variability (how much climate can vary from natural causes not including changes in the sun) derived from models are reasonably consistent with the pre-industrial variability deduced from paleo-climate data. Together, the estimates from model and paleo-climate observations provide more reliable estimates of the natural variability.
- Consequently, given the better sense of natural climate variability, detection of climate change is much clearer now than it was five years ago. Hence, it is very unlikely that recent climate change is natural in origin.

• The natural forcing agents (e.g., solar and volcanoes) over the last two to four decades are likely to have had a net cooling effect and, thus, cannot be a cause of the recent increase in temperature.

• A combination of internal climate variability, natural forcing, and perhaps small anthropogenic forcing can account for the increases in the observed globally averaged surface temperature up until about 1970. Increases in solar radiation may account, in part (perhaps 0.15 to 0.2°C), for the warming between about 1920 and 1940, even though solar changes are poorly known before 1979 when satellite observations began. . . . However, it is also probable that a natural component related to changes in North Atlantic Ocean circulation may have played a role.

• The rate and magnitude of the warming over the last few decades cannot be explained unless the net human influence is one of warming over the last 30 years. Uncertainties in cooling by aerosol forcing (especially the effects on clouds) are therefore constrained.

• The nearer the "balance" or the offset between positive anthropogenic greenhouse gas forcing and negative anthropogenic aerosol forcing over the last 50 years, the larger the climate responsiveness needs to be to explain warming over recent decades. For instance, if the net warming is small, the climate system must be quite sensitive to that warming to produce the observed temperature change. But if the warming is larger, the climate system must be less sensitive to produce the same temperature change. This has implications for future predictions.

The line of argument shown by these points is open to the criticism that there is some circular reasoning involved. The objective of attributing climate change to specific causes is to account for the change in temperature, but the temperature change itself is invoked as part of the argument. Ideally, only the knowledge of forcings and responsiveness of the system, as given by models, are used to replicate the observed temperature. Neither the forcings nor the true sensitivity of the systems are known well enough to proceed in this manner. Climate modelers attempt to avoid such a trap by basing their models on sound physical principles.

However, many parameters have to be chosen when developing models. Although the choices are based on knowledge of the processes, and the parameters are physically based, there is ample scope for unintentional tuning. For example, the brightness of clouds depends on the size and number of cloud droplets but varies from cloud to cloud and is not known well. Choice of a particular value for the model clouds may compensate for shortcomings in the amount of clouds in the model. Inevitably, running a model with two different sets of parameters yields different results, and the set that brings the model into best agreement with observations is chosen for further use in the model. It is important, therefore, to recognize that the procedure is not as objective as it might appear and that uncertainties remain.

The most contentious section in the *Summary for Policy Makers* proved to be the concluding paragraph on attribution. After much debate, a carefully crafted statement was agreed upon: "In the light of new evidence, and taking into account the remaining uncertainties, most of the observed warming over the last 50 years is likely to have been due to the increase in greenhouse gas concentrations." Moreover, although not highlighted by IPCC, increasing evidence suggests that the signal of human influence on climate emerged from the noise of natural variability in about 1980 and will only get larger.

The implications of these findings may be felt in the near future. The models predict that global temperature increases of 0.1 to 0.2°C over the next decade are likely unless volcanic eruptions interfere.[10] Time will tell whether the assessment is correct, perhaps within a decade.

Prediction of Climate Change

Climate models have been used to project the effects of future global warming to the year 2100. Because human activities are not predictable in any deterministic sense, "predictions" based on human influences necessarily contain a "what if" emissions scenario. IPCC presumes that these predictions will be used for planning purposes, including actions to prevent undesirable outcomes, consistent with the

Framework Convention on Climate Change. Such actions, which are a consequence of the prediction, may change the outcome and thus make the prediction wrong. Accordingly, they are not truly predictions but rather projections that are tied to particular emissions scenarios. This is an important point, because some skeptics have ignored the distinction and misused it to challenge findings. For example, in 1990, only scenarios with increasing greenhouse gases were used. Then, in 1995, the first primitive scenarios with aerosols were included, which produced a cooling. Some skeptics, pointing to this difference, claimed that the models had changed and were therefore suspect, when, in fact, it was the scenarios that had changed, not the models. In addition, for a given scenario, the rate of temperature increase depends on the model used and how, for instance, the model depicts features such as clouds. It is for this reason that a range of possible outcomes exists. About half of the spread in range of values at 2100 is due to uncertainties in models. The spread in values is unrelated to the scenarios and should not be considered as representative of anything real. The rest of the spread in range can be accounted for by the different scenarios.

In 2001, the future emissions scenarios were set up by the *Special Report on Emissions Scenarios* (SRES)[11]. . . and included 35 scenarios. . . . For each emissions scenario, IPCC calculates expected concentrations of CO_2. In the year 2100, the projected values range from about 550 ppm to almost 1,000 ppm, compared with 367 ppm at present. . . . When the range of uncertainties is factored in and the projections for 2100 across all 35 scenarios are analyzed, there is an increase in the global mean temperature from 1.4°C to 5.8°C. . . . Most increases fall between 2°C to 4°C. These numbers exceed those in the 1995 IPCC report, which showed temperature changes ranging from about 1°C to 3.5°C.[12] The increase is higher mainly because the new emissions scenarios include lower sulfur emissions (which are likely to be reduced for air quality reasons). The 35 scenarios also expand the range of possibilities from the last report and contribute to the range in temperature projected in 2100. Modifications in carbon cycle models that convert emissions to concentrations and in climate models account for less than 20 percent of the deviation between the 1995 IPCC report and this year's report and thus do not account for much change in the range.

. . . Because heat penetrates slowly into the voluminous oceans, sea-level rise is expected to be manifested over a longer period of time than temperature change. Because the heat inputs that have already occurred will only work their way through the system slowly, even in the unlikely scenario of a massive reduction in greenhouse gas emissions, sea-level rise will continue unabated. Note again that though these projections include crude estimates of the effects of sulfate aerosol, they deliberately omit other possible human influences, such as changes in land use.[13] A major concern is that the projected rates of climate change . . . exceed anything seen in nature in the past 10,000 years.

An increase in global mean temperature logically follows increased heating. But temperature increase, often thought of as the sole indicator of "global warming," is not the only possible outcome. For example, rising concentrations of greenhouse gases enhance the hydrological cycle by furnishing additional energy for evaporation of surface moisture. Because the water-holding capacity of the atmosphere is greater at higher temperatures, increased atmospheric moisture should accompany global temperature increases. Because water vapor is also a powerful greenhouse gas, it contributes a strong positive feedback, amplifying global warming. Naturally occurring droughts are also liable to be exacerbated by enhanced drying. Thus droughts, such as those set up by El Niño, are likely to take hold more quickly, wilt plants sooner, and become more extensive and longer-lasting with global warming. When the land is dry, the energy that would ordinarily drive the hydrological cycle goes into raising temperatures, bringing on sweltering heat waves. Further, globally there will have to be an increase in precipitation to balance the enhanced evaporation. More moisture in the atmosphere implies stronger moisture flow converging into all precipitating weather systems—such as thunderstorms or extratropical rain or snow storms—and rain or snow events of greater intensity.[14]

For any change in mean climate, there is likely to be an amplified change in extremes. Because of the wide range of natural variability associated with day-to-day weather, most small climate changes will probably go unnoticed; the extremes, however, will be easily detected. Extremes play an exceedingly important role for natural and human systems and infrastructure. All living organisms are adapted to a range of natural weather variations. New extremes could be devastating to ecosystems. Extremes that exceed tolerances of a system can cause nonlinear effects: the so-called "straw that breaks the camel's back." For instance, floods that historically have had an expected return period of 100 years may now recur in 50 or 30 years.[15] More frequent extreme floods may overstress dams and levees, causing breaks and the consequent damage to infrastructure, loss of human life, and contamination of drinking water.

The changes in extremes of weather and climate observed to date have only recently been compared to the changes projected by models, many of which agree with recent observed trends. Models project that higher maximum temperatures, more hot days, and more heat waves are all likely. The largest temperature increases are expected mainly in areas where soil moisture decreases are apt to occur. Increases of daily minimum temperatures are projected to occur over most land areas and are generally larger where snow and ice retreat. A decreased number of frost days and cold waves is likely. Changes in surface air temperature and surface humidity will mean increases in the heat index and increased discomfort. Increases in surface air temperature will lead to a greater number of days during which cooling (such as from air conditioning) might be considered desirable for comfort and fewer days during which space heating is required for comfort. Precipitation extremes are expected to increase more than the mean, as will the frequency of extreme precipitation events. A general drying is projected for the mid-continental areas during summer, as a result of higher temperatures and increased drying not offset by increased precipitation in these regions. Theoretical and modeling studies project increases in the upper limit of intensity of tropical cyclones in addition to appreciable increases in their average

and peak precipitation intensities. Changes in El Niño are also likely, but their nature is quite uncertain.[16]

Humans Are Changing the Climate

In 1995, the IPCC assessment concluded that "the balance of evidence suggests a discernible human influence on global climate."[17] Since then the evidence has become much stronger—the recent record warmth of the 1990s, the historical context provided by the improved paleo-record, improved modeling and simulation of the past climate, and improved statistical analysis. Thus the headline in the new IPCC report states, "There is new and stronger evidence that most of the warming observed over the last 50 years is attributable to human activities."[18] The best assessment of global warming is that the human contribution to climate change first emerged from the noise of background variability in the late 1970s. Hence, climate change is expected to continue into the future. The amplification of extremes is likely to cause the greatest impact. Although some changes arising from global warning may be benign or even beneficial, the economic effects of more extreme weather will be substantial and clearly warrant attention in policy debates.

Because of the long lifetime of CO_2 in the atmosphere and the slow heat penetration and equilibration of the oceans, there is already a substantial commitment to further global climate change, even in the absence of further emissions of greenhouse gases. IPCC considered implications for stabilizing CO_2 and greenhouse gases at various concentrations up to four times pre-industrial levels and concluded that substantial reductions in emissions, well below current levels, would be required sooner or later in all cases. Even full implementation of the Kyoto Protocol would merely slow the time of doubling of CO_2 concentrations from pre-industrial values by perhaps 15 years (for instance from 2060 to 2075).[19] Moreover, these projections emphasize that even stabilizing concentrations would not stop climate change because of the slow response of the system; for this reason, temperature increases and especially sea-level rise would continue for many decades thereafter. As we begin to understand that our geophysical experiment might turn out badly, we are also discovering that it cannot be turned off abruptly.

The IPCC report provides the evidence that global warming is happening and now the question arises, *What, if anything, should be done about these findings?* The options include: do nothing, mitigate or stop the problem, adapt to the changes as they happen, or find some combination of these options. Different value systems come into play in deciding how to proceed. Considerations include those of population growth, equity among developed and developing countries, intergenerational equity, stewardship of the planet, and the precautionary principle ("better to be safe than sorry"). Those with vested interests in the current situation frequently favor the first option, extreme environmentalists favor the second, and those who have a belief that technology can solve all problems might favor the third. In rationally discussing options, it is helpful to recognize the legitimacy of these different points of view. This problem is truly a global one because the atmosphere is a global commons. These immense problems cannot be solved by one nation acting alone. Unfortunately, to date, international progress toward mitigating and preparing for the possible outcomes of global warming is inadequate.

The evidence presented by the IPCC report suggests that there is a strong case for slowing down the projected rates of climate change caused by human influences. Any climate change scenario is fraught with uncertainties. But a slowing in the warming process would allow researchers to improve projections of climate change and its impacts. Actions taken to slow down climate change would provide time to better prepare for and adapt to the changes as they appear. Natural systems and human systems, many of which have long amortization lifetimes (e.g., power stations, dams, and buildings), are then less likely to be dislocated or become obsolete quickly. Therefore, we must plan ahead. Greater energy efficiency and expanding use of renewable resources, such as solar power, are clearly key steps toward slowing the rate of climate change.

NOTES

1. IPCC, *Climate Change 2001: The Scientific Basis*, J. T. Houghton et al., eds. (Cambridge, U.K.: Cambridge University Press. 2001) (in press).

2. R. Revelle and H. E. Suess, "Carbon Dioxide Exchange between Atmosphere and Ocean and Question of an Increase of Atmospheric CO_2 during the Past Decades." *Tellus* 9 (1957): 18–27.

3. F. S. Rowland, "Climate Change and Its Consequences: Issues for the New U.S. Administration," *Environment*, March 2001, 28–34.

4. Reconstructions of temperature and rainfall make use of multiple proxy indicators at individual sites around the world but have to be merged, reconciled, and combined to give regional and larger area averages. Sufficient data with annual resolution now exist to do this for the Northern Hemisphere for the past 1,000 years but not for the Southern Hemisphere or for beyond the past millennium. See M. E. Mann, R. S. Bradley, and M. K. Hughes, "Global-scale Temperature Patterns and Climate Forcing over the Past Six Centuries," *Nature* 392, 23 April 1998, 779–87; and M. E. Mann, R. S. Bradley, and M. K. Hughes, "Northern Hemisphere Temperatures during the Past Millennium: Inferences, Uncertainties, and Limitations," *Geophysical Research Letters* 26 (1999): 759–62.

5. J. W. Hurrell, "1995: Decadal Trends in the North Atlantic Oscillation Regional Temperatures and Precipitation," *Science* 269 (1995): 676–9; K. E. Trenberth and T. J. Hoar, "The 1990–1995 El Niño-Southern Oscillation Event: Longest on Record," *Geophysical Research Letters* 23 (1996): 57–60; and K. E. Trenberth and T. J. Hoar, "El Niño and Climate Change," *Geophysical Research Letters* 24 (1997): 3057–60.

6. J. T. Kiehl and K. E. Trenberth, "Earth's Annual Global Mean Energy Budget," *Bulletin of the American Meteorological Society* 78 (1997): 197–208.

7. Recent evidence highlights the possible importance of this effect, although the magnitude is very uncertain. See J. M. Hansen, M. Sato, A. Lacis, and R. Ruedy, "The Missing Climate Forcing,"

Philosophical Transactions of the Royal Society of London 352 (1997): 231–40.

8. K. E. Trenberth, J. T. Houghton, and L. G. Meira Filho, "The Climate System: An Overview," in J. T. Houghton et al., eds., *Climate Change 1995: The Science of Climate Change* (Cambridge, U.K.: Cambridge University Press, 1996), 51–64.

9. K. E. Trenberth, "The Use and Abuse of Climate Models in Climate Change Research," *Nature* 386, 13 March 1997, 131–33.

10. IPCC, note 1 above.

11. IPCC, *Special Report on Emissions Scenarios, Summary for Policy Makers* (2000).

12. IPCC, *Climate Change 1995: The Science of Climate Change*, J. T. Houghton et al., eds. (Cambridge, U.K.: Cambridge University Press, 1996). For a review of the second IPCC assessment, see *Climate Change 1995: The Science of Climate Change*, reviewed by W. C. Clark and J. Jälger, *Environment*, November 1997, 23–8; *Climate Change 1995: Impacts, Adaptations, and Mitigation*, reviewed by R. W. Kates, *Environment*, November 1997, 29–33; and *Climate Change 1995: Economic and Social Dimensions*, reviewed by T. O'Riordan, *Environment*, November 1997, 34–39.

13. It is estimated that conversion from forests to agriculture in the United States makes the surface much brighter, especially in the late summer and fall after crops are harvested. This means more solar radiation is reflected, which results in cooling.

14. K. E. Trenberth, "Atmospheric Moisture Residence Times and Cycling: Implications for Rainfall Rates with Climate Change," *Climatic Change* 39 (1998): 667–94.

15. K. E. Trenberth, "The Extreme Weather Events of 1997 and 1998," *Consequences* 5 (1999): 2–15.

16. The 1997–1998 El Niño is the biggest recorded event by several measures. The last two decades have been marked by unusual El Niño activity. See Trenberth and Hoar, 1996 and 1997, note 5 above. A key question is how is global warming influencing El Niño? Because El Niño is involved with movement of heat in the tropical Pacific Ocean, it is conceptually easy to see how increased heating from the build up of greenhouse gases might interfere. Climate models certainly show changes with global warming, but none simulate El Niño with sufficient fidelity to have confidence in the results. So the question of how El Niño may change with global warming is a current research topic.

17. Trenberth, note 14 above.

18. IPCC, note 1 above.

19. T. M. L. Wigley, "The Kyoto Protocol: CO_2 [CH_4] and Climate Implications," *Geophysical Research Letters* 25 (1998): 2285–8.

II.18   JANET SAWIN

Charting a New Energy Future

Although more advanced nations have often exploited less fortunate regions of the world, many of those less developed countries are experiencing rapid technological change. As these shifts occur, demands are being made by these nations for a greater role in determining their future as well as a larger share of the economic pie. In addition, some of these countries have recognized the importance of both producing and utilizing energy differently from what has been the practice. Janet Sawin, a senior researcher and director of the Energy and Climate Change program at the World Watch Institute, examines how the increasing energy appetite in the formerly neglected regions of the world might force all countries to produce and consume energy in more efficient and environmentally friendly ways. The increasing worldwide demand for power has the potential not only to deplete our reserves of fossil fuels more quickly than was originally anticipated but also to increase atmospheric pollution and the likelihood of more global warming. As the demand for

more and more inexpensive, convenient energy grows, the rationale for faster development and assimilation of renewable energy produced by wind turbines, photovoltaic cells,
and other new technologies becomes increasingly compelling. Although economics is
often mentioned as a reason to continue relying on the more traditional resources such as
coal and petroleum, which seem cheap and plentiful, Sawin presents a more realistic picture of the true costs of various fuels by considering what she refers to as "external costs."
One beneficial economic aspect of increasing utilization of renewable energy often not
considered is the growth of manufacturing industries related to these new energy sources
and energy-related jobs. Many of these benefits accrue directly to the regions where such
employment growth is needed and also help protect the environment.

Focus Questions

1. Discuss how the consideration of external costs makes sustainable energy more attractive and competitive from a cost-benefit perspective as compared with the more traditional forms of energy.
2. Consider our globalized world as discussed by Bhagwati (selection II.3) and the IFG
   article (selection II.4) and the potential economic benefits discussed in this article. Do
   you think our market-based economy would find Sawin's conclusions reasonable and
   economically viable? What are the likely consequences of not moving in the direction
   she suggests?
3. To what extent do you believe the proposals of this article are supported by the
   Trenberth article (selection II.17)? In what ways do you feel the two authors agree
   or disagree?
4. How might the "commons" concept discussed in both the IFG reading (selection II.4)
   and the Hardin article (selection II.16) relate to how we generate and consume energy?
   Discuss the ethical questions related to this issue. Do you think you have any personal
   responsibility toward resolving this dilemma?

Keywords

biomass, climate change, developing world, fossil fuels, Greenpeace, photovoltaics,
renewable energy

FOR EIGHT YEARS, PEOPLE in the Thai province of
Prachuap Khiri Kan have fought proposals to build
two large coal-fired power plants in the region out
of concern for the environmental and health impacts of the plants. When Thailand's Prime Minister
visited one possible site in January 2002, he was
met by 20,000 protesters. With help from the international environmental organization Greenpeace,
people of this province have begun installing what

they really want—wind and solar power. Meanwhile, halfway around the world, the state legisla-
ture in California passed a groundbreaking law in
September 2002 that sets a target of generating
20 percent of electricity from new renewable sources
by 2017. From Southeast Asia to California, leaders
in business, government, and civil society are calling
for a transition to a renewable energy economy.[1]

Between the late 1990s and 2020, global energy
consumption is projected to rise nearly 60 percent
due to population growth, continued urbanization,
and economic and industrial expansion. Consumption of electricity, the most versatile form of energy,

will increase even more sharply by most esti- mates—nearly 70 percent. The largest share of this growth is expected to occur in the developing world, where some 2 billion people have no access to modern forms of energy such as electricity and piped gas. And most of the additional energy is projected to come from fossil fuels, according to national and international agency forecasts. But meeting these demands with conventional fuels and technologies will further threaten the natural environment, public health and welfare, and inter- national stability.[2]

Renewable energy technologies have the poten- tial to meet world energy demand many times over and are now ready for use on a large scale. Wind and solar power are the fastest-growing energy sources in the world. By some estimates, "new re- newables" (which excludes large-scale hydropower and traditional biomass) already account for more than 100,000 megawatts (MW) of grid-connected electric capacity. Globally, new renewable energy supplies the equivalent of the residential electricity needs of more than 300 million people.[3]

In 1999, the International Energy Agency noted that "the world is in the early stages of an inevitable transition to a sustainable energy system that will be largely dependent on renewable resources." This is a bold statement for an organization that repre- sents North America, Europe, and Japan—areas that depend so heavily on fossil fuels. But it seems logical, given the many problems associated with the use of conventional energy and the tremendous surge in renewable energy investments over recent years. The world now uses 10 times as much wind energy as it did only a decade ago, and solar power consumption has risen sevenfold. Political support for renewables is on the rise as well. Several coun- tries have recently passed strong new legislation to support renewable energy, opening markets in a rapidly growing list of countries.[4]

Yet change is never easy, and there are strong forces—including politically powerful industries— that wish to maintain the status quo. The forces for and against change were on full display at the World Summit on Sustainable Development, held in Johannesburg, South Africa, in summer 2002. The European Union and Brazil proposed the adoption

of specific numerical targets for the use of new re- newable energy worldwide. Strong opposition arose from the fossil fuel industry and from the govern- ments of most oil-producing nations and major fossil fuel users such as China and the United States. The battle in Johannesburg ended in a watered- down, non-numerical goal to increase renewable energy use. But the fact that the issue even arose at a global summit was highly significant. While the world is sharply divided on what kind of energy fu- ture must lie ahead, many nations now view renew- able energy as a credible alternative to fossil fuels.[5]

Resistance to change is inevitable, but the world cannot afford to be held back indefinitely by those who are wedded to energy systems of the past. Each year new power plants, refineries, pipelines, and other forms of conventional infrastructure—facilities that will be around for at least a half-century—are added to the global energy system to replace exist- ing capital stock and to meet ever-rising demand, much of it in the developing world. An estimated $200–250 billion is invested in energy-related infra- structure every year, and another $1.5 trillion is spent on energy consumption, with nearly all of this in- vestment going to conventional energy. As a result, societies are in the process of further locking them- selves into indefinite dependence on unhealthy, unsustainable, insecure energy structures.[6]

We have a brief window of opportunity to start down the path to a more sustainable world—one in which rising demand for energy is met without sac- rificing the needs of current and future generations and the natural environment. Nongovernmental organizations, working with local communities, can make a difference on a small scale, as in Thai- land, but alone they will not bring about the trans- formation necessary for movement toward a re- newably powered world.

The rapid expansion of renewable technologies over the past decade has been fueled by a handful of countries that have adopted ambitious and deliber- ate government policies aimed to advance renew- able energy. These successful policy innovations have been the most important drivers in the ad- vancement and diffusion of renewable technologies such as wind and solar photovoltaics (PVs). By ex- amining the policies that have worked toward this end over the past two decades, as well as those that have failed, we can get some idea of what is required to launch a global takeoff in renewables in the decade ahead.

The Case for Renewables

New renewable resources provide only a small share of global energy production today. (See Figures 1 and 2.) Yet the advantages of shifting away from fossil fuels and nuclear energy and toward greater reliance on renewables are numerous and enormous. Several countries have begun this transition in response to rising demand for energy, increasing concerns about fuel supplies and global security, the growing threat of climate change and other environmental crises, and significant advances in renewable technologies and the benefits they offer.[7]

Global oil production is expected to peak early in this century. "In 20–25 years the reserves of liquid hydrocarbons are beginning to go down so we have this window of time to convert over to renewables," according to Harry Shimp, president and chief executive officer of BP's solar division. But of greater concern to many is not when or if economically recoverable fossil fuel reserves will be depleted, but

the fact that the world cannot afford to use all the conventional energy resources that remain.[8]

The Intergovernmental Panel on Climate Change, a body of approximately 2,000 scientists and economists who advise the United Nations on climate change, has concluded that global carbon dioxide (CO_2) emissions must be reduced at least 70 percent over the next 100 years to stabilize atmospheric CO_2 concentrations at 450 parts per million (ppm), which would be 60 percent higher than pre-industrial levels. The sooner societies begin to make these reductions, the lower the impacts and the associated costs—of both climate change and emissions reductions—will be. (See Box 1.) Because more than 80 percent of human-made CO_2 emissions are due to the burning of fossil fuels, such reductions are not possible without significant and rapid improvements in energy efficiency and a shift to renewable energy.[9]

Additional environmental costs of conventional energy production and use include destruction wrought through resource extraction; air, soil, and water pollution; acid rain; and biodiversity loss. Conventional energy requires vast quantities of fresh water. Mining and drilling affect the way of life and the very existence of indigenous peoples worldwide. In China, the environmental and health costs of air pollution, due mainly to coal burning,

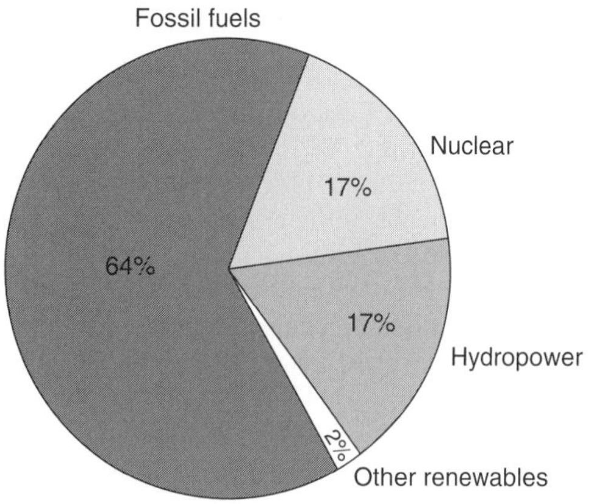

FIGURE 2

World Electricity Generation by Type, 2000

SOURCE: IEA.

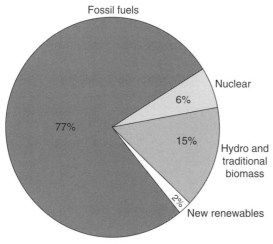

FIGURE 1

World Energy Consumption by Source, 2000

SOURCE: IEA.

Box 1.   Climate Change and the Kyoto Protocol

In its 2001 report, the Intergovernmental Panel on Climate Change found that "there is new and stronger evidence that most of the warming observed over the last 50 years is attributable to human activities" that have increased atmospheric concentrations of CO_2. Preindustrial concentrations were 280 ppm; today they are 371 ppm. Between 1990 and 2100, global temperatures are projected to increase between 1.4 and 5.8 degrees Celsius, and land areas will likely warm faster than the global average. To stabilize CO_2 "at 450 . . . ppm would require global anthropogenic [human-made] emissions to drop below 1990 levels, within a few decades." Even if greenhouse gas emissions were to stabilize at present levels, it is expected that average temperatures and sea level would continue rising for centuries, but the rate of change will slow once stabilization is achieved.

Under provisions of the Kyoto Protocol to the U.N. Framework Convention on Climate Change, industrial countries must reduce their CO_2 emissions an average 5.2 percent below their 1990 levels by the end of the first "commitment period" (2008–12). The protocol will enter into force 90 days after ratification by 55 countries accounting for at least 55 percent of industrial-country 1990 CO_2 emissions. As of mid-October 2002, 96 nations had ratified Kyoto, including the European Union and Japan, representing 37.4 percent of industrial-country emissions. Russia (17.4 percent) and Poland (3 percent) have officially declared their intention to ratify it soon—which would raise the total to 57.8 percent and thus bring the protocol into effect.

The United States represents 25 percent of current global emissions, and 36.4 percent of industrial-country 1990 emissions. Its March 2001 withdrawal from negotiations on the protocol dealt a blow to international efforts to battle climate change, but it also pushed the rest of the world to move forward and reach final agreement on the treaty in July 2001.

SOURCE: See endnote 9.

---

totaled approximately 7 percent of gross domestic product (GDP) in 1995. The World Bank estimates that under business as usual, these costs could rise to 13 percent of China's GDP by 2020. After a decade-long study, U.S. and European researchers calculated that the environmental and health costs associated with conventional energy are equivalent to 1–2 percent of the European Union's annual GDP, and that the price paid for conventional energy is significantly lower than its total costs. (See Table 1.) These estimates do not include the costs of climate change—potentially the most expensive consequence. Global economic losses due to natural disasters, which are in line with events anticipated as a result of global warming, appear to be doubling with each decade, and annual losses from such events are expected to approach $150 billion over the next 10 years.[10]

The direct economic and security costs associated with conventional energy are also substantial. Nuclear power is one of the most expensive means of generating electricity, even without accounting for the risks of nuclear accidents, weapons proliferation, and problems associated with nuclear waste.

TABLE 1. Costs of Electricity With and Without External Costs

Electricity Source	Generating Costs[1]	External Costs[2]	Total Costs
	(cents per kilowatt-hour)		
Coal/lignite	4.3–4.8	2–15	6.3–19.8
Natural gas (new)	3.4–5.0	1–4	4.4–9.0
Nuclear	10–14	0.2–0.7	10.2–14.7
Biomass	7–9	1–3	8–12
Hydropower	2.4–7.7	0–1	2.4–8.7
Photovoltaics	25–50	0.6	25.6–50.6
Wind	4–6	0.05–0.25	4.05–6.25

[1]For the United States and Europe.
[2]Environmental and health costs for 15 countries in Europe.
SOURCE: See endnote 10.

Political, economic, and military conflicts over limited resources such as oil will become more significant as demand increases worldwide. Similarly, the price of fossil fuels will become increasingly erratic as demand rises and conflicts rage in oil-rich regions, which in turn would affect the stability of economies around the world. The economic costs of relying on imported fuels are extremely high—it is estimated that African countries spend 80 percent of their export earnings on imported oil. Likewise, the benefits of reducing imports can be significant. If not for Brazil's 25-year ethanol program, which now displaces 220,000 barrels of oil per day, the country's foreign debt would be about $140 billion higher, according to one estimate.[11]

Renewable resources are generally domestic, pose no fuel or transport hazards, and are much less vulnerable to terrorist attack. They can be installed rapidly and in dispersed small- or large-scale applications—getting power quickly to areas where it is urgently needed, delaying investment in expensive new electric plants or power lines, and reducing investment risk. All renewables except biomass energy avoid fuel costs and the risks associated with future fuel price fluctuations. They pose significantly lower social, environmental, and health costs than conventional energy fuels and technologies do.

Further, "renewables is not just about energy and the environment but also about manufacturing and jobs." This ringing endorsement came from U.K. Energy Minister Brian Wilson in July 2002, after the commissioning of a new 30-megawatt wind farm atop Beinn an Tuirc, a hill in the northern reaches of Argylle, Scotland. The Kintyre Peninsula of Argylle once thrived on its fisheries, whiskey production, and textile manufacture. These traditional sources of employment are in decline, and now wind power is breathing new life into the region's economy, generating enough electricity to supply 25,000 homes. A new turbine manufacturing plant on the peninsula will provide steady jobs and produce the first large-scale wind turbines ever built in Britain.[12]

Using renewables stimulates local economies by attracting investment and tourist money and by creating employment not only in northern Scotland but elsewhere around the world. Renewable energy provides more jobs per unit of capacity of output and per dollar spent than conventional energies do. Many of the jobs are high-wage and high-tech, and require a range of skills, often in areas that are rural or economically depressed. Economic woes and high unemployment rates influenced Spain's 1994 decision to invest in renewable

energy. In Germany, the wind industry has created 40,000 jobs, compared with 38,000 in nuclear power—an industry that generates 30 percent of Germany's electricity.[13]

A recent study in California concluded that increasing renewable energy technologies in that state would create four times more jobs than continued operation of natural gas plants, while keeping billions of dollars in California that would otherwise go to out-of-state power purchases. According to Governor Gray Davis, over a five-year period the net benefits of renewable energy, compared with business as usual, include $11 billion in economic development benefits for California because of associated job creation and instate investments.[14]

In developing countries such as Brazil and India, where millions of people lack access to power, renewables can provide electricity more cheaply and quickly than the extension of power lines and construction of new plants could, and can aid in economic development. Renewables are also sources of reliable power for businesses in countries such as India where power cuts are common. M. Kannappan, India's Minister of Non-Conventional Energy Sources, has stated that renewables have "enormous potential to meet the growing requirements of the increasing populations of the developing world, whilst offering sustainable solutions to the threat of global climate change."[15]

The energy services delivered by renewables provide communities with access to education, clean water, improved health care, communications, and entertainment. These resources, in turn, improve the quality of life (particularly for women), raise living standards, increase productivity, and reduce the potential for economic and political instability. In Inner Mongolia, thousands of people now have access to education, information, and other benefits for the first time thanks to the use of televisions and radios powered by small wind and solar systems. As a result, they have become more productive and increased their monthly household incomes by as much as $150. (The average per capita annual net income in Inner Mongolia ranges from about $120 to $240.)[16]

Many of the components if not the entire systems for solar homes, wind farms, and other renewable technologies are now manufactured or assembled in developing countries, creating local jobs, reducing costs, and keeping capital investments at home. China and India have both developed domestic wind turbine industries. Brazil's ethanol program, begun in 1975, has created more than 1 million jobs while also bringing the nation's CO_2 emissions 20 percent below what they would have been otherwise. Brazil now exports ethanol fuel and will soon begin exporting its technologies as well. And in Kenya, more than 100 firms (6 of them domestic) provide PV systems or service, with numerous companies selling solar home systems in almost every town.[17]

Developing countries that invest in renewables will discover that they are energy-rich—that they can leapfrog over dirty technologies relied on earlier in industrial countries and can develop their economies with clean, domestic, secure sources of energy that avoid long-term and costly imports.

In light of the many advantages of renewables, the Task Force on Renewable Energy of the Group of Eight industrial countries concluded in 2001 that "though there will be a higher cost in the first decades, measured solely in terms of the costs so far reflected in the market, successfully promoting renewables over the period to 2030 will prove less expensive than taking a 'business as usual' approach within any realistic range of discount rates."[18]

State of the Technologies 2003

Since the 1970s and 1980s, renewable technologies have improved significantly in both performance and cost. Some are experiencing rates of growth and technology advancement comparable only to the electronics industry. Global clean energy markets exceeded $10 billion in 2001 and are expected to surpass $82 billion by 2010, and major corporations are entering the renewables marketplace—including Royal Dutch/Shell, BP, and General Electric. Technical progress of many renewables—particularly wind power—has been faster than was anticipated even a few years ago, and this trend is expected to continue. While costs are still a concern with some technologies, these are falling rapidly due to technological advances, learning by doing,

automated manufacturing, and economies of scale through increased production volumes.[19]

Solar and wind are the most commonly known renewables, but inexhaustible energy supplies are also offered by biomass; geothermal; hydropower; ocean energy from the tides, currents, and waves; and ocean thermal energy. This chapter principally focuses on wind power and solar photovoltaics—which produce electricity from sunlight—because they are the fastest-growing renewables and have the greatest potential for helping all countries achieve more sustainable development.

During the past 15–20 years, wind energy technology has evolved to the point where it competes with most conventional forms of power generation. In many instances, wind is now the cheapest option on a per-kilowatt-hour (kWh) basis. The main trends in wind energy development are toward lighter, more flexible blades, variable speed operation, direct-drive generators, and taller machines with greater capacity. The average turbine size has increased from 100–200 kilowatts (kW) in the early 1990s to more than 900 kW today, making it possible to produce more power with fewer machines. (One 900 kW machine can provide the electricity needed for about 540 European homes.) Turbines with capacity ratings of 2,000–5,000 kW (2–5 MW) are being manufactured for use offshore. At the same time, small wind machines that can be installed close to the point of demand—atop buildings, for example—are also under development. (See Box 2.) Advances in turbine technology and power electronics, along with a better understanding of siting needs and wind energy resources, have combined to extend the lifetime of today's wind turbines, improve performance, and reduce costs.[20]

Since the early 1980s, the average cost of wind-generated electricity has fallen from about 44¢ (in 2001 dollars) per kilowatt-hour to 4–6¢ at good wind sites. Costs vary from one location to the next due primarily to variations in wind speed and also to different institutional frameworks and interest rates. Globally, wind costs have declined by some 20 percent over just the past five years, and the Danish turbine manufacturer Vestas predicts that the generating costs of wind energy will continue to drop annually by 3–5 percent. As this happens, it

- At the Rocky Flats test site in Colorado, the U.S. Department of Energy is testing a lightweight turbine with two blades rather than the usual three. It is expected to be 40 percent lighter than today's standard turbines, require less material, and thus be 20–25 percent cheaper.
- Vestas is now equipping offshore turbines with sensors to detect wear and tear on components, along with backup systems in case of power electronic system failures.
- A turbine developed in Germany can desalinate water, generate electricity, or make hydrogen by electrolysis.
- Mathematical climatic models have been developed in Germany and Denmark to predict wind resources 24–36 hours in advance with reasonable accuracy. This will be important for managing wind power as it reaches a high percentage of the total electric system.

SOURCE: See endnote 20.

will become economical to site turbines in regions with lower wind speeds, increasing the global potential for wind-generated electricity.[21]

Global wind capacity has grown at an average annual rate over 30 percent during the past decade. (See Figure 3.) An estimated 6,824 MW of wind capacity were added worldwide in 2001, bringing the

total to more than 24,900 MW—enough to provide power to approximately 14 million households. While Europe accounts for more than 70 percent of total capacity, wind is now generating electricity in at least 45 countries. Sales in 2001 surpassed $6 billion, nearly double the total two years earlier, and it is estimated that more than 100,000 people are now employed in the wind industry worldwide.[22]

The majority of turbines operating today are on land, but wind power is now moving offshore. This is due to a shortage of sites on land, particularly in Europe, and the fact that wind speeds offshore are significantly higher and more consistent. Stronger winds generate more electricity, while consistency reduces wear and tear on machines. More than 80 MW of turbines are now spinning offshore, all of them in Europe, with an additional 5,000 MW in the pipeline worldwide and more than 20,000 MW proposed for areas surrounding northern Europe.[23]

Experts estimate that onshore wind resources could provide more than four times global electricity consumption. Offshore resources are substantial as well. While some of that potential is too costly to exploit over the near term, the promise of large amounts of wind power at competitive prices is enormous.[24]

As with all energy technologies, there are disadvantages associated with wind power. The environmental factor that has caused the most controversy and concern is bird mortality. This is a site-specific problem, however, and it is relatively low compared with other threats to birds such as vehicles, buildings, and cell phone towers. Further, such problems have been mitigated in recent years through the use of painted blades, slower rotational speeds, tubular turbine towers, and careful siting of projects.[25]

Both wind and sun are intermittent resources, meaning they cannot be turned on and off as needed. But there is no guarantee that any resource will be available when it is required, and utilities must have backup power for generation every day. Assessments in Europe and the United States have concluded that intermittent sources can account for up to 20 percent of an electric system without posing technical problems; higher levels might demand minor changes in operational practices. The wind already provides electricity to the grid

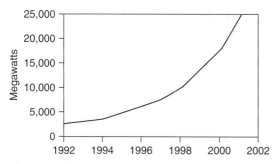

FIGURE 3

Cumulative Global Wind Capacity, 1992–2001

SOURCE: BTM, EWEA, AWEA, press report.

(transmission lines) that greatly exceeds 20 percent in regions of Germany, Denmark, and Spain, and distributed generation—for example, the use of solar panels on rooftops, or clusters of turbines along the path of a power line—can improve electric system reliability.[26]

The challenges posed by intermittency are not of immediate concern in most countries and will be overcome with hybrid systems, improvements in wind forecasting technology, and further development of storage technologies. New storage technologies could also help tap renewable resources that are far from demand centers. Furthermore, what is most significant is the per kilowatt-hour cost of electricity generated. Wind power is already cost-competitive with most conventional technologies. Solar PVs are likely to see dramatic cost reductions, and they produce power in the middle of hot summer days when demand is greatest and electricity costs are highest.[27]

According to the U.S. National Renewable Energy Laboratory (NREL), PVs have the "potential to become one of the world's most important industries." The potential PV market is huge, ranging from consumer products (such as calculators and watches) and remote standalone systems for electricity and water pumping to grid-connected systems on buildings and large-scale power plants.[28]

Each year the sun delivers to Earth more than 10,000 times the energy that humans currently use. While PVs account for a small share of global electricity generation, they have experienced dramatic growth over the past decade. Since 1996, global PV shipments have increased at an average annual rate of 33 percent. It took nearly 30 years, up until 1999, for the world to produce its first gigawatt (GW) of solar PVs (see Figure 4), but some experts expect a doubling as soon as 2003. The PV industry generates business worth more than $2 billion annually and provides tens of thousands of jobs. More than a million households in the developing world now have electricity for the first time from solar PVs, while more than 100,000 households in industrial countries supplement their utility power with PV systems.[29]

The production of solar cells is concentrated in Japan, Europe, and the United States, but there are

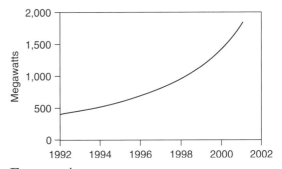

FIGURE 4

Cumulative Global Photovoltaic Capacity, 1992–2001

SOURCE: Maycock.

growing markets and manufacturing bases in developing countries as well, including China and India. Global PV output is expected to increase at annual rates of 40–50 percent over the next few years. As larger factories come into operation, manufacturers can increase the degree of automation.[30]

Such evolving industrial processes, along with technological advances in PVs and economies of scale, have led already to significant cost reductions. Since 1976, costs have dropped 20 percent for every doubling of installed PV capacity, or about 5 percent annually. PVs are now the cheapest option for many remote or off-grid functions. When used for facades of buildings, PVs can be cheaper than other materials such as marble or granite, with the added advantage of producing electricity. Currently, generating costs range from 25¢ to $1 per kWh, which is still extremely high, and cost remains the primary barrier to more widespread use of solar PVs. But companies around the world are in a race to create future generations of products to make PVs cost-competitive even for on-grid use. (See Box 3.)[31]

In addition to cost, one of the primary concerns regarding PVs' ability to meet a major portion of global electricity demand is the length of time they must operate to produce as much energy as was used to manufacture them. The energy "pay-back" period for today's cells in rooftop systems is one to four years, with expected lifetimes of up to 30 years, depending on the technology. The manufacture of PVs also requires a number of hazardous materials, including many of the chemicals and heavy metals

---

Box 3.   The Solar Race

- An Australian company is the first to manufacture solar PVs that can be incorporated into glass walls of buildings. When light falls on the glass from any angle, it will generate electricity.
- The U.S. National Renewable Energy Laboratory and Spectrolabs have developed a Triple-Junction Terrestrial Concentrator Solar Cell that is 34 percent efficient and that can be manufactured for less than $1 per watt, according to NREL (The maximum recorded laboratory efficiency is 24.7 percent, while the average cost of today's PVs is $5–12 per watt.)
- Spheral solar technology, being developed in Canada, will bond tiny silicon beads into an aluminum foil. While mass market application could take decades, this technology could halve the cost of power generation.

SOURCE: See endnote 31.

---

used in the semiconductor electronics industry. There are techniques and equipment to reduce environmental and safety risks, however, and these problems are minimal compared with those associated with conventional energy technologies.[32]

Global markets for renewables such as solar and wind power are only just beginning a dramatic expansion, starting from relatively low levels. It is useful to point out, however, that despite increasing concerns regarding safety and high costs, it took less than 30 years for nuclear power to develop into an industry that provides 16–17 percent of global electricity. The same can happen with renewable technologies. In fact, during 2001 the nuclear industry added only 25 percent as much capacity to the grid as wind did. If the average growth rates of wind and solar PV over the past decade were to continue to 2020, the world would have about 48,000 MW of installed solar PV capacity and more than 2.6 million MW of wind—equivalent to 78 percent of global electric capacity in 2000, or about 45 percent of projected 2020 capacity. Such continued growth is unlikely, but recent industry reports have concluded that if the necessary institutional framework is put in place, it is feasible for

wind to meet 12 percent of global electricity demand by 2020 and for PVs to meet 26 percent by 2040.[33]

The German Story

When the 1990s began, Germany had virtually no renewable energy industry, and in the view of most Germans the country was unlikely ever to be in the forefront of these alternative energy sources. Regulations governing the electricity sector, which dated from the 1930s, granted utilities monopoly rights to produce, distribute, and sell electricity. Utility opposition, entrenched nuclear and coal industries, and a general tendency to conservatism made Germany barren ground for renewable energy advocates. Jochen Twele, a German wind energy expert, recalls that, "when I started my job on wind energy in 1981, I thought that wind energy had only a chance in remote areas of developing countries. So I concentrated on Africa." Due to the strength of labor unions—traditionally strategic partners with the Social Democratic Party (known as SPD)—the indifference to renewables in the German left was at least as strong as it was among the industry-friendly and strongly pro-nuclear Christian Democrats. Even today, utilities and the government maintain strong ties. For example, in the state of North Rhine-Westphalia, many local political representatives are board members of the state utility company.[34]

Yet by the end of the 1990s, Germany had been transformed into a renewable energy leader. With a fraction as much potential in wind and solar power as the United States, Germany has almost three times as much installed wind capacity (more than one third of total global capacity) and is a world leader in solar PVs as well. In the space of a decade, Germany created a new, multibillion-dollar industry and tens of thousands of new jobs. This metamorphosis provides helpful lessons for the scores of countries that have not yet determined how to unleash the potential of their own indigenous renewable energy sources.

The German story began in the 1970s, when high oil prices sparked a growing interest in alternative sources of energy and the government began funding renewable energy research and development (R&D).

But the resulting sporadic efforts were unsuccessful in spurring commercial development. The major political parties remained comfortable with the strategy that nuclear power would be the long-run replacement for fossil fuel plants.

All of this changed with the Chernobyl nuclear power plant accident in 1986, which led the public to turn firmly against nuclear power and to begin a serious search for alternatives. For the first time, Germans began to question their energy supply system. Two years later, rising awareness of climate change, brought on by record high temperatures and mounting scientific evidence of human-induced warming, heightened people's concerns. In 1990, the German Bundestag prepared a study on protecting Earth's climate, with the goal of developing new strategies for a less risky (meaning less nuclear power) and less carbon-intensive energy future.[35]

In response to mounting public pressure, in late 1990 the Bundestag passed a new energy law that required utilities to purchase the electricity generated from all renewable technologies in their supply area, and to pay a minimum price for it—at least 90 percent of the retail price in the case of wind and solar power. This new "Electricity Feed-in Law" (EFL)—Stromeinspeisungsgesetz—provided fair access and standard pricing for new renewables. It was a dramatic break from past regulation as it enabled private producers to sell their renewably generated electricity to utilities at a competitive price, and it prevented electric utilities from further stalling development.[36]

The German law was inspired in part by similar policies that had proved effective in Denmark. It was strongly supported by owners of small hydropower plants in southern mountainous areas of Germany and by farmers on the northern plains who envied their Danish neighbors' ability to profitably install wind turbines and sell their power. These conservative Christian Democrat supporters of renewables were joined by Social Democrats and Greens who favored legislation to protect the environment and create a market for renewable energy. Hermann Scheer, a Social Democrat in the Bundestag who is considered one of the "fathers" of German renewable energy policy, also played an important role by helping to draft and push through the revolutionary one-page EFL. For their part, the coal industry and electric utilities did not take renewables seriously, and chose not to actively oppose the legislation, and the law was adopted unanimously by the German Bundestag.[37]

Wind energy development began a steady and dramatic surge soon after the EFL entered into force on 1 January 1991. Farmers, small investors, and start-up manufacturers created a new industry from scratch, and a growing number of turbines rose up from the flat plains of the northern coast where the wind blows strongest.

Because most of the initial wind development was in the north, the coastal states and their utilities bore the greatest financial burden for Germany's renewable energy projects. The strong regional variations fostered opposition to the law and to wind power itself among utilities and conservative factions of the German government, leading to efforts to declare the EFL unconstitutional. But there was increasing support for renewables as well. In September 1997, 5,000 people flocked to the streets of Bonn to rally in favor of wind power and continuation of the EFL. Opponents failed to overturn the law, although it was amended in 1998 to set a cap on electricity generated by renewable energy.[38]

The 5 percent cap, combined with falling electricity prices (and thus declining payments for renewable electricity) due to deregulation of the market, threatened the viability of existing and planned renewable energy projects. This was of great concern not only to renewable energy developers and producers, but also to major German financial institutions that were underwriting these projects. In response, the Bundestag adopted the Renewable Energy Law (REL) in April 2000.[39]

The Renewable Energy Law removed the cap on renewables, and required that renewable electricity be distributed among all suppliers based on their total electricity sales, ensuring that no one region would be overly burdened. The law also required companies that operate the transmission system to pay the costs of connection to the electric grid, eliminating barriers that arose when utilities discouraged wind development through inflated connection charges. Perhaps most important, it established specific per kilowatt-hour payments for each renewable technology based on the real costs of generation. Electric utilities qualify for these payments as well, a change driven by liberalization of the electricity sector, which the government correctly expected would reduce utility opposition while further stimulating the renewables market.[40]

Although the vote on this new law was not unanimous, broad support from the German public—including labor unions, farmers, environmentalists, and renewable industries—enabled the SPD-Green coalition to push it through Parliament. Again, utilities challenged the law, claiming that it was a subsidy and not legal within the European Union. The government responded that preferential payments for renewable energy were intended to internalize the costs of conventional energy and compensate for the benefits of renewables. In March 2001, the European Court of Justice ruled that the payments were not state aid and therefore not a subsidy. Utilities have since realized that they, too, can benefit from the REL.[41]

After the first access and pricing law was enacted, some barriers to wind energy remained. A major obstacle to German wind development in the mid-1990s was lengthy, inconsistent, and complex procedures for siting wind turbines. As the number of turbines installed in some regions began to skyrocket, local opposition to wind power started to emerge as well. The German government responded by encouraging communities to zone specific areas for wind—a step that both addressed issues that created opposition to wind power, such as noise and concern about aesthetic impacts, and assured prospective turbine owners that they would find sites for their machines.

Worldwide, one of the major barriers to renewable technologies has been the high initial capital costs of these projects. Thus the cost of borrowing plays a major role in the viability of renewable energy markets. Germany addressed this through low-interest loans offered by major banks and refinanced by the federal government. In addition, income tax credits granted only to projects and equipment that meet specified standards have enabled people to take tax deductions against their investments in renewable energy projects. Over the years, these credits have drawn billions of dollars to

the wind industry. The combination of these two policies and the access and pricing laws has enabled a diverse group of Germans to invest in wind power, leading to significant increases in installed capacity, associated jobs, and a broad base of political support for the industry.[42]

In the late 1980s, before the access and pricing laws and investment tax credits, the German government established a small, subsidized demonstration program that was inspired by Denmark's experiences, in an effort to change its approach to R&D. The program offered a one-time investment rebate or an on-going production payment to people who installed wind turbines, in exchange for participation in a long-term measurement and evaluation effort. It funded the installation of only 350 MW, a fraction of today's total wind capacity, but was significant because it encouraged wind development and enabled German manufacturers to sell their machines at higher prices to finance internal R&D. The program has also made it possible for the German government to track and publish years of useful data on capacity, generation, and operation of wind machines, which continues to this day.[43]

Several state governments have offered incentives for renewable projects, have funded studies of onshore wind potential, and have established institutes to collect and publish wind energy data. The federal government recently carried out an offshore resource study, and has advanced awareness about renewable technologies through architectural, engineering, and other relevant vocational training programs, as well as through publications on the potential of renewables and available subsidies.[44]

Although all these policies have played an important role, the fair access and standard pricing laws (EFL and REL) have had the greatest impact on Germany's renewables industries, particularly wind power. They ended uncertainties regarding whether producers could sell their electricity into the grid and at what price, and they provided investor confidence—making it easier for even small producers to obtain bank loans and drawing investment money into the industries. Increased investment drove improvements in technology, advanced learning and experience, and produced economies of scale that have led to dramatic cost reductions.

The average cost of manufacturing turbines in Germany fell by 43 percent between 1990 and 2000. As a result, it became more profitable to install turbines in areas with lower wind speeds, thereby distributing turbines more evenly around Germany and reducing conflicts with competing land uses.[45]

German wind capacity mushroomed from 56 MW at the beginning of 1991 to more than 6,100 MW a decade later, with additions increasing steadily each year. Wind capacity was expected to reach nearly 12,000 MW by the end of 2002, meeting 3.75 percent of Germany's electricity needs. In northern reaches of the country, where most of the development is concentrated, wind power provides as much as 26 percent of annual electricity needs, close to nuclear power's share for Germany as a whole. Some 40,000 people work in Germany's wind industry, producing turbines for domestic use and export. So many Germans own shares in turbines or work in the industry that there is now broad public support for wind power.[46]

Germany has promoted solar energy with policies similar to those for wind power. Incentives to encourage PVs began in 1991 with the 1,000 Roofs program, which like the early wind programs offered support in exchange for ongoing evaluation and monitoring of systems. It was upgraded in 1999 to 100,000 Roofs, a five-year program that offers 10-year low-interest loans to individuals and businesses for installation of solar PVs. Since 1992, PVs have experienced an average annual growth rate of nearly 49 percent. Germany surpassed the United States in 2001, ending the year with 192 MW of capacity, most of which is on-grid. When the 100,000 Solar Roofs program expires at the end of 2003, it is expected that Germany's PV capacity could reach nearly 440 MW.[47]

By lowering the cost of capital, the 100,000 Solar Roofs program effectively reduced the price of PV installation by 37 percent. Combined with the mandated payments of 45¢ per kWh under the REL, this program has had a major impact on the PV market. Total PV system prices have fallen 39 percent over the past decade, and full-time jobs in the PV industry have more than quadrupled, to 6,000, since 1995. To meet rapidly rising demand, major German manufacturers plan to expand PV manufacturing facilities significantly over the next five years, which will further reduce costs and increase employment.[48]

Germany has pledged to reduce its CO_2 emissions 21 percent below 1990 levels by 2010, and the nation will accomplish much of this through increased use of renewable energy. Total renewable energy revenues in Germany and electricity produced by renewable sources both increased 35 percent between 2000 and 2001. For the longer term, the German government aims for wind to generate 25 percent of electricity needs by 2025, with 20,000–25,000 MW of capacity offshore, and considers solar PVs as a viable long-term option for large-scale power generation.[49]

Policy Lessons from Around the World

It is difficult to claim that something is impossible once it has already occurred. This is why it is globally significant that the world's third largest economy, a country with no tradition of renewable energy development, was able to transform itself from laggard to leader in less than a decade. What Germany has accomplished can be replicated elsewhere—if a successful mix of policies is in place.

The main obstacles that have kept new renewables from producing more than a small share of energy in most of the world, despite their tremendous advantages and potential, are lack of access to the grid, high cost, lack of information, and biased, inappropriate, and inconsistent government policies. Germany's dramatic success over the past decade stems from a range of policies introduced to address all these barriers. The experiences of Germany and other countries provide an array of promising policy options that can be disseminated around the world.

There are five major categories of relevant policies:

- regulations that govern capacity access to the grid and utility obligations,
- financial incentives,
- education and information dissemination,
- stakeholder involvement, and
- industry standards and permitting.

There is not necessarily a direct link between these policy types and the four obstacles just described, as some of the policy options tackle a combination of barriers. An additional critical element is the need for a general change in government perspective and approach to energy policy.

As Germany's experience demonstrates, access to the grid is imperative for renewables to gain a foothold. Three main types of regulatory policies have been used to open the grid to renewables. One guarantees price, another ensures market share (mandated targets), and the third guarantees utility purchase of excess electricity from small-scale, distributed systems. The first is the fair access and standard pricing law. The marriage of a guaranteed market and long-term minimum payments has reduced the risks associated with investing in renewables, making it profitable to invest in wind, solar, and other technologies and easier to obtain financing. By creating demand for renewable electricity, the access and pricing law has attracted private investment for R&D, has spread the costs of technology advancement and diffusion relatively evenly across a nation's population, and has enabled the scale-up in production and experience in installation, operation, and maintenance needed to bring down the costs of renewable technologies and the power they produce.

Laws similar to Germany's access and pricing law have been enacted in Denmark, Spain, and several other European countries, including France, Italy, Portugal, and Greece. When Spain passed an access and pricing law in 1994, relatively few wind turbines were spinning in the Spanish plains or mountains; by the end of 2000, the country ranked third in the world for wind installations, surpassed only by Germany and the Untied States. Spain now generates 2 percent of its electricity with the wind—but more than 20 percent in some regions—and is home to the world's second largest wind turbine manufacturer.[50]

While fair access and standard pricing laws establish the price and let the market determine capacity and generation, mandated targets work in reverse—the government sets a target and lets the market determine the price. (See Box 4.) A mandated capacity target, called a Renewables Portfolio Standard (RPS), is primarily responsible for the

---

Box 4.   Renewable Energy Targets

Although no agreement was reached at the World Summit on Sustainable Development on numerical targets for new renewables with specific deadlines, countries around the world are setting their own targets. "Targets" can be goals or obligations. They can be highly effective if used to guide policies that encourage the use of renewables. But targets alone achieve little. For example, renewable energy targets for capacity and generation have been set in the United States since the mid-1970s, often in federal legislation, but rarely achieved. An extreme example is President Jimmy Carter's goal for wind energy to produce 500 billion kWh of electricity by 2000—actual wind generation reached only about 1 percent of this target.

Germany, on the other hand, has exceeded most if not all of its targets to date. Denmark has also set national targets, or goals, for wind and other renewables since the country's earliest national energy plans, nearly three decades ago. Time and again, Denmark's targets for wind energy have been surpassed: for example, in 1981, the national energy plan called for wind to generate 10 percent of the nation's electricity by 2000; this target was met three years early. In 1999 the government aimed to double the nation's share of electricity generated by renewables to 20 percent by the beginning of 2003, a goal that has been met with wind alone. The current energy plan aims for renewable resources to meet 35 percent of Denmark's energy needs by 2030 in order to meet ambitious CO_2 emissions reduction targets. Such policies send strong signals to the market, announcing that the wind industry is a good place to invest for the long term. But targets in Denmark and Germany have had meaning only because appropriate, consistent, long-term policies have been enacted to achieve them. Unfortunately, changes in Danish policies since 1999 could jeopardize existing targets.

SOURCE: See endnote 51.

rapid growth of wind energy in Texas since 1999, when the state required that 2,000 MW of additional renewable capacity be installed within a decade. Texas was more than halfway there with wind alone by mid-2002, and the target will likely be met before 2009. But the mandates have done little to encourage the use of more expensive technologies such as solar PVs, despite vast solar resources in Texas. Nationwide, about a third of the 50 states have RPS laws, many of them with less success than Texas.[51]

The United Kingdom passed legislation on mandated targets in 1989. Between 1990 and 1998, renewable energy developers competed for contracts to provide electric capacity in a series of bidding rounds. While this system made it easier to obtain financing and drove wind costs down through competition, it created major problems. The bidding system led to flurries of activity followed by long lulls with no development, making it difficult to build a domestic turbine manufacturing industry and infeasible for small firms or cooperatives to take part. In addition, competition to reduce costs and win contracts led developers to seek sites with the highest wind speeds, which are often also areas of scenic beauty. This increased public opposition to wind energy and made it more difficult to obtain project permits. When the program ended in late 1999, more than 2,670 MW of wind capacity were under contract, but only 344 MW had been installed.[52]

Another option used in a number of countries, including Japan, Thailand, Canada, and several states in the United States, permits consumers to install small renewable systems at their homes or businesses and then to sell excess electricity into the grid. This "net metering" is different from the access and pricing laws in Europe primarily in scale and implementation. In the United States, 36 states—including California and Texas—had net metering laws by mid-2002, with varying degrees of success. Neither California nor Texas saw much benefit for wind power, let alone for more costly renewables like solar PVs, until other incentives were added to the mix. Success in attracting new renewable energy investments and capacity depends on limits set on participation (capacity caps, number of customers, or share of peak demand); on the price paid, if any, for net excess generation; on the existence of grid-connection standards; on enforcement mechanisms; and on other available incentives. Mandated targets and net metering can be used simultaneously.[53]

Of all these regulatory options, the fair access and standard pricing laws have consistently proved to be the most successful. While more than 45 countries have installed wind capacity during the 1990s, just three—Germany, Denmark, and Spain—accounted for more than 59 percent of total additions for the period 1991 through 2001. More than 80 percent of the 1,388 MW of wind capacity installed worldwide during the first half of 2002 was located in three countries with guaranteed minimum prices—Germany, Spain, and Italy. (See Figure 5.)[54]

Financial incentives, the second category of policies, directly reduce the costs of renewable energy. Market compensation in the form of tax credits, rebates, and payments subsidizes investment in a technology or the production of power. (See Box 5.) This has been used extensively in Europe, Japan, the United States, and India (the only developing country that has enacted tax credits to date).[55]

In the early 1980s, the initial capital costs of renewable projects were far higher than they are today. To encourage investment in renewables, the U.S. government and California offered investors credit against their income tax, making it possible for people to recoup a significant share of their money in the first few years and reduce their level of risk. The credits played a major role in a wind boom that many called California's second gold rush. The lessons learned and economies of scale gained through this experience advanced wind technology and reduced its costs. But enormous tax breaks and a lack of technology standards encouraged fraud and the use of substandard equipment. Inexperienced financial companies and former shopping center developers flocked to the wind business, and untested designs were rushed into production—all to take advantage of credits that enabled wealthy investors to recoup anywhere from 66 to 95 percent of their investment over the first few years, in some cases without even generating a kilowatt-hour of power.[56]

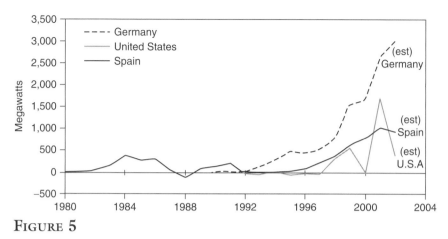

FIGURE 5

Wind Power Capacity Additions in Germany, Spain, and the United States, 1980–2002

SOURCE: Gipe, AWEA, BWE, Wagner, IDAE.

Box 5. The Case for Renewable Energy Subsidies

While some observers argue that incentives to encourage the development and use of renewables are costly and unnecessary, market compensation is warranted for several reasons. First, it begins to account for the environmental, social, and security costs of conventional energy that are not incorporated into the price of the energy. Second, nuclear power and fossil fuels have feasted on decades of subsidies, and in most cases continue to receive far more subsidies than renewables, creating an uneven "playing field." Renewables have been competing against moving targets, as continued subsidies and research for conventional energy have reduced their costs as well. As a result, renewables are behind on the learning curve and need compensation in order to close the gap. German parliamentarian Hermann Scheer has noted that "no energy source was ever established without political support. Policy support for the initiation of renewable energy is a matter of market fairness for abolishing the existing bias." Finally, the electricity sector in most countries is governed by regulations that were enacted to aid in the development of conventional electric systems and now favor them at the expense of renewables.

SOURCE: See endnote 55.

A decade later, India saw a similar boom, due to a combination of investment tax credits, financing assistance, and accelerated depreciation. India is now the world's fifth largest producer of wind power and has developed a domestic manufacturing industry. As in California, however, investment-based subsidies and a lack of turbine standards or production requirements led wealthy investors to use wind farms as tax shelters, and several projects experienced poor performance despite the significant technology advancements since the early 1980s. In both cases, wind energy markets and industries slowed considerably when investment credits expired.[57]

Japan has provided investment subsidies through rebates and has seen dramatic success with PVs. As with the early wind subsidies in Germany and a similar effort in Denmark, PV users receive a rebate in return for providing data about system operations. By 2000, the Japanese government was investing $200 million annually in this program. The goal was to create market awareness and stimulate PV production in order to reduce costs through economies of scale and technology improvements, and thereby enable large-scale power generation and the export of PVs to the rest of the world. And the policy has succeeded. Total capacity has increased an average of more than 41 percent annually since 1992, and Japan now leads the world in the manufacture and use of

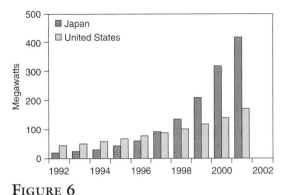

FIGURE 6

Cumulative Photovoltaic Capacity in Japan and the United States, 1992–2001

SOURCE: PVPS, EPI.

solar PVs, having surpassed the United States at both in the late 1990s. (See Figure 6.) To keep up with demand, Japanese PV manufacturers have dramatically increased their production capacity. As a result, PV system costs in Japan have dropped 75 percent since the mid-1990s, and Sharp is now the world's leading producer of solar cells.[58]

Since 1994, the U.S. government has offered a production tax credit for people who supply wind-generated electricity to the grid. The credit has encouraged wind development, but only in those states with additional incentives, and it provides greater benefit to those with higher income levels and tax loads. California has enacted a production incentive that awards a per kWh payment, rather than a tax credit, for existing and new wind projects. The program has kept 4,400 MW of existing renewable capacity online and led to the development of another 1,300 MW. It is financed through a small per kWh charge on electricity use, meaning that Californians share the cost of the program according to the amount of power they consume. Provided that such payments are high enough to cover the costs of renewable generation and are guaranteed over a long enough time period, this policy is a possible alternative to the fair access and standard pricing law—similar in effect and perhaps more politically feasible in some countries.[59]

Experiences to date demonstrate that payments and rebates are preferable to tax credits. Unlike tax credits, the benefits of payments and rebates are equal for people of all income levels. In addition, investment grants result in more even growth over time rather than encouraging people to invest at the end of tax periods (as tax credits tend to do). Further, production incentives are generally preferable to investment subsidies because they promote the desired outcome—generation of electricity. They are most likely to encourage optimum performance and a sustained industry. However, policies must be tailored to particular technologies and stages of maturation. Investment subsidies in the form of tax credits or, preferably, rebates can be helpful when a technology is still maturing and relatively expensive, as seen with PVs in Japan.[60]

Financing assistance in the form of low-interest, long-term loans and loan guarantees is also essential to overcome barriers due to the high up-front capital costs of renewables. Lowering the cost of capital can bring down the average cost of electricity and reduce the risk of investment, as seen in Germany. Even in the developing world, all but the very poorest people are able and willing to pay for reliable energy services, and the rate of on-time payment is extremely high. But the poor also need access to low-cost capital and the opportunity to lease systems.[61]

One of the most successful means for disseminating household-scale renewable technologies in rural China has been through local public-private bodies that offer such services as technical support, materials sale, subsidies, and government loans for locally manufactured technology. These bodies frequently provide revolving credit, with repayment linked to the timing of a household's income stream—for example, payments come due after crops have been harvested. As a result of this program more than 140,000 small wind turbines, producing power for more than a half-million people, have been installed in Inner Mongolia—the greatest number of household-scale wind plants operating anywhere in the world. In India, the terms of long-term, low-interest loans vary by technology, with the most favorable ones being for PVs. Through small-scale lending programs, even low-income people are able to purchase small systems. In addition, the national government has worked to obtain bilateral and multilateral funding for large-scale projects, particularly wind.[62]

Information dissemination is the third key policy component. Even if a government offers generous incentives and low-cost capital, people will not invest in renewable energy if they lack information regarding resource availability, technology development, the numerous advantages and potential of renewables, the fuel mix of the energy they use, and the incentives themselves. During the 1980s, several states in the United States offered substantial subsidies for wind energy—including a 100 percent tax credit in Arkansas, a state with enough wind to generate half of its electricity. But these subsidies evoked little interest due to a lack of knowledge about wind resources. By contrast, it was wind resource studies in California, Hawaii, and Minnesota that led to interest in wind energy there.[63]

Past experiences—from failed Californian wind projects in the 1980s to early development projects in Africa—or lack of experience have left people in much of the world with a perception that renewables do not work, are inadequate to meet their needs, are too expensive, or are too risky as investments. Above all, it is essential that government leaders recognize the inherent value of renewable energy. Then governments, nongovernmental organizations, and industry must work together to educate labor organizations about employment benefits, architects and city planners about ways to incorporate renewables into building projects and their value to local communities, agricultural communities about their potential to increase farming incomes, and so on. In India, the government's Solar Finance Capacity Building Initiative educates Indian bank officials about solar technologies and encourages them to invest in projects. The Indian government has also used print, radio, songs, and theater to educate the public about the benefits of renewable energy and government incentives, and has established training programs.[64]

Knowledge is power, as the saying goes, and disseminating information about renewables far and wide will beget more renewable power. At the local, national, and international levels, it is essential to share information regarding technology performance and cost, capacity and generation statistics,

and policy successes and failures in order to increase awareness and to avoid reinventing the wheel each time. While several countries now do this on a national level, a centralized global clearinghouse for such information is clearly needed.

A fourth strategy that has increased support for renewables—particularly wind power—is encouraging individual and cooperative ownership. In Germany and Denmark, where individuals singly or as members of cooperatives still own most of the turbines installed, there is strong and broad public support for wind energy. Farmers, doctors, and many others own turbines or shares of wind farms, and stand beside labor and environmental groups in backing policies that support wind power. The largest offshore wind farm in the world as of late 2002—the 40 MW Middelgrunden project off the coast of Copenhagen—is co-owned by a utility and several thousand Danes who have purchased shares in the project. Through cooperatives, people share in the risks and benefits of wind power; often avoid the problems associated with obtaining financing and paying interest; play a direct role in the siting, planning, and operation of machines; and gain a sense of pride and community. Several surveys have demonstrated that those who own shares of projects and those living closest to wind turbines view wind power more positively than those who have no economic interest or experience with it.[65]

Public participation and a sense of ownership are as important in the South as in the North. When technologies are "forced" on people without consultation regarding their needs or desires or are donated as part of an aid package, people often place little value on them and do not feel they have a stake in maintaining them. On the flip side, when individuals and communities play a role in decisionmaking and ownership, they are literally empowered and become invested in the success of the technologies.

The fifth essential ingredient in the policy package is industry standards—ranging from technology certification to siting and permitting requirements. Germany established an investment tax credit for wind energy in 1991, and while it too has been abused as a tax loophole for the wealthy, Germany has avoided the quality control problems experienced in California and India by enacting turbine standards and certification requirements. Standards can include everything from turbine blades, electronics, and safety systems to performance and compatibility with the transmissions system. Denmark adopted wind turbine standards in 1979, largely due to pressure from the wind industry itself. The sharing of information among turbine owners and manufacturers and the Danish technology standards program have combined to enable manufacturers to recognize and address problems with their technologies and to create pride in Danish machines. Standards prevent substandard technologies from entering the marketplace and generate greater confidence in the product, reducing risk. They are credited with playing a major role in Denmark's rise to become the world's leading turbine manufacturer. Eventually, technology standards should be established at the international level.[66]

Standards and planning requirements can also reduce opposition to renewables if they address other potential issues of concern, such as noise and visual or environmental impacts. Siting or planning laws can be used to set aside specific locations for development or to restrict areas at higher risk of environmental damage or injury to birds, for example. Both Germany and Denmark have required municipalities to reserve specific areas for wind turbines and have set restrictions on proximity to buildings and lakes, among other things. These policies have been extremely successful, reducing uncertainty about if and where turbines can be sited and expediting the planning process. The United Kingdom offers the best example of how the lack of planning regulations can paralyze an industry. Despite having the best wind resources in Europe, the nation added little wind capacity under its renewables obligation regulations, in great part because a lack of planning regulations virtually halted the process for obtaining planning and environmental permits.[67]

Perhaps the most important step governments can take to advance renewables is to make a comprehensive change in their perspective and approach to energy policy. Governments need to eliminate inappropriate, inconsistent, and inadequate policies that favor conventional fuels and technologies and that fail to recognize the social,

environmental, and economic advantages of renewable energy. Fossil fuels and nuclear power have received the lion's share of government support to date, and continue to get $150–300 billion a year in subsidies worldwide. Most of these subsidies—80–90 percent by some estimates—are found in the developing world, where the price for energy is often set well below the true costs of production and delivery. Even relatively small subsidies in developing countries for kerosene and diesel can discourage the use of renewable energy.[68]

Mature technologies and fuels should not require subsidization, and every dollar spent on conventional energy is a dollar not invested in clean, secure renewable energy. These subsidies should either be eliminated or shifted to wind, solar PVs, and other renewable technologies. Pricing structures must account for the significant external costs of conventional energy and the advantages of renewable energy, as Germany has begun to do through the Renewable Energy Law and other countries are doing with energy or carbon taxes. As the single largest consumers of energy in most, if not all, countries, governments should purchase ever-larger shares of energy from renewables and thereby set an example, increase public awareness, reduce perceived risks associated with renewable technologies, and reduce costs through economies of scale.

At the international level, the Global Environment Facility has allocated $650 million to renewable energy projects in developing countries since 1992. However, this is but a small fraction of global investments in carbon-intensive energy projects through international financial institutions like the World Bank and taxpayer-funded export credit agencies. According to one study, between 1992 and 1998, the World Bank Group put 100 times more money into fossil fuels than it did in renewables. Even a small shift in resources would have a tremendous impact on renewables industries and markets, although more than a small shift is needed.[69]

Policies enacted to advance renewable energy can slow the transition if they are not well formulated or are inconsistent, piecemeal, or unsustained. For example, because early investment credits in California were short-lived and extensions were often uncertain, many equipment manufacturers

---

Box 6.   Forging a New Energy Future

- Enact renewable energy policies that are consistent, long-term, and flexible, with enough lead time to allow industries and markets to adjust.
- Emphasize renewable energy market creation.
- Provide access to the electric grid and standardized payments that cover the costs of generation with policies similar to the fair access and standard pricing laws used in much of Europe.
- Provide financing assistance to reduce up-front costs through long-term, low-interest loans, through production payments for more advanced technologies, and through investment rebates for more expensive technologies such as solar PV, with gradual phaseout.

- Disseminate information regarding resource availability, the benefits and potential of renewable energy, capacity and generation statistics, government incentives, and policy successes and failures on local, national, and international levels.
- Encourage individual and cooperative ownership of renewable energy projects, and ensure that all stakeholders are involved in the decisionmaking process.
- Establish standards for performance, safety, and siting.
- Incorporate all costs into the price of energy, and shift government subsidies and purchases from conventional to renewable energies.

---

could not begin mass production for fear that credits would end too soon. When incentives expired, interest waned and the industries and markets died with them. In the case of wind power, the impact was felt as far away as Denmark, which relied on selling its turbines in California. The U.S. Production Tax Credit for wind energy has been allowed to expire several times, only to be extended months later. As a result, the credit has stimulated wind capacity growth but has created cycles of boom and bust in the market.[70]

This on-and-off approach to renewables has caused significant uncertainties, bankruptcies, and other problems and has made the development of a strong industry in the United States a challenge, at best. Indeed, the United States is the only country to have seen a decline in total wind generating capacity over the last decade. In India, uncoordinated, inconsistent state policies and bottlenecks imposed by state electricity boards have acted as barriers to renewables development. Even in Denmark, years of successful wind energy growth ended in 1999 when the government changed course, and uncertainty overtook years of investor confidence. The future of some planned offshore wind farms is now uncertain, as is Denmark's target to produce half its electricity with wind by 2030.[71]

Consistent policy environments are necessary for the health of all industries. Consistency is critical for ensuring stability in the market, enabling the development of a domestic manufacturing industry, reducing the risk of investing in a technology, and making it easier to obtain financing. It is also cheaper. Government commitment to develop renewable energy markets and industries must be strong and long-term (see Box 6), just as it has been with fossil fuels and nuclear power.[72]

Unlocking Our Energy Future

Renewable energy has come of age. After more than a decade of double-digit growth, renewable energy is a multibillion-dollar global business. Wind power is leading the way in many nations, generating more than 20 percent of the electricity needs in some regions and countries, and is cost-competitive with many conventional energy technologies. Solar cells are already the most affordable option for getting modern energy services to hundreds of millions of people in developing countries. Renewable energy can generate electricity, can heat and cool space, can do mechanical work such as water pumping, and can produce fuels—in other words, everything that conventional energy does.[73]

Renewable technologies are now attracting the funds of venture capitalists and multinational corporations alike. The major oil companies BP and Royal Dutch/Shell have invested hundreds of millions of dollars in renewable energy development. While this is a fraction of what they devote to oil and gas, it is a move in the right direction. BP currently has 20 percent of the global market share for solar cells and plans to enlarge its solar business to $1 billion by 2007, while Shell intends to become an industry leader in offshore wind energy. Commitments from major firms to invest in renewable energy over the next few years total at least $10–15 billion, and clean energy investment worldwide is expected to increase more than eightfold between 2001 and 2010, to over $80 billion annually.[74]

As a result of such investments, the use of renewable energy is expanding rapidly. If current growth rates continue, economies of scale and additional private investments in R&D and manufacturing capability will achieve further dramatic cost reductions, making renewable energy even more affordable in both North and South America. A classic example of the impacts of scale economies and learning is Ford's Model T car, which declined in price by two thirds between 1909 and 1923 as production increased from 34,000 to 2.7 million. A simple calculation shows that if wind power continues to grow at the pace of the past decade, it will exceed 2.6 million MW by 2020. At that level, wind energy alone would provide nearly three times as much electricity as nuclear power does today.[75]

Whether growth continues at this level will hinge largely on policy decisions by governments around the world. The growth of the past decade has occurred because of substantial policy changes in a half-dozen countries, and those nations alone are not large enough to sustain the needed growth at the global level. But recent developments suggest that political support for renewables is rising around the world.

One example is Europe, where the wind power industry is now centered. Tony Blair, Prime Minister of the United Kingdom, which so far has been a European straggler on renewables, calls his nation's investment in renewable energy technology "a major down-payment in our future" that will "open up huge commercial opportunities." And the European Union has adopted the goal of having renewables generate 22 percent of Europe's electricity by 2010. Developing countries such as China and India have recently strengthened their renewable energy

policies, and Brazil is leading the way in Latin America with a comprehensive and ambitious renewable energy law. Even in the United States, despite an oil-oriented White House, nearly half the members of Congress have joined the Renewable Energy and Energy Efficiency Caucus. Although this political support has not yet translated into the needed federal legislation, many states—including Arizona, California, Nevada, and Texas—have enacted pioneering laws in recent years.[76]

Despite the substantial strides being made in technology, investment, and policy, renewables continue to face a "credibility gap." Many people remain unconvinced that renewable energy could one day be harnessed on a scale that would meet most of the world's energy needs. Renewable energy sources appear too ephemeral and sparsely distributed to provide the energy required by a modern post-industrial economy. But those assumptions are outdated. In the words of Paul Appleby of BP's solar division, "the natural flows of energy are so large relative to human needs for energy services that renewable energy sources have the technical potential to meet those needs indefinitely."[77]

The Group of Eight Renewable Energy Task Force projects that in the next decade up to a billion people could be served with renewable energy. BP and Shell have predicted that renewable sources could account for 50 percent of world energy production by 2050, and David Jones of Shell has forecast that renewables could emulate the rise of oil a century ago, when it surpassed coal and wood as the primary source of fuel.[78]

Not only is solar energy alone sufficiently abundant to meet all of today's energy needs thousands of times over, harnessing it is not particularly land- or resource-intensive. All U.S. electricity could be provided by wind turbines in just three states—Kansas, North Dakota, and South Dakota—or with solar energy on a plot of land 100 miles square in Nevada. Farming under the wind turbines could continue as before, while farmers enjoyed the supplementary revenues from spinning wind into electricity. In cities around the world, much of the local power needs could be met by covering existing roofs with solar cells—requiring no land at all. Additional energy will be provided by wind and ocean energy installations located several kilometers offshore, where the energy flows are abundant.[79]

The other credibility gap that must be filled is how to provide renewable energy when and where it is needed—how do you get wind or sunshine into a gas tank, for example, and on a still, dark night? That question, which has stumped generations of engineers, has now been answered by automobile and energy companies around the world. Hydrogen will be the fuel of choice—to be produced from renewable energy, stored underground, and carried to our cities and factories by pipeline. Major automobile manufacturers around the world are developing hydrogen fuel cell-powered cars that will emit only water from their tailpipes. DaimlerChrysler, BMW, General Motors, and Nissan plan to sell their first such cars in 2003, and in 2002 Toyota and Honda raced to see who would be first to put a fuel cell car on the road. Full commercialization of fuel cell cars is expected as soon as 2010.[80]

In early 2001, the Intergovernmental Panel on Climate Change released its most recent report, confirming that in order to stabilize the world's climate, "eventually CO_2 emissions would need to decline to a very small fraction of current emissions"—meaning close to zero. If the world is to achieve this—which it must—countries must begin today, not tomorrow, to make the transition to a renewable, sustainable energy future.[81]

We still have a long way to go to achieve these visions. Today most of the world is locked into a carbon-based energy system that is neither better nor necessarily cheaper than renewable energy—it is the product of past policies and investment decisions. Breaking the lock will not be easy. But Germany and other countries are proving that change is indeed possible. The key is ambitious, forward-looking, consistent government policies that drive demand for renewable energy and create a self-reinforcing market.

NOTES

1. Thailand from Grainne Ryder, "Coal-fired Power Is Obsolete," *The Nation*, 12 May 1999, and from Greenpeace, "Blessings Rain Down for a Solar Future," press release (Prachuap Khiri Kan Province, Thailand: 2 May 2002); U.S. Department of Energy (DOE), Office of Energy Efficiency and Renewable Energy (EREN), "California Mandates 20 Percent Renewable Power by 2017," at <www.eren.doe.gov/news/news_detail.cfm?news_id=325>, viewed 25 September 2002.

2. International Energy Agency (IEA), *World Energy Outlook, 2001 Insights: Assessing Today's Supplies to Fuel Tomorrow's Growth* (Paris: IEA, 2001), pp. 26–27; DOE, Energy Information Administration (EIA), *International Energy Outlook 2002* (Washington, DC: 2002), pp. 1, 4; 2 billion from José Goldemberg, "Rural Energy in Developing Countries," in U.N. Development Programme (UNDP), U.N. Department of Social and Economic Affairs (UN-DESA), and World Energy Council (WEC), *World Energy Assessment: Energy and the Challenge of Sustainability* (New York: UNDP, 2000), p. 348.

3. Eric Martinot, "The GEF Portfolio of Grid-Connected Renewable Energy: Emerging Experience and Lessons," cited in Group of Eight (G8) Renewable Energy Task Force, *G8 Renewable Energy Task Force Final Report* (July 2001), pp. 27–28; 300 million from Eric Martinot, Climate Change Program, Global Environment Facility, discussion with author, 4 October 2002.

4. IEA, *The Evolving Renewable Energy Market* (Paris: 1999), p. v.

5. Christopher Flavin, discussion with author, 11 October 2002.

6. Annual investments in energy infrastructure from UNDP, UN-DESA, and WEC, op.cit.note 2, and from Eric Martinot, Climate Change Program, Global Environment Facility, e-mail to author, 9 October 2002.

7. Figures 1 and 2 are calculated by World-watch with data from IEA, *World Energy Outlook 2002* (Paris: 2002), pp. 410–11.

8. Shimp quoted in "Feature—Solar Power to Challenge Dominance of Fossil Fuels," *Reuters*, 9 August 2002.

9. Intergovernmental Panel on Climate Change (IPCC), *Climate Change 2001: The Scientific Basis* (Cambridge, U.K.: Cambridge University Press, 2001), pp. 223–24; Box 1 based on ibid., pp. 10, 12–13, 17, with countries that have signed or ratified the Kyoto Protocol, ratification dates, and share of emissions available at <unfccc.int/resource/kpstats.pdf>.

10. Wu Zongxin et al., "Future Implications of China's Energy-Technology Choices," prepared for the Working Group on Energy Strategies and Technologies, China Council for International Cooperation on Environment and Development, 24 July 2001, p. 5; World Bank, *Clear Water, Blue Skies: China's Environment in the New Century,* China 2020 Series (Washington, DC: 1997); European Union (EU) from European Commission, "New Research Reveals the Real Costs of Electricity in Europe," press release (Brussels: 20 July 2001); losses due to natural disasters from U.N. Environment Programme (UNEP), "Financial Sector, Governments and Business Must Act on Climate Change or Face the Consequences," press release (Nairobi: 8 October 2002). Table 1 based on the following: low coal figure is for the United States, and the high figure is European average; generating costs for coal and wind from "On Track as the Cheapest in Town," *Windpower Monthly,* January 2002, p. 30; low natural gas cost (for Europe) from David Milborrow, e-mail to author, 18 September 2002; high natural gas cost (U.S.) from DOE, EREN, "Economics of BioPower," at <www.eren.doe.gov/biopower/basics/ba_econ.htm>, viewed 15 July 2002; nuclear is 1993 levelized costs in California, from California Energy Commission, *1996 Energy Technology Status Report: Report Summary* (Sacramento, CA: 1997), p. 73; direct-fired biomass low figure as of 1999 in the United States from Dallas Burtraw, Resources for the Future, "Testimony Before the Senate Energy and Water Development Appropriations Subcommittee, 14 September 1999; high figure for direct-fired biomass from U.S. DOE, EREN, "Biomass at a Glance," at <www.eren.doe.gov/biopower/basics/index.htm>, viewed 15 July 2002; hydropower low figure calculated by DOE based on 21 projects completed in 1993; high hydropower figure calculated using 30-year lifetime and real cost of capital from DOE, EIA, *Energy Consumption and Renewable Energy Development Potential on Indian Lands* (Washington, DC: April 2000); photovoltaics (PVs) (unsubsidized in favorable climates) from Paul Maycock, e-mail to author, 18 October 2002; external costs from EU EXTERNE Project and from European Commission, op. cit. this note.

11. Africa from Hermann Scheer, Member of German Parliament, cited in Alenka Burja, "Energy Is a Driving Force for Our Civilisation: Solar Advocate," 2002, at <www.foldecenter.dk/articles/Hscheer_aburja.htm>, viewed 8 October 2002; Brazil from J.R. Moreira and J. Goldemberg, "The Alcohol Program," *Energy Policy,* vol. 27, no. 4 (1999), pp. 229–45.

12. Quote and details on Kintyre from "Wind Energy Turns Kintyre Economy Around," *Environment News Service,* 8 July 2002.

13. Renewable energy jobs from Virinder Singh with BBC Research and Consulting and Jeffrey Fehrs, *The Work That Goes into Renewable Energy,* Research Report no. 13 (Washington, DC: Renewable Energy Policy Project, November 2001); John Whitman, "Unemployment in Spain Plummets to 21 Year Lows," The Spain-U.S. Chamber of Commerce, at <www.spainuscc.org/eng/publications/LinkFall2000/paro21.html>, viewed 6 August 2002; Wilson Rickerson, *Germany and the European Wind Energy Market* (Berlin: Bundesverband WindEnergie (BWE, German Wind Energy Association), 2002); Jochen Twele, *Windenergie—Technik & Repowering* (Berlin: BWE, 2002).

14. California Public Interest Research Group, "Developing Renewable Energy Could Mean More Jobs," *KTVU News,* 25 June 2002, at <www.bayinsider.com/partners/krvu/news/2002/06/25_solar.html>, viewed 16 July 2002; Steve Rizer, "Davis Supports Plan to Double State's Level of Renewable-Based Electricity," *Solar & Renewable Energy Outlook,* 1 April 2002, p. 73.

15. M. Kannappan, speech at 2002 Global Windpower Conference in Paris, cited in European Wind Energy Association (EWEA), "Think Paris, Act Global," *Wind Directions,* May 2002, p. 11.

16. Inner Mongolia from Eric Martinot et al., "Renewable Energy Markets in Developing Countries," in *Annual Review of Energy and the Environment 2002* (Palo Alto, CA: Annual Reviews, in press), p. 14 (draft); per capita annual net income in Inner Mongolia Autonomous Region from Debra Lew, National Renewable Energy Laboratory, e-mail to author, 4 October 2002.

17. India from Indian Ministry of Non-Conventional Energy Sources (MNES), *Annual Report 1999–2000,* at <mnes.nic.in/frame.htm?publications.htm>, viewed 29 July 2002; China from Debra Lew, "Alternatives to Coal and Candles: Wind Power in China," *Energy Policy,* vol. 28 (2000), pp. 271–86; ethanol in Brazil and carbon dioxide (CO_2) emissions from Monica Saraiva Panik, "Greenhouse Gases Are Global," *Sustainable Development International,* Edition 4, p. 112, at <www.sustdev.org/journals/edition.04/download/ed4.pdfs/sdi4_111.pdf>, viewed

27 July 2002, and from CO2e.com, "Environment: Brazil to Take Renewable Energy Plan to Johannesburg," *Inter Press Service,* 17 May 2002; Brazil exports from Suani T. Coelho, Executive Assistant for the Secretary of State for the Environment, São Paulo, Brazil, discussion with author, 25 July 2002; PV suppliers and service providers in Kenya from James & James World Renewable Energy Suppliers and Services, at <www.jxj.com/suppands/renerg/select_company/567_61.html>, viewed 7 September 2002; local Kenyan firms from John Perlin, "Electrifying the Unelectrified," *Solar Today,* November-December 1999.

18. G8 Renewable Energy Task Force, op. cit. note 3, pp. 5, 9.

19. Clean energy markets in 2001 from Eric Martinot, Climate Change Program, Global Environment Facility, e-mail to author, 19 September 2002; projection from Al Massey, "Staying Clean and Green in a Developing World," *Ethical Corporation Magazine,* 7 February 2002; speed of progress from IPCC, Working Group 3, *Climate Change 2001: Mitigation,* Summary for Policy Makers, p. 5, at <www.ipcc.ch/pub/wg3spm.pdf>, viewed 10 August 2002.

20. Wind as cheapest option from Daniel M. Kammen, "Testimony for the Hearing on the Role of Tax Incentives in Energy Policy," Committee on Finance, U.S. Senate, Washington, DC, 11 July 2001; technology trends from D. I. Page and M. Legerton, "Wind Energy Implementation During 1996," *Renewable Energy Newsletter,* CADDET, September 1997, at <www.caddet-re.org/html/397art6.htm>, viewed 22 September 1998, and from IEA, "Long-term Research and Development Needs for Wind Energy for the Time Frame 2000 to 2020," October 2001, at <www.afm.dtu.dk/wind/iea>, viewed 7 October 2002; average size installed worldwide in 2001 from BTM Consult, *International Wind Energy Development: World Market Update 2001,* cited in Paul Gipe, "Soaring to New Heights: The World Wind Energy Market," *Renewable Energy World,* July-August 2002, p. 34; turbines for offshore from Peter Fairley, "Wind Power for Pennies," *Technology Review,* July/August 2002, p. 43; small-scale turbines from "Building Integrated Wind Turbines," *RENEW: Technology for a Sustainable Future,* July/August 2002, p. 27. Box 2 based on the following: DOE lightweight turbine and Vestas offshore equipment from Fairley, op. cit. this note, pp. 42, 43; German

turbine from Eize de Vries, "Where to Next? Developments and Trends in Wind Turbines," *Renewable Energy World,* July-August 2002, p. 70; climatic models from Birger Madsen, BTM Consult, e-mail to author, 14 September 2002.

21. Cost in early 1980s calculated by Worldwatch Institute based on Paul Gipe, "Overview of Worldwide Wind Generation," 4 May 1999, at <rotor.fb12.tu-berlin.de/overview.html>, viewed 3 March 2000; current wind costs from "On Track as the Cheapest in Town," *Windpower Monthly,* January 2002, p. 30; 20 percent decline over five years from EWEA and Greenpeace, *Wind Force 12,* May 2002, p. 12, at <www.ewea.org/doc/WindForce12.pdf>, viewed 17 July 2002; Vestas from "Renewables: Expansion Plan Progress," *Energy Economist,* April 2002, p. 36.

22. Capacity and generation from BTM Consult, "International Wind Energy Development: World Market Update 2001—Record Growth!" press release (Ringkøbing, Denmark: 8 April 2002); Figure 5–3 from BTM Consult, EWEA, American Wind Energy Association (AWEA), *Windpower Monthly,* and *New Energy,* estimated number of households from EWEA and Greenpeace, op. cit. note 21, p. 5; 70 percent and 45 countries from "Operating Wind Power Capacity," *Windpower Monthly,* July 2002, p. 66; 2001 wind sales totaled $6–6.5 billion, with $6 billion from Søren Krohn, "Danish Wind Turbines: An Industrial Success Story," at <www.wind power.dk/articles/success.htm>, viewed 14 October 2002, and $6.5 billion from Peter Asmus, "Another Enron Casualty: Wind Power?" *Environmental News Network,* 29 January 2002; sales in 1999 from Christopher Flavin, "Wind Power Booms," in Lester R. Brown et al., *Vital Signs 2000* (New York: W.W. Norton & Company, 2000), p. 56; number employed worldwide is Worldwatch estimate, based on Andreas Wagner, GE Wind Energy and EWEA, e-mail to author, 18 September 2002, and on EWEA, Forum for Energy and Development, and Greenpeace, *Wind Force 10* (London: 1999).

23. British Wind Energy Association, "Europe's Seas: An Abundant Source of Clean Power," 6 December 2001, at <www.bwea.com/view/news/arc/eweaowec.html>, viewed 19 July 2002; EWEA and Greenpeace, op. cit. note 21, p. 5.

24. Onshore resources, estimated at 53,000 billion kilowatt-hours (kWh) (53,000 terawatt-hours) of electricity annually, from Michael Grubb and Niels Meyer, "Wind Energy: Resources, Systems and

Regional Strategies," in Laurie Burnham, ed., *Renewable Energy Sources for Fuels and Electricity* (Washington, DC: Island Press, 1993), pp. 186–87, 198; global net electricity consumption in 1999 at 12, 833 billion kWh, according to EIA, "International Energy Outlook 2002," at <www.eia.doe .gov/oiaf/ieo/tbl_20.html>, viewed 12 July 2002.

25. Bird deaths from Paul Gipe, *Wind Power Comes of Age* (New York: John Wiley & Sons, May 1995), from National Wind Coordinating Committee, "Avian Collisions with Wind Turbines: A Summary of Existing Studies and Comparisons to Other Sources of Avian Collision Mortality in the United States," August 2001, at <www.nationalwind.org/ pubs/avian_collisions.pdf>, viewed 3 September 2002, and from Danish Energy Agency, *Wind Power in Denmark: Technology, Policies and Results 1999* (Copenhagen: Ministry of Environment and Energy, September 1999), p. 21; mitigation from AWEA, "Proposed Repowering May Cut Avian Deaths in Altamont," *Wind Energy Weekly*, 28 September 1998.

26. Figure of 20 percent from R. Watson, M. C. Zinyowera, and R. H. Moss, eds., *Climate Change 1995—Impacts, Adaptations and Mitigation of Climate Change: Scientific Technical Analyses*, Contribution of Working Group II to the Second Assessment Report of the IPCC (New York: Cambridge University Press, 1996), and from Michael Grubb, "Valuing Wind Energy on a Utility Grid," Parts 1–3, *Wind Energy Weekly*, vol. 27, no. 350–53; need for only minor changes from David Milborrow, *Survey of Energy Resources: Wind Energy* (London: WEC, 2001), at <www .worldenergy.org/wec-geis/publications/reports/ser/ wind/wind.asp>, viewed 3 September 2002.

27. For information regarding wind prediction and forecasting tools and modeling, see <www.iset .uni-kassel.de>.

28. DOE, National Renewable Energy Laboratory (NREL), "The Photovoltaics Promise," NREL Report No. FS-210-24588, at <www.nrel.gov/ ncpv/pdfs/24588.pdf>, viewed 19 July 2002.

29. Sun's energy from Richard Corkish, "A Power That's Clean and Bright," *Nature*, 18 April 2002, p. 680; increase of PV cell and module shipments since 1996 from European Photovoltaics Industry Association (EPVA) and Green-peace, *Solar Generation*, October 2001, p. 3, at <archive.greenpeace .org/~climate/climatecountdown/solargeneration/ solargen_full_report.pdf>, viewed 26 July 2002;

doubling from Jon R. Luoma, "Beyond the Fringe," *Mother Jones*, July/August 2002, p. 42; $2 billion PV industry from U.S. National Center for Photovoltaics, cited in Ricardo Bayon, "Unenlightened? The U.S. Solar Industry May Be Eclipsed," *The American Prospect*, 15 January 2002, and from PV industry data from EPVA, 2001; job estimate based on Singh, BBC, and Fehrs, op. cit. note 13, pp. 11–12, on "Job Opportunities in Photovoltaic and Renewable Energy Engineering," at <www.pv .unsw.edu.au/bepv/jobopps.htm>, viewed 9 October 2002, and on 3,800 jobs for every $100 million in solar cell sales, according to the Solar Energy Industries Association; number of households from Martinot et al., op. cit. note 16, p. 3 (draft); Figure 4 from Paul Maycock, *PV News*, various issues.

30. Growth rates projected by Sharp, cited in "Solar Cell Production Continues to Grow in Japan," *Renewable Energy World*, July-August 2002, p. 18.

31. Drop in costs per doubling from EPVA and Greenpeace, op. cit. note 29, p. 14; 5 percent annual cost decline from Bernie Fischlowitz-Roberts, "Sales of Solar Cells Take Off," *Economy Update* (Washington, DC: Earth Policy Institute, 11 June 2002); building facades from Steven Strong, "Solar Electric Buildings: PV as a Distributed Resource," *Renewable Energy World*, July-August 2002, p. 171; generating costs from EPVA and Greenpeace, op. cit. note 29, p. 14. Box 3 based on the following: Australian company (Sustainable Technologies International) from "Feature—Solar Power to Challenge Dominance of Fossil Fuels," *Reuters*, 9 August 2002; NREL cell from "High Yield Solar Cell," *RENEW: Technology for a Sustainable Future*, May/June 2002, p. 27; maximum recorded efficiency (single crystalline cells) and costs from IEA, Photovoltaic Power Systems Programme (PVPS), 2000, cited in EPVA and Greenpeace, op. cit. note 29, pp. 8, 15; spheral solar technology, being developed by Automation Tooling Systems of Ontario, Canada, from Rajiv Sekhri, "Canadian Firm Says Set to Slash Solar Power Costs," *Reuters*, at <www.planetark.org/dailynewsstory .cfm/newsid/16934/story.htm>, viewed 18 July 2002.

32. DOE, NREL, "Energy Payback: Clean Energy from PV," at <www.nrel.gov/ncpv/pdfs/245 96.pdf>, viewed 19 July 2002; expected lifetime from BP Solar, at <www.bpsolar.com/ContentDetails.cfm?page=125>, viewed 18 September 2002; PV manufacture risks

from Larry Kazmerski, "Photovoltaics—Exploding the Myths," *Renewable Energy World,* July-August 2002, p. 176, and from U.K. Department of Trade and Industry, at <www.dti.gov.uk/renewable/photovoltaics.html>, viewed 3 September 2002.

33. Share provided by nuclear power in 1988 estimated from graph by the Uranium Information Centre, Ltd., "Nuclear Power in the World Today," July 2002, at <www.uic.com.au/nip07.htm>, viewed 24 September 2002; additional nuclear capacity in 2001 according to International Atomic Energy Agency, Power Reactor Information System, cited in "Another Record Year for European Wind Power," *Renewable Energy World On-Line,* March-April 2002, at <www.jxj.com/magsandj/rew/news/2002_02_03.html>, viewed 14 August 2002; wind and solar growth and share of current capacity calculated using average annual global growth rates of wind and solar PV between 1992 and 2001, year-end 2001 cumulative installed capacity, and total global installed electric capacity figure of 3,400 gigawatts; feasible growth in wind capacity from EWEA and Greenpeace, op. cit. note 21, p. 6; PV projection from EPVA and Greenpeace, op. cit. note 29, p. 5.

34. Quote and North Rhine-Westphalia from Jochen Twele, BWE, e-mail to author, 29 August 2002.

35. Andreas Wagner, GE and EWEA, discussion with author, 10 September 2002.

36. Ibid.

37. Ibid.

38. Opposition to EFL from Jochen Twele, BWE, discussion with author, 14 April 1999, and from Kevin Rackstraw, "Wind Around the World," Sustainable Business.com and Global Environment and Technology Foundation, December 1998, at <www.sustainablebusiness.com/insider/dec98/3-wind.cfm>, viewed 28 January 2000; pro-wind rally from BWE, "5,000 Supporters of Wind and Renewable Energies Out on the Street," press release (Berlin: September 1997).

39. Bundesministerium für Umwelt, Naturschutz und Reaktorsicherheit (BMU, Federal Ministry for the Environment, Nature Conservation and Nuclear Safety), *Act on Granting Priority to Renewable Energy Sources* (Bonn: April 2000).

40. Gerhard Gerdes, Deutches Windenergie Institut (DEWI, Germany Wind Energy Institute), discussion with author, 7 December 2000.

41. Wagner, op. cit. note 35.

42. Jochen Twele, BWE, discussion with author, 5 December 2000; Gerdes, op. cit. note 40; investment amount from Wagner, op. cit. note 22.

43. Wagner, op. cit. note 35; Gerdes, op. cit. note 40.

44. State programs from DEWI, *Wind Energy Information Brochure* (Wilhelmshaven, Germany: 1998), pp. 30, 35; federal resource studies from Roland Mayer, Bundesministerium für Wirtschaft (Federal Ministry of Economics), e-mail to author, 30 March 2001; training programs and publications from BMU, *Environmental Policy: The Federal Government's Decisions of 29 September 1994 on Reducing Emissions of CO2, and Emissions of Other Greenhouse Gases, in the Federal Republic of Germany* (Bonn: November 1994), p. 32.

45. Andreas Wagner, GE and EWEA, e-mails to author, 10 September and 18 September 2002.

46. German capacity at beginning of 1991 and 2001 from BWE, "Installationszahlen in Deutschland, 1988–Ende 2000," at <www.wind-energie.de/statistik/deutschland.html>, viewed 14 March 2001; 11,750 megawatts (MW) and 3.75 percent from "German Wind Generation to Rise 25 pct in 2002—Firms," *Reuters,* 5 September 2002; 12,000 MW and number employed from Wagner, op. cit. note 35; 26 percent of Schleswig-Holstein's electricity is generated with the wind, according to DEWI, "Wind Energy Use in Germany—Status 30.06.02," *DEWI Magazine,* August 2002; as of early 2002, 90 percent of turbines are owned by individuals or cooperatives and more than 200,000 Germans are involved in cooperatives, according to BTM Consult, *World Market Update 2001—Forecast 2002–2006* (Ringkøbing, Denmark: 2002).

47. Growth rate calculated with data from IEA, PVPS, *Statistics by Country, 2000,* at <www.oja-services.nl/iea-pvps/stats/home.htm>, viewed 18 September 2002, and with 2001 data from Peter Sprau and Ingrid Weiss, *National Survey Report of PV Power Applications in Germany 2001,* prepared for the German Federal Ministry of Economics and the Research Centre Jülich (as part of the IEA Cooperative Programme on Photovolatic Power Systems), WIP-Renewable Energies Division, Munich, Germany, June 2002, at <www.wip-munich.de/homepage/projects/pdf/Executive_German_Summary_2001.pdf>, viewed 24 September 2002; projected year-end 2003 capacity from EPVA and Greenpeace, op. cit. note 29, p. 18.

48. Figure of 37 percent from Patrick Mazza, "Europe, Japan Seize Clean Energy Lead," press release

(San Francisco: Earth Island Institute, Climate Solutions, 15 April 2000); 1,400 full-time jobs in 1995 and 39 percent price reductions from Ingrid Weiss and Peter Sprau, "100,000 Roofs and 99 Pfennig—Germany's PV Financing Schemes and the Market," *Renewable Energy World,* January-February 2002; 2002 employment figure from Sprau and Weiss, op. cit. note 47, p. 5; expected expansion from Reiner Gärtner, "Fatherland and Sun," *Red Herring,* 22 July 2002.

49. CO_2 reductions from "German Wind Generation to Rise 25 pct in 2002—Firms," *Reuters,* 5 September 2002; revenue and generation increases from "German Renewable Revenues Rose 35 Pct in 2001," *Reuters,* 16 July 2002; wind targets announced by German Environment Minister Jürgen Trittin and cited in EWEA, *Another Record Year for European Wind Power* (Brussels: 20 February 2002).

50. Year-end 1993 capacity (52 MW) from Instituto para la Diversificación y Ahorro Energético, Spain; Legislation Development of the Spanish Electric Power Act, Vol. 2, Royal Decree 2818/1998; "Renewable Energy: World Renewable Energy Outlook—Western Europe," at <environment.about .com/library/weekly/blrenew21.htm>, viewed 20 June 2002; wind's share of power generation from Michael McGovern, "Wind Weakening System Security," *Windpower Monthly,* July 2002, p. 27; manufacturer ranking from EWEA, "Company Profile: Gamesa Eolica and Energia," *Wind Directions,* January 2002, p. 12.

51. AWEA, "Texas Wind Energy Development," 19 June 2002, at <www.awea.org/projects/texas.html>, viewed 24 July 2002; number of states with Renewables Portfolio Standard laws from DOE, EREN, "California Mandates 20 Percent Renewable Power by 2017," at <www.eren.doe.gov/ news/news_detail.cfm?news_id=325>, viewed 25 September 2002. Box 4 from the following: Carter's goal from U.S. Government, Interagency Domestic Policy Review Committee, *Domestic Policy Review of Solar Energy—Final Report: Research, Design and Development Panel* (Washington, DC: October 1978); U.S. wind-generated electricity in 2000 from Paul Gipe, discussion with author, 23 March 2001; wind's share of early 2003 Danish electricity generation from Madsen, op. cit. note 20.

52. Problems with U.K. law from British Wind Energy Association, "Promoting Wind Energy in and Around the UK—The Government's Policy for Renewables, NFFO and the Fossil Fuel Levy," at <www.bwea.com/ref/nffo.html>, viewed 3 September 2002; problems for small firms and cooperatives from Rickerson, op. cit. note 13, p. 4; 1999 statistics from WEC, *Survey of Energy Resources: Wind Energy* (London: 2001).

53. PV4You National Consumer Project, "36 States with Net Metering," Interstate Renewable Energy Council, at <www.spratley.com/ncp/board2/?i= 882>, viewed 18 September 2002.

54. Share of wind capacity additions calculated by Worldwatch and including only the years when the feed-in laws were in force, based on BTM Consult, *World Market Update,* various years, on Danish power company statistics cited in Danish Wind Turbine Manufacturers Association, "Installed Wind Power Capacity in Denmark in MW," at <www.windpower.dk/stat/tab12.htm>, viewed 28 January 2000, on Lester R. Brown, "World Wind Generating Capacity Jumps 31 Percent in 2001," *Eco-Economy Update* (Washington, DC: Earth Policy Institute, 8 January 2002), on BWE, op. cit. note 46, and on Instituto para la Diversificación y Ahorro Energético (IDEA), Spain; 80 percent from "Danish Wind Stalled," *RENEW: Technology for a Sustainable Future,* May/June 2002, p. 12; Figure 5 from Paul Gipe, discussions with author and faxes, 1 October 1998 and 23 March 2001, from AWEA, "U.S. Wind Industry Ends Most Productive Year, More Than Doubling Previous Record for New Installations," press release (Washington: 15 January 2002), from BWE, op. cit. note 46, from Wagner, op. cit. note 35, from IDEA, Spain, and from IDAE, EHN, and APPA data supplied by José Santamarta, e-mail to author, 19 October 2002.

55. Box 5 from Hermann Scheer, Member of German Parliament and General Chairman of the World Council for Renewable Energy, Address to the American Council for Renewable Energy, Washington, DC, 11 July 2002.

56. Janet L. Sawin, "The Role of Government in the Development and Diffusion of Renewable Energy Technologies: Wind Power in the United States, California, Denmark and Germany, 1970–2000" (dissertation, The Fletcher School, Tufts University), September 2001 (Ann Arbor, MI: UMI, 2001), pp. 204–05; inexperienced investors in wind power from Randall Tinkerman, former wind entrepreneur, discussion with author, 12 May 1999;

rate of investment recovery and lack of generation from Alan J. Cox et al., "Wind Power in California: A Case Study of Targeted Tax Subsidies," in Richard J. Gilbert, ed., *Regulatory Choices: A Perspective on Developments in Energy Policy* (Berkeley: University of California Press, 1991), p. 349, and from Vincent Schwent, California Energy Commission, discussion with author, 6 May 1999; use of untested designs from Alfred J. Cavallo, Susan M. Hock, and Don. R. Smith, "Wind Energy: Technology and Economics," in Burnham, op. cit. note 24, p. 150.

57. MNES, op. cit. note 17; mid-2002 capacity from "Operating Wind Power Capacity," *Wind-power Monthly,* July 2002, p. 66; lower capacity factors and some nonfunctioning turbines from Martinot et al., op. cit. note 16, pp. 11, 20 (draft).

58. Mazza, op. cit. note 48; growth rate calculated by Worldwatch with data from IEA, PVPS, op. cit. note 47, with 2001 capacity additions from Fischlowitz-Roberts, op. cit. note 31; system cost reductions from EPVA and Greenpeace, op. cit. note 29, p. 23; Figure 6 from IEA, PVPS, cited at <www.bp.com/centres/energy2002/page downloads/solar.pdf>, viewed 24 September 2002, and from Fischlowitz-Roberts, op. cit. note 31; production increases by Kyocera and Sharp from Curtis Moore and Jack Ihle, *Renewable Energy Policy Outside the United States,* Issue Brief 14 (Washington, DC: Renewable Energy Policy Project, October 1999), and from Fischlowitz-Roberts, op. cit. note 31.

59. Benefits to those with higher income from Sawin, op. cit. note 56, p. 151; impact of California incentive from Rizer, op. cit. note 14.

60. Sawin, op. cit. note 56, pp. 151, 340–41.

61. Goldemberg, op. cit. note 2, p. 381.

62. China and number of turbines in Inner Mongolia from Martinot et al., op. cit. note 16, pp. 8, 22 (draft); number of people from L. Wu, "Inner Mongolia: One of the Pioneers of Chinese Wind Power Development," in Proceedings of the Beijing International Conference on Wind Energy (Beijing: Organizing Committee of the Beijing International Conference on Wind Energy, 1995), cited in Goldemberg, op. cit. note 2, p. 377; Indian loans from MNES, op. cit. note 17, p. 53; funding in India from "Why Renewables Cannot Penetrate the Market," *Down to Earth,* 30 April 2002, p. 35.

63. Tax credit in Arkansas from Robert Righter, *Wind Energy in America: A History* (Norman: University of Oklahoma Press, 1996), p. 205; wind's

potential share of Arkansas' electricity calculated by Worldwatch with consumption data from EIA, at <www.eia.doe.gov/cneaf/electricity/st_profiles/arkansas/ar.html>, viewed 7 September 2002, and with wind potential from Battelle/Pacific Northwest Laboratory, *Assessment of Available Windy Land Area and Wind Energy Potential in the Contiguous United States* (Battelle/PNL, August 1991), cited in Jan Hamrin and Nancy Rader, *Investing in the Future: A Regulator's Guide to Renewables* (Washington, DC: National Association of Regulatory Utility Commissioners, February 1993), p. A-11.

64. Indian programs from MNES, op. cit. note 17.

65. Middelgrunden from EWEA and Greenpeace, op. cit. note 21, p. 20; benefits of cooperatives from Sawin, op. cit. note 56, p. 377; surveys from Andersen et al., *Rapport om hvordan en dansk kommune blev selvforsynende med ren vindenergi og skabte ny indkomst til kommunens borgere,* Nordvestjysk Folkecenter for Vedvarende Energi, 1997, cited in Steffen Damborg and Soren Krohn, "Public Attitudes Towards Wind Power," Danish Wind Turbine Manufacturers Association, 1998, at <www.windpower.dk/articles/surveys.htm>, viewed 13 April 1999.

66. Impact of standards in Denmark from Sawin, op. cit. note 56, pp. 261–62, 375; dominance of Danish turbine manufacturers from Søren Krohn, "Danish Wind Turbines: An Industrial Success Story," 21 January 2000, at <www.windpower.dk/articles/success.htm>, viewed 28 January 2000, and from Birger Madsen, BTM Consult, discussion with author, 8 December 2000.

67. Denmark and Germany from Sawin, op. cit. note 56, p. 375; United Kingdom from Madsen, op. cit. note 20.

68. Low figure for conventional energy subsidies from Thomas Johansson, UNDP, quoted in Margot Roosevelt, "The Winds of Change," *Time,* 26 August 2002, p. A-44; high figure from UNDP, "UNDP Initiative for Sustainable Energy—Summary," at <www.undp.org/seed/energy/unise/summary.html>, viewed 4 October 2002, and from Scheer, op. cit. note 55; 80–90 percent from International Energy Agency and from Martinot, op. cit. note 6.

69. Global Environment Facility funding from Martinot, op. cit. note 6; World Bank Group investments from Institute for Policy Studies (IPS), "The World Bank and the G-7: Changing the Earth's

Climate for Business," June 1997, cited in Kate Hampton, *Banking on Climate Change: How Public Finance for Fossil Fuel Projects is Short Changing Clean Development* (Washington, DC: IPS, 17 November 2000), p. 6.

70. Manufacturers' fears from California Energy Commission, *Wind Energy Program Progress Report* (Sacramento, CA: 1982), p. 23.

71. Decline in U.S. capacity from Gipe, op. cit. note 54; India from "Renewables Deserted?" *Down to Earth,* 30 April 2002, from MNES, op. cit. note 17, p. 69, and from "Why Renewables Cannot Penetrate the Market," op. cit. note 62, p. 33; Torgny Møller, "Government Closes Door in Denmark," *Windpower Monthly,* July 2002, p. 22.

72. Lower cost of consistent policies from Sawin, op. cit. note 56, pp. 360–63, 379.

73. Watson et al., op. cit. note 26.

74. BP from Amanda Griscom, "Got Sun? Marketing the Revolution in Clean Energy," *Grist Magazine,* 29 August 2002; Shell from Platts Global Energy, 2001, at <www.platts.com/renewables/investment.shtml>, viewed 10 October 2002; $10–15 billion from World Bank, *Global Development Finance 2000* (Washington, DC: 2000); eightfold increase from Martinot, op. cit. note 19, and from Massey, op. cit. note 19.

75. Model T from William J. Abernathy and Kenneth Wayne, "Limits of the Learning Curve," *Harvard Business Review*, September-October 1974, cited in Christopher Flavin and Nicholas Lenssen, *Power Surge* (New York: W.W. Norton & Company, 1994), p. 304; wind generation by 2020 calculated to be about 6,833 billion kWh by Worldwatch, assuming capacity factor of 30 percent; global nuclear power generation in 2001 from International Atomic Energy Agency, cited in Nuclear Energy Institute, "World Nuclear Power Generation and Capacity," at <www.nei.org/documents/World_Nuclear_Generation_and_Capacity.pdf>, viewed 11 October 2002.

76. Prime Minister Tony Blair, speech entitled "Environment: The Next Steps," *Reuters*, 6 March 2001, cited in G8 Renewable Energy Task Force Report, op. cit. note 3, p. 16; European Union goal from European Wind Energy Association, "European Renewable Electricity Directive: The Final Version," *Wind Directions,* January 2002, pp. 10–11; China and India from Christoper Flavin, discussions with author, September 2002; Brazil from Coelho, op. cit. note 17; members of Congress from Susanna Drayne, Coordinator, Sustainable Energy Coalition, e-mail to author, 11 October 2002; U.S. states from Interstate Renewable Energy Council, Database of State Incentives for Renewable Energy, at <www.dsireusa.org>, viewed 14 October 2002.

77. Paul Appleby, Director of Strategy and Planning, BP Solarex, United Kingdom, cited in Greenpeace, *Breaking the Solar Impasse* (Amsterdam: September 1999), p. 2.

78. G8 Renewable Energy Task Force, op. cit. note 3, p. 9; BP from Griscom, op. cit. note 74; Shell from Simon Tuck, "Royal Dutch/Shell Taking Minority Stake in Iogen," *Globe & Mail*, at <www.gogreenindustries.com/Clippings/RoyalDutchShell8May02.pdf> viewed 10 October 2002; Jones from Platts Global Energy, op. cit. note 74.

79. Meeting U.S. needs with wind calculated with data from Battelle/Pacific Northwest Laboratory, op. cit. note 63; solar in Nevada from U.S. Department of Energy, "Concentrating Solar Power Technologies Overview," at <www.energlan.sandia.gov/sunlab/overview.htm>, viewed 25 January 2002.

80. Fuel cell cars from "Factbox—What Are Carmakers Doing to Cut Emissions?" *Reuters,* 24 September 2002.

81. IPCC, op. cit. note 9, p. 12.

AMORY B. LOVINS, L. HUNTER LOVINS, AND PAUL HAWKEN   II.19

A Road Map for Natural Capitalism

The first two authors of this reading, Amory and Hunter Lovins, are the founders and directors of the Rocky Mountain Institute (*www.rmi.org*), a Colorado-based environmental policy think tank, and Paul Hawken is the founder of the Smith & Hawken retail and catalogue company. In this reading, which originally appeared in *Harvard Business Review,* they describe some ways for businesses to rethink their current wasteful and inefficient strategies and replace them with more profitable and sustainable alternatives.

The popular mind-set of most businesses today is to utilize natural resources as if they were unlimited, ignoring the long-term implications caused by these actions. However, this article provides several examples of ways in which natural design alternatives have proved more profitable in the long run. The authors argue that businesses should strive to increase the productivity of natural resources and utilize production systems modeled on biological ones. Businesses should emphasize creating solutions, not products.

The authors believe that technological innovation, not government regulation, will produce technological solutions that will enable us to better protect the biosphere, provide for a higher standard of living, and also produce profits for entrepreneurs. The key to making industrial capitalism sustainable is to transform it into "natural capitalism" that reinvests in and expands "the planet's ecosystems so that they can produce their vital services and biological resources even more abundantly."

Focus Questions

1. What are the four key elements of "natural capitalism" as the authors describe it?
2. The authors give several examples of designers who have implemented "whole-system design" technologies that have netted substantial savings over conventional designs. Do you think these examples can be generalized to other kinds of technology? Discuss the potential for this new approach in several industry sectors.
3. Compare the view of the authors of this reading with those of Feenberg (selection I.8) and Dyson (selection I.11). Do you think it likely that environmental values can provide the basis for the development of more sustainable technological solutions, or is it necessary to impose regulations that force industries to limit damage to the environment? Discuss.

Keywords

biomimicry, capitalism, closed-loop manufacturing, ecosystems, industrialism, innovation, pollution, regulation, whole-system design

ON SEPTEMBER 16, 1991, A SMALL group of scientists was sealed inside Biosphere II, a glittering 3.2-acre glass and metal dome in Oracle, Arizona. Two years later, when the radical attempt to replicate the earth's main ecosystems in miniature ended, the engineered environment was dying. The gaunt researchers had survived only because fresh air had been pumped in. Despite $200 million worth of elaborate equipment, Biosphere II had failed to generate breathable air, drinkable water, and adequate food for just eight people. Yet Biosphere I, the planet we all inhabit, effortlessly performs those tasks every day for 6 billion of us.

Disturbingly, Biosphere I is now itself at risk. The earth's ability to sustain life, and therefore economic activity, is threatened by the way we extract, process, transport, and dispose of a vast flow of resources—some 220 billion tons a year, or more than 20 times the average American's body weight every day. With dangerously narrow focus, our industries look only at the exploitable resources of the earth's ecosystems—its oceans, forests, and plains—and not at the larger services that those systems provide for free. Resources and ecosystem services both come from the earth—even from the same biological systems—but they're two different things. Forests, for instance, not only produce the resource of wood fiber but also provide such ecosystem services as water storage, habitat, and regulation of the atmosphere and climate. Yet companies that earn income from harvesting the wood fiber resource often do so in ways that damage the forest's ability to carry out its other vital tasks.

Unfortunately, the cost of destroying ecosystem services becomes apparent only when the services start to break down. In China's Yangtze basin in 1998, for example, deforestation triggered flooding that killed 3,700 people, dislocated 223 million, and inundated 60 million acres of cropland. That $30 billion disaster forced a logging moratorium and a $12 billion crash program of reforestation.

From "A Road Map for Natural Capitalism," by Amory B. Lovins, L. Hunter Lovins, and Paul Hawken, *Harvard Business Review.* May/June 1999, pp. 145–158. Copyright © 1999 by the Harvard Business School Publishing Corporation. Reprinted by permission of Harvard Business Review. All rights reserved.

The reason companies (and governments) are so prodigal with ecosystem services is that the value of those services doesn't appear on the business balance sheet. But that's a staggering omission. The economy, after all, is embedded in the environment. Recent calculations published in the journal *Nature* conservatively estimate the value of all the earth's ecosystem services to be at least $33 trillion a year. That's close to the gross world product, and it implies a capitalized book value on the order of half a quadrillion dollars. What's more, for most of these services, there is no known substitute at any price, and we can't live without them.

This article puts forward a new approach not only for protecting the biosphere but also for improving profits and competitiveness. Some very simple changes to the way we run our businesses, built on advanced techniques for making resources more productive, can yield startling benefits both for today's shareholders and for future generations.

This approach is called *natural capitalism* because it's what capitalism might become if its largest category of capital—the "natural capital" of ecosystem services—were properly valued. The journey to natural capitalism involves four major shifts in business practices, all vitally interlinked:

• *Dramatically increase the productivity of natural resources.* Reducing the wasteful and destructive flow of resources from depletion to pollution represents a major business opportunity. Through fundamental changes in both production design and technology, farsighted companies are developing ways to make natural resources—energy, minerals, water, forests—stretch 5, 10, even 100 times further than they do today. These major resource savings often yield higher profits than small resource savings do—or even saving no resources at all would—and not only pay for themselves over time but in many cases reduce initial capital investments.

• *Shift to biologically inspired production models.* Natural capitalism seeks not merely to reduce waste but to eliminate the very concept of waste. In closed-loop production systems, modeled on nature's designs, every output either is returned harmlessly to the ecosystem as a nutrient, like compost, or becomes an input for manufacturing another product. Such systems can often be designed to eliminate the use of toxic materials, which can hamper nature's ability to reprocess materials.

• *Move to a solutions-based business model.* The business model of traditional manufacturing rests on the sale of goods. In the new model, value is instead delivered as a flow of services—providing illumination, for example, rather than selling lightbulbs. This model entails a new perception of value, a move from the acquisition of goods as a measure of affluence to one where well-being is measured by the continuous satisfaction of changing expectations for quality, utility, and performance. The new relationship aligns the interests of providers and customers in ways that reward them for implementing the first two innovations of natural capitalism—resource productivity and closed-loop manufacturing.

• *Reinvest in natural capital.* Ultimately, business must restore, sustain, and expand the planet's ecosystems so that they can produce their vital services and biological resources even more abundantly. Pressures to do so are mounting as human needs expand, the costs engendered by deteriorating ecosystems rise, and the environmental awareness of consumers increases. Fortunately, these pressures all create business value.

Natural capitalism is not motivated by a current scarcity of natural resources. Indeed, although many biological resources, like fish, are becoming scarce, most mined resources, such as copper and oil, seem ever more abundant. Indices of average commodity prices are at 28-year lows, thanks partly to powerful extractive technologies, which are often subsidized and whose damage to natural capital remains unaccounted for. Yet even despite these artificially low prices, using resources manyfold more productively can now be so profitable that pioneering companies—large and small—have already embarked on the journey toward natural capitalism.[1]

Still the question arises—if large resource savings are available and profitable, why haven't they all been captured already? The answer is simple: scores of common practices in both the private and public sectors systematically reward companies for wasting natural resources and penalize them for boosting resource productivity. For example, most companies expense their consumption of raw materials through the income statement but pass resource-saving investment through the balance sheet. That distortion makes it more tax efficient to waste fuel than to invest in improving fuel efficiency. In short, even though the road seems clear, the compass that companies use to direct their journey is broken. Later we'll look in more detail at some of the obstacles to resource productivity—and some of the important business opportunities they reveal. But first, let's map the route toward natural capitalism.

Dramatically Increase the Productivity of Natural Resources

In the first stage of a company's journey toward natural capitalism, it strives to wring out the waste of energy, water, materials, and other resources throughout its production systems and other operations. There are two main ways companies can do this at a profit. First, they can adopt a fresh approach to design that considers industrial systems as a whole rather than part by part. Second, companies can replace old industrial technologies with new ones, particularly with those based on natural processes and materials.

IMPLEMENTING WHOLE-SYSTEM DESIGN

Inventor Edwin Land once remarked that "people who seem to have had a new idea have often simply stopped having an old idea." This is particularly true when designing for resource savings. The old idea is one of diminishing returns—the greater the resource saving, the higher the cost. But that old idea is giving way to the new idea that bigger savings can cost less—that saving a large fraction of resources can actually cost less than saving a small fraction of resources. This is the concept of expanding returns, and it governs much of the revolutionary thinking behind whole-system design. Lean manufacturing is an example of whole-system thinking that has helped many companies dramatically reduce such forms of waste as lead times, defect rates, and inventory. Applying whole-system thinking to the productivity of natural resources can achieve even more.

Consider Interface Corporation, a leading maker of materials for commercial interiors. In its new Shanghai carpet factory, a liquid had to be circulated through a standard pumping loop similar to those used in nearly all industries. A top European company designed the system to use pumps requiring a total of 95 horsepower. But before construction began, Interface's engineer, Jan Schilham, realized that two embarrassingly simple design changes would cut that power requirement to only 7 horsepower—a 92% reduction. His redesigned system cost less to build, involved no new technology, and worked better in all respects.

What two design changes achieved this 12-fold saving in pumping power? First, Schilham chose fatter-than-usual pipes, which create much less friction than thin pipes do and therefore need far less pumping energy. The original designer had chosen thin pipes because, according to the textbook method, the extra cost of fatter ones wouldn't be justified by the pumping energy that they would save. This standard design trade-off optimizes the pipes by themselves but "pessimizes" the larger system. Schilham optimized the *whole* system by counting not only the higher capital cost of the fatter pipes but also the *lower* capital cost of the smaller pumping equipment that would be needed. The pumps, motors, motor controls, and electrical components could all be much smaller because there'd be less friction to overcome. Capital cost would fall far more for the smaller equipment than it would rise for the fatter pipe. Choosing big pipes and small pumps—rather than small pipes and big pumps—would therefore make the whole system cost less to build, even before counting its future energy savings.

Schilham's second innovation was to reduce the friction even more by making the pipes short and straight rather than long and crooked. He did this by laying out the pipes first, *then* positioning the various tanks, boilers, and other equipment that they connected. Designers normally locate the production equipment in arbitrary positions and then have a pipe fitter connect everything. Awkward placement forces the pipes to make numerous bends that greatly increase friction. The pipe fitters don't mind: they're paid by the hour, they profit from the extra pipes and fittings, and they don't pay for the oversized pumps or inflated electric bills. In addition to reducing those four kinds of costs, Schilham's short, straight pipes were easier to insulate, saving an extra 70 kilowatts of heat loss and repaying the insulation's cost in three months.

This small example has big implications for two reasons. First, pumping is the largest application of motors, and motors use three-quarters of all industrial electricity. Second, the lessons are very widely relevant. Interface's pumping loop shows how simple changes in design mentality can yield huge resource savings and returns on investment. This isn't rocket science; often it's just a rediscovery of good Victorian engineering principles that have been lost because of specialization.

Whole-system thinking can help managers find small changes that lead to big savings that are cheap, free, or even better than free (because they make the whole system cheaper to build). They can do this because often the right investment in one part of the system can produce multiple benefits throughout the system. For example, companies would gain 18 distinct economic benefits—of which direct energy savings is only one—if they switched from ordinary motors to premium-efficiency motors or from ordinary lighting ballasts (the transformer-like boxes that control fluorescent lamps) to electronic ballasts that automatically dim the lamps to match available daylight. If everyone in America integrated these and other selected technologies into all existing motor and lighting systems in an optimal way, the nation's $220-billion-a-year electric bill would be cut in half. The after-tax return on investing in these changes would in most cases exceed 100% per year.

The profits from saving electricity could be increased even further if companies also incorporated the best off-the-shelf improvements into their building structure and their office, heating, cooling, and other equipment. Overall, such changes could cut national electricity consumption by at least 75% and produce returns of around 100% a year on the investments made. More important, because workers would be more comfortable, better able to see, and less fatigued by noise, their productivity and the quality of their output would rise. Eight recent case studies of people working in well-designed, energy-efficient buildings measured labor productivity gains of 6% to 16%. Since a typical office pays about 100 times as much for people as it does for energy, this increased productivity in people is worth about 6 to 16 times as much as eliminating the entire energy bill.

Energy-saving, productivity-enhancing improvements can often be achieved at even lower cost by piggybacking them onto the periodic renovations that all buildings and factories need. A recent proposal for reallocating the normal 20-year renovation budget for a standard 200,000-square-foot glass-clad office tower near Chicago, Illinois, shows the potential of whole-system design. The proposal suggested replacing the aging glazing system with a new kind of window that lets in nearly six times more daylight than the old sun-blocking glass units. The new windows would reduce the flow of heat and noise four times better than traditional windows do. So even though the glass costs slightly more, the overall cost of the renovation would be reduced because the windows would let in cool, glare-free daylight that, when combined with more efficient lighting and office equipment, would reduce the need for air-conditioning by 75%. Installing a fourfold more efficient, but fourfold smaller, air-conditioning system would cost $200,000 less than giving the old system its normal 20-year renovation. The $200,000 saved would, in turn, pay for the extra cost of the new windows and other improvements. This whole-system approach to renovation would not only save 75% of the building's total energy use, it would also greatly improve the building's comfort and marketability. Yet it would cost essentially the same as the normal renovation. There are about 100,000 twenty-year-old glass office towers in the United States that are ripe for such improvement.

Major gains in resource productivity require that the right steps be taken in the right order. Small changes made at the downstream end of a process often create far larger savings further upstream. In almost any industry that uses a pumping system, for example, saving one unit of liquid flow or friction in an exit pipe saves about ten units of fuel, cost, and pollution at the power station.

Of course, the original reduction in flow itself can bring direct benefits, which are often the reason changes are made in the first place. In the 1980s, while California's industry grew 30%, for example, its water use was cut by 30%, largely to avoid increased wastewater fees. But the resulting reduction in pumping energy (and the roughly tenfold larger saving in power-plant fuel and pollution) delivered bonus savings that were at the time largely unanticipated.

To see how downstream cuts in resource consumption can create huge savings upstream, consider how reducing the use of wood fiber disproportionately reduces the pressure to cut down forests. In round numbers, half of all harvested wood fiber is used for such structural products as lumber; the other half is used for paper and cardboard. In both cases, the biggest leverage comes from reducing the amount of the retail product used. If it takes, for example, three pounds of harvested trees to produce one pound of product, then saving one pound of product will save three pounds of trees—plus all the environmental damage avoided by not having to cut them down in the first place.

The easiest savings come from not using paper that's unwanted or unneeded. In an experiment at its Swiss headquarters, for example, Dow Europe cut office paper flow by about 30% in six weeks simply by discouraging unneeded information. For instance, mailing lists were eliminated and senders of memos got back receipts indicating whether each recipient had wanted the information. Taking those and other small steps, Dow was also able to increase labor productivity by a similar proportion because people could focus on what they really needed to read. Similarly, Danish hearing-aid maker Oticon saved upwards of 30% of its paper as a by-product of redesigning its business processes to produce better decisions faster. Setting the default on office printers and copiers to double-sided mode reduced AT&T's paper costs by about 15%. Recently developed copiers and printers can even strip off old toner and printer ink, permitting each sheet to be reused about ten times.

Further savings can come from using thinner but stronger and more opaque paper, and from designing packaging more thoughtfully. In a 30-month effort at reducing such waste, Johnson & Johnson saved 2,750 tons of packaging, 1,600 tons of paper, $2.8 million, and at least 330 acres of forest annually. The downstream savings in paper use are multiplied by the savings further upstream, as less need for paper products (or less need for fiber to make each product) translates into less raw paper, less raw paper means less pulp, and less pulp requires fewer trees to be harvested from the forest. Recycling paper and substituting alternative fibers such as wheat straw will save even more.

Comparable savings can be achieved for the wood fiber used in structural products. Pacific Gas and Electric, for example, sponsored an innovative design developed by Davis Energy Group that used engineered wood products to reduce the amount of wood needed in a stud wall for a typical tract house by more than 70%. These walls were stronger, cheaper, more stable, and insulated twice as well. Using them enabled the designers to eliminate heating and cooling equipment in a climate where temperatures range from freezing to 113°F. Eliminating the equipment made the whole house much less expensive both to build and to run while still maintaining high levels of comfort. Taken together, these and many other savings in the paper and construction industries could make our use of wood fiber so much more productive that, in principle, the entire world's present wood fiber needs could probably be met by an intensive tree farm about the size of Iowa.

ADOPTING INNOVATIVE TECHNOLOGIES

Implementing whole-system design goes hand in hand with introducing alternative, environmentally friendly technologies. Many of these are already available and profitable but not widely known. Some, like the "designer catalysts" that are transforming the chemical industry, are already runaway successes. Others are still making their way to market, delayed by cultural rather than by economic or technical barriers.

The automobile industry is particularly ripe for technological change. After a century of development, motorcar technology is showing signs of age. Only 1% of the energy consumed by today's cars is actually used to move the driver: only 15% to 20% of the power generated by burning gasoline reaches the wheels (the rest is lost in the engine and drive-train) and 95% of the resulting propulsion moves the car, not the driver. The industry's infrastructure is hugely expensive and inefficient. Its convergent products compete for narrow niches in saturated core markets at commoditylike prices. Auto making is capital intensive, and product cycles are long. It is profitable in good years but subject to large losses in bad years. Like the typewriter industry just before the advent of personal computers, it is vulnerable to displacement by something completely different.

Enter the Hypercar. Since 1993, when Rocky Mountain Institute placed this automotive concept in the public domain, several dozen current and potential auto manufacturers have committed billions of dollars to its development and commercialization. The Hypercar integrates the best existing technologies to reduce the consumption of fuel as much as 85% and the amount of materials used up to 90% by introducing four main innovations.

First, making the vehicle out of advanced polymer composites, chiefly carbon fiber, reduces its weight by two-thirds while maintaining crashworthiness. Second, aerodynamic design and better tires reduce air resistance by as much as 70% and rolling resistance by up to 80%. Together, these innovations save about two-thirds of the fuel. Third, 30% to 50% of the remaining fuel is saved by using a "hybrid-electric" drive. In such a system, the wheels are turned by electric motors whose power is made onboard by a small engine or turbine, or even more efficiently by a fuel cell. The fuel cell generates electricity directly by chemically combining stored hydrogen with oxygen, producing pure hot water as its only by-product. Interactions between the small, clean, efficient power source and the ultralight, low-drag auto body then further reduce the weight, cost, and complexity of both. Fourth, much of the traditional hardware—from transmissions and differentials to gauges and certain parts of the suspension—can be replaced by electronics controlled with highly integrated, customizable, and upgradable software.

These technologies make it feasible to manufacture pollution-free, high-performance cars, sport utilities, pickup trucks, and vans that get 80 to 200 miles per gallon (or its energy equivalent in other fuels). These improvements will not require any compromise in quality or utility. Fuel savings will not come from making the vehicles small, sluggish, unsafe, or unaffordable, nor will they depend on government fuel taxes, mandates, or subsidies. Rather, Hypercars will succeed for the same reason that people buy compact discs instead of phonograph records: the CD is a superior product that redefines market expectations. From the manufacturers' perspective, Hypercars will cut cycle times, capital needs, body part counts, and assembly effort and space by as much as tenfold. Early adopters will have a huge competitive advantage—which is why dozens of corporations, including most automakers, are now racing to bring Hypercar-like products to market.[2]

In the long term, the Hypercar will transform industries other than automobiles. It will displace about an eighth of the steel market directly and most of the rest eventually, as carbon fiber becomes far cheaper. Hypercars and their cousins could ultimately save as much oil as OPEC now sells. Indeed, oil may well become uncompetitive as a fuel long before it becomes scarce and costly. Similar challenges face the coal and electricity industries because the development of the Hypercar is likely to accelerate greatly the commercialization of inexpensive hydrogen fuel cells. These fuel cells will help shift power production from centralized coal-fired and nuclear power stations to networks of decentralized, small-scale generators. In fact, fuel-cell-powered Hypercars could themselves be part of these networks. They'd be, in effect, 20-kilowatt power plants on wheels. Given that cars are left parked—that is, unused—more than 95% of the time, these Hypercars could be plugged into a grid and could then sell back enough electricity to repay as much as half the predicted cost of leasing them. A national Hypercar fleet could ultimately have five to ten times the generating capacity of the national electric grid.

As radical as it sounds, the Hypercar is not an isolated case. Similar ideas are emerging in such industries as chemicals, semiconductors, general manufacturing, transportation, water and wastewater treatment, agriculture, forestry, energy, real estate, and urban design. For example, the amount of carbon dioxide released for each microchip manufactured can be reduced almost 100-fold through improvements that are now profitable or soon will be.

Some of the most striking developments come from emulating nature's techniques. In her book, *Biomimicry,* Janine Benyus points out that spiders convert digested crickets and flies into silk that's as strong as Kevlar without the need for boiling sulfuric acid and high-temperature extruders. Using no furnaces, abalone can convert seawater into an inner shell twice as tough as our best ceramics. Trees turn sunlight, water, soil, and air into cellulose, a sugar stronger than nylon but one-fourth as dense. They then bind it into wood, a natural composite with a higher bending strength than concrete, aluminum alloy, or steel. We may never become as skillful as spiders, abalone, or trees, but smart designers are already realizing that nature's environmentally benign chemistry offers attractive alternatives to industrial brute force.

Whether through better design or through new technologies, reducing waste represents a vast business opportunity. The U.S. economy is not even 10% as energy efficient as the laws of physics allow. Just the energy thrown off as waste heat by U.S. power stations equals the total energy use of Japan. Materials efficiency is even worse: only about 1% of all the materials mobilized to serve America is actually made into products and still in use six months after sale. In every sector, there are opportunities for reducing the amount of resources that go into a production process, the steps required to run that process, and the amount of pollution generated and by-products discarded at the end. These all represent avoidable costs and hence profits to be won.

Redesign Production According to Biological Models

In the second stage on the journey to natural capitalism, companies use closed-loop manufacturing to create new products and processes that can totally prevent waste. This plus more efficient production processes could cut companies' long-term materials requirements by more than 90% in most sectors.

The central principle of closed-loop manufacturing, as architect Paul Bierman-Lytle of the engineering firm CH2M Hill puts it, is "waste equals food." Every output of manufacturing should be either composted into natural nutrients or remanufactured into technical nutrients—that is, it should be returned to the ecosystem or recycled for further production. Closed-loop production systems are designed to eliminate any materials that incur disposal costs, especially toxic ones, because the alternative—isolating them to prevent harm to natural systems—tends to be costly and risky. Indeed, meeting EPA and OSHA standards by eliminating harmful materials often makes a manufacturing process cost less than the hazardous process it replaced. Motorola, for example, formerly used chlorofluorocarbons for cleaning printed circuit boards after soldering. When CFCs were outlawed because they destroy stratospheric ozone, Motorola at first explored such alternatives as orange-peel terpenes. But it turned out to be even cheaper—and to produce a better product—to redesign the whole soldering process so that it needed no cleaning operations or cleaning materials at all.

Closed-loop manufacturing is more than just a theory. The U.S. remanufacturing industry in 1996 reported revenues of $53 billion—more than consumer-durables manufacturing (appliances; furniture; audio, video, farm, and garden equipment). Xerox, whose bottom line has swelled by $700 million from remanufacturing, expects to save another $1 billion just by remanufacturing its new, entirely reusable or recyclable line of "green" photocopiers. What's more, policy makers in some countries are already taking steps to encourage industry to think along these lines. German law, for example, makes many manufacturers responsible for their products forever, and Japan is following suit.

Combining closed-loop manufacturing with resource efficiency is especially powerful. DuPont, for example, gets much of its polyester industrial film back from customers after they use it and recycles it into new film. DuPont also makes its polyester film ever stronger and thinner so it uses less material and costs less to make. Yet because the film performs better, customers are willing to pay more for it. As DuPont chairman Jack Krol noted in 1997, "Our ability to continually improve the inherent properties [of our films] enables this process [of developing more productive materials, at lower cost, and higher profits] to go on indefinitely."

Interface is leading the way to this next frontier of industrial ecology. While its competitors are "down cycling" nylon-and-PVC-based carpet into less valuable carpet backing, Interface has invented a new floor-covering material called Solenium, which can be completely remanufactured into identical new product. This fundamental innovation emerged from a clean-sheet redesign. Executives at Interface didn't ask how they could sell more carpet of the familiar kind; they asked how they could create a dream product that would best meet their customers' needs while protecting and nourishing natural capital.

Solenium lasts four times longer and uses 40% less material than ordinary carpets—an 86% reduction in materials intensity. What's more, Solenium is free of chlorine and other toxic materials, is virtually stainproof, doesn't grow mildew, can easily be cleaned with water, and offers aesthetic advantages over traditional carpets. It's so superior in every respect that Interface doesn't market it as an environmental product—just a better one.

Solenium is only one part of Interface's drive to eliminate every form of waste. Chairman Ray C. Anderson defines waste as "any measurable input that does not produce customer value," and he considers all inputs to be waste until shown otherwise. Between 1994 and 1998, this zero-waste approach led to a systematic treasure hunt that helped to keep resource inputs constant while revenues rose by $200 million. Indeed, $67 million of the revenue increase can be directly attributed to the company's 60% reduction in landfill waste.

Subsequently, president Charlie Eitel expanded the definition of waste to include all fossil fuel inputs, and now many customers are eager to buy products from the company's recently opened solar-powered carpet factory. Interface's green strategy has not only won plaudits from environmentalists, it has also proved a remarkably successful business strategy. Between 1993 and 1998, revenue has more than doubled, profits have more than tripled, and the number of employees has increased by 73%.

Change the Business Model

In addition to its drive to eliminate waste, Interface has made a fundamental shift in its business model—the third stage on the journey toward natural capitalism. The company has realized that clients want to walk on and look at carpets—but not necessarily to own them. Traditionally, broadloom carpets in office buildings are replaced every decade because some portions look worn out. When that happens, companies suffer the disruption of shutting down their offices and removing their furniture. Billions of pounds of carpets are removed each year and sent to landfills, where they will last up to 20,000 years. To escape this unproductive and wasteful cycle, Interface is transforming itself from a company that sells and fits carpets into one that provides floor-covering services.

Under its Evergreen Lease, Interface no longer sells carpets but rather leases a floor-covering service for a monthly fee, accepting responsibility for keeping the carpet fresh and clean. Monthly inspections detect and replace worn carpet tiles. Since at most 20% of an area typically shows at least 80% of the wear, replacing only the worn parts reduces the consumption of carpeting material by about 80%. It also minimizes the disruption that customers experience—worn tiles are seldom found under furniture. Finally, for the customer, leasing carpets can provide a tax advantage by turning a capital expenditure into a tax-deductible expense. The result: the customer gets cheaper and better services that cost the supplier far less to produce. Indeed, the energy saved from not producing a whole new carpet is in itself enough to produce all the carpeting that the new business model requires. Taken together, the 5-fold savings in carpeting material that Interface achieves though the Evergreen Lease and the 7-fold materials savings achieved through the use of Solenium deliver a stunning 35-fold reduction in the flow of materials needed to sustain a superior floor-covering service. Remanufacturing, and even making carpet initially from renewable materials, can then reduce the extraction of virgin resources essentially to the company's goal of zero.

Interface's shift to a service-leasing business reflects a fundamental change from the basic model of most manufacturing companies, which still look on their businesses as machines for producing and selling products. The more products sold, the better—at least for the company, if not always for the customer or the earth. But any model that wastes natural resources also wastes money. Ultimately, that model will be unable to compete with a service model that emphasizes solving problems and building long-term relationships with customers rather than making and selling products. The shift to what James Womack of the Lean Enterprise Institute calls a "solutions economy" will almost always improve customer value *and* providers' bottom lines because it aligns both parties' interest, offering rewards for doing more and better with less.

Interface is not alone. Elevator giant Schindler, for example, prefers leasing vertical transportation services to selling elevators because leasing lets it capture the savings from its elevators' lower energy and maintenance costs. Dow Chemical and Safety-Kleen prefer leasing dissolving services to selling solvents because they can reuse the same solvent scores of times, reducing costs. United Technologies' Carrier division, the world's largest manufacturer of air conditioners, is shifting its mission from selling air conditioners to leasing comfort. Making its air conditioners more durable and efficient may compromise future equipment sales, but it provides what customers want and will pay for—better comfort at lower cost. But Carrier is going even further. It's starting to team up with other companies to make buildings more efficient so that they need less air-conditioning, or even none at all, to yield the same level of comfort. Carrier will get paid to provide the agreed-upon level of comfort, however that's delivered. Higher profits will come from providing better solutions rather than from selling more equipment. Since comfort with little or no air-conditioning (via better building design) works better and costs less than comfort with copious air-conditioning, Carrier is smart to capture this opportunity itself before its competitors do. As they say at 3M: "We'd rather eat our *own* lunch, thank you."

The shift to a service business model promises benefits not just to participating businesses but to the entire economy as well. Womack points out that by helping customers reduce their need for capital goods such as carpets or elevators, and by rewarding suppliers for extending and maximizing asset values rather than for churning them, adoption of the service model will reduce the volatility in the turnover of capital goods that lies at the heart of the business cycle. That would significantly reduce the overall volatility of the world's economy. At present, the producers of capital goods face feast or famine because the buying decisions of households and corporations are extremely sensitive to fluctuating income. But in a continuous-flow-of-services economy, those swings would be greatly reduced, bringing a welcome stability to businesses. Excess capacity—another form of waste and source of risk—need no longer be retained for meeting peak demand. The result of adopting the new model would be an economy in which we grow and get richer by using less and become stronger by being leaner and more stable.

Reinvest in Natural Capital

The foundation of textbook capitalism is the prudent reinvestment of earnings in productive capital. Natural capitalists who have dramatically raised their resource productivity, closed their loops, and shifted to a solutions-based business model have one key task remaining. They must reinvest in restoring, sustaining, and expanding the most important form of capital—their own natural habitat and biological resource base.

This was not always so important. Until recently, business could ignore damage to the ecosystem because it didn't affect production and didn't increase costs. But that situation is changing. In 1998 alone, violent weather displaced 300 million people and caused upwards of $90 billion worth of damage, representing more weather-related destruction than was reported through the entire decade of the 1980s. The increase in damage is strongly linked to deforestation and climate change, factors that accelerate the frequency and severity of natural disasters and are the consequences of inefficient industrialization. If the flow of services from industrial systems is to

be sustained or increased in the future for a growing population, the vital flow of services from living systems will have to be maintained or increased as well. Without reinvestment in natural capital, shortages of ecosystem services are likely to become the limiting factor to prosperity in the next century. When a manufacturer realizes that a supplier of key components is overextended and running behind on deliveries, it takes immediate action lest its own production lines come to a halt. The ecosystem is a supplier of key components for the life of the planet, and it is now falling behind on its orders.

Failure to protect and reinvest in natural capital can also hit a company's revenues indirectly. Many companies are discovering that public perceptions of environmental responsibility, or its lack thereof, affect sales. MacMillan Bloedel, targeted by environmental activists as an emblematic clear-cutter and chlorine user, lost 5% of its sales almost overnight when dropped as a U.K. supplier by Scott Paper and Kimberly-Clark. Numerous case studies show that companies leading the way in implementing changes that help protect the environment tend to gain disproportionate advantage, while companies perceived as irresponsible lose their franchise, their legitimacy, and their shirts. Even businesses that claim to be committed to the concept of sustainable development but whose strategy is seen as mistaken, like Monsanto, are encountering stiffening public resistance to their products. Not surprisingly, University of Oregon business professor Michael Russo, along with many other analysts, has found that a strong environmental rating is "a consistent predictor of profitability."

The pioneering corporations that have made reinvestments in natural capital are starting to see some interesting paybacks. The independent power producer AES, for example, has long pursued a policy of planting trees to offset the carbon emissions of its power plants. That ethical stance, once thought quixotic, now looks like a smart investment because a dozen brokers are now starting to create markets in carbon reduction. Similarly, certification by the Forest Stewardship Council of certain sustainably grown and harvested products has given Collins Pine the extra profit margins that enabled its U.S. manufacturing operations to survive brutal competition. Taking an even longer view, Swiss Re and other European reinsurers are seeking to cut their storm-damage losses by pressing for international public policy to protect the climate and by investing in climate-safe technologies that also promise good profits. Yet most companies still do not realize that a vibrant ecological web underpins their survival and their business success. Enriching natural capital is not just a public good—it is vital to every company's longevity.

It turns out that changing industrial processes so that they actually replenish and magnify the stock of natural capital can prove especially profitable because nature does the production; people need to just step back and let life flourish. Industries that directly harvest living resources, such as forestry, farming, and fishing, offer the most suggestive examples. Here are three:

• Allan Savory of the Center for Holistic Management in Albuquerque, New Mexico, has redesigned cattle ranching to raise the carrying capacity of rangelands, which have often been degraded not by overgrazing but by undergrazing and grazing the wrong way. Savory's solution is to keep the cattle moving from place to place, grazing intensively but briefly at each site, so that they mimic the dense but constantly moving herds of native grazing animals that coevolved with grasslands. Thousands of ranchers are estimated to be applying this approach, improving both their range and their profits. This "management-intensive rotational grazing" method, long standard in New Zealand, yields such clearly superior returns that over 15% of Wisconsin's dairy farms have adopted it in the past few years.

• The California Rice Industry Association has discovered that letting nature's diversity flourish can be more profitable than forcing it to produce a single product. By flooding 150,000 to 200,000 acres of Sacramento valley rice fields—about 30% of California's rice-growing area—after harvest, farmers are able to create seasonal wetlands that support millions of wildfowl, replenish groundwater, improve fertility, and yield other valuable benefits. In addition, the farmers bale and sell the rice straw, whose high silica content—formerly an air-pollution hazard when the straw was burned—adds insect resistance and hence value as a construction material when it's resold instead.

• John Todd of Living Technologies in Burlington, Vermont, has used biological Living Machines—linked tanks of bacteria, algae, plants, and other organisms—to turn sewage into clean water. That not only yields cleaner water at a reduced cost, with no toxicity or odor, but it also produces commercially valuable flowers and makes the plant compatible with its residential neighborhood. A similar plant at the Ethel M Chocolates factory in Las Vegas, Nevada, not only handles difficult industrial wastes effectively but is showcased in its public tours.

Although such practices are still evolving, the broad lessons they teach are clear. In almost all climates, soils, and societies, working with nature is more productive than working against it. Reinvesting in nature allows farmers, fishermen, and forest managers to match or exceed the high yields and profits sustained by traditional input-intensive, chemically driven practices. Although much of mainstream business is still headed the other way, the profitability of sustainable, nature-emulating practices is already being proven. In the future, many industries that don't now consider themselves dependent on a biological resource base will become more so as they shift their raw materials and production processes more to biological ones. There is evidence that many business leaders are starting to think this way. The consulting firm Arthur D. Little surveyed a group of North American and European business leaders and found that 83% of them already believe that they can derive "real business value [from implementing a] sustainable-development approach to strategy and operations."

A Broken Compass?

If the road ahead is this clear, why are so many companies straying or falling by the wayside? We believe the reason is that the instruments companies use to set their targets, measure their performance, and hand out rewards are faulty. In other words, the markets are full of distortions and perverse incentives. Of the more than 60 specific forms of misdirection that we have identified,[3] the most obvious involve the ways companies allocate capital and the way governments set policy and impose taxes. Merely correcting these defective practices would uncover huge opportunities for profit.

Consider how companies make purchasing decisions. Decisions to buy small items are typically based on their initial cost rather than their full life-cycle cost, a practice that can add up to major wastage. Distribution transformers that supply electricity to buildings and factories, for example, are a minor item at just $320 apiece, and most companies try to save a quick buck by buying the lowest-price models. Yet nearly all the nation's electricity must flow through transformers, and using the cheaper but less efficient models wastes $1 billion a year. Such examples are legion. Equipping standard new office-lighting circuits with fatter wire that reduces electrical resistance could generate after-tax returns of 193% a year. Instead, wire as thin as the National Electrical Code permits is usually selected because it costs less up-front. But the code is meant only to prevent fires from overheated wiring, not to save money. Ironically, an electrician who chooses fatter wire—thereby reducing long-term electricity bills—doesn't get the job. After paying for the extra copper, he's no longer the low bidder.

Some companies do consider more than just the initial price in their purchasing decisions but still don't go far enough. Most of them use a crude payback estimate rather than more accurate metrics like discounted cash flow. A few years ago, the median simple payback these companies were demanding from energy efficiency was 1.9 years. That's equivalent to requiring an after-tax return of around 71% per year—about six times the marginal costs of capital.

Most companies also miss major opportunities by treating their facilities costs as an overhead to be minimized, typically by laying off engineers, rather than as profit center to be optimized—by using those engineers to save resources. Deficient measurement and accounting practices also prevent companies from allocating costs—and waste—with any accuracy. For example, only a few semiconductor plants worldwide regularly and accurately measure how much energy they're using to produce a unit of chilled water or clean air for their clean-room production facilities. That makes it hard for

them to improve efficiency. In fact, in an effort to save time, semiconductor makers frequently build new plants as exact copies of previous ones—a design method nicknamed "infectious repetitis."

Many executives pay too little attention to saving resources because they are often a small percentage of total costs (energy costs run to about 2% in most industries). But those resource savings drop straight to the bottom line and so represent a far greater percentage of profits. Many executives also think they already "did" efficiency in the 1970s, when the oil shock forced them to rethink old habits. They're forgetting that with today's far better technologies, it's profitable to start all over again. Malden Mills, the Massachusetts maker of such products as Polartec, was already using "efficient" metal-halide lamps in the mid 1990s. But a recent warehouse retrofit reduced the energy used for lighting by another 93%, improved visibility, and paid for itself in 18 months.

The way people are rewarded often creates perverse incentives. Architects and engineers, for example, are traditionally compensated for what they spend, not for what they save. Even the striking economics of the retrofit design for the Chicago office tower described earlier wasn't incentive enough actually to implement it. The property was controlled by a leasing agent who earned a commission every time she leased space, so she didn't want to wait the few extra months needed to refit the building. Her decision to reject the efficiency-quadrupling renovation proved costly for both her and her client. The building was so uncomfortable and expensive to occupy that it didn't lease, so ultimately the owner had to unload it at a firesale price. Moreover, the new owner will for the next 20 years be deprived of the opportunity to save capital cost.

If corporate practices obscure the benefits of natural capitalism, government policy positively undermines it. In nearly every country on the planet, tax laws penalize what we want more of—jobs and income—while subsidizing what we want less of—resource depletion and pollution. In every state but Oregon, regulated utilities are rewarded for selling more energy, water, and other resources, and penalized for selling less, even if increased production would cost more than improved customer efficiency. In most of America's arid western states, use-it-or-lose-it water laws encourage inefficient water consumption. Additionally, in many towns, inefficient use of land is enforced through outdated regulations, such as guidelines for ultrawide suburban streets recommended by 1950s civil-defense planners to accommodate the heavy equipment needed to clear up rubble after a nuclear attack.

The costs of these perverse incentives are staggering: $300 billion in annual energy wasted in the United States, and $1 trillion already misallocated to unnecessary air-conditioning equipment and the power supplies to run it (about 40% of the nation's peak electric load). Across the entire economy, unneeded expenditures to subsidize, encourage, and try to remedy inefficiency and damage that should not have occurred in the first place probably account for most, if not all, of the GDP growth of the past two decades. Indeed, according to former World Bank economist Herman Daly and his colleague John Cobb (along with many other analysts), Americans are hardly better off than they were in 1980. But if the U.S. government and private industry could redirect the dollars currently earmarked for remedial costs toward reinvestment in natural and human capital, they could bring about a genuine improvement in the nation's welfare. Companies, too, are finding that wasting resources also means wasting money and people. These intertwined forms of waste have equally intertwined solutions. Firing the unproductive tons, gallons, and kilowatt-hours often makes it possible to keep the people, who will have more and better work to do.

Recognizing the Scarcity Shift

In the end, the real trouble with our economic compass is that it points in exactly the wrong direction. Most businesses are behaving as if people were still scarce and nature still abundant—the conditions that helped to fuel the first Industrial Revolution. At that time, people were relatively scarce compared with the present-day population. The rapid mechanization of the textile industries caused explosive economic growth that created labor shortages in the factory and the field. The Industrial Revolution, responding to those shortages and mechanizing one industry after another, made people a hundred times more productive than they had ever been.

The logic of economizing on the scarcest resource, because it limits progress, remains correct. But the pattern of scarcity is shifting: now people aren't scarce but nature is. This shows up first in industries that depend directly on ecological health. Here, production is increasingly constrained by fish rather than by boats and nets, by forests rather than by chain saws, by fertile topsoil rather than by plows. Moreover, unlike the traditional factors of industrial production—capital and labor—the biological limiting factors cannot be substituted for one another. In the industrial system, we can easily exchange machinery for labor. But no technology or amount of money can substitute for a stable climate and a productive biosphere. Even proper pricing can't replace the priceless.

Natural capitalism addresses those problems by reintegrating ecological with economic goals. Because it is both necessary and profitable, it will subsume traditional industrialism within a new economy and a new paradigm of production, just as industrialism previously subsumed agrarianism. The companies that first make the changes we have described will have a competitive edge. Those that don't make that effort won't be a problem because ultimately they won't be around. In making that choice, as Henry Ford said, "Whether you believe you can, or whether you believe you can't, you're absolutely right."

NOTES

1. Our book, *Natural Capitalism*, provides hundreds of examples of how companies of almost every type and size, often through modest shifts in business logic and practice, have dramatically improved their bottom lines.

2. Nonproprietary details are posted at http://www.hypercar.com.

3. Summarized in the report "Climate: Making Sense *and* Making Money" at http://www.rmi.org/catalog/climate.htm.

II.20   ROBERT W. KATES

The Nexus and the Neem Tree

In this reading, Robert W. Kates, University Professor Emeritus at Brown University and co-convener of the Initiative on Science and Technology for Sustainability, examines the concept of sustainable development in light of what he regards as the failures of the contemporary pattern of globalization. Kates characterizes sustainable development as an oxymoron that "seeks to finesse the real conflicts between economy and environment and between the present and the future." Finding the correct balance between these ends requires that we examine the current system of globalization to determine whether or not it is enabling us to meet the goals of reducing the numbers of chronically hungry people while at the same time preserving the earth's life-support system for future generations. On both of these counts, Kates believes that the current form of globalization is failing to meet these goals overall, even though there are important and hopeful signs of progress in some areas. Instead of being opposed to globalization, the challenge, as he sees it, is to "humanize" it by changing the way in which the current system of globalization is governed in the direction of greater local control and democracy at the grass-roots level. Only by "civilizing" globalization in this way can we ensure that the benefits of economic development will be fairly distributed and used to address human needs.

Focus Questions

1. How does the U.S. National Academy of Sciences—National Research Council define the concept of *sustainable development*? To what extent are the basic human needs identified in this concept adequately satisfied for the approximately 6 billion humans living today? Discuss.
2. In what respects does the Neem tree stand as a metaphor for globalization? What are the defining characteristics of globalization? Has globalization as it has been developed thus far helped to reduce the number of chronically hungry people in the world? Why or why not?
3. What does the IPAT formula tell us about the causes of environmental degradation? Why does the author believe that this formula is only partially accurate? What factors need to be added to improve it? Explain.
4. Compare Kates's view of globalization with those of Bhagwati (selection II.3) and the International Forum on Globalization (selection II.4). Which of these authors presents the most balanced and informed assessment of globalization's benefits, risks, and costs?

Keywords

consumption, globalization, governance, population, risk assessment, sustainable development

THE WORLD OF THIS NEW CENTURY is in transition— becoming more crowded and more consuming, warmer and more stressed, more interconnected, yet diverse and divided. Can this transition also be a transition for sustainability, in which the more than 9 billion people of the next half century meet their wants and needs in ways that do not further degrade the planet's life-support systems?

In this chapter, I explore this transition to sustainability, the context in which it will take place, and the ways in which the new-old phenomenon of globalization affects it. My title is a play on the title of what may be the best-known book on globalization—Tom Friedman's *The Lexus and the Olive Tree*.

Friedman describes his title as follows:

> So there I was speeding along at 180 miles an hour on the most modern train in the world, reading this story about the oldest corner of the world. And the thought occurred to me that these Japanese, whose Lexus factory I had just visited and whose train I was riding, were building the greatest luxury car in the world with robots. And over here, on the top of page 3 of the *Herald Tribune*, the people with whom I had lived for so many years in Beirut and Jerusalem, whom I knew so well, were still fighting over who owned which olive tree. It struck me then that the Lexus and the olive tree were pretty good symbols of this post–Cold War era: half the world seemed to be emerging from the Cold War intent on building a better Lexus, dedicated to modernizing, streamlining and privatizing their economies in order to thrive in the system of globalization. And half the world—sometimes half the same country, sometimes half the same person—was still caught up in the fight over who owns which olive tree (p. 31).

But unlike this Lexus, which stands for all that is modern and different in globalization, and the olive tree for all that resists it, the nexus I explore is that of environment and development and the context

in which it will play out over the coming two generations. And the Neem tree symbolizes the globalizing world where the elements of both the Lexus and the olive tree coexist in an uneasy tension of mutual attraction and repulsion.

I use three critical goals required for a successful sustainability transition—meeting human needs, reducing hunger and poverty, and preserving the life-support systems of the planet—to ask how globalization might help or hinder achieving these. For globalization to help more than hinder, it will need to be "civilized," and I conclude with an analog of how that might take place.

Sustainable Development: The Nexus of Environment and Development

The nexus of society's developmental goals with its environmental limits over the long term comes together in "sustainable development," which is only the most recent effort to link together the collective aspirations of the peoples of the world. Over my adult life, four aspirations emerged: first, for peace in the postwar world of 1945; then for freedom, in the struggles in the late 1940s and 1950s to end imperialism; followed by development for the poorest three-fourths of the world; and last, in the final quarter of the century, a concern for a healthy environment for humankind, the earth itself, and its complex systems that support life. As global aspirations develop, good people try to bring them together in a characteristic pattern of international high-level commissions (Brandt, Palme, Brundtland), followed by great international conferences. Such was the 1987 report of the World Commission on Environment and Development (WCED, also known as the Brundtland Commission) widely disseminated as *Our Common Future* (WCED, 1987), followed by the United Nations Conference on Environment and Development (UNCED) in Rio de Janeiro in 1992, and now a decade later in South Africa as the World Summit for Sustainable Development.

"Sustainable development" is now central to the mission of countless international organizations, national institutions, "sustainable cities" and locales,

From *Worlds Apart: Globalization and the Environment*, ed. by James Gustave Speth, pp. 85–107. Copyright © 2003 Island Press. Reprinted by permission of Island Press, Washington, D.C.

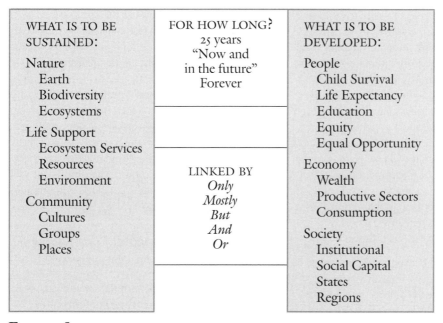

WHAT IS TO BE SUSTAINED:	FOR HOW LONG?	WHAT IS TO BE DEVELOPED:
Nature	25 years	People
Earth	"Now and	Child Survival
Biodiversity	in the future"	Life Expectancy
Ecosystems	Forever	Education
		Equity
Life Support		Equal Opportunity
Ecosystem Services		
Resources		Economy
Environment	LINKED BY	Wealth
	Only	Productive Sectors
Community	*Mostly*	Consumption
Cultures	*But*	
Groups	*And*	Society
Places	*Or*	Institutional
		Social Capital
		States
		Regions

FIGURE 1

Sustainable Development: Common Concerns, Differing Emphases.

transnational corporations, and nongovernmental organizations. The genius of the oxymoron of sustainable development lies in its essential ambiguity that seeks to finesse the real conflicts between economy and environment and between the present and the future. While sharing a common concern for the fate of the earth, proponents of sustainable development differ in their emphases on what is to be sustained, what is to be developed, how to link environment and development, and for how long a time (see Figure 1). Thus, proponents differ on what is to be sustained: Is it nature itself, or nature in the utilitarian life support of humankind, and does it include sustaining the community of the olive tree, as Friedman (2000) describes it: "everything that roots us . . . family, a community, a tribe, a nation, a religion or, most of all, a place called home" (p. 31)? Proponents differ on what is to be developed: Is it the economy, some broader notion of society, or is it people themselves? And how shall we link the two: sustain only, develop mostly, develop only but sustain somewhat, sustain or develop? — these and many more permutations are found. Finally, over what time horizon will this occur? The Brundtland report employs the usefully ambiguous and widely accepted time horizon as "now and in the future." But in a future of a single generation, twenty-five years, almost any development appears sustainable. Over an infinite forever, none does, as even the smallest growth extended indefinitely creates situations that seem surely unsustainable. And over the century, now encompassed in many assessments such as that of climate change, the large and the long future is both remote and uncertain.

While a major political success, sustainable development has not been a significant scientific focus beyond the earliest days of its conceptualization. While originating in the scientific activities of the early 1980s, particularly the work of the International Union for the Conservation of Nature (IUCN), as sustainable development gained greater political adherence, organized science found less to address. This has now changed, and a focus on a transition toward sustainability has made sustainable development scientifically manageable, and measurable for the world academies of science (IAP, 2000), for the international organizations of science (ICSU/WFEO, 2002), and increasingly for an emergent sustainability science (Kates et al., 2001).

In 1995, the Board on Sustainable Development of the U.S. National Academy of Sciences–National Research Council (NAS-NRC) sought to resolve some of the ambiguity I have described by focusing on a transition to sustainability over the next fifty years. By focusing on a transition, we took as our starting point the best understood of future trends—the demographic transition from a world with a population that grew by many births and many deaths to one that stabilized with few births and few deaths. With such a transition well under way, we can with some confidence project a declining or steady state population by the end of this century, with the bulk of that population born by 2050 (perhaps 9 billion of an eventual 10 billion). Thus, the human development needs of that population will surely increase, compared to the more than 6 billion alive today, but probably not more than by half again as much as that of today. The board defined a sustainability transition as one that would meet the human needs for food, nurture, housing, education, and employment of that larger but finite population, significantly reducing hunger and poverty, while still maintaining the essential life-support systems of the planet (NRC-BSD, 1999). These human needs are unmet today; for example, in 1995, 16 percent of the world population was hungry, 24 percent had unsafe water to drink, and 24 percent were illiterate (Raskin et al., 1998).

For these three normative goals, we found ample consensual support and measurable targets in the deliberations and subsequent treaties of international conferences and summits of leaders. For example, for the amount of reduction in hunger and poverty we used international consensus statements that call for reducing hunger and poverty by half within one to two decades (IMF et al., 2000) and suggested a target of reducing hunger by half in each of the next two generations.

Compared to meeting human needs, quantitative targets for preserving life-support systems are fewer, more modest, and more contested. Global targets now exist for reducing ozone-depleting substances, greenhouse gases, and, regionally, for some air pollutants. Absolute prohibitions (zero targets) exist for ocean dumping of radioactive wastes and some toxics (persistent organic pesticides), for the taking and/or sale of a few large mammals (whales, elephants, seals), migratory birds when breeding or endangered, and certain regional fishing stocks. International standards exist for many toxic materials, organic pollutants, and heavy metals that threaten human health, but not for ecosystem health. Water, land, and vegetative resources, such as arid lands or forests, have at best qualitative aspirations for sustainable management or restoration.

The Neem Tree: The New and Old Globalization

The 1992 NAS-NRC report *Neem: A Tree for Solving Global Problems* begins:

> Neem is a fascinating tree. On the one hand, it seems to be one of the most promising of all plants, and may eventually benefit every person on the planet. Probably no other yields as many strange and varied products or has as many exploitable by-products. Indeed, as foreseen by some scientists, this plant may usher in new era in pest control, provide millions with inexpensive medicines, cut down the rate of human population growth, and perhaps even reduce erosion, deforestation, and the excessive temperature of an overheated globe.

The Neem tree, *Azadirachta indica,* is an attractive broad-leafed evergreen that grows tall and broad and can live for a century or more. Native to South Asia, it has been carried over the last century to the rest of tropical and semitropical Asia, Africa, and increasingly to the Caribbean and Central America and is now well established in thirty countries and has been introduced to many more.

Everywhere it grows, it is prized for its ability to grow in marginal soils, to provide shade, firewood, oil for lamps, cosmetics, soaps, lubrication, and medicinals that date back several millennia, twig toothbrushes that prevent gum disease, and as a natural insecticide. Even where it does not grow, word of its wonders are carried on numerous Web sites, many dedicated to the Neem itself.

But it is for its pesticidal qualities—as a safer alternative to dangerous neurotoxins, effective across a large range of insects, fungi, nematodes, and the like, and seemingly safe for humans, birds, and animals—that Neem has attracted considerable scientific and commercial interest. More than seventy patents for uses or processes related to Neem products exist, and in May 2000 in an important decision, the European Patent Office revoked the patent given to W. R. Grace company for a fungicidal product, a decision hailed by Vandana Shiva, who had challenged the original patent, as "a great day for all who have been fighting to take back control of their resources and knowledge-systems from the patent regimes of the North" (Anon., 2000).

Thus, the Neem shares three major characteristics of globalization. It is not new, but quite ancient, as is globalization. In ancient Sanskrit it is known as *aristha,* or reliever of sickness. As with previous globalizations, it spread with religion and with empire. Part of traditional ayurvedic medicine, the Neem is found wherever Hinduism is found and often where the British Empire ruled. But as with globalization, there is much that is new in its dispersal and product development, as Neem seeds are now an international commodity. Modern science is close to synthesizing its major insecticidal properties, international nongovernmental organizations encourage its usage for impoverished rural peoples, and Web sites huckster its cosmetic and medicinal values. Finally, as with globalization, it is full of unrealized promise and currently realized discord. For except as a source of shade, firewood, toothbrushes, oil, or home remedies, it is not widely used beyond its South Asian home; and its most promising commercial products—refined or synthesized and standardized pesticides, medicinals, or contraceptives—are either underdeveloped or contested as to their efficacy and safety, as well as ethically in relation to the commercialization of an ancient legacy of nature and humankind.

Contemporary Globalization

As to globalization in general, I prefer the simplified definition by Held, McGrew, Goldblatt, and Perraton (1999) in *Global Transformations: Politics, Economics, and Culture,* a study that some think is currently the best academic book on the subject. Held et al. say that "in its simplest sense globalization refers to the widening, deepening and speeding up of global interconnectedness . . ." (p. 14). But, of course, as good academics they are not content with such simplicity and go on to describe a set of technical terms and criteria to mirror these items as extensiveness, intensiveness, velocity, and the impacts of interconnections.

Globalization, as noted, is not new, and Held et al. recognize four major periods of globalization: the premodern period of early empires and world religions, the early modern period of Western expansion, the modern industrial era, and the contemporary period from 1945 to the present. I would add two others: the earliest prehistoric period in which humans spread out of Africa around the world, and the future, especially that of the first half of the twenty-first century.

Reviewing the contemporary period and projecting to the future, our academy study (NRC-BSD, 1999) identified some major dimensions of contemporary globalization. The first is global interconnectedness with the much larger population of the future more closely connected by ties of economic production and consumption, migration, communication, and interlinked technologies. Since 1950, trade between nations has grown at more than twice the rate of the economy, and now some 20 percent of the world's goods and services pass over a border. Trade in money and capital—a hundred times the volume of world trade—now moves at a dizzying pace with electronic movement of funds, worldwide currency markets, and twenty-four-hour financial markets.

Words, images, and ideas also outpace the flow of products. New information technologies and mass communication techniques will continue to penetrate many different linguistic, cultural, and political barriers. Flows of people—temporary, permanent, and forced—have also increased, although most movements are poorly measured. The rate of increase in refugees is more rapid than that of world trade.

The rapid movement of peoples and products also makes possible the rapid transmission of infectious diseases of people, crops, and livestock and the biological invasions so destructive of native biota. Environmental harms are exported to countries with weak environmental standards. Most feared of all may be the rapid increases in consumption fueled by aggressive marketing and rapid cultural change. But as communication carries a culture of consumption, it also carries a culture of universal concern with the fate of the earth and links to common international efforts, shared information, and growing numbers of environmental groups.

But the academy study also considered the persistence of diversity, how connectedness, while increasing the similarity of places, can also increase diversity, particularly in urban areas that attract migrants. Places of wealth or opportunity toward which people and products are drawn actually become more diverse. There are also strong countercurrents to global culture that emphasize ethnic, national, and religious distinctiveness.

Finally, connectedness and diversity are also reflected in institutional innovation and power shifts (Mathews, 1997). At a global level, new institutions of governance have emerged, transnational corporate and financial institutions grow and consolidate, and networks of nongovernmental institutions collaborate and expand. At the subnational level,

government has devolved, privatization is common, and civic society in many places has been strengthened. Power has shifted from the national state—upward to the global level and downward to the local level—and at all levels from the public to the private.

How does globalization affect a transition toward sustainability in meeting human needs, reducing hunger and poverty, and preserving life-support systems? It helps in some ways, hinders in others, and for many important characteristics, it does both. In this exploration of a highly complex subject, I present two illustrative examples using qualitative, but ordered, judgments. For one, I combine the first two human needs, feeding and nurturing, with the related goal of reducing hunger. In the second, I explore the determinants of threats to the life-support systems.

Feeding, Nurturing, and Reducing Hunger

There are three major types of hunger: chronic household hunger, episodic hunger, and special-needs hunger. Each responds somewhat differently to globalization.

GLOBALIZATION AND REDUCING CHRONIC HUNGER

Current estimates find some 800–900 million people who are chronically hungry—living in households with insufficient income or its equivalent to provide for health, children's growth, and ability to work. The numbers of hungry people differ greatly between regions of the world, with the largest numbers in Asia and the greatest proportion in Africa (Table 1).

TABLE 1. **Numbers and Proportion of Chronically Hungry Population, 1996–1998**

Regions	% Total Population	Hungry Population (millions)
Sub-Saharan Africa	34	186
Near East/North Africa	10	36
Latin America and the Caribbean	11	55
China and India	16	348
Other Asia	19	166
Developing countries: Total	18	791

SOURCE: FAO, 2000.

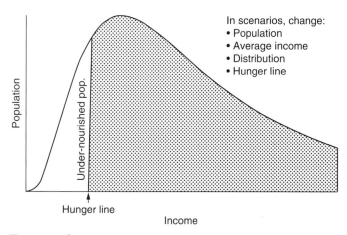

FIGURE 2

Hunger and Income.

TABLE 2. Trends in Regional GDP Per Capita, 1950, 1973, and 1992

World Regions	1950 GDP/capita (in 1990 $)	GDP/capita/ 1950 GDP/capita		U.S. GDP/capita/ REGIONAL GDP/capita		
		1973	1992	1950	1973	1992
United States	9573	1.7	2.3	1.0	1.0	1.0
Western Europe	5513	2.1	3.2	1.7	1.4	1.2
East Europe	2235	2.4	2.0	4.3	3.1	4.7
Latin America	3478	1.4	1.7	2.8	3.3	3.6
Asia	863	2.8	6.1	11.1	6.8	4.1
Africa	893	1.5	1.5	10.7	12.5	16.2

SOURCE: Madison, 1995.

The number of chronically hungry people can be approximately estimated by using four variables: the size of the population, the average income per person, the distribution of income across the population, and the definition of a hunger line of income, or its equivalent, below which the population is thought to be hungry (see Figure 2).

It is useful to examine some differences in these major determinants over the period of contemporary globalization beginning in 1950. World *population* grew over a half century from 2.5 billion to 6 billion, but the peak growth rate was in the 1960s and has been slowing ever since. Nonetheless, about 80 million people are added each year, increasing the numbers of chronically hungry even as the proportion of hungry people diminishes. Examining trends in *income* (Table 2) in this period, per capita gross domestic product (GDP) grew in all world regions between 1950 and 1973, but between 1973 and 1992, GDP in Eastern Europe declined, and it stagnated in Africa and Latin America.

Inequality in the *distribution of income* occurs both between countries and regions and within countries and regions. Between regions, Africa,

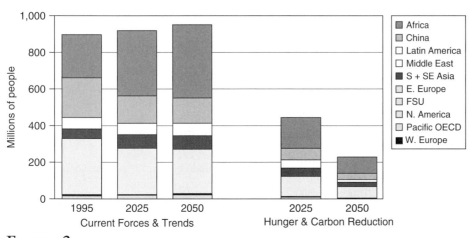

Figure 3

Reducing Chronic Hunger by Halves.

Eastern Europe, and Latin America (Table 2) show growing inequality with the United States (ratio of U.S. GDP per capita to regional GDP per capita), even as the rest of Europe converged with the United States and the ratio of U.S. per capita GDP to Asia declines from sevenfold in 1973 to fourfold in the course of two decades. Using a different data set (Deininger and Squire, 1996), within-region inequality of income (as measured by the Gini coefficient, a standard measure of inequality) differs almost twofold with the greatest inequality found in Latin America and the least found among the former socialist countries of Eastern Europe. Over time, for most regions, within-region inequality has been generally diminishing except in Africa and in Eastern Europe with the end of socialism. Finally, the *hunger line* grows over time as income increases, access to informal sources of food declines, food purchases increase, and diets change.

The NAS-NRC Board on Sustainable Development commissioned a study on the feasibility of reducing hunger by half in each of the two generations before 2050 using these variables and contrasting two different scenarios. The reference scenario projected major current trends, institutional continuity, economic globalization, and the slow convergence of developing countries toward the socioeconomic norms of developed countries. In this scenario, the number of hungry actually increased by 2050, although the proportion of hungry people declined. The "policy reform" scenario assumed that a proactive set of initiatives is instituted to achieve sustainability goals. In this scenario, hunger is cut in half with a small change in the speed of the demographic transition leading to less population, with growth in income at the higher end of plausible income growth rates, and most important, a convergence of equity to the current levels of Europe. The contrasting scenarios are shown in Figure 3 for the world as a whole and by region.

For these contrasting scenarios and the four major causal elements that underlie them, what are the impacts of globalization? In Table 3, I set out my

TABLE 3. Globalization's Impacts on Reducing Chronic Hunger

Causal Element	HELP	HINDER
Population Growth Decrease	++	
Increase in Income per capita	++	++ In Africa
Decrease in Inequity	+ Between Nations	+++ Within Nations
Decrease in Hunger Line		+

qualitative judgments (using a scale of one plus sign [+] for small impact and four plus signs [++++] for very large impacts) as to how globalization helps or hinders the causal elements linked to chronic hunger. For *population,* globalization probably helps through a population growth rate decline by influencing all three important determinants for reducing fertility: making contraception more accessible; providing opportunities for education and work for women; and encouraging postponement of marriage through such opportunities for education and work, as well as through diffused Western lifestyle concepts.

For *income,* globalization helps increase per capita income in some parts of the world, but practices not-so-benign neglect in others. The development of an export-oriented industry in Southeast Asia, accompanied by significant public sector actions, led to major reductions in hunger in that region until the recent financial crisis slowed and even reversed some of those gains. But in Africa, where hunger will increase most, globalization has exacerbated some of the region's problems, its export trade in such products of affluence as oil or diamonds fueling corruption and conflict, while development aid has diminished without an equivalent growth in private investment. But most of all, it has suffered not-so-benign neglect and has been marginalized from the globalized world system.

While globalization will probably decrease *inequity* overall between countries, globalization will, for some time at least, increase inequity within countries, particularly affecting the poorest of the poor. This is so because rapid export-oriented growth in developing countries reduces somewhat the differences in income with developed countries, but within countries opportunities vary greatly. Thus, for example, China, which had made enormous gains in reducing hunger, might well suffer an increase in hunger as the income gap between regions increases, as employment opportunities expand in export manufacturing and services but decline in local manufacturing and agriculture, and overall, the safety net system diminishes. Finally, the *hunger line* shifts relatively as diets expand (by preferences for both animal products and imported products or brands), more and more basic food

TABLE 4. Globalization's Impacts on Reducing Episodic Hunger

Causal Element	HELP	HINDER
Famine	+++	+
War	+	+
Financial Crisis		+++
Structural Adjustment		++

enters the market, and the income requirement to meet these new needs increases.

GLOBALIZATION AND REDUCING EPISODIC HUNGER

Applying similar judgments to episodic hunger (Table 4), the reduction of famine-determined hunger from natural hazards is a great recent success story of a globalized emergency food aid system that relies on both public and private efforts. Today, famine-inspired hunger exists only where war and violent conflict persist. Globalization, however, increases famine vulnerability in the sense of entitlement shifts, as Sen (1981) has shown, especially in cases where the availability of food and purchasing power of rural landless workers can be diminished by far-off events. Globalization has increased the incidence of war and civil conflict both by making weapons easily available (the ubiquitous Kalashnikov) and by diminishing the impacts of war by providing emergency food aid. Recent financial crises often triggered by globalized movements of capital have created sudden episodic hunger in countries where such episodes were rare—as in Southeast Asia, which had made marked progress in reducing hunger prior to the crises. Finally, structural adjustment efforts initiated either internally or at the behest of the IMF almost always lead to an increase in hunger from a decrease in social services and programs, despite some counterefforts.

GLOBALIZATION AND REDUCING SPECIAL-NEEDS HUNGER

Concerning special needs hunger (Table 5), global efforts to address some major causes of child undernutrition, especially from sickness and disease, by addressing immunization, treatment of diarrhea,

TABLE 5. Globalization's Impacts on Reducing Special Needs Hunger

Hunger Type	HELP	HINDER
Mothers and Children	+++	+
Iron, Iodine, Vitamin A	+++	+

and breast-feeding have helped to reduce the rate of wasting and stunting of children (although the actual numbers have increased as a result of population growth centered in the youngest ages). Similarly, the major micronutrient deficiencies of iodine, vitamin A, and iron have been reduced by international programs to encourage iodizing salt, to increase intakes of vitamin A through vitamin A–rich foods and through vitamin A supplementation, and to a much lesser extent, to reduce anemia by iron supplements. In some cases the diversification of diets has helped as well—for example, by providing greater access to iodized salt. The major countercurrent related to globalization is similar to the previous case: Structural adjustment and diminished development aid have severely constrained many programs directed at addressing these special needs.

Preserving Life-Support Systems

The life-support systems of the planet are often factored into major media: atmosphere, freshwater, oceans, and the biota as biomes, ecosystems, and species. The major threats to atmosphere, freshwater, oceans, and the biota are threefold: (1) the large-scale introduction of pollutants, such as acid rain and chlorofluorocarbons in the atmosphere, heavy metals in the soil, or chemicals in groundwater; (2) the massive assault on biota, such as deforestation in the tropics and the mountains, desertification in dry lands, overfishing of marine resources, and species extinction everywhere; and (3) human-induced climate change.

These threats are incredibly recent. In nine of twelve indicators of global environmental change, half of all the change that took place over the last ten thousand years occurred in our lifetime (Table 6).

Driving Forces of Environmental Change

These changes coincide but are not necessarily caused by the most recent wave of globalization. A general consensus among scientists posits that growth in population, in affluence, and in technology are jointly major driving forces for such change and related environmental problems. This has become enshrined in a useful, albeit overly simplified, identity known as IPAT, first published in 1972 by Ehrlich and Holdren in *Environment* magazine in response to a more limited version by Commoner et al. (1971). In this identity, various forms of environmental or resource impacts (I) equals population (P) times affluence (A), usually income per capita, times the impacts per unit of income as determined by technology (T) and the institutions that use it. Academic debate has now shifted from the greater or lesser importance of each of these driving forces of environmental degradation or resource

TABLE 6. 10,000 Years of Environmental Change: Selected Indicators

10,000 Years of Environmental Change	Selected Indicators	
	Rate of Change Still Accelerating	Rate of Change Now Decelerating
Half Occurred before Our Lifetimes	Deforested area Soil area loss	Terrestrial vertebrate diversity
Half Occurred during Our Lifetimes	Carbon releases Nitrogen releases Floral diversity Sediment flows Water withdrawals	Carbon tetrachloride releases Lead releases Marine mammal diversity Sulphur releases

SOURCE: Turner et al., 1990.

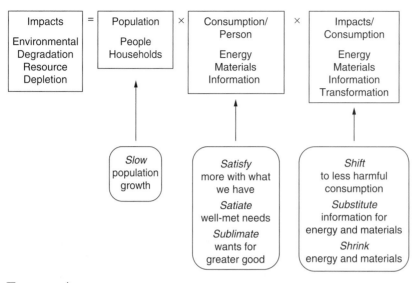

FIGURE 4

Variant of IPAT Identity.

depletion, to debate about their interaction and the ultimate forces that drive them.

Let me introduce a variant of the IPAT identity (Figure 4)—which might be called the PC version—and restating that identity in terms of population and consumption, it would be I = P*C/P*I/C. I equals environmental degradation and/or resource depletion; P equals the number of people or households; and C equals the consumption per person of energy, materials, and information.

With such an identity as a template and with the goal of reducing environmentally degrading and resource-depleting influences, there are at least seven major directions for research and policy. To reduce the level of impacts per unit of consumption, separate more damaging consumption from less harmful forms and *shift* to these, *shrink* the amounts of environmentally damaging energy and materials per unit of consumption, and *substitute* information for energy and materials. To reduce consumption per person or household, *satisfy* more with what is already had, *satiate* well-met consumption needs, and *sublimate* wants for a greater good. Finally, *slow* population growth and then stabilize population numbers as indicated earlier.

Before using these proximate determinants of the identity, a bit of caution is in order. IPAT is very useful, but is more complex than a simple identity. The PAT terms are only proximate, each in turn is driven by diverse underlying processes. Nor are the PAT terms independent of each other; for example, income (or affluence) influences the rate of population growth and consumption, as well as the technologies used to produce it. Indeed, the supposed technology term is really a catch-all of all the diverse items that determine a different set of impacts per unit of consumption— including technology, but also all kinds of ideas and institutions. Nor do I think the PAT terms are sufficient to examine the impact of globalization on Earth's life-support systems.

To add to the classic determinants, let me borrow from an analysis by Clark (2000) of environmental globalization, one that includes not only the globalization of environmental "stuff"—the energy, materials, biota transformed by production and consumption—but also the globalization of environmental ideas and governance. Specifically, Clark notes three major ideas: planetary management, risk assessment, and sustainable development; along with

TABLE 7. **Globalization's Impacts on Preserving Life-Support Systems**

Causal Element	HELP	HINDER
Population	++	
Consumption		++++
Technology	+++	+
Ideas	+++	++
Governance	++	++

three forms of governance: by governments; by nongovernmental organizations, both profit and nonprofit; and by coalitions and networks that bring them together.

Globalization and Preserving Life-Support Systems

Thus, there are five causal elements related to globalization's impact on preserving the life-support systems of the planet: population, consumption, technology, ideas, and governance. Examining these five causal elements (Table 7), beginning with *population*, globalization, as noted, will encourage a decline in the population growth rate thus lessening future human impacts on the environment. But globalization also accelerates *consumption* in three ways. Insofar as globalization increases income and to a degree inequity, it encourages greater production and consumption. Insofar as it extends the reach of trade and transport, it makes possible consumption of distant resources that would not be consumed locally and the import of goods not available locally. With the spread of ideas and images of "Western material standards of living," it further encourages consumption. Much of this enhanced consumption is desperately needed and desired by the poorer peoples of the world, but much of it will be in the form of material and energy transformations that are environmentally degrading and resource-depleting.

At the same time, globalization facilitates both the creation and the diffusion of *technologies* that lessen the need for energy and materials per unit of production or consumption, that create fewer toxics and pollutants, or that substitute information for energy and material use. Countering these helpful technologies are trickle-down technologies that export secondhand or second-rate technologies, buildings, and toxic or polluting processes to regions heretofore relatively free of degrading or depleting activities.

In the realm of *ideas*, there are also dual impacts. Development is seen as a good to be pursued, with environmental concerns a luxury that developing countries cannot readily afford. Countering this has been the rapid spread of the major environmental ideas of planetary and risk management and sustainable development, to the extent that while rhetoric persists as to differences between the North and the South, international surveys show little difference in the high environmental aspirations among the people of both North and South.

As to *governance*, while there are some 180 international environmental treaties in force to date, they are insufficient to counter the major threats to the atmosphere, oceans, and biota, with the possible exception of the Montreal protocol on ozone depletion. But as Clark notes, governance is greater than governments, and the governance activities of advocacy coalitions and the discourses between transnational corporations and international environmental groups can be very substantial in helping to maintain the planet's life-support system. Indeed, it is often the ability to draw global attention to some local threat that leads to mitigative or preventive actions. All of these forms of governance will grow with globalization. Substantially countering these forms are the notions of free trade unhindered by environmental constraint or regulation currently ensconced in the operation of the World Trade Organization and in various regional trade treaties.

Globalization and Two-Armed Scientists

The Maine version of a well-known story has Senator Edmund Muskie listening to testimony on the need for clean-air legislation. After a series of cautious scientific testimonies by scientists, he asks whether anyone in the room is a "one-armed scientist" who can testify without the endless academic qualifications of "on the one hand . . . then on the other hand . . ?"

It is obvious that I must plead guilty to being a two-armed scientist. But it is difficult for anyone thoughtfully confronting globalization not to be. Indeed, whether you sing paeans to globalization as Tom Friedman (2000) does or fear "the manic logic of global capitalism" as Bill Grieder (1997) does, the other hand, whichever it might be, is always present. What may separate the two more is that Friedman thinks that globalization itself will in time deal with its many harms, whereas Grieder believes in the need for radical revision and strong local to international action.

So, what can the two-armed scientist conclude from this first, tentative attempt to assess the impact of globalization on a sustainability transition: meeting human needs, reducing hunger and poverty, preserving the life-support systems of the planet? In this brief assessment I have focused on how globalization has affected the reduction of hunger and meeting the human needs for food and nurture and on the driving forces of global environmental change.

In sum, globalization to date has not helped reduce the numbers of chronically hungry in the world, although the proportion decreases as population grows. The shifts in investment, income, and job opportunities in some parts of the world are matched by the growth of hunger elsewhere. Episodic and special-needs hunger have benefited more as globalized public and private programs have expanded to respond rapidly to famine, to the special needs of children, and to two of the three major micronutrient diseases. Finally, the increase in hunger from globalized financial crises and policy decisions argues for new sources of instability for the fragile existence of the poorest of the poor. Short-run and long-run simulations of halving hunger argue for these trends to persist.

In preserving the life-support systems, the crucial issue is globalization's impact on current and projected production and consumption of energy and materials that are environmentally degrading and resource depleting. To date, despite major gains in technologies that reduce the use of energy and materials per unit of production, the absolute growth in consumption overwhelms the steady global technological progress. The globalization of environmental ideas has been truly remarkable, and these, along with feminism and human rights, constitute the major ideological revolutions of the contemporary period of globalization. The spread of these ideas has been well facilitated by global interconnections. Similarly, the rise of environmental governance writ large to include corporate behavior and local and international popular initiatives is facilitated by the interconnectedness of globalization and is a great portent for the future. But to date, these have all been insufficient to counter the major threats to the life-support systems, and when projected to address the extraordinary increases in the consumption of the future, such helpful developments may fail as well.

Civilizing Globalization

If the goods of globalization are to be realized for most of the world's peoples, and if its ills are to be reduced for those people and natural systems most vulnerable, then globalization itself must change in significant ways. Gerry Helleiner (2000), the Canadian economist, as well as Held et al. (1999), call this process "civilizing" globalization. All of them focus on changing governance. Helleiner asks, "Can the global economy be civilized?" "Globalized markets," he argues "operate within politically defined rules and governance institutions. The current global rules and economic governance institutions are in need of repair, updating and relegitimization," and he goes on to suggest some of those initiatives.

Held et al. (1999) focus not on economy but on politics and three major approaches to civilizing and democratizing contemporary globalization: a liberal-internationalism approach to reform global governance; a cosmopolitan, democratic approach to reconstruct global governance; and a radical republican approach to create alternative structures of governance. Exploring these issues are well beyond the scope of this chapter, but I conclude with my own thoughts on the efforts to "civilize" globalization.

Civilizing U.S. Capitalism: 100 Years

As I contemplate the varied efforts to understand globalization and how to reform or reconstruct it, I am struck by the similarity of contemporary globalization to an earlier period of American history. I perceive an analog to the current global situation in the U.S. economic history of the post–Civil War era. At the time, a truly integrated and nationalized industrial capitalism was created, spurred by the growth of interconnections of railroad and telegraph. Reading of this age of "robber-baron" capitalism, I am struck by the parallels with current globalization; for example, the great uncertainty at the time, even by the major participants, in understanding the new and different systems that had emerged.

Whatever emerged from the fierce competition and growing monopolization of economic power was initially marred by an absence of law and regulation. Much early regulatory effort was needed around what today are called "rule of law" and "transparency" issues, such as those that make contracts enforceable or stock certificates verifiable. These initial efforts were followed by numerous attempts to control monopoly power and maintain genuine competitiveness.

Almost parallel to these efforts, but much slower, were those that recognized the victims, harms, inequities, and externalities generated by the new integrated industrial system. The initial focus, as it is currently, was on child labor, followed by other working conditions, and then the essentials of a social safety net including disability insurance, unemployment insurance, pensions, and the like. Efforts to gain workers' rights began early and were repeatedly rebuffed, and it was not until 1935 that they were basically recognized. Finally, environmental issues were not really recognized until Earth Day 1970, thus capping a century of effort to civilize U.S. capitalism. Throughout this whole period the individual states of the United States served as the focus for innovative leadership and the testing ground for appropriate regulation that only later was emulated or taken over by the federal government.

The challenge for civilizing globalization is to reduce this century-long efforts to, at most, two decades. The good news is that this effort is well under way, again with a push for "humanizing globalization" or "globalization from the bottom." I illustrate with Bangor, Maine, population 35,000.

Civilizing Globalization: In Bangor, Maine

Beginning in 1991, Bangor became a sister-city to Carasque, a small village in the highlands of El Salvador, as part of a group of twenty-nine such sister-cities all trying to support returned populations who had been refugees from the civil war. From Bangor, Carasque has received a rebuilt truck, pedal sewing machines, school and health materials, and when needed, support for human and economic rights in the form of communications expressed to both the U.S. and El Salvador governments. From Carasque, Bangor has received an opportunity to learn of the realities of poor people in the developing world, a model of how young people can exercise leadership in their own communities, and instructive experience as to what alternative schooling might provide.

Trying to find an issue in common to both communities, people in Bangor identified sweatshop- or *maquiladora*-made clothes, the making of which takes jobs from Mainers and exploits Salvadorans. Today, there are a thousand consumers and thirty businesses in Bangor displaying the "clean clothes" sweatshop-free logo, and four Maine communities are now committed to selective sweatshop-free city purchasing. This has led to a statewide selective purchasing act for textiles and footwear that is now being implemented. The "clean clothes" criteria for such selective purchasing—protecting children and workers, providing a living wage, and giving workers rights to bargain—is an agenda for civilizing globalization. Finally, many of the same Mainers recently took a five-hour trip to Quebec City, Canada, for the so-called Americas Summit to protest a free trade area until it incorporates children's, workers', and environmental concerns.

Globalization and a Transition toward Sustainability

The very notion of a transition toward sustainability, and the concept of sustainable development from which it derives, are products of the widening, deepening, and speeding up of the interconnectedness that characterizes globalization. To think of humankind as a whole, to see its links to the fate of the blue planet, has been an essential part of the globalization process. Thus, those of us who aspire to a transition toward sustainability, to meet human needs while preserving the life support of the planet, cannot be "against globalization." But what we can say (and are saying) is that for globalization to continue to encourage such a transition, it will need to redouble those aspects of this complex movement in our collective lives that help a sustainability transition and to dampen those that hinder such a transition. It is this nexus that will make real the promise of the Neem tree.

REFERENCES

Anon. 2000. "Neem tree free," *The Ecologist*, 30/4:8.

Clark, William C. 2000. "Environmental globalization." In Joseph S. Nye Jr. and John D. Donahue, eds., *Governance in a Globalizing World*. Washington, D.C.: Brookings Press.

Commoner, B., M. Corr, and P. Stamler. 1971. "The causes of pollution," *Environment*, April, pp. 2–19.

Deininger, Klaus, and Lyn Squire. 1996. "A new data set measuring income inequality," *World Bank Economic Review* 10(3):565–591.

Ehrlich, Paul, and John Holdren. 1972. "Review of *The Closing Circle*," *Environment* 14(3):24–39.

Food and Agriculture Organization of the United Nations (FAO). 2000. *Agriculture: Towards 2015/30*. Technical Interim Report. Rome: FAO.

Friedman, Thomas L. 2000. *The Lexus and the Olive Tree*. New York: Anchor Books.

Grieder, William. 1997. *One World Ready or Not: The Manic Logic of Global Capitalism*. New York: Simon and Schuster.

Held, David, Anthony McGrew, David Goldblatt, and Jonathan Perraton. 1999. *Global Transformations: Politics, Economics, and Culture*. Stanford, Calif.: Stanford University Press.

Helleiner, Gerald K. 2000. "Markets, politics and globalization: Can the global economy be civilized?" The Tenth Raúl Prebisch Lecture, Geneva, 11 December.

InterAcademy Panel (IAP) on International Issues. 2000. *Transition to Sustainability in the 21st Century*. Conference of the World's Scientific Academies. 15–18 May 2000, Tokyo, Japan. http://interacademies.net/intracad/tokyo2000.nsf/all/home.

International Council for Science (ICSU) and the World Federation of Engineering Organizations (WFEO). 2002. *Role and Contributions of the Scientific and Technological Community (S&TC) to Sustainable Development*. World Summit on Sustainable Development. Secretary-General's Note for the Multi-Stake Holder Dialogue Segment of the Second Preparatory Committee. Addendum No. 8: Dialogue Paper by Scientific and Technological Communities. United Nations Economic and Social Council E/CN.17/2002/PC.2/6.Add.8. Advance Copy, 28 January 2002.

International Monetary Fund (IMF), Organisation for Economic Cooperation and Development (OECD), United Nations (UN), and World Bank Group (WB). 2000. *A Better World for All: Progress towards the International Development Goals*. Washington, D.C.: IMF, OECD, UN, WB.

Kates, Robert W., William C. Clark, Robert Corell, J. Michael Hall, Carlo C. Jaeger, Ian Lowe, James J. McCarthy, Hans Joachim Schellnhuber, Bert Bolin, Nancy M. Dickson, Sylvie Faucheux, Gilberto C. Gallopin, Arnulf Gruebler, Brian Huntley, Jill Jäger, Narpat S. Jodha, Roger E. Kasperson, Akin Mabogunje, Pamela Matson, Harold Mooney, Berrien Moore III, Timothy O'Riordan, and Uno Svedin. 2001. "Sustainability science." *Science* 292:641–642, April 27. http://sustainabilityscience.org/keydocs/fulltext/wssd_stc_020128.pdf.

Madison, Angus. 1995. *Monitoring the World Economy 1820–1992*. Paris: Organization for Economic Cooperation and Development.

Mathews, Jessica. 1997. "Power shift," *Foreign Affairs* 76(1):50–66.

National Research Council, Board on Science and Technology for International Development (BOSTID). 1992. *Neem: A Tree for Solving Global Problems*. Washington, D.C.: National Academy Press.

National Research Council, Board on Sustainable Development (NRC-BSD). 1999. *Our Common Journey: A Transition Toward Sustainability*. Washington, D.C.: National Academy Press.

Raskin, Paul, Gilberto Gallopin, Pablo Gutman, Alan Hammond, and Rob Swart. 1998. *Bending the Curve: Toward Global Sustainability, a Report of the*

Global Scenario Group. Polestar Series, Report No. 8. Boston: Stockholm Environmental Institute.

Sen, Amartya. 1981. *Poverty and Famines: An Essay on Entitlement and Deprivation*. New York: Oxford University Press.

Turner, B. L. II, William C. Clark, Robert W. Kates, John F. Richards, Jessica T. Mathews, and William B. Meyer, eds. 1990. *The Earth as Transformed by Human Action: Global and Regional Changes in the Biosphere over the Past 300 Years*. Cambridge: Cambridge University Press.

World Commission on Environment and Development (WCED). 1987. *Our Common Future*. New York: Oxford University Press. (Brundtland Report).

Bibliography

Aiken, W. E. (1977). *Technocracy and the American Dream: The Technocratic Movement 1900–1941*. Berkeley: University of California Press.

Appleyard, B. (1998). *Brave New Worlds: Staying Human in the Genetic Future*. New York: Viking Press.

Arterton, F. C. (1987). *Teledemocracy: Can Technology Protect Democracy?* London: Sage.

Baden, J. A., Noonan, D. S., and Ruckelshaus, W. D. (Eds.). (1998). *Managing the Commons,* 2nd ed. Bloomington: Indiana University Press.

Barnet, R. J., and Cavanagh, J. (1994). *Global Dreams: Imperial Corporations and the New World Order*. New York: Touchstone.

Bartlett, D., and Steele, J. (1992). *America: What Went Wrong?* Kansas City, MO: Andrews and McMeel.

Beniger, J. (1986). *The Control Revolution: Technological and Economic Origins of the Information Society*. Cambridge, MA: Harvard University Press.

Bijker, W. E., Hughes, T. P., and Pinch, T. (1990). *The Social Construction of Technological Systems*. Cambridge, MA: MIT Press.

Bolter, J. D. (1984). *Turing's Man*. Chapel Hill: University of North Carolina Press.

Boorstin, D. J. (1978). *The Republic of Technology*. New York: Harper & Row.

Borgmann, A. (1984). *Technology and the Character of Contemporary Life: A Philosophical Inquiry*. Chicago: University of Chicago Press.

Brand, S. (1987). *The Media Lab: Inventing the Future at MIT.* New York: Viking Press.

Braun, E. (1984). *Wayward Technology*. Westport, CT: Greenwood Press.

Bright, C. (1998). *Life Out of Bounds: Bioinvasion in a Borderless World*. New York: Norton.

Brod, C. (1984). *Techno Stress: The Human Cost of the Computer Revolution*. Reading, MA: Addison-Wesley.

Brook, J., and Boal, I. A. (Eds.). (1995). *Resisting the Virtual Life: The Culture and Politics of Information*. San Francisco: City Lights Books.

Brown, L., et al. (1998). *State of the World 1998: A Worldwatch Institute Report on Progress toward a Sustainable Society*. New York: Norton.

Brzezinski, Z. (1989). *The Grand Failure: The Birth and Death of Communism in the Twentieth Century*. New York: Scribner's.

Burke, J., and Ornstein, R. (1997). *The Axmaker's Gift: Technology's Capture and Control of Our Minds and Culture*. New York: Putnam Group.

Bush, C. G. (1983). *Machina Ex Dea*. New York: Teachers College Press.

Carnegie Commission on Science, Technology, and Government. (1992). *Enabling the Future: Linking Science and Technology to Societal Goals*. New York: Carnegie Commission on Science, Technology, and Government.

Carson, R. (1962). *Silent Spring*. Boston: Houghton Mifflin.

Cavanagh, J., and Mander, J. (2004). *Alternatives to Economic Globalization: A Better World Is Possible*, 2nd ed. San Francisco: Berrett-Koehler.

Chandler, A. D., Jr. (1977). *The Visible Hand: The Management Revolution in American Business*. Cambridge, MA: Belknap Press.

Chomsky, N. (1996). *World Orders Old and New*. New York: Columbia University Press.

Clark, A. (2004). *Natural-Born Cyborgs: Minds, Technologies, and the Future of Human Intelligence*. New York: Oxford University Press.

Commoner, B. (1971). *The Closing Circle: Nature, Man and Technology*. New York: Knopf.

Corn, J. (Ed.). (1986). *Imagining Tomorrow: History, Technology, and the American Future*. Cambridge, MA: MIT Press.

Cothran, H. (Ed.). (2002). *Energy Alternatives: Opposing Viewpoints*. San Diego, CA: Greenhaven Press.

Cowan, R. S. (1983). *More Work for Mother: The Ironies of Household Technology from the Open Hearth to the Microwave*. New York: Basic Books.

Cowan, R. S. (1997). *A Social History of American Technology*. New York: Oxford University Press.

Cross, G. (1993). *Time and Money: The Making of Consumer Culture*. New York: Routledge.

Daly, H. E., and Cobb, J. B., Jr. (1994). *For the Common Good: Redirecting the Economy toward Community, the Environment, and a Sustainable Future*. New York: Beacon Press.

Davies, P. (2004). *What's This India Business? Offshoring, Outsourcing, and the Global Services Revolution*. London: Nicholas Brealey International.

Dawkins, R. (1990). *The Selfish Gene*. Oxford: Oxford University Press.

Desmond, K. (1986). *The Harwin Chronology of Inventions, Innovations, Discoveries*. London: Constable.

Diamond, J. (1999). *Guns, Germs, and Steel: The Fates of Human Societies*. New York: Norton.

Diamond, J. (2004). *Collapse: How Societies Choose to Fail or Succeed*. New York: Viking Adult.

Dobbs, L. (2004). *Exporting America: Why Corporate Greed Is Shipping American Jobs Overseas*. New York: Warner Business.

Donaldson, T. (1989). *The Ethics of International Business*. New York: Oxford University Press.

Douglas, M., and Wildavsky, A. (1982). *Risk and Culture: The Selection of Technical and Environmental Dangers*. Berkeley: University of California Press.

Dreyfus, H. (1979). *What Computers Can't Do: The Limits of Artificial Intelligence*, 2nd ed. New York: Basic Books.

Dreyfus, H. (1992). *What Computers Still Can't Do: A Critique of Artificial Reason*. Cambridge, MA: MIT Press.

Drucker, P. (1993). *Post-Capitalist Society.* New York: HarperCollins.

Dunn, L. (1965). *A Short History of Genetics.* New York: Plenum.

Durning, A. (1989). *Action at the Grassroots: Fighting Poverty and Environmental Decline.* Washington, DC: Worldwatch Institute.

Dyson, F. (1985). *Origins of Life.* Cambridge: Cambridge University Press.

Dyson, F. (1999). *The Sun, the Genome, and the Internet: Tools of Scientific Revolutions.* New York: Oxford University Press.

Dyson, G. B. (1997). *Darwin among the Machines: The Evolution of Global Intelligence.* New York: Perseus.

Easton, T. A. (Ed.). (1998). *Taking Sides: Clashing Views of Controversial Issues in Science, Technology, and Society,* 3rd ed. Guilford, CT: Dushkin/McGraw-Hill.

Edgar, S. (1997). *Morals and Machines: Perspectives in Computer Ethics.* New York: Jones and Bartlett.

Ellul, J. (1964). *The Technological Society,* J. Wilkenson trans. New York: Knopf.

Elster, J. (1983). *Explaining Technical Change.* Cambridge: Cambridge University Press.

Ermann, M. D., Williams, M., and Shauf, M. (Eds.). (1997). *Computers, Ethics, and Society,* 2nd ed. New York: Oxford University Press.

Feenberg, A. (1999). *Questioning Technology.* New York: Routledge.

Feenberg, A., and Hannay, A. (Eds.). (1995). *Technology and the Politics of Knowledge.* Bloomington: Indiana University Press.

Feeré, F. (1995). *Philosophy of Technology.* Athens: University of Georgia Press.

Fishman, T. (2005). *China, Inc.: How the Rise of the Next Superpower Challenges America and the World.* New York: Scribner's.

Fox, M. (1992). *Superpigs and Wondercorn: The Brave New World of Biotechnology and Where It May Lead.* New York: Lyons and Burford.

Frenkel, S. (Ed.). (1999). *On the Front Line: Organization of Work in the Information Age.* Ithaca, NY: Cornell University Press.

Friedman, T. L. (1999). *The Lexus and the Olive Tree.* New York: Farrar, Straus & Giroux.

Friedman, T. (2005). *The World Is Flat: A Brief History of the Twenty-first Century.* New York: Farrar, Straus & Giroux.

Gates, B. (1995). *The Road Ahead.* New York: Viking Penguin.

Gimpel, J. (1977). *The Medieval Machine: The Industrial Revolution of the Middle Ages.* New York: Penguin.

Gordon, D. (1996). *Fat and Mean: The Corporate Squeeze of Working Americans and the Myth of Managerial "Downsizing."* New York: Kessler Books.

Gordon, J. (2004). *An Empire of Wealth: The Epic History of American Economic Power.* New York: HarperCollins.

Hardin, G. (1993). *Living within Limits: Ecology, Economics, and Population Taboos.* New York: Oxford University Press.

Hardison, O. B., Jr. (1989). *Disappearing through the Skylight: Culture and Technology in the Twentieth Century.* New York: Viking Press.

Heidegger, M. (1977). *The Question Concerning Technology and Other Essays,* W. Lovitt, trans. New York: Harper & Row.

Henry, D. (1989). *From Foraging to Agriculture.* Philadelphia: University of Pennsylvania Press.

Hofstetter, R. (1997). *Mobius.* New York: Vantage Press.

Hughes, T. P. (1989). *American Genesis: A Century of Invention and Technological Enthusiasm.* New York: Viking Press.

Ihde, D. (1990). *Technology and the Lifeworld: From Garden to Earth.* Bloomington: Indiana University Press.

Jonas, H. (1974). *Philosophical Essays: From Ancient Creed to Technological Man.* Englewood Cliffs, NJ: Prentice Hall.

Jonas, H. (1984). *The Imperative of Responsibility: In Search of an Ethics for the Technological Age.* Chicago: University of Chicago Press.

Karliner, J. (1997). *The Corporate Planet: Ecology and Politics in the Age of Globalization.* San Francisco: Sierra Club Books.

Kennedy, P. (1993). *Preparing for the Twenty-first Century.* New York: Random House.

Kevles, D. (1995). *In the Name of Eugenics: Genetics and the Uses of Human Heredity.* Cambridge, MA: Harvard University Press.

Keynes, J. (1989). *General Theory of Employment, Interest and Money.* New York: Harcourt Brace.

Kidder, T. (1982). *The Soul of a New Machine.* London: Allen Lane.

Kitcher, P. (1996). *The Lives to Come: The Genetic Revolution and Human Possibilities.* New York: Touchstone.

Koestler, A. (1964). *The Act of Creation.* New York: Macmillan.

Korten, D. C. (1995). *When Corporations Ruled the World.* West Hartford, CT: Kumarian Press.

Kuhn, T. (1970). *The Structure of Scientific Revolutions,* 2nd ed. Chicago: University of Chicago Press.

Kurzweil, R. (1990). *The Age of Intelligent Machines.* Cambridge, MA: MIT Press.

Kurzweil, R. (1999). *The Age of Spiritual Machines: When Computers Exceed Human Intelligence.* New York: Viking Press.

Landes, D. (1983). *Revolution in Time: Clocks and the Making of the Modern World.* Cambridge, MA: Harvard University Press.

Latour, B. (1987). *Science in Action.* Cambridge, MA: Harvard University Press.

Longman, P. (2004). *The Empty Cradle: How Falling Birthrates Threaten World Prosperity and What to Do about It.* New York: Basic Books.

Lovins, A. B. (1977). *Soft Energy Paths: Towards a Durable Peace.* Cambridge, MA: Ballinger.

Lyons, J., and Gorner, P. (1966). *Altered Fates: Gene Therapy and the Retooling of Human Life.* New York: Norton.

Mackenzie, D., and Wajcman, J. (Eds.). (1999). *The Social Shaping of Technology.* Philadelphia: Open University Press.

Maisels, C. (1990). *The Emergence of Civilization: From Hunting and Gathering to Agriculture, Cities, and the State in the Near East.* London: Routledge & Kegan Paul.

Marx, L. (1964). *The Machine in the Garden: Technology and the Pastoral Ideal in America.* New York: Oxford University Press.

McCorduck, P. (1979). *Machines Who Think.* San Francisco: W. H. Freeman.

McGee, G. (1997). *The Perfect Baby: A Pragmatic Approach to Genetics.* Lanham, MD: Rowman & Littlefield.

McLuhan, M. (1964). *Understanding Media: The Extensions of Man.* New York: McGraw-Hill.

McPhee, J. (1989). *The Control of Nature.* New York: Farrar, Straus & Giroux.

Mesthene, E. (1970). *Technological Change: Its Impact on Man and Society.* New York: New American Library.

Meyerowitz, J. (1985). *No Sense of Place: The Impact of Electronic Media on Sociable Behavior.* New York: Oxford University Press.

Mills, S. (Ed.). (1997). *Turning Away from Technology: A New Vision for the 21st Century.* San Francisco: Sierra Club Books.

Mitcham, C. (1994). *Thinking through Technology: The Path between Engineering and Philosophy.* Chicago: University of Chicago Press.

Mitcham, C., and Mackey, R. (Eds.). (1973). *Biography of the Philosophy of Technology.* Chicago: University of Chicago Press.

Mitcham, C., and Mackey, R. (Eds.). (1983). *Philosophy and Technology: Readings in Philosophical Problems of Technology.* New York: Free Press.

Morevec, H. (1989). *MindChildren: The Future of Robot and Human Intelligence.* Cambridge, MA: Harvard University Press.

Morevec, H. (1999). *Robot: Mere Machine to Transcendent Mind.* New York: Oxford University Press.

Mumford, L. (1934). *Technics and Civilization.* New York: Harcourt, Brace, and World.

Mumford, L. (1966). *Technics and Human Development.* New York: Harcourt Brace Jovanovich.

Naisbitt, J. (1984). *Megatrends: Ten New Directions Transforming Our Lives.* New York: Warner Books.

Negroponte, N. (1995). *Being Digital.* New York: Vintage Books.

Noble, D. F. (1979). *America by Design: Science, Technology, and the Rise of Corporate Capitalism.* New York: Oxford University Press.

Noble, D. F. (1984). *Forces of Production: A Social History of Industrial Automation.* New York: Knopf.

Noble, D. F. (1997). *The Religion of Technology: The Divinity of Man and the Spirit of Invention.* New York: Knopf.

Nye, D. E. (1994). *American Technological Sublime.* Cambridge, MA: MIT Press.

Oakley, A. (1984). *The Captured Womb: A History of the Medical Care of Pregnant Women.* Oxford: Blackwell.

Pacey, A. (1983). *The Culture of Technology.* Cambridge, MA: MIT Press.

Perrin, N. (1979). *Giving Up the Gun: Japan's Reversion to the Sword, 1543–1879.* Boston: David R. Godine.

Peterson, B. (Ed.). (2002). *Rethinking Globalization: Teaching for Justice in an Unjust World.* Milwaukee, WI: Rethinking Schools Ltd.

Petrovski, H. (1985). *To Engineer Is Human: The Role of Failure in Successful Design.* New York: St. Martin's Press.

Petrovski, H. (1996). *Invention by Design: How Engineers Get from Thought to Thing.* Cambridge, MA: Harvard University Press.

Pitt, Joseph C. (2000). *Thinking about Technology: Foundations of the Philosophy of Technology.* New York: Seven Bridges Press.

Pool, R. (1997). *Beyond Engineering: How Society Shapes Technology.* New York: Oxford University Press.

Postman, N. (1985). *Amusing Ourselves to Death: Public Discourse in the Age of Show Business.* New York: Viking Press.

Postman, N. (1992). *Technopoly: The Surrender of Culture to Technology.* New York: Knopf.

Postrel, V. (1998). *The Future and Its Enemies: The Growing Conflict over Creativity, Enterprise, and Progress.* New York: Free Press.

Reich, R. (1992). *The Work of Nations: Preparing Ourselves for 21st Century Capitalism.* New York: Random House.

Renner, M. (1996). *Fighting for Survival: Environmental Decline, Social Conflict, and the New Age of Insecurity.* Washington, DC: Worldwatch Institute.

Rheingold, H. (1991). *Virtual Reality.* New York: Summit Books.

Rifkin, J. (1983). *Algeny.* New York: Viking Press.

Rifkin, J. (1995). *The End of Work: The Decline of the Global Labor Force and the Dawn of the Post-Market Era.* New York: Putnam.

Rifkin, J. (2002). *The Hydrogen Economy: The Creation of the World-Wide Energy Web and the Redistribution of Power on Earth.* New York: Jeremy P. Tarcher.

Roberts, J. M. (1993). *A Short History of the World.* New York: Oxford University Press.

Roberts, P. (2004). *The End of Oil: On the Edge of a Perilous New World.* Boston: Houghton Mifflin.

Rosenberg, N. (1982). *Inside the Black Box: Technology and Economics.* Cambridge: Cambridge University Press.

Roszak, T. (1994). *The Cult of Information: A Neo-Luddite Treatise on High Tech, Artificial Intelligence, and the True Art of Thinking,* 2nd ed. Berkeley: University of California Press.

Russo, E., and Cove, D. (1995). *Genetic Engineering: Dreams and Nightmares.* New York: Viking Press.

Rybczynski, W. (1985). *Taming the Tiger: The Struggle to Control Technology.* New York: W. H. Freeman.

Sachs, J. (2005). *The End of Poverty: Economic Possibilities for Our Time.* New York: Penguin.

Sahal, D. (1981). *Patterns of Technological Innovation.* Cambridge: Cambridge University Press.

Schick, K. D., and Toth, N. (1993). *Making Silent Stones Speak: Human Evolution and the Dawn of Technology.* New York: Simon & Schuster.

Schor, J. (1991). *The Overworked American: The Unexpected Decline of Leisure.* New York: Basic Books.

Schumacher, E. F. (1973). *Small Is Beautiful: Economics as if People Mattered.* New York: Harper & Row.

Sclove, R. E. (1995). *Democracy and Technology.* New York: Guilford Press.

Shaiken, H. (1985). *Work Transformed: Automation and Labor in the Computer Age.* New York: Holt, Rinehart & Winston.

Shrader-Frechette, K., and Westra, L. (Eds.). (1997). *Technology and Values.* Totowa, NJ: Rowman & Littlefield.

Silver, L. (1997). *Remaking Eden: Cloning and Beyond in a Brave New World.* New York: Avon Books.

Simons, G. (1992). *Robots: The Quest for Living Machines.* New York: Sterling.

Singer, P. (2002). *One World: The Ethics of Globalization.* New Haven, CT: Yale University Press.

Smith, A. (1937). *An Inquiry into the Nature and Causes of the Wealth of Nations.* New York: Modern Library.

Speth, J. (2004). *Red Sky at Morning: America and the Crisis of the Global Environment.* New Haven, CT: Yale University Press.

Stover, C. (Ed.). (1963). *The Technological Order: Proceedings of the Encyclopaedia Brittanica Conference.* Detroit: Wayne State University Press.

Strasser, S. (1989). *Satisfaction Guaranteed: The Making of the American Mass Market.* New York: Pantheon.

Strobel, F. (1993). *Upward Dreams, Downward Mobility: The Economic Decline of the American Middle Class.* Lanham, MD: Rowman & Littlefield.

Strong, D. (1995). *Crazy Mountains: Learning from Wilderness to Weigh Technology.* Albany: State University of New York Press.

Teich, A. H. (1997). *Technology and the Future,* 7th ed. New York: St. Martin's Press.

Tenner, E. (1997). *Why Things Bite Back: Technology and the Revenge of Unintended Consequences.* Cambridge, MA: Harvard University Press.

Thurow, L. C. (1996). *The Future of Capitalism: How Today's Economic Forces Shape Tomorrow's World.* New York: William Morrow.

Tiles, M., and Oberdiek, H. (1995). *Living in a Technological Culture: Human Tools and Human Values.* New York: Routledge.

Toffler, A. (1970). *Future Shock.* New York: Random House.

Toffler, A., and Toffler, H. (1990). *Powershift.* New York: Bantam Books.

Turkle, S. (1982). *The Second Self: The Human Spirit in a Computer Culture.* New York: Simon & Schuster.

Turney, J. (1998). *Frankenstein's Footsteps: Science, Genetics and Popular Culture.* New Haven, CT: Yale University Press.

Van Creveld, M. (1989). *Technology and War: From 2000 BC to the Present.* New York: Free Press.

Vandermeer, J., and Goldberg, D. (2003). *Population Ecology: First Principles.* Princeton, NJ: Princeton University Press.

Volti, R. (1992). *Society and Technological Change,* 2nd ed. New York: St. Martin's Press.

Wajcman, J. (1991). *Feminism Confronts Technology.* University Park: Pennsylvania State University Press.

Weeks, J. (2001). *Population: An Introduction to Concepts and Issues (with InfoTrac),* 8th ed. Belmont, CA: Wadsworth.

White, L., Jr. (1966). *Medieval Technology and Social Change.* New York: Oxford University Press.